# The Book of Guy Fawkes Day And its BONFIRE NIGHT
## Volume VIII
### Guy Fawkes in America from Pope Night to Pork Day

Conrad Jay Bladey, Hutman Productions, 2020

The Book of
Guy Fawkes Day
And its Bonfire Night
Volume VIII
Guy Fawkes in America
from Pope Night to
Pork Day

©Conrad Jay Bladey,
Hutman Productions, 2020

ISBN: 978-1-7352875-2-2

Image: Pierre Eugene Du Simitière, Pope Day in Boston, 1767, sketch of the South End cart company, detail, The Library Company of Philaelphia.

# Dedication: To "Alfred F. Young, a Giant of a Historian" ~ J.L. Bell

Alfred F. Young, historian, died November 6, 2012 at the age of 87. He wrote important books about the American Revolution,

*(Image: Alfred F. Young. NIU College of Liberal Arts and Sciences.*

*The Shoemaker and the Tea Party: Memory and the American Revolution.*
*Masquerade: The Life and Times of Deborah Sampson, Continental Soldier.*
*Liberty Tree: Ordinary People and the American Revolution.*

And collections of essays

*The American Revolution: Explorations in the History of American Radicalism. Beyond the American Revolution: Explorations in the History of American Radicalism.*
*Whose American Revolution Was It? Historians Interpret the Founding.*
*We the People: Voices and Images of the New Nation.*
*Revolutionary Founders: Rebels, Radicals, and Reformers*

"South End Forever North End Forever", Broadside, Boston, 1768, Library of Congress.

"They cannot indeed wish for a finer Opportunity of recommending themselves to the publick Favour, and gaining infinite Applause; for a long Series of ill Success has created such an Appetite for good News, that a small Victory obtain'd would be magnify'd to a great one, and the Man who procures us a Bonfire and a Holiday, would be almost ador'd as a Hero."

−Letter: "From Benjamin Franklin to Joseph Galloway, 17 February 1758.", Yale University.

"Procession", Elkanah Toisdfale, 1795, New York

Pope Night (also called Pope's Night, Pope Day, or Pope's Day) was an holiday celebrating independence from foreign military and political intervention in the affairs of the colonies and later United States of which the Gunpowder Plot was the most famous example: that is it was a secular plot, a part of the political counter reformation and sought to impose external political control in England. It was celebrated annually on November 5 in the colonial United States. As in England in 1605 the colonists in Boston and New York knew the Pope in his political role as head of state, of the Papal States, who, along with his strong allies represented a significant threat to the isolated colonies. (You will find a record of military actons involving the Papal States in Appendix 1)

The celebration evolved from the British Guy Fawkes Night, which commemorates the failure of the Gunpowder Plot of 1605. Although involving Catholics, including officials of the church, including the pope; the attempted revolt was primarily political in nature: "Regime Change". The plot became a trademark for foreign intervention. Pope Night was most popular in the seaport towns of New England, especially in Boston, where it was an occasion for drinking, mobocracy, and protest by all classes. Image:

~Conrad Bladey 2020

We can not at this time confirm
Nor deny
how our celebrations work in the
"World Unseen."
With work we will.
Meanwhile we must not be
 "Druv"!!
-Conrad Bladey, 2020

-Image: Robert Sayer and John Bennett, "The Bostonins Paying the Exciseman", 1795.

# 1623- November 5: Earliest recorded celebration of Pope's Day in New England. Bonfire at Plymouth Plantation
~Goes out of control and burns several homes.

But after he was gone, M$^r$. Weston in lue of thanks to y$^e$ Gov$^r$ and his freinds hear, gave them this quib (behind their baks) for all their pains. That though they were but yonge justices, yet they wear good beggers. Thus they parted at this time, and shortly after y$^e$ Gov$^r$ tooke his leave and went to y$^e$ Massachusets by land, being very thankfull for his kind entertainemente. The ship stayed hear, and fitted her selfe to goe for Virginia, having some passengers ther to deliver; and with her returned sundrie of those from hence which came over on their perticuler, some out of discontente and dislike of y$^e$ cuntrie; others by reason of a fire that broke out, and burnt y$^e$ houses they lived in, and all their provisions [106[BF]] so as [182] they were necessitated therunto. This fire was occasioned by some of y$^e$ sea-men that were roystering in a house wher it first begane, making a great fire in very could weather, which broke out of y$^e$ chimney into y$^e$ thatch, and burnte downe 3. or 4. houses, and consumed all y$^e$ goods & provissions in y$^m$. The house in which it begane was right against their store-house, which they had much adoe to save, in which were their comone store & all their provissions; y$^e$ which if it had been lost, y$^e$ plantation had been over-throwne. But through Gods mercie it was saved by y$^e$ great dilligence of y$^e$ people, & care of the Gov$^r$ & some aboute him. Some would have had y$^e$ goods throwne out; but if they had, ther would much have been stolne by the rude company y$^t$ belonged to these 2. ships, which were allmost all ashore. But a trusty company was plased within, as well as those that with wet-cloaths & other means kept of y$^e$ fire without, that if necessitie required they might have them out with all speed. For y$^{ey}$ suspected some malicious dealling, if not plaine treacherie, and whether it was only suspition or no, God knows; but this is certaine, that when y$^e$ tumulte was greatest, ther was a voyce heard (but from whom it was not knowne) that bid them looke well aboute them, for all were not freinds y$^t$ were near them. And shortly after, when the vemencie of y$^e$ fire was over, smoke was seen to arise within a shed y$^t$ was joynd to y$^e$ end of y$^e$ storehouse, [183] which was watled up with bowes, in y$^e$ withered leaves wherof y$^e$ fire was kindled, which some, runing to quench, found a longe firebrand of an ell longe, lying under y$^e$ wale on y$^e$ inside, which could not possibly come there by cassualtie, but must be laid ther by some hand, in y$^e$ judgmente of all that saw it. But God kept them from this deanger, what ever was intended. -Bradford, William, <u>Bradford's History of Plymouth Plantation</u>, Boston, 1898, (1623).

# Table of Contents

The Liberty Tree

Dedication: To "Alfred F. Young, a Giant of a Historian"- J.L. Bell ........................... 3
    1623- November 5: Earliest recorded celebration of Pope's Day in New England. Bonfire at Plymouth Plantation ........................... 7

Table of Contents ........................... 8
........................... 8

Preface ........................... 16
    Evolution ........................... 17
  Volleyball/ Force Field Analogy ........................... 19

Introduction ........................... 21
    Definition: Heteroglossia ........................... 21
    Definition: Dark Matter~ ........................... 23

Orientation ........................... 25

Structure and Analysis ........................... 27
    Definitions: Pope Night and Popes ........................... 28
    Pope Night/ Day ........................... 28
  Some Uses of the Term in England ........................... 30
    Popes ........................... 32

Disclosures ........................... 34
    Disclosure of Seasonal Change ........................... 34
    Disclosure and Maximization of Providence/ Thanksgiving and Sermons ........................... 35
    Thanksgiving Act, James I, 1605 ........................... 37
    Liturgy ........................... 39
  Liturgy for Gunpowder Treason Day Book of Common Prayer 1606 ........................... 40
    Sermons ........................... 52

  1668, John Flavel- Tydings from Rome or England's alarm. Wherein several grounds to suspect the prevalency of the popish interest are seasonably suggested; Londons ruine pathetically lamented; arguments to disswade from the popish religion, are urged; and the duties of Christians in this time of common danger, and distraction perswaded. Cambridge, Mass.: Printed [by Samuel Green], in the year 1668. ... 52

1719, Cotton Mather - Mirabilia Dei: An Essay on the Very Seasonable & Remarkable Interpositions of the Divine Providence, to Rescue & Relieve Distressed People, Brought Unto the Very Point of Perishing; Especially Relating to That Twice-Memorable Fifth of November ... 54

Cotton Mather ... 63

Some thoughts about this sermon... ... 63

1745- The folly and perjury of the rebellion in Scotland, display'd: in a sermon preach'd at Portsmouth, in New-Hampshire, February the 23d 1745-6. Arthur Browne. ... 65

1746- The presence of the great God in the assembly of political rulers. A sermon preached before his Excellency William Shirley, Esq; governour; the Honourable His Majesty's Council; and the Honourable House of Representatives of the province of Massachusetts Bay in New-England, May 28th. 1746. Being the day for the election of His Majesty's Council for the said province. John Barnard, Massachusetts. General Court. ... 66

1755-Popish zeal inconvenient to mankind and unsuitable to the law of Christ: a sermon preached in St. Barnabas Church, Queen-Anne Parish on the fifth of November 1754 by William Brogden, rector of the said parish, in Prince-George's County. Brogden, William, d. 1770, Annapolis: Printed and sold by Jonas Green, 1755. ... 77

William Brogden ... 79

Some thoughts about this Sermon ... 79

## The Evolution of American Thanksgiving ... 81

The Gunpowder Plot and Thanksgiving in the USA ... 81

1678- October 2-Boston: A Proclamaton for a Day of Fasting and Prayer November 21, 1678. ... 82

BY THE HONORABLE Jonathan Trumbull, Esq; Governor of the English Colony of Connecticut, in New-England, in America A Proclamation ... 84

### One Of vs Institutionalized Dates ... 84

1630-1651 William Bradford, Of Plymouth Plantation ... 85

1620-1621 Edward Winslow, Mourt's Relation ... 85

William Bradford, Plymouth 1623, Harvest and Thanksgiving Day ... 86

### Institutionalized Celebration ... 86

By the United States in Congress Assembled, PROCLAMATION ... 86

1778 By the United States in Congress assembled. A PROCLAMATION ... 87

1780 By the United States in Congress assembled. A PROCLAMATION ... 89

1781 By the United States in Congress assembled. A PROCLAMATION ... 90

1782 By the United States in Congress assembled. A PROCLAMATION ... 91

1783 By the United States in Congress assembled. A PROCLAMATION ... 91

1784 By the United States in Congress assembled. A PROCLAMATION. ... 92

### First Presidential Proclamation ... 94

1789- THANKSGIVING DAY, BY THE PRESIDENT OF THE UNITED STATES OF AMERICA - A PROCLAMATION, George Washington ... 94

### National Holiday- Lincoln ... 95

1863- By the President of the United States of America, A Proclamation ... 95

### Disclosing the Seasonal Mysteries ... 96

    Puritans The fifth and Thanksgiving ........................................................... 98
William DeLoss Love, The Fast and Thanksgiving Days of New England, 1895 ........................ 98
1675? - UNCLE TRACY'S THANKSGIVING ........................................................... 112
    Thanksgivings Day Parades and Fantasticals ........................................................... 113
The Fantasticals and Target Compnies, N.Y. Times Nov. 28, 1873, p.8 ........................ 114
1909- (1870) The Surviving Fantasticals ........................................................... 114
New York boys in a wide range of curious garments, 1911. ........................................................... 116
1999- Elizabeth Pleck, "The making of the domestic occasion: The history of Thanksgiving in the United States" ........................ 117
1898- William Shepard Walsh, "Curiosities of popular customs and of rites, ceremonies, observances". ........................ 117
1833-Grand Fantastical Parade, New-York, Dec 2d. ........................................................... 119
1867- Holiday Street, Fantasticals, New York ........................................................... 120
1897-Thanksgiving Parade, New York ........................................................... 121
1910-15- Thanksgiving Maskers, New York ........................................................... 122
1910- Thanksgiving Maskers, New York ........................................................... 123
The River Press, Montana, November 29, 1911, Ma ........................................................... 124
The Transition from Ragammuffin to Halloween and Thanksgiving ........................................................... 125
1896- New York ........................................................... 125
    Conclusion ........................................................... 127
    The Theology of the Effigy ........................................................... 128
The Mock Execution and Burning of the Effigy of Haman ........................................................... 129
Emblem VII. The Powder-Plot Anon., 1680. ........................................................... 131
    Charivari/ Skimmington ........................................................... 133
    The Evil Ones ........................................................... 136
The Devil ........................................................... 136
Popes ........................................................... 136
Nancy Dawson ........................................................... 139
The Old Pretender ........................................................... 142
........................................................... 142
The Young Pretender ........................................................... 143
Henry Benedict Cardinal Stuart (1725-1807) ........................................................... 143
Admiral Byng ........................................................... 144
Ld. [Frederick] North ........................................................... 145
........................................................... 145
Gov. [Thomas] Hutchinson ........................................................... 145
Gen. [Thomas] Gage ........................................................... 146
Lord Bute ........................................................... 147
Lord Mansfield ........................................................... 148
Judge Andrew Oliver ........................................................... 149
John Mein ........................................................... 149
Henry Hulton ........................................................... 150
Coronet Joyce ........................................................... 151

    Charles Paxton ............................................................................................................................................. 151

# Complex Primary Accounts ..................................................................................................... 152

    1735: Diary of Samuel Checkley ................................................................................................... 152

    1753- CHAPTER 18. AN ACT FOR FURTHER PREVENTING ALL RIOTOUS, TUMULTUOUS AND DISORDERLY ASSEMBLIES OR COMPANIES OF PERSONS, AND FOR PREVENTING BONFIRES IN ANY OF THE STREETS OR LANES WITHIN ANY OF THE TOWNS OF THIS PROVINCE. .................................................................................... 161

    1760s- Henry Knox .................................................................................................................... 163

    1765- Benjamin Carp ................................................................................................................. 163

    1765- Charge to the Grand Jury, 1765 Boston ............................................................................ 165

    1768- New London, Connecticut ................................................................................................. 166

    1775- George Washington, Enemy of the Bonfire ....................................................................... 168

    1751-1752- George Washington Diary from Barbados referring to Celebration of Guy Fawkes Day ......... 171

    1823- James Otis, (1725-1783), Plymouth .................................................................................. 172

    1831- Popes Day Folklore: The North American Review ............................................................. 175

    1842- Pope Night, ANNETTE, (Harriet Jane Farley) .................................................................... 176

    1845- Joshua Coffin, A SKETCH THE HISTORY NEWBURY, NEVBURYPORT, MD WEST NEWBURY .......... 178

    1856- Samuel G. Drake ............................................................................................................. 180

    1885 (1724)- Concerning New England New York and Virginia ................................................... 183

    1867- Harpers Weekly: The Pumpkin Effigy ................................................................................ 183

    1888- POPE-DAY IN AMERICA., By John Gilmary Shea. ............................................................. 187

    1891, Nov. 15, How Pope Night is Celebrated in Portsmouth An Old English Custom, The New York Times. ......... 191

    1893- John, Albee, "Pope Night: Fifth November: New England. ................................................. 194

    1894- Harpers Weekly: The Fifth of November and Its Ancient Associations ................................ 195

    1895-Gorge E. Ellis, Pope's Day, .............................................................................................. 199

# Legislation .................................................................................................................................. 200

    The Law of 1753, Massachusetts .............................................................................................. 200

    Directive of 1761 Masachusetts ................................................................................................. 201

    1768- New Hampshire Legal Action ........................................................................................... 202

# Artifacts of Celebration ............................................................................................................ 204

    ................................................................................................................................................ 205

        Pageantry-Carts ................................................................................................................... 205

    A Silver Beaker ......................................................................................................................... 206

    Du Simitière's Sketches of Pope Day in Boston, 1767 ................................................................ 207

    A Representation of the Figures Exhibited and Paraded Through the Streets of Philadelphia, on Saturday, the 30th of September 1780 ........................................................................................................................ 215

        British Parallels .................................................................................................................... 216

    Devil Cart .................................................................................................................................. 216

Giant Guy London 19th century .................................................................................................................. 216

Pageantry, 1680 ........................................................................................................................................ 219

## Music–Rough Music .............................................................................................. 223

1620- Bermuda: "Musicke ...................................................................................................................... 223

1689-1776, Boston: Drums ................................................................................................................... 223

1765- November 11, Boston: "Musick" .................................................................................................. 223

1765- Caribbean, Drums and Horns ...................................................................................................... 223

1767- Boston: Nancy Dawson Dance tune ............................................................................................ 224

1776- Monday, November 6th, Drums and Fifes .................................................................................. 224

1821- *Columbian Centinel*, Stage Music and Dance .......................................................................... 224

1821- Bells ............................................................................................................................................. 224

1893- John Albee "Blowing Horns" ........................................................................................................ 225

(1973)- Sherwood Collins "Dancers and Musicians" ............................................................................. 225

   1768- Music Depicted In: "South End Forever North End Forever", Broadside, Boston, Library of Congress. And: .................................................................................................................................. 226

   Pierre Eugene Du Simitière, "Pope Day in Boston, 1767 ................................................................ 226

Horns ..................................................................................................................................................... 226

Horn and Conch Trumpet ...................................................................................................................... 228

Speaking Trumpet ................................................................................................................................. 229

1765- Bernard Describes Uniforms and Speaking Trumpets ................................................................ 230

## Costume ................................................................................................................ 233

1707-1708- Silver Beaker ...................................................................................................................... 233

1767-Pierre Eugene Du Simitière, Pope Day in Boston, ...................................................................... 234

1768- South End Forever North End Forever", Broadside, Boston. ..................................................... 238

## Poetry And Amphibrachs ..................................................................................... 241

Amphibrach ........................................................................................................................................... 241

A Poem from Newfoundland ................................................................................................................. 241

1669- Thomas Bailey, "In Quintum Novembris," November 5, 1669 .................................................... 241

1735- Samuel Checkley ........................................................................................................................ 242

"Description of the Pope, 1769" ............................................................................................................ 244

1766- Boston News Boy, New Years Ode ............................................................................................ 246

1766-New-Year's Wish From the Carrier of the Boston Post-Boy, &c. ................................................ 248

1766- New Year's Ode for the Year 1766. New York .......................................................................... 248

South End Forever North End Forever ................................................................................................. 249

1771, 1772, 1773, and 1774- LATIN VERSES PRESENTED BY STUDENTS OF WILLIAM AND MARY COLLEGE TO THE GOVERNOR OF VIRGINIA, 1771, 1772, 1773, and 17741 ............................. 252

Norwich Conn. USA .............................................................................................................................. 259

1660-1800- Perkins, Mary E.: Old Houses of the Antient [sic] Town of Norwich, ................................ 259

Pope Night ............................................................................................................................................. 260

Ame's Almanac 1735 ............................................................................................................................ 260

Ame's Almanac 1746 ............................................................................................................................ 260

| | |
|---|---|
| Otis 1823 | 260 |
| 1845- Joshua Coffin | 261 |
| 1856- Drake | 262 |
| 1888- POPE-DAY IN AMERICA, By John Gilmary Shea | 262 |
| 1899- William Barton | 262 |
| 1930, NOVEMBER 5- LATIN VERSES PRESENTED TO THE GOVERNOR OF VIRGINIA, | 263 |
| The Center for Fawkesian Pursuits: Linthicum Maryland | 264 |

## Bonfire ........................................................... 265

| | |
|---|---|
| 1620-Captain John Smith | 265 |
| 1623- Mariners celebrated the day in Massachusetts, at Plymouth | 265 |
| 1662- Middlesex County Court | 266 |
| 1662- Samuel Maverick, | 266 |
| 1704- In early 1704, the Common Council of New York | 267 |
| 1714- New York, | 267 |
| 1731&1737- The legislature of Rhode Island | 267 |
| 1735- Samuel Checkley wrote: | 268 |
| 1751-1752, George Washington | 268 |
| 1753- Anti-Bonfire Legislation | 268 |
| 1768- New Hampshire Law | 268 |
| 1895- Mary Elizabeth Perkins | 269 |

## Fireworks ........................................................... 271

| | |
|---|---|
| 1731&1737- The legislature of Rhode Island | 271 |
| 1735- Dorchester Neck | 271 |

## Theatre ........................................................... 272

| | |
|---|---|
| The Anti-Theatre/Pageantry Law of 1753 | 272 |
| 1761- Suffolk County Directive | 273 |
| 1877-Samuel Breck Describes "Antics" | 274 |
| 1685, 1775, 1776- Samuel Sewell Observed | 274 |
| 1735- Samuel Checkley Wrote | 276 |
| 1766- John Rowe Observed | 276 |
| 1845- Joshua Coffin Describes Performance | 276 |
| Isaiah Thomas c. 1749-1831, Describes One of the Larger Popes | 277 |
| 1973- Sherwood Collins Describes Popes Day Theatre | 277 |
| Plays on Relevant Topics Performed in America | 279 |
| Comprehensive List of Relevant British Plays | 280 |
| 1823, January: American Performances | 280 |

## Mummers Plays ........................................................... 281

- Mummer's Poem In Newburyport, Massachusetts (1760 ?) .................... 281
- The Memorial History Of Boston .................... 282
  - Food Ways .................... 284
- 1735: Diary of Samuel Checkley .................... 284
- Wine .................... 284
- 1750-The diary of Captain Francis Goelet .................... 285
- 1821- Supper .................... 285
- 1864 Reminiscences by Gen. Wm. H. Sumner. P. 191 .................... 286

# Chronology-Short Entries .................... 287

# Dissolution-Spin Offs .................... 364
- Guy Fawkes/Bonfire becomes Election Celebration in the U.S.A. .................... 364
- 1896- Election Day in New York .................... 365
- 1954--From "The Yearbook of English Festivals" .................... 365

# Commentary .................... 366
- 1609- Robert Johnson .................... 366
- 1742- William Stephens .................... 368
- 1748- James Burgh .................... 369
- 1765- November 11, Boston Gazette, Monday #55 Boston .................... 369
- 1768- New Hampshire Legal Action .................... 370
- 1770-1882- Boston, Isaiah Thomas .................... 371
- 1792- Norwich [Conn.] .................... 374
- c. 1771- Samuel Breck .................... 374
- 1774- Rokeby, Matthew Robinson-Morris, Baron .................... 376
- 1852- Nathaniel Hawthorne .................... 379
- 1854- John Greenleaf Whittier, .................... 379
- 1907- Martin I.J. Griffin, Pope Day in the Colonies .................... 383
- 1933- R.S Longley, Pope Day, Massachusetts .................... 385
- 1962- Edmund s. & Helen M. Morgan .................... 386
- 1979- Gary B. Nash .................... 387
- 1973- Alfred F Young .................... 389
- 1981-Peter Shaw .................... 391
- 1982- Robert Middlekauff .................... 395
- 1987- Gilje, Paul, A. .................... 396
- 1989- David Cressy .................... 398
- 1995- Francis D. Cogliano .................... 402
- 1995- Peter D. Apgar .................... 405
- 2002- Peter Benes .................... 409
- 2006- Brendan McConville .................... 410
- 2013-Kevin Q. Doyle .................... 412

# Revival .................... 415

The Center For Fawkesian Pursuits Bonfire Society .................................................. 415
1997-Bonfire Celebration, Linthicum, Maryland, U.S.A .................................................. 418
# Conclusion ............................................................................ 424
# Bibliography .......................................................................... 426
# Appendix I - Papal Wars ...................................................... 448
# Appendix II The Gunpowder Plot Prepares the Colonists at Jamestown ............ 457
# Appendix III, 1769, Price, "Great Town of Boston" Map ................ 459

Boston Mummer? C.1900

# Preface

A powerful network of artifacts of celebration of all kinds emanated from the national horror of the intended treason in England known as the Gunpowder Plot. (See Volume I). It permeated all dimensions of society. Following the horror came the wonder of the mysterious Great Deliverance. The nation, the government, the culture, the people, had all been saved and no one knew how or why. Artifacts of celebration were created, retrieved from storage or were adapted. The network of artifacts, sharing constituent parts, integrated with society, extended outward serving potentially as many interpretations, meanings and functions as there could be participants or ideas. The network began immediately with a traditional "off the shelf" cultural response to the horror and deliverance--bonfires and bells. Then it was given energy by government mandates and theology along with the primal drumbeat from coincidental seasonal change. Yet throughout, the most important motivating force was the horror and awe felt by the people in general. How did they miss the evil lurking in their midst? Why did God deliver them? How could they reveal evil, remember to do so and maintain the favor of the Deity? This all motivated them, despite their local and regional cultures to unite to "Remember and Remember."

As Anne James noted:

." Joel Hurstfield's contention that the Gunpowder Plot is not merely "the story of an explosion which never took place" but has in it "the basic ingredients of the whole human order" is strikingly echoed in David Quint's observation that Milton revisited the event throughout his literary career because in it he "had found the recurring plot of history itself." Seventeenth-century English persons frequently viewed the Gunpowder Plot as a kind of microcosm of English history. But how they understood that history depended upon the narrative they constructed around it. Some saw England attacked repeatedly from outside by international Catholicism, while others saw it undermined from within by those who appeared to be English but subscribed to foreign religions, whether viewed as the founding moment for a new Protestant Britain or merely a step on the road towards apocalypse, the plot continued to echo in the English historical and literary consciousness well beyond the seventeenth century."

-James, Anne, *Poets, Players and Preachers, Remembering the Gunpowder Plot in Seventeenth Century England*, University of Toronto Press, 2016, p.252.

A Deliverance well worth commemoration, even in our time.

Celebration was never religious, but politicaly informed and founded by theology. The purpose was nationalistic existentialism. It became much more than mere celebration as discloser of the dark folkloric landscape; it became a shadow government a "mobocracy" that served to address greviences to keep imperfect institutions in check. It kept nationalism focused. No other celebration accomplished this important mission. Though drastically reduced it continues though fighting for its life to this day. When imported to the American Colonies it was called "Pope Day".

# Evolution

As the world turned away from national and cultural tradition via Reformation, Renasance and "Awakening" toward personal reason and Science, regional and ideological diversity of expression would broaden the base of celebration. This root in diversity, the confusng shifting sands of public opinion, cultural preferences and trends would not provide the strongest footing. With the Great Chain of Being untethered and replaced by a "tower of Philosophical and Theological Babel" so configured the celebrations faced constant reassessment and renegotiation which continues to this day. The wonder of Deliverance and the mysteries such as seasonal change and the existence of good and evil provided universal purposes and would have provided a much stronger foundation.

1579 drawing of the great chain of being, Didacus Valades, Rhetorica Christiana

The concept of celebration has its origins in a pre-Renaissance, Pre-Reformation world. a time when the world and society were examined on the basis of tradition. This was a world unified by the concept of The Great Chain of Being in which the natural world, the state, religion and the people were one ordered whole. With one God, and a one unified, conservative, slowly evolving almost: "scientific" theology based closely upon tradition and the Old Testament, the one people utilized a unified concept of celebration to communicate up through the chain of being to the Deity in order to give thanks for deliverance and prepare for favorable outcomes in the future. Celebration was an integral part requiring no further justification. Celebration was managed within the Great Chain by theologians. Once the Great Chain became untethered at the top by the Reformation and and by the Science of Renaissance at the bottom, management of celebration drifted from one special interest to another and sometimes went unmanaged forgotten. In this way elements of celebration lost their original relevance. Extreme behavior, such as feasting, street theatre and" mobocracy," economic re-distribution or, begging, threshold crossing or house visitation, was no longer understood. Justification became hotly debated. As the 17th century unfolded a transition was made from a society examined by tradition to one examined by reason. Pope Night celebrations began in this transition. As they moved into the 18th century they became less like disclosures of universal truths and more like temporal, popular, rational arguments–essentially fewer popes and devils and more tax collectors and politicians. Essentially it is a transition from religious, theologically–

based liturgy to street theatre and circus. This transition may have occurred, marked by the appearance of effigies of Coronet Joyce in processions, beginning in 1770.

It is interesting that the monarch, a player in the old chain of being, never or rarely if at all appears, while Parliament's officials are common.

If celebration is to be understood and efficiently managed, we must relate back from later forms to its origins.

Caution! It is of great importance to avoid at all cost inflicting modern value judgements or even the values of contemporary nay-sayers upon analysis. The celebrations, from their beginning, have elicited many reactions from all points of view. Our obligation is to focus upon original intent and configuration of the complex artifact. Pejorative terms such as riot, extortion, theatre etc. are not helpful, even when used by some contemporaries. Additionally, we can never understand how celebrations reflect their world until we can explain their configuration, structure and original intent. A good source for the understanding of the significance of wht we might consider "extreme" behavior can be found in: Excess and the *Mean in Early Modern English Literature* by: Joshua Scodel, 2002. Theological foundations for celebratory acts can be found in: Volume V, *Gunpowder Treason Sermons and Liturgy* of this series.

In a post Great Chain of Being world celebration while preserved in essence, in shared cultural consciousness as described by Doyle (2013) lacked logistical stability and constant, consistent relevance. Perhaps it may help to consider it as a volleyball game where the goal was to keep a complex ball up in the air:

# Volleyball/ Force Field Analogy

-Created over centuries by theologian engineers.

-Designed to keep the ball in the air=communication of thanksgiving to God.

-The game comes disassembled, boxed, encoded in strange language without instructions- set aside sometimes hidden- sometimes decays when not in use.

-When needed the game must be assembled by only one available force- two teams of non-communicative individually competitive volleyball players.

-Once operating shield is kept operating by keeping volleyball (created from a collected of loosely interlocking artifacts of celebration (masks, effigies, music, foods...) in the air and together.

-Following condemnation of a single player the whole thing falls to bits is boxed.

-It is stored in the proverbial "safe place" –its location recorded only by memory.

Therefore, it is difficult to keep everything in working order--the wheel needs constant reinvention. Most scholars tend to focus on the progress of specific games and game plays rather than upon the nature and original purpose of the game itself.
In order to restore and manage celebration we must see it as it relates to its original form.

Through history emphasis upon founding concepts would shift. To avoid this constant uncertainty and to create more durable celebrations, celebrants would be well advised to focus as much as possible on purposes that do not change, those rooted in the disclosure of universal wonders and mysteries. This work points out how those universals appear subtly, disclosed by artifacts of celebration with the hope that focus upon them might be intensified while also maintaining the diverse footing provided by a wide network founded upon a cultural and political diversity such that the celebrations might proceed more efficiently and reliably.

The roots of the network of supporting paradigms once extended to all levels of society and permeated all aspects of culture both in the United Kingdom and worldwide.

This work is designed to gather together artifacts created from those of the Gunpowder Plot. It brings them from many obscure and hard- to access places. This makes of many one; *E pluribus unum* so to speak. I encourage further in-depth analysis and progress toward greater understanding beyond that which is suggested here.

The collection of artifacts presented here is just a start. The celebration continues in a world in which the danger of terrorism looms large and where flaws in the administration of justice by imperfect institutions result more often than not, in painful, dangerous, unregulated street violence rather than the structured operation of "mobocracy". The record shows that Pope Day "mobocracy" was effective and reltively safe.

I hope you will find some of these artifacts of assistance for your own expressions and celebrations. Don't stop there. Compose some of your own. Re-visit the concept.

This is only the first step toward meaningful analysis and explanation. I hope it facilitates future work.

# Introduction
## Definition: Heteroglossia

In order to understand the ability of celebrants to bring many individual purposes of or functions for celebration it is helpful to apply the concept of "Heteroglossia." The concept answers the questions of political and economic historians as to the levels upon which Popes Day functioned with a resounding: All of them!

The term heteroglossia describes the merged coexistence of distinct varieties within a single "language," or for our purposes, celebration (in Greek: hetero- "different" and glōssa "tongue, language"). The term translates the Russian разноречие [raznorechie] (literally "different-speech-ness"). It was introduced by the Russian linguist Mikhail Bakhtin in his 1934 paper Слово в романе [Slovo v romane], published in English as Discourse in the Novel.

Bakhtin argues that the power of the novel begins in the coexistence of, and conflict between, different types of speech: the speech of characters, the speech of narrators, and even the speech of the author. He defines heteroglossia as "another's speech in another's language, serving to express authorial intentions but in a refracted way." Bakhtin identifies the direct narrative of the author, rather than dialogue between characters, as the primary location of this conflict.

In celebration, these different languages, or organized paradigms of celebration, often peacefully coexist, at times remaining quiet in the minds of the celebrants. At other times, violent vocal conflicts can erupt putting the celebration at risk. Any language, in Bakhtin's view, breaks down into layers, into many voices: "social dialects, characteristic group behavior, professional jargons, generic languages, languages of generations and age groups, tendentious languages, languages of the authorities, of various circles and of passing fashions." This diversity of voice is, Bakhtin asserts, the defining characteristic of the novel as a genre. It also defines complex celebration.

While the coexistence of the greatest number of paradigms of celebration, "something for everyone," thus provides the strongest foundation for events, it must be remembered that some paradigms are stronger, more eternal than others. It is important that priority be given to paradigms rooted deeply in the universal mysteries resident in the dark folkloric landscape which will not be susceptible to changing times, fashion or opinion. They act, for example, as the central pole of the bonfire supporting the whole. Because of heteroglossia scholars should not despair when one dimension of celebration for example that of the historical narrative of the plot appear to fade weaken or disappear. On the other hand, the decline of dimensions of celebration relating to the eternal mysteries of the dark folkloric landscape should be of great concern as without them the existence of celebration which should be eternal, as was once the great chain of being, becomes open to debate which threatens all other dimensions ranging from warmth and pure fun to nationalism and commerce. This sort of implosion occurred when the purposes of mobocracy dominated celebration in the United States in the late 18th century and in Britain prior to Victorian reforms. In the United States in 1783 Mobocracy was made obsolete by the more perfect Democracy, while in Britain it was displaced by the reformed Victorian government by the revocation of the official holiday in 1859. (See below)

The situation is not hopeless; once constructed, paradigms like artifacts of celebration can be curated and may appear in use in another time. Weakening and disappearance are to some degree reversible. The image below by Paul Sandby, an Aquatint with etching entitled: <u>Windsor Castle from the lower court on the 5th of November</u>, published in 1776, illustrates well the "heteroglossia" of bonfire. What appears to be a single event is actually a storm of many

events co-existing, networked together each of which involved some degree of planning, possible financial investment, and perhaps manufacture or curating of props and costumes. Some activities cost money, some were speculative ventures designed to make money. Most of the complex artifacts had been constructed long ago and were implemented by trained specialists who hauled them out often at a moment's notice such as for victories, annaversaries, accession dates and special visits as needed. Celebrations of the Great Deliverance were in this regard no different. What set them appart is their link to fundimental disclosure of so many universal aspects of the dark historical landscape.

Note the presence of soldiers. No dimension can exist without some sort of permission or sanction/tolerance from others. Apprentices in New England could not celebrate without the consent of masters. Masters had to have the consent of government officials. The public at large judged the pageantry ~condemning the losers to the bonfire. Groups working on dimensions/levels of celebration are represented by artifacts of celebration which they bring to the whole, are interdependent, at equilibrium, within levels of tolerance. The configuration of any dimension is set by both internal negotiation within the sub-group of celebrants and negotiation with the entire community including law enforcement by government.

> "The question remains how does such a heterogeneous group of individuals come to cooperate on such mutually agreeable terms?
> Cross cultural and cross class cooperation had long been practiced in the colonies in the form of festivals. Many festivals allowed the lower classes to take control and reverse, albeit temporarily, their social position with betters. Festivals provided common experiences and the opportunities for otherwise unrelated groups the chance for cooperation. Popular culture found festivals as forums of expression, where other forums in society such as politics and newspapers excluded the masses."
>
> *(Re. Pope Night)*
>
> -Apgar, Peter, *Festivals of Colonial America: From Celebration to Revolution,* M.A. Thesis. 1995, p. 26.

The answer is in the concept that the primary unifying foundation lies in the universal dark folkloric landscape, and methods for its disclosure.

## Definition: Dark Matter-

"Dark matter is a kind of matter that accounts for most of the matter in the entire universe. Dark matter is one of the greatest mysteries in modern astrophysics. It cannot be seen directly with telescopes; evidently it neither emits nor absorbs light or other electromagnetic radiation at any significant level. It is otherwise hypothesized to simply be matter that is not reactant to light. Instead, the existence and properties of dark matter are inferred from its gravitational effects on visible matter, radiation, and the large-scale structure of the universe. According to the Planck mission team, and based on the standard model of cosmology, the total mass−energy of the known universe contains 4.9% ordinary matter, 26.8% dark matter and 68.3% dark energy Thus, dark matter is estimated to constitute 84.5% of the total matter in the universe, while dark energy plus dark matter constitute 95.1% of the total content of the universe."

-Wikipedia (verified)

I propose that the dark folkloric landscape is disclosed or inferred by artifacts of celebration, customs, spirits etc....... It is proven by the existence of certain causal dimensions such as deliverance, seasonal change and the existence of good and evil. If people do not take evasive action these dimensions can cause negative effects, therefore, the need for disclosure.

A concept similar to my concept of" the dark folkloric world is found in the Nicene Creed, a profession of faith widely used in Christian liturgy. It is called Nicene because originally adopted in the city of Nicaea (present day Iznik, Turkey) by the First Council of Nicaea in 325. In 381, it was amended at the First Council of Constantinople, and the amended form is referred to as the Nicene or the Niceno Constantinopolitan Creed.
The relevant parts of the creed are below:

First Council of Nicea (325)
We believe in one God, the Father Almighty, Maker of all things visible and **invisible**.

First Council of Constantinople (381)
We believe in one God, the Father Almighty, Maker *of heaven and earth, and* of all things visible and **invisible.**

Note that the unseen "invisible" world is distinct from both the material world "visible" and from "Heaven".

In the Bible the following passages refer to the unseen world: . First Corinthians 12 and 14, Gospel of John (sending of the Spirit), Acts 2, 1 Peter 1:12, Didache 11, Shepherd of Hermas, Mandate 11, and the accounts of Montanism. For a good discussion of the Pneuma and spirit world see: Clint Tibbs, <u>Religious Experience of the Pneuma: Communication with the Spirit World in 1 Corinthians 12 and 14</u>, 2007.

One way disclosure is advanced is by the construction and maintenance of artifacts of disclosure, cumulatively using the broadest range of human experience rather than selectively based upon the received views of the present.

Practice makes perfect!" Without practice and implementation of artifacts of disclosure, understanding and, explanation will be limited. Curation and storage are necessary but not sufficient.

# Orientation

"All right," said Susan. "I'm not stupid. You're saying humans need... *fantasies* to make life bearable."

REALLY? AS IF IT WAS SOME KIND OF PINK PILL? NO. HUMANS NEED FANTASY TO BE HUMAN. TO BE THE PLACE WHERE THE FALLING ANGEL MEETS THE RISING APE.
"Tooth fairies? Hogfathers? Little—"
YES. AS PRACTICE. YOU HAVE TO START OUT LEARNING TO BELIEVE THE LITTLE LIES.
"So we can believe the big ones?"
YES. JUSTICE. MERCY. DUTY. THAT SORT OF THING.
"They're not the same at all!"
YOU THINK SO? THEN TAKE THE UNIVERSE AND GRIND IT DOWN TO THE FINEST POWDER AND SIEVE IT THROUGH THE FINEST SIEVE AND THEN SHOW ME ONE ATOM OF JUSTICE, ONE MOLECULE OF MERCY. AND YET—Death waved a hand. AND YET YOU ACT AS IF THERE IS SOME IDEAL ORDER IN THE WORLD, AS IF THERE IS SOME...SOME RIGHTNESS IN THE UNIVERSE BY WHICH IT MAY BE JUDGED.

"Yes, but people have got to believe that, or what's the point—"

MY POINT EXACTLY."

--Terry Pratchet: <u>Hogfather.</u>

But, if elements of the dark are "lies and fantasies" why then is their role causative, and why is knowledge of them through disclosure so useful?

We live in a world filled with abstract, unseen, eternal mysteries and wonders. We are tempted to believe in "Pratchett's Grinder", described above, -- even though in everyday life the abstract mysteries can be as causal as any physical entities. They would probably destroy "Pratchett's Grinder". They make up the dark landscape of the human conditions filled with dark matter made visible only indirectly through folklore and celebration. To make it visible we cover it, disclose it, with artifacts-just as Vaughn Williams does with music:

"Before going any further may we take it that the object of art is to obtain a partial revelation of **that which is beyond human senses and human faculties – of that, in fact, which is spiritual?** And that the means which we employ to induce this revelation are those very senses and faculties themselves?"

-Vaughan Williams, Ralph "The Letter and the Spirit", In: <u>Music and Letters</u>, vol. 1 (1920) p. 88.

Once disclosed we can make our way more efficiently avoiding the dark folkloric landscape's swamps, pitfalls, and mountains, to go about our life's journey.

The "physics" of the relationships between our disclosing artifacts and the underlying landscape -the black folkloric matter, if you will- has not been explored. Folklorists have been distracted by history and physical description, collection and recording. Our challenge is to explore this new frontier. The goal of celebration is to help us to live in the dark, invisible, yet strangely tangible, causal, and physical landscape of the human conditions.

Why did celebrants create these artifacts of disclosure, celebration and instruction? How did they manipulate them? Were their attempts at disclosure successful? I encourage you to explore the dark folkloric landscape, but also to take the artifacts off the pages and share them with others. Try your own hand at the work of disclosure.

# Structure and Analysis

Guy Fawkes Day celebrations have always been composed of many cultural artifacts stitched together by many individuals and groups, maintained by a spectrum of supporting forces ranging from the changing seasons to universal human tendencies to political whim. These items are created in order to disclose eternal mysteries. Why are we still here? Why are there divisions in society? Why did life unfold as it has? There have been many course corrections and design changes. There are always elements of the Commercial, the Religious, and the Secular as well as of Un-rule, a benevolent anarchy. The world paused through unrule and waived the rules in favor of a breath of decompression, of venting and of the exercise of exuberance. In this way "Mobocracy" is born as a way to overcome the humanity of imperfect institutions and cultural preasures and stresses.

The celebration has traveled a complex and often rocky road over the centuries, disclosing the dark folkloric landscape to us by the many artifacts of celebration which we have attached to it. The question is- Do we still see it through all the manmade accretion? Are there enough artifacts of disclosure? Do we still value them? Can we celebrate with the artifacts we have and avoid the consequences of a life in the dark landscape without them?

We should all realize that our celebrations exist to reveal and disclose universal mysteries so we might negotiate our way around them as we travel between the immensities of birth and death. In this light our celebrations are not arbitrary or optional. They are essential and mandatory. Without them we are at risk.

It is not so much the presence of commercialism or conservatism that matters, but the dominance of the superficial manmade artifacts of celebration at the expense of the disclosure and adaptation to the underlying mysteries of the universe that should concern us. We achieve balance by carefully considering our universal human physical and emotional needs. When these are being met -when all are provided for -we then will have a holiday that renews, cures and re-creates our universal humanity.

# Definitions: Pope Night and Popes

## Pope Night/ Day

Popes day was a complex celebration in North America, inspired by the celebration of the Great Deliverance of 1605 (The Gunpowder Plot, Guy Fawkes Day, Bonfire Night) in the British Isles which was possibly supported by the celebration of fire and of seasonal change of British and other cultures resident in the American colonies. The celebration served primarily to use artifacts of celebration in order to disclose the mysteries of the dark folkloric landscape of seasonal change, evil, providential deliverance, and evasion of justice, among others. As the power of the Great Chain of Being as an organizing and belief enforcement structure waned beginning with the Renaissance and Reformation, the meaning and "ownership" of the celebration drifted from its essential purposes to functions centered upon pursuits such as politics, theatre and entertainment. Without its founding structure the purposes of the celebration became confused and essential artifacts were discredited and condemned. Following collapse of the celebration its major parts are generally agreed to have been re-tooled to support Election Day (bonfires), 4th of July (fireworks) and Thanksgiving (costume parades). Without the structured rituals of celebration, the emergent nation lacked a formal structure for dealing ritually with failures of government and justice in the community and on the streets.

With reference to the history of Pope Day I cite an expert whose judgement here reflects an important missed opportunity:

1763- Thomas Hutchinson:

Thomas Hutchinson, Portrait by Edward Truman, 1741

*(Gov. Thomas)* Hutchinson wrote, July 27, 1763, "Four of the commissioners of the customs thought themselves in danger, and took shelter in the castle. Some people were so foolish as to say that they might be taken from thence, and we have had the castle surrounded ever since with men-of-war. We have such people among us: but an attempt upon the castle would be the most consummate piece of Quixotism; and, mad as we are, I cannot think we are mad enough for it, if there had not been a man-of-war in America. Mobs, a sort of them at least, are constitutional, and we have reason enough to fear mobs; and our misfortune is, that the authority of Government is so weak, that we are not able to check them when they rise, but are forced to leave them to their natural course. We cannot continue a great while in this state. Government must be aided from without, or else it must entirely subside."

-Cited in: Frothingham, Richard, *life and Times of Joseph Warren,* 1865, p.74.

(Hutchinson's Boston home was looted in 1765 during Stamp Act protests. As acting governor in 1770, he helped to inspire mob attack after the Boston massacre, after which he ordered the removal of troops from Boston to Castle William.)

One might suggest a third path: institutionalization in the form, perhaps, as "shadow government" rather than either dominance by power or "subsiding" via neglect. It is tempting to muse that Had Popes

Day/Night evolved we would, by now, have a rich culture of perhaps even economically profitable street theatre protest.

Both the government of the early United States in the 18th century; reacting to the power of the ritual celebrations in bringing about independence, and the government of Victorian England, reacting to the threats of events such as the Guilford riots of 1866 and 1868, condemned Pope Day and related rituals as obsolete and dysfunctional, in the context of "enlightened" governance. Thus, we are left today without theologically enforced and organized rituals for counteracting dysfunctional governance and must suffer chaotic and destructive street violence and the frustrations of the miscarriage of justice. With this in mind, a reconsideration of Pope Day rituals appears promising.

Tax Stamp

# Some Uses of the Term in England

"Pope Day" was used as equivalent to Guy Fawkes Day/Bonfire Night/Fifth of November. "Pope" refers to an effigy which may be constructed to resemble either The Devil, the Pope or Guy Fawkes. Possibly due to the frequency of the Pope being referenced in celebrations due to his appearance in current events, participants may have used Pope as a collective term referencing all effigies.

1841- Wednesday, November, 10

"Pope's Day- Serious Accidents. Friday night Thomas Taylor, a youth of 14 years of age, was taken the London Hospital, in dreadful state. Owing to a quantity of fireworks in his pocket exploding his arm was frightfully burnt. -George Roberts, aged 41, of No. 4, Mount Pleasant, Liemehouse, was also admitted into the same institution, with a fractured leg, through the bursting of a small cannon, overcharged, and lies in a dangerous state."

- *Taunton Courier, and Western Advertiser* – Wednesday, November 10, 1841.

1841- November 12, Friday

Hone, in his Everyday Book, observes in reference to this memorable day: — " It is not to be expected that poor boys should be well informed as to Guy's history, or be particular about his costume. With them "Guy Fawkes day," or, as they often call it, "Pope day "is a holiday, and as they reckon their year by their holidays, this, on account of its festivous enjoyment, is the greatest holiday of the season."

- *Essex Standard*, 1841, November 12, Friday, p.4.

1852- March 13, Saturday, "There were lots of Guys carried about in Dymchurch on every Pope Day…

-*Kentish Mercury* – Saturday, March 13, 1852, p.7.

1856-November 8, Saturday-

Pope Day. —On Wednesday last, from a very early hour, the little boys were out, disguised as ugly as they could make themselves, for the purpose of collecting halfpence from those who were silly good natured enough in such a way to "Remember the Pope." Later in the day bigger boys were out with bigger guys, and towards dusk, overgrown boys and men were out with hanging popes, drawn about in carts; and, according to olden custom, the "Regular Watermans' Pope" paraded the streets of the borough, levying black mail on the inhabitants. The modern rival from the upper parts of the town was out, as usual, but meeting with the originals," an encounter took place, which terminated in the flight of the rivals," and the total destruction of their guy. From dusk till midnight, complete fusilade of squibs was kept up in the streets, particularly in that part of the town lying between High Street and Hartner Street; and the mischievous ones were not content with merely firing these squibs, but they threw about those most dangerous combustibles, the fire balls. There was also lighted tar barrel rolling amongst crowd. We must say that it is to be regretted that the offenders with the fire balls could not brought to justice, for it really can be little else than wanton mischief, that can find amusement with such.

-Kentish Independent - Saturday 8, 1856, p6.

1898, Saturday November 12 –

The Argus Letters

To the Editor of the Advertiser. Croydon. Friday.

 Dear Sir. — The Fifth Is an excuse all round for wheedling the unwilling copper out of the British breeches pocket. Croydon was no exception to this rule last Saturday, when what is left of the celebration of Gunpowder Plot was on view. In this part of the world, with the exception of private displays of fireworks in the evening. Guy Fawkes Day, or "Pope Day," as it is called in some places, consisted principally of the dressing of children, boys and girls, in more or less hideous costumes and their touting for coppers in and out of the shops and in the streets…."

-*Croydon Advertiser and East Surrey Reporter*, Saturday November 12, 1898.

# Popes

The term "Pope" first referred to the effigies of particular Roman pontiffs involved in the Gunpowder Plot of 1605 (Innocent VIII, Pope Leo XI, Pope Paul V) which was an aspect of the political Counter Reformation. These effigies were therefore originally designed, displayed, processed and destroyed as political rather than religious objects following the British tradition, not to harm individuals, as in Voodoo, but to remind God of the identification of evil doers and that his deliverance from them was appreciated, (See Volume VII) just as incense conveys intentions to heaven. Eventually due to the frequent appearances of the historical and political popes and the very real threat posed by the Pope, Vatican, Papal States, and their surrogates (often France and Spain) to political liberty and freedom (see Appendix-1) the name was given to the entire event even though Pope effigies were almost always joined by others such as devils, and other historical figures.

Effigies of popes were not always named or identified as specific historical popes. They appear

symbolically as the conduit by which evil influence flows from the Devil to humans, leading them astray. The popes are half human, half devil. They are transitional. This follows from the insistence of theology that we should not regard fellow humans who follow other religions as evil sub-humans but as ordinary humans who have been led astray~who have the potential to be reformed, forgiven. (See: Volume V, Gunpowder Treason Sermons and Liturgy) In European iconography Fawkes is shown being followed by the Devil, and the Pope playing cards with him. (Image left: Anon. After Samuel Ward, "The Papists' Powder Treason" c. 1689) In this way, evil doers identified from contemporary events can be inserted in place of Fawkes. This aspect is of great importance as it allows the ritual to continue through time, renewed by current events. One may suggest that the ritual has relevance even today.

Dutch print c. 1605 showing Fawkes being directed by the Devil ( British Museum, Political and Personal Satires, 63).

Devil Playing cards with Pope. (Anon. After Samuel Ward, "The Papists' Powder Treason" c. 1689)

# Disclosures

## Disclosure of Seasonal Change

In North America as in Europe, seasonal change prior to scientific weather prediction and accurate calendars was an important mystery. Even with modern methods and aids. preparation for seasonal celebration is felt "in the air" well before calendars are consulted. Until a season is upon you it is abstract. You can't see it or feel it until it is too late to plan for it. It can be dangerous, especially the November transition to winter in the northern hemisphere. Disclosure of this important feature of the dark landscape is therefore essential especially for agrarian societies. Therefore the date is disclosed by artifacts of celebration and administration. Around the fifth of November temperatures begin to drop and killing frosts intensify. From this time onward travelers confront deadly weather and work outside becomes more difficult. It is important to note that the harvest should be long past and that celebrations of the harvest occur earlier. The Harvest Home celebration generally occurs in the British Isles around September 24. Following the growing season and harvest fields, pastures and, orchards are littered with foliage, fruit, vegetables and pruned branches which if it is not burned breeds fungus and pests. Fires would clean this all up and at the same time provide light and heat. When fires were over ash could be used for many purposes including killing organisms that infest the hoofs of livestock~which is why they were ceremoniously walked through the cold bonfire site. The Celtic season of Samhain which starts on November 1 is more closely related and is a celebration of the transition from light to darkness, life to death. Note however, that the celebration of the great deliverance on November 5 was chosen purely by accident~the original plotters had planned to blow up Parliament much earlier in the year but were forced to re-schedule, thus making the important date selected to be even more of a wonder! The first week of November was a time that, once the crops were safely in, could be used for gatherings such as court and legislative sessions. It was a time for reassessing of employment arrangements to be ready for Spring planting. Hiring fairs were scheduled. It was the mid-term break for the Michaelmass term for educational institutions. In the liturgical year the first of November, would begin the last month before the onset of the advent fast which began around November 30 during which celebration would be difficult. All of these activities were artifacts that disclosed the period so that consequences of a lack of preparation could be avoided. Courts, legislatures and fairs brought people together thus reinforcing celebration.

# Disclosure and Maximization of Providence/ Thanksgiving and Sermons

Our continued deliverance from evil is an important mystery. The deity is abstract, invisible. The process needs to be disclosed so we can avoid God's wrath and get out of the way! Why are we saved and not others? Theology was created to figure this out. Theologians agreed that deliverance from evil cannot be taken for granted—even by a chosen people. They instruct us to follow the good life, live righteously, seek forgiveness for our sins and most importantly plant trees of thanksgiving in the orchards of deliverance so as to have a good chance of being saved in the future. God's positive intervention was not guaranteed.

Sermons served to orient, unify and guide the nationed. They reached both the illiterate and all levels of society via public presentation and accessible publication. As Anne James noted:

> "…the development of the occasional political sermon recognized that ordinary people, even the illiterate, contributed, through thanksgiving and obedience, to ensuring their nation's peace and spiritual health. Between 1606 and 1641 writers and translators of Anglo-Latin Gunpowder epics increasingly reinforced this role, as their faith in the will and ability of a godly monarch to sustain God's favor declined.

-James, Anne, *Poets, Players and Preachers, Remembering the Gunpowder Plot in Seventeenth Century England*, University of Toronto Press, 2016, p.252.

There was not the concept of "master race". Though oft chosen the people could only do their mortal best to be chosen again. Thanksgiving was taken seriously. This called for prayer and thanksgiving such that our bones would ache. Sacrifice included righteous gluttony and expenditures of all kinds. Risks could be taken!

The celebration in the colonies had the same structure as that in Britain.

1. Bonfire
2. Sermons and liturgy
3. Red Letter Days, feasting, consumption of alcohol
4. Pageantry, procession, tableaux
5. Commercial and individual house visitation with effigies
6. Intrusive Mummer's play, threshold crossing
7. "Mobocracy" – Addressing of outstanding grievances via extra formal judicial means
8. Rough music and chants

All of these were to be pursued fervently and righteously as sacrifices as defined by theologins. Participation was to be taken to the limit. For more, see the S,ermons volume: Volume V, *Gunpowder Treason Sermons and Liturgy*

Prayers communicate to the deity but smoke also works. Incense can be burned, candles lit but for our purposes effigies of evil doers can be burned to send them to the deity to indicate that we know who is responsible. In so doing deliverance is acknowledged. Bell ringing also sent important messages of thanksgiving.

Sermons, liturgies and prayers all bring people together. Church dinners and "ales" are scheduled and soon enough you have a celebration. Most importantly, in the English tradition liturgies and prayers of thanksgiving were required by law well into the 19th century.

From Gunpowder Treason Liturgy 1662, Book of Common Prayer

# Thanksgiving Act, James I, 1605

1605- Thanksgiving Act

In the Third Year of King *James*

An ACT for a publicke Thanks-giving to Almighty God, on the fifth day of November every Year.

For as much as Almighty God hath in all Ages shewed his Power and Mercy, in the miraculous and gracious deliverance of his Church, and in the protection of Religious Kings and States And that no Nation of the earth hath been blessed with greater benefits then this Kingdom now enjoyeth, having the true and free protection of the Gospel under our most Soveraigne Lord, King James, the most Great, Learned, and Religious King that ever reigned therein, inriched with a most hopeful and plentiful Progenie, proceeding out of his Royal loynes, promising continuance of this happiness and possession to all posterity: the which many Malignant and Devillish Papists, Jesuites and Seminary Priests much envying and fearing, conspired most horribly, when the kings most excellent Majesty, the Queen, the Prince, and all the Lords Spiritual and Temporal, and Commons would have been assembled in the Upper-house of Parliament upon the fifth of November, in the year of our Lord one thousand six hundred and five, suddenly to have blown up the said whole house with Gun-powder; an invention so inhumane, barbarous, and cruel, as the like was never before heard of, and was (as some of the principal Conspirators hereof confess) purposely devised and concluded to be done in the said house, that where sundry, necessary, and Religious Laws for preservation of the Church and State were made, which they falsely and slanderously term cruel Laws, enacted against them and their Religion, both place and persons should all be destroyed and blown up at once, which would have turned to the utter ruine of this whole kingdom, had it not pleased Allmighty God, by inspiring the Kings most excellent Majesty with a Divine Spirit, to interpret some dark phrases of a Letter shewed to his Majesty, above and beyond all ordinary construction, thereby miraculously discovering this hidden treason not many hours before the appointed time for the Execution thereof: Therefore the Kings most excellent Majesty, the Lords Spiritual and temporal, and all his Majesties faithful and loving Subjects, do most truly acknowledge this great and infinite Blessing to have proceeded meerly from God his great mercy, and to his most holy name do ascribe all honor, Glory and Praise: and to the end, this unfeigned thankfulness may never be forgotten, but be had in a perpetual remembrance, that all ages to come may yield praises to his Divine Majesty for the same, and have in perpetual memory, This joyful day of deliverance.

Be it therefore enacted by the Kings most excellent Majesty, the Lords Spiritual and Temporal, and the Commons in this present Parliament assembled, and by the Authority of the same, that all and singular Ministers in every Cathedral and Parish Church or other usuall place for common Prayer, within this Realm of England, and the Dominions of the same, shall always upon the fifth day of November, say morning Prayer, and give unto Almighty God, thanks for this most happy Deliverance.

And that all and every Person and Persons inhabiting within this Realm of England, and the Dominions of the same, shall always upon that day, diligently and faithfully resort to the Parish Church or Chappel accustomed, or to some usual Church or Chappel where the said Morning Prayer, preaching or other service of God shall be used, then and there to abide orderly and soberly, during the time of the said Prayers, preaching or other service of God there to be used and ministered.

And because all and every person may be put in mind of this Duty, and be the better prepared to the said holy Service, Be it enacted by authority aforesaid, that every Minister shall give warning to his Parishoners publickely in the Church at Morning Prayer, the Sunday before every such fifth day of November, for the due observation of the said Day. And that after Morning Prayer or preaching upon the said fifth day of November, they read distinctly and plainly this present ACT.
F I N I S.

-As cited in:  England's warning-peece: or The History of the gun-powder treason:inlarged with some notable passages not heretofore published.  Whereunto is annexed the Act of Parliament for publick thanksgiving upopn the fifth day of November yearly. By T.S

# Liturgy

Celebrated on the eve of the holiday, the holiday liturgy laid the foundation for celebration. It is in Liturgy and sermons that we find the original justification, intent and structure of the holiday. We must measure and interpret subsequent celebration in terms of this model.

# Liturgy for Gunpowder Treason Day Book of Common Prayer 1606

Prayers and Thanksgiving;

To be used by all the Kings Majesties loving Subjects for the happy Deliverance of his Majestie, the Queene, Prince, and States of Parliament, from the most Traiterous and Bloudy intended Massacre by Gun-Powder the fifth of November 1605

I exhort you therefore, that first of all, prayers, supplications, intercession, and giving of Thankes be made for all men: For Kings, and for all that are in authoritie, that we may lead a quiet and peaceable life, in all godlinesse and honesty. For that is good and acceptable in the sight of God our Sauviour.

First the minister shall with a lowd voice pronounce one of these three sentences following.
TURN thy face away from our sinnes, O Lord; and blot out all our offences. Psal. 51. 9

Correct us, O Lord, and yet in thy judgment, not in thy fury, lest we should be consumed and brought to nothing. Jere. x, 14

I will goe to my Father, and say unto him; Father, I have sinned against Heaven, and against thee; and am no more worthy to be called thy sonne. S. Luke xii. 18, 19.


Dearly beloved brethren, the Scripture moveth us in sundry places, to acknowledge and confesse our mainifold sinnes and wickeness, and that wee should not dissemble nor cloke them before ht face of Almighty God our heavenly Father, but confesse them with an humble, lowly, penitent, and obedient heart, to the end that we may obtaine forgivenesse of the same, by his infinite goodnesse and mercie. And although we ought at all times humbly to acknowledge our sinnes before God, yet ought we most chiefly so to do when we assemble and meete together, to render thanks for the great benefits that we have received at his hands, to set forth his most worthy prayse, to heare his most holy worde, and to aske those things which be requisite and necessary, as well for the body as the soule. Wherefore I pray and beseech you, as many as bee here present, to accompany mee with a pure heart and humble voyce, unto the throne of the heavenly grace, saying after me.

A Generall confession to be said of the whole congregation after the Minister, kneeling.

Almighty and most merciful Father, we have erred and strayed from the wayes like lost sheep. We have followed too much the devices and desires of our own hearts. We have offended against thy holy Lawes. We have left undone the things which wee ought to have done, and wee have done those things which we ought not to have done, and there is no health in us, but thou, O Lord, have mercy upon us miserable offenders. Spare thou them, O God, which confesse their faults, restore thou them that bee penitent, according to their promises declared unto mankinde in Christ Jesu our Lord. And graunt, O most mercifull Father, for his sake, that wee may hereafter live a godly, righteous, and sober life, to the glory of his holy Name. Amen

The absolution or remission of sinnes to be pronounced by the Minister alone.

Almightie God, the Father of our Lord Jesus Christ, which desireth not the death of a sinner, but rather that hee may turne from his wickedness and live, and hath given power and commandement to his ministers, to declare and pronounce to his people, being penitent, the absolution and remission of their sinnes, he punisheth and absolveth all them which truly repent, and unfainedly believe his holy Gospel. Wherefore wee beseech him to grant us true repentence and his holy Spirit, that those things may please him which we do at this present, and that the rest of our life hereafter may be pure and holy, so that at the last wee may come to his eternal joy, through Jesus Chrsit our Lord.

The people shall answere, Amen.

Then shall the Minister begin the Lords prayer with a lowde voice.

Our Father, which art in Heaven, hallowed be thy Name. Thy Kingdome come, thy will be done in earth as it is in heaven. Give us this day our dayly bread. And forgive us our trespasses, as we forgive them that trespasse against us. And lead us not into temptation, but deliver us from evil, Amen.


   Then likewise he shall say.
O Lord open thou or lips.
    Answere.
And our mouth shall shew for thy praise.
    Minister.
O God make speed to save us.
    Answere.
O Lord make haste to helpe us.
    Minister
Glory be to the father, &c.
As it was in the beginning, &c.
Praise ye the Lord.
Then shall be said or sung this Psalme following.

   O come, let us sing unto the Lord: let us heartily rejoyce in the strength of our salvation.
   Let us come before his presence with thanksgiving: and shew our selves glad in him with Psalmes.
   For the Lord is a great God: and a great King above all gods.
   In his hand are all the corners of the earth: and strength of the hilles is his also.
   The sea is his, and hee made it: and his handes prepared the dry land.
   O come, let us worship and fall down: & kneele before the Lord our master.
   For hee is the Lord our God, and wee are the people of his pasture, and the sheep of his hands.
   Today, if yee will hear his voice, harder not your hearts: as in the provocation, and as in the day of temptation in the wildernesse.
   When your fathers tempted me: prooved mee, and saw my workes.
   Fourty yeares long was I grieved with this generation, and said: It is a people that do erre in their hearts, for they have not knowen my waies.
   Unto whom I sware in my wrath: that they should not enter inot my rest.
   Glory be to the Father, &c.
   As it was in the beginning, &c.

The other Psalmes to be read are the 35,68,69.

Iudica me Domine, Psal. 35
Plead thou my cause, O Lord…..

Exurgat Deus, Psal. 68.
Let God arise,….

Salvum me fac. Psal. 69
Save me, O God, ….

The first Lesson, is the xxii Chapter of the second Booke of Samuel.
And David spake the words of this song unto the Lord, what time the Lord had delivered him out the hand of all his enemies…

Then read, or sing.


We praise thee, O God: we knowledge thee to be the Lord.
   All the earth doth worship thee: the father everlasting.
   To thee all angels crie aloud: the heavens and all the powers therein.
   To thee Cherubin and Seraphin: continually do crie.
   Holy, holy. Holy: Lord God of Sabaoth.
   Heaven and earth are full of the Majestie: of thy glory.
   The glorious company of the Apostles: prayse thee.
   The goodly fellowship of the Prophets: prayse thee.
   The noble army of Martyrs: praise thee.
   The holy Church throughout all the world: doeth acknowledge thee.
   The Father: of an infinite Majestie.
   Thy honourable: true, and onely Sonne.
   Also the holy Ghost: the Comforter.
   Thou art the King of glory: O Christ.
   Thou art the everlasting Sonne: of the Father.
   When thou tookest upon thee to deliver man: thou diddest not abhore the virgins womb.
   When thou haddest overcome the sharpenesse of death: thou diddest open the kingdome of heaven to all beleevers.
   Thou sittest at the right hand of God: in the glory of the Father.
   We beleeve that thou shalt come: to be our Judge.
   We therefore pray thee helpe thy servants: who thou hast redeemed with thy precious blood.
   Make them to bee numbered with thy Saints: in glory everlasting.
   O Lord save thy people: and blesse thine inheritance.
   Govern them: and lift them up for ever.
   Day by day: we magnify thee.
   And wee worship thy name: ever world without end.
   Vouchsafe (O Lord): to keep us this day without sinne.
   O Lord have mercy upon us: have mercy upon us.
   O Lord let thy mercy lighten upon us: as our trust is in thee.
   O Lord, in thee have I trusted: let mee never be confounded.

The seconde Lesson is the xxiii Chapter of the Actes of the Apostles.
And Paul earnestly beholding the Councill, said, Men and brethren, I have lived in all good conscience before God until this day…

Then read, or sing.

   Blessed be the Lord God of Israel: for he hath visited and redeemed his people.
   And hath raised up a mighty salvation for us: in the house of his servant David.
   As he spake by the mouth of his holy prophets: which have been since the world began.
   That wee should be saved from our enemies: and from the hands of all that hate us.
   To perfourm the mercie promised to our forefathers: and to remember his holy Covenant.
   To perfourme the oath which hee sware to our forefather Abraham: that hee would give us.
   That wee being delivered out of the handes of our enemies: might serve him without feare.
   In holinesse and righteousnesse before him: all the dayes of our life.

And thou Childe shalt bee called the Prophet of the Highest: for thou shalt go before the face of the Lord, to prepare his wayes.

To give knowledge of salvation to his people: to the remission of their sinnes.

Through the tender mercie of our God: whereby the dayspring from an high has visited us.

To give light to them that sit in darkenesse, and in the shadow of death: and to guide our feete into the way of peace.

Glory be to the Father, &c.

As it was in the beginning, &c.

Or this 100 Psalme. Iubilate Deo.
O be joyfull in the Lord…

Then shall be said the Creed, by the Minister and the people, standing.
I beleeve in God, the Father Almighty…

And after that, these prayers following, all devoutly kneeling, the Minister first pronouncing with a loude voyce.
The Lord be with you.
   Answere
And with thy spirit.
   The Minister
Let us pray.
Lord have mercy upon us.

Christ have mercy upon us

Lord have mercy upon us.
Our father which art in heaven &c.

Then the Minister standing up shall say.
O Lord shew thy mercie upon us
   People
And grant us thy salvation.
   Minister.
O Lord, save the King;
   People.
Who putteth his trust in thee.
   Minister
Send him help from thy holy place
   People.
And evermore mightily defend him.
   Minister
Let his enemies have no advantage against him.
   People.
Let not the wicked approach to hurt him.
   Minister
Indue thy Ministers with righteousnesse.
   People.
And make thy chosen people joyfull.

*Minister*
O Lord save thy people.
    *People.*
And blesse thine inheritance.
    *Minister*
Give peace in our time, O Lord.
    *People.*
Because there is none other that fighteth for us, but onely thou, O God.
    *Minister*
O God make cleane our hearts within us.
    *People.*
And take not thy holy Sprit from us.

ALMIGHTY God, who hast in all ages shewed thy power and mercy in the miraculous and gracious deliverances of thy Church, and in the protection of righteous and religious Kings and States, professing thy Holy and Eternal truth, from the wicked conspiracies and malicious practices of all the enemies thereof; We yield unto thee from the very ground of our hearts all possible praise and thanks for the wonderful and mighty deliverance of our gracious Sovereign King James, the Queene, the Prince, and all the Royal Branches, with the Nobility, Clergy, and Commons of this Realme, assembled together at this present in Parliament, by Popish treacherie appointed as sheep to the slaughter, and that in most Barbarous, and Savage manner, no age yeelding example of the like cruelty intended towards the Lords Anointed, and his people. Can this thy goodnesse, O Lord, be forgotten, worthy to be written in a pillar of Marble, that wee may ever remember to praise thee for the same, as the fact is worthy a lasting monument, that all posteritie may learn to detest it. From this unnatural conspiracy, not our merit, but thy mercy; not our foresight, but thy providence, delivered us, not our love to thee, but they love to thine Anointed Servant, and thy poore Church, with whom thou hast promised to be present to the end of the world. And therefore, not unto us, O Lord, not unto us; but to thy Name be ascribed all honour, and glory in all Churches of the saints, throughout all generations: for thou Lord hath discovered the snares of Death, thou hast broken them, and we are delivered; Be thou still our mighty Protectour, and scatter our cruel enemies, which delight in blood: infatuate their counsels, and root out that Babylonish and Anti-Christian Sect, which say of Jerusalem, Downe with it, downe with it, even to the ground.  And to that end, strengthen the handes of our gracious King, the Nobles and Magistrates of the Land with judgment and justice to cut off these workers in iniquitie, (whose Religion is Rebellion, whose Faith is Faction, whose practise is murthering of soules and bodies) and to root them out of the confines and limits of this Kingdome, that they may never prevaile against us, and triumph in the ruine of thy Church, and to give us grace by true and serious repentance, to avert these & the like judgements from us. This Lord we earnestly crave at thy mercifull hands, together with the continuance of thy powerfull protection over our dread Soveraigne, the whole Church, & these Realmes, and the speedy confusion of our implacable enemies, and that for thy deare Sonnes sake, our onely Mediatour and Advocate.
Almighty God and heavenly Father, which of thy everlasting providence and tender mercy towards us, hast prevented the extreme malice and mischievous imagination of our enemies, revealing and confounding their horrible and devilish enterprise plotted against our Soveraigne Lord the King, his Royall house, and the whole State of the Realme, for the subversion thereof, together with the truth of the Gospel and pure Religion amonst us, and for the reducing into the Church and land of Popish superstition and tyranny: we most humbly praise and magnifie thy glorious Name, for thine infinite gracious goodnesse in this our marvelous deliverance; we confesse it was and is thy mercy, thy mercy alone, (most mercifull father) that we are not consumed, that their snare is broken, and our soule is escaped. For our sinnes cried to heaven against us, and our iniquities justly called for judgment upon us: but thy great Mercy owards us hath exalted itselfe above Judgement, not to deale with us after our sinnes, to give us over (as we deserved) to be a prey to our enemies, but taking our correction into thine owne hands, to deliver us from their blood-thirstie malice, and preserve from death & destruction our King and State, with the holy Gospel and true Religion amongst us. Good Lord give us true repentance, and unfained conversion unto thee, to prevent further judgements: increase in us more and more a lively faith and fruitfull love in all obedience, that thou maiest continue thy loving favour with the light of thy Gospel, to us and our posteritie for evermore. Make us now and always truely thankefull in heart, word and deed, for all thy gracious mercies, and this our speciall devliverance. Protect and defend our Soveraigne Lord the King, with the

Queene and Prince, and all the Royall progenie, from all treasons and conspiracies, preserve them in thy faith, feare and love, under the shadow of thy wings against all evill and wickedness, prosper their raigne with long happiness on earth, & everlating glory following in the kingdome of heaven. Blesse the whole State and Realme with grace and peace, that with one heart and mouth we may praise thee in thy Church, and always sing joyfully, that thy mercifull kindnesse is ever more and more towardes us, and the truth of the Lord endureth for ever, through Jesus Christ our onely Saviour and Redeemer. Amen.

The second Collect for peace.
O God, which art authour of peace, and lover of concord, in knowledge of whom standeth our eternall life, whose service is perfect freedome, defend us thy humble servants in all assaults of our enemies, that we surely trusting in thy defence, may not feare the power of any adversaries, through the might of Jesus Christ our Lorde, Amen.
The third Collect for grace.

O Lord our heavenly father, almightie and everlasting God, which hath lately brought us to the beginning of this day, defend us in the same with thy mightie power, and grant that this day we fall into no sinne, neither runne into any kind of danger, bu that all our doings may be ordered by thy governance, to doe alwayes that is righteous in thy sight, through Jesus Christ our Lord, Amen.

May God the Father of heaven: have mercy upon us miserable sinners.
    O God the Father of Heaven: &c.
O God the Sonne redeemer of the world: have mercy upon us miserable sinners.
    O God the Sonne redeemer of the world: &c.
O God the holy Ghost proceeding from the Father and the Sonne: have mercy upon us miserable sinners.
    O God the holy Ghost proceeding, &c.
O holy, blessed and glorious Trinity, three persons and one God: have mercy upon us miserable sinners.
    O holy, blessed and glorious Trinity, &c.
Remember not, Lord, our offences, nor the offences of our forefathers, neither take thou vengeance of our sinnes: spare us good Lord, spare thy people whom thou hast redeemed with thy most precious blood, and be not angry with us for ever.
    Spare us good Lord.
From all evil and mischiefe, from sinne, from the craftes and assaults of the devill, from thy wrath, and from everlasting damnation,
    Good Lord, deliver us.
From all blindness of heart, from pride, vaineglory, and hypocrasie, from envie, hatred, and malice, and all uncharitablenesse.
    Good Lord, deliver us.
From fornication, and all other deadly sinne, and from all the deceits of the world, the flesh and the devill.
    Good Lord, deliver us.
From lightning and tempest, from plague, pestilence and famine, from battell and murder, and from sudden death,
    Good Lord, deliver us.
From all sedition and privie conspiracie, from all false doctrine and heresie, from hardnesse of heart, and contempt of thy word and commandement.
    Good Lord, deliver us.
By the mystery of thy holy incarnation, by thy holy nativity and circumcision, by thy baptism, fasting, and temptation.
    Good Lord, deliver us.

By thine agony and bloody sweat, by thy crosse & passion, by thy precious death and burial, by thy glorious resurrection and ascension, and by the coming of the holy Ghost.

    Good Lord, deliver us.

In all time of our tribulation, in all time of our wealth, in the houre of death, and in the day of judgement.

    Good Lord, deliver us.

We sinners doe beseech thee to heare us (O Lord God) and that it may please thee to rule and governe thy holy Church universally in the right way.

    We beseech thee to heare us good Lord.

That it may please thee to keepe and strengthen in the true worshipping of thee, in righteousnesse and holinesse of life, the servant James, our most gracious King and governour.

    We beseech thee to heare us good Lord.

That it may please thee to rule his heart in thy faith, feare, and love, and that he may evermore have affiance in thee, and ever seeke thy honour and glory.

    We beseech thee to heare us good Lord.

That it may please thee to bee his defender and keeper, giving him the victorie over all his enemies.

    We beseech thee to heare us good Lord.

That it may please thee to blesse and preserve our gracious Queene Anne, Prince Henry, and the rest of the King and Queenes royall issue.

    We beseech thee to heare us good Lord.

That it may please thee to illuminate at Bishops, Pastors, and Ministers of the Church, with true knowledge and understanding of thy word, and that both by their preaching and living they may set it forth, and shew it accordingly.

    We beseech thee to heare us good Lord.

That it may please thee to endue the Lords of the Counsell and all the Nobilitie, with grace, wisedome, and understanding.

    We beseech thee to heare us good Lord.

That it may please thee to blesse and keepe the Magistrates, giving them grace to execute justice and to maintain truth.

    We beseech thee to heare us good Lord.

That it may please thee to blesse and keepe all thy people.

    We beseech thee to heare us good Lord.

That it may please thee to give to all Nations, unitie, peace, and concord.

    We beseech thee to heare us good Lord.

That it may please thee to give us an heart to love and dread thee, and diligently to live after thy commandements.

    We beseech thee to heare us good Lord.

That it may please thee to give to all thy people increase of grace, to heare meekely thy word, and to receive it with pure affection, & to bring forth the fruits of the Spirit.

    We beseech thee to heare us good Lord.

That it may please thee to bring into the way of truth, all such as have erred, and are deceived.

    We beseech thee to heare us good Lord.

That it may please thee to strengthen such as doe stand, and to comfort and heal the weake hearted, and to raise up them that fail, and finally to beate downe Satan under our feete.

    We beseech thee to heare us good Lord.

That it may please thee to succour, helpe, and comfort all that bee in danger, necessitie, and tribulation.

    We beseech thee to heare us good Lord.

That it may please thee to preserve all that travaile by land or by water, all women labouring of childe, all sicke persons and young children, and to shew thy pitie upon all prisoners and captives.

    We beseech thee to heare us good Lord.

That it may please thee to defend and provide for the fatherlesse children and widowes, and all that be desolate and oppressed.

    We beseech thee to heare us good Lord.

That it may please thee to have mercie upon all men.

    We beseech thee to heare us good Lord.

That it may please thee to forgive our enemies, persecutours and slaunderers, and to turne their hearts.
    We beseech thee to heare us good Lord.
That it may please thee to give and preserve to our use the kindly fruits of the earth, so as in due time we may injoy them.
    We beseech thee to heare us good Lord.
That it may please thee to give us true repentance, to forgive us all our sinnes, negligences and ignorances, and to endue us with the grace of thy holy Spirit, to amend our lives according to thy holy word.
    We beseech thee to heare us good Lord.
Sonne of God: we beseech thee to heare us.
    Sonne of God: we beseech thee to heare us.
O Lambe of God, that takest away the sinnes of the world
    Have mercie upon us.
O Christ heare us.
    O Christ heare us.
Lord have mercie upon us.
    Lord have mercie upon us.
Christ have mercie upon us.
    Christ have mercie upon us.
Lord have mercie upon us.
    Lord have mercie upon us.
Our Father which art in heaven, &c.

And leade us not into temptation,
But deliver us from evill. Amen.
    The Versicle.
O Lord deale not with us after our sinnes.
    The Answere.
Neither reward us after our iniquities.

Let us pray.

O God mercifull Father, that despiseth not the sighing of a contrite heart, nor the desire of such as be sorowfull, mercifully assist our prayers that we make before thee, in all our troubles and adversities, whenever they oppresse us: and graciously heare us, that those evils which the craft of subtiltie of the devill or man worketh against us be brought to nought, and by the providence of the goodnesse they may be dispersed, that wee thy servants being hurt by no persecutions, may evermore give thanks unto thee in thy holy Church, through Jesus Christ our Lord.


O Lord arise, helpe us, and deliver us for thy Names sake.
O God, we have heard with our eares,
and our fathers have declared unto us,
the noble workes that thou diddest in their dayes,
and in the olde time before them.
    O Lord arise, helpe us, and deliver us for thine honour.
Glory be to the Father, and to the Sonne, &c.
    As it was in the beginning, is now, &c.
From our enemies defend us, O Christ.
    Graciously look upon our afflictions.

Pitifully behold the sorrowes of our hears.
    Mercifully forgive the sinnes of thy people.
Favourably with mercy heare our prayers.
    O Sonne of David have mercy upon us.
Both now and ever vouchsafe to heare us, O Christ.
    Graciously heare us, O Christ,
      Graciously heare us, O Lord Christ.
        The Versicle.
O Lord let thy mercy be shewed upon us.
      The answere.

As we do put out trust in thee.

Eternall God, and our most mighty protectour, wee thy people of this Land, confesse our selves, above all the Nations of the earth, infinitely bound unto thy heavenly Majestie, for thy many unspeakeable benefits conferred and heaped upon us, especially for planting thy Gospel among us, and placing over us a most gracious King, a faithfull professor and defender of the same; both which exasperate the enemies of true Religion and enrage their thoughts to the invention of most dreadfull designes: All which notwithstanding it hath pleased thee hitherto either to prevent or overthrow, at this time principally thou hast most strangely discovered an horrible and cruel plot and device, for the massacring as well of the deare Servant and our dread Soveraigne, as of the chiefe States, assembled in thy feare, for the continuance of the truth and good of this Realme. Wee humbly present our selves at thy feete, admiring thy might and wisedome, and acknowledging thy grace and favour, in preserving them and the whole Realme, by their safetie, beseeching thee for thy Sonne Jesus Christ his sake. To continue still thy care over us, and to shield our gracious King under the shadow of thy wings, that no mischievous attempt may come neere, nor the sonnes of wickedness may hurt him, but that under him we may still enjoy this his peaceable government, with the profession of the Gospel of thy Sonne Chirst Jesus, to whom with thee and the holy Ghost, &c.

O God, infinite in power and of endlesse mercie, wee give thee all possible thankes, that it hath pleased thee so miraculously to discover, and defeat the mischievous plots of thine and our enemies: thou hast delivered our dread Soveraigne from the snare of the fowler, and his Nobles from the fire and the fury of the wicked: hee shall rejoice in thy salvation and we his people shall triumph in this thy wonderfull deliverance, thy Gospel shall prosper, and thine adversaries shall bee confounded. And multiply (good Lord) wee beseech thee, thy great goodnesse towards our grcious King, and his kingdoms, from this time forth, through Jesus Christ our Lord, Amen.

Wee humbly beseech thee, O Father, mercifully to looke upon our infirmities, and for the glory of thy Names sake, turne from us all those evils that wee most righteously have deserved: and grant that in all our troubles wee may put our whole trust and confidence in thy mercy, and evermore serve thee, in holinesse and purenesse of living, to thy glory through our onely mediatour and Advocate Jesus Christ our Lord, Amen.

Almighty and everlasting God, which onely workest great marveiles, sende downe upon our Bishops and Curates, and all Congregations committed to their charge, the healthfull Spirit of thy grace, and that they may truely please thee, poure upon them the continuall dewes of thy blessing: Graunt this, O Lord, for the honour of our Advocate and Mediatour Jesus Christ, Amen.

A Prayer of Chrysostome

Almightie God, which hast given us grace at this time with one accord to make our common supplications unto thee, and doest promise that when two or three bee gathered together in thy Name, thou wilt grant their requests: fulfill now, O Lord, the desires and petitions of thy servants, as may be most expedient for them, graunting us in this world knowledge of thy truth, and in the world to come life everlating, Amen.

The grace of our Lord Jesus Christ, and the love of God, and the fellowship of the holy Spirit, be with us all evermore, Amen.

If there be a Communion, then let the Epistle, Gospel, and Prayers of thanksgiving newly appointed for the present occasion, be used in the places as they are here following set downe, to be used when there is no Communion.

Our Father which art in heaven, &c.

Almighty God, unto whom all hearts are open, all desires known, and form whom no secrets are hid: cleanse the thoughts of our hearts by the inspiration of the holy Spirit, that wee may perfectly love thee, and worthily magnifie thy holy Name, through Christ our Lord, Amen.
    Minister
God spake these wordes, and sayd, I am the Lord thy God: thou shalt have none other gods but me.
    People
Lord have mercy upon us, and incline our hearts to keepe this law.
Minister
Thou shalt not make to thyself any graven image…
…
    People
Lord have mercy upon us, and write all these thy laws in our hearts, we beseech thee.

Almighty God, whose kingdome is everlasting, and power infinite, have mercy upon the whole Congregation, and so rule the heart of thy chosen servant James our King and governour, that he (knowing whose minister he is) may above all things seeke thy honour and glory, and that wee his subjects (duely considering whose authority he hath) may faithfully serve, honour, and humbly obey him, in thee, and for thee, according to thy blessed word and ordinance, through Jesus Christ our Lord, who with thee and the holy Ghost, liveth and reigneth ever one God, world without end, Amen.

    The Epistle    Rom. 13
Let every soule be subject unto the higher powers…


The Gospel    Matth. 17
When the morning was come, all the chiefe priests and Elders of the people helde a counsell against Jesus to put him to death…

I beleve in one God. &c.

Whatsoever yee would that men should doe unto you, even so do unto them, for this is the Law and the Prophets.

Let us pray for the whole state of Christes Church militant here in earth.

Almighty and everlasting God, which by thy holy Apostle hast taught us to make prayers and supplications, and to give thanks for all men: wee humbly beseech thee, most mercifully to receive these our prayers, which wee offer unto thy divine Majestie, beseeching thee to inspire continually the universall Church with the Spirit of truth, unity and concord: and grant that all they that doe confesse thy holy Name, may agree in the truth of thy holy Word, and live in unity and godly love. Wee beseech thee also to save and defend all Christian Kings,

Princes, and Governours, and specially thy servant James our King, that under him we may be godly and quietly governed. And graunt unto his whole Counsaile, and to all that bee put in authority under him, that they may truly and indifferently minister justice, to the punishment of wickednesse and vice, and to the maintenance of Gods true Religion and vertue. Give grace (O heavenly Father) to all Bishops, Pastours, and Curates, that they may both by their life and doctrine set forth thy true and lively word, and rightly and duely administer thy holy Sacraments. And to all thy people give thy heavenly grace, and especially to this Congregation here present, that with meeke heart and due reverence, they may heare and receive thy holy word, truly serving thee in holynesse and righteousnesse all the dayes of their life. And wee most humbly beseech thee of thy goodnesse (O Lord) to comfort and succour all them which in this transitory life bee in trouble, sorrow, neede, sickenesse, or any other adversitie. Grant this, O Father, for Jesus Christes sake, our onely Mediatour and Advocate. Amen.

Assist us mercifully, O Lord, in these our supplications and prayers, and dispose the way of thy servants toward the attainement of everlasting salvation, that among all the changes and chances of this mortall life they may bee ever defended by thy most gracious and readie helpe, through Christ our Lord, Amen.

Almightie God, which hast promised to heare the petitions of them that aske in thy sonnes name, we beseech thee mercifully, to incline thine eares to us that have made now our prayers and supplications unto thee, and grant that those things which we have faithfully asked according to thy will, may effectually be obtained, to the reliefe of our necessitie, and to the setting fourth of thy glory, through Jesus Christ our Lord, Amen.

The peace of God which passeth all understanding, keepe your hearts and mindes in the knowledge and love of God, and of his Sonne Jesus Christ our Lorde, and the blessing of God Almighty, the Father, the Sonne, and the holy Ghost, bee among you, and remaine with you alwayes. Amen.

FINIS


O LORD, who didst this day discover the snares of death that were laid for us, and didst wonderfully deliver us from the same; Be thou still our mighty Protector, and scatter our enemies that delight in blood. Infatuate and defeat their counsels, abate their pride, assuage their malice, and confound their devices. Strengthen the hands of our gracious King Charles, and all that are put in authority under him, with Judgment and justice, to cut off all such workers of iniquity, as turn religion into rebellion, and faith into faction; that they may never prevail against us, or triumph in th ruine of thy Church among us: But that our gracious Soveraign and his Realms, being preserved in thy true Religion, and by thy merciful goodness protected in the same, we may all duly serve thee, and give thee thanks in thy holy congregation, through Jesus Christ our Lord. Amen.

In the end of the Litany (which shall always this day be used) after the Collect [We humbly beseech thee, O Father, &c.], shall this be said which followeth.

ALMIGHTY God and heavenly Father, who of thy gracious providence, and tender mercy towards us, didst prevent the malice and imaginations of our enemies, by discovering and confounding their horrible and wicked enterprize, plotted, and intended this day to have been executed against the King, and whole State of this Realm, for the subversion of the Government, and Religion established among us; We most humbly praise and magnify thy glorious Name for this thine infinite gracious goodness towards us, expressed in both these acts of thy mercy. We confess, it was thy mercy, thy mercy alone, that we were not then consumed. For our sins cried to heaven against us; and our iniquities justly called for vengeance upon us. But thou hast not dealt with us after our sins, nor rewarded us after our iniquities; nor given us over, as we deserved, to be a prey to our enemies; but didst in mercy delivered us from their malice, and preserved us from death and destruction. Let the consideration of this thy goodness, O Lord, work in us true repentance, that iniquity may not be our ruine. And increase in us more and more a lively faith, and fruitful love in all holy obedience, that thou maist continue thy favour, with the light of thy Gospel to us and our posterity for evermore; and that for thy dear Sons sake, Jesus Christ our only Mediator and Advocate. Amen.

In the Communion Service, instead of the Collect for the Day, shall this which followeth, be used.

ETERNAL God, and our most mightly protector, we thy unworthy servants do humbly present ourselves before thy Majesty, acknowledging thy power, wisdom, and goodness in preserving the King, and of the Three Estates of this Realm assembled in Parliament, from the destruction this day intended against them. Make us, we beseech thee, truly thankful for this thy great mercy towards us. Protect and defend our Sovereign Lord the King, and all the Royal Family from all treasons and conspiracies: Preserve them in thy faith, fear and love; prosper his Reign with long happiness here on earth; and crown him with everlasting glory hereafter in the kingdom of heaven; through Jesus Christ our only Saviour and Redeemer. Amen.

The Epistle. Rom. xiii. 1.

LET every soul be subject unto the higher powers. For there is no power but of God: the powers that be, are ordained of God. Whosoever therefore resisteth the power, resisteth the ordinance of God; and they that resist, shall receive to themselves damnation. For rulers are not a terrour to good works, but to the evil. Wilt thou then not be afraid of the power? Do that which is good, and thou shalt have praise of the same: For he is the minister of God to thee for good. But if thou do that which is evil, be afraid; for he beareth not the sword in vain: for he is the minister of God, a revenger to execute wrathe upon him that doth evil. Wherefore ye must needs be suject, not only for wrath, but also for conscience sake. For, for this cause pay you tribute also: for they are Gods ministers, attending continually upon this very thing. Render therefore to all their dues; tribute to whom tribute is due, custom to whom custom, fear to whom fear, honour to whom honour.

The Gospel. S. Matth. xxvii. 1.

WHEN the morning was come, all the chief priests and elders of the people took counsel against Jesus to put him to death. And when they had bound him, they led him away, and delivered him to Pontius Pilate the governour. Then Judas which had betrayed him, when he saw that he was condemned, repented himself, and brought again the thirty pieces of silver to the chief priests and elders, saying, I have sinned, in that I have betrayed the innocent Bloud. And they said, What is that to us? see thou to that. And he cast down the pieces of silver in the temple, and departed, and went and hanged himself. And the chief priests took the silver pieces, and said, It is not lawful for to put them into the treasury, because it is the price of bloud. And they took counsel, and bought with them the potters field, to bury strangers in. Wherefore that field was called, The field of bloud unto this day. Then was fulfilled that which was spoken by Jeremy the prophet, saying, And they took the thirty pieces of silver, the price of him that was valued, whom they of the children of Israel did value; and gave them for the potters field, as the Lord appointed me.

After the Creed, if there be no Sermon, shall be read one of the six Homilies against Rebellion.

This Sentence is to be read at the Offertory.
WHATSOEVER ye would that men should do to you, do ye even so to them; for this is the law and the prophets. St. Matth. vii. 12.

# Sermons

Sermons were carefully constructed according to prescriptions composed scientifically by theologians to assist the people live lives which had a high proability of obtaing favor with God. Celebrations were founded upon the customs of the people of Israel found in the Old Testament of the Bible. Sermons are important sources for documenting the evolution of theological thought. Printed sermons crossed the ocean to the North America and werer reprinted there, forming an important cultural link.

*Ed. Note: Flavel emphasizes the importantce of a fervent celebration of the deliverance in the colonies.*

## 1668, John Flavel- Tydings from Rome or England's alarm. Wherein several grounds to suspect the prevalency of the popish interest are seasonably suggested; Londons ruine pathetically lamented; arguments to disswade from the popish religion, are urged; and the duties of Christians in this time of common danger, and distraction perswaded. Cambridge, Mass.: Printed [by Samuel Green], in the year 1668.

EVery faithful Minister of Christ, sustains the relation of a Watchman unto the nation wherein he lives,* as well as of a Pastor to the particular flock over which the Holy Ghost hath set him; and therefore not only ought to be of a publick spirit, to observe the first approaches of National calamities; but also of a couragious and faithful spirit, to give warning of them. Being thus a debtor to my dear native Country, and hearing round about me the noise of bloody *Papists* rallying together, and preparing themselves to make a slaughter; and finding the fears and jealousies of the Nation (lately awakened by the flames of *London*; and the instrument of cruelty there discovered) beginning to abate, though their dangers are still encreasing upon them; I could not but present to the publick view, these awakening *considerations* and *counsels* following; if happily thereby true zeal for the *Protestant interest* might be provoked; and the growing design of the common enemy detected and retarded. For alas!*How can I endure to see the evil that shall come upon my people, and upon my kindred?* As *Esther* said in a like case of common danger: yea, were I sure of personal safety in such a day of slaughter and desolation, yet how terrible a thing would it be to stand upon the shoar and see so glorious a Vessel as *England* is, to be cast away! the Golden Candlestick removed, and the Doctrines of Devils preached and professed in those places where Jesus Christ hath been so purely and sweetly worshipped.

O *England*! God hath set watchmen upon thy walls who will not hold their peace day nor night:* and though men have....

...It is not hid from Your Majesty what a pe...fidi...us and bloody Enemy this is whose principles as well as pr...ct...se tend to the subversion both of Kings and Kingdoms. One of them affirms it lawful to murder any one (though his own Prince) if the Pope hold him excommunicted; and another sets down rules how it may be done,* and thinks poysoning to be the best way What but Treason and Rebellion can flow from those bloody Doctrines of the Popes, temporal Jurisdiction over Princes; and his power to dissolve all Gathes and...yes of Allegiance? so that neither Your Person no... Honour can be safe in their hands; or should Your Royal Person be exempt from danger, yet if this Enemy prevail, How many... innocent Subjects may fall by their merciless hands? what a field of blood will they make Your Kingdom? and surely *the ...can never countervail the Kings* *damage herein* Esth. 6.16. Most gladly at Your Command, would we offer our lives on the high places of the field against them, but to fall by treachery, and be butchered in our beds, is horrible to think.

*And O that God would make our Honourable Representatives in Parliament still vigilant to observe… and zealous to oppose the motions of this Enemy! we bless the Lord for what you have already done, in detecting them so far; but yet we cannot think our danger over, whilst they swarm in such numbers among us. *Hannibal* was wont to say, *Magis se a non pugnant Fabio, quam a pugnante Marcello timere.* he more feared *Fab…us* not fighting, then fighting, *Marceus*. O be as zealous for the Protestant Interest, as they are against it; if they dare to smite with the fist of wickedness, we hope You will not be afraid to smite them with the Sword of Justice. Remember what a matchless salvation was once given to our English Parliament, I mean from the Powder Plot, that *Catholick Villany*, as one aptly calls it: Such a deliverance as ages past cannot parrellel in any Hystory, and of which we may say, as the Hystorian in another case, *Sin analibus non foret fabula videreur*. Had it not been recorded in our own Annals posterity would never believe it: They have indeed studiously endeavoured in their late *Bold Rmonstrance* to hide from your eyes the goodness of God in that deliverance, that so by forgetting his goodness, they might bury in silence their own wickedness; we hope none of your actings against this enemy, will be stained with lukewarmness; if justice be sprinkled with a favourable hand, like a few drops of water upon fire; we doubt instead of quenching, it will rather increase the flame. *Rome* is a •ettle, the more gently it's handled the more it stings. My Lords and Gentlemen, here is an enemy that deserves your hottest zeal and greatest vigilance, much better then honest, loyal *Nonconformists*, who plead with God night and day on your behalf.

'Tis acknowledged they differ in lesser matters, from the established worship of the Nations, but from the tolleration of such differences no publick danger can arise. Some differences in Opinion (saith an Honourable Author) are as the striving of one *Israelite* with another;* and those *Moses* quiets and parts them fairly; and some are …ke the *Egyptian strivng* with the *Israelites*, whom *Moses* smites down.

# 1719, Cotton Mather - Mirabilia Dei: An Essay on the Very Seasonable & Remarkable Interpositions of the Divine Providence, to Rescue & Relieve Distressed People, Brought Unto the Very Point of Perishing; Especially Relating to That Twice-Memorable Fifth of November

## *Mirabilia DEI.*

An ESSAY On the very SEASONABLE & REMARKABLE Interpositions OF THE *Divine Providence,* TO Rescue & Relieve *Distressed People,* Brought unto *the very Point* of Perishing; Especially relating to that TWICE-Memorable FIFTH of *November.* Offered in the Audience of His EXCELLENCY the GOVERNOUR and the GENERAL ASSEMBLY of the *Massachusetts* Province, NEW-ENGLAND, On the FIFTH of NOVEMBER. 1719. By COTTON MATHER D.D. & F.R.S.

*BOSTON:* Printed by *B. Green,* Printer to His Excellency the GOVERNOUR & COUNCIL. 1719. Published by Order of His Excellency the GOVERNOUR & COUNCIL.

*Josiah Willard,* Secr.

*BOSTON,* Novemb. 11th. 1719.

*Ed. Note: Mather places the success of the colony within the context of divine providence and urges celebration and remembrance to maximize future benefits. This sermon bridges the old and new worlds.*

Genesis XXII. 14

It is said unto THIS DAY, In the Mount of the LORD it shall be seen.

AND upon THIS DAY, What remarkable, What admirable Occasions, has our Glorious God given us to Repeat this Proverb of Israel!
As there never was any Man on the Face of the Earth, whose Name has been so universally known among the Children of Men as the Patriarch Abraham, to whom a Great Name had been Promised by our God, so there is nothing more known about this Renowned Patriarch, than this, *By Faith Abraham, when he was tried, offered up Isaac and he that had received the Promises, offered up his only begotten Son; Accounting that GOD was able to Raise him up even from the Dead.* This Memorable Friend of GOD, after many previous Trials, at last had his Faith tried unto the uttermost, with an Order from the Sovereign Lord of Life, making His usual Descent in the *Shechinah* unto him; an order whereof every Word was a Thunderbolt; It was, *Take now thy Son, thine only Son, Isaac, whom thou lovest, and get thee into a Land, forty miles off, and offer him for a Burnt offering upon a Mountain there.* The Obedience which our Father paid unto this astonishing Order, has been celebrated in all Succeeding Ages, and with very many Nations. The Ancients, who have employ'd their Pens in the celebration, have also told us, that the Story was rarely beheld in a Picture, without Weeping Eyes among them. The Pagans had their famous Traditions of the Matter; Especially that of Saturn Sacrificing of his Feoud (?). The Jews tell us, That the Two Sons of Sennacherib had like to have been a Sacrifice to the Traditions of Abraham's. I am not sure, That Satan took Advantage from hence, to draw the poor Pagans into Humane Sacrifices, particularly of their Children unto Moloch. But I find ?hilo, notably censuring and confuting the envious Detractions of those who would go to compare them with the Piety of our Incomparable Abraham.

The Action you know. The Action of binding Isaac on the Altar on the Account whereof the whole Business is by the Jews called, *G---dab Yitzchah,* Or; *The Binding of Isaac.* The brave Young Man, tho' above Twenty

Years of Age, readily Submitted unto this Action of his Father. Doubtless the same Earth which was in his Excellent Father, filled and acted the Soul of this wonderful Youth! But what was the Issue of the Action?

Our Glorious God would see the Triumph of the Faith, with which He had Enriched the Soul of the Patriarch; and at the same time give in his Isaac a Lively and Lovely Type of what was afterwards to be done unto our Saviour. Abraham does as firmly Believe, that God would Raise his Isaac from the Dead, yea, out of his Ashes, as if he had seen it with his Eyes. Isaac is laid on the Altar. Everything is ready for the Mortal Stroke. The Father gives his Last Kiss to the Resigning Victim. The Knife is in his hand. His hand is lifted up. One Second of a Minute more, and the deadly Stab reaches the Heart that lay exposed unto it; Isaac is a Dead Man without any more ado. But behold, God by an Angel from Heaven, Steps in at the very Moment: The Voice of God by an Angel, calls to him *Stop, Stay, Lay not thy hand upon the Sacrifice!*-O most Seasonable Interposition! What a Deliverance, in what an Extremity! Abraham could not but settle a Memorial of this Miraculous Deliverance in the Name of, JEHOVAH JIREH, on the Place where he received it. *GOD will provide*; This was the English of it. You know, That the Mountain was also called Moriah, which is of the like Importance. And you know what was afterwards done upon that Exalted Mountain of the House of the Lord. And now Don't wonder, that we now hear of a Proverb which from this amazing Occurrence obtained among the People of God, in the Succeeding Ages. A Proverb which has been called, *Proverbium Tribulatorum*: A Sentence fitted for the People of God, in every Extremity of Adversity: A saying with which the People of God should animate their Expectation of Help to come from Heaven, when any Adversity comes to an Extremity upon them. The Proverb is, In *the Mount of the Lord it shall be seen*. O People of God, when a Perplexity comes upon you to an Extremity like what Abraham and Isaac saw in the Mont which the Lord led them to, then *it shall be seen*, what God will do for you; *it shall be seen*, how God will appear for your Deliverance. Sooner shall the Mountains of Moriah depart, and the Hill of God be removed, than this Proverb grow into a Desuetude.

Behold, The Entertainment that is now provided for you. A Relation of Seasonable Interpositions from Heaven, for the Relief of the Distressed, is what is now to Entertain you.

A Seasonable Interposition of the Divine Providence to prevent the Destruction of each as are upon the very Point of being Destroyed; This is a Dispensation, made to be wondered at, and still to be looked for.

'Tis no Rare Thing for the Glorious God, Seasonably to Step in, and prevent the Sacrifice, which we are upon the Point of being brought unto. 'Tis no Rare Thing, for the Glorious God Seasonably to Step in, and put by a Deadly Blow, which is upon the very Point of being Struck at our dearest Interests.

The Succour which our God has for us in our Distresses, is often deferr'd until we even Despair of a Deliverance. But when things are come to an Extremity, Then 'tis that He steps in to Succour us.

We read of our God and Saviour, Heb. IV. 16. That from Him, we *obtain Mercy and find Favour, to Help in a Time of Need*. But the Time of Need, wherein the Only Wise GOD chooses to help us, is, when our Necessity comes to an Extremity. And then He takes as we say, the very Nick of Time, to send in His Help unto us.

We may give this DOCTRINE of Seasonable Interpositions, in the Terms of an Old saying very common among the People of God, *Mans Extremity is GOD's Opportunity*. Is there not such a Promise as That, Zech. XIV. 7 *At Evening it shall be light*. At Evening! Who would have expected a breaking forth of Light in the Evening? A Morning of Salvations in an Evening of Distresses! But God will Perform what he does promise. And the Upright shall in their Darknesses have Light arising to them.

We will Declare, first, THAT it has been so.

Let us for a few Minutes walk about the Field of History, and gather here and there a Rose of Sharon; Make a brief Collection of Instances, wherein GOD has with Seasonable Interpositions, come in for the Relief of the Faithful, when Extreme Dangers of Ruine have sorely terrified them.

And here, Oh! Let it not be forgotten,-- indeed, I cannot go on with my Collection till I first make this Introduction to it!--it must be Remembered, That Mankind upon our First Fall, that was just upon the very Point, of being made a Sacrifice, unto the Infinite justice of GOD. The out-stretched Arm of Infinite justice was ready to give the Stroke. The Powers of Heaven shook; None of them could see how it could be diverted. But GOD then did Provide a Sacrifice. The Son of GOD with a most Seasonable Interposition did then Step in; and say, I will be the Sacrifice. Christians, behold your SAVIOUR sacrificed on Mount Calvary; [ Yea, some look on Mount Calvary as an Appendage to Mount Moriah!] and then cry out, *The Lord seen in the mount! The Lord seen in the Mount!* \The World has never seen any thing equal to this Dispensation. *The Son of GOD, Saw, and there was no Man, and wondered that there was no Intercessor. Therefore His Arm did bring Salvation;* HE Step'd in, and Saved at this Extremity! It has been indeed for the sake of this Appearance of the Great GOD our SAVIOUR, that we have been made able to go on unto the Instances which we now proceed unto.

First. The People of GOD in Associated Bodies; These have all along seen the Seasonable Interpositons of His Providence, when Distresses have grown Extream upon them. Let us Consider the Days of old, and the Years of Ancient Generations; The condition of, the Bush all on a Light Fire, but yet not consumed. When was it, that our Compassionate GOD *Look'd on the Affliction* of His People in Egypt? Things were come to an Extremity; And it is said unto this day, *Cum duplicantur Lateres, venit Moses.* The Tasks are Doubled, the Pains are Doubled: Then comes the Deliverer! Anon, the People are brought unto a *Pi-habiroth*; A *Mouth of Perils*; Where they cannot escape, except they Eat up a vast Army behind them or Drink up the Reedy Sea before them. *Well, Fear not, stand still, See the Salvation of the Lord!* How seasonably and Remarkably the Blessed GOD appeared on that Memorable Day! and *Opened a Way in the Sea, and Made a Path in the Mighty Waters!* ---IN the Difficulties of the Wilderness, When the People were come to the Last Pinch, were on the very Point of Starving; how strangely does the Mighty GOD of Jacob, cause the Angels to drop down Bread from Heaven upon them, and the very Rock to yield Rivers of Waters unto them? And be of a Good Heart, O NEW-ENGLISH Israel; Neither will thy God suffer thee to be Starved in thy Wilderness! IN the Book of Judges, how often does our God Raise up a Deliverance for His People when Israel is sorely distressed, and has no Prospect of any Deliverance? What was the Distress of Asia, and his People, when a Million of Rapacious Arabians Invade him? What was the Distress of Jehoshaphat, and his People, when united Moabites and Ammorites, and Edomites, Invade him? There was another time, *When the Lord saw the Affliction of Israel that it was very bitter; for there was not any shut up, nor any Left, nor any Help for Israel*; But, Then! GOD found, I will rather say, GOD made an *Hand, by which He saved them*. Oh! the Distress of the People, in the Days of Hezekiah, when the Assyrian Invasion was carrying all before it! The Captial City invested, and all on the very Point of Perishing by a Blast of the Terrible Ones! But Now, GOD sends down His Angel from Heaven; *Judgment was heard from Heaven*; God shewed Himself *Glorious and Excellent on the Mountains of Prey*. A Thunder-storm is raised, in which the *Stout-hearted are spoiled*. Oh! The Joy of the Deliverance! When was a Deliverance wrought for the Church under the Babylonian Captivity? It was, when the People found themselves in the very Grave; Their Harts were hung on the Willows; They were in as disparate Circumstances as the Dry Bones of the Dead; their Cry was, Ezek. XXXVII:11, *Our Hope is gone.* After This, what a Design was there formed, for the Utter Extinction of all the People which our God then had in the World; When Haman had obtained a Bloody Decree to cut off every Mothers Child of 'em; all in one day; and the Lucky Day fixed for the Execution! Was Isaac ever in such a Mount before? But,--*Between the Cup and the Lip!* O the Wonder-working Providence of our Glorious God! And what became of Haman, and his Ten Sons? Antichrist and his Ten Sons, have cause to think of That! Unto what a Low Ebb was Christianity reduced when such incredible Numbers of Christians had been Martyred by Dioclesian, and imagining that he had burnt all the Bibles as well as kill'd all the Christians in the World, he set up his Triumphal Pillars, with that Inscription upon them, *Christiana Superstitione deleta,*--There's an End of Christianity, thought he. No, Sir, You're mistaken! The Next News is, A Christian Emperour on the Throne; and a greater Number of Christians appearing, than had ever been in the World before! IN what a forlorn Condition was the Church, on the very

Point of giving up the Ghost, when the hidden Remains of the Taborites, dispatched Four Men to travel into all Parts, upon Discovery, and they returned with sorrowful Tidings, that the Church was Lost in hideous Idolatries; only they were told, that there was a few Remains of the Piemontese, which were Scattered & Concealed; no body knew where they were, But this Darkest Time of the Night, was just before Break of Day! Presently, a certain Monk, who had until then made none of the greatest figure, fell out with a Knave about the price of his Indulgences; and this brought on the Reformation, wherein Half Europe embraced the Religion which had been just on the very Point of being banished out of the World.

Secondly; The People of God in Particular Persons; These also have all along seen the Seasonable Interpositions of His Providence, when Distresses have grown Extreme upon them. *Call now, if there be any that will not answer thee*, and will not say, *I was brought Low, and then my GOD helped me! Unto which of the Saints wilt thou turn*, and not find them still saying, *When I was brought very Low, then the Tender Mercies of my GOD speedily prevented me!* All the Cases of the Hundred and Seventh PSALM, are still renewed with Believers; in every Generation. Who is there to be found among the People of God, but what may have the Report of the Hundred and Seventh PSALM given of them; *Their Soul fainted in them; They fell down and there was none to help; They drew near to the Gates of Death; Their soul was melted because of Trouble, and they were at their Wits End.* But THEN! *They Cry unto the Lord in their Trouble; and He brings them out of their distresses.* How frequent a Spectacle This! A Tragedy carried on to an Extremity; And then, God on a sudden, makes a Descent from the Machin of Heaven, and all goes off more comfortably than any one could have dreamed of! Our Father Noah, in the Darkness, & the vast Labour and Fatigue of the Ark; Doubtless he was even spent, with waiting for on Outgate. Anon God remembers him, and fetches him out of his Melancholy Coffin. Was not Sarah, thrown into the Jaws of a Wild-beast, who was just ready to bring an Endless confusion upon her? God then steps in and says to the Raptor, *Thou art a Dead Man, if thy prey be no presently delivered up!* Jacob can see nothing else, but his Brother Esau just upon the very Point of doing upon him, all that the Hound can do; to the Deer that comes up withal. But THEN,--Lo, God steps in, to change the Heart of the Beast, and bring him to Fawning on him, instead of Biting of him. No doubt Joseph reckoned himself shut up in a Perpetual Prison, when an Ungrateful and Forgetful Butler, left him there, and his *Feet were hurt with Fetters*. But NOW is the Time, that *the Word of the Lord Purges him;* The revelation which God made unto him, Vindicates him, Advances him, and he becomes the Ruler of a Mighty Nation. The Rescues of David, how often were these, When the poor Partridge on the Mountains, was just upon the very Point of being Siezed by the Talons of the Vulture! But God was ever seen in those Mountains! At last he cries out, *I shall one day perish. Ziklag* is burn't and all he had is carried away and his very Friends talk of Stoning him. Here is what we may with Good Sense call, The last Extremity! Well, O David, Now *Encourage thy self in the Lord thy GOD:* Thou shalt be upon the Throne immediately! When has the Poor Widow, her Supplies brought in unto her? Truly When She is come to the Last Handful of Meal in the Barrel, the Last Spoonful of Oyl in the Cruse. The Three Worthies are thrown into the tremendous Furnace. How seasonably does the SON of GOD step down to cover them? Daniel is thrown down to the hungry Lions. How Seasonably does the Messenger of God step down to Muzzle them? Is it possible for Peter to be delivered! Why He is to Dy the Next Day; Heavy Fetters are upon him; cruel Keepers are about him; A strong Prison holds him in the Straitest Custody. But God sends down from Heaven; and Peter is on the Next Day Preaching to the People of God. Who would have imagined it? How often is Paul *just upon the very Point* of being offered up? Once he says, Act. XXVII 20. *All hope that we should be saved, was then taken away.* But still, Paul when thus Dying Daily, yet, Behold, He Lives! Doubtless, Many of those who felt the Healing Miracles of our Saviour, were Healed, with very Unexpected Cures. A learned Physician, has written an Essay of much Erudition, to prove, *That they were all Incurable by any other Hand, but our SAVIOURS.* Ask among the People of God: How many will you find, who have had the Mercy of God coming unto them, when like Epaphroditus, they have been just Nigh unto Death? How many have been brought into the comfort of a Calm, when the Tempest caused 'em to cry, with the Disciples in theirs, *Lord, Save us or we perish in a Moment*! How many brought out of Perplexity, when the

Extremity has been such as to throw them into an uncommon Agony? Of our GOD and SAVIOUR we may say, *These are part of His ways; But how little a portion is heard of them!*

We will Enquire, Secondly; WHY it must be so?

'Tis with Seasonable Interpositions, that our GOD will Step in to Relieve the Faithful, when things are gone so far that they can see none but Extreme Dangers of Ruine before them.

It must be so; Because a Glorious GOD will give a Manifestation of his Perfections, and will be greatly Glorified in such Dispensations. An Extremity of Distress, brings Men to that strain, 2 Chron. XX. 12. *O our GOD, we know not what to, but our Eyes are upon Thee.* Our GOD will have All other Help to fail us; Then will He step in for our Help; 'Tis to manifest the Greatness of His Excellencies. *NOW, Help me, O Lord my GOD, That it may be known that this is thy Hand, and that thou, Lord, art the Doer of it!* It compels us to say, *The Finger of GOD is here.* We are compell'd now to say, *If it had not been the Lord that was on our side, our Souls must have gone to dwell in the Place of Silence!* Why will GOD our SAVIOUR do such Things? 'Tis, *That Men may see, and know, and consider, and understand, that the Hand of the Lord has done these things.* We are told, *In the Mount it shall be seen.* What shall be seen? It shall be seen, that our GOD is a Powerful, Merciful, Faithful GOD. Yea, It shall be seen, That our GOD has Angels at His Command. For 'tis usually in their Instrumentality that He Commands these Deliverances. NOW the Saved of the Lord, will cry out, *O Lord, I know, that thou canst do every thing!* Now they cannot but cry out, *O give Thanks unto the Lord, who remembers us in our Low Estate, because His Mercy endureth for ever!* They will go to *Mahanaim*, and add, *There is no Number of His Armies.*

But then, It must be so, Because the Prayers, and the Frames, and the Steps, of the Distressed Ones in their Extremities, are often such as prepare them to *See the Salvation of GOD.* Our GOD brings us into Extreme Dangers. 'Tis to bring us down upon our Knees. In such Exegencies our Prayers will be Cries: The Voice of the Prayers will pierce the Clouds, will reach the Heavens. It may be said, as in Psal. XXXIV. 6. *This poor man cried, and the Lord heard!* GOD will be so Acknowledged, and all Dependencies on Creatures will be so renounced in these Cries, that now our SAVIOUR says, *'Tis now Seasonable for me to step in, & save them!* Oh! Nothing like the Prayer of the Afflicted, when he is overwhelmed! --The Importunity of it, gives those Knocks at the Gates of Mercy, which they cannot continue any longer shut upon.

And why may it not be said, It must be so, Because our SAVIOUR will in this way keep Alive, our Faith for the Resurrection of the Dead. Seldom is a Good Thing bestowed upon us, till we first have had a Sentence of Death written upon it. Extreme Dangers must bring us to That, 2 Cor. XII. 9. *We have the Sentence of Death in our selves, that we may Trust in GOD who Raises the Dead.* The Faith of a Resurrection for the Dead, is the Life of our Souls. Our GOD keeps killing of us, and causing us to have nothing but a black Death in our view; but then He gives us to see, all Alive again. We Live, and say, *The Lord has done things for us, which we looked not for!* 'Tis to Illustrate, yea, to Demonstrate this thing unto us. The SAVIOUR who does these things, will one day Shew Wonders to the Dead.

In the mean time, Oh! How Happy, How Happy, they that are in Good Terms with the Glorious GOD! What an Happiness to have such a Friend always ready to step in with Seasonable Interpositions, when we have any Extreme Distress upon us! My Friend, Embrace and Obey thy Saviour, and make sure of such an Happiness.

And now, *What shall we say to these things*? There will e're long arrive a Day, where-in that word will be fulfilled, Rev.XX.12. *The Books were opened.* No doubt, some of the Things to be found in those Glorious Books, will be the Seasonable Appearances of our Good God, for the help of his People, when distresses have been growing into an extremity upon them. And among the rest, no doubt, the Divine Appearances, which have now been given you, will be found in those Books of Remembrance, with a much more ample Record of them, in all their Beautiful and Engaging Circumstances.

But I am oblig'd at this time to proceed no farther in the Mention of those Things, whereof I must use the Expression of the Apostle, upon the Things that occur'd in the Lives of the Ancient Hero's, *The Time would suit me to mention them.*

Hitherto the Things wherewith I have Entertained you, must have this title upon them, *These are Ancient Things.* But what remains for me is, to make some Remarks upon more Modern Occurrences wherein the Divine Appearances, for our Nation in general, and for this Province in Particular; have been such Seasonable Interpositions to Relieve in an Extremity, as we have hitherto observed in the more Ancient Operations of God.

I am to put you in Mind, of some Things done in Later Times, wherein, *Thou hast Awoke, O Arm of the Lord, Awoke as in the Ancient Days, as in the Generations of Old!* Strange Things done for our Nation, in the Critical Moments wherein we had been all Undone, if They had not been Done just when they were, and if the Mercies of our God had not *Speedily flown down unto us* Christians, *Whoso is wise and will observe these things, even they shall understand the Loving-kindness of the Lord.*

You are all sensible, That our Nation does on THIS DAY, make an Anniversary Commemoration of a National Deliverance from a PLOT, just Ripe for Execution, which cannot be Realized and Considered, without a Shuddering Horror at the Thought,--That ever any Thing in Human Shape could become guilty of so Matchless a Villany! The wish of the Infamous Emperour, to see the Romans United all so together, that One Blow at the Neck, might behead them all at Once, was now very near obtained by a crue of horrid Romans. Incredible! Impossible! One of the most famous among our New-English Divines, who was born on that very Signalized Fifth of November, his Father call'd him Thomas; For, said he, *It will hardly be believed, and this Child will have much ado to Believe it, that ever such a Thing should be found among the Children of Men.* But what is it that Popery cannot be guilty of? How Abominable, How Execrable, must Popery become unto all that will not utterly divest themselves of all Humanity? Certainly, When the Days of Intoxication, continue to this Day upon, as it is judged, about Fourscore Millions of People, abandoned by the Unsearchable Judgments of God unto it, are over, it will be so!

There having been, by a Probable & moderate Computation, at least a Million of Sermons Preached on this Day since the first Act of Parliament for the Anniversary Commemoration, I may be Excused, from any Amplications upon it. But, tho' we come not into a Religious Observation of Stated Days, not appointed of God, yet I am not willing to let THIS DAY pass, without making at least this One Remark upon it, That the Bloody Destruction intended by the more Immediate Plotters to be brought at once upon the King, Lords, and Commons of our Nation, was all to bring in a Popish Pretender. And how any can think to Set a Popish Pretender on the British Throne, without Shedding of more Blood, yea, and this with the more open explosions of Gunpowder too, than the Fifth of November would have shed, if it had gone on, an hundred and fourteen Years ago,--it appears an Unintelligible Mystery!

:How the Old Plotters came to think of Gunpowder, as the most agreeable Tool for them to work withal, Some have wondered, who forgot the Fate of him who had been a Father to the King then designed for a Sacrifice. This however may be said upon it: It is very Surprising, that a Spanish Writer, whose Name was Del Rio, Publishing a Book of Magical Disquisitions, and the Powers of Evil Spirits, Two or Three Years before our Celebrated Fifth of November, puts thereto the very Case of the Gun-Powder Plot, and his Decision of the Case, is, That a Father Confessor made Privy to such a Plot in a Confession, ought by no means to discover it. And now, whatever Hidden works of Darkness relating to that Hellish Plot may remain Undiscovered, until the Day of our Saviours Revelation, we may without any Scruple say, The Evil Spirits which Del Rio treated of, used their Instigation to push on the Conspirators to their infandous Enterprize. Could my Sermon reach to any of those, who are at this Day hoping to Blow up, whole Kingdoms, and more than Three Nations, that so they may see what their Fathers, Garnet and Company, miss'd of, I would Entreat these New Plotters, to Examine seriously, Whose instigation it is, that they are Moved withal, when they have so little Fear of GOD before their Eyes; And they should hear me saying, *Surely, Thou wilt slay the wicked, O GOD; and therefore, ye Bloody men Depart from me!* I would Expostulate with such Unhappy People. When the Just and Necessary Oathes, are by the best of Governours from a Tender concern for the Publick Safety proposed unto you, with what loud Vociferations do you Complain & Exclaim That your Conscience is imposed upon? May Conscience then be hearken'd to. To swallow Oathes against a Dissatisfyed Conscience is what no Good Man would advise you to. But, That you impartially Labour for a Better Conscience, a Wiser Conscience, One more Enlightened; This is the Best Advice that we can give you. 'Tis nothing but a due Regard unto the Publick Safety, that makes these Oathes to be required of you: the Publick Safety, for the Disturbance whereof, no Plea of a pretended Conscience is to be admitted of. And, Sirs, Can your Conscience tell you, That three Nations lying in Blood, and the British Islands in Desolations which would requirte the Pen of another Gildas to describe them, would be a Desirable Spectacle? Can your Conscience tell you, That every Protestant in the World ought to have his Throat Cut, or be condemned unto Louisian Dungeons and Galleys? Can your Conscience tell you, That the Religion which your Bible has taught you, should be Extirpated by Fire and Sword, and the Romish Idolatries established with the most Barbarous and Inhumane Cruelties? Are you aware, that you Really are in a Plot, for the Accomplishment of such Horrible Things, while you abet the cause of a Popish Pretender, who must needs go to do them all! Certainly, 'Tis a fearful Judgment of God, for any Man to be abandoned unto such a Conscience. Or, Can your Conscience tell you, That if a Man be an Ideot or Lunatick, the People are not worse than so, who do not provide (as not long ago, they did in Portugal, ) that such an one shall not Sit & Act of the Throne of the Kingdom? Whereas, a Roman Catholick, bound by Principle to Betray and Ruine his Kingdom, is a thousand times more Disqualified, (as being more Unrestrainable) than such an One! Does your Conscience tell you a Story of Hereditary Right? But, you cannot but know, That hereditary Right, has been many times disclamed, m any times diverted, often Superseded in the Succession of the British Monarchy. If an Act of Parliament may not Limit and Alter, the Succession of the Crown, Those from and thro' whom you derive the Right of your Pretender, had no Right at all; and so by consequence He has no Right at all, The Hereditary Right which you insist upon, (the Line whereof has been so often Interrupted!) vanishes into Nothing. You cannot in any Conscience insist upon it. Thus may they be argued with! But these are a sort of People that NEW ENGLAND is very much a stranger to! Our Soyl don't agree with People that have that Venom in them.

And now, was what our Nation saw in the Seasonable Deliverance, which caused our Ancestors to make this Day like the Days of Purim, the only Instance wherein GOD our SAVIOUR, has after an astonishing manner Step'd in, to rescue us, when we were on the very Precipice of a Perdition to be trembled at? No; There was a Marvellous Deliverance wrought for the Nation, Forty Seven Years before, by a swift change upon the Publick Affairs; A CHANGE which if it had been delay'd a few Months longer, England might have been a Province to Spain; And something like the Spanish Inquisition had been Established in it; But the PROTESTANT RELIGION,--*Whither must thou have made thy Flight, O thou Daughter of GOD!*

But I will not insist on a Fifth of November that shone Fifteen Years before this Country was born. I will rather Stir up your Minds to the Remembrance, of what has been done in Our Days, yea, in the very Year that is now passing over us.

And I pray, How much does the Fifth of November, in the Days of King James the first, outshine the Fifth of November, in the Days of King James the second; on which Twice-memorable Day, there landed on the English Shore, that Illustrious PRINCE, whom GOD rais'd and sent for the Deliverance of our Nation, from a Return of Popery and Slavery, the Two Grand Plagues of a woful World, and of Europe from the Chains that France was laying upon it. How Near, how very Near!-- was the whole PROTESTANT interest in the World, unto an Apparent Ruine?-- Verily, It lay bound on the Altar, and the Knife was just Ready to Strike, when a Great King was for that purpose United with France, and had a Standing Army at his command, and there only remained the Experiment of some New Creations in the House of Lords, and bold Returns for an House of Commons; to introduce at Once the Horrible Stroke!

But the Rebuilder of the Romish Jericho, found the Curse of our Glorious Jesus, to Blast the Enterprize. That unhappy King, had no sooner boasted in a Proclamation, *That there was nothing left now to disturb the future Tranquility of his Reign* but a sudden REVOLUTION chased him from his Throne; An Eighty Eight brought unto the Nation a Deliverance not inferiour to that of the Eighty Eight in the Century that went before it; and a Change came on, whereof he must be very Insensible, who does not make that Acclamation, *The Lords doing, and Marvellous in our Eyes!*

That Fifth of November, is the more to be kept in thy Remembrance, O NEW ENGLAND, Because among the Things afterwards brought into the Light, it was found That the Establishment of Popery in these Colonies, was an Article that had been very particularly provided for.

Thus was our God *seen in the Mount*! And it shall no more be said, *The Lord Liveth*, who Saveth the Parliament-House, and all that was in it, from a Desolation *in a Moment*, and an *Utter Consumption with Terrible Things*: But it shall be said, *The Lord Liveth*, who Step'd in, at the Moment, when all that is dear to us, was on the very Point of going from us, and by an Happy REVOLUTION Enabled us to sing *Our Soul is Escaped as a Bird out of the Snare of the Fowlers; The Snare is broken, and we are Escaped.*

The Memory of the Never-to-be-forgotten King WILLIAM, will be for ever precious to all True Protestants, but none more than the New English ones, on a Thousand Accounts; But very particularly for the Influence which he had on that All of Parliament, by which the Succession of the British Crown has been Settled on the Illustrious House of Hanover, and we see therein, what is most Valuable to a Christian and an English-man secur'd unto us.

Behold, What a New Field of Wonders we are brought unto! And what wonderful Interpositions of God our Saviour, to make Things Turn well for us, when we have been upon the very Point of being made a Sacrifice, we are invited now to take into our contemplation!

Every body now knows, That there was a Design with a Strong Hand carried on, to put by that Succession to the Crown, which all the Good Men in the Nations wish'd well unto. One cannot look back on the Story, without being ever now and then in pain for the Next Events! Without being Surprized & Amazed at the Strange Things which fell out One after another, to disappoint the Design which the Men that betray'd the Nations to France, had brought so near, so very near!--to an Execution!

Our Lawful & Rightful King GEORGE, being Peaceably and Wondrously Settled on the Throne of Great BRITAIN, to the Joy of all the Good Men in the World, it was not long before the Popish Pretender made an Invasion upon the British Nations, and an Infatuated Party of Self-destroyers made Violent Efforts to bring him in. A Seasonab'e Death gave a Mortal Wound unto the Undertaking; very much Dispirited the Undertakers, Disconcerted all their Measures! The Leviathan at Versailles being Smitten of God, Putrified into a most loathsome Carcase, and Left off to *Make the World a Wilderness, and to destroy the Cities thereof.* The Tree that sheltered and cherished the Birds of Prey was most Seasonably hewn down by the Order of God. And the GOD of Battel, in One day, gave a Double Defeat unto the Insurrections of the workers of Iniquity. In One Day did the Lord of Hosts powerfully defeat them, and both Dunblain and Preston saw the Treading down of all their Strength. But He Step'd in, how Opportunely, how much at the very Nick of Time, which Dispensations to be for ever wondered at!

The Last Winter the Men who are like *the troubled Sea,* prepared for another Invasion. A seasonable Death again gave a Mortal Wound unto the Undertaking; and withdrew the Assistences which the Undertakers mightily relied upon. A Monarch who had caused *Terror in the Land of the Living*, was most Seasonably taken off; And therby, as the Oppressed Swedes have had their Gothick Liberties Miraculously Restor'd unto them, so there was a Thing of Great Consequence done towards the Preserving of ours. The Embarcation from Spain indeed went on. But, when there was above an hundred and thirty Years ago, a Descent From Spain upon our Fore-fathers, with a Navy that called itself, Invincible, GOD Fought against it, and by the *Stormy Wind fulfilling*

*His Word*, confounded that Expedition. And now another Descent from Spain was making upon us, God who holds the *Wind in His Hand*, by His own Irresistible Hand, brought all the costly Expedition to Nothing. But He Step'd in, how Opportunely, how much at the very Nick of Time, with Dispensations to be for ever wondered at!

O the Triumphs of Soveraign Grace, in these Divine Appearances, for our most Unworthy Nations! *I will sing unto our most Gracious God for he has triumphed gloriously!*

NEW ENGLAND is Thankfully sensible of the share which it has in the Seasonable Salvations wherewith our Nation had been thus.

But then, How many Peculiar Salvations hath NEW-ENGLAND seen, wherein our Glorious Lord has most Seasonably Interposed for us, in our Extremities? Those *Magnalia CHRISTI*, even the Seasonable Interpositions of God our Saviour, to deliver us, when Extreme Hazards of Ruine look'd very dark upon us; These are Things which the History of NEW ENGLAND is filled withal. *Many a Time,* let NEW-ENGLAND now say, *Many a Time, in Affliction, from my Youth, had the Destroyers prevailed against me, if my Glorious Lord had not Seasonably Steped in to rescue me.* Verily, NEW-ENGLAND continues to this Day, having obtained Help from GOD, in such Seasonable Dispensations!

One Time above the rest, cannot but be Rememberd by many that remain to this Day. Some who did then *Jeopard their Lives in the High Places of the Field,* are now in this very Auditory. There was a Time Three and Forty Years ago, when the fierce Indian Salvages, having Spred the Flame of a Dubious War, from One End of the Country to the Other, Every One thought, the Summer then coming on, would be fill'd with Desolatons, that would very near have broke Up the Colonies. But Behold when Things were come to that Extremity GOD Step'd in, and made bare His Almighty Arm for our Deliverance. The Enemy distracted like Beasts that to the People inhabiting the Wilderness. Yea, Sword and Sickness in a few Months consumed whole Nations of them!

This has indeed been the way of God our Saviour all along Appearing for us.

What a Seasonable Provision did our God make for us, by a Friend on the Spot, appearing at the Court for us, at the Revolution that we might be delivered from a Total and Final Deprivation of all the Privileges which distinguished us, from the rest of the Plantations!

How often have we been upon the very Point, of being made the *Prey of the Terrible*? Those which are called, *The wild-beasts of the Earth,* have been just coming upon us! But the Great GOVERNOUR of the World, Seasonably Stepping in, has very Unespectedly more than Twice done the Things, which have enabled us to say, *Blessed be the Lord, who has not given us as a prey to their Teeth!*

How often have our Churches been upon the very Point of doing Things which would have been attended with an Unknown Train of Disturbances? But their Glorious HEAD Seasonably Stepping in, has put a Stop unto them, and the feared Storms have all blown over.

But, *Who can Utter the mighty Acts of the Lord? Who can shew forth all His Priase?* How long a work would it be to Recapitulate the Seasonable Interpositions, wherewith He has rescued us from Grevious Things, when we have been upon the very Point of being overwhelmed with them! *Lo, God hath sent from above; He hath drawn us out of many Waters.*

The Improvement, which we are to make of this Experience, must be to Encourage our Prayers and our Hopes for the continuance of it. Sirs, Let us Improve our Experience, unto that Argument; 2 Cor. I. 10. GOD *who raises the Dead, has Delivered us from so great a Death, and He doth Deliver; and we trust in Him, that He will still deliver us.* The Syllogism, I confess, is not of any such form as our common Logick allows of; But Faith Legitimates this way of Arguing, and can Remove Mountains with it!

You will allow me to use the Language of the Day; and say, There may be Things which may threaten to Blow up the Country, and Blow up the Churches, which have the Beauty and the Safety of the Country in them. Let thy *watchmen set upon thy Walls*, O NEW-ENGLAND, give thee yet more faithful & more solemn Warnings of them and may their Visons prevent thy Perishing!

But now, Why may we not Hope, that before the Distresses which the Exportation of our Coin thro' the Extravagancy of our Living has brought upon us, be brought an to much greater Extremity, the Methods which the Men of Thought have to offer for the Stopping of that Hemorrhage, will be yet more thoroughly Digested, will be hearkened unto, will be complied withal: And all foolish Animosities that may hinder this Felicity, be entirely Extirpated?

Why may we not Hope, That the Intentions of those, who may be willing to see us a Miserable People, yea, of those Treacherous Men from among our selves, who, to recommend themselves unto preferments, propose and pursue things that would make our Miseries Unsupportable; may by the Hand of our God Seasonably Interposing for us, and with them that help us, have their Chariot-Wheels taken off, so that they shall drive heavily, and anon be all Abortive?

Why may we not Hope, That if any Rash Doings may be likely to Discompose our Churches, our Strong Redeemer Seasonably Interposing, may cause those things to fall out, that will put an End unto Days of Temptation, an give them to Walk on in the Right Ways of the Lord, and in our Good Old Ways, in the Fear of GOD, and in the comforts of the Holy Spirit, and be Multiplied?

O Thou Hope of NEW-ENGLAND (?), thou SAVIOUR thereof in the Times of Trouble, with Encouraged Hopes will we Keep (?) Looking up unto thee!

FINIS

## Cotton Mather

Cotton Mather was born in 1663 and died in 1728. Mather attended Boston Latin school. He received a B.A. from Harvard College in 1678, a M.A. in 1681 and an honorary doctorate from University of Glasgow in 1710. Mather was in important Puritan leader, minister and author. He is remembered for his involvement in the persecution of witches. He became Pastor of North Church, Boston in 1723 and encouraged the people to return to the conservative roots of Puritanism. His most important book was *Magnalia Christi Americana.* published in 1702. Mather believed that texts were important for the understanding of history. In 1688 Mather helped to lead the revolt against Sir Edmund Andros, Governor of the Dominion of New England. Mather was also a scientist and worked with the hybridization of corn. He was instrumental in the development of the practice of inoculation against Smallpox. Mather had three wives and fifteen children. He is buried on Copp's Hill. His last wife and two children survived him.

## Some thoughts about this sermon…

"Abraham does as firmly Believe, that God would Raise his Isaac from the Dead, yea, out of his Ashes, as if he had seen it with his Eyes. Isaac is laid on the Altar. Everything is ready for the Mortal Stroke. The Father gives his Last Kiss to the Resigning Victim. The Knife is in his hand. His hand is lifted up. One Second of a Minute more, and the deadly Stab reaches the Heart that lay exposed unto it; Isaac is a Dead Man without any more ado. But behold, God by an Angel from Heaven, Steps in at the very Moment: The Voice of God by an Angel, calls to him Stop, Stay, Lay not thy hand upon the Sacrifice! -O most Seasonable Interposition! What a Deliverance, in what an Extremity!"

This sermon focuses upon the tendency of God to step in at just the last minute with his deliverances. One has to be true to God and patient right up to the line. This feeling reflects Mather's experiences in New England far away from the mother land, on the edge of the known world, in a hostile environment. Despite all threats, God had protected the people of New England just as he had brought deliverances to the people of the Old Testament-- in the nick of time.

" And be of a Good Heart, O NEW-ENGLISH Israel; Neither will thy God suffer thee to be Starved in thy Wilderness!...."

At the time, it was quite clear that God's actions were the only way to explain the survival of the colonists. It is interesting to note how Mather saw the sickness of the Indians as a deliverance provided by God.

NEW ENGLAND is Thankfully sensible of the share which it has in the Seasonable Salvations wherewith our Nation had been thus.

"But then, How many Peculiar Salvations hath NEW-ENGLAND seen, wherein our Glorious Lord has most Seasonably Interposed for us, in our Extremities?  Those *Magnalia CHRISTI*, even the Seasonable Interpositions of God our Saviour, to deliver us, when Extreme Hazards of Ruine look'd very dark upon us; These are Things which the History of NEW ENGLAND is filled withal. *Many a Time,* let NEW-ENGLAND now say, *Many a Time, in Affliction, from my Youth, had the Destroyers prevailed against me, if my Glorious Lord had not Seasonably Steped in to rescue me.*  Verily, NEW-ENGLAND continues to this Day, having obtained Help from GOD, in such Seasonable Dispensations!"

"One Time above the rest, cannot but be Rememberd by many that remain to this Day. Some who did then Jeopard their Lives in the High Places of the Field, are now in this very Auditory.  There was a Time Three and Forty Years ago, when the fierce Indian Salvages, having Spred the Flame of a Dubious War, from One End of the Country to the Other, Every One thought, the Summer then coming on, would be fill'd with Desolatons, that would very near have broke Up the Colonies.  But Behold when Things were come to that Extremity GOD Step'd in, and made bare His Almighty Arm for our Deliverance.  The Enemy distracted like Beasts that to the People inhabiting the Wilderness.  Yea, Sword and Sickness in a few Months consumed whole Nations of them!

This has indeed been the way of God our Saviour all along Appearing for us.

What a Seasonable Provision did our God make for us, by a Friend on the Spot, appearing at the Court for us, at the Revolution that we might be delivered from a Total and Final Deprivation of all the Privileges which distinguished us, from the rest of the Plantations!

How often have we been upon the very Point, of being made the Prey of the Terrible? Those which are called, The wild-beasts of the Earth, have been just coming upon us!  But the Great GOVERNOUR of the World, Seasonably Stepping in, has very Unespectedly more than Twice done the Things, which have enabled us to say, Blessed be the Lord, who has not given us as a prey to their Teeth!"

# 1745- The folly and perjury of the rebellion in Scotland, display'd: in a sermon preach'd at Portsmouth, in New-Hampshire, February the 23d 1745-6. Arthur Browne.

*Ed. Note: Arthur Browne was a missionary for the Society for the Propagation of the Gospel in Foreign Parts and a minister of the Anglican church of Portsmouth, New Hampshire. Browne mentioned the plot in a sermon that attacked both Catholicism and Jacobitism. He called the Church of Rome "ravenous Wolves"; a "savage" thing. He supported the celebration.*

*Proverbs the twenty fourth, 21st verse.*

My Son, fear thou the Lord and the King, and meddle not with th [...] that are given unto change.

"…The fifth of November is still celebrated among us, and fit it is at the Memorial of it should be handed down from Generation to Generation. I may be bold to affirm, that no good Man unacquainted with the hellish Conspiracy of that Day, could with the utmost Stretch…Invention, form to himself such a complicated Piece of Villany. … t tho' such wicked Designs Could not have even been suspected more they were in Reality detected; yet after repeated Deliverances from the same Quarter, not to be apprehensive of Danger from such human Adversaries, is Infatuation; not to be awake and upon our …ard, is Distraction. Catholicks (as they are pleased to call themselvs, with the utmost Impropriety) are the same ravenous Wolves …, retain the same savage Disposition to the Flock of Christ, which •••y (according to their charitable Principles) think proper to stigmatise with the odious Apellation of Hereticks; and as such, think it not only lawful, but necessary to exterpate them off the Face of the Earth.

Thus I have examined the most plausible Pleas that can be urged in Favour of the Rebels; and tho' I have supposed them founded in Reason and Religion, yet you see they are all strongly in Favour of his Majesty, and directly against the Pretender. The Disturbers the,.. of our native Country's Peace, must have Recourse to some other extenuating Pleas; and what can these be but Ambition, Avarice, Disappointment, Revenge, Vanity, Self-conceit, patching up bad Fortunes, Levity, Fickleness of Temper, scheming Heads, a love o• innovating in Religion and Government? It is not at all then to be wondered at, that Wretches should be given to change, who are influenced by such abominable Motives, from which I pray God of his Mercy to deliver us…"

# 1746- The presence of the great God in the assembly of political rulers. A sermon preached before his Excellency William Shirley, Esq; governour; the Honourable His Majesty's Council; and the Honourable House of Representatives of the province of Massachusetts Bay in New-England, May 28th. 1746. Being the day for the election of His Majesty's Council for the said province. John Barnard, Massachusetts. General Court.

PSALM LXXXII. 1. First Clause.
*GOD standeth in the Congregation of the Mighty.—*

IT was a very foolish Assertion, and grosly reproachful to the infinite GOD, which was uttered by the *Ancients* of *Israel,* That *the Lord hath forsaken the Earth.*[a]

Such a Conclusion, as it is highly *blasphemous,* so it subverts the Foundation of religious Duties resulting from the Circumstances of particular Persons, and Condition of Societies. It destroys *Affiance* in the *Almighty,* utterly discourages *Prayer* to Him for *temporal* Mercies, leaves no Place for the Exercise of *Repentance* and *Submission* to His Will, in a Day of *Adversity;* nor for devout and holy Joy and Gratitude, in a Time of *Prosperity.* It robs every sober and considering Mind of the Comfort and Satisfaction among from an Apprehension of GOD's universal *Presidency* over His Creatures. How much soever the abandon'd Sons of Vice might be gratified with a Persuasion, that the *Deity* is confin'd to the *Third Heaven,* and not concern'd about Persons and Things in this lower *World:* It is certain, this Thought would overspread the Souls of the wise and serious Part of *Mankind* with Clouds and Darkness.

But Thanks be to GOD; notwithstanding the many and great *Apostacies* of this *Land,* our Degeneracy hath not proceeded to this Degree and Pitch of *Atheism:* We yet believe there is a glorious *Providence* managed by the sovereign, unerring, powerful, righteous, faithfull and merciful Hand of the *Most High.*

What but the Consideration of *this* induceth us religiously to *assemble* in this *sacred* Place, upon the joyful Return of our Anniversary Solemnities? Is not a Sense of our Dependance upon GOD, the great Motive of our coming into His *House,* this Morning? Is not the Belief, that He interests Himself in the Concerns of Men on Earth; that it is with Him graciously to continue us in the Enjoyment of the invaluable *Privileges,* which He hath given us; to direct and influence in the momentous Transactions of *this Day,* and the Affairs of Government the *Year* ensuing: Is not this *Belief* the Reason of the …*Supplications* we present unto Him, and the Oblation of *Praise* we pay Him, for *publick* Blessings?

The inspired Book of *Psalms,* out of which I have chosen the Passage, now read in your Audience, abounds in a peculiar Manner, in the Displays of the matchless Glory and Grandeur of the blessed GOD, as the supream Ruler and Governour of the World; it is fruitful in the Exhibitions of His boundless and everlasting Dominion and Kingdom; gives us Assurance, that His Angels, those Ministers whom He hath made Flames of Fire, *do His Commandment, and hearken to the Voice of His Word*[b]. That He doth what He pleaseth in the *Realms of Light above,* and Governs in the inferior *Heavens*[c]. That His *Footstool* is not below His Cognizance and Concern; but that He extends His Inspection and providential *Influences* to all Parts of this lower Creation[d].—And, that the *Legions of Darkness* are under His Government[e].

But not to be too *general,* I shall contract and confine my Thoughts to one particular Branch of Divine *Providence,* plainly directed to in the Words of the *Psalmist, GOD standeth in the Congregation of the Mighty.*

The heavenly *Intelligencies* have the Stile *Mighty* given them in the sacred Oracles. The great *Apostle* declares, That *the Lord Jesus Christ will be revealed from Heaven with His Mighty Angels*[f]: And *St. John* in his *Visions,* saw a *mighty Angel* make his Descent from the upper World[g]: But the *Mighty,* whom the sacred

Penman speaks of, are, in the Context, charged with judging unjustly, and accepting Persons, are exhorted to defend the Poor and Fatherless, and do Justice to the Afflicted and Needy; and tho' they are called Gods, yet were obliged to die like Men: Characters utterly incompatible to those spotless and immortal Creatures who surround the Throne of GOD.

It is evident then, That by the *Mighty,* in the Congregation of whom GOD is said to stand, we are to understand *Men* that are concerned in the Government of a People, those that sustain high Posts, who have the *Legislative* Power in their Hands, who assemble and sit to consider, determine and resolve upon what will be for the Relief and Good of particular Persons, and Bodies and Societies of Men under their Jurisdiction; and the Defence, Peace and Happiness of the People in general, committed to their Charge: These are the Persons, I conceive, whom the Psalmist means, when he says, *GOD standeth in the Congregation of the Mighty.*

In this great Congregation GOD standeth: I suppose every one will easily conceive, that bodily Parts and Postures are by no means strictly and properly to be ascribed unto Him, who is an immense *Spirit;* but without any Difficulty will see a *Figure* in the Word. Should we take it strictly and literally it would be to debase the *Godhead,* and make Him such an one as ourselves[h]: When it is said then, *GOD standeth in the Congregation of the Mighty,* we are to understand (as I apprehend) His inspecting and affording this honourable and important Assembly His protecting Presence and gracious Influence.

I shall endeavour to discourse upon the Words under the two following PROPOSITIONS.

- I. *IT is most fit and suitable, that there should be a* Number *concern'd in the* Civil Government *of a People.*
- II. *THE great GOD is present in the Assembly of* Political *Rulers.*

I. *It is most fit and suitable, that there should be a* Number *concer••d in the* Civil Government *of a People.*

The *Congregation of the Mighty,* says the Text, implying there was a *Number* invested with Power and Authority convened for the Exercise thereof. Now that it is most fit and suitable it should be, will appear from the three following Things.

1st, Such is the *Infirmity* and *Darkness* of the human Understanding in Man's present Condition, as to render Government managed by a *Number* of Men most eligible.

In this State of Imperfection, the intellectual Powers of Mankind labour under great Disadvantages; tho' they may be greatly improv'd, strengthned and brightned by Use, Study, Education and Conversation: The wisest Man is not always wise; his Mind is subject to *Inadvertency,* and his Memory needs a *Monitor:* Tho' his Capacity be large and extensive, yet there may be some Things relating to the publick Good, that have escaped his Observation, that others may take Notice of; and for this Reason 'tis best there should be an Assembly of Rulers: The Welfare of a People may be more promoted by having *many* Heads employ'd for it, than One only.

When there is a *Number* concern'd in *Government,* setting to deliberate and resolve upon Measures proper to be taken for the Safety, Peace and Advantage of a People, or the Relief and Happiness of particular Men; the Debates, in such an Assembly, are productive of *Light,* which tends to prepare and ripen the Thoughts of *Rulers* for coming to a Determination upon the weighty Matters that call for their Consideration.

2dly, The *Burden* of Government, if faithfully attended, is too great for a *single* Person to bear.

It is a Business that is very ponderous; the Cares and Fatigues of it are too painful and heavy to be sustained by *one* Man; his Strength had need be the Strength of Scones, and his Flesh ⟨...⟩ , or he will sink under them. Apprehensive of …. was *Jethro,* Father-in-law to *Moses;* when he saw him sit alone, from Morning to Evening, to judge the People; he was concern'd for him, and said, *the Thing that thou doest is not good, thou wilt surely wear away; this Thing is too heavy for thee, thou art not able to perform it thyself alone;* and then he gives him this prudent *Advice,* to *provide out of all the People able Men, such as feared GOD: Men of Truth, hating Covetousness, and to place them over the People.*\*

There is a Multiplicity of arduous Concerns that he upon the Hands, and fill the Head of a *Civil Ruler;* and it is so especially at some particular *Junctures.* The Safety and Defence of his People is to be intensely regarded, when Enemies make *War* against them: Their Trade is to be protected; it may be, they are fallen into perplext and distressing Circumstances, and, if it can be, are to be extricated and delivered out of them: Good Laws must be supported, and new ones occasionally made; meet Persons to *execute* them are to be chosen, and put into Commission: *Religion* and *Learning* are to be upheld, and Measures taken to promote the flourishing of these great Interests: The *Grievances* of particular Persons and Societies must, if it be practicable, be redress'd. It is not enough, that a Ruler take Care, that the People don't suffer in their Persons and Interests; but he must lay himself out to advance their *Prosperity:* And it may be further observed, that sometimes a People are grievously out of *Frame;* and this renders the Difficulties of Government so much the greater. The composed, meek and patient Leader of *Israel,* found the Discontent and Uneasiness of his People to be more than he could bear,

*How can I myself alone,* said he, *•ear your Cumbr•nce, and your Burden, and your Strife?*ᵏ And he than expostulated with the glorious GOD,ˡ *Have I conceived all this People, have I begotten them? that Thou shouldst say unto me, Carry them in thy Bosom, (as a nursing Father carrieth the sacking Child) unto the Land which Then •••rest unto the•• Fathers: I am not able to •ear all this People alone, because it is too heavy for me.* The compassionate GOD heard the Complaint of his dejected Servant, and provided Assistance for him, said unto him, *Gather unto Me seventy of the Elders of* Israel, *whom thou knowest to be the* Elders *of the People, and Officers over them, and bring them unto the Tabernacle of the Congregation, that they may stand there with thee, and I will come down, and talk with thee there; and I will take of the Spirit, that is upon thee, and I will put it upon them, and they shall bear the Burden of the People with thee, that thou bear it not thyself alone.* It is very evident then, that the *Government* of a People is too great a Labour and Burden for One to bear; and consequently it is most fit and suitable, that a Number should be employed and concerned therein, that there should be *an Assembly* of Rulers to share the Labours, Cares and Troubles which attend it.

3ᵈˡʸ, For one Person alone to have the Government of a People in his Hands, would be too great a Temptation.

It tends to excite and draw forth the Pride of Man, to make him unsufferably haughty; it gives him too much Liberty to exert his *Corruptions;* and it encourages him to become a *Tyrant* and an *Oppressor,* to *dispense* with Laws, and break the most solemn Oaths; to proceed so far in his unrighteous Practices, that his Subjects, weary of the Doctrine of *passive Obedience* and *Non-resistance,* are necessitated to plead their own Cause, and vindicate

their Rights by Measures which for a long Time they were loth to make Use of.—Thus King *James the Second,* tir'd with *Parliaments,* and thirsting after a despotick Power, set them aside; and such *arbitrary* Courses did he take, that his injured, provoked Subjects, arm'd themselves in Defence of their *Religion* and *Liberties;* the Consequence of which was his *abdicating* the Throne, which, by all his Attempts and the Endeavours of his Friends, he could never afterwards recover. So let the Efforts of his *pretended Son* to seat himself upon the *British Throne,* be blasted by Heaven, and rendered abortive, as (blessed be GOD) they have hitherto been.

From the Whole then, it appears, that it is most fit and suitable that a *Number* should be concern'd in *Civil Government,* that it is best for a People to be under such a Constitution and Establishment, whether it be a mixt *Monarchy,* that excellent Form which *our Nations,* and the *British Plantations* are happily in the Enjoyment of, who are governed by a KING, House of *Peers,* and *Commons,* the latter of which are chosen by the People; or an *Aristocracy,* which is the Government of a *Commonwealth,* by *Nobles;* or a *Democracy,* wherein *Magistrates* are elected from among and by the People.

- I pass now to take the *Second Proposition* under Consideration.
- II. *The great GOD is present in the* Assembly *of Political Rulers.*

To illustrate this *Head,* I shall consider in what Respects He is present in this *Assembly.*

It would be too great a Departure from the Intention of the Text, should I observe, that He is present in it *Representatively,* although 'tis so in *Fact,* for Rulers are his Vicegerents, his Agents, and exhibit some Image of His Authority and governing Power: For this Reason they are called Gods in Scripture, they are stiled so twice in the *Psalm* that contains my *Text: He judgeth among the Gods: I said ye are Gods:* But not to dwell upon this Thought.

1$^{st}$, The *inspecting Presence* of the great GOD is always in this Assembly.

He is an immense *Being,* and therefore Omniscient: *Is He a GOD at hand, and not afar off; and can any hide themselves in secret Places, that He should not see them? He fills Heaven and Earth with His Presence;* and nothing escapes His Observation[m].

Hath not He, who governs and will judge the World, a universal Knowledge of Men, their Actions and Behaviour? Besure His *Eyes are in every Place, beholding the Evil and the Good*[n]; He *pandereth Men's Goings*[o]; and *all Things are open and naked unto Him*[p]: Who can doubt then of His *inspecting Presence,* it's being in the Assembly of *Political Rulers?* He takes a particular and critical View of them, seeth who they are who compose the Congregation of the *Mighty,* and sit in this *Honourable Assembly;* He calls them all by Name: *His Eyes are like a Flame of Fire;* and penetrate into the Hearts of Rulers: *The Lord seeth not as Man seeth; Man looketh at the outward Appearance, but the Lord looketh at the Heart*[q] If any of the Members that compose this *Society* are govern'd by low, mean, base and selfish Principles in their Proceedings; if they are influenced by a Party-Spirit, and have no Regard for the publick Good, any further than is consistent with their private Interests, the Omniscient GOD remarks it: Are there any *careless, indolent Members,* contented with the Honours and Emoluments of their advanced Seats, not attending to the weighty Concerns of *Government,* the great GOD is privy to it: He is conscious of it, if there be any who indulge themselves in letting their Minds be absent from the Business of their exalted Stations, who depend upon their *Brethren* to think for them; and by an *implicit Faith,* will give their *Votes* with the Majority, not weighing and examining Matters themselves, which they act upon: If *Iniquity* should be established by a Law, in this Assembly, the righteous LORD, who loveth Righteousness, has a perfect Knowledge of it.

If obvious Measures to promote the Honour of GOD, the Interests of Religion, and the Relief and Prosperity of his People be neglected, it comes under his Observation: He was able, from His own Knowledge, thus to expostulate with the Congregation of the Mighty of old, *How long will ye judge unjustly?*[r] And this was His Complaint, *They know not, neither will they understand, they walk in Darkness, all the Foundations of the Earth are out of Course.* In short, He is thoroughly acquainted with all the Sins of this *Assembly,* whether of Omission or Commission.

And indeed, this His *Inspection* is very *awful;* for it is in order to a *future Account,* which He will exact of the Rulers of the Earth: *The Great, as well as Small, must stand before His enlightned Tribunal:*[s] Though Rulers are called Gods, yet they *must die like Men*[t]. *The Breath even of Princes goeth forth, and after Death is the Judgment*[u]. The exalted Potentates of the Earth are accountable to Him, who is higher than the highest: And with GOD there will be no Respect of Persons: He will judge *impartially;* and none of the *Distinctions,* which make a Difference between Men in this World, will be regarded at the *last Day;* but every Man shall be treated according to his Works, whether he be high or low, rich or poor.

And if the *Great GOD* takes Cognizance of what is *amiss* in the Assembly of *Civil Rulers,* besure He doth of what is *pleasing* to Him. He observes the Integrity, the Diligence and the Faithfulness of those who sit in the Assembly of the Mighty: He beholds their Patience and Self-denial, their publick Spirit, and the agreeable Application of their Talents; the good Improvement they make of their superior Accomplishments, and their peculiar Opportunities to do Good, and singular Advantages to serve the Honour of His Name in their exalted Stations, and to approve themselves publick Blessings: They may address Him in the Words of Governour *Nehemiah, Think upon me, my GOD, for good, according to all that I have done for this People*[w]. He keeps a Record of their Fidelity and Serviceableness; and will gloriously Reward them therefor in the World to come: They shall have Boldness in the Day of Judgment, and rejoice with Joy unspeakable; when Shame shall cover the Face, and Regret and Anguish fill the Soul of the unfaithful, unprofitable and mischievous Ruler.

2[dly], The great GOD is present in the Assembly of Political Rulers *influentially.*

He has a tender Regard for *human Societies;* and in order to their Safety, Peace and Prosperity, establishes and preserves *Government* in them: He furnishes them with Rulers: The raising up Persons of this Character is His Work, *The Powers that be, are ordained of Him*[x]. *The Shields of the Earth are His*[y]. *By Him Kings reign, and Princes decree Justice: By Him Princes rule, and Nobles, yea, all the Judges of the Earth*[z]. He vouchsafes His favourable Influences in the Assembly of Rulers; otherwise how could His kind Intention and Purpose in setting up and continuing a good Form of Government among a People be ever accomplished?

(1.) The great GOD is present with *Political Rulers,* when they have sufficient *Light,* for their Direction in the important Work they are called unto.

*Light* proceeds from Him, He is the *Father* of it:[a] He giveth Understanding, Wisdom and Prudence: He made King *David* wise as an *Angel,* to discern both Good and Evil; gave his Son *Solomon* an understanding Heart, so that there was none like him, before nor after him; and furnished *Daniel* with extensive Measures of Wisdom.

When He, who dwelleth between the *Cherubims, shines forth,* affords Light, gives Counsel and Direction in this Assembly, He is present in it by His Influences upon the Minds of His Servants. And is it not oftentimes so? Don't He lead them in a right and plain Path? He is the GOD of *the Spirits of all Flesh*[b]; and has an easy Access to the Souls, which He hath made; strengthens Men's thinking Powers and Faculties; scatters the Clouds which darken the Minds of Rulers, and irradiates their Understandings; leads them into such wise and prudent Measures as answer the great Purposes of *Government:* Under the illuminating Influences of Heaven they make good Laws, do *Justice* to Persons who complain to them of Grievances; project such *Schemes,* as greatly tend to the Peace, Safety and Prosperity of a People; are directed to Means conducive to their *Defence,* from the Insults and Depredations of their Enemies; and which issue in the *Annoyance* of those that rise up against them: We have had a late Instance of a great and good Projection of this Kind, form'd by the *Government* we are *immediately* under.

(2.) The great GOD is present in the Assembly of Political Rulers by His *animating Influences.*

*Courage* is an Endowment necessary in the *Leaders* of a People. Rulers should not be Cowards. When the LORD advanced *Joshua* to be Successor to His Servant *Moses,* He bid him *be strong, and of good Courage*[c]. Unhappy is it for a People when they have Women and Children to govern them; those who are not only void of Political Wisdom, but Persons who are apt to be disheartened at the Sight of Difficulties, and affrighted at the Appearance of Dangers: But happy is it when GOD provides strong Rods for the Scepter of them that bear Rule over a People. Civil Rulers should be steady and unmoveable, as the great *Mountains,* in just and good Proceedings, stedfast in the Discharge of the Duties of their superior Places, and ought with Intrepidity to pursue what makes for the Welfare of the Publick, though they incur the ill Resentments of particular Men, and expose themselves to the Malignity of some People.

Now when they are resolute and couragious in the Discharge of their weighty *Betrustments,* it proceeds from the divine *animating* Influences: Being vigorously moved hereby, they had rather offend *Men* than the great and mighty Ruler of the Universe, whose *Trustees* they are; had rather preserve a good Conscience, than gratify ill Humours, and keep in good Terms with those who impertinently meddle with State-Affairs, and addict themselves to inspect the publick Administration, and find Fault with every Thing almost, which they themselves have not a Hand in. Being thus influenced by *Heaven,* the Pilots of a *Province* won't baulk their Duty, thro' a base Fear of being dropt out of their publick Character at the next *Election:* They had rather live *neglected,* and in an obscure private Capacity, than omit doing what appears to them to be for the publick *Weal,* or have a Hand in what they they think will be an *Encroachment* upon the *Royal Prerogative,* or Detrimental to the *People,* with whose Interests they are betrusted.

As ⟨...⟩ which they have received from above will restrain them from lavishing away the Publick Money, so they won't let a Projection drop, if they can help it, when the common Safety and Prosperity makes the Prosecution of it necessary. They will engage in chargeable Enterprizes, in Behalf of their People, trusting in GOD to give them an Ability in Time, to discharge the Expences arising therefrom. The *Outcries* of inconsiderate People will not terrify them so much as to prove a Temptation to Unfaithfulness.

(3.) The great GOD is *present* in the *Assembly* of Political Rulers by His *pacifick* Influences.

When there is Peace among the Heads of a People it proceeds from Him: He is the GOD of Peace. He maketh Peace in the *high Places* of the Earth, and preserves it among Rulers: By an *Impression* upon the Souls of Men, He creates and upholds a *Harmony* among them. When Love and a good Agreement subsists among Rulers, in their Essays to promote the common Welfare, it is evident, GOD is with them in a gracious Manner. How favourable is He to them, and to those who are under their Authority, when one Spirit and Soul appears to animate this Body of Men; and they are united in employing their *Talents* for the Honour of Him, from whom they have derived them, and the Good of the People, who are their Care and Charge? But on the other Hand, when there are Jars and a Misunderstanding among Rulers, GOD absents Himself from them, as to His *gracious* Presence; and it bodes ill to this Assembly, and has a dark Aspect upon the Circumstances of a People. Where there is Envy and Strife among Persons of *low Life,* there is Confusion; but much worse is a *Fire* kindled and blown up in the Bowels of a *Political* Body: 'Tis a bad *Omen,* when this is the State of the *Congregation of the Mighty:* It presages ill to Rulers and Ruled: The Contrary is a Token for Good,

that GOD has a gracious Design and Purpose …respect to those who are in Authority, and them who are subject to them. A good Harmo…is the Strength, the Beauty and Glory of Societies, and especially of *political Assemblies.* A House divided against itself is a Place of *Confusion,* and in Danger of falling; and 'tis well if a *Kingdom* divided against itself is not brought to Ruin.[d]

(4.) When Rulers are *patient* and *resigned,* the great GOD is *influentially present* with them.

They have need of Patience and Resignation: The Occasions for the Exercise of these *Vertues* are many and various. The *Labours and Fatigues* of Government are very heavy, if it be faithfully attended: Sometimes the *Schemes and Projections,* which they form to promote the Publick Good, don't succeed according to their Hope and Expectation; the Smiles of Divine Providence don't accompany them, although they are most wisely adapted to bring about the End they are design'd for: This Disappointment calls for their Patience and Resignation to the Will of GOD. Sometimes their *Way* is so dark, encumbered and embarassed that they can't proceed with *Satisfaction* of Mind: And let them be never so diligent and faithful in serving the Publick, many will fault and reproach them: This is too often the Case. *Moses* was a Ruler of rare Accomplishments, he was a wise Man, and learned in all the *Learning of the Egyptians,* and was eminently faithful in his Post; yet were there some that disliked him, and were uneasy under his *Conduct;* their discontented Spirits moved them to an Insurrection against this excellent Servant of the LORD; there was a Confederacy to throw off his *Government:* The great Cry was, that *he took too much upon him;* but GOD awfully rebuked these bold and wicked *Men.*[e] When Civil Rulers are patient and resign'd under the uneasy and difficult they meet with, from a Consciousness of the *Divine over-ruling Providence,* and their own *Integrity,* the great GOD is *graciously present* with them by His Influences upon their Spirits. He is the *GOD of Patience*[f]. They are the Words of the Apostle, *Strengthned with all Might, according to His glorious Power unto all Patience and Longsuffering, with Joyfulness.*[g]

I have considered, that the *inspecting and influential Presence* of the great GOD is in the Assembly of Political Rulers: I would observe,

3[dly], That His *safe-guarding Presence* is in this Assembly.

The *Congregation of the Mighty* is sometimes exposed to great Dangers. There are secret Plots and Devices, form'd against it by the Enemies of the *Government,* the Execution of which would be fatal and destructive to it. When GOD, who is knowing to all the Works of Darkness, and has the wicked Contrivances of Men and Devils under His Observation, brings to Light *treasonable Machinations* against Government, He is *graciously* present with the Assembly of the Mighty: Thus was He *present* with the great Convention *of our Nations,* in the *Reign of King* JAMES *the First;* He wonderfully discovered the *Gunpowder Treason,* when it was ripe for Execution: In the *Mount* was GOD seen; the *sudden* Design was in an astonishing Manner detected, and the wicked Instruments of it were brought to condign Punishment.

Sometimes the Enemies of a *Government* seek its Ruin by *open Violence,* by hellish *Insurrections* and *Rebellions:* But the supreme Ruler of the World, who sitteth in the *Heavens,* laugheth at their Attempts, maketh them as *Chaff before the Wind; and His Angel chaseth them.*

This was the Case in our Nations, *A. D.* 1715. And we have had a *late Instance* of it: GOD's People have seen the *Rebels* in *Scotland* fleeing before the *Mighty* and *Puissant* DUKE of CUMBERLAND: Their Hands have not been able to perform their Enterprize. Blessed be the most high GOD, who *granteth Deliverance, and giveth Salvation unto Kings,* that the horrid *Rebellion,* conceived and formed in the *Conclave* of *Hell* and *Rome,* fostered and spirited up by the Courts. of *France* and *Spain,* hath been so far obstructed in its *Progress:* May it be utterly discouraged, and all the Sparks of it extinguished!

It remains now that I make some *Application* of what has been said.

## APPLICATION.

1st. Is it most *sit* and suitable, that a *Number* should be concerned in the Civil Government of a People, what Cause have We to bless GOD, for the agreeable Political *Establishment* which we are under.

The *supream* Government at Home, which we are the Subjects of, calls for our most hearty Gratitude to *Heaven.* That Form of Government is thought by many wise Men to be the Best, which is lodg'd in the Hands of a KING and *Parliament;* the best adapted for the Security and Advantage of a People: Should we not be very thankful for so good a *Constitution?* It has been once and again struck at, and the Subversion of it has been greatly attempted, the Liberties and Privileges of the *British Realm* have been in great Hazard; but the *Gates of Hell,* and Men of arbitrary Principles, have not been able to prevail against them: Being safe guarded by the kind and watchful Providence of GOD, they have continued unto this Day.

And what Reason have we to bless the great Ruler of the World, for the *Charter-Privileges* which we enjoy? That the Form of *Government* we are *immediately* under, is not oppressive. We are ruled by a GOVERNOUR who represents the KING, a Board of *Councellers,* chosen by and from among our-selves; and by a House of *Representatives,* elected by the *Freeholders* of the respective *Towns* of the *Province.* It is of GOD, that our *political* Circumstances are so comfortable; We should rejoice in them, and give Him Praise, that it is our

Lot to be subject to such a desireable Constitution: May we never be so imprudent and ungrateful to GOD and the KING, as to take any *Steps,* which may expose us to the Loss of our *Charter;* but let us be solicitous that we may enjoy it all our Days, and leave it as a most rich and valuable Inheritance to our *Children.*

2[dly], Is the *inspecting Presence* of the great GOD in the Assembly of political Rulers, then they ought to be greatly *influenced* by the Consideration hereof in all their Proceedings.

They should act up to *Conscience,* as remembering they are under His Eye, who is a *Being* of consummate *Righteousness* and *Goodness.* These divine Perfections, which He displays in the Government of the World, they should be concern'd to *Copy.* They should be Followers of Him, in the Exercise of the same Virtues and Perfections; hereby their Administrations will be highly pleasing to Him: But if they are conducted by Principles that are corrupt and vicious, He will behold it with Displeasure. The Presence of such a GOD, the Virtues which He discovers in the Government of His Creatures, should keep the Gods of the Earth under a proper *Regimen.* Shall not these Excellencies make them afraid? Shall not the Dread of a just and good GOD fall upon and influence them in all their Transactions? Shall it not engage them to the greatest Fidelity in the

Services He requires of them? Shall not the Intention for which He takes *Notice* of their Actions, have a mighty Force to make them sincere and conscientious? Doth He *inspect* them, in order to the calling them to an Account, and rendering to them according to their Behaviour in the publick Capacity they sustain; and should not the Thought hereof oblige them to acquit themselves well in their exalted Stations, that they may escape His tremendous Rebuke, and through Grace, receive His transporting *Well done, good and faithful Servant?* Faithful Rulers shall receive a great and blessed Reward from Him, who knows their Services, and is acquainted with the Integrity of their Hearts: And when we lament the Loss we sustain by the Deaths of our wife, faithful and serviceable *Patriots,* may we not rejoice in their superior and peculiar Felicity; and particularly should we not refresh our Souls, in the midst of our *Sorrow,* by thinking of the distinguishing Glory, which is already, and will at the *last Day* be assigned, by the Grace of our Lord JESUS CHRIST, to the lately deceas'd Honourable *Thomas Cushing,*Esq; who uprightly employed his *rare and sanctified Political Talents* for the *Honour* of the great GOD, and in the Service of His People?

And will the Honourable *Gentlemen,* who are to be concern'd in the important *Elections* of this Day, suffer me to say, Let the Consideration of GOD's *inspecting Presence* make a powerful Impression upon your Hearts, and govern you in the great Affair before you. Let me entreat your *Honours,* to consider yourselves in the Sight of GOD, and accountable unto Him: He will cite us all before His Bar in a little Time, and treat us according to our Demeanour in the respective Relations and Stations we are now in: Let a Sense of this guide you in your *Elections,* and make you studious of electing those into His *Majesty's Council* who are most likely to be serviceable, and who come nearest to the Scripture-Character

of those who are meet to be introduced into high Places of Trust, Power and Authority.

And need I be your *Monitor,* that they should be Men of *Knowledge and Wisdom?* Did not the *Head* of the Tribes of *Israel* direct to Persons thus qualified? *Take ye wise Men,* says he, *understanding and known among your* Tribes, *and I will make them Rulers over you*[h]. A Councellor should be a good *Thinker:* Not that it be necessary he should be a great *Philosopher;* but he should understand his Duty as a *Magistrate,* in such an elevated Station, be well acquainted with the State of his *Country,* and be *understanding in the Times.* So necessary was Wisdom thought to be in a *Ruler* by the *Egyptians,* that their *Kings* had their *Crowns and Diadems* twisted with *Serpents,* as an *Emblem* of this excellent Endowment.

And doth not *Justice and Honesty* enter into the Character of a good Ruler? Every one, I hope, will acknowledge these Virtues should be found in all those that fit at the *Council-Board; He that ruleth over Men,* must be Just[i]. *Machiavel* would have a Ruler be a cunning Deceiver; but such a vicious Man is not be trusted with private Concerns, much less with the Affairs and Interests of the *Publick*. A Ruler should deserve the Commendation that was given to a *Heathen Emperor,* that he was *Wise without Improbity.*

And ought they not to be Men of a *publick generous Spirit?* Moses was advised to appoint Men *bating Covetousness,* for Rulers[k]. The Emperor *Adrian's* Motto was, *Non mihi, sed Populo,* I am not for myself, but for my People. *Mordecai* was a bright Example of this Spirit,

would not he who is chosen to sit at the *Council-Board,* be wanting in his Character, should he be destitute of *Zeal, Courage and Magnanimity? Jethro* advised *Moses* to chuse able M••, and set them over the People: According to the *Hebrew* it is Men of *Strength* or *Courage.* The Steps of *Solomon's Throne* were on both Sides supported with *Lions:* They were design'd, no doubt, to be *Symbols* of that *Courage* which should be in a Ruler. *A King, that sitteth in the Throne of Judgment, scattereth away all Evil with his Eyes,* says the wise Man.[m]

And is not *Mercy,* as well as *Zeal and Justice,* essential to a good Ruler? In Government *Mercy* must be mixt and blended with Justice. We read the *Throne is established by Righteousness*[n]. We also read, *it is established by Mercy.*[o] *Summum Jus, summa injuria,* is a true Maxim. Mercy makes a Ruler's Face to shine. I remember, the *Roman* Orator in an Oration which he made to *Julius Caesar,* in Behalf of one who had been on *Pompey's* Side, says, That Men resemble the Gods in nothing more than in Goodness and Mercy. It was the Advice of *Maecenas* to the Emperor *Augustus,* that he would not abuse his Power, nor think it any Diminution of it, *if he did not do all that he could do.*

Finally, Is it not of great Importance that those who are chosen into His *Majesty's Council,* be Gentlemen of *Sobriety and Religion?* Are those so fit to govern others who don't govern their Passions and Appetites? Rulers should be able to rule their own Spirits, to restrain their criminal Inclinations. It was a poor *Character* given of an *Assyrian* Monarch, *That he was the best Man alive at Eating and Drinking.* Is an Epicure or a Debauchee a meet Person to be a Senator? And is it not to be wished, that all who sit at this *Honourable Board* might be of a *Religious Character?* The stronger the Ties of Conscience are, the better qualified are Persons (caeteris paribus) for a publick Trust, King *David* thought so, he could not bear with irreligious Courtiers[p].

3[dly], Are the Divine gracious *Influences* so necessary in the Assembly of Political Rulers, we see where their *Dependance* should be placed.

A great *Trust* is reposed them, they need Help from above, for the right and acceptable Discharge of it: Being sensible hereof, it is of Consequence that they exercise Faith in the allsufficient GOD, through the great *Mediator.* GOD is able to guide the *Guides* of a People, to lead their *Leaders,* and give their *Senators* Wisdom; to animate and inspire them with *Resolution* and *Courage;* to fill their Souls with *Patience* and *pacifick Dispositions;* and carry them through the weighty Affairs they are engaged in. And have they any Reason to suspect His *Inclination* to afford them His gracious influential Presence? If they make Him the Object of their *Trust,* with a sincere Regard to His Glory, and are found in a Way of Well-doing.

4[thly], What we have heard, suggests to us the great *Duty of Gratitude* to a gracious GOD, when Things *go well* in the *Assembly* of our Rulers.

When it is so, GOD is with them of a *Truth,* by His favourable Influences; and we should observe and gratefully acknowledge it, to His Praise and Glory.

And hath He not appeared to smile upon the *Administrations* of Government in this *Province,* from Time to Time? Have we not had good *Laws* enacted by our Political *Fathers?* Laws well calculated to prevent Irreligion; and for the promoting of Virtue and Piety; to deter Persons from profaning the *Sabbath;* from needlessly absenting themselves from the *publick Worship;*

and to guard the adorable Name of GOD, from the Abuses of the *Tongues;* and to defend our *Persons, Names* and *Interests;* to curb Men's licentious *Passions* and *Appetites;* to maintain our *Peace,* and advance our *Prosperity?* Have not Means been used to protect us from an *Invasion* of our Enemies by Sea; and have not our exposed inland *Frontiers* been the Care of our *Honourable Rulers?* And have they not carried on the Business of the Publick with a great Measure of Peace and good Agreement?

And here I cannot pass by in *Silence,* the late ever-memorable successful *Expedition,* first plan'd, concerted and resolved upon in the *General Assembly* of this *Province:* An Enterprize of the greatest Consequence, in its prosperous Event to our *Merchandize and Fishery!* A Design succeeded by such a Series of astonishing *Providences,* that we need not doubt, that He who hath the Hearts of all Men at His Disposal, influenced our Honourable Rulers to form and prosecute this wonderful Scheme.

When the News was first brought us of the very remarkable Success, that attended that great *Affair,* every *Mouth was filled with Laughter, and Tongue with Singing: Then said we, The Lord hath done great Things for as, The Lord hath done great Things for us, whereof we are glad.* Our Obligations to be thankful to the GOD of *Armies* and Victory, still remain as strong as ever: Though alas! We are called to mourn the Deaths of many Hundreds of our *brave Men,* cut down in the *surrendered City,* by the Sword of the destroying *Angel!* What shall we say? The Ways of Divine Providence are *unsearchable!* But GOD is always infinitely Wise, Just and Holy, when Clouds and Darkness are round about His Throne. The awful *Scene* of Death, which has been in that *Place,* should not make us unthankful for the Conquest of it.

Will your EXCELLENCY now permit me humbly and thankfully to take Notice of the observable gracious Presence of *Heaven,* that has been with you since your Access to the *Chief Seat* of Government among us: Through the good Hand of GOD upon you, your Administrations have (as we trust) been easy to your *own Mind;* besure they have been *Satisfactory* to your *People.*

And here let me congratulate your EXCELLENCY, upon the Reduction of *Cape-Breton,* to the Obedience of the *British Crown;* a great Event, which your Heart was much set upon; and in the Accomplishment of which you have (under Divine Providence) been the principal Leader.

We have Reason also to bless the *Heart-disposing GOD,* that, when your Presence was so needful at *Louisbourg,* your Self-denial was so great, as to reconcile you to a *Voyage* to that Place; where your Essays to regulate Matters were, in a good Measure, succeeded; and, that you were contented to make so *long a Stay* there, in a Time of raging Sickness: And we would gratefully acknowledge the Goodness of the great Preserver of Men, in returning you to your Government in Safety.

As your EXCELLENCY has been favour'd with GOD's gracious Influences hitherto, so may that GOD, who has been with you, be so for the future, and render you a great and lasting *Blessing* to us; enable you successfully to use your Interest at *Home,* as well as your best Endeavours here, for the Good of *this People;* and, in due Time, gloriously Reward you for your faithful Services.

5[thly], Is the great GOD willing to be *influentially* present in the Assembly of *Political Rulers,* this should be a great *Motive to Prayer.*

It should be so with those who have a Seat in this superiour *Convention.* Rulers should be moved by this Consideration, often to repair to the Prayer-hearing GOD, who is both able and willing to supply all their Needs, according to his Riches in Glory thro' JESUS CHRIST[p]. We read of Rulers in *Scripture,* how were Men of Prayer, *David* was so, *Solomon* prayed for Wisdom, that he might know how *to go out and come in* before the great People, whom he had the Charge of. *Nehemiah,* Governour of *Judah,* was a Man of Prayer, so was *Moses, Samuel* and *Jehos..ph...t:* But not to insist upon this, I hope our ⟨...*Rulers,* have such a Sense of their Dependance upon GOD, as not to need any Excitations to Prayer from me.

I …apply myself to you, my Brethren, who are not of the Legislature, I would do it to all the People of GOD in the *Province,* were they within hearing, and beseech you and them to be excited, by what has been said, to pray for your Rulers GOD is willing to afford them His Help, to afford them His gracious Presence, and what an Encouragement is this to their People to pray for them Is not their Work attended with Difficulties, and especially in this *tempestuous & dark* Time of War? Don't our Prosperity depend very much upon the Divine favourable Presence with them? Are they not betrusted with our invaluable Interests, and shall we not seek the Prosperity of this *important* Assembly by our Prayers? Is it not agreable to the Apostolick Direction, to pray for our Rulers? *I exhort,* says St. *Paul, that first of all Supplications, Prayers, giving of Thanks be made for all Men; for Kings, and for all that are in Authority, that we may lead a quiet and peaceable Life, in all Godliness and Honesty*[q]. But let us not confine our *Prayers* to the Government we are more *immediately* under, but let us offer up our Supplications for our rightful, lawful and gracious King

GEORGE, His *Council,* the *Ministers of State,* and *both Houses of Parliament,* That the great GOD would be in these *Assemblies* of the Mighty, graciously influencing of them; affording Protection from the secret Attempts, and open Violence of all the Adversaries of our happy Establishment.

And that our Prayers in Behalf of our Rulers may be effectual, we must be concern'd that we be *obedient* to the Holy GOD: Will He attend to our Supplications, if we do not cleanse our Hands, and purify our Hearts? *If we turn away our Ear from hearing the Law,* Will our Prayers be heard, though they be many?[s] GOD may be provoked by the Sins of a People, to fill the Way of their Rulers with Darkness; and though they abound in Prayer for them, they shall not be heard. When He was angry with His ancient People, for their Iniquities, He denounced this *Commination* against them, that *He would do a marvellous Work amongst them, a marvellous Work, and a Wonder, the Wisdom of their wise Men should perish, and the Understanding of their prudent Men should be hid*[t]: On the contrary, having promised His People to pour out His *Spirit* upon them, He gives them Assurance of His Favour with Regard to their *Political* Government,[u] *I will turn my Hand upon thee, and purely purge away thy Dross, and take away all thy Tin; and I will restore thy Judges as at the First, and thy Counsellors as at the Beginning: Afterward thou shalt be called, the City of Righteousness, the faithful City.*

FINIS.

*Ed. Note: This sermon illustrates the importance of the Deliverance of the 5th of November for all subjects of the crown no matter where they were.*

# 1755-Popish zeal inconvenient to mankind and unsuitable to the law of Christ: a sermon preached in St. Barnabas Church, Queen-Anne Parish on the fifth of November 1754 by William Brogden, rector of the said parish, in Prince-George's County. Brogden, William, d. 1770, Annapolis: Printed and sold by Jonas Green, 1755.

*Ed. note: Maryland, U.S.A.*

Galatians, Chap. iv. Ver. 17, and Part of the 15th
They zealously affect you, but not well; yet they would exclude you, that you might affect them. But it is good to be zealously affected always in a good Thing.-

We have been called upon this Day to render a Tribute of Praise and Thanksgiving to our gracious GOD, for one of the most signal Deliverances that is recorded of any Nation.---The high Opinion which our Forefathers had of the Mercy of that Deliverance, appears by their appointing a Day of Thanksgiving, to be annually observ'd in Commemoration of it. And, though we live at some Distance from the Time, wherein the bloody Design was laid to enslave us, yet if we rightly understand the Deliverance between a free Protestant Government, and Popish arbitrary Dominion, in regard both of civil and religious Rights, we can't but believe, that the Issue of that horrid Attempt is as much our Concern, as it was theirs: For had it succeeded according to the Jesuit's subtil Plan, in all Probability, we should at this Time be Slaves to the Pests of human Nature; groaning under the Iron Rod of some merciless Tyrant; or of the more merciless Tyrants the Roman Clergy, whose Name, for Numbers and Cruelty, is Legion.

It is easy to imagine, both from what we hear daily of their Cruelties, where they bear a Sway, and from what pass'd formerly in our own Nation, that if Providence had not seasonably interposed for our Rescue, from the horrible Contrivance of this Day's Treason, we must have been now the Subject of Popish bitter Rage; our Tortures made the Diversion of a Priesthood reeking with Blood, or a Mob set mad upon Cruelty, by their Instigation; our Families torn to Pieces; our Children shut up in Convents against our Will, or sent out to starve in the World; and our Substance seiz'd on to the Use of our very Destroyers, to render them still more able to execute their pernicious Schemes and to do more Mischief in the World---This, indeed, might be avoided byour taking Part in their Errors, but then our Condition would be a Thousand Times more deplorable: For, if we joined with them in Appearance only, such Hypocrisy would be damning; it is earnest we should be in extreme Danger of missing Salvation, seeing that the Doctrines and Practices of the Popish Religion, are at the utmost Distance from those Qualification which the Scriptures require, in order to Salvation. It belongs not to us to determine any Thing concerning Men's future Condition; yet the highest Charity, if it hath any Knowledge of the true Nature and Design of Christianity, can have hardly any Hope of the Salvation of papists, but by supposing them to depart from some of those Doctrines and Practices, that aare inculcated b y their Religion; which, is certain, some of the best and most learned do, even while they hold Communion with the Roman Church. If Charity for Papists goes further than this, it can be only to hope, that it may please GOD to do more for them, than his written Word stands engaged for: But to forego a Certainty for an Uncertainty, is alike dangerous nad unwise.

In every Respect, therefore, our Deliverance from the Machinations of Rome, is a Mercy we can never be thankful enough for, nor sufficiently Value. Every Return of this Day should renew our Sense of the Obligation, and increase our Abhorrence of Popery, without lessening our Charity for the Men who are unhappily captivated to that Way. Past Experience should make us more Zealous in Defence of a righteous Cause, and more watchful against Encroachments upon our civil and religious Libertry, (the Overthrowing of which is the constant Spirit and Endeavour of the Adherents of Rome), without prompting us to entertain such personal Abhorrence and Malice against them, on Account of religious Differrence, as they do against us.

In several late Discourses I have laid open the roman Religion, as far as my Compass would allow; wherein I kept designedly to doctrinal Points, I mean, such as immediately respect religious Faith and Practice. If, at this Time, I shall make any Mention of secular and civil Matters, 'tis what the Nature of the present Subject requires, seeing the attempt of this Day was made to destroy our civil as well as religious Rights, by setting a Prince bred up in the arbitrary Notions of the Spanish Nation, upon the British Throne. However, though the Discoursing of civil Rights and Duties may not be seasonable at all Times, I am far from acknowledging that they are foreign to Religion. Every Condition of Life has it's Rules of Conduct laid down in the Gospel; and therefore, whatever is repugnant to those Rules in any Condition, whether it be as Superiors or Equals, it pertains properly to Religion, and is a fit Subject for this Place. And though the Black-friends of our Constitution, as well as it's avowed Enemies, are pleased to call it Preaching Politics, it is because they are determined to blame, though it be at the Expense of known Truth; for any one might see, if he was willing, that the Character is ill-placed, and has more of Ill-will than of Judgment. And of all People it least becomes Papists to find fault with Politics, whose Religion is no other. But whatever they are pleased to make of it, the Reproach will not affect me, as I shall meddle, not at all with Politics, and as little with Matters that are entirely secular, as I can; but where civil Right happens to be blended with religious Duty, they must excuse me if I am not altogether to complaisant, as to separate them…..

…Therefore, my Bretheren, while I argue for Peace and moderation, I must heartily recommend Zeal and Wariness too.---Remember who it was that said, I send you forth as Sheep in the midst of Wolves, be ye therefore wise as serpents and harmless as Doves. As Papists are by their very Principles, restless and unquiet, we ought to be upon our Guard. GOD and our Religion requires us not to be indifferent. Our Families, our Posterities, and our own Souls, in a manner, cry to us to defend our Cause with Courage. In such a Cause, Dangers and Ill-usage do but whet a brave mind, while the timorous and lukewarm sink poorly under their Fears. We have Truth and Right on our Side, let us unite, my Bretheren, in it's Defense. Papists can have no Advantage against us, but what our Differences give them; and it has always been their Policy to torment them. This was the express Design of their instituting Schools at S. Omer's, and some other Towns in Flanders,---But yet, with all their Policy, Wealth and Numbers they want Truth.---In this we have an Advantage over them, let us join heartily in maintaining it. And, Let the Experience of former Mercies engage us to depend on GOD's Providence for further Protection, No Nation upon the Earth, has been more signally favour'd that the English nor any of it's Affairs so remarkably as the Reformation.---K. Henry, after renouncing the Pope's Supremacy, which laid the Foundation of the Reformation, was upon the very Point of annulling all hat had been done, when the Pope himself, in his mistaken Policy, made the Breach irreparable by an unseasonable Sentence.-- Though the many Murders done in Q. Mary's Reign seem'd to promise nothing less than Extirpation, yet the Reformation increased; so as it might be said of that trying Time, as of the Primitive Church, the Blood of the Martyrs is the Seed of the Church.---And when every Thing seem'd to be agreed on for setting up the Inquisition in England it pleased GOD to remove that bigoted Queen, and blast the Papist's bloody Hopes.--Q. Elizabeth was visibly defended at many Times; and in her long Reign, the Protestant Religion was established. The Deliverance of the Kingdom from the vast Preparations of the Spaniards, wherein the very Elements seem'd to fight against them, was very extraordinary; insomuch that it is said, the Spanish Admiral exclaimed, in a Fit of Dispair, that JESUS CHRIST, is believed, was become a Protestant.--Need I again make mention of our wonderful Escape from the Powder Conspiracy? An Excape next to Miraculous!--A Letter without a Name was written by one of the Conspirators to a Friend, and conceive'd in such dark and ambiguous Terms that none could comprehend the Meaning, 'til it pleased GOD to put it into the King's Heart. A discovery so extraordinary confounded Rome and her Sons. One of their own Preachers, when he woiuld account for the Disappointment to his Congregation, let fall the Truth unwittingly, that it was, because GOD had a Love for the English.---And this Day is further memorable to Protestants, by the coming of the Prince of Orange into

England. An Event never to be forgotten by us, who have been rescued thereby from Popish Treachery, Tyranny, and Cruelty, coming in upon the Nation, like a Flood.

These Things, if rightly considered, can't fail to fill our Souls with Thanks, and our Mouths with Praise, to that gracious GOD, who has so often interposed on our Behalf, Let us not slight his Mercy, either by Ingratitude, or by looking on with Indifference, while our Enemies are endeavouring to destroy his Work. As our Cause is better than theirs, let us at least be as Zealous, and as United as they, in Defence of it; whilst we shun and detest their Manner, by Force and Flames, Malice and Cruelty.

And to conclude, let us be particularly attentive to the Demands of this pure Religion which we profess, and labour to live holy to the LORD. This is the best Way to express our Gratitude for the Devine Mercies, and the suresst Ground to expel the Continuance of his Favour.----By this will be consuted the mean Reproaches of our Adversaries and their Faction, in Time, be weaken'd. The first Reformed gained upon the World by the Holiness of their Lives, and the same Argument will be always prevailing, being easily understood of all, being demonstrative and experimental,--We justly boast of our Liberty to look into the Scriptures, let us not neglect that Liberty; for if we do, we fall into the very Error that we condemn in Papists; though with this deifference, Their Church in Fault in their Ignorance, but your church is not in your's.---We boast of J e s u s   C h r i s t as our only Head and Lord, let us then observe and do what Things he commands, both as to Faith and Piety towards GOD, and Good-will and Charity to Men.

Which he, of his infinite Mercy grant, through the same of our Lord  J e s u s   C h r i s t, to whom, with the Father and the Holy Ghost, be all Houour and Glory, Love and Obedience, for ever and ever.

A M E N.

## William Brogden

William Brogden was the son of William Brogden. He lived in Calvert County, Maryland, on the Patuxent River, and was a merchant and a shipper of tobacco. He died in 1735, the same year that his son William took Holy Orders. William, the son, is mentioned in his Letters of Deacon's Orders. This document notes that he was ordained by Rt. Rev. Edmund Gibson, Lord Bishop of London in 1735, in the Chapel Royal, Whitehall, Westminster, Middlesex County. Soon thereafter he is the rector of All Hallow's Parish in Anne Arundel County, Maryland. After becoming Rector of All Hallow's, Brogden married Mrs. Haddock, of Prince George County, who soon died. He then married Miss Elizabeth Chapman in 1741. The next year he purchased a farm near Annapolis. Brogden became Rector of Queen Anne's Parish, Prince George's County in 1751. He was known as a man of piety and an independent and unflinching spirit as well as a historian, classical scholar and conversant in French. As Major Brogden, he served in the American army in a volunteer company in the Revolutionary war but remained within the church. He served as a member of the Diocesan Convention several times signing the ratification of the Constitution, and Cannons of the Diocese. Brogden died in 1770 after thirty-five years of ministry. He was known as one of the lights of the church of Maryland.

## Some thoughts about this Sermon

The mystery of Deliverance changed history in a positive way.

And, though we live at some Distance from the Time, wherein the bloody Design was laid to enslave us, yet if we rightly understand the Deliverance between a free Protestant Government, and Popish arbitrary Dominion, in regard both of civil and religious Rights, we can't but believe, that the Issue of that horrid Attempt is as much our Concern, as it was theirs: For had it succeeded according to the Jesuit's subtil Plan, in all Probability, we should at this Time be Slaves to the Pests of human Nature; groaning under the Iron Rod of some merciless Tyrant; or of the more merciless Tyrants the Roman Clergy, whose Name, for Numbers and Cruelty, is Legion.

It is important not to criticize people but rather to criticize religions when they demonstrate intolerance or are actively hostile and threatening.

In every Respect, therefore, our Deliverance from the Machinations of Rome, is a Mercy we can never be thankful enough for, nor sufficiently Value. Every Return of this Day should renew our Sense of the Obligation, and increase our Abhorrence of Popery, without lessening our Charity for the Men who are unhappily captivated to that Way.

In order for churches to co-exist they must exercise the right of self-defense of their liberty.

…Therefore, my Bretheren, while I argue for Peace and moderation, I must heartily recommend Zeal and Wariness too. ---Remember who it was that said, I send you forth as Sheep in the midst of Wolves, be ye therefore wise as serpents and harmless as Doves. As Papists are by their very Principles, restless and unquiet, we ought to be upon our Guard. GOD and our Religion requires us not to be indifferent.

This last statement concerning liberty reflects the context of the sermonizer writing in an American colony before the revolution.

We justly boast of our Liberty to look into the Scriptures, let us not neglect that Liberty; for if we do, we fall into the very Error that we condemn in Papists; though with this difference, Their Church in Fault in their Ignorance, but your church is not in your's.---We boast of J e s u s   C h r i s t as our only Head and Lord, let us then observe and do what Things he commands, both as to Faith and Piety towards GOD, and Good-will and Charity to Men.

When discussing churches, it is essential to consider them as distinct. Sermonizers are entitled to defend as superior their "game," their "constitution" because others cannot and should not be held as equally correct as they are distinct. At the same time sermonizers can ask the auditory to do a better job playing the game and maintain righteousness within its structure.

# The Evolution of American Thanksgiving

## The Gunpowder Plot and Thanksgiving in the USA

When the American colonies were being explored and settled only a few years after the great Deliverance from the Gunpowder Plot of 1605, the only day of Thanksgiving on the Official Calendar of Customs of England was November 5 when thanks were given for deliverance from the horrors of the plot. The Government required that prayers were said, a sermon given, and the official liturgy followed, so it was appropriate that as the culture and the government was transferred to the colonies, so too were the liturgy and the observation of the day. The celebration of the 5th persisted into the 18th century.

In the new colonies, existing precariously on the edge of the frontier, the celebration of the deliverance of November 5, 1605, was exceptionally heartfelt and relevant. For the colonists, God's deliverance was a daily occurrence as they were protected from the Native Americans, rebellions, bad weather and crop failure. Later as political ties with England were broken the date of the Thanksgiving changed. Even so, proclamations recognizing the day continued to be issued on November 5 highlighting the date's continuing importance. Here are two proclamations of Colonial New England:

The First Thanksgiving, Ferris, Jean Leon Gerome, 1863-1930, artist, c. 1932.

# 1678- October 2-Boston: A Proclamaton for a Day of Fasting and Prayer November 21, 1678.

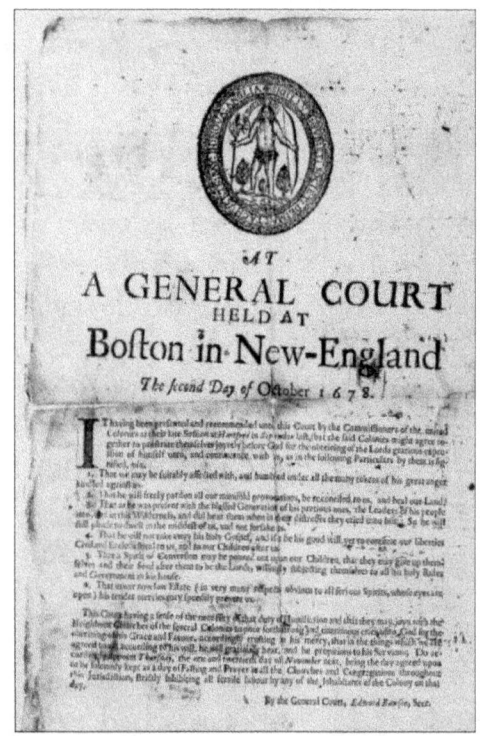

AT A GENERAL COURT HELD AT Boston in New-England

The Second Day of October 1678. It having been presented and recommended until this Court by the Commissioner of the united Colonies at their late Sessions at Hartford in September last, that the said Colonies might agree together to prostrate themselves jointly before God for the obtaining of the Lords gratious expression of himself unto, and continuance with us, as in the following Particulars by them is signified, viz.

1. That we may be suitably affected with, and humbled under all the many tokens of his great anger kindled against us.

2. That he will freely pardon all our manifold provocations, be reconciled to us, and heal our Land.

3. That us he was present with the blessed Generation of his pretious ones, the Leaders of his people into, and in this Wilderness, and did hear them when in their distresses they cried unto him: So he will still please to dwell in the middest of us, and not forsake us.

4. That he will not take away his holy Gospel, and if it be his good will, yet to continue our liberties Civil and Ecclesiastical to us, and to our Children after us.

5. That a Spirit of Convection may be poured out upon our Children, that they may give up themselves and their Seed after them to be the Lords, willingly subjecting themselves to all his holy Rules and Government in his house.

6. That in our now low Estate (in very many respects obvious to all serious Spirits, whose eyes are open) his tender mercies may speedily prevent us.

This Court having a sense of the necessity of that duty of Humiliation that they may join with the Neighbour Churches of the several Colonies to pour for the strong and unanimous cries unto God for obtaining of this Grace and Favour, accordingly crafting in his mercy, that in the things which we agreed to ask accordingly to his will, he will gratiously hear, and be propitious to his Servants; Do accordingly appoint Thursday, the once and twentieth day of November next, being the day agreed upon to be solemnly kept as a day of fasting and Prayer in all the Churches and Congregations throughout this Jurisdiction, strictly Inhibiting all servile labour by any of the Inhabitants of the Colony on that day.

By the General Court, Edward Ramson, Secr.

- "At a General Court held at Boston in New England the second day of October 1678." [A proclamaton for a day of fasting and prayer November 21, 1678] [Cambridge, Printed by Samuel Green 1678], Library of Congress.

# 1724- By the Honourable, Wiliam Dummer Esq; Lieutenant Governour & Commander in Chief, in and over His Majesty's Province of the Massachusetts Bay in New-England. A Proclamation for a General Thanksgiving

Whereas it hath pleased Almighty God of his Great Goodness, to Favour us with many undeserved Blessings in the Course of this Year, Respecting as well our Nation, as our land; More especially, For that He hath preserved the persons of our Sovereign Lord the King, and Their Royal Highnesses the Prince and Princess of Wales, with the rest of the Royal Family, and has graciously directed & succeeded His Majesty's wise councils for preserving the tranquility of Europe that he hath granted us a good measure of Health and in many instances, a plentiful harvest, Notwithstanding the Scorching Drought in the Summer past; That he hath so far protected our Sea-Coasts from the Merciless Pirates, (some of whom it hath pleased God in a remarkable Manner to deliver into our Hands, ) and Defended our In-Land frontiers from the Rage and Violence of the bloody Salvages, and

Granted us a very signal Victory over the Eastern Indians at Norridgewock.; And that He is pleased hitherto to Continue to us our invaluable Privileges Civil and Ecclesiastical; All which, with innumerable other Instances of the Divine Favour and Goodness demand our grateful and publick Acknowledgements:

I have thought fit, with the advice of his Majesty's Council, to Order and Appoint, That Thursday the Fifth of November next, be Observed as a Day of General Thanksgiving throughout this Province; Exhorting both Ministers and people in their respective Assemblies, Religiously to Celebrate the same by Offering up their Cheerful Praises and unfeigned Thanks to Almighty God the Author and Bestower of all our Mercies; And all Servile Labour is forbidden on the said Day.

Given at Boston the Seventeenth of October, 1724. In the Eleventh Year of the Reign of Our Sovereign Lord George by the Grace of God of Great Britain, France and Ireland, King, Defender of the Faith, etc.
By Order of the Hounourable the Lieut. Governour, with the Advice of the council,

Josiah Willard,
Secr. W. Dummer
God Save the King

-Boston, Printed by B. Green, Printers to His Hounour the Lieut, Governour & Council 1724.

# BY THE HONORABLE Jonathan Trumbull, Esq; Governor of the English Colony of Connecticut, in New-England, in America A Proclamation

As is the Will of GOD that we should ask all Mercy we need, from Him who is the Father of Lights, from whom cometh down every good and perfect Gift; so it is our Duty in every Thing to give Thanks, and render to Him the Glory of all the Good we receive. And as He has been pleased to vouchsafe to us in this Colony new and gracious Influences of his Blessing in the Course of the Year past:

I HAVE therefore thought fit, by and with the Advice of the Council, and at the Desire of the Representatives, in General Court assembled, to appoint, and do hereby appoint, Thursday the Fifth Day of November next, to be observed as a Day of public Thanksgiving throughout this Colony; directing and exhorting both Ministers and People in all their religious Societies and Assemblies, to give Praise and Glory to GOD for all the Instances of his Goodness shewn to us in the past Year: Particularly, that He has preserved the Life of our gracious Soverign King George the Third, of his Royal Consort, and so many of his illustrious House: That we still enjoy the blessed Gospel, the unsearchable Riches of Christ, and so many of our precious civil and religious Rights and Liberties: That He continues Peace to our Nation and Land: That He has blessed us with general Health in the Course of the Year; and dealt with us much better than our Fears, in bestowing upon us a competent former and later Harvest. And to offer up our sincere and hearty Prayers to the great Preserver of Men, for the Continuance of the Life of his sacred Majesty the King; of our gracious Queen Charlotte; the Prince of Wales; and the Rest of the Royal Family. That He would graciously direct and bless the King's Administrations: Give his Counselors and Ministers Wisdom and Understanding in the Things of the King's Honour, and the Prosperity and Happiness of all his People; Continue to this Colony our civil and religious Privileges; Bless our civil Rulers with Wisdom and Firmness in a righteous and happy Administration of Government; Bless and succeed the Gospel Ministry and Ordinances; Grand His Smiles and Favour to the College, and Means of Education, and abundantly prosper them to promote useful Knowledge, real Religion and Virtue: That He would greatly bless us with the influence of His holy and good Spirit and cause Religion to flourish in Power and Purity among us: Give us to enjoy Health and Peace: Enable and incline us with our Lips, our Hearts and Lives to give Him the Glory due to His great and blessed Name.

And all Servile Labour is forbidden on said Day.

GIVEN under my Hand, at the Council-Chamber in New-Haven, the Thirteenth Day of October, in the Twelfth Year of the Reign of our Sovereign Lord GEORGE the Third, of Great-Britain, France, and Ireland, KING, Defender of the Faith, &c. Anoq; domini, 1772.

-Jonth Trumbull

One Of vs Institutionalized Dates

The Thanksgiving celebrated by the Pilgrims in Plymouth was a one-of event which took place from c. Sept. 21 to Nov. 11, 1621. It was not called a thanksgiving in contemporary accounts. It followed the harvest, herefore it should be considered a "Harvest Home" celebration.

## 1630-1651 William Bradford, Of Plymouth Plantation

They began now to gather in the small harvest they had, and to fit up their houses and dwellings against winter, being all well recovered in health and strength and had all things in good plenty. For as some were thus employed in affairs abroad, others were exercised in fishing, about cod and bass and other fish, of which they took good store, of which every family had their portion. All the summer there was no want; and now began to come in store of fowl, as winter approached, of which this place did abound when they can be used (but afterward decreased by degrees). And besides waterfowl there was great store of wild turkeys, of which they took many, besides venison, etc. Besides, they had about a peck a meal a week to a person, or now since harvest, Indian corn to the proportion. Which made many afterwards write so largely of their plenty here to their friends in England, which were not feigned but true reports.

## 1620-1621 Edward Winslow, Mourt's Relation

Our harvest being gotten in, our governor sent four men on fowling, that so we might after a special manner rejoice together after we had gathered the fruits of our labor. They four in one day killed as much fowl as, with a little help beside, served the company almost a week. At which time, amongst other recreations, we exercised our arms, many of the Indians coming amongst us, and among the rest their greatest king Massasoit, with some ninety men, whom for three days we entertained and feasted, and they went out and killed five deer, which we brought to the plantation and bestowed on our governor, and upon the captain and others. And although it be not always so plentiful as it was at this time with us, yet by the goodness of God, we are so far from want that we often wish you partakers of our plenty.

The Pilgrims held a thanksgiving celebration in 1623 after a fast, and a refreshing 14-day rain which resulted in a larger harvest.

## William Bradford, Plymouth 1623, Harvest and Thanksgiving Day

"Inasmuch as the great Father has given us this year an abundant harvest of Indian corn, wheat, peas, beans, squashes, and garden vegetables, and has made the forests to abound with game and the sea with fish and clams, and inasmuch as he has protected us from the ravages of the savages, has spared us from pestilence and disease, has granted us freedom to worship God according to the dictates of our own conscience. Now I, your magistrate, do proclaim that all ye Pilgrims, with your wives and ye little ones, do gather at ye meeting house, on ye hill, between the hours of 9 and 12 in the day time, on Thursday, November 29th, of the year of our Lord one thousand six hundred and twenty-three and the third year since ye Pilgrims landed on ye Pilgrim Rock, there to listen to ye pastor and render thanksgiving to ye Almighty God for all His blessings."

## Institutionalized Celebration

# First institutionalized Congressional proclamations:

The Continental-Confederation Congress, the legislative body that governed the United States from 1774 to 1789, issued several "national days of prayer, humiliation, and thanksgiving". This proclamation was published in The Independent Gazetteer; or, the Chronicle of Freedom on November 5, 1782, the first being observed on November 28, 1782. By the United States in Congress Assembled, PROCLAMATION

It being the indispensable duty of all nations, not only to offer up their supplications to Almighty God, the giver of all good, for His gracious assistance in a time of distress, but also in a solemn and public manner, to give Him praise for His goodness in general, and especially for great and signal interpositions of His Providence in their behalf; therefore, the United States in Congress assembled, taking into their consideration the many instances of Divine goodness to these States in the course of the important conflict, in which they have been so long engaged, – the present happy and promising state of public affairs, and the events of the war in the course of the year now drawing to a close; particularly the harmony of the public Councils which is so necessary to the success of the public cause, – the perfect union and good understanding which has hitherto subsisted between them and their allies, notwithstanding the artful and unwearied attempts of the common enemy to divide them, – the success of the arms of the United States and those of their allies, – and the acknowledgment of their Independence by another European power, whose friendship and commerce must be of great and lasting advantage to these States; Do hereby recommend it to the inhabitants of these States in general, to observe and request the several states to interpose their authority, in appointing and commanding the observation of THURSDAY the TWENTY-EIGHTH DAY OF NOVEMBER next as a day of SOLEMN THANKSGIVING to GOD for all His mercies; and they do further recommend to all ranks to testify their gratitude to God for His goodness by a cheerful obedience to His laws and by promoting, each in his station, and by his influence, the practice of true and undefiled religion, which is the great foundation of public prosperity and national happiness.

Done in Congress at Philadelphia, the eleventh day of October, in the year of our LORD, one thousand seven hundred and eighty-two, and of our Sovereignty and Independence, the seventh.

-JOHN HANSON, President. CHARLES THOMSON, Secretary.

## 1778 By the United States in Congress assembled. A PROCLAMATION.

It having pleased Almighty God, through the course of the present year, to bestow great and manifold mercies on the people of these United States; and it being the indispensable duty of all men gratefully to acknowledge their obligations to Him for benefits received: Resolved, That it be, and hereby is recommended to the legislative or executive authority of each of the said states, to appoint Wednesday, the 30th day of December next, to be observed as a day of public thanksgiving and praise, that all the people may, with united hearts, on that day, express a just sense of his unmerited favors; particularly in that it hath pleased him, by his overruling providence, to support us in a just and necessary war, for the defense of our rights and liberties, by affording us seasonable supplies for our armies, by disposing the heart of a powerful monarch to enter into alliance with us, and aid our cause; by defeating the councils and evil designs of our enemies, and giving us victory over their troops; and, by the continuance of that union among these states, which, by his blessing, will be their future strength and glory. And it is further recommended, that, together with devout thanksgiving, may be joined a penitent confession of our sins, and humble supplication for pardon, through the merits of our Savior; so that, under the smiles of Heaven, our public councils may be directed, our arms by land and sea prospered, our liberty and independence secured, our schools and seminaries of learning flourish, our trade be revived, our husbandry and manufactures encreased, and the hearts of all impressed with undissembled piety, with benevolence and zeal for the public good. And it is also recommended, that recreations unsuitable to the purpose of such a solemnity may be omitted on that day. Done in Congress, this 17th day of November 1778, and in the third year of the independence of the United States of America.

# 1779 By the United States in Congress assembled. A PROCLAMATION

Whereas it becomes us humbly to approach the throne of Almighty God, with gratitude and praise for the wonders which his goodness has wrought in conducting our forefathers to this western world; for his protection to them and to their posterity amid difficulties and dangers; for raising us, their children, from deep distress to be numbered among the nations of the earth; and for arming the hands of just and mighty princes in our deliverance; and especially for that he hath been pleased to grant us the enjoyment of health, and so to order the revolving seasons, that the earth hath produced her increase in abundance, blessing the labors of the husbandmen, and spreading plenty through the land; that he hath prospered our arms and those of our ally; been a shield to our troops in the hour of danger, pointed their swords to victory and led them in triumph over the bulwarks of the foe; that he hath gone with those who went out into the wilderness against the savage tribes; that he hath stayed the hand of the spoiler, and turned back his meditated destruction; that he hath prospered our commerce, and given success to those who sought the enemy on the face of the deep; and above all, that he hath diffused the glorious light of the gospel, whereby, through the merits of our gracious Redeemer, we may become the heirs of his eternal glory: therefore, Resolved, That it be recommended to the several states, to appoint Thursday, the 9th of December next, to be a day of public and solemn thanksgiving to Almighty God for his mercies, and of prayer for the continuance of his favor and protection to these United States; to beseech him that he would be graciously pleased to influence our public councils, and bless them with wisdom from on high, with unanimity, firmness, and success; that he would go forth with our hosts and crown our arms with victory; that he would grant to his church the plentiful effusions of divine grace, and pour out his holy spirit on all ministers of the gospel; that he would bless and prosper the means of education, and spread the light of Christian knowledge through the remotest corners of the earth; that he would smile upon the labors of his people and cause the earth to bring forth her fruits in abundance; that we may with gratitude and gladness enjoy them; that he would take into his holy protection our illustrious ally, give him victory over his enemies, and render him signally great, as the father of his people and the protector of the rights of mankind; that he would graciously be pleased to turn the hearts of our enemies, and to dispense the blessings of peace to contending nations; that he would in mercy look down upon us, pardon our sins and receive us into his favor, and finally, that he would establish the independence of these United States upon the basis of religion and virtue, and support and protect them in the enjoyment of peace, liberty and safety. as long as the sun and moon shall endure, until time shall be no more. Done in Congress, || the 20th day of October, one thousand seven hundred and seventy-nine, and in the 4th year of the independence of the United States of America.

Samuel Huntington, President. Attest, Charles Thomson, Secretary.

# 1780 By the United States in Congress assembled. A PROCLAMATION

Whereas it hath pleased Almighty God, the Father of all mercies, amidst the vicissitudes and calamities of war, to bestow blessings on the people of these states, which call for their devout and thankful acknowledgments, more especially in the late remarkable interposition of his watchful providence, in rescuing the person of our Commander in Chief and the army from imminent dangers, at the moment when treason was ripened for execution; in prospering the labors of the husbandmen, and causing the earth to yield its increase in plentiful harvests; and, above all, in continuing to us the enjoyment of the gospel of peace; It is therefore recommended to the several states to set apart Thursday, the seventh day [of December next, to be observed as a day of public thanksgiving and prayer; that all the people may assemble on that day to celebrate the praises of our Divine Benefactor; to confess our unworthiness of the least of his favors, and to offer our fervent supplications to the God of all grace; that it may please him to pardon our heinous transgressions and incline our hearts for the future to keep all his laws that it may please him still to afford us the blessing of health; to comfort and relieve our brethren who are any wise afflicted or distressed; to smile upon our husbandry and trade and establish the work of our hands; to direct our public councils, and lead our forces, by land and sea, to victory; to take our illustrious ally under his special protection, and favor our joint councils and exertions for the establishment of speedy and permanent peace; to cherish all schools and seminaries of education, build up his churches in their most holy faith and to cause the knowledge of Christianity to spread over all the earth.

Done in Congress, the lath day of October 1780, and in the fifth year of the independence of the United States of America.

# 1781 By the United States in Congress assembled. A PROCLAMATION

Whereas, it hath pleased Almighty God, the supreme Disposer of all Events father of mercies, remarkably to assist and support the United States of America in their important struggle for liberty, against the long continued efforts of a powerful nation: it is the duty of all ranks to observe and thankfully acknowledge the interpositions of his Providence in their behalf. Through the whole of the contest, from its first rise to this time, the influence of divine Providence may be clearly perceived in many signal instances, of which we mention but a few. In revealing the councils of our enemies, when the discoveries were seasonable and important, and the means seemingly inadequate or fortuitous; in preserving and even improving the union of the several states, on the breach of which our enemies placed their greatest dependence; in increasing the number, and adding to the zeal and attachment of the friends of Liberty; in granting remarkable deliverances, and blessing us with the most signal success, when affairs seemed to have the most discouraging appearance; in raising up for us a powerful and generous ally, in one of the first of the European powers; in confounding the councils of our enemies, and suffering them to pursue such measures as have most directly contributed to frustrate their own desires and expectations; above all, in making their extreme cruelty of their officers and soldiers to the inhabitants of these states, when in their power, and their savage devastation of property, the very means of cementing our union, and adding vigor to every effort in opposition to them. And as we cannot help leading the good people of these states to a retrospect on the events which have taken place since the beginning of the war, so we beg recommend in a particular manner that they may observe and acknowledge to their observation, the goodness of God in the year now drawing to a conclusion: in which a mutiny in the American Army was not only happily appeased but became in its issue a pleasing and undeniable proof of the unalterable attachment of the people in general to the cause of liberty since great and real grievances only made them tumultuously seek redress while the abhorred the thoughts of going over to the enemy, in which the Confederation of the United States has been completed by the accession of all without exception in which there have been so many instances of prowess and success in our armies; particularly in the southern states, where, notwithstanding the difficulties with which they had to struggle, they have recovered the whole country which the enemy had overrun, leaving them only a post or two upon on or near the sea: in which we have been so powerfully and effectually assisted by our allies, while in all the conjunct operations the most perfect union and harmony has subsisted in the allied army: in which there has been so plentiful a harvest, and so great abundance of the fruits of the earth of every kind, as not only enables us easily to supply the wants of the army, but gives comfort and happiness to the whole people: and in which, after the success of our allies by sea, a General of the first Rank, with his whole army, has been captured by the allied forces under the direction of our illustrious Commander in Chief. It is therefore recommended to the several states to set apart the 13th day of December next, to be religiously observed as a Day of Thanksgiving and Prayer; that all the people may assemble on that day, with grateful hearts, to celebrate the praises of our gracious Benefactor; to confess our manifold sins; to offer up our most fervent supplications to the God of all grace, that it may please Him to pardon our offenses, and incline our hearts for the future to keep all his laws; to comfort and relieve all our brethren who are in distress or captivity; to prosper our husbandmen, and give success to all engaged in lawful commerce; to impart wisdom and integrity to our counselors, judgment and fortitude to our officers and soldiers; to protect and prosper our illustrious ally, and favor our united exertions for the speedy establishment of a safe, honorable and lasting peace; to bless all seminaries of learning; and cause the knowledge of God to cover the earth, as the waters cover the seas.

## 1782 By the United States in Congress assembled. A PROCLAMATION.

It being the indispensable duty of all nations, not only to offer up their supplications to Almighty God, the giver of all good, for his gracious assistance in the a time of public distress, but also in a solemn and public manner to give him praise for his goodness in general, and especially for great and signal interpositions of his Providence in their behalf; therefore, the United States in Congress assembled, taking into their consideration the many instances of divine goodness to these states, in the course of the important conflict in which they have been so long engaged; and the present happy and promising state of public affairs; and the events of the war in the course of the last year now drawing to a close, particularly the harmony of the public councils, which is so necessary to the success of the public cause; the perfect union and good understanding which has hitherto subsisted between them and their allies, notwithstanding the artful and unwearied attempts of the common enemy to sow dissension between them divide them; the success of the arms of the United States and those of their allies, and the acknowledgment of their independence by another European power, whose friendship and commerce must be of great and lasting advantage to these states; and the success of their arms and those of their allies in different parts do hereby recommend it to the inhabitants of these states in general, to observe, and recommend it to the executives of request the several states to interpose their authority in appointing and requiring commanding the observation of the last Thursday, in the 28 day of November next, as a day of solemn thanksgiving to God for all his mercies: and they do further recommend to all ranks, to testify their gratitude to God for his goodness, by a cheerful obedience to his laws, and by promoting, each in his station, and by his influence, the practice of true and undefiled religion, which is the great foundation of public prosperity and national happiness. Given, &c.

## 1783 By the United States in Congress assembled. A PROCLAMATION

Whereas it hath pleased the Supreme Ruler of all human events, to dispose the hearts of the late belligerent powers to put a period to the effusion of human blood, by proclaiming a cessation of all hostilities by sea and land, and these United States are not only happily rescued from the dangers distresses and calamities which they have so long and so magnanimously sustained to which they have been so long exposed, but their freedom, sovereignty and independence ultimately acknowledged by the king of Great Britain. And whereas in the progress of a contest on which the most essential rights of human nature depended, the interposition of Divine Providence in our favor hath been most abundantly and most graciously manifested, and the citizens of these United States have every possible reason for praise and gratitude to the God of their salvation. Impressed, therefore, with an exalted sense of the magnitude of the blessings by which we are surrounded, and of our entire dependence on that Almighty Being, from whose goodness and bounty they are derived, the United States in Congress assembled do recommend it to the several States, to set apart the second Thursday in December next, as a day of public thanksgiving, that all the people may then assemble to celebrate with one voice grateful hearts and united voices, the praises of their

Supreme and all bountiful Benefactor, for his numberless favors and mercies. That he hath been pleased to conduct us in safety through all the perils and vicissitudes of the war; that he hath given us unanimity and resolution to adhere to our just rights; that he hath raised up a powerful ally to assist us in supporting them, and hath so far crowned our united efforts with success, that in the course of the present year, hostilities have ceased, and we are left in the undisputed possession of our liberties and independence, and of the fruits of our own land, and in the free participation of the treasures of the sea; that he hath prospered the labor of our husbandmen with plentiful harvests; and above all, that he hath been pleased to continue to us the light of the blessed gospel, and secured to us in the fullest extent the rights of conscience in faith and worship. And while our hearts overflow with gratitude, and our lips set forth the praises of our great Creator, that we also offer up fervent supplications, that it may please him to pardon all our offenses, to give wisdom and unanimity to our public councils, to cement all our citizens in the bonds of affection, and to inspire them with an earnest regard for the national honor and interest, to enable them to improve the days of prosperity by every good work, and to be lovers of peace and tranquillity; that he may be pleased to bless us in our husbandry, our commerce and navigation; to smile upon our seminaries and means of education, to cause pure religion and virtue to flourish, to give peace to all nations, and to fill the world with his glory. Done by the United States in Congress assembled, witness his Excellency Elias Boudinot, our President, this 18th day of October, in the year of our Lord one thousand seven hundred and eighty-three, and of the sovereignty and independence of the United States of America the eighth.

1784 By the United States in Congress assembled. A PROCLAMATION.

Whereas it hath pleased the Supreme Ruler of the universe, of his infinite goodness and mercy, so to calm the minds and do away the resentments of the powers lately engaged in a most bloody and destructive war, and to dispose their hearts towards amity and friendship, that a general pacification hath taken place, and particularly a Definitive Treaty of peace between the said United States of America and his Britannic Majesty, was signed at Paris, on the 3d day of September, in the year of our Lord 1783; the instruments of the final ratifications of which were exchanged at Passy, on the 12th day of May, in the year of our Lord 1784, whereby a finishing hand was put to the great work of peace, and the freedom, sovereignty and independence of these states, fully and completely established: And whereas in pursuit of the great work of freedom and independence, and the progress of the contest in which the United States of America have been engaged, and on the success of which the dearest and most essential rights of human nature depended, the benign interposition of Divine Providence hath, on many occasions, been most miraculously and abundantly manifested; and the citizens of the United States have the greatest reason to return their most hearty and sincere praises and thanksgiving to the God of their deliverance; whose name be praised: Deeply impressed therefore with the sense of the mercies manifested to these United States, and of the blessings which it hath pleased God, to shower down on us, of our future dependence, at all times, on his power and mercy as the only source from which so great benefits can be derived; we, the United States of America, in the Committee of the States assembled, do earnestly recommend to the supreme executives of the several states, to set apart Tuesday, the 19th day of October next, as a day of public prayer and thanksgiving, that all the people of the United States may then assemble in their respective churches and congregations, to celebrate with grateful hearts, and joyful and united voices, the mercies and praises of their all-bountiful Creator, most holy, and most righteous! for his innumerable favors and mercies vouchsafed unto them; more especially that he hath been graciously pleased so to conduct us through the perils and dangers of the war, as finally to establish the United States in freedom and independence, and to give them a name and place among the princes and nations of the earth; that he hath raised up great captains and men of war from amongst us, to lead our armies, and in our greatest difficulties and distresses hath given us unanimity to adhere to and assert our just rights and privileges; and that he hath been most graciously pleased also, to raise up a most powerful prince and magnanimous people, as allies, to assist us in effectually supporting and maintaining them; that he hath been pleased to prosper the labor of our husbandmen; that there is no famine or want seen throughout our land: And above all, that he hath been pleased to continue to us the light of gospel truths, and secured to us, in the fullest manner, the rights of conscience in faith and worship. And while our hearts overflow with gratitude, and our lips pronounce the praises of our great and merciful Creator, that we may also offer up our joint and fervent supplications, that it may please him of his infinite goodness and mercy, to pardon all our sins and offenses; to inspire with wisdom and a true sense of public good, all our public councils; to strengthen and cement the bonds of love and affection between all our citizens; to impress them with an earnest regard for the public good and national faith and honour, and to teach them to improve the days of peace by every good work; to pray that he will, in a more especial manner, shower down his blessings on Louis the Most Christian King our ally, to prosper his house, that his son's sons may long sit on the throne of their ancestors, a blessing to the people entrusted to his charge; to bless all mankind, and inspire the princes and nations of the earth with the love of peace, that the sound of war may be heard of no more; that he may be pleased to smile upon us, and bless our husbandry, fishery, our commerce, and especially our schools and seminaries of learning; and to raise up from among our youth, men eminent for virtue, learning and piety, to his service in church and state; to cause virtue and true religion to flourish, to give to all nations amity, peace and concord, and to fill the world with his glory. Done by the United States, in the Committee of the States assembled, witness the honbl Samuel Hardy, chairman, this-- day of--, in the year of our Lord, &c. and in the 9th of the sovereignty and independence of the United States of America.

# First Presidential Proclamation

## 1789- THANKSGIVING DAY, BY THE PRESIDENT OF THE UNITED STATES OF AMERICA - A PROCLAMATION, George Washington

Whereas it is the duty of all Nations to acknowledge the providence of almighty God, to obey his will, to be grateful for his benefits, and humbly to implore his protection and favor - and Whereas both Houses of Congress have by their joint Committee requested me "to recommend to the People of the United States a day of public thanksgiving and prayer to be observed by acknowledging with grateful hearts the many signal favors of Almighty God, especially by affording them an opportunity peaceably to establish a form of government for their safety and happiness." Now therefore I do recommend and assign Thursday the 26th day of November next to be devoted by the People of these States to the service of that great and glorious Being, who is the beneficent Author of all the good that was, that is, or that will be – That we may then all unite in rendering unto him our sincere and humble thanks – for his kind care and protection of the People of this country previous to their becoming a Nation – for the signal and manifold mercies, and the favorable interpositions of his providence, which we experienced in the course and conclusion of the late war –for the great degree of tranquillity, union, and plenty, which we have since enjoyed – for the peaceable and rational manner in which we have been enabled to establish constitutions of government for our safety and happiness, and particularly the national One now lately instituted, for the civil and religious liberty with which we are blessed, and the means we have of acquiring and diffusing useful knowledge; and in general for all the great and various favors which he hath been pleased to confer upon us. And also that we may then unite in most humbly offering our prayers and supplications to the great Lord and Ruler of Nations and beseech him to pardon our national and other transgressions – to enable us all, whether in public or private stations, to perform our several and relative duties properly and punctually – to render our national government a blessing to all the People, by constantly being a government of wise, just, and constitutional laws, discreetly and faithfully executed and obeyed – to protect and guide all Sovereigns and Nations (especially such as have shewn kindness unto us) and to bless them with good government, peace, and concord – To promote the knowledge and practice of true religion and virtue, and the increase of science among them and Us – and generally to grant unto all mankind such a degree of temporal prosperity as he alone knows to be best. Given under my hand at the City of New York the third day of October in the year of our Lord 1789.

-GO. WASHINGTON.

# National Holiday- Lincoln

1863- By the President of the United States of America, A Proclamation

Washington, D.C.
October 3, 1863

The year that is drawing towards its close, has been filled with the blessings of fruitful fields and healthful skies. To these bounties, which are so constantly enjoyed that we are prone to forget the source from which they come, others have been added, which are of so extraordinary a nature, that they cannot fail to penetrate and soften even the heart which is habitually insensible to the ever watchful providence of Almighty God. In the midst of a civil war of unequalled magnitude and severity, which has sometimes seemed to foreign States to invite and to provoke their aggression, peace has been preserved with all nations, order has been maintained, the laws have been respected and obeyed, and harmony has prevailed everywhere except in the theatre of military conflict; while that theatre has been greatly contracted by the advancing armies and navies of the Union. Needful diversions of wealth and of strength from the fields of peaceful industry to the national defence, have not arrested the plough, the shuttle or the ship; the axe has enlarged the borders of our settlements, and the mines, as well of iron and coal as of the precious metals, have yielded even more abundantly than heretofore. Population has steadily increased, notwithstanding the waste that has been made in the camp, the siege and the battle-field; and the country, rejoicing in the consciousness of augmented strength and vigor, is permitted to expect continuance of years with large increase of freedom. No human counsel hath devised nor hath any mortal hand worked out these great things. They are the gracious gifts of the Most High God, who, while dealing with us in anger for our sins, hath nevertheless remembered mercy. It has seemed to me fit and proper that they should be solemnly, reverently and gratefully acknowledged as with one heart and one voice by the whole American People. I do therefore invite my fellow citizens in every part of the United States, and also those who are at sea and those who are sojourning in foreign lands, to set apart and observe the last Thursday of November next, as a day of Thanksgiving and Praise to our beneficent Father who dwelleth in the Heavens. And I recommend to them that while offering up the ascriptions justly due to Him for such singular deliverances and blessings, they do also, with humble penitence for our national perverseness and disobedience, commend to His tender care all those who have become widows, orphans, mourners or sufferers in the lamentable civil strife in which we are unavoidably engaged, and fervently implore the interposition of the Almighty Hand to heal the wounds of the nation and to restore it as soon as may be consistent with the Divine purposes to the full enjoyment of peace, harmony, tranquillity and Union.

In testimony whereof, I have hereunto set my hand and caused the Seal of the United States to be affixed.

Done at the City of Washington, this Third day of October, in the year of our Lord one thousand eight hundred and sixty-three, and of the Independence of the United States the Eighty-eighth.

By the President: Abraham Lincoln

William H. Seward,
Secretary of State

-*Collected Works of Abraham Lincoln*, edited by Roy P. Basler et al.

## Disclosing the Seasonal Mysteries

In North America as in Europe seasonal change prior to scientific weather predicting and accurate calendars was an important mystery. Even with modern methods and aids preparation for seasonal celebration is felt "in the air" well before calendars are consulted. Until a season is upon you it is abstract. You can't see it or feel it until it is too late to plan for it. It can be dangerous especially the November transition to winter in the northern hemisphere. Disclosure of this important feature of the dark folkloric landscape is therefore essential especially for agrarian societies therefore the date is disclosed by artifacts of celebration and administration. Around the fifth of November temperatures begin to drop and killing frosts intensify. From this time onward travelers confront deadly weather and work outside becomes more difficult. It is important to note that the harvest should be long past and that celebrations of the harvest occur earlier. The Harvest Home celebration generally occurs in the British Isles around September 24. Following the growing season and harvest fields pastures and orchards are littered with foliage, fruit, vegetables and pruned branches which if it is not burned breed fungus and pests.

The Celtic season of Samhain which starts on November 1 is more closely related and is a celebration of the transition from light to darkness, life to death. Note however, that the celebration of the great deliverance on November 5 was chosen purely by accident-the original plotters had planned to blow up parliament much earlier in the year but were forced to re-schedule thus making the important date selected to be even more of a wonder! The first week of November was a time that once the crops were safely in, could be used for gatherings such as court and legislative sessions. It was a time for reassessing of employment arrangements to be ready for Spring planting. Hiring fairs were scheduled. It was the mid-term break for the Michaelmass term for educational institutions. In the liturgical year the first of November would begin the last month before the onset of the advent fast which began around November 30 during which celebration would be difficult. All of these activities were artifacts that disclosed the period so that consequences of a lack of preparation could be avoided. Courts, legislatures and fairs brought people together thus reinforcing celebration.

-The Book of Bonfire Night, C. Bladey, c. 2017.

# Puritans The fifth and Thanksgiving

## William DeLoss Love, The Fast and Thanksgiving Days of New England, 1895

THE

FAST AND THANKSGIVING DAYS

OF

NEW ENGLAND

BY

W: DELOSS LOVE, JR., PH.D.

p. 48 …The discovery of the Gunpowder Plot in 1605 brought out the common sentiment. A diabolical scheme had been formed — it was thought by the Papists — to blow up the Parliament House on the 5th of November, the first day of the session. Vast quantities of gunpowder and inflammable material were found concealed in the vaults underneath. The traitors were arrested and executed.3 In consequence of this deliverance the day was ordered to be kept as a " public thanksgiving to Almighty God " every year, " that unfeigned thankfulness may never be forgotten,

[3] Knight's Hist. of England, chap, bcxxi. ; Fuller's Chh. Hist., iii. 212-219; Neal's Hist. of Puritans, U. 52-54.

and that all ages to come may yield praises to God's

divine Majesty for the same." All ministers were ordered to say prayers thereon, for which special forms were for many years provided, and the people were commanded to attend worship. Thomas Fuller, writing years afterwards, expressed a regret that this " red letter day" had fallen into decay. But throughout most of the term of the exodus to New England it was generally esteemed, except by the Papists, and esteemed, too, by some who were abused at its services.[1] The custom of burning at night the image of Guy Fawkes the conspirator, which had been paraded through the streets during the day by boys who begged and sang, was continued in England to within a century : —

" Pray to remember

The fifth of November,

Gunpowder treason and plot,

When the King and his train

Had nearly been slain,

Therefore it shall not be forgot."

This annual thanksgiving, together with the one established

later on the 29th of May, was abolished in 1833, though both had previously fallen into disuse. Both were recognized in New England, to some extent among the Congregationalists, but chiefly in the Episcopal Church on account of their place in the calendar.

[1] The prayer for the day had this inspiring petition: "Root ont that Anti-christian and Babylonish sect which say of Jerusalem, Down with it even to the ground. Cut off those workers of Iniquity, whose Religion is Rebellion, whose Faith is Faction, whose Practice is murdering both Soul and Body." In 1633 this was altered by the archbishop so as to turn it against the Puritans (Neal. ii. 254). " On the 5th of November we as well as the Churchmen bless God for our deliverance from the Gunpowder Plot."—Peirce's Vindication, etc., p. 505....

p.219-......It was impossible to resist the hilarious proceedings on the Fifth of November, — " Guy Fawkes's Day." They dared not if they would. The Royal Commissioners in 1665 had proposed the permanent establishment of the 5th of November, the 29th of May, and the 30th of January, — the first two as thanksgivings, the last as a fast. [1] Only the first was celebrated to any extent, and that because it was " Pope's Day," — a suitable time, it was thought, for mocking pageants and bonfires. The Church of England kept it with religious services, but it never became popular except with riotous youths. Still the bonfire and cannon firing, by this means, became later a form of celebrating thanksgiving, especially during and after the Revolution. Such demonstrations had been tolerated a century before this on Guy Fawkes's Day, and some other English holidays, though the fathers protested against them if these chanced to fall on the Sabbath. We can understand how English ships in port would think it proper to commemorate the New England thanksgiving in the same manner. At all events they did so, and certain divines uttered their protest against it. Upon one occasion, in 1662, a public thanksgiving for a good harvest notwithstanding a drought chanced to be appointed on the 5th of November, and then there was a combination of religious services and bonfires which could not have been

[1] Mass. Col. Rec., iv. pt. 2. p. 212.

agreeable to all,[1] though they did the same thing in 1667, two years after the proposal of the Royal Comissioners, which might have been one cause for it.

The celebration of the Fifth of November was at its

height in England about that time, and was afterwards revived in connection with the wars against France. It was the same in New England, and so great was the disturbance and danger of the customary riotous pageants that it became necessary to enact laws prohibiting them.[2] As the Revolution drew near they died out altogether, and whatever customs were appropriate passed over to the Thanksgiving Day, or the Fourth of July.

The customs which have clustered round the New England Thanksgiving are by far the most interesting. An autumn harvest festival has a relation to social life which generates them. Since the Pilgrim Fathers celebrated their feast at Plymouth, the same forces which then inspired it have been at work, gradually creating a festival peculiarly adapted to preserve the savor of early New England life. In this respect it is unique among our holidays. Others are of later date. They do not reach back into those adventurous experiences in the wilderness, nor introduce us to the households of our simple, hearty, pious forefathers as this does. Here alone do we meet with customs which can claim originality and antiquity, more wholesome if less fantastic than those which have made England's holidays

[1] Felt was led to give quite an erroneous impression concerning this " Pope's Day," because he overlooked the fact that it was also a public thanksgiving. Annals of Salem, ii. 45 ; Frothingham's History of Charlestown, p. 204.

[2] Acts and Resolves, iii. 647, 664, 997; Am. Antiq. Soc. Coll., v. p. xxviii.

a blessing to her people. The harvest festival was developed by home life. Its power is social rather than religious. The feast has been from the first the sustaining element, not so much on its own account, as because it furnished the occasion for family gatherings, and this we must follow in tracing the growth of customs. The germ is found in such social repasts as we have witnessed among the Pilgrims in Holland and the Seituate flock, which we have noted as kept after the Pequot war, and which were officially recognized in 1645 by the Westminster Assembly of Divines in the " Directory for Public Worship." It was a seed that fell into good ground among those who were dependent upon harvests and were stripped of their ancient holidays. So it grew, thriving especially in the Plymouth Colony. As the household became the self-sustaining unit of their life, it was better that the family should feast together, rather than that the richer should invite the poorer, or that they should divide into three companies as Lothrop's church did. So in a few years this became a distinctive feature of thanksgiving days. At the same time it was no such feast as interfered with the religious features of the day, which were dominant, particularly in the Massachusetts Bay Colony and in Connecticut. Amusements were contrary to the law everywhere. The Puritan family met at the noontime meal in a spirit of deep gratitude, and worship was the expression of their feelings rather than recreation. They would not have thought of indulging in those hilarious customs which arose after a century, only to be rebuked by their ministers, and at last became common because the Puritan fervor had waned. That which is now usually esteemed as the early celebration of thanksgiving does not date back into the lives of the first comers. It was no such occasion as that festival week at Plymouth in 1621 has led many writers to suppose. The feast itself was not an elaborate affair, — no Puritan meal was. Extra fare was provided, perhaps occasionally a wild turkey or a haunch of venison,1 and there was an assembly of the family, with sometimes invited guests, but they did not abandon themselves to feasting nor forget that the day was holy unto the Lord. The father was wont to read aloud some thanksgiving sermon, either the evening before in preparation for the day, or as the family gathered about the fireside after the second service. The theme of conversation was the mercies of God to the first settlers, — such reminiscences as we meet with from the pen of Johnson, Roger Clap, and Mather, — and there were recitals of providential deliverances, which the hero might well have made thrilling stories

---

[1] An interesting incident, professing to relate to a thanksgiving dinner, was recorded by Rev. Lawrence Conant, of Danvers, in 1714 as follows : —

" When ye services at ye meeting house were ended ye council and other dignitaries were entertained at ye house of Mr. Epes, on ye hill near by, and we had a bountiful Thanksgiving dinner with bear's meat and venison, the last of which was a fine buck, shot in ye woods near by. Ye bear was killed in Lynn woods near Reading.

" After ye blessing was craved by Mr. Garrich of Wrentham, word came that ye buck was shot on ye Lord's day by Pequot, an Indian, who came to Mr. Epes with a lye in his mouth like Ananias of old.

" Ye council therefore refused to eat ye venison, but it was after ward decided that Pequot should receive 40 stripes save one, for lying and profaning ye Lord's day, restore Mr. Epes ye cost of ye deer, and considering this a just and righteous sentence on ye sinful heathen, and that a blessing had been craved on ye meat, ye council all par took of it but Mr. Shepard, whose conscience was tender on ye point of ye venison."

of hairbreadth escapes, to be remembered by the children, even if they forgot the moral. The proclamations themselves encouraged the people to such occupations, being a presentation of their causes for gratitude, and possibly those extended dissertations may have grown out of this ancient custom. Indeed, there were generally two services on the day for nearly a century, and the feast, crowded in between them, had no great chance to expand. It finally made war against the second service and overcame it. We find Samuel Sewall in 1721 discussing the matter with Colonel Townsend in the Council Chamber at Boston, and the latter would not " move a jot towards having two," though he would consent on that particular occasion.[1] Evidently the colonel was of those who felt that the latter part of the day should be devoted to social enjoyments in the home, giving more time to the feast, which had been a feature in Sewall's family life for at least twenty-five years, many instances being noted in his diary. Even before this the evening exercise had been put at a later hour than usual, or in some towns, where the people found it inconvenient to return to it, altogether abandoned. At first even special thanksgivings, whatever the time of year, were honored by a dinner, but after the days became annual, and more particularly associated with the harvest, the high festival was reserved for the autumn. The bounties of the season favored the feast, and that in turn warmed the social circle. So it came about that ere the first quarter of the eighteenth century had passed, the autumn harvest festival was a fully grown and established institution. As they might have

[1] Sewall's Diary, iii. 294.

expected, advantage was taken of this social license, particularly among such as made the inn their evening resort and had a fondness for the sizzling " flip." A thanksgiving, too, which commemorated a victory in war, offered special inducements to celebrate by noisy demonstrations. Rev. Daniel Wadsworth, of Hartford, in his manuscript sermon preached July 25, 1745, closes with this caution : " Take heed yt after ye public exercise of ye day is over yt none of you run into those follies and indecencies yt are unbecoming such a solemnity as this, let not this solemnity be dishonored by any disorders committed on this day or in ye evening following, let there be no carousing at publick houses nor unseemly noises or clamors in ye streets." [1] This was the common attitude of the ministers at the time, but such demonstrations occurred, nevertheless. The harvest thanksgiving was not so liable to them. It was a quiet day, the service at the meeting-house in the morning being attended by all, and the feast, followed by social fireside pleasures, filling the remainder of the day. After the Revolution, — which was the greatest force of the century for the development of our social life, — these latter features were very greatly expanded. In some respects they were liberalized. The farmer and his grown-up sons thought it a proper time to hunt the wolf which had raided his flock. In the home, games were indulged in by the younger members of the family, such as "Hunt the slipper," " Fox and geese," and " Blind man's buff." Pilgrimages to the old home, which had long been customary, were more highly regarded. Some thought even

[1] MS. Ser. in Conn. Hist. Soc.

then that too much pleasure was a desecration of the day. They did not see how it was all the work of healthy and natural forces. That had survived which was fittest. The sabbatical thanksgiving of the forefathers could not have lived. It could never have been made such a festival as Christmas, for the truth was lacking. Their calamities and adventures in the wilderness were over. So the family consecrated the day anew to its own religious and social uses, honoring alike the worship of the Puritan and the feast of the Pilgrims; and, as years pass, it becomes more and more evident that the family life alone, which has saved the day, can preserve it for coming generations. There are those now living who have heard their fathers tell of the New England Thanksgiving Day a hundred years ago. In the great red farmhouse on the hill, preparations were begun long before the day. The turkey that stalked about the dooryard had been watched with hungry eyes, and fattened with urgent care. Pumpkins had been brought from the cornfield to sun themselves on the woodpile. Ah! it was a sure sign of the day's approach; and they might have defended their right to be there without being laughed at by the ancient chronicler's words: " Let no man make a jest at pumpkins, for with this fruit the Lord was pleased to feed his people to their good content till corne and cattel were increased." [1] A goodly supply of all garden vegetables was at hand. Apples and pears, the best in the orchard, had been gathered and hidden away in the dark to mellow. Alas for the feast, if there was not molasses enough

[1] Johnson's Wonder- Working Providence, p. 56.

to be had ; there could be none without it.[1] Stores of raisins and citron had been laid in, so there was something for the girls to do, while the boys looked after the popcorn, which had been seasoning in the wood shed chamber, or picked up walnuts under the old shagbark-tree in the pasture. Then there was a deal of work necessary within the house, — the wedding china to be brought out, the brasses all around to be polished, especially the ancestral andirons, and the spare chambers to be set in order, with extemporized beds in every available corner, — all ready for the home-coming.

[1] The town of Colchester, Conn., in 1705, voted to put off the Thanksgiving from the first to the second Thursday in November;

and the tradition is well supported that the cause was a delay in receiving a supply of molasses

- — Barber's Conn. Hist. Coll., p. 305.
- Love, William, DeLoss, <u>The fast and Thanksgiving Days of New England,</u> 1895.

# 1675? - UNCLE TRACY'S THANKSGIVING

There can be no doubt but that this queer song runs back in time to the end of the first century of the colony. It is purely traditional. I heard it as early as 1825, and I do not believe it has ever been printed until now.

I have no doubt as to its antiquity. It belongs before 1689 and after 1661.

UNCLE TRACY'S THANKSGIVING. 1675?

'T Was up to Uncle Tracy's  
The Fifth of November,  
Last Thanksgiving night  
As I very well remember  
And there we had a Frolic,

A Frolic indeed,  
Where we drank good full Glasses  
Of old Anise-seed.

And there was Mr. Holmes  
And there was Peter Drew,

And there was Seth Gilbert  
And Seth Thomas too

And there were too many  
Too many for to name,

And by and by I'll tell you how  
They carried on the Game.

They carried on the Game

Till't was late in the night,  
And one pretty Girl  
Almost lost her Eyesight .  
No wonder, no wonder

No wonder indeed,  
For she drank good full Glasses  
Of old Anise-seed.

-Hale, Edward, Everett, <u>New England History in Ballads,</u> 1903. p.29.

# Thanksgivings Day Parades and Fantasticals

It is widely acknowledged that a point in the 19th century that the guising/house visitation/procession aspects of Guy Fawkes Day/ Bonfire Night/ Popes Day/ Night celebrations in the United States morphed into the traditions of Thanksgiving Day parades and Fantasticals.

Remember that the Pilgrim/Puritan thanksgiving was an anti-celebration observance on behalf of a small group and never a national celebration". They would have opposed such a concept.

The moving of Popes Day to Thanksgiving was brought about by reforms promised by the new nation after the Revolutionary War and the need to distance celebrations from British tradition substituting "rule of law" for "Mobocracy".

The Fantasticals and Target Compnies, N.Y. Times Nov. 28, 1873, p.8

## THE FANTASTICALS AND TARGET COMPANIES.

Thanksgiving would not be Thanksgiving without the Fantasticals, alias the ragamuffins, exhibited themselves in the streets and performed their accustomed pranks for the delectation of the youngsters throughout the City. These people turned out yesterday in good force, and in every variety of costume. The target companies were not at all behindhand in turning out, and one could not travel half a-dozen blocks without encountering one of them with the inevitable accompaniments of a flaming torchlight and a band of musicians that managed to make day and night hideous with their discordant strains. Each target company was invariably attended by a crowd of boisterous urchins, who cheered and shouted frantically, doubtless in the vain hope of drowning the music of the bands.

## 1909- (1870) The Surviving Fantasticals

New York Times, Nov. 23, 1909, pg.8.

Brooklyn clergyman, preaching to children on Sunday, made some extraordinary misstatements about the custom among ill-bred children, now tolerated by the police and encouraged by the undiscriminating citizen, of disguising themselves in cast-off clothing on Thanksgiving Day and begging for pennies in the streets. It is an abominable custom, amounting to a public nuisance, and it should be suppressed, but it is unmistakably a survival of an ancient if grotesque ceremony whose meaning has been forgotten. The clergyman we have mentioned told the children that the custom belongs to the Puritan festival of Thanksgiving. He said, according to The Tribune's report:

About the year 1870, on Thanksgiving Day, the different societies in New York, dressed in elegant costumes, paraded the streets and made social calls.

As a matter of fact, the fantastical are related more closely to the Guy Fawkes Day grotesqueries in old England. Thanksgiving Day was never a day of parades of any sort, or of social calls, though what social calls have to do with the disguised children begging in the streets and invading the areaways with their clamor for money is not easily understood. In 1870, and long before, Thanksgiving was a day for churchgoing in the morning and home dinners, with family reunions in the afternoon. Coincident with Thanksgiving this year will be the anniversary of the evacuation of New York by the British troops in 1783. Evacuation Day was for many years a holiday kept with a show of great public spirit in Manhattan. There was generally a military parade with public meetings and dinners in the evening.

The parade of the so-called Fantasticals was one of the features of the day. They were not children, and they were not beggars. They were members of target companies and chowder clubs, generally, and their parades were finished with some sort of banquet and much drinking. The origin of the Fantasticals is dubious. They may have been intended to perpetuate remembrance of the ragged and forlorn appearance of the Continental troops when they marched victoriously into the city the British had surrendered. Certainly they had some sort of historical association with the Horribles who parade in New England towns on Bunker Hill Day, and the Bummers in Philadelphia. But no historian of New York has thought it worth while to trace their origin. They were a rowdy lot from the beginning, frowned upon by the respectable people. But they paraded on Thanksgiving Day only when that revered festival fell on Nov. 25, the anniversary of evacuation.

The celebration of Evacuation Day has been disregarded in recent years. As a festival it expired in a blaze of glory when its centenary was celebrated in 1883. There was a time when its military spectacle rivaled that of the Fourth of July, when a reminder to the people of the strength of the country and State in arms was considered appropriate and inspiring on both those anniversaries. The child beggars of Thanksgiving are the survival of the Evacuation Day Fantasticals. They have no historic association with the Puritan feast of the harvest. The Brooklyn clergyman's idea that the children should be encouraged to blacken their faces or wear masks, don cast-off rags, and beg pennies in the streets Thanksgiving morning, in order that they may have money to put in the collection box for the poor, is creditable enough to his heart, but not to his head. The little beggars are not making nuisances of themselves for charity's sake. (*typos in original*)

# New York boys in a wide range of curious garments, 1911.
(Photo courtesy of the Library of Congress)

## 1999- Elizabeth Pleck, "The making of the domestic occasion: The history of Thanksgiving in the United States"

In: Journal of Social History (Summer 1999) Vol. 32, Iss. 4; pg. 773, 17 pgs).

Pleck writes,

'As William Dean Howells put it, "The poor recognize [Thanksgiving] as a sort of carnival," a masculine escape from the family, a day of rule breaking, and spontaneous mirth . . . Drunken men and boys, often masked, paraded from house to house and demanded to be treated. Boys misbehaved and men committed physical assaults on Thanksgiving as well as on Christmas."

"Groups of men, crossdressing, who called themselves the Fantastics or Fantasticals, masqueraded on Thanksgiving beginning in the 1780s.. . Subsequently the Fantastics copied these and other elements of English mumming, such as drunkenness and ridiculing authority . . . An editorial in a Pennsylvania newspaper in 1870 defended the Fantastics, on the grounds that "it is better to be merry than sad, and if, as some genial writer asserts, a good hearty laugh takes a nail out of your coffin, a parade of the fantasticals can not fail to lessen the bills of mortality."

## 1898- William Shepard Walsh, "Curiosities of popular customs and of rites, ceremonies, observances"

In: Social Science (1897), p. 924:

Curiosities of popular customs and of rites, ceremonies, observances, and miscellaneous antiquities by Walsh, William Shepard, 1898

…Another and somewhat strange way of observing the holiday in New York has been, up to very recent years, to dress one's self in the most fantastic costume imaginable and parade the streets. This was undoubtedly a survival of the old Pope Day or Guy Fawkes's Day (q. v.) mummeries translated to a later day in the same month. Hundreds of companies of these motley persons, under some such name as the " Square Back Eangers," the " Slenderfoot Ai-my," or the " Original Hounds," and dressed chiefly, as an old account says, as "clowns, Yankees, Irishmen, kings, washerwomen, and courtiers," thronged the streets all day. These "ragamuffin parades" have fallen into disuse except for a few small boys, but as recently as 1885 they were in full swing, as the following paragraph, printed in the Sun on November 27,1885, testifies:
" Fantastic processions burst out all over the town in unusual abundance and filled the popular eye with a panorama that looked like a crazy-quilt show grown crazy and filled the popular ear with the din of thumping drums and blaring trumpets. Thirty-six companies of fantastics had permits to

march around making an uproar, and they did it with great success. Local statesmen went around with the down-town paraders and helped them whoop things up. There were lots and lots of fantastics who hadn't any permit, and who didn't care either. They were the thousands and thousands of small boys who put on their sisters' old dresses, smeared paint on their faces, pulled on red, yellow, brown, black, and indiscriminate wigs, and pranced round their own particular streets, without the least fear of police interference." These fantastic parades sometimes attained the dignity of a political demonstration. In 1870 the chief feature of Thanksgiving Day observances in New York was a parade of the Shandley Legion. The route was from Essex Market to Irving Hall, and the whole town turned out to see it. The newspapers the day before announced that " Senator Tweed will review the troops from the parlor windows of the Blossom Club, and not from the balcony of his residence at Forty-First Street and Fifth Avenue." Prizes worth over ten thousand dollars were distributed among the paraders. The list of those contributing towards the prizes makes rather interesting reading at this time. Here are a few

extracts from the list : Senator William M. Tweed, $500 in gold ; Assistant District Attorney Fellows, a diamond ring, worth $75 ; James Timoney, of Wallack's, silver, $20 ; E. D. Bassford, set of crockery, worth $175 ; the Hon. Tim J. Campbell, check for $50 ; Mr. William Edelstein (law partner of young Tweed), $50 ; a friend of Commissioner Shandley, a set of harness ; General Miles, president of the Sixpenny Savings Bank, gold, $100 ; the Stable Gang, bills, $100 ; W. J. Florence, the comedian, check for $50. The Sun, in concluding its list of these donations, says, " And so on to an almost interminable length, the list comprising everything from a piano to a shirt-stud."

# 1833-Grand Fantastical Parade, New-York, Dec 2d.

Image above-

Title: Grand fantastical parade, New-York, Dec 2d. 1833

Summary

Another burlesque parade (see no. 1833-11), satirizing Andrew Jackson as a military hero and President and the local militia displays of the period. The print apparently portrays one of the mock processions actually held in New York during the 1830s. A motley array of characters, some of them on horseback and carrying banners, swords, and lances, proceeds from left to right. They include mainly clowns and other carnival-type figures, with some literary and historical characters such as Don Quixote and Napoleon. The procession is led by a clown-like general resembling Jackson. The banners read:

"Our General!! May he "soon" meet his "reward" in Heaven for his "everlasting" services on "earth." "Death to the Militia System." "Soldiers in "peace. Citizens in "War."" The print is labeled "Part 1st" in the upper left corner. Below the title are the following lines: "Come get thee a sword, tho' made of lath. There's Best's son the tanner, and Dick the Butcher, and Smith the weaver, as ragged as Lazarus. No eye hath seen such scarecrows. I'll not march with them that's flat. Shakespeare."

   -Library of Congress

# 1867- Holiday Street, Fantasticals, New York

# 1897-Thanksgiving Parade, New York

## Curiosities of Popular Customs and of Rites, Ceremonies, Observances, and ... William Shepard Walsh, Published 1897, J.B. Lippincott Co.

The New York Gazette of November 7, 1737, affords a glimpse of how the festival was celebrated at that time: "Saturday last, being the fifth of November, it wus observed here in memory of that horrid and Treasonable Popish Gun-Powder Plot to blow up and destroy King, Lords, and Commons, and the Gentlemen of his Majesty's Council. The Assembly and Corporation and other the principal Gentlemen and Merchants of this City waited upon his Honor the Lieutenant-Governor at Fort George, where the Royal Healths were drunk, as usual, under the discharge of the Cannon, and at the Ni^ht the City was illuminated." All through the English provinces bonfires were burned, volleys were fired, The celebration of Guy Fawkes's Day was brought over from England to America by the early colonists, and still has local survivals in several of the original thirteen States. In New York, the code known as the Duke's Laws, given to the province in 1665, ordered that every minister should on November 5 preach a sermon commemorative of the English deliverance from Guy Fawkes and his effigies were carried in procession, and mummers and maskers singing No Popery songs importuned passers-by for a gratuity. Giant Pope came in time to be substituted for Guy Fawkes, and the 5th of November was known as Pope Day. Under this name it survives in Newburyport, Massachusetts, and Portsmouth, New Hampshire. In Newcastle, New Hampshire, it is corrupted into Pork Night. In other New England towns fires are still lighted on the 5th of November by boys who know not what they commemorate. In New York and Brooklyn there is a feeble and divided survival of Pope Day sports in the bonfires kindled on election night, and in the bedraggled parades of begging child maskers on Thanksgiving Day.

# 1910-15- Thanksgiving Maskers, New York

-Library of Congress

# 1910- Thanksgiving Maskers, New York

-Library of Congress

The River Press, Montana, November 29, 1911, Maskers

# THANKSGIVING MASKERS

### Many Children and Some Grown-ups Parade In Costume.

#### By WILTON MARKHAM.

IN addition to eating turkey and incidentally being grateful for past mercies, New York has a Thanksgiving day custom that is observed in few if any other communities in America. It is a masker's parade, indulged in chiefly by the children, but also enjoyed and in many cases participated in by the grownups.

The custom is believed to have been originated by the foreign born population of the big city, who, while they have no Thanksgiving in their own lands, make use of other holidays for carnival masquerades and seized upon Thanksgiving for that purpose after coming to America. From them it spread to some extent to the native Americans and now is generally observed throughout Greater New York.

On that one day at least the children literally take possession of the streets, ride all over the street cars, even on the fenders; impersonate Uncle Sam, George Washington and other characters that suit their fancy; dress in all sorts of costumes, that of the ragamuffin having the preference; mask, black their faces, parade, blow horns, ride sorry horses, prance astride of broomsticks and generally enjoy themselves to the limit of their temporary liberty.

New York children have something to be thankful for on Thanksgiving day, even though they have not all the rest of the year. They have no limit set on their hilarity short of the actual commission of crime. Thanksgiving thus becomes to New York what New Year's is to Philadelphia, Christmas eve is in southern cities and Halloween is throughout the country.

The human animal takes to revelry as naturally as the sparks fly upward. This is true whether the animal in question is an inhabitant of Japan, Italy or America and whether he belonged to the first century or boasts himself an up to date product of the twentieth.

Above all, however, it is a day of freedom for the children. They are out as gamins and are permitted to play at begging in the streets and at houses. Horns and rattles are worked overtime. The throwing of confetti and even of flour on pedestrians is an allowable pastime. At some of the open squares cakewalks are given by the children in the presence of thousands and usually with a big cake, presented by a baker in the neighborhood, as a prize. Wearing masks or with their faces stained, the youngsters roam through the streets by thousands

---Library of Congress

## The Transition from Ragammuffin to Halloween and Thanksgiving

"By 1930, the library blog reports, some New Yorkers were ready to move on. School Superintendent William J. O'Shea instructed administrators that "modernity is incompatible with the custom of children to masquerade and annoy adults on Thanksgiving Day" by asking for gifts and money.

Others kept the tradition alive. The Madison Square Club for Boys and Young Men, for instance, put on Ragamuffin Parades in an attempt to bring order to the occasion. The 1940 parade, according to the library blog, featured more than 400 children and touted the group's motto: "American boys do not beg."

Ragamuffin parades continued to be popular into the 1950s, but they were eventually overpowered by another burgeoning tradition catapulted into prominence by the 1947 movie *Miracle on 34th Street*. The new symbol of Thanksgiving also showcased people in fantastic masks and costumes and, in addition, hoisted giant character-based balloons. It was called:

Macy's Thanksgiving Day Parade"

--https://www.npr.org/sections/theprotojournalist/2014/11/19/365195079/when-thanksgiving-was-weird

## 1896- New York

### COLONIAL DAYS IN OLD NEW YORK, ALICE MORSE EARLE, NEW YORK, CHARLES SCRIBNER'S SONs, 1896.

The English brought a political holiday to New York. In the code of laws given to the province in 1665, and known as "The Duke's Laws," each minister throughout the province was ordered to preach a sermon on November 5, to commemorate the English deliverance from Guy Fawkes and the Gunpowder Plot in 1605. From an early entry in the "New York Gazette" of November 7, 1737, we learn how it was celebrated that year, and find that illuminations, as in England, formed part of the day's remembrance. Bonfires, fantastic processions, and "burning a Guy" formed, in fact, the chief English modes of celebration.

"Saturday last, being the fifth of November, it was observed here in Memory of that horrid and Treasonable Popish Gun-Powder Plot to blow up and destroy King, Lords and Commons, and the Gentlemen of his Majesty's Council; the Assembly and Corporation and other the principal Gentle- men and Merchants of this City waited upon his Honor the Lieutenant-Governor at Fort George, where the Royal Healths were drunk, as usual, under the discharge of the Cannon, and at the Night the city was illuminated."

All through the English provinces bonfires were burned, effigies were carried in procession, mummers and masqueraders thronged the streets and invaded the houses singing Pope Day rhymes, and volleys of guns were fired. In some New England towns the boys still have bonfires on November 5th. In the year 1765 the growing feeling with regard to the Stamp Act chancing to come to a climax in the late autumn, produced in New York a very riotous observance of Pope's Day. The demonstrations really began on November 1st, which was termed "The Last Day of Liberty." In the evening a mob gathered, "designing to execute some foolish ceremony of burying Liberty," but it dispersed with noise and a few broken win- dows. The next night a formidable mob gathered, "carrying candles and torches in their hands, and now and then firing a pistol at the Effigy which was carried in a Chair." Then the effigy was set in the Governor's chariot, which was taken out of the Fort. They made a gallows and hung on it an effigy of the Governor and one of the Devil, and carried it to the Fort, over which insult soldiers and officers were wonderfully patient. Finally, gallows, chariot and effigies were all burnt in the Bowling Green. The mob then ransacked Major James's house, eating, drinking, destroying, till £1500 of damage was done. The next day it was announced that the delivery and destruction of the stamps would be demanded. In the evening the mob started out again, with candles and a barber's block dressed in rags. The rioters finally dispersed at the entreaties of

many good citizens, - among them Robert R. Livingstone, who wrote the letter from which this account is taken. In 1774, November 5th was still a legal holiday. There still exists in New York a feeble and divided survival of the processions and bonfires of Guy Fawkes Day. The police- prohibited bonfires of barrels on election night, and the bedraggled parade of begging boys on Thanksgiving Day are our reminders to-day of this old English holiday.

# Conclusion

The history of the transition of the celebration of the Great Deliverance from the Plot of 1605 to Official State Celebration in the Colonies, to Popes Day, to Revolutionary War Protest then to Protest Processions of Fantasticals, to Thanksgiving Day Maskers and then to Halloween processions and Guising, demonstrates how celebrations experienced at the time as timeless, and traditional are infact constantly in play, their forms shifting and struggling for the critical mass of relevance, meaning and support, both political and economic, from various interest groups and sub-culures. Without a foundation in the eternal structures of the dark folkloric landscape and with relevance no longer firmly teathered by the Great Chain of Being, the elements of celebration drifted, blown by the winds of popular culture into the orbits of other celebrations: Independence, Elections, Halloween, redistributive house visitation. Even so, the trnsformed celebrations maintained a vestigial whisper of their eternal roots sufficient to address some of the disclosures of their original intent. The unfortunate divisions between groups, the imperfections of government and the fire of hope in Democracy were disclosed and flickered, still inviting reform and mittigation.

It is quite amusing that Halloween Guising and House Visitation criticized by the British as Ameican impositions are nothing more than Guy Fawkes/Gunpowder Treason celebrations returning to their shores!

# The Theology of the Effigy

When the plot was discovered in 1605, theologians were tasked with the production of a commemorative response which served both the deity and the state. Immediately they turned to off-the-shelf artifacts of celebration; bonfires and bells. To these was added others such as the burning of effigies, prayer, feasting and sermonizing. All of these choices were in accordance with practices of the people of Israel as recorded in the Old Testament of the Bible. The task was to communicate messages of thanksgiving to the deity across the boundary dividing our world from the unseen world of the dark folkloric landscape. Those responsible for evil acts needed to be identified. However, the disclosure of evil was the primary focus; this created a unified general cultural framework which proved to be durable while public opinion concerning specific individuals, changed. Because the focus of celebration was upon evil, and not the individual others associated with evil in other contexts and times could be interchanged as effigy identity from year to year thus giving the celebrations renewed life and purpose. Guy Fawkes could be burned again each time with a new focus derived from current events. In Pope Day wagons the devil is shown confounding a generic pope disclosing an evil partnership while specific named individual "evil ones" are inserted as needed.

The smoke of incense, the sound of bells, the sounds of the human voice all start out in our world but do not persist in it, therefore it was thought that they traveled to the dark folkloric world and to the deity in much the same way as did the burnt offerings of the people of Israel.

The effigy was created for the purpose of remembrance of the deliverance and to identify the perpetrator. On earth, the purpose was to put a physical face on the evil ones so that the people would be vigilant. Effigy burning was never originally intended to harm anyone. (See Volume V)

Tennyson inserted as Fawkes, <u>Punch Magazine</u>, May 2, 1885.

# The Mock Execution and Burning of the Effigy of Haman

The deliverance from Gunpowder Treason has often been called "our Purim" in sermons (See: Volume V, Gunpowder Treason Sermons and Liturgy). The festival of Purim is celebrated every year on the 14th of the Hebrew month of Adar (late winter/early spring). It commemorates the salvation of the Jewish people in ancient Persia from Haman's plot

As Rabbi Prof. David Golinkin writes:

"to destroy, kill and annihilate all the Jews, young and old, infants and women, in a single day. Haman (Also known as Haman the Agagite האגגי המן, or Haman the evil הרשע המן) was the subject of a custom observed by many Jews throughout history to burn Haman in effigy on Purim. This custom may have stemmed from a literal interpretation of the verse in Deuteronomy to blot out the memory of Amalek/Haman. On the other hand, it may have been an outlet for Jews to blow off steam at their current persecutors by taking revenge on a puppet (see Horowitz). In any case, this was a widespread custom which may have started as early as the fourth century and continues until our day.

1. In the tractate of Sanhedrin 64a Rava (ca. 325 c.e.) says that the custom of passing one's son through the fire in order to worship Molekh is like "mashvarta d'furia", "like the jumping of Purim". This is the only place where this expression appears in all of Talmudic literature. The Geonim and Rashi explain that there was a custom in Babylon and Elam that young boys/men would hang Haman in effigy on their roofs 4-5 days before Purim. On Purim they would make a big bonfire and throw the effigy in the fire and jump through the fire. (1)

2. On May 29, 408 c.e., Emperor Theodosius II promulgated a law forbidding the Jews to burn an effigy of Haman on the cross on the holiday of Purim (Codex Theodosian 16:8:18 and see Linder and Rabello) The purpose of that custom, says the law, was to hold Christianity in contempt."

--http://www.schechter.edu/responsa.aspx?ID=58, BLOTTING OUT HAMAN ON PURIM
Volume 5, Issue No. 5, March 2011 Rabbi Prof. David Golinkin

"The children especially enjoy this time. They receive presents of toys and sweets, but most of all they enjoy wearing grotesque masks; and on the feast days small companies of boys parade the streets dressed in fantastic clothes collecting alms exactly as was the custom with boys in England on November 5, "Guy Fawkes's Day." The similarity is still closer by reason of the shooting of firecrackers, and the burning of colored lights at night."
-The Biblical World, University of Chicago Press, 1904.

The celebration of the Deliverance of 1605 was constructed by a government and church which generally founded its practices upon those of the Jewish people as detailed in the Old Testament of the Bible. It may be expected, therefore, that ancient Jewish practice may have influenced the formulation of Gunpowder Treason Day celebrations. Although Purim is celebrated in March, it was celebrated by Jews in Britain, therefore its artifacts of celebration would have been readily available for re-purposing. Direct evidence for this crossover has not yet been discovered.

The Mock Execution and Burning of the Effigy of Haman is important because, as in Guy Fawkes effigy rituals, the soul of Haman is not attacked. It is his evil that is "blotted out," not his being. If his being was under attack his name could easily had been removed entirely--as if he had never existed. Instead, celebrants remember his evil while not attacking his person. In this way the two celebrations have much more in common.

# Emblem VII. The Powder-Plot Anon., 1680.

The last line of this "Emblem" sums up the theology of effigy of the 17th century.

Mischief on mischief doth from Rome proceed,
Yet all is blasted in the very deed,
And Heav'n still helps when there is any need.

In the dark they dig through houses, which they had marked for themselves in the day-time; they know not the light. -JOB, Chap. 24 v.16.

Has Hell ungorg'd and from its entrails thrown
Into the lap of Rome this Plot alone?
Has the dark Consult of the gloomy part,
Unbosom'd now the utmost of their Art,
And writ it in the Center of the heart?
Still hand in hand cannot the Nation see
A Pope and Devil, but false Rome in thee!
Falser than Hell, nay, falser than its chief;
He sins as Devil; few allow belief
To him, whom we all know to be a thief
But cloath'd in Holiness, great Pope, like you,
He may essay another world t'undo.
Like him at first, y'assault the weakest part,
And dart Rebellion in a woman's heart.
Hell keeps an Annal, registers you there,
And dines upon a Pope twice every year.
Sated with such a damn'd luxurious crue,
He vomits all his Treasons out on you.
The then dull Pope, he in Religion rouls,
Whose only business is to damn their souls.
You're but an Agent here within the world;
Hell's business done, and all its banners furl'd.
Loaden with sins, you're to its Kingdom hurl'd.
Cease, cease for shame, lay all your plotting by,
For once again you've lost the Victory,
So great a Cheat and base a Gilt you're grown,
That for Religion I'le allow you none.
Your self, I guess, did you but often trace,
And view the yawning wrinkles in your face,

The dry parch'd furrows of the *Romish* Clay,
You would in spite of Hell our God obey.
Behold, you strange, you Irreligious Crue,
And look upon the mischiefs caus'd by you.

Look from a far, how through the Eastern sky,
The Beams of Heav'd have made discovery;
Then look again, and in the West you'll see
The under-Agents of this villany;
See 'em suspended, and at once look pale,
And then consider if you can prevail,
Blood requires blood, this has our Maker taught,
And yet it is your ev'ry minutes fault.
If Murder be no sin, why should not we,
That have both strength and hands, act cruely?
Were that the way to prove Religion good,
We could exhaust a Nation of its Blood.
But you have got the knack to save, forgive,
Nay, to damn those you would not have to live.
Did you e'r read, or can you all maintain,
That God commanded *Abel* should be slain?
Or had its great Omnipotence decreed,
That for some secret reason he should bleed?
Yet he curs'd *Cain,* who presently was driv'n,
And made a vagabond on Earth and heav'n;
A secret mark was on the Murth'rer set.
Which did to al, his villany detect.
So to your cause the fatal Brand is giv'n,
Which keeps you from the path which leads to Heav'n.

**"Tis plainly seen Heav'n has a careful eye,**
**And guards his Church from *Romish* vanity.**
**He has forbid, nor will he e'r allow**
**That man should to a graven image bow.**
**Ill grounded sure the Faith of Man must be,**
**That courts Salvation by offending thee,**
**And Christ forgets---**
**Unless he's put in mind by Effigie**.

- Anon: Emblem VII. "The Powder-Plot." From: <u>Emblem Books Epigrams and Formal Satires, 1500-1850: The Protestants Vade Mecum,</u> 1680.

# Charivari/ Skimmington

When it came time for the celebration of deliverance from the Gunpowder Treason of 1605 it is not surprising that celebrants turned to ancient traditional "ready-made" "off the shelf" familiar paradigms and artifacts of celebration.

Image: "Rough Music" utilized in Pope Day celebrations, South end forever [cut] North end forever. Extraordinary verses on Pope-night. or, A commemoration the fifth of November, giving a history of the attempt, made by the papishes, to blow up king and Parliament, A. D. 1588. Together with some account of the Pope himself, and his wife Joan: with several other things, worthy of notice, too tedious to mention. Sold by the printer's boys in Boston [1768].☐

"'Rough music" is the term which has been generally used in England since the end of the seventeenth century to denote a rude cacophony, with or without more elaborate ritual, which usually directed mockery or hostility against individuals who offended against certain community norms. It appears to correspond, on the whole, to charivari in France, to the Italian scampanate, and to several German customs: haberfeld-treiben, thierfjagen and katzenmusik. There is, indeed, a family of ritual forms here, which is European-wide, and of great antiquity, but the degree of kinship within this family is open to enquiry. In international scholarship "charivari" has won acceptance as the term descriptive of the whole genus. In 1972 I followed this example by entitling a study published in France ' "Rough Music": Le Charivari anglais'. The difficulty of this assimilation soon became apparent. For the very term 'charivari' arouses inappoite expectations and constructs the subject according to a French problematic, with its strong emphasis upon charivari as occasioned by second marriages, and also upon the role of unmarried youths."

"'Rough music' is also a generic term, and even within the British islands, the ritual forms were so various that it is possible to view them as distinct species. Yet beneath all the elaborations of ritual certain basic human properties can be found: raucous, ear-shattering noise, unpitying laughter, and the mimicking of obscenities. It was supported, in Thomas Hardy's description, by 'the din of cleavers, tongs, tambourines, kits, crouds, humstrums, serpents, ram's horns, and other historical kinds of music'. But if such 'historical' instruments were not to hand, the rolling of stones in a tin kettle-or any improvisation of draw-tins and shovels-would do. In a Lincolnshire dialect glossary (1877) the definition runs: 'Clashing of pots and pans."

- Thompson, E. P., "Rough Music Reconsidered", In: <u>Folklore</u> vol. 103: i, 1992 3, p. 4.

Charivari (or shivaree or chivaree, also called "rough music") is the term for folk customs in which the community gave a noisy, discordant mock serenade, also pounding on pots and pans. The origin of the word is charivari likely from the Roman caribaria, meaning "headache", or the Greek kerebaria—keras (head), barys (heavy)—most likely to represent the effect of the cacophony on the victim. Often these performances related to community disapproval of extra marital relationships, but as a generalized artifact of celebration charivari could be used for other applications including Gunpowder Treason Day tormenting of effigies and related retribution of mobocracies upon perceived evil-doers who had escaped justice. The loud, public ritual therefore evolved to a form of social coercion, for instance, to force an as-yet-unmarried couple to wed or politician to reform. It would certainly be appropriate treatment for the evil-doer Fawkes. Often charivari did bring about change and extract compensation, thus contributing to the maintenance of the equilibrium of the social order. As an artifact of celebration charivari contributed to the general theme of disclosure of evil, and Fawkes certainly qualified as a subject.

A skimmington is a rowdy procession with effigies of victims or people dressed up to represent them. It was designed to make a public demonstration of moral disapproval of the individual or individuals. Fawkes therefore was worthy of a skimmington ride. In some cases, the individual(s) themselves were forced to participate. Skimmingtons were typically noisy affairs, with rough music made by the banging of pots and pans. Francis Grose described a skimmington as: "Saucepans, frying-pans, poker and tongs, marrow-bones and cleavers, bull's horns, etc. beaten upon and sounded in ludicrous processions" (A Classical Dictionary of the Vulgar Tongue, 1796).

Skimmingtons are recorded in England as early as the 17th century. The practice is recorded in colonial America from around the 1730s. The term is particularly tied to the West Country region of England. It has been suggested that it derived from the ladle used in that region for cheesemaking, which was used by a woman to beat a weak or henpecked husband.

To "ride such a person skimmington" involved ridiculing them or their effigy on a cart, pole, or on the back of a horse or donkey.
The noisy parade served as a punishment to the offender and a warning to others to follow community norms;

> "They are coming up Corn Street after all! They sit back to back!"
>
>> "What--two of 'em—are there two figures?"
>> "Yes. Two images on a donkey, back to back, their elbows tied to one another's! She's facing the head, and he's facing the tail."
>> "Is it meant for anybody in particular?"
>> "Well--it mid be. The man has got on a blue coat and kerseymere leggings; he has black whiskers, and a reddish face. 'Tis a stuffed figure, with a falseface." (...)
>
> The numerous lights round the two effigies threw them up into lurid distinctness; it was impossible to mistake the pair for other than the victims.
>
>> "Come in, come in," implored Elizabeth; "and let me shut the window!"

"She's me—she's me—even to the parasol—my green parasol!" cried Lucetta with a wild laugh as she stepped in. She stood motionless for one second—then fell heavily to the floor. "—Thomas Hardy, The Mayor of Casterbridge

However, it is not always clear whether Fawkes was in or out of favor. What then does his chairing represent?

William Hogarth, "Hudibras Encounters the Skimmington," 1726.

# The Evil Ones
## The Devil

Image- "South End Forever North End Forever", Broadside, Boston, 1768, Library of Congress.

"Effigies of the Pope and the Devil, the imputed instigators of the plot, were placed on a Stage, placed on cart wheels and Drawn by horses, at least some of them, for there were numerous exhibitions of this kind annually on that day in Boston." …. behind him was the imaginary representation of the Devil, standing Erect, with extended arms. In one hand was placed another small Lanthorn. The other grasped a pitchfork." …" . The Effigy of the Devil was always well tarred in order to hold a thick coat of feathers. The tar and feathers extended from his neck to his heels. Why tar and feathers were selected as proper clothing for his satanic Majesty I have never learned." …" The Great Lanthorn of the large Ones was 6 or 9 feet high, as wide as the stage, covered with oiled paper, on which were various labels, ugly and uncouth figures, on the sides, but on the front invariably was wrote or painted in as large Letters as the biggness of the Lanthorn would permit, 'The Devil take the Pope" …

-- Thomas, Isaiah, *"Three Autobiographical Fragrnents; Now First Published Upon the 150th Anniversary of the Founding of the American Antiquarian Society*, (Worcester, Mass.: American Antiquarian Society, 1962), 22—25. Submitted by Ross W. Beales Jr -p. 218. Note in: Bell, J. L. "Du Simitière's Sketches of Pope Day in Boston, 1767." *The Worlds of Children, 1620-1920* (2002): 209-217.

The king of them all! The most popular effigy in early celebrations. Guy Fawkes was known as "The Devil in the Vault." Being personified, or possessed by the devil enables disclosure of evil as the most important aspect. The Devil appears to reveal the ones possessed by evil, confused, led astray. The theologins taught that flawed, weak, imperfect, humans were not inherently evil. In this way, the devil often accompanied by his imps was an essential part and reflects that the whole process is that of disclosure.

## Popes

The popes represent the confused leaders of humans led astray. Throughout the period the popes possessed significant military power and along with their surrogates, represented even more of a threat to the freedom and liberty of the colonists than did Britain. If anything, the motherland attracted these powers to North America through its political entanglements. A prime example is the French and Indian War. (The French and Indian War (1754-1763) was the North American theater of the worldwide Seven Years' War of 1754-1763. The war pitted the colonies of British America against those of New France. Both sides were supported by military units from their parent countries of Great Britain and France, as well as by Native American allies.) For more on papal power see Appendix 1. One should never equate the presence of the pope in celebrations with bigotry. It is also important to note that the title "Pope" is aways used generically. Individual popes are never identified, literally or symbolically.

Popes of the Roman Catholic Church during Pope Night celebrations in Boston:

**Benedictus XIV-** (in office 1740-1758)- Prospero Lorenzo Lambertini's papacy began in a time of difficulties, caused by the disputes between Catholic rulers and the papacy about governmental demands to nominate bishops istead of leaving the appointment to the Church. He overcame most of these problems — the Holy See's disputes with the Kingdom of Naples, Sardinia, Spain, Venice, and Austria were settled. -Wikipedia, verified

**Clemens XIII-** (1758-1769) His pontificate was dominated by constant pressure to suppress the Society of Jesus. Despite this, he championed their order and also was their greatest defender. He was one of the few early popes who supported dialogue with Old Catholic Protestants and hoped to mend the schism with the Catholic Church that existed in England and the low countries. These effortswere not successful. In France, the Parlement de Paris, with a strong upper bourgeois background and Jansenist sympathies, began to expel the Jesuits from France in the spring of 1761, and excerpts from Jesuit writings, the *Extrait des assertions*, provided anti-Jesuit ammunition. Though a congregation of bishops assembled at Paris in December 1761 recommended no action, Louis XV of France (1715–74) promulgated a royal order permitting the Society to remain in France, with the proviso that certain essentially liberalising changes in their institution satisfy the Parlement with a French Jesuit vicar-general who would be independent of the general in Rome. When the Parlement by the *arrêt* of 2 August 1762 suppressed the Jesuits in France and imposed untenable conditions on any who remained in the country, Clement XIII protested this invasion of the Church's rights and annulled the *arrêts*. Louis XV's ministers could not permit such an abrogation of French law, and the King expelled the Jesuits in November 1764.

Clement XIII warmly espoused the Jesuit order in a papal bull *Apostolicum pascendi*, 7 January 1765, which dismissed criticisms of the Jesuits as calumnies and praised the order's usefulness; it was largely ignored: by 1768 the Jesuits had been expelled from France, the Two Sicilies and Parma. In Spain, they seemed safe, but Charles III of Spain (1759–88), aware of the drawn-out contentions in Bourbon France, decided on a more peremptory efficiency. During the night of 2–3 April 1767, all the Jesuit houses of Spain were suddenly surrounded, the inhabitants arrested, shipped to the ports and loaded onto ships for Civitavecchia. The question of the investiture of Parma aggravated the Pope's troubles. The Bourbon Kings espoused their relative's quarrel, seized Avignon, Benevento and Pontecorvo, and united in a demand for the total suppression of the Jesuits (January 1769).

-Wikipedia, verified.

**Clemens XIV (1769-1774)**- born Giovanni Vincenzo Antonio Ganganelli, was Pope from 19 May 1769 to his death in 1774. When elected, he was the only Franciscan friar in the College of Cardinals. King Louis XV of France's (1715–74) minister, the duc de Choiseul, had former experience of Rome as the French ambassador and was Europe's most skilled diplomat. Choiseul's suggestion was that they should press, in addition to the Jesuit issue, territorial claims upon the Patrimony of Peter, including the return of Avignon and the Comtat Venaissin to France, the duchies of Benevento and Pontecorvo to Spain, an extension of territory adjoining the Papal States to Naples, and final settlement of the question of Parma and Piacenza that had caused a diplomatic rift between Austria and Pope Clement XIII.

Eventually the suppression of the Jesuit order was urged by the faction called the "court cardinals", who were opposed by the diminished pro-Jesuit faction, the *Zelanti* ("zealous"), who were generally opposed to the encroaching secularism of the Enlightenment

-Wikiperdia, verified.

**Pius VI (1775-1799)**- born Count Giovanni Angelo Braschi, reigned as Pope from 15 February 1775 to his death in 1799.

Pius VI condemned the French Revolution and the suppression of the Gallican Church. French troops commanded by Napoleon Bonaparte defeated the papal troops and occupied the Papal States in 1796. In 1798, upon his refusal to renounce his temporal power, Pius was taken prisoner and transported to France. He died one year later in Valence. His reign is the fourth-longest in papal history, being over two decades.

-Wikipedia, verified.

## The political aspects drew them in.

# Nancy Dawson

Nancy Dawson, Anon.

English actress, former prostitute, celebrated in a well-known ballad. Played by a man "dressed in female attire": danced, caressed the pope, and kissed the devil. "Nancy Dawson (1730? –1767) was born Ann Newton and published her memoirs in 1764. See Selma Jeanne Cohen, *There's none like Nancy Dawson! Containing the Authentic memoirs of the celebrated Miss Nancy D-ws-n* (New York, Dance Perspectives, 1966)."

-Benes, Peter, *Night Processions: Celebrating the Gunpowder Plot in England and New England, (unpublished Mss.)*

"…Dawson had a popular dance named after her, and that seems to have prompted Bostonians to dub this dancing female figure with her name. Hezekiah Niles, compiler, Principles and Acts of the Revolution in America (Baltimore: William Ogden Niles, 1822), p. 490, quoting from the Boston Gazette. Boston merchant William Palfrey's daughter Polly had learned the "Nansy Dawson" dance by the time she was seven, in 1772; Mary Beth Norton, Liberty's Daughters: The Revolutionary Experience of American Women, 1750—1800 (New York: Harper, 1980), p. 90. The tune was earlier titled "Piss upon the grass," and is now known as "Here we go 'round the mulberry bush"; Joy Van Cleef and Kate Van Winkle Keller, "Selected American Country Dances and Their English Sources," in Music in Colonial Massachusetts, 1630—1820—1: Music in Public Spaces, Colonial Society of Massachusetts Publications, 53 (Boston: Colonial Society of Massachusetts, 1980), pp. 53, 57."

-Bell, J. L. "Du Simitière's Sketches of Pope Day in Boston, 1767." *The Worlds of Children, 1620-1920* (2002): 209-217

# Piss Upon The Grass

ABC Notation

Piss upon the grass
X: 1
T: Piss Upon The Grass
R: jig
M: 6/8
L: 1/8
K: Gmaj
:G2G G2Bd2B G2GA2B A2BA2B AFD
G2G G2Bd2B G2BA2G F2ED3 D3:
:A2A A2BA2B AFDG2A B2cd2e dBG
c2B c2de2f gfedcB AGFG3 G3:

Dance: NANCY DAWSON

Country dance: Longways set for 4 couples.

| | | |
|---|---|---|
| A1 | 1-8 | 1st Couple: Cast Off down outside and back. |
| A2 | 1-8 | 1st Couple: Cross and Cast, Cross and Cast, Lead Up to face 1st Corners. |
| | | 2nd couple move up on bars 3 & 4. |
| B1 | 1-8 | Set* to 1st Corners and dance around them by the left shoulder. |
| | | Meet partner in the middle, clap hands [own, own, partner's] |
| | | and two-hand Turn to face 2nd Corners. |
| B2 | 1-8 | Repeat B1 with 2nd Corners. |

* Setting step is the Rigadoon.

-From "No Kissing Allowed in School! A Virginia Dancing School in 1784." by Kate Van Winkle Keller & George A. Fogg.

"Her early life is unclear; she may have been born at Axminster, Devon…
In October 1759, during the run of the Beggar's Opera, the man who danced the hornpipe among the thieves fell ill, and his place was taken by Nancy Dawson. From that moment she became a celebrity.

Nancy Dawson was induced by an increase of salary to move to Drury Lane, where she appeared for the first time on 23 September 1760 in the Beggar's Opera. Here for the next three years she dance in its frequent revivals, and in a variety of Christmas entertainments.

Her death took place at Haverstock Hill on 26 May 1767. She was buried in the graveyard belonging to the parish of St George the Martyr, Bloomsbury, behind the Foundling Hospital.

## Ballad

The hornpipe by which she danced into fame was performed to a tune (thought to be probably by Thomas Arne) which then had words set, a song called Ballad of Nancy Dawson attributed to George Alexander Stevens. Miss Dawson's hornpipe, was introduced in Carey's and Bickerstaffe's opera 'Love in a Village,' and is mentioned as 'Nancy Dawson' by Oliver Goldsmith in the epilogue to She Stoops to Conquer.

The Ballad of Nancy Dawson

Of all the girls in our town,
The red, the black, the fair, the brown,
That dance and prance it up and down,
There's none like Nancy Dawson.

Her easy mien, her shape so neat,
She foots, she trips, she looks so sweet;
Her every motion's so complete,
I die for Nancy Dawson.

See how she comes to give surprise,
With joy and pleasure in her eyes:
To give delight she always tries,
So means my Nancy Dawson.

Was there no task, t'obstruct the way,
No shutter old, no house so gay,
A bet of fifty pounds I'd lay,
That I gained Nancy Dawson.
See how the opera takes a run
Exceeding Hamlet, Lear and Lun
Though in it there would be no fun,
Was't not for Nancy Dawson.

Though beard and brent charm ev'ry night
And female peachum's justly right,
And filch and lockit please the sight,
'Tis kept by Nancy Dawson.

See little davey strut and puff,
'Confound the opera and such stuff,
My house is never full enough,
A curse on Nancy Dawson".

Though G[arric]k he had has his day

And forced the town his laws t'obey,
With Jonny Rich is come in play,
With the help of Nancy Dawson."

-Wikipedia, verified.

## The Old Pretender

James Francis Edward Stuart (1688–1766) a baby when his father, James II, was forced to leave England. He spent his life in exile in Europe working to regain te throne, but he did not give up his Catholic faith. He is known as "James III" by supporters and "the Old Pretender" by enemies.

-Wikipedia, verified

James Francis Edward Stuart

# The Young Pretender

Charles Edward Louis John Casimir Sylvester Severino Maria Stuart

"Charles Edward Louis John Casimir Sylvester Severino Maria Stuart (31 December 1720 – 31 January 1788), commonly known in Britain during his lifetime as The Young Pretender and The Young Chevalier, and often known in retrospective accounts as Bonnie Prince Charlie, was the second Jacobite pretender to the thrones of England, Scotland, France and Ireland (as Charles III) from the death of his father in 1766. This claim was as the eldest son of James Francis Edward Stuart, himself the son of James VII and II. Charles is perhaps best known as the instigator of the unsuccessful Jacobite uprising of 1745, in which he led an insurrection to restore his family to the throne of Great Britain, which ended in defeat at the Battle of Culloden that effectively ended the Jacobite cause. Jacobites supported the Stuart claim due to hopes for religious toleration for Roman Catholics and a belief in the divine right of kings. Charles's flight from Scotland after the uprising has made him a romantic figure of heroic. In 1759 he was involved in a French plan to invade Britain which was abandoned following British naval victories."

-Wikipedia, verified

## Henry Benedict Cardinal Stuart (1725-1807)

Charles Edward Stuart's brother/heir. He was a Catholic priest and a cardinal. Losing his property during the wars following the French Revolution, he was given a pension by George III.

-Wikipedia, verified

Left, Henry Benedict Cardinal Stuart

# Admiral Byng

Admiral Byng

" who was suspended from a gibbet; he represented the naval officers who enforced revenue laws. However, as the newspaper soon reported, "thinking our Deliverance from the Stamp-Act somewhat analogous in its Consequences to the Escape from the Popish Plot, it was thought necessary by the Conductors of the Pageantry, to increase the Pope's Retinue."[i] On 5 November 1766, Dedham diarist William Ames noted: "Pope Devil and Stampman exhibited together."

-Benes, Peter, *Night Processions: Celebrating the Gunpowder Plot in England and New England, (unpublished Mss.)* "

"Admiral John Byng (baptised 29 October 1704 – 14 March 1757)[1] was a Royal Navy officer. After joining the navy at the age of thirteen, he participated at the Battle of Cape Passaro in 1718. Over the next thirty years he built up a reputation as a solid naval officer. He also served as Commodore-Governor of Newfoundland Colony in the 1740s, and was a Member of Parliament from 1751 until his death.

Byng is best known for failing to relieve a besieged British garrison during the Battle of Minorca at the beginning of the Seven Years' War. Byng had sailed for Minorca at the head of a hastily assembled fleet of vessels, some of which were in poor condition. He fought an inconclusive engagement with a French fleet off the Minorca coast, and then returned to Gibraltar to repair his ships. Upon return to Britain, Byng was court-martialled and found guilty of failing to "do his utmost" to prevent Minorca falling to the French. He was sentenced to death and shot by firing squad on 14 March 1757."

-Wikipedia, verified.

# Ld. [Frederick] North

"Frederick North, 2nd Earl of Guilford, KG, PC (13 April 1732 – 5 August 1792), more often known by his title, Lord North, which he used from 1752 until 1790, was Prime Minister of Great Britain from 1770 to 1782. He led Great Britain through most of the American War of Independence. He also held a number of other cabinet posts, including Home Secretary and Chancellor of the Exchequer.

North's reputation among historians has swung back and forth. He was depicted as a creature of the king and an incompetent who lost the American colonies. -Wikipedia, verified.

Frederick North, 2nd Earl of Guilford

# Gov. [Thomas] Hutchinson

"Thomas Hutchinson (9 September 1711 – 3 June 1780) was a businessman, historian, and a prominent Loyalist politician of the Province of Massachusetts Bay before the American Revolution. He has been referred to as "the most important figure on the loyalist side in pre-Revolutionary Massachusetts." He was a successful merchant and politician, and was active at high levels of the Massachusetts government. He served as lieutenant governor and then governor from 1758 to 1774. He was a proponent of hated British taxes, despite his initial opposition to Parliamentary tax laws directed at the colonies. He was blamed by Lord North (the British Prime Minister at the time) for being a significant contributor to the tensions that led the outbreak of the American Revolutionary War.

Hutchinson's Boston mansion was ransacked in 1765 during protests against the Stamp Act, damaging his collection of materials on early Massachusetts history. As acting governor in 1770, he exposed himself to mob attack in the aftermath of the Boston massacre, after which he ordered the removal of troops from Boston to Castle William. Letters of his calling for abridgement of colonial rights were published in 1773, further intensifying dislike of him in the colony. He was replaced as governor in May 1774 by General Thomas Gage, and went into exile in England, where he advised the government on how to deal with the Americans."

-Wikipedia, verified.

# Gen. [Thomas] Gage

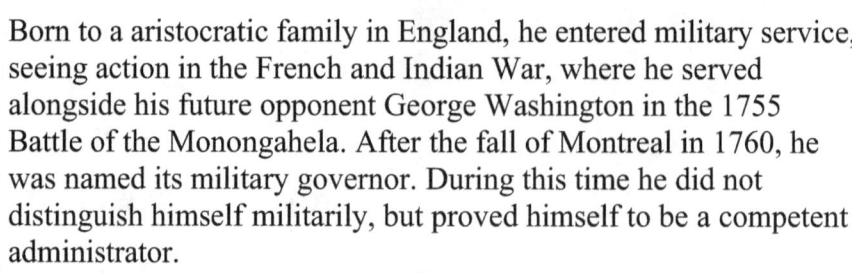

"Thomas Gage (10 March 1718/19– 2 April 1787) was a British general best known for many years of service in North America, including his role as military commander in the early days of the American Revolution.

Born to a aristocratic family in England, he entered military service, seeing action in the French and Indian War, where he served alongside his future opponent George Washington in the 1755 Battle of the Monongahela. After the fall of Montreal in 1760, he was named its military governor. During this time he did not distinguish himself militarily, but proved himself to be a competent administrator.

Gen. [Thomas] Gage

From 1763 to 1775 he served as commander-in-chief of the British forces in North America, overseeing the British response to the 1763 Pontiac's Rebellion. In 1774 he was also appointed the military governor of the Province of Massachusetts Bay, with instructions to implement the Intolerable Acts, punishing Massachusetts for the Boston Tea Party. His attempts to seize military stores of Patriot militias in April 1775 sparked the Battles of Lexington and Concord, beginning the American War of Independence. After the Pyrrhic victory in the June Battle of Bunker Hill he was replaced by General William Howe in October 1775, and returned to Great Britain"

-Wikipedia, verified.

# Lord Bute

John Stuart, 3rd Earl of Bute, KG, PC (25 May 1713 – 10 March 1792) was a Scottish nobleman who served as Prime Minister of Great Britain (1762–1763) under George III. He was the first Prime Minister from Scotland following the Acts of Union in 1707. Bute succeeded to the Earldom of Bute (named after the Isle of Bute) upon the death of his father, James Stuart, 2nd Earl of Bute, in 1723. He was brought up thereafter by his maternal uncles, the 2nd Duke of Argyll and Archibald Campbell, 3rd Duke of Argyll, 1st and only Earl of Ilay, Viscount and Earl of Hay. In 1737, due to the influence of his uncles, he was elected a Scottish representative peer, but he was not very active in the Lords and was not reelected in 1741. For the next several years he retired to his estates in Scotland to manage his affairs and indulge his interest in botany.

During the Jacobite Rising of 1745, Bute moved to Westminster, London, and two years later met Prince Frederick, the Prince of Wales there, soon becoming a close associate of the Prince. Upon the Prince's death in 1751, the education of his son, Prince George, the new Prince of Wales, became a priority and in 1755 Bute was appointed as his tutor.

-Wikipedia, verified

Lord Bute

# Lord Mansfield

William Murray, 1st Earl of Mansfield, PC, SL (2 March 1705 – 20 March 1793) was a British barrister, politician and judge noted for his reform of English law. He gained a reputation as an excellent barrister.

He became involved in politics in 1742, beginning with his election as a Member of Parliament for Boroughbridge, and appointment as Solicitor General. In the absence of a strong Attorney General, he became the main spokesman for the government in the House of Commons, and was noted for his "great powers of eloquence" and described as "beyond comparison the best speaker" in the House of Commons. With the promotion of Sir Dudley Ryder to Lord Chief Justice in 1754, he became Attorney General, and when Ryder unexpectedly died several months later, he took his place as Chief Justice.

William Murray, 1st Earl of Mansfield

The most powerful British jurist of the century, his decisions reflected the Age of Enlightenment and moved England on the path to abolishing slavery and the slave trade. He advanced commercial law in ways that helped establish the nation as the world leader in industry, finance and trade. For his work in *Carter v Boehm* and *Pillans v Van Mierop*, he has been called the founder of English commercial law. He is perhaps best known for his judgment in Somersett's Case (1772), where he held that slavery had no basis in common law and had never been established by positive law (legislation) in England, and therefore was not binding law (although this did not end slave trafficking altogether).

-Wikipedia, verified

# Judge Andrew Oliver

"Andrew Oliver (March 28, 1706 – March 3, 1774) was a merchant and public official in the Province of Massachusetts Bay. Born into a wealthy and politically powerful merchant

family, he is

Judge Andrew Oliver

best known as the Massachusetts official responsible for implementing the provisions of the Stamp Act, for which he was burned in effigy. He never actually carried out those duties, and was later commissioned as the province's lieutenant governor."

-Wikipedia, verified.

# John Mein

Controversial Tory publisher was forced to flee Boston on board an English ship after his name was featured in the 1769 procession.

-Benes, Peter, *Night Processions: Celebrating the Gunpowder Plot in England and New England, (unpublished Mss.)* "

John Mein was a Scottish bookseller who came to in Boston in 1764. In 1767 he and printer John Fleeming founded the Boston Chronicle. They became the printers of the Customs service, and were soon linked to support of the royal government.

When Boston's merchants protested taxes with the "non-importation" boycott 1769, Mein printed Customs office documents noting that some leaders of that cause were receiving goods from London. He criticized the movement's leaders using names like "Muddlehead" (James Otis, Jr.) and "Johny Dupe, Esq" (John Hancock).
On October 28, 1769, gentlemen approached Mein on King Street near the Old State House. He pulled out pistols and escaped into a British army barracks. That night a waterfront crowd accomplished Boston's first tar-and-feathering, of a sailor who worked for the Customs service.

The next week, Pope Night gangs made John Mein their target. A verse painted on a wagon's lantern spelled out his name as an acrostic poem:

"Mean is the Man, M—n is his Name,
Enough he's spread his hellish Fame,
Infernal Furies hurl his Soul,
Nine Million Times from Pole to Pole."

--Wikipedia, verified.

# Henry Hulton

Hulton was an English bureaucrat who came to Boston as a new Commissioner of Customs in 1767. He was tgo responsible for collect the Townshend duties. He landed on 5 November, in Boston:"Pope-Night".

Lord George Sackville noted:

"They landed on the 5th of November, and the populace were then carrying in procession the Pope, the Devil, and the Pretender, in order to commit them to the flames in honour of Protestantism. . . . these figures met the Commissioners at the water side and were carry'd before them without any insult through the streets, and whenever they stopped to salute an acquaintance, the figures halted and faced about till the salutation was over, and so accompany'd them to the Governor Hutchinson's door, where the Devil, &c. took their leave with loud huzzas from the mob...

-Vol. 49th vol. Historic Manuscripts Commission, U.K.

"the Mob carried twenty Devils, Popes, & Pretenders, thro the Streets, with Labels on their breasts, Liberty & Property & no Commissioners," but Commissioner Hulton "laughed at 'em with the rest."

- Ann Houlton, Letters of a Loyalist Lady, (1927).

-J.L. Bell, http://boston1775.blogspot.com/search/label/Henry%20Hulton

# Coronet Joyce

1764-1776- Coronet Joyce who arrested Charles I before the execution added as parade effigy. Custom continues beyond independence.

-Matthews, "Joyce Junior Once More," in: Colonial Society of Massachusetts, Publications, XI, 294n

"Cornet George Joyce (born 1618) was an officer in the Parliamentary New Model Army during the English Civil War

Between 2 and 5 June 1647, while the New Model Army was assembling for rendezvous at the behest of the recently formed Army Council, George Joyce seized King Charles I from Parliament's custody at Holdenby House and brought him to Thomas Fairfax's headquarters on Triplo Heath (8 miles south of Cambridge, and now spelled Thriplow Heath), a move that weakened Parliament's position and strengthened the Army's"

1 Cornet George Joyce (Jacob Huysmans

-Wikipedia, verified.

# Charles Paxton

(1708-1788) Unpopular Boston Customs official. He was known for exaggerated, old-fashioned manners. It is said that he greeted a merchant as "Your humble servant," and the man answered: "Everybody's humble servant, and nobody's friend." At the time of the Stamp Act protests of 1765, a crowd was to attack Paxton's home due to the intervention of his landlord.

In 1767 the South End gang chose Paxton as their effigy. On the figure and the wagon they put signs saying, "EVERYBODY'S HUMBLE SERVANT, & NOBODY'S FRIEND," and "POOR CHARLES THE BATCHELOR." Bostonians thought that Paxton did not have manly qualities. In 1769, the *Boston Gazette* made fun of him for hiding himself in a woman's cape in order to escape a mob and being afraid of "unruly Boys" playing football..

# Complex Primary Accounts

## 1735: Diary of Samuel Checkley

The third royal celebration took place on October 11 in honor of the King's coronation, and is thus described in the News-Letter of Thursday, October 16:

*Last Saturday being the Anniversary of His Majesty's Coronation, the same was observed by the Discharge of the Guns at Castle William; those on board His Majesty's Ship Scarborough, &c. with other Demonstrations of Loyalty and Rejoycing.*

Closely following the coronation came the King's birthday on October 30, and this, in spite of the snow and cold, was celebrated by a bonfire and fireworks on Dorchester Neck, and one poor fellow, losing his way in the storm, was frozen to death. In the Weekly Journal of Tuesday, November 4, we read:

*Thursday last the 30th of October, being the Birth Day of His Majesty King GEORGE the Second, our most gracious Sovereign, when His Majesty entred the Fifty Third Year of his Life, the same was observed here with all possible Demonstrations of Loyalty and Joy. At Noon, the Guns were discharged at His Majesty's Castle William, and His Excellency's Troop of Guards, with two other Troops from the County were muster'd on the Occasion, and drawn up in King-Street. At Night His Excellency's Seat, with divers others, were finely Illuminated on this joyfull Occasion.*

The account of this affair in the News-Letter of November 6 concludes as follows:

*A large bonfire was made at Dorchester-Neck, and many curious Fire-Works play'd off; but by reason of thick Weather and a great Fall of Snow, the Splendor thereof was much diminish'd, being scarce visible in Town.*

*The same Night, one Joseph Green of this Town, a labouring Man, who had been employed the Day before to assist in erecting a Mast for the Bonfire at Dorchester Neck, lost his Way as he was going from the Fire to some House or Barn, and the next Morning was found dead in the Snow.*[1]

---

1 In these days such a death seems extraordinary.

The following extract is taken from the Boston Evening Post of Monday, January 24, 1737:

*Friday last one Richard Williams, a Chimney-Sweeper at the South End of the Town, was found in his Bed froze to Death, where in all probability he had lain since Tuesday Night, having never been seen by the Neighbours since that Time.*

Shortly after this, on November 5, came a similar celebration at the same place, it being the anniversary of the famous Gunpowder Plot of 1605 in which Guy Fawkes was the active figure; and this day too was followed by fatalities, for four young men crossing the harbor in a canoe were drowned. The Weekly Journal of Tuesday, November 11, says:

*On Wednesday, last being the 5th of November, the Guns were fired at Castle William, in Commemoration of the happy and remarkable Deliverance of our Nation from Popery and Slavery, by the Discovery of the Gun Powder Plot in the Year 1605; and in the Evening there were Bonfires, and other Rejoycings.*

*The same Evening four young Men of this Town went in a Canoe (as we are informed) to see the Bonfire on Dorchester Neck, and have not been heard of since; which makes it fear'd they were drowned in their return home.*

A further account of this fatality is contained in the News-Letter of Thursday, November 20:

*Four Youths that went over from this Town, in a small Boat, to Dorchester Neck, to see the Diversions There in the Evening after the 5th Instant, having not been heard of for some Time after, People had various Conjectures concerning them; but it was most generally tho't they were drowned in their return Home; and accordingly it now appears that they were, the Bodies of two of them having been found, one on Monday and the other on Tuesday last; The Name of one was John Darling,1 an Apprentice belonging to Mr. Salt the Cooper, and Son of Mrs. Darling a Widow in Charlstown; the other's Name was John Hemmenway of this Town, an Apprentice to Mr. Joseph Hill, Rope-maker: The Bodies of the other Two are not yet found.*

This anniversary had been celebrated since the early days of the colony, and as the eighteenth century advanced the celebrations became more boisterous and the turbulent spirits of the community caused the authorities much anxiety. At first there were processions in which effigies of the Pope and the Devil were carried about the streets and finally burned, but near the time of the Revolution, when

---

[1] In the Weekly Journal of November 25, the name given is James Darling. This is correct. He was the son of George and Abigail (Reed) Darling. See Wyman, Genealogies and Estates of Charlestown, i. 276.

---

popular feeling against the English ran high, the images of unpopular officials like Governor Hutchinson, General Gage, and others were added. Just how early these celebrations began in New England is hard to say, but Judge Sewall speaks of one in 1685 as if it were a regular occurrence, for he says:

*Mr. Allin preached Nov. 5. 1685 finished his Text 1 Jn? 1. 9. mentioned not a word in Prayer or Preaching that I took notice of with respect to Gun-powder Treason. . . . Although it rained hard, yet there was a Bonfire made on the Comon, about 50 attended it. Friday night [ November 6] being fair, about two hundred hallowed about a Fire on the Comon.*[1]

Most of the almanacs mentioned the day, as this very one of Bowen's, where against November 5 is found "Powder Plot;" and Ames's almanac for 1735 has under November the lines —

*Gun Powder Plot
We ha'nt forgot.*

In his issue for 1740 Ames says:

*N.OW for the Old Plot, the POPE goes to Pot
The curst Pope stands in the Way, or I had told you the Day.
What Heaven decrees, no Prudence can prevent.*

And in the issue for 1746 we read:

*Powder-Plot is not forgot; '
T will be observed by many a Sot.*

In the issue of 1767 he has so much to say about the growing political troubles that he merely adds the line — "Powder plot most forgot;" while in the issue for 1772 his allusion brings in the name of Captain Preston of the British troops engaged in the Boston Massacre:

To burn the Pope, is now a joke,
for a design he miss't on,
to sap that mansion
which dares pension
Your famous Butcher Preston I*

---

1 Diary, i. 102, 235, 368, 462. *
8. Briggs, Essays, Humor and Poems of Nathaniel Ames, pp. 139, 440.

Dr. Nathaniel Ames the younger in his Diary under November 5, 1765, says, "Pope Devil and Stampman exhibited together."[1] Captain Francis Goelet, a New York merchant visiting Boston in 1750, was evidently amused and impressed by what he saw on Pope Night, for he records in his Journal:

*After dinner went with some of the Compy to ye North End the Towne Bo\* Some Limes &c where we saw the Devil and the Pope &c Carried ab\* by the Mob represented in Effegy very drole soone after see two more, but the Justices feareing some Outrages may be Committed Put a Stop to them.*[2]

It seems that as the custom grew, in Boston there became two rival processions, one from the North End and one from the South End, each carrying images of the Pope and the Devil, and that they marched towards each other and had a skirmish in which the mob joined and the victorious band then burned both sets of images. In 1765 the popular leaders of the town put a stop to this useless quarrel, pacified the two factions, formed them into a Union, and brought to an end the noisy and turbulent celebration. This Union observed the day in a quieter manner with a supper at night; and in this was a nucleus that was of service to the patriots in the approaching struggle.[3] John Boyle mentions this same occurrence:

*1765, Nov. 5. A Union established between the South and North End Popes. Capt. M° Intosh on the Part of the South, and Capt. Swift, on the Part of the North. It.has heretofore been the Practice on the even'g of the 5th of November, for the two Popes to engage, by which means many Persons have been greatly maimed. This Union and one other more extensive, may be looked upon as the only happy Effecte arising from the Stamp Act.*

This Union was undoubtedly hastened by the fatalities of the year before, for Boyle in his Journal for November 5, 1764, says:

*A Child of Mr. Brown's at the North-End was run over by one of the Wheels of the North-End Pope and Killed on the Spot. Many others were wounded in the evening.*[4]

1 Dedham Historical Register, ii. 27. '
New England Historical and Genealogical Register, rriv. 61. •
Palfrey, History of New England, v. 339; Snow, History of Boston (1825), p. 263.
4 John Boyle's Journal,
p. 87. For these extracts from this imprinted Journal,

This accident impressed others, for John Howe mentions it in his Diary, as well as the fact that it took place in the forenoon:

*1764 Nov. 5. A sorrowful accident happened this forenoon at the North End—the wheel of the carriage that the Pope was fixed on run over a Boy's head & he died instantly. The Sheriff, Justices, Officers of the Militia were ordered to destroy both S° & North End Popes. In the afternoon they got the North End Pope pulled to pieces. they went to the S° End but could not Conquer upon which the South End people brought out their pope & went in Triumph to the Northward and at the Mill Bridge a Battle begun between the people of Both Parts of the Town. The North End people having repaired their pope, but the South End people got the Battle (many were hurt & bruised on both sides) & Brought away the North End pope & burnt Both of them at the Gallows on the Neck. Several thousand people following them, hallowing &ct.[1]*

Several years ago Mr. Albert Matthews' made some mention of the observances of Pope Day and quoted from articles in Boston newspapers of 1821 written by some man who remembered the celebrations of the day, though it is probable that after the outbreak of the Revolution the day was less frequently celebrated in New England.[1] Perhaps the one place where it lingered longest is in the old town of Portsmouth, New Hampshire, which clings to many an ancient custom, and there even to the present time something is done on the evening of November fifth, though the performance has changed to the blowing of horns and the carrying about of pumpkin lanterns by boys, none of whom know the origin of the celebration,4 and even the name has been changed to Pork Night.

John Albee of New Castle, New Hampshire, in 1892 bore testimony to the survival of the custom in Portsmouth up to that year, saying that he had been a resident of New Castle for the preceding twenty-six years and that he remembered a celebration in that town each of those years.[8] He also furnished clippings from two of the local newspapers which told of the doings of 1892, as follows:

owned by a member of the Palfrey family, I am indebted to Professor George L. Kittredge.
Letters and Diary, p. 67.
I am indebted to Mr. Matthews for aid in the preparation of this paper.
Publications of this Society, viii. 90, 91, 92 104.
Dialect Notes, i. 18, 217.
Journal of American Folk-Lore, v. 335.

*The celebration of the anniversary of Guy Fawkes' night on Saturday by the young people of this city was not so extensive as in former years, no doubt owing to the condition of the streets, but nevertheless small bands paraded the streets and made the early part of the evening hideous with music (?) from the tin horns they carried for the occasion. Some carried the usual pumpkin lanterns. The ringing of door-bells was also extensively indulged in. Very few of the paraders knew that the celebration was in keeping of the old English custom of observing the anniversary of the discovery of the famous gunpowder plot to blow up the House of Commons.[1]*

*Chaps in this city had their annual blow-out on Guy Fawkes' night, and in parts of the city the toot of the horns was something terrific. Some grotesque pumpkin lanterns were seen, and altogether the celebration was evidently enjoyed by the boys. Portsmouth is not alone in this peculiar observance, for down at Marblehead the night of the 5th of November is remembered by a huge bonfire on the neck, around which the chaps with horns dance in fantastic glee. The blaze Saturday night on the M. N. was a bigger one than usual.*

It's a queer custom the youths of Portsmouth and Marblehead have.[2] In the early times the day was observed in most of the large New England towns as well as in Boston, and there are many casual references to it.

The Rev. Samuel Deane of Portland makes mention of it twice in his Journal:

"1770 November 5 Several popes and devils tonight;" "1771 November 5 No popes nor devils here tonight at my house."

The Rev. Ezra Stiles speaks of it at Newport in 1771, saying "Powder Plot, — Pope &ct carried about;"

and again on November 5, 1774, he says,

"This Afternoon three popes &ct. paraded thro' the streets, & in the Evening they were consumed in a Bonfire as usual — among others were Ld. North, Gov. Hutchinson & Gen. Gage."

[4] John Adams, attending court at Salem on Wednesday, November 5, 1766, says:

Spent the evening at Mr. Pynchon's, with Farnham, Sewall, Sargeant, Col. Saltonstall &ct. very agreeably. Punch, wine, bread and cheese, apples,

pipes and tobacco. Popes and bonfires this evening at Salem, and a swarm of tumultuous people attending.[1]

1 Portsmouth Republican News, Monday, November 7, 1892. '
Portsmouth Daily Evening Times, November 7, 1892. '
Journals of the Rev. Thomas Smith and the Rev. Samuel Deane, pp. 329, 331.
4 Literary Diary, i. 182, 470.

Coffin gives an excellent account in much detail of the way the day was celebrated in Newbury and says that the last celebration was in 1775, the principal cause of its discontinuance being an unwillingness to displease the French, whose assistance was deemed so advantageous at that time. As the observance of the day at Newburyport was probably typical of those in other large New England towns, it is interesting to quote what Coffin says of it:

*In the day time, companies of little boys might be seen, in various parts of the town, with their little popes, dressed up in the most grotesque and fantastic manner, which they carried about, some on boards, and some on little carriages, for their own and others' amusement. But the great exhibition was reserved for the night, in which young men, as well as boys, participated. They first constructed a huge vehicle, varying at times, from twenty to forty feet long, eight or ten wide, and five or six high, from the lower to the upper platform, on the front of which, they erected a paper lantern, capacious enough to hold, in addition to the lights, five or six persons. Behind that, as large as life, sat the mimic pope, and several other personages, monks, friars and so forth. Last, but not least, stood an image of what was designed to be a representation of old Nick himself, furnished with a pair of huge horns, holding in his hand a pitchfork, and otherwise accoutred, with all the frightful ugliness that their ingenuity could desire. Their next step, after they had mounted their ponderous vehicle on four wheels, chosen their officers, captain, first and second lieutenant, purser and so forth, placed a boy under the platform, to elevate and move round, at proper intervals, the moveable head of the pope, and attached ropes to the front part of the machine, was, to take up their line of march through the principal streets of the town.- Sometimes in addition to the images of the pope and his company, there might be found, on the same platform, half a dozen dancers and a fiddler, whose*

[1] 'Hornpipes, jigs, strathspeys, and reels
Fat life and mettle in their heels,'

*together with a large crowd who made up a long procession. Their custom was, to call at the principal houses in various parts of the town, ring their bell, cause the pope to elevate his head, and look round upon the audience, and repeat the following lines.*

1 Works, ii. 201.

The fifth of November,
As yon well remember.
Was gunpowder treason and plot;
I know of no reason
Why the gunpowder treason
Should ever be forgot.
When the first King James the sceptre swayed,
This hellish powder plot was laid.
Thirty-six barrels of powder placed down below
All for old England's overthrow :

> Happy the man, and happy the day
> That caught Guy Fawkes in the middle of his play.
> You'll hear our bell go jink, jink, jink j
> Pray madam, sirs, if you 'll something give,
> We 'll burn the dog and never let him live.
> We'll burn the dog without his head,
> And then you 'll say the dog it dead.
> From Rome, from Rome, the pope is come,
> All in ten thousand fears;
> The fiery serpent's to be seen,
> All head, month, nose and ears.
> The treacherous knave had go contrived,
> To blow king parliament all np alive.
> God by his grace he did prevent
> To save both king and parliament.
> Happy the man, and happy the day,
> That catched Guy Fawkes in the middle of his play.
> Match touch, catch prime,
> In the good nick of time.
> Here is the pope that we have got,
> The whole promoter of the plot.
> We 'll stick a pitchfork in his back
> And throw him in the fire.'

*After the verses were repeated, the purser stepped forward and took up his collection. Nearly all on whom they called, gave something. Esquire Atkins and Esquire Dalton, always gave a dollar apiece. After perambulating the town, and finishing their collections, they concluded their evening's entertainment with a splendid supper; after making with the exception of the wheels and the heads of the effigies, a bonfire of the whole concern, to which were added, all the wash tubs, tar barrels, and stray lumber, that they could lay their hands on. With them the custom was, to steal all the stuff. But those days have long since passed away.[1]*

When we read such accounts as this, what wonder is it that towns should pass ordinances against bonfires on the night of November fifth? Even as early as 1753 these celebrations had caused enough

---

1 History of Newbury, pp. 249-251.

---

anxiety for the Province to pass "An Act for further preventing all riotous, tumultuous and disorderly Assemblies or Companies of Persons, and for preventing Bonfires in any of the Streets or Lanes within any of the Towns of this Province."[1] Finally, in many places all the sport was obliged to take place in the day time. And in Boston,

where just before the Revolution the two rival processions with
hostile intentions towards one another created such a tumult, leading
citizens used their influence to unite the two factions and then
subscribed money for a supper and a more peaceful entertainment
for the would-be participants. And so this old New England celebration
gradually died out except in Portsmouth and possibly one or
two other places, and even there it has undergone so great a change
that none of its original features are left, and few if any of the participants
know the significance of the day or even its old-time name.


July 17, August 21, 23, 30, September 4, 18, 23, 29, 30, October 17, November 3,


- Checkley, Samuel, "Diary of the Rev. Samuel Checkley", 1735  In: <u>Publications of the Colonial Society of Massachusetts Colonial Society of Massachusetts,</u> pp. 292-295.

# 1753- CHAPTER 18. AN ACT FOR FURTHER PREVENTING ALL RIOTOUS, TUMULTUOUS AND DISORDERLY ASSEMBLIES OR COMPANIES OF PERSONS, AND FOR PREVENTING BONFIRES IN ANY OF THE STREETS OR LANES WITHIN ANY OF THE TOWNS OF THIS PROVINCE.

Whereas many and great disorders have of late year's been committed by tumultuous companies of men, children and negroes, carrying about with them pageants and other shews through the streets and lanes of the town of Boston, and other towns within this province, abusing and insulting the inhabitants, and demanding and exacting money by menaces and abusive language ; and besides the horrid profaneness, impiety and other gross immoralities usually found in such companies, a person has lately been killed when orderly walking in the streets of the town of Boston, by one or more belonging to such tumultuous company ; and the aforesaid practices have been found by experience to encourage and cultivate a mobbish temper and spirit in many of the inhabitants, and an opposition to all government and order,

---

\* These acts were only revived and continued by 1745-46, chap. 17; but they were passed as in the margin.

648 Province Laws. —1752-53. [Chap. 18.]

*Margin notes:*

Persons disguised to go about with pageants and armed with any weapons, exacting money, &c.,— to be punished by fine or imprisonment.
Negroes, &c., may be punished by whip, ping.
Persons carrying pageants, &c., in the night, though unarmed, to be punished.
Bonfires in streets or lanes forbidden.
Masters and parents liable for their servants and children.
Limitation.

Be it therefore enacted by the Lieutenant Governour, Council and House of Representatives,

[Sect. 1.] That if any persons, being more than three in number, and being arm'd all or any of them with sticks, clubs or any kind of weapons, or disguised with vizards, so called, or painted or disco[u]lour[e]d faces, or being in any other manner disguis[e]'d, shall assemble together, having any kind of imagery or pageantry with them, as a publick shew, in any of the streets or lanes of the town of Boston or any other town within this province, or if any person or persons being of or belonging to any company having any imagery or pageantry for a publick shew, shall, by menaces or otherwise, exact, require, demand or ask any money or other thing of value from any of the inhabitants or other persons, in the streets, lanes or houses of any town within this province, every person being of or assembled with such company, shall for each offence forfeit and pay the sum of forty shillings, or suffer imprisonm[ew]t not exceeding one month ; or if the offender shall be a negro servant, in lieu of the imprisonm[ew]t, he may be whip['t][ped] not exceeding ten stripes, at the discretion of the justice before whom the trial shall be.

And be it further enacted,

[Sect. 2.] That if any persons to the number of three or more, between sun-setting and sun-rising, being assembled together in any of the streets or lanes of any town within this province, shall have any kind of imagery or pageantry for a publick shew, altho none of the company so assembled shall be arm'd or disguis[e]'d, or exact, demand or ask any money or thing of value, every person being of such company shall forfeit and pay the sum of forty shillings, or suffer imprisonment not exceeding one month, or if the offender shall be a negro servant, in lieu of the imprisonment he may be whip'[t][d] not exceeding ten stripes, at the discretion of the justice before whom the trial shall be. And whereas bonfires have been sometimes kindled in the streets, lanes and other parts of several of the towns of this province, to the endangering of the lives and estates of the inhabitants,

—

Be it further enacted,

[Sect. 3.] That if any person or persons shall set fire to any pile, or any combustible stuff, or be anyways concern[e]'d in causing or making a bonfire in any street or lane, or any other part of any town within this province, such bonfire being within ten rods of any house or building, every person so offending shall for each offence forfeit the sum of forty shillings or suffer imprisonment not exceeding one month, or if the offender shall be a negro servant, in lieu of the imprisonment, he may be whip'[t][d] not exceeding ten stripes, at the discretion of the justice before whom the trial shall be : the several fines in this act to be applied, when recovered, one half to the poor of the town where the offence shall be committed, and the other half to him or them that shall inform and sue for the same ; and all masters are hereby made liable to the payment of the several fines as afores[ai]d, for the offences of their servants, and all parents for the offences of their children under age, not being servants.

[Sect. 4.] This act to continue and be in force for three years from the publication thereof, and to the end of the session of this court then next after, and no longer.

Passed January 5, published January 6, 1753

- "Chap. 0018 AN ACT FOR FURTHER PREVENTING ALL RIOTOUS, TUMULTUOUS AND DISORDERLY ASSEMBLIES OR COMPANIES OF PERSONS, AND FOR PREVENTING BONFIRES IN ANY OF THE STREETS OR LANES WITHIN ANY OF THE TOWNS OF THIS PROVINCE.," *Special acts and resolves passed by the General Court of Massachusetts.*

# 1760s- Henry Knox

1848- (1760s), July, 21, George Ingersoll, Letter to Charles Daveis from Account of "Mr. Charles Hayward of Boston from Eye-witness Mr. Richard Chamberlain

*The South & North ends of Boston were, in old times, (that is that exceedgly wise & important [?] portion of the Population the <u>boys</u>) in decided and unceasing opposition to each other. In celebration of that immortal day the fifth of Nov. each Party had its Pope accompanied by the "gentleman in black"—there were thus the South End Pope & the North End Pope.*

*These two parties always continued to meet at some half way spot where a regular fight ensued (an annual battle)—which lasted until one Party drove off the other & took possession of its Pope—the victorious Party then took both Popes to some particular place—generally the Mill Pond, & then burnt them both together.*

*On the present occasion, one of the wheels which supported the Platform of the **South** End Pope came off—or broke down—this, of course, would tend to Slide off his Holiness into the Street or at least compel him to lower his head before the rival Pope which would be regarded as a Sign of Submission.*

*To prevent this awful catastrophe,(Henry) Knox immediately placed his Shoulder under the platform & kept the Sacred image erect until the fight was over. Which way the victory turnd Mr. Hayward does not remember.*

*Knox at the time was not—properly speaking—a boy, but rather as Mr. Chamberlain said, a dashing young man, about 18 or so. The belligerents—by the way—on these occasions were not by any means mere boys only, but were composed also of young men.*

*The South End Party was then commanded by a certain Abraham Foley—usually known as Niddy-Noddy, a nickname given him from a peculiar motion of the head. This man afterwards became a Servant and at last died in the Hospital [i.e., was poor and possibly insane]. Knox as Pope man was Subject to his orders—among others of the South End Party. And here, as the Showman says, is the illustration which the anecdote affords— Foley the comander, dying in the Hospital—Knox, the dashing young man, at last the Major-General.*

-Joseph Willard Papers, <u>Massachusetts Historical Society</u>,  Francis S. Drake, Life *and Correspondence of Henry Knox, 1873.*

# 1765- Benjamin Carp

Many enginemen in New York and Boston had relatives or in-laws in the fire department, often in the same company, and sometimes sons replaced their fathers. In Salem, Mass., there was a specific provision that if a member of the engine company were to die, "his son [was] to succeed him as a member"; Dennis, "Fire Clubs of Salem,". describing the Pope Day celebration of November 5, 1765, an anti-pope demonstration that whig leaders had adopted for patriotic purposes. In order to circumvent further rioting during the celebrations, the Loyal Nine and future fireward John Hancock had furnished the two parade "captains," Mackintosh and Henry Swift, with fancy uniforms and speaking trumpets (often used to convey commands at a fire), and Oliver was impressed with Mackintosh's ability to keep the paraders in line. Later Mackintosh boasted of being an active participant in the Boston Tea Party. By the spring of 1774 the press reported a rumor that the British had "orders to bring to England, in irons, Messrs. Hancock, Row, [Samuel] Adams and McIntosh; the latter has been very active among the lower order of people, and the other among the higher." Although the rumor was incorrect, it is noteworthy that an engineman and three firewards were purported to be the most dangerous whig leaders in Boston, and that together they were politically active among all orders of people. Boston's other enginemen were probably not idle during the Stamp Act crisis. On August 27, the Governor's Council had Greenleaf (now the sheriff) arrest Mackintosh, his former engineman, although he later released him in deference to public opinion. Meanwhile, the selectmen ordered two of the engine companies to assist the magistrates in suppressing crowd action. These enginemen faced a dilemma. One historian believes that they were inclined to side with the rioters, so a force of upper-class volunteers ended up providing protection instead. Yet there is little evidence to suggest what the Boston firefighters did. Perhaps they stood with Mackintosh, a fel- low fireman; there were probably several enginemen in the crowds, although none were among the eleven identified participants in the August 26 riots. The Boston firefighters may have played a critical role in the history of crowd action during the eighteenth century. Firemen, after all, knew how to tear down a building with axes and hooks, often in the dark, with dexterity, speed, strength, and organization. They were familiar with fire, and they had experience removing property; hence another historian finds it difficult to ignore the suspicion that firemen used their "special talents" and equipment for extralegal projects like the Stamp Act riots. Yet some Boston enginemen may have sided instead with the author- ties. Whatever their opinions on the Stamp Act, quite a few firemen were prosperous, respectable artisans with their own property to protect, and Mackintosh was the South End captain, and Swift, the North End captain, was a ship- wright who became an engineman…

-Carp, Benjamin L. "Fire of Liberty: Firefighters, Urban Voluntary Culture, and the Revolutionary Movement." *The William and Mary Quarterly*, vol. 58, no. 4, 2001, pp. 781–818.

# 1765- Charge to the Grand Jury, 1765 Boston

"A Government always thinks itself happy when the Grand Jury can find no Offenders to present. This is not our Case. There has been a most scandalous nad notorious Riot, not only against Common Law, Natural Law, that is ,the Law which every Man has implanted in him, but directly against a Law of this Province; (2) nay the Offenders had Notice of the very Law , and warned against a Violation of it; and I question whether there is any Law of this Province more universally known than this . for your Direction, Gentlemen-Riots, Routs, and unlawful Assemblies are where there are any Number not less than three, where they come with an Intent to commit some unlawful Act—if they take not one Step they ought to be punished for this Intent; if they move forward, it is a Rout; if they commit any one Act, it is a Riot; every Man ought to use his utmost Endeavor for the Suppression of such scandalous Breaches of the Public Peace; and I am informed that the Magistrates and others of this Town did their utmost to prevent that Insult upon Government in this notorious Riot, but it seems all proved ineffectual.  You cannot be insensible that I have Reference to that lawless Mob who assembled on the 5th of last November, (3) most atrociously broke the peace put every

---

Anc. Chart. 595. This statute was for the suppression of disorders caused by "tumultuous companies carrying about with them pageants and other shows through the streets and lanes of the town of Boston." See note (3) infra.

The anniversary of the Gunpowder Plot, known as "Pope Day," had been for many years the occasion of an annual riot between the "north-enders" and "south-enders" in the town of Boston.  Each of these rival factions celebrated the day by a procession carrying the effigies of the Pope, the Devil and the Pretender upon a platform, under which small boys, by means of rods connected with the figures, caused them to rise up and look into chamber windows as they passed. The householders were called upon for contributions for the celebration under the penalty of broken windows; and the two processions, after parading the town, met in Union Street, where they fought for the figures, which were afterwards burnt, either on Copps' Hill or the Common, according as victory remained with the north or south end. See Drake's History of Boston, p. 661.

Before the next anniversary in 1765, the general indignation occasioned by the Stamp Act had caused a reconciliation to be effected, and both parties joined in the escort of a "Union Pope," together with several additional figures representing Tyranny, Oppression, Slavery, &c. Mass. Gazette, Nov. 7, 1765; Boston Evening Post, Nov. 11,1765.  The description of this celebration which appeared in both the above papers, concludes as follows: —"This union and one other more extensive may be looked upon as the (perhaps the only) happy effects arising from the S——p A——t"

Members of this Town in Confusion, and many in the utmost Hazard of their Lives; and I would mention for the Benefit of all present, as they are a pretty large Concourse of People, that Persons in general do not know what a Danger they run, in mixing in such a Mob; if there had been any Person killed, every Man there would have been ilable to be tried for his Life, and by a rigorous Construction of the Law, might have lost it: It would have lain upon every Person to have proved how he came there and what was his Business; and every Person who could have been proved to have been aiding before the Fact, encouraging and assisting after it was begun, and actually doing, or protecting and screening after it was committed, must have come to his Trial, and for aught I see must have been convicted; for there are no Accessories in Murder; all are Principals.

– Miller, Samuel, Quincy, , Josiah Quincy, Horace Gray, Massachusetts Superior Court of Judicature, Reports of Cases Argued and Adjudged in the Superior Court of Judicature of the Province of Massachusetts Bay Between 1761 and 1772.1865 Little, Brown, "Charge to the Grand Jury, 1765" pp. 113-114.

# 1768- New London, Connecticut

In town meeting December 27th, 1768, the inhabitants exhibited a commendable zeal to eradicate two distinct evils from their bounds....The second denunciatory vote was directed against an evil of a different kind no less doubtfully pernicious, though it was to be visited with only an equal penalty. (fifteen shillings lawful money...) This was the mock celebration of Pope-day, which had been for some time annually celebrated on the 5th of November, the anniversary of the Gunpowder plot. The edict was as follows:

"Whereas the custom that has late years prevailed in this town of carrying about the Pope, in celebration of the 5th of November, has been attended with very bad consequences, and pregnant mischief and much disorder, which therefore to prevent for the future, voted that every person or persons that shall be any way concerned in making or carrying about the same, or shall knowingly suffer the same to be made in their possession, shall forfeit fifteen shillings to the town treasury of New London, to be recovered by the selectmen of said town, for the use aforesaid."

Descriptions of this obsolete custom may still be obtained from persons whose memories reach back to a participation in the ceremonies. The boys of the town, apprentices, sailors, and that portion of the inhabitants which come under the denomination of the populace, were the actors. The effigies exhibited were two, one representing the pope and the other the devil; each with a head of hollow pumpkin, cut to represent a frightful visage, with a candle inside to make it "grin horribly a ghastly smile," and the only differences between the two, consisting in a paper crown upon the head of the pope, and a monstrous pair of horns to designate the other personage. These were fixed upon a platform, and lifted high on the shoulders of a set of bearers, who in the dusk of evening, with boiserous shouts and outcries, marched in procession through the principal streets, stopping at every considerable house to levy pennies and six-pence's, or cakes and comfits upon the occupants. When arrived opposite a door, where they expected largesses, the cavalcade halted, the shouts ceased, and a small bell was rung, while some one of the party mounted the door-step and sung or recited the customary doggerels, of which the refrain was,

"Guy Fawkes and the 5th of November,
The Pope and the Gun-powder plot,
Shall never be forgot."

At the conclusion of the orgies, the two images were thrown into a bonfire and consumed, while the throng danced around with tumultuous shouts.

The ban of authority issued as above related, in December, 1768, against this celebration, had no effect. In defiance of the law, Guy Fawkes and the Pope made their annual procession through the streets, until after the destruction of the town by the British, saving only two or thee years in which it was interrupted or greatly modified, through an unwillingness to give offence to our French allies, who were loyal subjects of the Pope. Washington, in one of his general orders, prohibited the army from making their usual demonstrations on this day, out of respect to the generous power that had come to our aid in the great contest, and the New London boys were too magnanimous in their patriotism not to follow such an example.

After the Revolution, Pope-day, or rather Pope-night, revived in all its details and the restrictive acts of the town being entirely disregarded, Messrs. Shaw and Miller, and other magistrates, determined to try what could be done by indirect measures. Judging that the most effectual method of destroying a custom so ancient and deep-rooted, would be to supersede it with a new one, which not being so firmly established in usage, might be assailed at any time, they suggested to the populace the substitution of Arnold for the Pope, and the 6th of September for the 5th of November. This was eagerly adopted, and the ditty now sung at the doors, ran in this manner:

Don't you remember, the 6th of September,
When Arnold burnt the town,
He took the buildings one by one,
And burnt them to the ground,
And burnt them to the ground.

And here you see these crooked sticks,
For him to stand upon,
And when we take him down from them,
We'll burn him to the ground,
We'll burn him to the ground.

Hark! my little bell goes chink! chink! Chink!
Give me some money to buy me some drink.
We'll take him down and cut off his head,
And then we'll say the traitor's dead,
And burn him to the ground,
And burn him to the ground."

After a few annual Jollifications in this form, the whole custom fell into desuetude.

-Caulkins, Frances, Manwaring, and Cecelia Griswold, History of New London, Connecticut: From the First Survey of the Coast in 1612 to 1860 .1895.pp. 480-482.

# 1775- George Washington, Enemy of the Bonfire

The father of our country one of the intolerant! Although this is generally taken as an order to ban the celebration in the army, Washington at this time had no power to inflict his will upon the nation as a whole. Perhaps more searches will uncover congressional activity along these lines. Some scholars have none the less traced the disappearance of Pope Day celebrations to this document.
Below you willalso find a record of Washington's celebration of the day while in Barbados in 1751-52.

Head Quarters, Cambridge, November 5, 1775.

Parole Montgomery. Countersign Chamblee.

Samuel Huntington, and John Englis, soldiers in the 34th Regt. of foot, tried at a late General Court Martial for "Mutiny"--The Court upon mature consideration, are of opinion that the Evidence against the prisoners, is not sufficient to convict them of Mutiny, but they are each of them guilty of assisting and encouraging Mutiny, therefore adjudge that each of them pay a fine of fifteen Shillings, and suffer each of them fifteen days fatigue.

The General approves the Sentence and orders it to be put in execution.

As the Commander in Chief has been apprized of a design form'd for the observance of that ridiculous and childish custom of burning the Effigy of the pope--He cannot help expressing his surprise that there should be Officers and Soldiers in this army so void of common sense, as not to see the impropriety of such a step at this Juncture; at a Time when we are solliciting, and have really obtain'd, the friendship and alliance of the people of Canada, whom we ought to consider as Brethren embarked in the same Cause. The defence of the general Liberty of America: At such a juncture, and in such Circumstances, to be insulting their Religion, is so monstrous, as not to be suffered or excused; indeed instead of offering the most remote insult, it is our duty to address public thanks to these our Brethren, as to them we are so much indebted for every late happy Success over the common Enemy in Canada.

# 1751-1752- George Washington Diary from Barbados referring to Celebration of Guy Fawkes Day

-The Diaries of George Washington. Vol. 1. Donald Jackson, ed.; Dorothy Twohig, assoc. ed. The Papers of George Washington. Charlottesville: University Press of Virginia, 1976. Voyage to Barbados 1751--52
Page 36.

The captain's name, if he had just debarked from it after several weeks on the "fickle & Mirciless Ocean" (p. 69). Also, it is not likely that a vessel arriving in port on 2 Oct. would be preparing to sail by 6 Oct. MRS. CLARKE & MISS ROBTS.: Mrs. Mary Clarke, wife of Gedney Clarke, and her niece Elizabeth Roberts. TO COME & SEE THE SERPTS. FIR'D: Serpents, or fireworks discharged in commemoration of Guy Fawkes Day, 5 Nov. This remark enables us to correct the dating of the diary entries made during this period.

(*Editor's Note: he got the date wrong!*)

# 1823- James Otis, (1725-1783), Plymouth

He espoused a cause gratuitously at Plymouth, that arose out of a frolic on a "Pope day;" some details of which, furnish characteristics of the times. A custom of English origin, prevailed in Boston, and occasionally in other seaports of Massachusetts, of celebrating the fifth of November, the day of the well known Gunpowder plot, which was called Pope day. It was attended here with extravagances and pasquinades, not unlike, by a whimsical approximation, the satirical and burlesque licentiousness, that is practiced during certain days of the Carnival in some Catholic countries. On one of these occasions at Plymouth, there was a great deal of noisy turbulence. The inhabitants had been forced to illuminate their windows, some of which had been broken, which excited a good deal of ill temper, and led to a prosecution of the offenders. Mr. Otis was applied to by the defendants some thoughtless young men, to plead their cause. Thinking the prosecution to have been ill natured and vindictive, he kindly engaged in their defense, exerted all his powers of humour and argument, described it as a common, annual frolic, undertaken without malice, and conducted without substantial injury; obtained their acquittal and refused all fees.

This anniversary, which was got up originally with political views, to keep alive hatred and distrust towards the Catholics in England;* was commemorated in this country in a solemn way, and finished a topic for occasional sermons and prayers, against popery. It sometimes included in its denunciations, a covert reference to the hierarchy in England; which in succeeding to many of the possessions, and some of the ceremonies of the papal church, was also thought by our puritan forefathers to have retained a good share of its cruel intolerance; an intolerance, that, with marvelous inconsistency, they practiced on others, while grieving themselves under its effects. Boston was always the headquarters of the celebration, which was indeed seldom practiced beyond the limits of Massachusetts; but in process of time it degenerated into a turbulent, licentious frolic. The town was divided into two parties, called the North-end and South-end, who had each their "pope," as it was called. One of the party ringing a hand bell knocked at every house, and recited a short ballad,** to get some gratuity for

---

*Pope burning was first introduced in England on the anniversary of Elizabeth's coronation. In Scott's edition of Dryden, there is a curious account of the ceremony, with a plate representing a procession that was made November 17, 1679. See Vol. 6, p. 222, and vol. 10, p. 370

**don't you remember
The fifth of November,
The Gunpowder treason and plot;
I see no reason,
Why gunpowder treason
Should ever be forgot.

---

a common purse, to defray the expense of a jovial supper for the principal performers.

The pageant was exhibited on a stage, mounted on wheels and drawn by horses. In front of the stage, was a lantern six or eight feet high, made with oiled paper, and covered with satirical inscriptions, alluding to the political characters or events of the day; and sometimes a boy was placed inside of it, accoutered and dancing in an antic manner. Next to the lantern, was a small figure meant for the Pretender, suspended to a gibbet. In the centre was the Pope preposterously dressed, and made as corpulent as possible; and in the rear was a figure of the Devil, with an enormous tail, a pitchfork in one hand, and a lantern in the other. Beneath the floor, boys were placed, who held poles that went up through the principal figures into the head, so that they could turn the heads round, or raise them up to a level with the chamber windows of the houses. Occasionally some political character, obnoxious to the popular ill will, was exhibited between the figures of the Pope and the Devil. thus the Marquis of Bute was caricatured by a boot suspended

---

From Rome to Rome the Pope is come,
Amid ten thousand fears,
With fiery serpents to be seen
At eyes, nose, mouth, and ears,
Don't you hear my little bell
Go chink, chink, chink,
Pleas to give me a little money,
To buy my Pope some drink.

---

to a gallows: Commissioner Paxton, *** who was a remarkably polite man, but very unpopular, was represented by a figure with this label-"every man's humble servant but no man's friend"--Governor Bernard was personified by a tomcod, a small fish he was very fond of catching and consuming in his family, a fondness that was attributed to his parsimony. The pageants of the two parties were paraded about in the day time quietly; but in the evening they met in Union Street, which was the line of demarcation between them. A struggle ensued with all the force they could respectively muster, and the object was to capture the "Pope" of the other. This was commonly effected at the expense of some broken heads; and if the South succeeded, the trophies of the contest were carried to the Common and thre consumed; if the North was victorious, they were taken to Copps Hill, where a bonfire was had, followed by a jovial supper. The sailors, mechanics, young men and boys of all classes, took part in these scenes. A story is related of one of them, that interested the feelings of the whole town at the time, and was productive of much chagrin to one side, and many a hearty laugh to the other. The South-end had been unlucky for several years in the contests, when some young men, resolved to retrieve its reputation. This they effected

---

****Charles Paxton was one of the Commissioners of the Customs, and actively discharged the duties of a very unpopular office. He was remarkable for the finished politeness and courtesy of his manners: but this, which might have been considered a merit at other times, was in the bitterness of party struggles turned sarcastically against him.

---

chiefly by stratagem. They went down in considerable numbers in the evening to the lower part of Middle Street, and vociferated the usual cry, "North-end forever!" Deceived by this watch-word, the North end Pope was brought out, when only a few of its real partisans were present, who joined this convoy of the enemy, as soon as they had carried it a little way, the disguised party, being joined by a number of their friends, threw off the concealment, assumed their own cry of South-end forever! and carried the prize to a triumphal bonfire in the Common.

The termination off these Pope days, exhibits a characteristic trait of those times, and the docility of what might be considered a thoughtless, mob. The patriots of the town saw the mischief of these dissensions, when they wanted the feelings of the citizens to be united in the great object of opposition to the measures of the British ministry: they therefore brought about a reconciliation, and in 1774, had what was called an Union Pope, when the two parties, after great preparations, met with their pageants, and exchanging amicable salutes, proceeded to make a common bonfire, and terminated the frolic by supping together. This was in November, 1774. The next spring, the affairs of Lexington and Bunker Hill took place, and this foolish and turbulent practice, a striking mark of colonial subserviency, was never repeated.

-Tudor, William, <u>The Life of James Otis, Of Massachusetts…,</u> 1823. 25-29.

# 1831 - Popes Day Folklore: The North American Review

Before the revolutionary war, it was customary to celebrate the fifth of November, or the anniversary of what was called the 'Gunpowder Plot.' The custom was borrowed from England, where Guy Fawkes, who seems to have received rather more than his share of popular honor, was the hero of the occasion; his effigy, with a dark lantern in one hand, and a bundle of matches in the other, being borne round in solemn procession during the day, to the music of an appropriate song, and burnt with great pomp in the evening. The practice is not yet wholly forgotten by the boys of London; though the police of that city regularly threaten both the usage, and the lawless youth who pursue it, with a fate not unlike that which Guy himself intended for the Parliament. When it came to this country, it seems to have received a material improvement by the addition of certain ceremonies, which in England were appropriated to the seventeenth of November, the anniversary of Queen Elizabeth's accession; when the effigies of the Devil and the Pope were regularly carried about and burnt in the same manner as Guy Fawkes, until, in the time of Queen Anne, that of the Pretender was added to the group. Here they were united on the fifth of
November; and it was not unusual for various parties to have their separate Popes, who were used as standards to animate them to battle, as were the Guys in the mother country. There was nothing very romantic in the celebration, and the hereditary prejudice against the Catholic faith alone would have induced the community to tolerate it so long; for it seems to have been tolerated, though it was at best nothing more than a rude amusement of young men and boys. The whole was laid aside prior to our Revolution, when this prejudice had in a great degree subsided, and the memory of the Pretender began to be looked upon with a more favorable eye.

-The North American Review, "Popular Sports and Festivals": pp. 191-216  p. 206  Volume 33, Issue 72 Publisher: University of Northern Iowa Publication Date: July 1831 City: Cedar Falls, Iowa, etc.

# 1842- Pope Night, ANNETTE, (Harriet Jane Farley)

SKETCHES OF THE PAST, No. 4

ANNETTE, (Harriet Jane Farley (m. John I. Donlevy))

*The Lowell Offering (1840-1845)*; Jan, 1, 1842; 2, APS Online
Pg. 111

SKETCHES OF THE PAST, No. 4
POPE NIGHT

How very few are the days kept in New England, as festivals, compared with those observed by other nations! Thanksgiving Day, and the Fourth of July, are with us the *great* days, and the only ones celebrated universally. Election Day is sometimes *elected,* by country girls, as a proper time for an afternoon party, and much attention is generally bestowed upon the election cake. Muster Day is a *great* day with the little *boys*, yet seldom aught but a season of vexation to their anxious mammas and sisters. Forefathers' Day (the 22nd of December) is very unfrequently alluded to; and Christmas Day is, by many descendants of the ascetic Puritans, considered a day of unhallowed rites and religious mockery. New Year's Day is, to be sure, thought a day when every body must say, "I wish you a happy new year," though the conduct of the well-wisher may, in every other respect, sadly refute his expressed desire to contribute to his neighbor's happiness. The First of April is sacred to Momus, and is perhaps as consistently and invariably observed as any of those previously mentioned.

But the little boys of Amesbury and Salisbury, have a celebration which, so far as I know, is peculiar to themselves. It is the observance of Pope Night, or the Fifth of November, by bonfires upon the hills, shoutings, and all such demonstrations of rejoicing. The fifth of November, 1605, it will be remembered, was the ever-memorable era of the Gunpowder Plot; but from whom our young friends learned this, and their mode of celebrating it, I have never yet ascertained. But it is most certainly considered one of their *white* days, or rather nights; and is anticipated with much impatience, for months previously to its arrival.

Preparations are made for it long before the forgetful shipbuilders have recalled the interesting fact, that there will be a Pope Night this year also; but in due season they are effectually reminded of it, by finding that their tar-barrels have, in sine pleasant, star-lit evening, most generously bestowed half their supplies upon some intruder, or quietly eloped, barrel and all; and, snugly ensconced under some old wharf, barn, or projecting rock, are patiently awaiting the time when their grand *debut* will make ample amends for this temporary seclusion.

And a truly splendid appearance they sometimes present, when, after the thick shades of evening have descended upon hill, vale, and river, their bright light streams up into the dark firmament, mingled with the brighter but more flickering and evanescent flames of the other materials for the illumination. I remember well the first time I ever witnessed it. Dark and cloudy were the heavens above, and still and quiet the earth beneath. Suddenly, from a neighboring hill, a spire of light, like a signal flame, sprung into the murky atmosphere, and

"Rocked through the dark skies to and fro,
Then shot forth another, another still;
And see! How they answer from hill to hill!

> Tossing, like pines in the tempest's sway,
> Joyously, wildly, the bright spires play;
> And each is hailed with a pealing shout,"

from the throngs of little fellows, whose mothers all know that 'they are out,' and are often out also, admiring their *brilliant* exploits. Bridge's, Brown's, Swett's, Whittier, and Powow hills, are each thronged with their juvenile patriots; but all this effervescence among the youngsters, has little to do with Protestantism or Popery. Very few of them know what a vast and terrible plot was many years ago conceived by the Catholics of England to revenge themselves on their oppressors. Nor do they know what cruel persecutions had maddened them to such horrible retaliation. Very few of them, I fear, would care if King James, Guy Fawkes, the Pope, Parliament, and all, had been blown up together—though they would have liked to see the explosion.

I have said that few of the members of these active little bands are aware of what they are commemorating; and you will quite as often hear the younkers call it *Poke* Night, as anything else—and *poke* night it assuredly is. There they are, hopping and screaming, shouting and clapping, and *poking* together their piles of brush, and all sorts of combustibles. Nothing comes amiss that will make a blaze—corn-stalks, pumpkin vines, bean-poles, and everything which can be raked and scraped, far and near, lend their "shining light" in this good cause.

But the old fragments from the ship-yards, and more especially the remnants of the tar-barrels, which they have either begged or stolen, form their chief dependence. I say begged—for they do sometimes condescend to *ask* for them, and the man who presents them with a barrel which is not entirely emptied, is thenceforth entitled to their everlasting gratitude.

It takes considerable to furnish them with 'tar-mops,' as they call them, or bunches of corn-stalks, or something of that kind, which they fasten upon the end of a long stick, then dip it in the tar, and when they have fired it, they run around, brandishing it in the air, and swinging it far above their heads. Strange and imp-like do their little forms appear, when revealed by the deep red glare of the crackling flames, as they sing and yell around them, sporting with that element which has been deemed a fit plaything for demons, and reminding a classic observer of "the carnival of the Fairies." Surely Powow hill could seldom have exhibited a wilder scene, in those savage festivals from which it derived its cognomen, than it sometimes does on the night of the fifth of November.

AS the materials for the illumination diminish, the fires of course die away; but before they are entirely extinguished, the reserved tar-barrels are fired, and when well enveloped in flame, are, by a well-developed blow, sent whirling, bounding and hissing down the hill. Those huge red fire-balls are truly worthy of a painter's delineation, as they come rolling and tearing down the hills; and, after their mad leaps into the valleys, it takes but a short time of uninterrupted combustion to reduce them to ashes. Then the little boys stand and watch the smoldering relics of their toil and materials, until their mothers call the home.

ANNETTE

# 1845- Joshua Coffin, A SKETCH THE HISTORY NEWBURY, NEVBURYPORT, MD WEST NEWBURY

p.249

"Other facts and incidents demand a passing notice. Among them, maybe mentioned, the annual celebration of an event, which, from the first settlement of New England, till this year, was deemed worthy of public commemoration. I allude to the discovery of the ' gunpowder plot,' which took place November fifth, 1605. The last public celebration of ' pope day,' so called, in Newbury and Newburyport, occurred this year. ' To prevent any tumult or disorder taking place during the evening or night,' the town of Newburyport voted, October twenty-fourth, 1774, ' that no effigies be carried about or exhibited on the fifth of November only in the day time.' Motives of policy afterward induced the discontinuance of this custom, which has now become obsolete. This year, the celebration went off with a great flourish. In the day time, companies of little boys might be seen, in various parts of the town, with their little popes, dressed up in the most grotesque and fantastic manner, which they carried about, some on boards, and some on little carriages, for their own and others' amusement. But the great exhibition was reserved for the night, in which young men, as well as boys, participated. They first constructed a huge vehicle, varying, at times, from twenty to forty feet long, eight or ten wide, and five

\* New York Gazette and Weekly Messenger, September eleventh, 1775, and October fifth, 1775. 33

or six. high, from the lower lo the upper platform, on the front of which, they erected a paper lantern, capacious enough to hold, in addition to the lights, five or six persons. Behind that, as large as life, sat the mimic pope, and several other personages, monks, Friars, and so forth. Last, but not least, stood an image of what was designed to be a representation of old Nick himself, finished with a pair of huge horns, holding in his hand a pitchfork, and otherwise accoutered, with all the frightful ugliness that their ingenuity could devise. Their next step, after they had mounted their ponderous vehicle on four wheels, chosen their officers, captain, first and second lieutenant, purser, and so forth, placed a boy under the platform, to elevate and move round, at proper intervals, the movable head of the pope, and attached ropes to the front part of the machine, was, to take up their line of march through the principal streets of the town. Sometimes, in addition to the images of the pope and his company, there might be found, on the same platform, half a dozen dancers, and a fiddler, whose

' Hornpipes, jigs, strathspeys, and reels,
Put life and mettle in their heels,'

together with a large crowd, who made up a long procession. Their custom was, to call at the principal houses in various parts of the town, ring their bell, cause the pope to elevate his head, and look round upon the audience, and repeat the following lines.

' The fifth of November,
As you well remember.
Was gunpowder treason and plot;
I know of no reason
Why the gunpowder treason,
Should ever be forgot.
When the first king James the scepter swayed,
"I'his hellish powder plot was laid.
Thirty-six barrels of powder placed down below,
All for old England's overthrow:
Happy the man, and happy the day.
That caught Guy Fawkes in the middle of his play.
You 'll hear our bell go jink, jink, jink

Pray madam, sirs, if you'll something give,
We'll burn the dog. and never let him live.

Well burn the dog without his head,
And then you'll say the dog is dead.
From Rome, from Rome, the pope is come,
All in ten thousand fears;
The fiery serpents to be seen
All head, mouth, nose, and ears
The treacherous knave had so contrived,
To blow king Parliament all up all alive.
God by his grace he did prevent
To save both king and parliament.
Happy tlie man, and happy the day.
That catchcd Guy Fawkes in the middle of hi« play.
Match touch, catch prime.
In the good nick of time.
Here is the pope that we have got,
The whole promotor of the plot.
We'll stick a pitchfork in his back,
And throw him in the fire.'

After the verses were repeated, the purser stepped forward, and took up his collection. Nearly all on whom they called, gave something. Esquire Atkins and esquire Dalton, always gave a dollar apiece. After perambulating the town, and finishing their collections, they concluded their evening's entertainment with a splendid supper; after making, with the exception of the wheels, and the heads of the effigies, a bonfire of the whole concern, to which were added, all the wash tubs, tar barrels, and stray lumber, that they could lay their hands on. With them, the common custom was, to steal all the stuff. But those days have long since passed away. The last exhibition of this kind, took place this year. The principal cause of its discontinuance, was, an unwillingness to displease the French, whose assistance was deemed so advantageous during the revolution.

# 1856- Samuel G. Drake

*The History and Antiquities of Boston* (Boston, 1856), 662.

The anniversary of the discovery of the " Popish Gunpowder Treason" was celebrated with all the licentiousness which long continued recurrences of such celebrations are calculated to produce. This important era in the history of England had been observed by the people of New England from its first settlement, but nowhere with such an enthusiasm as in Boston, especially of late years. The day was always sure to invite all the frolicsome, wayward and turbulent young men as participants ; and hence the termination was an extravagant and, some

times, a riotous affair. The manner of proceeding on these anniversaries was to form a pro

cession at certain head-quarters, thence to proceed through the streets. At the head of the procession went one with a bell in his hand, which notified the people in their houses that the procession was in motion, and that they were to be called upon to contribute something to carry out the celebration.* Those who did not contribute were in danger of having their windows broken, or of receiving some other injury. The money thus obtained was to defray the expense of a supper provided for the leaders. An imposing pageant was carried along with the procession. It consisted of a figure, or figures, upon a platform, or stage, mounted upon wheels, and drawn by horses. On the front part of the stage a lantern was elevated some six or eight feet, constructed with transparent paper, upon which were inscriptions suited to the occasion; usually significant of some obnoxious political characters of the day. The Pretender, † on a gibbet, stood next the lantern, and in the centre of the platform stood the Pope, grotesquely attired, exhibiting a corresponding corpulency.

In the rear stood a devil, with a superabundance of tail, with a trident in one hand, and a dark lantern in the other. Under the platform were placed boys, or persons of small size, who, with rods which extended up through the figures, caused them to perform certain motions with their heads, — as making them face to the right or left, according to circumstances, or rise up as though to look into chamber windows. Pope Day originated on the accession of Queen Elizabeth, in 1558. At first the Pope and the Devil were the only pageantry, which were burnt as soon as they had been satisfactorily exhibited. After the detection of the Gunpowder Plot, in 1605, Guy Fawkes figured conspicuously. Hence, in process of time, the pageantry became considerably changed, as it respected its subordinate characters. In this country the conductors of the celebration took such liberties in the production and arrangement of characters as suited their fancies. At what time Boston first produced two celebrations, upon the same day and occasion, does not appear. But there were two about this time, occasioned, no doubt, by the rivalry which had grown up between the inhabitants of the North End

---

\* The bellman chanted a ballad as he proceeded, which, according to Tudor, in his life of Otis, ran thus :

"Don't you remember
The fifth of November,
The Gunpowder treason and Plot?
I see no reason
Why gunpowder treason
Should ever be forgot.
From Rome to Rome
The Pope is come,
Amid ten thousand fears,
With fiery serpents to be seen
At eyes, nose, mouth and ears.
Don't you hear my little bell
Go chink, chink, chink?
Please give me a little money,
To buy my Pope some drink."

† The effigy of the Pretender was added after the accession of Queen Anne. An epigram used on the occasion has been preserved :

"Three Strangers blaze amidst a bonfire's revel,
The Pope, and the Pretender, and the Devil;
Three Strangers hate our faith, and faith's defender,
The Devil, and the Pope, and the Pretender;
Three Strangers will be strangers long, we hope,
The Devil, the Pretender, and the Pope;
Thus in three rhymes three Strangers dance the lay,
And he that chooses to dance after 'em may."

---

and those of the South End. The two celebrating parties, after having marched about to their content, used to meet in and about Union-street, and then would commence a disgraceful fight for the possession of all the effigies. These fights ended in bloodshed, broken bones, and sometimes broken heads. The victors, if South-Enders, carried the trophies to the Common, and there burnt them. If the North-Enders gained the day, they took the trophies to Copp's Hill, and burnt them there. These celebrations were kept up till 1774, when the patriot leaders of the Revolution found means to reconcile the North and South Ends, and to unite both in the common cause of the Country. So in November of that year both parties joined in one celebration, which they called the Union Pope, and this was the last Pope Day in Boston. There were now four Newspapers published regularly, namely, the News-Letter, The Evening Post, The Gazette, and The Advertiser, or Post-Boy".

p. 709
…On the morning of the same day, November the first, Nathaniel Hurd, " near the Town-house," issued an extraordinary caricature, designed to increase the contempt in which the Stamp Act and its promoters were held. **F**

The Tuesday following was the anniversary of the Powder Plot. " When the day arrived the morning was all quietness. About noon the Pageantry, representing the Pope, Devil, and several other Effigies, signifying Tyranny, Oppression, Slavery, etc., were brought on stages from the North, and South, and met in King-st., where the Union,**FF** previously entered into by the leaders, was established in a very ceremonial manner, and, having given three huzzas, they interchanged ground ; the South [men] marched to the North, and the North [men] to the South, parading through the streets until they again met near the Court-house. The whole then proceeded to the Tree of Liberty, under the shadow of which they refreshed themselves for a while, and then retreated to the northward, agreeably to their plan. They reached Copp's Hill before six o'clock, where they halted, and having enkindled a fire, the whole Pageantry was committed to the flames and consumed. This being finished, every person was requested to retire to their respective houses. And it must be noticed, to the honor of all those concerned in this business, that everything was conducted in a most regular manner, and such order observed as could hardly be expected among a concourse of several thousand people. All seemed to be joined agreeably to their principal motto, 'Lovely Unity.' The leaders, Mr. Mcintosh,**FFF** from the South, and Mr. Swift, from tlie North, appeared in military habits, with small canes resting on their left arms, having music in front and flank ; their assistants appeared also distinguished with small reeds. Then the respective corps followed ; among whom were a great number of persons in rank. These, with the spectators, filled the streets. Not a club was seen among the whole, nor was any Negro allowed to approach near the stages. After the conflagration the people retired, and the Town remained the whole night in better order than it had ever been on this occasion. Many gentlemen, seeing the affair so well conducted, contributed to make up a handsome purse to entertain those that carried it out."

"This union," the writer in the Gazette adds, " and one other more extensive,* may be looked upon as the (perhaps the only) happy effects arising from the Stamp Act." About this time there was published in London, and not long after republished in Boston, an ingenious account of the proceedings which had grown out of the Stamp Act. It was in Scripture style, and consisted of ninety-one verses, and was divided into three chapters. The commencement of the second runs thus : " Now tidings came to the men of America that the decree had gone forth for them to pay the Stamp tribute. 2. And they were greatly amazed thcrcat, and they cried Vith a loud voice, saying, 3. Now is fulfilled that which was spoken of the Prophet ; America shall howl ; on all their heads shall be baldness, and every beard cut off. 4. In their streets they shall gird themselves with sackcloth ; on the tops of their houses, and in their streets, every one shall howl, weeping abundantly. " 5. And many of the men of America waxed exceeding WToth, and they took unto them garments and stuffed them with stuffing, yca, with filthy rags did they sluff them, and they fashioned them till they did represent men. 6. And they called them the representations of Stamp Masters, and they hung them upon trees and gallowses, and they were mocked by men until evening, when they were taken down and burned with fire. 7. And they burned also a Jack Boot, but what they meant by that is unknown at this day. 8. Yea, and they made likewise a stuffed figure with horns to represent Satan ; for they said, ' Go to, for surely Satan himself was the deviser of this tribute.' 9. And in like manner did they act all over the whole land." f The whole was of this tenor, which showed that the Stamp Act found adversaries at home as well as elsewhere.

On the eighth of November, Gov. Bernard prorogued the General Court to the fifteenth of January. This gave much dissatisfaction to the inhabitants, who had been looking to that body for some relief from the distresses which surrounded them. But, as has been before detailed, the Assembly was prorogued while the Bill intended for their relief was in the hands of a Committee. Soon after this several vessels went to sea without stamped clearances ; the Custom-house Officers giving the Masters certificate's that no Stamps could be procured in their jurisdiction. The first ship to venture under such circumstances, was the Boston Packet, Capt. John Marshall, owned and sent out by John Hancock, Esquire. She was bound for London, where she safely arrived, and passed the Custom-house without her certificate being questioned. But, in general, business was at a stand. A Town-meeting was called to see what could be done. It was appointed to take place on the eighteenth of December. In the mean time, new arrivals from England brought further advices of the opposition to the Stamp Act in that country. This gave the "Sons of Liberty " new courage, and caused them to give the Government a further proof of their firmness in the cause they had espoused. They were determined to compel Mr. Oliver to make a new and public declaration that he would not act as Stamp Distributor under any circumstances. And it is surprising that a high-minded and honorable man, as Mr. Oliver certainly was, should ever have submitted to the gross indignity. However, he thought it best to yield to the demands of the people; considerably influenced, no doubt, by the news from England, that the Ministry had been turned out, chiefly because they had, by their imprudence, caused measures to be adopted which could not be carried out.

---

\* "The Government party inferred that this was an evidence of an influence the mob was under, and that they might be let loose or kept up, just as their leaders thought fit." —*Hutchinson*.

† I have never met with a copy of this caricature, and do not know that a copy exists. It is described at length in the Gazette of Nov. 7th. The description closes thus: "On the other side [on the other hand of the picture] is a Gallows with this inscription, 'Fit entertainment for St[am]p M[e]n.' A number of these gentlemen, with labels, expressing various sentiments on the occasion. At the bottom is a Coat of Arms proper for the Stamp Man."

‡ Deploring the bad effects of former celebrations of Pope Days, many of the better sort of inhabitants had, by their prudent intercession with the Chiefs or Leaders, brought about a union, as mentioned in the text. Those Chiefs met on the day of the Stamp-Act demonstration, namely, Nov. 1st, "and conducted that affair in a very orderly manner. In the evening the Commander of the South entered into a treaty with the Commander of the North, and, after making several overtures, they reciprocally engaged in a UNION, the former distinctions to subside. At the same time the Chiefs with their assistants engaged, upon their honor, no mischiefs should arise by their means, and that they would prevent any disorders on the fifth." — *Mass. Gaz.* 7 *Nov.* 1765. Tudor, in his *Life of Otis* (whose date is followed *ante*, p. 663), is probably wrong as to the time when this pageant ceased, or the two parties united in one.

§ The same person mentioned before, probably.

# 1885 (1724)- Concerning New England New York and Virginia

*Social Life in the Colonies*, by Edward Eggleston: pp. 387-408
p. 400 The Century; a popular quarterly. / Volume 30, Issue 3 The Century Company July, 1885, New York.

"It was complained in 1724 that the Virginians paid little attention to the two anniversaries of the gunpowder treason — the 5th of November and the 3oth of January. But the former of these was celebrated in some of the northern colonies by fire-works, by burning an effigy of Guy Fawkes, or by carrying about the village two hideous pumpkin faces, supposed to represent the Pope and the devil, and then consigning them to a bonfire. The pale shadow of this old celebration reaches to our time; boys in some New England coast towns still light their bonfires on the 5th of November, though quite unable to tell what for. In the region about New York forgetfulness has gone further; stacks of barrels are burned, not on the 5th, but on the evening of the November election day, by lads both Catholic and Protestant, none of whom have any interest in the gunpowder plot, or any suspicion that they are perpetuating in dis- guise a custom handed down to them from ancestors loyal to the throne and Parliament of England."

# 1867- Harpers Weekly: The Pumpkin Effigy

## Harpers Weekly \Volume: 1867 Issue: 11/23 Page Range: 0737ad-0737ad "THE PUMPKIN EFFIGY."

Many of the quaint old customs prevalent in New England a few years ago are now almost forgotten, and many of the old autumn out-of- door and winter fireside sports are no longer observed by the rising generation, the majority of them being abandoned for the more popular "bees," in which such numbers of the country- folks throughout all parts of the land engage. Among the minor sports now but seldom prac- ticed by the urchins of the country is that which we illustrate on this page, under the title of "The Pumpkin Effigy," and to which Whittier has alluded in his beautiful poem of "The Pumpkin," which we also give complete. The sport of the pastime con-

"THE PUMPKIN EFFIGY."—[Drawn by L. W. Atwater.]

sists in paring a pumpkin to resemble a human head, and placing a light within to illuminate it, suddenly expose the monster thus created to the view of passing persons, frequently to the very considerable horror of more youthful and more timid persons. The pastime came to this country from England, whence we naturally derive, with our blood and language, many others of our customs. The Fifth of November—"Guy Fawkes's Day"—is annually observed in England with something like this custom as it prevails here, though the effigies, which are called "Guy Fawkeses," are made of turnips instead of pumpkins, and being placed on a long stick, and attired in a long coat, are paraded about the streets. The "pumpkin effigies" as used in this country had no particular design, as those of England, and no other purpose than amusement, though the writer of this can remember an instance in which the use of one produced much terror and pain. "Pumpkin effigies" were little known in the South fifteen years ago, and the first appearance of one in the little country town in which the writer resided was, owing to certain unfortunate circumstances, long remembered and talked of. It was known that what was there called a "gang of negroes"—literally a chain gang of slaves on their way further South—were to pass through the town that evening, and a number of mischievous urchins prepared a "pumpkin effigy," with which to frighten them and amuse themselves. The negroes had never seen such an object, and when it was suddenly displayed as they were passing they were panic-stricken, and fled in great fright. As they were handcuffed together at the wrist—men, women, and children alike—and united by a strong chain which ran the whole length of the file, they soon became confused in their flight, and the weaker ones were thrown to the ground and much bruised and injured. Their overseers, or "drivers" as they were called, on securing them, abused and maltreated them still further. "Pumpkin effigies" became thereafter very unpopular in that re- gion of the South; but few seemed to think the originator of the evil was the individual who had thus bound the helpless creatures together.

The following is the poem by Whittier to which we have alluded. It is entitled.

THE PUMPKIN.

Oh! greenly and fair in the lands of the sun,
The vines of the gourd and the rich melon run,
And the rock and the tree and the cottage enfold,
With broad leaves all greenness and blossoms all gold,
Like that which o'er Nineveh's prophet once grew,
While he waited to know that his warning was true,
And longed for the storm-cloud, and listened in vain
For the rush of the whirlwind and red fire-rain.

On the banks of the Xenil the dark Spanish maiden
Comes up with the fruit of the tangled vine laden;
And the Creole of Cuba laughs out to behold
Through orange-leaves shining the broad spheres of gold;
Yet with dearer delight from his home in the North,
On the fields of his harvest the Yankee looks forth,
Where crook-necks are coiling and yellow fruit shines,
And the sun of September melts down on his vines.

Ah! on Thanksgiving Day, when from East and from West,
From North and from South come the pilgrim and guest,
When the gray-haired New Englander sees round his board
The old broken links of affection restored,
When the care-wearied man seeks his mother once more,
And the worn matron smiles where the girl smiled before,
What moistens the lip and what brightens the eye?
What calls back the past, like the rich Pumpkin pie?

Oh!—fruit loved of boyhood!—the old days recalling,
When wood-grapes were purpling and brown nuts were falling!
When wild, ugly faces we carved in its skin,
Glaring out through the dark with a candle within;

When we laughed round the corn-heap, with hearts all in tune,
Our chair a broad pumpkin—our lantern the moon,
Telling tales of the fairy who traveled like steam,
In a pumpkin-shell coach, with two rats for her team!

Then thanks for thy present!—none sweeter or better
E'er smoked from an oven or circled a platter!
Fairer hands never wrought at a pastry more fine,
Brighter eyes never watched o'er its baking than thine!
And the prayer, which my mouth is too full to express,
Swells my heart that thy shadow may never be less;
That the days of thy lot may be lengthened below,
And the fame of thy worth like a pumpkin-vine grow,
And thy life be as sweet, and its last sunset sky
Golden-tinted and fair as thy own Pumpkin Pie!

Our artist has chosen for the subject of his charming illustration the fruit as it is "loved of boyhood," and represented a merry group gathered around the "pumpkin effigy" in the barn-yard; and it is the fourth verse of the poem which refers more particularly to the pumpkin in this form.

# 1888- POPE-DAY IN AMERICA., By John Gilmary Shea.

*(Editor's Note: Mr. Shea was a prominent American Catholic and he brings with him a strong Catholic Perspective)*[Read before the United States Catholic Historical Society, January 19, 1888.]

The present Pope has recently had a day--a day of Jubilee, commemorated in all parts of the world. The faithful testified their joy at the celebration of his sacerdotal Jubilee, and renewed the protestation of their heartfelt allegiance to the See of Unity, to the one whom Christ has set to govern His kingdom. Princes and rulers of all lands, Mohammedan and heathen, as well as Christian, sent their courteous offerings and congratulations to His Holiness, Pope Leo XIII.
The Pope has just had a day, and a glorious day. But is this my topic? No, I am going back into the past.

There was a time when, in New England and other colonies, the Pope had his day, which was very enthusiastically celebrated. This, as a matter of history, will doubtless be new to most of my hearers, for it is not brought into prominence in the current histories of the country, and few would trace the only remnant left of the old-time celebration--the Fourth-of-July firecracker--to its real origin.

The celebration of Pope-Day arose in a curious way. After the overthrow of the English commonwealth, and the restoration of Charles II., New England was in a dilemma.
The English Crown was asserting its rights over New England, and State holidays had to be observed. But how were the Puritans to keep Guy Fawkes' Day, the 5th of November? A few misguided Catholics, driven to desperation by the penal laws, had plotted to blow up King James I. and his Parliament, led on by government detectives, in all probability. But how could the Puritans, who, as a body, drove the son of James from the throne, and sent his head rolling from the executioner's block--how could they hold up Guy Fawkes to public execration for an unaccomplished crime, when their own hands were reeking with royal blood?
The case was indeed a puzzling one. But New England shrewdness saw a way out of the difficulty. A clergyman of the Established Church in England, when he found his flock growing listless and indifferent, or, what was worse, inclined to criticize him, used to give them what he called "Cheshire Cheese"; he began a series of philippics against the Pope. This always roused them to zeal and friendly feeling.

New England, in the same way, resorted to "Cheshire Cheese," and by a happy device pleased Court and people. They would celebrate the 5th of November with all due noise and honor; but they had the Pope carried around in effigy, instead of Guy Fawkes, amid the noise of firecrackers, and finally committed it to the flames amid loud huzzas.

Thus, though they sang

"Let's always remember The fifth of November," the day became, on this side of the Atlantic, not Gunpowder Treason, but Pope-Day. The contrast between that annual insult of the last century, and the recent ovation of all loyal hearts, the tributes paid by the rulers of English-speaking lands, is striking enough. "Viva il Papa-re"

Boston, being a city of great cultivation and refinement, took the lead in celebrating Pope-Day. An effigy of the Pope was made, and generally one of the Devil; these were placed on a platform, and carried by the crowd, who kept firing crackers, home-made at first, but when New England enterprise opened intercourse with China, the Chinese firecrackers were imported for use on Pope-Day. On the front of the stage was a huge transparency, with inscriptions suited to the temper of the times. Boys below the platform worked strings, causing the figures to face toward the houses and make gestures. At the head of the procession went a man ringing a bell, and bawling a song, which ended:

"Don't you hear my little bell Go chink, chink, chink? Please give me a little money, To buy my Pope some drink."

Every house on the route of the procession was required to contribute to the expense of the show, under penalty of having the windows broken, or being otherwise damaged. The procession passed through the Common, past the State House, and often ended on Copp's Hill, where the effigies were consumed in a bonfire. Such was Pope-Day in Boston, which never dreamed in that day of the Old South Church existing to see Boston ruled by a Catholic mayor, the see of a Catholic archbishop, or its celebrating with loud acclaim an anniversary of a Pope. The newspapers of the day sometimes described these processions on Pope-Day as being carried on "with great decency and decorum"! But it was not always so. In the course of time, one quarter of Boston thought itself badly treated in the arrangements for the procession. Then North End and South End each had a Pope, and the processions generally met on Union Street, where a fight took place for the possession of all the figures; the North Enders burning them on Copp's Hill if they won the day, while their antagonists, when successful, burned the Pope on the Common. In 1745, the celebration of Pope-Day was especially disgraceful. A paper of the time says:

Tuesday last being the Anniversary of the Gunpowder Plot, two Popes were made and carried thro' the Streets in the evening, one from the North, the other from the South End of the Town, attended by a vast number of negroes and white servants, armed with clubs, staves and cutlashes, who were very abusive to the Inhabitants, insulting the Persons and breaking the windows,&c., of such as did not give them money to their satisfaction, and even many of those who had given them liberally; and the two Popes meeting in Corn-hill, their followers were so infatuated as to fall upon each other with the utmost Rage and Fury. Several were sorely wounded and bruised, some left for dead, and rendered incapable of any business for a long time to the great Loss and Damage of their respective Masters.

And he prints a letter from a subscriber, condemning the supineness of the authorities. This letter was as follows:

I hope you will not suffer the grand fray, not to say bloody, that happen'd before your Door last Tuesday evening to pass off without a public rebuke; and such an one as becomes a person zealous as well for the Peace and Good Order of the State as the Church. What a scandal and Infamy to a Protestant Mob, be it of the rudest and lowest Sailors out of Boston, or even of the very negroes of the Town, to fall upon one another with Clubs and Cutlashes in a Rage and Fury which only Hell could inspire or the Devil broke loose from chains there could represent! Is this a meet or sufferable show of Protestant zeal against Popery? Is this to honor the Protestant religion to the few French prisoners of war that are left among us? Or can our children or servants be safe in the streets at such a time if such Rioters be permitted? Or in a word, what madness must seize the two mobs, united Brethren, as they would appear against Popery, to fall upon each other, break one another's Bones or dash one another's Brains out?
Why this enormity above all others should be winked at, and the Inhabitants of the Town with their Dwellings left to the mercy of a rude and intoxicated Rabble, the very Dregs of the People, black and white, and why no more has been done to prevent or suppress such Riotous proceedings, which have been long growing upon us, and as long bewailed by all sober Persons, must be humbly left to our betters to say. *

But the voice of "decency and decorum" could not stop the celebration of Pope-Day. As politics grew fierce, first the Pretender, then obnoxious English statesmen, were burned in effigy with the Pope.
In 1755, "the Devil, the Pope, and the Pretender, at night were carried about the city on a bier, their three effigies hideously formed, and as humorously contrived, the Devil standing close behind the Pope, seemingly paying his compliments to him, with a three-pronged pitchfork in one hand, with which at times the was made to thrust his Holiness on the Back, and a lanthorn in the other, the young Pretender standing before the Pope, waiting his commands."

The newspaper which gives these details adds: "In their route through the Streets, they stop't at the French General's Lodgings,"--this was General Dieskau, then lying wounded and a prisoner in Boston,--"where a guard was ordered to prevent mischief by the Mob. The General sent down some silver by the carriers, with which after giving three huzzas, they marched off to a proper place, and set fire to the Devil's tail, burning the three to cinders."†

The passage of the Quebec Act, by which Catholics in Canada and the country northwest of the Ohio were maintained in the exercise of their religion, as it was under French rule, excited a bitter feeling in the Thirteen Colonies. This revived the Pope-Day celebration, and gave it new zest.

We have accounts of the observance of the day in several places in the year 1774:
The last public celebration of "Pope Day," so called in Newbury and Newburyport (Mass.), occurred this year. To prevent any tumult or disorder taking place during the evening or night, the town of Newburyport voted October 24, 1774, "that no effigies be carried

* "Weekly Post-Boy," Nov. 18, 1745.
† "Annapolis Gazette," Dec. 4, 1755.

about or exhibited on the 5th of November, only in the day-time." Motives of policy afterwards induced the discontinuance of this custom which has now become obsolete. This year (1774) the celebration went off with a great flourish. In the day-time companies of little boys might be seen in various parts of the town, with their little popes dressed up in the most grotesque and fantastic manner, which they carried about, some on boards and some on little carriages for their own and others' amusement. But the great exhibition was reserved for the night, in which young men as well as boys participated. They first constructed a huge vehicle, varying at times, from 20 to 40 feet long, 8 or 10 wide, and 5 or 6 high, from the lower to the upper platform, on the front of which they erected a paper lantern, capacious enough to hold in addition to the lights, five or six persons. Behind that as large as life sat the mimic Pope and several other personages, monks, friars and so forth. Last but not least stood an image of what was designed to be a representation of old Nick himself, furnished with a pair of huge horns, holding in his hands a pitchfork and otherwise accoutred, with all the frightful ugliness that their ingenuity could devise. Their next step after they had mounted their ponderous vehicle on four wheels, chosen their officers, captain, first and second lieutenant, purser and so forth, placed a boy under the platform to elevate and move around at proper intervals the movable head of the Pope.*

This same year, the two rival factions in Boston united in one celebration of what they called a Union Pope.

Even down in the Carolinas the day was observed, feeling being very strong there, as we may see by the fact that South Carolina alone, of all the States, made Protestantism the established religion in her first Constitution.

A letter from Charleston in November, 1774, says:

We had great diversion the 5th instant in seeing the effigies of Lord North, Governor Hutchinson, the Pope and the Devil, which were erected on a moving machine, and after having been paraded about the town all day, they were in the evening burnt on the common with a large bonfire, attended by a numerous crowd of people.†

* "History of Newburyport," p. 249.
† "New York Journal," Dec. 15, 1774.

General and enthusiastic as was the celebration of Pope-Day in 1774, it was the last occasion of that crafty means to excite the ignorant and brutal to hatred and violence against Catholics, though it needs no philosopher to see in Pope-Day the genesis of some events in our own time.

Pope-Day ended with 1774.

The next year the din of arms sounded through the land. Protestant and Catholic alike shouldered their muskets, and marched side by side in the cause of America. Yet in the very camp of Washington, in the army where Catholic soldiers from Maryland and Pennsylvania were gallantly facing the foe, it was proposed to celebrate Pope-Day. But from the headquarters of the Army of Freedom came the words of George Washington, already strong in the attachment of his fellow-citizens:

November 5th.--As the Commander-in-Chief has been apprised of a design formed for the observance of that ridiculous and childish custom of burning the effigy of the Pope, he cannot help expressing his surprise that there should be officers and soldiers in this army so void of common sense as not to see the impropriety of such a step at this juncture; at a time when we are soliciting, and have really obtained the friendship and alliance of the people of Canada, whom we ought to consider as brethren embarked in the same cause,--the defence of the Liberty of America. At this juncture and under such circumstances, to be insulting their religion, is so monstrous as not to be suffered or excused; indeed, instead of offering the most remote insult, it is our duty to address public thanks to these our brethren, as to them we are indebted for every late happy success over the common enemy in Canada.*

This was the funeral oration on the celebration of Pope-Day. It was heard of no more.
It would be presumption in me to continue, after George Washington has spoken.
But I will merely add that the firecrackers of Pope-Day have been transferred to the Fourth of July.
* Washington's Works, iii., p. 144.

# 1891, Nov. 15, How Pope Night is Celebrated in Portsmouth An Old English Custom, The New York Times.

In Remembrance of the Discovery of the Gunpowder Plot of 1605-
Former fierce hostilities between bands of boys.
Portsmouth, N. H. Nov. 14.—

It is believed that this is the only place in the United States where the old English custom of celebrating Pope Night is continued yearly in remembrance of the discovery of the plot of Guy Fawkes to blow up the Parliament House in London, with the King, Lords, and Commons, on Nov. 5, 1605, in revenge for the penal laws against Roman Catholics. The anniversary was formerly celebrated in England by the carrying and burning of effigies of Fawkes, and until a few years ago it was a legal holiday there. The youthful descendants of the English settlers on the banks of the Piscataqua have never relinquished the custom, and the anniversary was celebrated last week by boys parading in the streets, blowing tin horns and carrying pumpkin lanterns. The occasion ws not marked by an outbreak of hostilities although there was considerable emulation in having the biggest and most pumpkins and making the most noise.

The custom can be traced back in the records to the early days of the town, the name of which changed in 1653 from Strawberry Bank to Portsmouth. In 1603, or two years before the discovery of the Gunpowder Plot, as it is known in history, the Piscataqua was explored by Martin Ping, who came here with thirty men in the ship Speedwell, of 50 tons, and thirteen men in the bark Discoverer, of 26 tons. But the name of Capt. John Smith is more closely connected with that of the Pisataqua, because he came here in 1614, discovered the Isles of Shoals off the coast, drew a map of the coast, and presented it to Prince Charles, who called the newly-discovered country New-England.

The first settlers came here from England in 1623, landing at Odiorne's Point, and as they were loyal Englishmen, bringing in their vessel the materials for building the manor house on a manor to be established according to the English custom-the occupants of the land to be held as tenants by the proprietors under the grant-it is more than likely that they celebrated an event of as much importance as the plot, Fawkes and other conspirators having been hanged only seventeen years previous to their arrival. The names signed to the petition for changing the name of the "toune at present called Strabery Banke" to that of Portsmouth, " being a name most suitable forthis place, it being the river's mouth, and good as any in this land," are good old English names, the petitioners being the representatives of the fifty or sixty families in the limits, and as the records indicate that the growing colony observed the old English customs, it is probable that anniversary of the discovery of the plot was celebrated in some mild way.

Any person born in Portsmouth can bring to mind the hostilities between the Northenders, Southenders, and Westenders on former anniversaries of Pope Night. It appears in the old records that Northenders nad Southenders were recognized parties long before 1800. In his "Rambles About Portsmouth," the late Charles W. Brewster referes to the parties in describing the agitation of the subject of laying side pavements between 1790 and 1800. The town had none except very narrow ones in Paved Street, so called, and they had been laid only for the accommodation of ladies who desired to trade in the principal dry goods store. The residents could not agree on the location for the commencement of the pavements, and the difficulty was increased by the attitude and belligerency of the boys of the town who had made Buck Street the dividing line between the Northenders and the Southenders, and had made the street, by common consent, neutral ground on which decorations of war were made and parleys held. The Whigs and the Torys had taken sides on the question, and influenced the boys to take part in the agitation.

But at an annual town meeting a wise and farseeing townsman took advantage of the influence that the boys had created in regard to neutral ground in Buck Street and moved that the northwest side be paved with Durham flat stones….The most intense strive, however, was between the Northenders and Sputhenders, and during and for some time after the rebellion the boys took sides with the Republicans and the Democrats, the celebration of the victory of either on election night being an additional occasion for hostilities.  Any middle-aged resident can remember the days when he as an intense partisan, prepared to venture forth for the fray on election night or Pope Night.  Pockets were filled with horse chestnuts, and, with a cord or belt around the waist, the inside of one's jacket was jammed full also.

The gathering of chestnuts was begun as soon as they began to fall, and reserve stocks were stored in secret places. Under the steps of the. Universalist Church, within a block and a half of the dividing line, was a favorite hiding place for some of the reserve stock of the Southenders until it was raided one night by venturesome Northenders.  A dried chestnut propelled by a lusty arm has a stinging effect on the cheek of an opponent.  It will break windows, also, but the residents in the neighborhood of the scene of hostilities learned by experience to close their blinds early on the nights of the attacks.  Each force was divided into squads for approaching in different directions.  The plans of a battle were carefully prepared, the natural leaders among the boys having command.  Overcoats were discarded, fleetness being essential in the attack and the retreat.  Pickets were posted early in the day to guard against the secreting of squads for attacks in the rear, and toward nightfall it was not wise for any one of either party to be seen beyond the dividing line.  Boys who had errands in their opponent's district hurried through them in the afternoon, and only a brave lad could be induced to go over the line after dark.

One night a Southend boy was sent by his mother, who knew nothing of the fray, to summon a physician to the bedside of a sick sister. The physician lived over the line, but the boy had spunk enough to start on the errand before the time for the beginning of the battle.  He put on his lightest shoes, jammed his cap on hard, filled his pockets with the biggest chestnuts, and without calling for aid, as that would attract attention, he by keeping in the shadows of the houses, reached the physician's house.  While he was waiting at the door he saw flitting shadows near the trees on the opposite side, and suspecting that the Northenders were approaching.  It was a hurry call for the physician from that minute, and as the boy started to return he heard the challenging whistle.  He pretended not to have heard but quickened his pace.  The challenge was answered ahead of him, and he stepped behind a tree to reconnoiter.  Half a block away was a corner by turning which he could head for home. He dashed for it. A Northender sprang at him from a darkend doorway, but was tripped. Another sprung from the shadow of a high doorstep and caught him by the neck, but he twisted away and started again on a dead run.  He reached the corner in a hail of chestnuts one of which split one of his ears, but he took an extra breath and fled down the hill.  He kept in the middle of the street to avoid being tripped, and with head down took the volleys of chestnuts.  He reached the line, but he had to go to bed as soon as he reached home, and his body was covered with blue spots for a week or more.

There being several ways of approach, and as each party would not show its strength any earlier than possible, the first part of a battle consisted of skirmishes, the shadows flitting from tree to tree or dropping over fences, with the occasional ping of a chestnut against the side of a house.  Signals, generally in imitation of the voices of animals, passed from squad to squad, and sorties for the capture of prisoners enlivened the proceedings, although captures were rare, the boys dreading the treatment dealt out to prisoners.

Once a boy was kept bound and secreted for two days with hardly anything to eat.  To attack the flanks squads had to go through back yards, climb fences, cut across swamps, wade through streams, and save themselves from attacking dogs, but they got there somehow, and then the real battle began.  Chestnuts flew in all directions switches were used in close conflicts, and rough-and-tumble wrestling was indulged in where spaces permitted.  The chances of victory changed continually, until one party swept the field and drove the other far beyond the dividing line.  The largest force did not win always.  When the mill boys joined the Northenders toughness counted for more the numbers.  In the course of time the feeling ran so high that pebbles instead of chestnuts, and hickory sticks instead of switches, were used in the conflicts and the wounds and bruises were serious.  For a while the animosity was so extended that a boy who ventured at any other time of the year than

Pope Night too far beyond the boundary was likely to be assaulted. A Northender could not skate on the South mill Pond, and Southenders would not dare to be seen on the North mill Pond. At length the parents took notice of the extent of the enmity and by threats and punishments stopped the yearly attacks.

The making of pumpkin lanterns by scooping out the pulp and seeds, cutting openings to represent eyes, nose, and mouth in the rind, and using a short length of candle inside was always a part of the preparations for the celebration of the victories. The defeated force always made use of its lanterns, after the great bother of making them, but with not so much hilarity as the victorious force. Any boy who ventured too near the line with his lantern after the battle had it smashed on general principles, and the lanterns of the goody-goody boys who had to stay at home suffered the same treatment in the course of the celebrations. The moderate celebrations of the anniversary in recent years have been marked contrasts with those of twenty-five years ago and the rising-generation may drop the custom before many years.

-1891, Nov. 15, "How Pope Night is Celebrated in Portsmouth An Old English Custom", *The New York Times*.

# 1893- John, Albee, "Pope Night: Fifth November: New England.

POPE NIGHT: FIFTH NOVEMBER. - It is said there are only three places left in New England in which Pope Night continues to be celebrated. These are Newburyport, in Massachusetts, and Portsmouth and New Castle, in New Hampshire. In regard to Newburyport I can only speak from common report; but of Portsmouth and New Castle I can bear eye-witness, or rather ear-witness, for it is a celebration in which noise is the main element. It is boys, however, and rather young boys who maintain a custom once pretty general in the cities and larger towns of New England, and the small boy's enjoyment and way of manifesting himself is and ever has been by making a noise, helping himself thereto by every sort of instrument that will produce the loudest sound with the least music. It has been said that human beings in the various stages of growth, from infancy to manhood, pass through and typify the progressive stages in the development of races. The so-called music of the barbarian and half-civilized man corresponds to the strange and rude sounds which seem to delight the ears of boyhood. Pope Night, in Portsmouth and New Castle, which is a seaside village below and very near to Portsmouth, is at present celebrated by boys from six to fourteen years of age by the blowing of horns and the carrying of lights of all kinds. They march through the streets in procession, or in small bands, gathering in, as they march, single groups, or dividing again and sending off detachments, so as to leave no street unvisited. The horns are of all sorts, from the penny whistle to those of two and three feet in length. Whence the origin of the custom of blowing horns on Pope Night I am uncertain. But the lanterns and other devices for lighting the darkness of the November night have evidently something to do with the discovery of Guy Fawkes under the chambers of Parliament in the act of blowing them up with gunpowder. In childhood I remember well looking at pictures of the scene which represented armed men with lanterns search ing about in a subterranean place while the dwarfish Guy crouched among great casks of supposed gunpowder. Formerly the lights used by the boys in their observance of Pope Night were candles set in hollowed-out pump kins, the light showing through holes in the shells of the pumpkins, cut to represent a very squat human face. To the lighted pumpkin-heads have now been added all sorts of illuminations, chiefly lanterns and torches. There is no doubt that in Portsmouth at least Pope Night has been ob served from the earliest times, and formerly by older boys than at present; those indeed who knew what they were celebrating and in which they took a serious interest. It is doubtful if the children who now take a part in it know what their own act signifies or commemorates. I shall presently produce a curious proof of this in the case of the boys of New Castle. It is a very singular fact that in Portsmouth, which long since outgrew its early local boundaries, the observance of Pope Night is entirely confined to the ancient portion of the town. This portion has remained substantially unchanged since the colonial period; and along with its antique houses, streets, alleys and docks, there remain the remnants of old families, many local names and traditions, and this historic survivor of the observance of the Gunpowder Plot. But it will not apparently survive much longer in Portsmouth. Every year the interest grows less and less and the boys who take part in it fewer and of a younger age. The same may be said of New Castle, where even the name, Pope Night, has become confounded and the whole meaning of the celebration obliterated. It sufficiently attests the easy loss of the primitive significance of customs and observances and the complete transformation of their names, to note that in this obscure village the name Pope Night has undergone the absurd change to Pork Night.

-John Albee.

-Albee, John, "Pope Night: Fifth November", In: *The Journal of American Folklore*, Vol. 6, No. 20 (Jan. - Mar., 1893), pp. 68-69.

# 1894 - Harpers Weekly: The Fifth of November and Its Ancient Associations

## THE FIFTH OF NOVEMBER, AND ITS ANCIENT ASSOCIATIONS.

"Which, like a waxen image 'gainst a fire Bears no impression of the thing it was." —Two Gentlemen of Verona, Act II., Scene IV. Mr. Brander Matthews, in his "Americanisms and Briticisms." calls attention to the fact that many established and accepted Americanisms are but Briticisms in disguise: and he cites, particularly, certain November customs of ours as coming directly from our ancestors over the ocean. On the evening of the Tuesday following the first Monday of November, he says, the boys of New York, in accord with their immemorial custom on Election nights, illumine the city with countless bonfires, not knowing, any of them, that they are thus commemorating Guy Fawkes and the dis- covery of the Gunpowder Plot. In like manner the "dressing up of a Guy" still survives among us on Thanksgiving Day, the last Thursday of the same negative month. Thus do we, on two memorable feasts, imitate in the new land the celebration of a permanent festival which the old land has, in a measure, forgotten.

It is hardly necessary here to relate all the well-known de- tails of the British Gunpowder Plot of 1605. The accession of the son of a Roman Catholic mother to the throne of a Protestant Queen had, naturally, raised in the breasts of the adherents of the old faith some hopes of an unrestricted toleration, on the part of the government, towards them. But James, whatever his personal feelings may have been, was too much under the dominion of the Commons to resist; and many, and certainly cruel and oppressive, were the severities practised, by statute, upon the Papists who lived in England during the early part of his reign. The result was a fanatical scheme to blow up, by gunpowder, the House of Lords and the House of Commons, with everybody in them, including the King, the Queen, the Prince of Wales, and all the rest of the royal family. The explosive material was stored in a cellar under the Upper Chamber, and everything was ready for a grand and unique celebration of the original 5th of November when the plot was discovered. Guy Fawkes and his fellow-conspirators were hoisted into an unexpected and unpleasant notoriety with their own petar, and James and his Court were saved, for one generation at least; Charles I. living to die at the hands of the very party of enthusiasts who were condemned to die with his father and his brother.

In the Tower of London is still preserved a catalogue of those royal persons who were to have gone up with the Houses of Parliament. It is said to have been the composi- tion of the King himself; and as an exhibition of royal modesty in the beginning of the Seventeenth Century, it may be quoted in part. The first on the list was: "James the Great, King of Great Britain, illustrious for piety, justice, fore- sight, learning, hardihood, clemency and other regal virtues; Champion and Patron of the Christian Faith, of the public safcty, and of universal peace; author most subtle, most au- gust and most auspicious." The Queen is described as "the most serene daughter of Frederick the Second, invincible King of the Danes." Prince Henry is designated as "the ornament of nature, strengthened with learning, blest with grace, born and given to us from God"; while we are told that Charles, Duke of York, afterwards Charles I., was "divinely disposed to every virtue."

One Jeffrey Charlton, at his shop at the Great North Door of St. Paul's, published in 1606 a now very rare pamphlet entitled: "Gunpowder Plot. Arraignment and Execution of the late Traytors, the 27th January, last past." A paragraph from this work, as exhibiting the clemency and other royal virtues of the Champion and Patron of the Christian Faith, is here set down in full:

"Last of all came the great Devil of all, Fawkes alias Johnson, who should have put fire to the powder. His body being weak with torture and sickness, he was scarce able to go up the ladder, but with much ado, by the help of the hangmen, went high enough to break his neck by the fall: who made no long speech, but, after a sort, seeming to be sorry for his offence, asked a kind of forgiveness of the King and the State for his bloody intent, and with his cross- es and his idle ceremonies made his end upon the gallows and the block, to the great joy of the beholders, that the land was ended of so wicked a villany."

We manage such things better in our own days. Dynamiters get reprieves now, and notoriety and cakes and ale, and ask no sort of forgiveness of anybody.

A relic of Mr. Fawkes is said to exist in the Bodleian Library at Oxford, although the present chronicler, who has spent many studious hours in that delightful institution, has no recollection of ever having seen it. It is described as a curiously constructed affair, and as "a fine specimen of ancient workmanship, both as regards secrecy and orna- ment, possessing at the bottom a mechanical movement by which the candle can be instantaneously crushed by the hand and completely extinguished. It turns with great facility, so as speedily to render it a dark lantern ….And [it] has a very strong reflector."

Guy Fawkes was designated the "Damned-to everlasting-fame man"; and his name I find thus variously spelled by his contemporaries: "Fawks," "Fawkes,""Fowks," "Faukes,""Faux," and "Vaux"; and from this last do certain etymologists derive the appellation of Vauxhall Gardens, because of their displays of fireworks, and because of the intimate association between fireworks and Guy Fawkes. But Vauxhall Gardens were so called a century before fireworks became a feature of their entertainments.

In reply to Hazlitt's very ingenious and subtle defence of Guy Fawkes and his conspiracy, published anonymously in 1823, Charles Lamb wrote a humorous essay in which he tried to imagine the successful results of a similar attempt in his own days; and he thus describes the scene in the terms of a Parliamentary reporter— the italics and small capitals being his own: "A motion was put and carried that this House do adjourn; that the Speaker do quit the chair. The House ROSE amid clamors for order." And he concludes by an urgent appeal to the people of England "by means less wholesale than Guido's, to ameliorate, with- out extinguishing. Parliaments; to hold the lantern to the dark places of corruption; to apply the match to the rotten places of the system only; and to wrap themselves up, not in the muffling mantle of conspiracy, but in the warm hon- est cloak of integrity and patriotic intention." These are words which the gentle Elia might have applied seventy years later, not only to the British Parliament, but to the American Congress as well.

The fact that a distant kinsman of the hero of the 5th of November honored America by his presence for a short time during the first half of the present century is preserved in a historical volume written by the late Charles Dickens. In the opening chapter of the work in question the author says that there was unquestionably a Chuzzlewit in the Gunpowder Plot, if, indeed, the archtraitor himself were not a scion of this remarkable stock, as he might easily have been, supposing another Chuzzlewit to have emigrated to Spain in the previous generation, and there to have inter- married with a Spanish lady by whom he had issue, one olive-complexioned son. If this fact had been generally known upon the arrival of Martin Chuzzlewit in America, no one can say what would have been the result; and how far it would have affected his life and nature it is difficult to imagine. A man with the blood of Guy Fawkes in his veins might have been triumphant on any Election day. He might, even, as Governor of his State, have issued Thanksgiving Day proclamations, signed by his own hand; and he might have lived to repeat history by being hanged to a telegraph pole or a lamp-post, or by being burned in effigy for his political delinquencies, thus uniting a Briticism and an Americanism in his own person.

It was not until well into the present reign that the special services for the 5th of November were taken from the ritual of the English Book of Common Prayer by an ordi- nance of the Queen in Council; while at the same time were abolished those for the Martyrdom of Charles I. and the Restoration of Charles II. But no special ordinance and no Queen in Council have been able to restrain the British juvenile from his celebration of Guy Fawkes day. All over the kingdom he dresses up scarecrow figures on that joyful anniversary, clothes *[text is unclear]* in such cast-off garments as he can steal, or beg, or borrow, parading them by day on chairs through the principal streets of the town he honors by his citizenship, and then burning them up with great ceremony and barbaric rejoicing in some very public place at night, to the air of the familiar tune and with solemn chant of the well-known words:

"Remember! Remember! The Fifth of November, The Gunpowder treason and plot; For there is no reason Why Gunpowder Treason Should ever be forgot."

The lines are faulty, but the sentiment is laden with love of country, and it gives the small boy a chance to make a noise and a disturbance which under no circumstances does he ever willingly or wittingly neglect. The invariable and universal custom of the small boy in England to solicit money from door to door in order to make his elders pay for the annoyance he causes them, still survives in America, where the English small boy's cousin goes about from area to area for subscriptions for his fantastic foolery on Thanksgiving Day, and rings basement bells furiously until his de- mands are complied with.

One Guy Fawkes day rhyme is preserved in the pages of Notes and Queries for November 3, 1855. It is a harmless parody upon Wolfe's admirable ballad, "The Death of Sir John Moore," and it evidently refers to some unpopular municipal regulation. The first and the last verse read as follows:

"Not a squib went fiz nor a rocket whiz As the Guy to the gallows was hurried; The mob was afraid of the New Police, And therefore were deucedly flurried.

"Slowly and sadly the bonfire burned Till it reached to his upper story; They fired not a gun nor a pistol, but turned, And they left him alone in his glory."

Again the feet are faltering. But "his upper story" is good. And it sounds like the author of "The Song of the Shirt," although his name is not generally associated with it.

In earlier times the celebration of Guy Fawkes day was not confined to boys and rowdies, but was accompanied by most important and portentous ceremonies on the part of grave and reverend seniors, especially in London. Two hundred cart-loads of fuel have been consumed in the feed- ing of a single fire in Lincoln's Inn Fields, while no less than thirty Guys were hung and burned there on one particu- larly successful night. The uproar is said to have been deafening and blinding, the mobs shouted, the church bells rang, the fireworks blazed and spluttered, and the gun- powder flashed and banged. In later days contemporary figures of unpopular celebrities were exchanged for those of Guy Fawkes. Cardinal Wiseman was hanged and burned in effigy in London on the 5th of November, 1850, because the Pope had made him Archbishop of Westminster; and on the same day, seven years afterwards, a similar honor was conferred upon Nana Sahib, because of his atrocities at Cawnpore. It is to be presumed that this gentle church- man and the brutal Indian did not mind this any more than does Guy Fawkes himself.

In the early part of the present century it is said that on Guy Fawkes day, in Lincolnshire, any person who could procure a gun was at liberty to shoot it, not only to make a noise, but to kill the game which was carefully preserved on every other day of the year; and there used to be a tra- dition in the North Country that executions were prohibited on that sacred anniversary, but out of respect for whom or for what nobody can find out.

A writer in Notes and Queries calls attention to a very old custom existing in the West Riding of Yorkshire in 1857, which he considers as apparently coeval with the annual bonfires and fireworks. It consists of the baking, and partaking of a "kind of oatmeal gingerbread," on that dread- ful day, the local name of which is "Parkin."

Still another correspondent contributes the following: "A singular custom was observed on Thursday last [November 5, 1857], at Durham. The Dean and Chapter of the venerable cathedral supplied themselves with twenty shillings' worth of coppers, which they scattered among as many of the juvenile citizens as chose to attend, and [naturally] many availed themselves of the privilege." The writer adds that this highly appropriate game for a venerable ecclesiastical body is known as "Push-penny," and that it has existed very far beyond the memory of the oldest in- habitant. But no hint is given as to its origin, and no explanation is made as to what it has to do with Guy Fawkes or his nefarious scheme.

The connection between bonfires and Election day, or even Guy Fawkes day, is not very apparent, unless we accept Dr. Johnson's derivation and definition— "From bon and fire. Fr.—A fire made for some publick cause of triumph" and consider them as an expression of good feeling at the receipt of good news. But Election-night bonfires are usually lighted before news of any kind is received; and not infrequently they are kept lighted by enthusiasts to whom the news, when it does come, is apt to be bad.

Bonfires in England upon occasion of rejoicing of any kind are as old as history. But fireworks seem to have been little known until the days of Elizabeth; although when Anne Bullen was conveyed to her coronation, before Elizabeth was born, we read of one of the royal barges as containing a great red dragon continually moving and cast- ing forth wild fire, and 'round about stood terrible monsters and wilde men, casting of fire, and making a hideous noise. Strutt preserves many records of pyrotechnic displays in honor of the Virgin Queen, such as blazing, burning darts flying to and fro, beams of stars, coruscant streams and hail of fire, sparks, lighting of wild fire on the water and on the land, flight and shot of thunder-bolts, etc.

Concerning the 5th of November, Pepys had almost nothing to say, except an occasional expression of annoyance at the bonfires which frightened the horses who dragged his coach. But on the 14th August, 1666, which was celebrated as a thanksgiving day in honor of recent naval successes, he alludes to fireworks in a way so characteristic—not of Pepys but of fireworks—that his words will well bear quoting. "About nine to Mrs. Mercer's, where the fire and boys expected us, and her son had provided abundance of serpents and rockets; and there mighty merry, my Lady Pen and Pegg going thither with us, till about twelve at night, flinging our fireworks, and burning one another, and the people over the way!"

The italics and small capitals in this instance are my own.

-Laurence Hutton.

# 1895-Gorge E. Ellis, Pope's Day,

November 5, with its rival North End and South End processions, and their contest or " battle," sometimes at Mill Bridge on Hanover Street, is described by Rowe. In 1764 the sheriff, justices, and militia undertook to destroy the figures, but the populace was too much for them. Several thousand people were in attendance, and there was a fatal in jury. This " foolish custom," as Rowe calls it, became in later years, as in 1769, 1773, and 1774, less of an affair, and then died out altogether. The lottery still existed in this Puritan community, legalized for public objects. Rowe bought, March 19, 1767, seven tickets of John Ruddock, and sold one, kept two for himself, and gave the rest to Mrs. Rowe and the Inmans. The fashion of duelling still lingered, Feb. 23,1765: " …Boston does not seem to have been the orderly and well governed town which our fathers sometimes proclaimed it to be. There was no constabulary force which amounted to anything when such a force was required. The mobs of Pope's Day, as already seen, had their own way, defying even the militia. The populace arrested at pleasure the infliction of public punishments judicially ordered, and sometimes superadded discretionary pelting of their own (Sept. 11, Oct. 4, 1764; Jan. 11,1770; March 28,1771). When the political troubles came, they sacked and destroyed the houses of unpopular citizens and magistrates. They stripped the offender naked, covered him with tar, decked him with feathers, and transported him in this plight, without hindrance, through the main thoroughfares …One cannot help asking where at such times were the selectmen, the twelve constables, the militia, Hancock and his Cadets, and the principal citizens who were so effective when fires were to be extinguished or patriotic enterprises to be executed. On the whole, Boston is now a safer place to live in for one who asserts the right to differ with his neighbors than it was in those good old days… (1773)… Nov. 4. ? The town very quiet this day. I dined at Bracketts on Boston Neck on turtle. . . . Spent the evening at the Possee. . .. Thos. Palmer P]sq. had his ball to-night at the Concert Hall. Nov. 5. ? This day there is to be a town meeting. Mr. Palmer's ball was very brilliant; there were upwards of two hundred gentlemen and ladies. Very quiet for a Pope Night. Nov. 6. ? Town meeting again this forenoon. Nov. 11. ? The geese flew to the s?ward yesterday. Nov. 12. ? The Govr sent Colo. Hancock an order for him to hold his company in readiness in case of any riot or tumult happening…

-Adams, Charles Francis et al. "March Meeting, 1895. Will of Dr. George E. Ellis; A Century of the United States Senate; Diary of John Rowe; Samuel Skelton; Alice Blower." *Proceedings of the Massachusetts Historical Society*, vol. 10, 1895, pp. 1–115.

# Legislation

A Massachusetts Bay Colony law of 1750 indicates an early formal origin of theatre. Cultural or Folk informal theatre is a different matter.  Theatre in forms such as mumming, guising, and ritual performance were integral parts of the folk cultures of Europe brought with the first colonists.  In 1686 Cotton Mather, in his *Testimony Against Profane and Superstitious Customs*, wrote "there is much discourse now of beginning stage plays in New England." In 1699, the Governor and Council banned, both variety acts and more formally theatrical activity. Laws in both 1753 and 1761 were specifically designed to ban Pope day theatre.

The law of 1753 states the prohibition of: "tumultuous companies of men, children and negroes, carrying about with them pageants and other shews through the streets and lanes of the town of Boston and other towns within this Province"

## The Law of 1753, Massachusetts

CHAPTER 18.
AN ACT FOR. FURTHER PREVENTING ALL RIOTOUS, TUMULTUOUS AND DISORDERLY ASSEMBLIES OR COMPANIES OF PERSONS, AND FOR PREVENTING BONFIRES IN ANY OF THE STREETS OR LANES "WITHIN ANY OF THE TOWNS OF THIS PROVINCE.

Whereas many and great disorders have of late years been commit- Preamble, ted b}' tumultuous companies of men, children and negroes, carrying about with them pageants and other shews through the streets and lanes of the town of Boston, and other towns within this province, abusing and insulting the inhabitants, and demanding and exacting money by menaces and abusive language ; and besides the horrid profaneness, impiet}' and other gross immoralities usually found in such companies, a person has lately been killed when orderly walking in the streets of the town of Boston, by one or more belonging to such tumultuous company ; and the aforesaid practices have been found by experience to encourage and cultivate a mobbish temper and spirit in man}' of the inhabitants, and an opposition to all government and order,

---

\* These acts were only revived and continued by 1745-46, chap. 17; but they -were passed as in the margin.

Persons disguised to go about with pageants and armed with any weapons, exacting money, &c.,—
to be punished by fine or imprisonment.
Negroes, &c., may be punished by whipping.
Persons carrying pageants, &c., in the night, though unarmed, to be punished.

Bonfires in streets or lanes forbidden.
Penalty.
Masters and parents liable for their servants and children.
Limitation.

Be it therefore enacted by the Lieutenant-Governour, Council and House of Representatives, [Sect. 1.] That if an}- persons, being more than three in number, and being arm'd all or any of them with sticks, clubs or any kind of weapons, or disguised with vizards, so called, or painted or disco[u]lour[e]d faces, or being in any other manner disguis[e]'d, shall assemble together, having any kind of imager}' or pageantiy with them, as a publick shew, in an}- of the streets or lanes of the town of Boston or any other town within this province, or if any person or persons being of or belonging to any company having any imagery or pageantry for a publick shew, shall, by menaces or otherwise, exact, require, demand or ask any money or other thing of value from any of the inhabitants or other persons, in the streets, lanes or houses of any town within this province, every person being of or assembled with such com)any, shall for each oftence forfeit and pay the sum of forty shillings, or suffer imprisonm[en]t not exceeding one month; or if the offender shall be a negro servant, in lieu of the imprisonm[e/i]t, he may be whip['t][j9ed] not exceeding ten stripes, at the discretion of the justice before whom the trial shall be.

And be it further enacted, [Sect. 2. J That if any persons to the number of three or more, between sun-setting and sun-rising, being assembled together in any of the streets or lanes of any town within this province, shall have any kind of imagery or pageantry for a publick shew, altho none of the company so assembled shall be arm'd or disguis[e]'d, or exact, demand or ask any money or thing of value, every person being of such company shall forfeit and pay the sum of forty shillings, or suffer imprisonment not exceeding one month, or if the offender shall be a negro servant, in lieu of the imprisonment he may be whip'[t][(dJ not exceeding ten stripes, at the discretion of the justice before whom the trial shall be. And lohereas bonfires have been sometimes kindled in the streets, lanes and other parts of several of the towns of this province, to the endangering of the lives and estates of the inhabitants,

Be it further enacted, [Sect. 3.]
That if any person or persons shall set fire to any pile, or any combustible stuff, or be anyways concern[e]'d in causing or making a bonfire in any street or lane, or any other part of any town within this province, such bonfire being within ten rods of any house or building, every person so offending shall for each offence forfeit the sum of forty shillings or suffer imprisonment not exceeding one month, or if the offender shall be a negro servant, in lieu of the imprisonment, he may be whip'[t][d] not exceeding ten stripes, at the discretion of the justice before whom the trial shall be : the several fines in this act to be applied, when recovered, one half to the poor of the town where the offence shall be committed, and the other half to him or thorn that shall inform and sue for the same ; and all masters are hereby made liable to the payment of the several fines as afores[ai]d, for the offences of their servants, and all parents for the offences of their children under age, not being servants.
[Sect. 4.] This act to continue and be in force for three years from the publication thereof, and to the end of the session of this court then next after, and no longer. \_Passed January 5; 2
Published January 6,1753, [2d Sess.] Province Laws. —1752-53. 64
-*Acts and Resolves, Massachusetts Bay Colony, 1742-1756*, Vol. III (Boston, 1878.), pp. 647-48. 6 Court Files,

## Directive of 1761 Masachusetts

The law of October 1761 acted to: "prevent the carrying of Pageantry or Imagery in any of the Streets and Lanes of the town of Boston."

In October of 1761, the authorities wrote in the directive:

"To the Sheriff of the County of Suffolk his Under-sheriff & Deputies, and to the Constables of the Town of Boston, & Each & Every of them Greetings." The directive emphasized the danger of "tumultuous companies, found by experience to encourage and cultivate a mobbish temper and spirit in many of the inhabitants, and an opposition to all government and order."

"These are therefore in His Majesty's Name to Direct and Require you and Each & Every of you, carefully to attend your Duties incumbent on you, by doing your utmost to prevent the practices aforesaid, & all Transgressions of the Laws now in force for prohibiting the same, and for that End, & for the better discovering the Breaches of the Law, and the offenders, you the Sheriff, Undersheriff & Deputy Sheriffs, & you & Each of you the Constables of the Town of Boston aforesaid, with your Staffs, are directed and requir'd, immediately upon the Setting of the Sun, on the fifth day of November next, to attend & wait at such places in Boston aforesaid, as carrying of any kind of Pageantry or Imagery in any of the Streets or Lanes in the Town of Boston aforesaid, & also prevent any person or persons making any Bonfires in said Streets or Lanes, & you are also required to give Information to all of His Majesty's Justices of the peace, of all such persons as shall offend in any of the particulars aforesaid, that so they may be punish'd as the Law in such Case directs. Hereof you are not to fail at your Perils. Dated at Boston the thirtyeth day of October, in the Second year of His Majesty's Reign Anno Dom 1761.

By order of the Court of General Sessions of the Peace begun & held at Boston the first Tuesday of October AD 1761.

Ezekiel Goldthwait, Clerk"

-*Suffolk County*, Vol. 487, August 1761-October 1761.

## 1768- New Hampshire Legal Action

New Hampshire Law
1768

[Chapter 9.]

An Act To Prevent the Disorders Commonly Committed on the Fifth of November & the Evening following under pretence of celebrating the anniversary of the deliverance from the Gunpowder Plot.

[Passed Oct. 28, 1768. 9 George III. Original Acts. Vol. 6, p. 21: recorded Acts, vol. 3, p. 90. This act is revived and extended for ten years by the act of Jan. 10, 1771.]

      Whereas it Often Happens that many Disorders & Disturbances are Occasioned and Committed by Loose Idle People under a Notion & Pretence of Celebrating and keeping a Memorial of the Deliverance from the Gunpowder Plot on the fifth of November & the Evening following as Servants & boys Tempted to Excessive Drinking & Quarreling – Surrounding Peoples doors with Clamor& rudely Demanding money or Liquor making mock Shows of the Pope & other Exhibitions making bonfires whereby buildings are in Danger in Populous places & Stealing Materials for such fires with many other Irregularities which Disturb the Peace of Such places & tend much to Corrupt the Manners of Youth – for Prevention whereof.

      Be it enacted by the Governor Council and Assembly That Henceforth all Such Clubs Companies & Assemblies for Celebrating or Commemorating the Day aforesaid with the usual shows & mock representations of the Pope & other Exhibitions usually Carried from place to place with the Rude Noisy speeches & Demands of Money or Liquor frequently made at Peoples Doors and the making of bonfires are hereby Strictly forbidden to be done, on the said Day or evening following or any other on the Account of & for the Cause Aforesaid on pain of Imprisonment for the Space of forty eight hours of all concernd in perpetrating any of the Offences aforesaid. And it shall be Lawful for any Justice of the peace Judge of the Superior Court of Judicature Inferior Court of Common pleas or the Sheriff of the Province upon their own View, or the Information of any Credible

Witness to Cause any such Offenders or Offender to be brought before him & on Conviction to Commit the Offender for the space aforesaid unless they shall upon warning & being forbid to proceed therein which shall be first given by any householder, they shall Immediately Disperse & Retire.

Provided that the Punishment of Imprisonment shall not be Inflicted on Boys under twelve years of Age.

This Act to Continue and be in force for three years and no Longer.

# Artifacts of Celebration

Thanksgiving barrel burning on Jail Hill, Norwich, Conn. Clarence E. Spalding

- Perkins, Mary Elizabeth, <u>Old Houses of the Antient Town of Norwich [Conn.] 1660-1800</u>, 1895, p,19.

# Pageantry-Carts

68, Library of Congress.

# A Silver Beaker

A silver beaker showing images of the Devil, the Young Pretender and the Pope. It was made by Hughes Lossieux in Saint Malo, 1707-1708 and engraved by Joseph Leddel in New York City in 1750. It is in the Museum of the City of New York. The text: "Three mortal enemies: The Devil, Pope and the Pretender. Most wicked damnable and evil. The Pope Pretender and the devil. I wish they were all hang'd in a rope. The Pretender Devil and Pope"

Image- A silver beaker showing images of the Devil, the Young Pretender and the Pope. Source- Gilje, Paul, A. *The Road To Mobocracy*, University of North Carolina Press, 1987.

"[The] head of [a] beast with jaws agape, flame emerging from mouth, smoke from eyes and nostrils; amid flames: "Hell" in roman letters (2) [a] full-length male figure with [a] hairy body, cloven feet, horns, and snakes for hair, a serpent entwined around his body; his left hand holds a flail with 3 snakes emerging from the end; the flail is directed toward the fires of hell; chain leads from this figure back through a gate of 2 fluted columns and an arch with a death's head and inscription: "DEATH" in roman letters (3) the chain from the gate is attached to the nose of a standing male figure, wearing a mi-ter and ecclesiastical garments, who carries a cross in his right hand and a rope in his left; (4) the rope runs from the mitered figure through a gallows to the neck of a standing male figure attired in tam-o'-shanter, plaid shawl, knee breeches, shoes, and a sword."

- Ian M. G. Quimby, American Silver at Winterthur (Winterthur: Henry Francis du Pont Museum, 1995), 230-32.

# Du Simitière's Sketches of Pope Day in Boston, 1767

Pierre Eugéne Du Simitiére, "Boston Affairs," November 5, 1767 (The Library Company of Philadelphia.)

In these sketches, the artist Pierre Eugéne Du Simitiére depicted Pope's Day in Boston in 1767, the day that a new customs officials arrived.

Drawings of North End and South End cart companies, the old State House in central King Street is in a light pencil. Both companies are shown with a two-wheeled cart pulled by horses with a large lantern at one end of each wagon, a tent of oiled paper painted with pictures and slogans and illuminated from inside. This may have been "six or eight feet high," and "sometimes a boy was placed inside of it, accoutred and dancing in an antic manner." The hanged man besides the traditional effigies on the South End wagon, with a note that reads "Sur le pendu everybody's humble servant & nobody's friend" and the slogan "liberty & property & no commissioners," identify the political target as Charles Paxton, a friend of vice governor Thomas Hutchinson and customs official. Paxton was known for his courtesy to higher-ups; he had just returned to Boston to serve as one of the new custom commissioners. The North End wagon was painted with slogans and symbols of unity with the British radical reformer John Wilkes in London

Above: Pierre Eugene Du Simitière, Pope Day in Boston, 1767, sketch of the South End cart company, detail, The Library Company of Philadelphia. On the South End wagon, the hanged man besides the traditional celebration effigies, like the tall devil with the lantern, is a reference to Charles Paxton, friend of the vice governor and customs official who had just returned to Boston.

The South End Pope (Figure 1).

Labeled "the South end" and '4 chevaux [horses]." At the left of the image is the wagon's lantern, a tent of oiled paper painted with pictures and slogans and lighted from inside. The lantern would be "six or eight feet high," and "sometimes a boy was placed inside of it, accoutred and dancing in an antic manner." The South End's lantern illuminated a coat of arms ("The Loyal Arms"), perhaps a personification of America ("the true american"), and a caricature of a profile ("TERROR / DESPAIR"). A note on this page says, "behind / true blue," which may refer to a motto visible only from the other side.

The major Pope Day figures appear, just as a Bostonian recalled in 1821, "on the stage, within the railing." (*Boston Daily Advertiser*, November 10,1821) Moving right from the lantern is an effigy on a gallows, with an effigy of the Pope and his cross, a female figure with two devils. The small devil is a child in costume. His gigantic counterpart has horns, pitchfork, lamp, and a tail which is held up with a wire—it is an effigy.

The female is a boy in a dress. He was to dance lovingly about the effigies, It was called "Nancy Dawson." Nancy Dawson was an actress. She died in 1767.

She was not related to Pope, Pretenders, or Guy Fawkes, or to the Stamp Act sponsors or customs commissioners. Dawson had a dance named after her. *(See the Nancy Dawson section.)*

On this sketch a label reads, "Sur le pendu [On the hanged man] everybody's humble servant & nobody's friend." Below the slogan reads: "liberty & property & no commissioners." A line to the right is: "poor charles the batchelor that was once master of the ceremonies."

These lines refer to Charles Paxton (1708—1788), a friend of Thomas Hutchinson, customs official. In 1767 Paxton, had returned to Boston as a new customs commissioner.

*(See the Paxton section)*

-Bell, J. L. "Du Simitière's Sketches of Pope Day in Boston, 1767." *The Worlds of Children, 1620-1920* (2002): 209-217.

"Boston Affairs Figure 3"

"Boston Affairs" (Figure 3).

This separate image shows boys steering a Pope Day wagon without horses. The wagon holds a large lantern and effigies of a seated Pope, a hanged man, and a gigantic devil. The wagon has decorations on its sides. A child rider blows a horn, so does a boy at the back.

Du Simitiére did not identify this wagon with either the South End or the North End, and it is not exactly the same as of his other sketches. This sketch might be of a lesser Pope Day wagon or one of another town.

All wagons Du Simitiére drew were two-wheeled. The Boston Broadside woodcut, published around 1765, depicts a four-wheeled cart. It had the advantage of staying level without horses or people to steady it. In

Newburyport the Pope Day wagon had four wheels, curated from one year to the next. Henry Knox was remembered for once holding up a corner of the Boston South End wagon when a wheel came off.

-Bell, J. L. "Du Simitière's Sketches of Pope Day in Boston, 1767." *The Worlds of Children, 1620-1920* (2002): 209-217.

Above Pierre Eugene Du Simitière, Pope Day in Boston, 1767, sketch of the North End cart company, The Library Company of Philadelphia. The North End wagon was painted with slogans and symbols of unity with the British radical reformer John Wilkes in London.

## The North End Pope (Figure 2).

The North Enders painted symbols on the front of their wagon. These words appeared on their lantern: "No. 45 / LOVE / AND / UNITI / the / north briton." Their pageantry supported Whig hero John Wilkes. Behind the lantern danced the North End's Nancy Dawson. It is hard to identify. There is a British flag, a seated Pope, a boy blowing a horn, and a large devil which is a different design from that of South End's. It did have horns, pitchfork, tail, and lamp. One child steers the wagon. The words "the north end" are below.

Near the North End wagon Du Simitières drew two horses ("2 che[vaux]") with a smaller lantern suspended above their heads.

On the upper right of this page the artist described the two processions: "le north end tender avec un tambour [the North End Pretender with a drum] / le South end dit la plus part avec des potences [the South End says more with a gallows?].

-Bell, J. L. "Du Simitière's Sketches of Pope Day in Boston, 1767." *The Worlds of Children, 1620-1920* (2002): 209-217.

## Could this be a "Jingling Johnny"?

Percussion instrument from the Jannissary tradition

"By the end of the century *(18th)* the British Royal Artillery Band had a bass drum, cymbals, and tambourine, later adding the Turkish crescent. In 1785 the band of the Coldstream Guards included two tambourines and a Turkish crescent [pole or baton with a crescent shape on the top to which bell are attached. Also, known as a "jingling johnny"].

- Adelson, Charles El, "The Turkish March", *Selmer Bandwagon* No. 57, p. 11.

Above Du Simitière also sketched celebrants: two young men in long coats and hats carrying a walking stick and a trumpet may be captains of the companies, with a larger group of boys wearing turbans or nightcaps, blowing horns or conch shells.

Youth holding pope on shingle-Note that the large figure is a devil.

"Men to boys of all sizes and ages exhibited [a host of] Effigies [of the Devil and the Pope] . . . Little boys had [the effigies] placed on shingles, bigger Boys [atop] a piece of a board no bigger than one boy could carry in his hands, others would require 2 or more boys, and so on."

-- Thomas, Isaiah, Three *Autobiographical Fragments; Now First Published Upon the 150th Anniversary of the Founding of the American Antiquarian Society* (Worcester: American Antiquarian Society, 1962), 22-25., Thomas, Isaiah and Benjamin Franklin Thomas, "Memoir of Isaiah Thomas," *The History of Printing in America: With a Biography of Printers, Vol. 1*, in *Transactions and Collections of the American Antiquarian Society*, Vol. V (Worcester: Printed for the Society, 1874), xxviii-xxxi., Marble, Annie Russell, *From 'Prentice to Patron: The Life Story of Isaiah Thomas* (New York: D. Appleton-Century, 1935); and, also, Clifford K. Shipton, *Isaiah Thomas: Printer Patriot and Philanthropist, 1749-1831* (Rochester, New York: Hart, 1948)

1821, Nov. 9 *Boston Daily Advertiser* wrote:

"Boys in petticoats...swarmed in the streets and ran from house to house with little Popes in their hands, on pieces of board and shingle, the heads of which were carved out of small potatoes."

# Pope Day Celebrants (Figure 4).

Du Simitiére also sketched two groups of celebrants. At top are two young men are dressed in long coats and hats. One holds a walking stick and trumpet, and the other is gesturing with a cane in his hand.

The upper pair of celebrants are described as: "officier bleu galonné enor. trompette. autre bleu tourne de rouge. [officer in blue braid huge trumpet. other in blue edged with red.]" In 1765 Boston's Whigs, had provided the town's Pope Day captains with red and blue uniforms, gold-laced hats, speaking trumpets, and rattan canes. Later there were new captains, but they seem to have done without new uniforms. In the lower group, the fourth boy from the left is dressed finely, his hat and coat are ornamented with braid. On the left, one boy blows a horn, both wear turbans or gentlemanly nightcaps.

The boy on the right of the lower demonstrate blowing of conch shells which added to the processions' noise. The boy in the middle of the lower group a tall conical hat, like figures in the Boston broadside woodcut. He carries a small Pope Day wagon, with a horned, lamp-holding devil; the Pope; and a lantern. Carrying miniature models of the wagons, on shingles and bits of board, was done by smaller boys.

-Bell, J. L. "Du Simitière's Sketches of Pope Day in Boston, 1767." *The Worlds of Children, 1620-1920* (2002): 209-217

# Biography-

Pierre Eugene du Simitiere (born Pierre-Eugène Ducimetière, 18 September 1737, Geneva – October 1784, Philadelphia, Pennsylvania) was a Swiss American member of the American Philosophical Society, naturalist, American patriot, and portrait painter.

Born in Geneva, du Simitiere's original name was Pierre-Eugène Ducimetière or Pierre-Eugène du Cimetière. After leaving Switzerland, he spent more than a decade in the West Indies before moving to New York and then Philadelphia. He spelled his name Pierre-Eugène du Simitière, Pierre Eugene du Simitiere or du Symitiere after settling in Philadelphia. Elected to the American Philosophical Society in 1768, he further became one of its curators (1777–81).

Du Simitiere served as the artistic consultant for the committees that designed the Great Seal of the United States, and in 1776 he submitted the first proposed design to include the Eye of Providence, which element was eventually adopted. Moreover, he suggested the adoption of the U.S. motto *E pluribus unum* ("Out of Many, One"). He also designed the Seal of New Jersey, of Delaware, and of Georgia. In 1779, du Simitiere painted the first known portrait of George Washington, later used for the 1791 one-cent coin. In 1781, he was conferred an honorary degree from Princeton University (which was still called College of New Jersey until 1896). Thomas Jefferson's daughter Martha took drawing lessons with du Simitiere. He created the first American museum of natural history from his personal collections constituted during his travels and through his purchases. He opened it to the public in 1782, over forty years before the Charleston Museum, which is generally considered the first of all American museum.

-*Wikipedia, verified.*

-Bell, J. L. "Du Simitière's Sketches of Pope Day in Boston, 1767." *The Worlds of Children, 1620-1920* (2002): 209-217. Peter Benes, "Night Processions: Celebrating the Gunpowder Plot in England and New England," in *New England Celebrates: Spectacle, Commemoration, and Festivity*, Dublin Seminar for New England Folklife Annual Proceedings 2000 (Boston: Boston University, 2002).

-Benes, Peter, and Jane Montague Benes. *The worlds of children, 1620-1920*. Boston University, 2004.

-Gian Domenico Iachini, *Pierre Eugene Du Simitière and The First American National Museum, RSA Jou r n a l, 23/2012*.

# A Representation of the Figures Exhibited and Paraded Through the Streets of Philadelphia, on Saturday, the 30th of September 1780

Pageantry depicting Benedict Arnold created in Philadelphia.

Anonymous (Charles Willson Peale?), A Representation of the Figures Exhibited and Paraded Through the Streets of Philadelphia, on Saturday, the 30th of September 1780 (Philadelphia: John Dunlap? 1780)

Arnold was processed, in effigy in "regimental" dress, with a mask, two faces "emblematical of . . . traitorous conduct," and a letter from Beelzebub that suggested suicide. Musicians played "The Rogue's March" using drums and fifes in front of a cart that held the traitor. The crowd noted that Arnold betrayed the country aqs well as "the laws of honour."

-*[Boston] Independent Chronicle*, October 19, 1780.

# British Parallels

## Devil Cart

Devil Cart: *Street life in London* 1877, John Thompson and Adolphe Smith.

From: Street Life in London, 1877, by John Thomson and Adolphe Smith:

"The accompanying photograph is that of a nondescript guy, somewhat clumsily built up by a costermonger who lives in the south-east of London. This meaningless monstrosity, together with the absurd appearance of the man in woman's clothes, amuses some persons, and the conductor of such an exhibition can hope to realize about thirty shillings the first day, a pound on the 6th of November, and ten or fifteen shillings on the 7th. With this money the cost of getting up the guy must be refunded, and a shilling or eighteen pence per day given to the boys who help to swell the cortege. The boys' share of the proceeds is consequently somewhat out of proportion with the time and cheers they devote to promoting the success of the enterprise; but it is argued that they enjoy the fun, while to their seniors the venture is attended with some risk, and is only considered as another form of labour for daily bread."

This Devil effigy represents a survival from the carted, standing effigy tradition. It is also an important example of the commercial dimension of the celebration. With dependent on these financial arrangements both the boys and the costermonger have an important stake in the maintenance of the celebration as a whole. Therefore it is not really "meaningless."

## Giant Guy London 19th century

GUY FAWKES.

-Mayhew, Henry, *London Labour and the London Poor; a cyclopaedia of the condition and earnings of those that will work, those that cannot work, and those that will not work*, 1851.

For a detailed description of Guying in London as a business see Volume VII

**And:** -Mayhew, Henry, *London Labour and the London Poor; a cyclopaedia of the condition and earnings of those that will work, those that cannot work, and those that will not work*, 1851.

1903- Kensington, London:

"The guy, an unusually large one, was mounted in a small cart drawn by a pony. It was preceded, first, by a man ringing a bell, and then by two dancers, wearing costumes resembling that of a clown and masks ot the common painted kind sold in the shops at this season, who danced up the street in front of the effigy in the real old style, lifting the arms in the air alternately, in time to the motion of the feet. (They did not sing or shout.) For musicians they had a man playing on a shrill long tin whistle or pipe, and another following the cart beating a drum. A man in women's clothes walked beside the cart, occasionally cutting a clumsy caper, as well s his clinging skirts would allow. The rear of the procession was brought up by the clown, capering and curveting and shaking his money-box. It was a poor vulgar show, no doubt, but it retained in its debased state several of the principal features of the old Morris-dance. There were the time honoured figures of the Fool and the Bessy, accompanying the dancers; the drum and penny whistle represented the ancient tabor and pipe; while the bell which the Fool formerly wore hung at his back, was now carried in the van to inform the householders of the passing of the show (very possibly the original purpose for which the bell was introduced)"

- Burne, Charlotte S., "Guy Fawkes Day", In: *Folk –Lore*, Vol. XXIII. December, 1912, No. IV, p.411-1.

# Pageantry, 1680

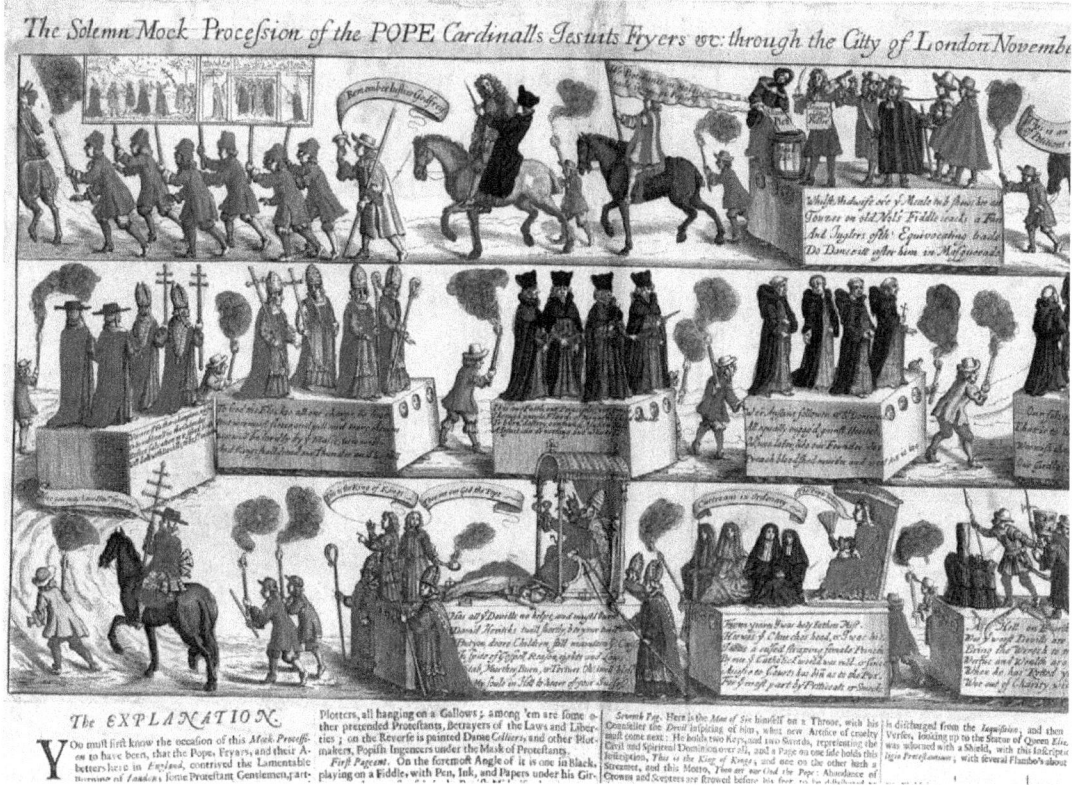

## The EXPLANATION

You must first know the occasion of this Mock-Procession to have been, that the Pope, Fryars, and their Abetters here in England, contrived the Lamentable Burning of London; some Protestant Gentlemen, partly in a thankful Commemoration of their Deliverance, and partly to raise a just Abhorrency of such Popish practices, do now bring these Incendiaries in Effigie to the Fire they have better deserved; and that rather on Queen Eliz. Coronation Day, for that in her Reign, the Protestant Religion, and the true English Interest, were more conspicuously and candidly minded, with admixture of crooked Ends, or Forreign Policies.

But not to prolong your expectation, this Popish Cavalcade or Procession, did march out of George's Yard without White-Chappel Bars, and so gravely came on thorough Allgate, Leaden-Hall Street, and straight along to Fleetstreet, and the Temple Gate. 1. Was a Leader on Horseback; after him marched Whisflers, clad like Pioneers, to clear the way. 2. A Bell-man ringing, and with a dolesome voice saying, Remember Justice Godfrey. 3. A Dead Body, representing Sir Edm. B. Godfrey Strangled and Bloody, and one of his Murtherers holding him up on Horseback, after the manner he was carried from Somerset-House to Green-Berry Hill. 4. A large Banner is born by four, where on the painted Cloth are exprest the Wild-House Consulters, viz. the Popish Clergy Plotters, all hanging on a Gallows; among 'em are some other pretended Protestants, Betrayers of the Laws and Liberties; on the Reverse is painted Dame Celliers, and other Plotmakers, Popish Ingeneers under the Mask of Protestants.

First Pageant. On the foremost Angle of it is one in Black, playing on a Fiddle, with Pen, Ink, and Papers under his Girdle; on the opposite side is the Popish Midwife, leaning on a Meal-Tub;

219

on the hinder part stand some Protestants in Masquerade, in pye-bald Habits: Then comes one born on an Ass, with his Face to the Tail, and in a black ghastful Hue, representing an Abhorrer of Petitions and Parliaments: After him one bears a Banner with this Motto, We Protestants in Masquerade Usher in Popery.

Second Pag. Here are born four Grey Fryars, some Franciscans, strictly so called; others Minimes, a diminutive sort of that Order.

Third Pag. This carries two Benedictines, or other black Fryars, and two Dominicans.

Fourth Pag. Bears forty Jesuits, a sore burden to the whole World, Corrupters of all Morality, Christianity, and Government, Opulent as Civitates, ubi sunt commoditates semper quarunt isti Patres, Clar…s aedes, bonum vinum, bonum panem, bonum linum, tanquam Sancti venerantur, tanquam Reges dominantur, tanquam fures depradantur, Martem norunt an imare, & Tumultus suscitare, Inter Reges & sedare: But hang 'em now on the—

Fifth Pag. Do stand two Popish Bishops, and two Arch bishops, who have not a Rag, but what they are beholding to the Pope for in their Pomp and Courts of Judicature, &c.

Sixth Pag. Here ride two Patriarchs, and two Cardinals; for as about Gods Throne, so about the Popes, and the Devils; these are the four Animals, or Beasts, with Eyes all before and behind; the Eyes of Pride and Covetousness. After this Pageant comes an Officer of the Popes, distributing of Pardons, and saying, Loe here you may have Heaven for Money.

Seventh Pag. Here is the Man of Sin himself on a Throne, with his Counseller the Devil inspiring of him, what new Artifice of cruelty must come next: He holds two Keys, and two Swords, representing the Civil and Spiritual Dominion over all, and a Page on one side holds this Inscription, This is the King of Kings; and one on the other hath a Streamer, and this Motto, Thou art our God the Pope: Abundance of Crowns and Scepters are strowed before his feet, to be distributed to those poor slavish Princes that will hold their Kingdoms in Villenage from him.

Eighth Pag. Carries Donna Olympia, and poor deluded Nuns, as Whores by Dispensation or necessity, following the Popes Camp.

Ninth Pag. In the foregoing ones you have seen the Charming Voice, Fineries of the Popish Circe and her Syrenes, now you have her Cruelties in this Pageant, representing the Fathers of the Inquisition, condemning a Martyr to the Stake for reading the Scripture, or judging by that Word of their new Forgeries.

Thus the whole Procession went along, and was attended by hundreds of Flamboes and Torches. Never were the Streets, Windows, and Balconies more throng'd with Spectators, who with Acclamations exprest their abhorrence of Popery; and that they would with their Lives and Fortunes strive to keep out that cruel foolish Religion. When it came to Temple-Bar, the Statue of Queen Eliz. in respect to the day was adorn'd with a Crown of Lawrel, and a Shield, on which was inscrib'd the Protestant Religion, and Magna Charta; before which the Pope and his Crew having received the Sentence to be burned by the like Flames they have kindled in the City, and the Temple, they were all tumbled down from their Grandeur into the impartial Element; abundance of Fuzes, like falling Stars, and Artificial Fires, in the meantime recreated the Spectators; a great store of Wine, and other Liquors, were profusely poured out to the Multitude, who unanimously of their own accord cryed, No Popery; God bless the King, Protestant Religion, the Church, and Dissenting Protestants, both whom God Unite. Amen.

The Pope, &c. being burnt, the Protestant (by them call'd Heretick) is discharged from the Inquisition; and then immediately repeats these Verses, looking up to the Statue of Queen

Elizabeth on Temple-Bar, which was adorned with a Shield, with this Inscription, Magna Charta, & Religio Protestantium; with several Flambo's about it.

1
Behold the Genius of our Land!
Englands Paladium! may this shrine
Be honour'd still, and ever stand,
Than Palas Statue more Divine.
2
Whilst we thy Praise in Songs repeat,
Whose Maiden Virtues fixt the State;
Made us unite, and made us great,
From whence all happiness we date.
3
Thou to the Root the Axe didst lay,
Both Popish Successor, and Plots;
At one brave stroak thou took'st away,
In spight of Rome, France, Spain, and Scots.
4
A course of glad and peaceful years
That did so happily ensue,
Shews us how we may ease our cares,
And the Conspirators subdue.
5
Nor need the English Senate dread
The Forts, the Fleet, the Scottish Host,
The Irish Friends, and Popish Head,
Apostate H— does boast.
6
The Fox, the Lyon, and the Goat,
Have labour'd to defame thy days;
But still thou hast our Senates Vote,
In London still thy Statue stays.
7
Fixt in our hearts thy Fame shall live,
And maugre all the Popish spight;
To honour thee our Youth shall strive,
And Yearly Celebrate this Night.

London, Printed for Nathaniel Ponder, at the Peacock near the Stocks Mark•t; Jonathan Wilkins, at the Star in Cheapside, next Mercers Chappel; and Samuel Lee, at the Feathers in Lumbard-Street, near the Post-Office."

-The Solemn mock procession of the Pope, Cardinalls, Jesuits, Fryers etc. through the Citty of London, November the 17th. 1680, (London : Printed for Nathaniel Ponder, at the Peacock near the Stocks Mark[e]t ; Jonathan Wilkins at the Star in Cheapside, next Mercers Chappel ; and Samuel Lee at the Feathers in Lumbard-Street, near the Post-Office, 1680) .

The date celebrated by this procession was the anniversary of Queen Elizabeth I's accession. The Whig party hijacked the celebration and moved it to the later date. The procession mocked the Papal

Coronation ceremony. The figure of the Pope was stuffed with live cats, and after the procession had paraded through the streets of London it finished at Temple Bar. The effigies were tossed onto a bonfire. The screams of the cats added to the effect. Political concerns had shifted emphasis from Gunpowder Treason day to the accession for a few years, therefore the tradition of procession of pageantry for both celebrations can be considered to be identical. At first there were no effigies of Fawkes. They were religious figures, Devils or persons from current events.

Refer to: Mayhew, Henry, London Labour and the London Poor, Volume 3. London. Griffen, Bohn and Company, Stationer's Hall Court, 1851.

# Music-Rough Music

## 1620- Bermuda: "Musicke

Captain John Smith records the first New World celebration in Bermuda:

"The fift[h] of No[v]ember the damnable plot of the powder treason was solemnized, with Praiers, Sermons, and a great Feast, whereto the Go[v]ernor in[v]ited the chiefe of the *Spaniards*, where drinking the Kings health, it was honored with a quicke volly of small shot, which was answered from the Forts with the great Ordnance, and then againe concluded with a second volley of small shot; neither was the afternoone without musicke and dancing, and at night many huge bone-fires of sweet wood.

- Smith, John, *The Generall Historie of Virginia, New-England, and the Summer Isles [1584-1624]* . . . (London: I.D. and I.H. . . ., 1624), 197. For more on Bermuda (the Summer Isles) in this time, see Jean de Chantal Kennedy, *Isle of Devils: Bermuda Under the Somers Island Company* (London: Collins, 1971). -

## 1689-1776, Boston: Drums

"All night long through Boston's unlighted, cobbled streets, nothing was heard but "a confused medley of the rattling of the Carriages, the noise of the Popes Drums, and the infernal yelling of those who are fighting for possession of the Devil." For twenty-four hours Boston was in the hands of a mob [a mob that practiced "hell-raising"] which custom, if not law, had legalized."

-Warden, G. B., *Boston, 1689-1776* (Boston: Little, Brown, and Company, 1970): 35.

## 1765- November 11, Boston: "Musick"

*Boston Gazette*, Monday #55 Boston

"…The Leaders, Mr. McIntosh from the South, and Mr. Swift from the North, appeared in Military Habits, with small Canes resting on their Left Arms, having Musick in front and Flank: their Assistants appeared also distinguished with small Reeds, then the respective Corps followed among whom were a great Number of Persons in Rank:" …

## 1765- Caribbean, Drums and Horns

" Nevis and St. Kitts demonstrated "the true loyal Spirit" burning effigies of the stamp deputy and the stamp master "in the Common Pasture" and holding a elegant dinner with drums, horns, and toasts of "Liberty, Property, and no Stamps."

- "Extract of a Letter from St. Kitts," *New-York [City] Mercury*, December 23, 1765.

# 1767- Boston: Nancy Dawson Dance tune

"…Dawson had a popular dance named after her, and that seems to have prompted Bostonians to dub this dancing female figure with her name. Hezekiah Niles, compiler, Principles and Acts of the Revolution in America (Baltimore: William Ogden Niles, 1822), p. 490, quoting from the Boston Gazette. Boston merchant William Palfrey's daughter Polly had learned the "Nansy Dawson" dance by the time she was seven, in 1772; Mary Beth Norton, Liberty's Daughters: The Revolutionary Experience of American Women, 1750—1800 (New York: Harper, 1980), p. 90. The tune was earlier titled "Piss upon the grass," and is now known as "Here we go 'round the mulberry bush"; Joy Van Cleef and Kate Van Winkle Keller, "Selected American Country Dances and Their English Sources," in Music in Colonial Massachusetts, 1630—1820—1: Music in Public Spaces, Colonial Society of Massachusetts Publications, 53 (Boston: Colonial Society of Massachusetts, 1980), pp. 53, 57."

-Bell, J. L. "Du Simitière's Sketches of Pope Day in Boston, 1767." *The Worlds of Children, 1620-1920* (2002): 209-217.

# 1776- Monday, November 6th, Drums and Fifes

"…. Some New England Masters of Vessels that lie here being the anniversary of the Gunpowder Plot, had the Pope, Lord North, Barnard, Hutchinson, and the Devil burnt in effigy after carting them through the town with Drums and fifes

-Cresswell, Nicholas, The Journal of Nicholas Cresswell, 1774-1777, 1925, p. 127-128.

- Harold B. Gill, Jr. and George M. Curtis, III, eds., *Nicholas Cresswell, a Man Apart: The Journal of Nicholas Cresswell, 1774-1781* (Lanham, Maryland: Lexington Books, 2009), 89.

# 1821- *Columbian Centinel,* Stage Music and Dance

An anonymous 70-year-old man is cited as he wrote to the *Columbian Centinel* in 1821: *"On the stage was music and something to drink-also boys, clad in frocks and trousers well covered with tar and feathers who danced around the Pope and frequently climbed up and kissed the devil"*-p26.

- Cogliano, Francis D., *No King No Popery*, (Greenwood Press, London 1995).

# 1821- Bells

"Not shown in the illustration are people with small bells who were commissioned to visit houses for contributions and at least one or two additional characters mentioned in the 1821 recollections who may have been either effigies or actors. One of these was "the Pretender, who presumably stood for the Catholic sovereign who was ready to assume England's throne if opportunity beckoned. Boys."

- Benes, Peter, "Night Processions: Celebrating the Gunpowder Plot in England and New England," in *New England Celebrates: Spectacle, Commemoration, and Festivity*, Dublin Seminar for New England Folklife Annual Proceedings 2000 (Boston: Boston University, 2002), p.21.

— From the *Portsmouth Republican News*, November 7, 1892.

## 1893- John Albee "Blowing Horns"

POPE NIGHT: FIFTH NOVEMBER. - It is said there are only three places left in New England in which Pope Night continues to be celebrated. These are Newburyport, in Massachusetts, and Portsmouth and New Castle, in New Hampshire. In regard to Newburyport I can only speak from common report; but of Portsmouth and New Castle I can bear eye-witness, or rather ear-witness, for it is a celebration in which noise is the main element. It is boys, however, and rather young boys who maintain a custom once pretty general in the cities and larger towns of New England, and the small boy's enjoyment and way of manifesting himself is and ever has been by making a noise, helping himself thereto by every sort of instrument that will produce the loudest sound with the least music. It has been said that human beings in the various stages of growth, from infancy to manhood, pass through and typify the progressive stages in the development of races. The so-called music of the barbarian and half-civilized man corresponds to the strange and rude sounds which seem to delight the ears of boyhood. Pope Night, in Portsmouth and New Castle, which is a seaside village below and very near to Portsmouth, is at present celebrated by boys from six to fourteen years of age by the blowing of horns and the carrying of lights of all kinds. They march through the streets in procession, or in small bands, gathering in, as they march, single groups, or dividing again and sending off detachments, so as to leave no street unvisited. The horns are of all sorts, from the penny whistle to those of two and three feet in length. Whence the origin of the custom of blowing horns on Pope Night I am uncertain.

- John Albee.

-Albee, John, "Pope Night: Fifth November", In: *The Journal of American Folklore*, Vol. 6, No. 20 (Jan. - Mar., 1893), pp. 68-69.

## (1973)- Sherwood Collins "Dancers and Musicians"

"Small boys frolicked and danced about, sometimes playing with the cards on the table, at other times sitting on the Pope's lap, kissing and fondling him as did the Nancy Dawson. The accounts also place dancers and musicians on this stage, though it would seem there would not be room for them unless the wagons were, after all, twenty to forty feet long. More than likely, the dancers performed on the ground before and around the wagon.

-- "Boston's Political Street Theatre: The Eighteenth-Century Pope Day Pageants", Sherwood Collins, Educational Theatre Journal, Vol. 25, No. 4 (Dec., 1973), p. 408.

1768- Music Depicted In: "South End Forever North End Forever", Broadside, Boston, Library of Congress. And:
Pierre Eugene Du Simitière, "Pope Day in Boston, 1767

## Horns

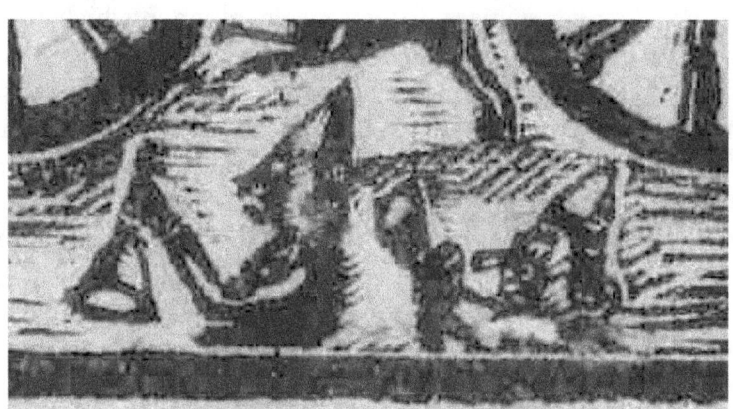

Bell Left, Horn? Right

Horn

Horn and musicians?

-"South End Forever North End Forever", Broadside, Boston, 1768, Library of Congress.

## Horn and Conch Trumpet

**Conch**, or **conque**, also known as a "seashell horn" or "shell trumpet", is a musical instrument, a wind instrument that is made from a seashell, the shell of several different kinds of very large sea snails. The shells of large marine gastropods are prepared by cutting a hole in the spire of the shell near the apex, and then blowing into the shell as if it were a trumpet, as in blowing horn. Sometimes a mouthpiece is used, but some shell trumpets are blown without one.

Various species of large marine gastropod shells can be turned into "blowing shells", but some of the best-known species are: the sacred chank or shankha *Turbinella pyrum*; the "Triton's trumpet" *Charonia tritonis*; and the Queen Conch *Strombus gigas*.

-Wikipedia, verified

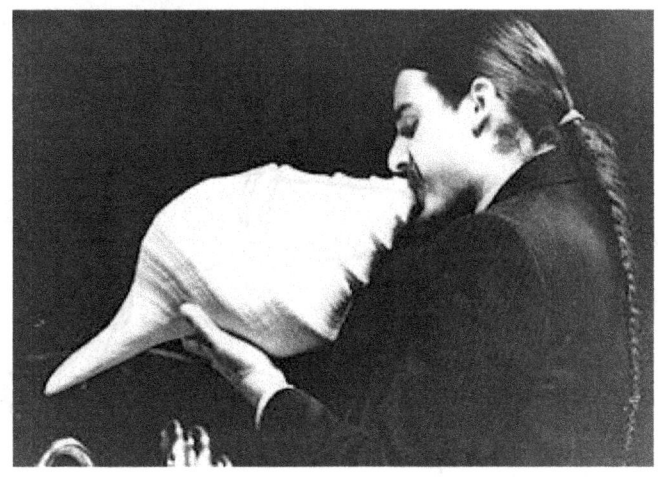

Steve Turre playing conch in 1976.-Wikipedia

## Speaking Trumpet

"Speaking Trumpet" unlike horns which were curved speeking trumpets were most always straight. Speaking trumpets also had flared mouth pieces and bells.

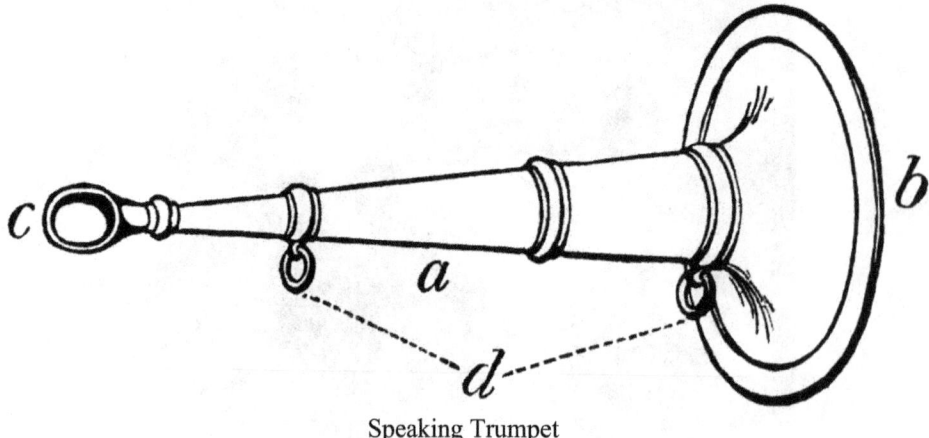
Speaking Trumpet

"In order to circumvent further rioting during the celebrations, the Loyal Nine and future fireward John Hancock had furnished the two parade "captains," Mackintosh and Henry Swift, with fancy uniforms and speaking trumpets (often used to convey commands at a fire), and Oliver was impressed with Mackintosh's ability to keep the paraders in line."

-Carp, Benjamin L. "Fire of Liberty: Firefighters, Urban Voluntary Culture, and the Revolutionary Movement." *The William and Mary Quarterly*, vol. 58, no. 4, 2001, pp. 781–818.

## 1765- Bernard Describes Uniforms and Speaking Trumpets

1765- Bernard observed: "Being "dresst in blue & red, in a gold lace Hat & a gilt Gorget on his breast, with a Rattan Cane hanging at his wrist," Mackintosh led the militia parade of two thousand, shouting orders from a megaphone, supervising a march that united both ends to protest of the Act. "Trumpet" in hand, the "general" led a mock officialdom carrying hats and wands through the streets of the town, ensuring that "no one else" in the procession carried sticks or weapons – and that "no Negro was suffered" to be in the ranks of this protest. Hancock financed the uniforms"

- Winslow, Isaac, Letter to [Unknown], November 15, 1765, in Robert Newsome, ed. and trans., *Family Memorial: The Winslows of Boston*, Vol. I: Isaac Winslow and Margaret Catherine Winslow, 1837? – 1873? (University of California, Irvine, and Massachusetts History Society, 2009-10), 66. Bernard, Letter to John Pownall, November 26, 1765, in Nicholson, ed., *The Papers of Francis Bernard*, II: 423.

-Pierre Eugene Du Simitière, "Pope Day in Boston, 1767", sketch of the South End cart company, detail, The Library Company of Philadelphia.

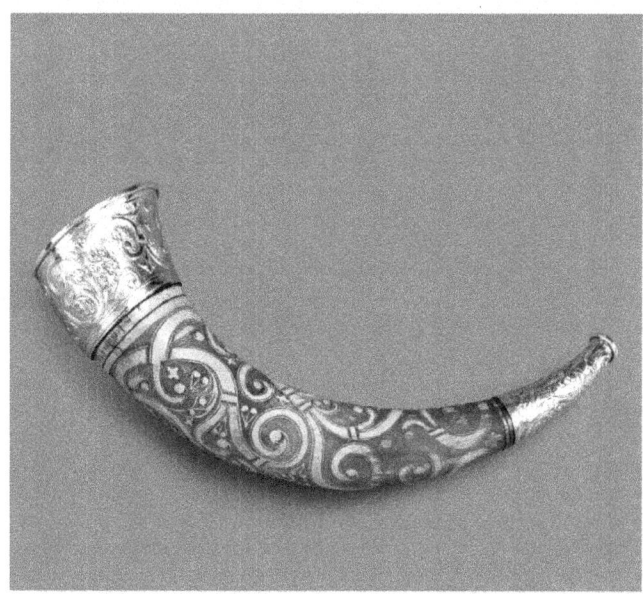

**Olifant** (an alternate spelling of the word elephant) was the name applied in the Middle Ages to ivory hunting horns made from elephants' tusks. One of the most famous olifants belonged to the legendary Frankish knight Roland, protagonist of *The Song of Roland*.

In *The Song of Roland*, Roland carries his olifant while serving on the rearguard of Charlemagne's army. When they are attacked at the Battle of Roncevaux, Oliver tells Roland to use it to call for aid, but he refuses. Roland finally relents, but the battle is already lost. He tries to destroy the olifant along with his sword Durendal, lest they fall into enemy hands. In the end, Roland blows the horn, but the force required bursts his temple, resulting in death.[1] The *Karlamagnussaga* elaborates (V. c.XIV) that Roland's olifant was a unicorn's horn, hunted in India.

Another famous olifant belonged to Gaston IV, viscount of Béarn, and is now preserved in the Spanish city of Saragosse, which he helped conquer from the Banu Hud

**Zobo Horn**

Kazoo like metal Horn c. 1800, An English Band instrument.

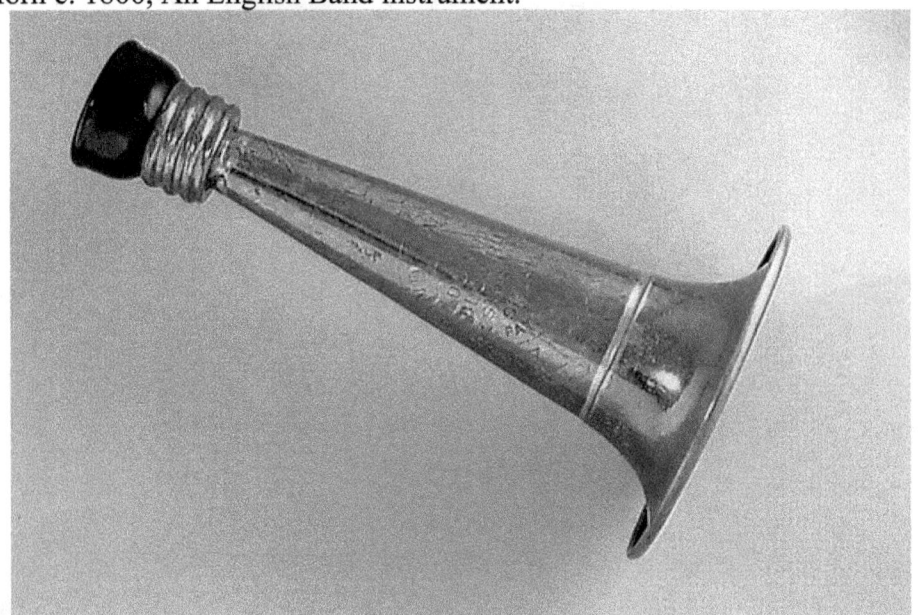

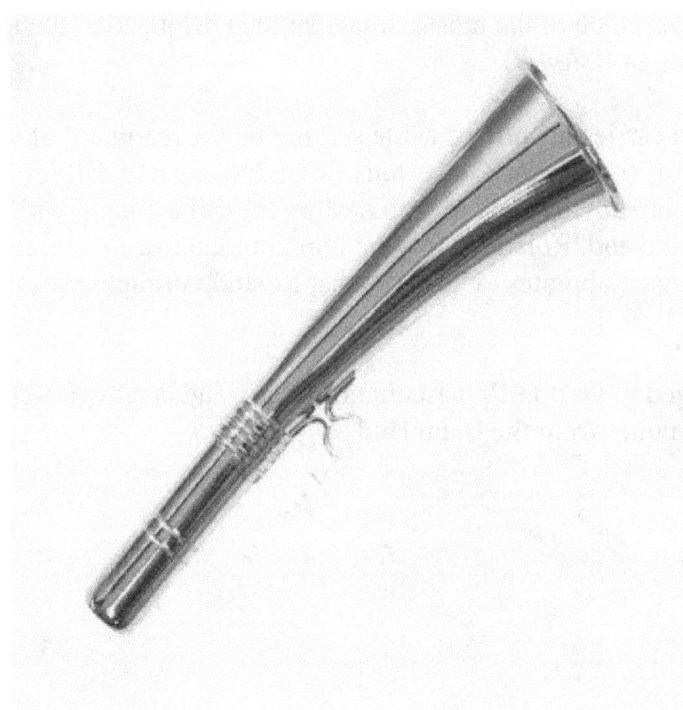

Acme Reed Horn (metal reed) Used for Fog Warnings

# Costume

## 1707-1708- Silver Beaker

Silver Beaker: Devil

Silver Beaker: Pope

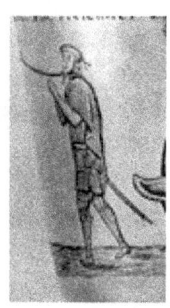

Silver Beaker: Pretender

-Made by Hughes Lossieux in Saint Malo, 1707-1708 and engraved by Joseph Leddel in New York City in 1750. It is in the Museum of the City of New York. The text: "Three mortal enemies: The Devil, Pope and the Pretender.

# 1767-Pierre Eugene Du Simitière, Pope Day in Boston,

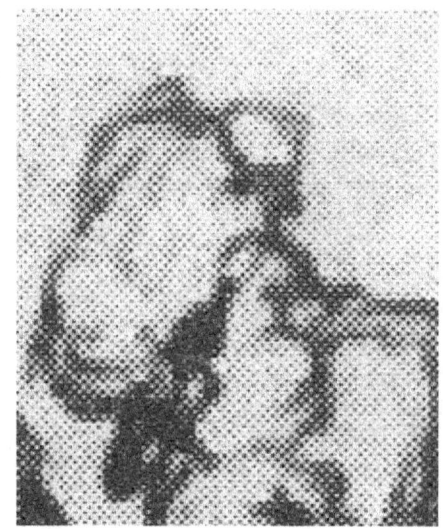

Turban?

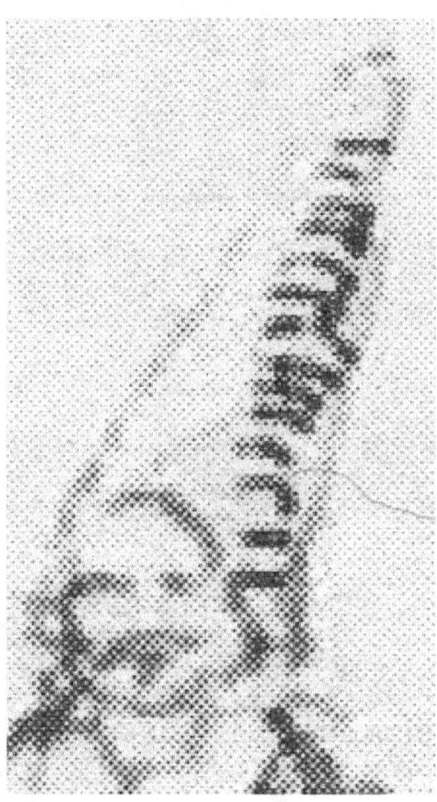

Conical Hat

Horned Devil

Horned Devil

Animal Mask

Horned Devil

- Pierre Eugene Du Simitière, Pope Day in Boston, 1767, sketch of the South End cart company, detail, The Library Company of Philadelphia. Below: Pierre Eugene Du Simitière, Pope Day in Boston, 1767.

# 1768- South End Forever North End Forever", Broadside, Boston.

Conical Hats

Pope and Devil-"South End Forever North End Forever", Broadside, Boston, 1768, Library of Congress

1765- Bernard observed: Being "dresst in blue & red, in a gold lace Hat & a gilt Gorget on his breast, with a Rattan Cane hanging at his wrist," Mackintosh led the militia parade of two thousand, shouting orders from a megaphone, supervising a march that united both ends to protest of the Act. "Trumpet" in hand, the "general" led a mock officialdom carrying hats and wands through the streets of the town, ensuring that "no one else" in the procession carried sticks or weapons – and that "no Negro was suffered" to be in the ranks of this protest. Hancock financed the uniforms

- Winslow, Isaac, Letter to [Unknown], November 15, 1765, in Robert Newsome, ed. and trans., *Family Memorial: The Winslows of Boston*, Vol. I: Isaac Winslow and Margaret Catherine Winslow, 1837? – 1873? (University of California, Irvine, and Massachusetts History Society, 2009-10), 66. Bernard, Letter to John Pownall, November 26, 1765, in Nicholson, ed., *The Papers of Francis Bernard,* II: 423. -

c. 1765-Harrison Gray Otis-

One such boy was Harrison Gray Otis, born in 1765. He experienced only a few Pope Days before the tradition was suppressed but passed down his memories of them. Every year, Harry's parents would 'give him a new pair of leather breeches which would be preserved for best until the next Fifth of November." In addition, "A few days before the anniversary, boys ran around to every front door in town ringing handbells and singing:

> 'Don't you hear my little bell
> Go chink, chink, chink?
> Please to give me a little money
> To buy my Pope some drink '"

-Bell, J. L. "Du Simitière's Sketches of Pope Day in Boston, 1767." *The Worlds of Children, 1620-1920* (2002): 209-217

It is noted that the pope is shown as the servant of Satan. The Hierarch of celebrants is noted. Officers were elected to oversee construction of the pope and to lead the procession. Ebenezer Mackintosh, a shoemaker who had risen from poverty is mentioned as such an elected officer. He was known as "General" Mackintosh and is described leading the South End Pope wearing a blue and gold uniform with a lace hat and holding a rattan cane and speaking trumpet (1760s). p.26.

-*No King No Popery,* Cogliano, Francis D., (Greenwood Press, London 1995).


Both the Pope and the Devil were dressed as the eighteenth-century Bostonians pictured them. The Devil's costume was covered with tar and feathers with a very grotesque mask. Some accounts indicate that the minor devils (the small boys) occasionally wore costumes covered with tar and feather, though more often they were dressed as monks and friars. The Pope was dressed in brilliant red robes "with a large white bush wig on, over which was an enormous gold laced hat. The wigs procured for this occasion had often adorned the pulpits of Churches." The men pulling the wagons usually wore dunce hats and their regular street clothing.

-- "Boston's Political Street Theatre: The Eighteenth-Century Pope Day Pageants", Sherwood Collins, Educational Theatre Journal, Vol. 25, No. 4 (Dec., 1973), p. 408.


1821-"Reminiscences" "A man used to ride on an ass, with immense jack boots, and his face covered with a horrible mask, and was called Joyce, Jr. His office was to assemble men and boys in mob style, and ride in the middle of them, and in such company to terrify adherents to Royal Government, before the Revolution. The tumults which resulted in the Massacre, 1770, was excited by that means.-Joyce Junior was said to have a particular whistle which brought his adherents, &c. whenever they were wanted. "*Publications of the Colonial Society of Mass. VIII (1903). 90-91. and Boston Daily Advertiser*, Nov 9 1821.

1877- Samuel Breck in: *Recollections* mentions Pope Day "Anticks" and the blackguards, who "disguised in filthy clothes and ofttimes with masked faces, went from house to house in large companies... obtruding themselves everywhere... ," He records a traditional Mummers play:

"There he lies But ere he dies
 A Doctor must be had."

He observed that there was more than one Mummers' company: "it happened not infrequently that the house would be filled by another gang when they [the first] had departed. There was no refusing admittance."

Samuel Breck, Recollections of..., ed. H. E. Scudder (Philadelphia, 1877), pp. 35-6

1782-

….I forget on what holiday it was that the Anticks, another exploded remnant of colonial manners, used to perambulate the town. They have ceased to do it now; but I remember them as late as 1782. They were a set of the lowest blackguards who disguised in filthy clothes and oftimes with masked faces went from house to house in large companies; and, bon gré, mal gré, obtruding themselves everywhere, particularly into the rooms that were occupied by parties of ladies and gentlemen, would demean themselves with great insolence. I have seen them at my father's, when his assembled friends were at cards, take possession of a table, seat themselves on rich furniture, and proceed to handle the cards, to the great annoyance of the company

-- Winsor, Justin ed.,*The Memorial History Of Boston*, Vol. III, Boston, 1881.

# Poetry And Amphibrachs

## Amphibrach

[ am-f uh-brak] NOUN [PROSODY.]

1. a trisyllabic foot, the arrangement of the syllables of which is short, long, short in quantitative meter, or unstressed, stressed, unstressed in accentual meter. Thus, together is an accentual amphibrach.-Dictionary.com

## A Poem from Newfoundland

1628, Robert Hayman, governor and poet of Newfoundland, "Of the Gunpowder Holly-day, the 5. of November,"

The Powder-Traytors, Guy Vaux, and his mates,
Who by a Hellish plot sought Saints estates,
Have in our Kalendar unto their shame,

A joyfull Holy-day cald by their Name.

-Robert Hayman, *Quodlibets Lately Come Ouer From New Britaniola, Old Newfound-land Epigrams and Other Small Parcels, Both Morall and Diuine . . . All of Them Composed and Done . . . in Britaniola, Anciently Called Newfound-Land . . .* (London: Elizabeth All-de [and Felix Kyngston], 1628), 27.

## 1669- Thomas Bailey, "In Quintum Novembris," November 5, 1669

"The Puritans, thought to Calumniate
O'th Plott and that they did participate...."

"Who sav'd us on 5th day of November
Which may us cause God still to remember.
. . .
But [?] Let us God celebrate
Who hath us freed from such a hellish fate.
To my exclaim that it shall bee
Praise be to God to all eternity.
Who hath thus far us kept, preserved always"
Render to him the glory and the praise.

- Bailey, Thomas, "In Quintum Novembris," November 5, 1669, Massachusetts Historical Society, MSS, Miscellaneous Bound Collection, 1657-1671.

# 1735- Samuel Checkley

…together with a large crowd who made up a long procession. Their custom was, to call at the principal houses in various parts of the town, ring their bell, cause the pope to elevate his head, and look round upon the audience, and repeat the following lines.

1 Works, ii. 201.

The fifth of November,
As yon well remember.
Was gunpowder treason and plot;
I know of no reason
Why the gunpowder treason
Should ever be forgot.
When the first King James the sceptre swayed,
This hellish powder plot was laid.
Thirty-six barrels of powder placed down below
All for old England's overthrow :
Happy the man, and happy the day
That caught Guy Fawkes in the middle of his play.
You'll hear our bell go jink, jink, jink j
Pray madam, sirs, if you 'll something give,
We '11 burn the dog and never let him live.
We'll burn the dog without his head,
And then you 'Ilsay the dog it dead.
From Rome, from Rome, the pope is come,
All in ten thousand fears;
The fiery serpent's to be seen,
All head, month, nose and ears.
The treacherous knave had go contrived,
To blow king parliament all up alive.
God by his grace he did prevent
To save both king and parliament.
Happy the man, and happy the day,
That catched Guy Fawkes in the middle of his play.
Match touch, catch prime,
In the good nick of time.
Here is the pope that we have got,
The whole promoter of the plot.
We 'll stick a pitchfork in his back
And throw him in the fire.'

After the verses were repeated, the purser stepped forward and took up his collection. Nearly all on whom they called, gave something. Esquire Atkins and Esquire Dalton, always gave a dollar apiece.

…In the issue of 1767 he has so much to say about the growing political troubles that he merely adds the line — "Powder plot most forgot;" while in the issue for 1772 his allusion brings in the, name of Captain Preston of the British troops engaged in the Boston

Massacre:

To burn the Pope, is now a joke,
for a design he miss't on,
to sap that mansion
which dares pension
Your famous Butcher Preston

… Most of the almanacs mentioned the day, as this very one of Bowen's, where against November 5 is found "Powder Plot;" and Ames's almanac for 1735 has under November the lines —

Gun Powder Plot
We ha'nt forgot.

In his issue for 1740 Ames says:

N.OW for the Old Plot, the POPE goes to Pot
The curst Pope stands in the Way, or I had told you the Day.
What Heaven decrees, no Prudence can prevent.

And in the issue for 1746 we read:

Powder-Plot is not forgot; '
T will be observed by many a Sot.

- Checkley, Samuel, "Diary of the Rev. Samuel Checkley", 1735 In: <u>Publications of the Colonial Society of Massachusetts Colonial Society of Massachusetts,</u> pp. 292-295.

## "Description of the Pope, 1769"

1. Toasts on the front of the large Lanthorn.
Love and Unity---The American Whig.---Confusion to the
Torries, and a total Banishment to Bribery and Corruption.
On the Right Side of the same.---An Acrostick.
I nsulting Wretch, we'll him expose,
O 'er the whole World his Deeds disclose,
H ell now gaups wide to take him in.
N ow he is ripe, O Lump of Sin.
M ean is the Man, M—n is his Name,
E nough he's spread his hellish Fame
I nfernal Furies hurl his Soul,
N ine Million Times from {Pole to "Pole.
        Labels of the Left Side.

2. Now shake, ye Torries! See the Rogue behind,
Hung up on a Scarecrow, to correct Mankind.
Oh had the Villain but received his Due,
Himself in Person would here swing in View:
But let the Traitor mend [?] within the Year,
Or by the next he shall be hanging here.

3. Now shake, ye Torries ! see the Rogue behind,
Hung up a Scarecrow, to correct Mankind.
Oh had the Villain but receiv'd his Due,
Himself in Person would here swing in View:
But let the Traitor mend within the Year,
Or by the next he shall be hanging here.
Ye Slaves! Ye Torries, who infest the Land,
And scatter num'rous Plagues on ev'ry Hand,
Now we'll be free, or bathe in honest Blood;
We'll nobly perish for our Country's Good,
We'll purge the Land of the infernal Crew,
And at one Stroke we'll give the Devil his Due.
Labels on each Side the small Lanthorn.
WILKEs and LIBERTY, No. 45.

See the Informer how he stands,
If any one now takes his Part,
An Enemy to all the Land,
He'll go to Hell without a Cart.
May Discord cease, in Hell be jam'd,
And factious fellows all be dam'd.
From B------, the veriest monster on earth,
The fell production of some baneful birth,
These ill proceed,---from him they took their birth,
The Source supreme, and Center of all Hate.
If I forgive him, then forget me Heaven,
Or like a WILKES may I from Right be driven.
Here stands the Devil for a Show,
With the I—p---rs in a row,
All bound to Hell, and that we know.
Go M—n lade deep with Curses on the head,
To some dark Corner of the World repair,
Where the bright Sun no pleasant dreams can shed,
And spend thy Life in Horror and Despair.
Effigies, ---M—n, his Servant, &c.—A Bunch of TOM-CODS.

- Anonymous, "Description of the Pope, 1769," Boston: S.N., 1769; and "From Tuesday, November 7 to Tuesday, November 14, 1769.

# 1766 - Boston News Boy, New Years Ode

*Vox Populi*
*Liberty, Property*
*and **No** Stamps*

The **News-Boy**
Who carries the **Boston Evening-Post**, with the greatest Submission begs Leave to present the following Lines to the Gentlemen and Ladies to whom he carries the NEWS.

ODE on the New Year.

What Time bears on his rapid Wing,
And of the doubtful Year I sing.
Say Monarch! why thy furrow'd brow
Frowns from thy Chariot on us now?
Thy Wheels, which sometimes seem'd to glide,
In smoother Current than the Tide,
Now lumber heavy as my Verse:
Why com'st thou to us in a Hearse?
As thy approach, when GEORGE first reign'd,
Fair Freedom wanton'd in thy Train:
I saw her move in graceful Dance,
One Foot on **Spain** and one on **France**.
But now she droops, deform'd with Fear;
From her dim Eye-ball starts the Tear.
Whence, too, that grisly Form that bears
Bonds made for Innocents to wear?
Will **British** Steel in GEORGE's Reign,
Bend for to form a Subject's Chain?
**Avert it**—————————
Methinks a mighty Hand I see,
That grasps thy Rein and governs thee.
Him, as in silent Pomp he rides,
No Pencil paints, no Pen describes:
An awful Veil his Body shrouds;
His Head lies hid in Golden Clouds.
When Captives long have groan'd in vain,
His single **touch** dissolves their Chain.
He over **King** and **Senate** rules;
Oppressors, sometimes, are his Tools.
Hail, KING supreme! thy mighty Hand,
Has, more than once, reliev'd this Land;
Descend, and bless the coming Year;
And humble Hope shall banish Fear.

Therefore—————
Ye Months foredoom'd to form th' ensuing Year,
With ev'ry happy Omen fraught appear:
Each Week, Day, Hour, in all the annual road.
With ev'ry prosperous Event be crown'd;

*Nor let one swiftly flying Minute move,*
*That shan't **New-England**'s happiness improve:*
*Oppressive SCHEMES let Disappointment brand,*
*Nor let one Tyrant in the Senate stand:*
*Let Study and Experience make us wise;*
*And as our Years extend, our Virtues rise:*
*Let Reason's Light gild Life's extremest gloom,*
*And Virtue's Lamp attend us to the Tomb;*
*And the Memorial that we leave behind,*
*To us be glorious—useful to Mankind.*

*Thus does the Carrier of your NEWS appear,*
*To wish you in the New, **a happy Year!***
*Time swiftly flying, hurl'd the Year away,*
*And once a Week produc'd **his** running Day,*
*And whether wet or cold, his Task he still maintains,*
*(In spite of **Stamps**) In hopes you'll now **reward him** for his Pains.*

- *Boston Evening-Post* as 1765/1766

# 1766-New-Year's Wish From the Carrier of the Boston Post-Boy, &c.

GEN'ROUS Customers, I run
To serve you as I begun,
With the freshest of News from the Press;
In Hot, and in Cold,
With News, new and old
I readily shall you address.
Ah! the Times are hard,
But we'll pay no regard
To the Stamps, Mobs, Devils, or Popes;
The freedom of Press
Will gain the Success,
And fully Accomplish our Hopes.---
The old Year is past,
The new come at last;
I wish you full Bumpers, and Bowls,
With every Thing good,
Which serveth for Food
For your Bodies, as well as your Souls,
Then while you are Eating,
And each other greeting,
With Things which you richly enjoy,
Pray freely dispense
Of some Shillings or Pence,
To your faithfull unwearied Boy.

## 1766- New Year's Ode for the Year 1766. New York

Dong Ding. Ding Dong.
 Long hve the KING,
The King hve long,
But the Devil may shoot.
Wicked G[renvUl]e and B[ute].

- Swinney, Lawrence, "New Year's Ode for the Year 1766." New York: Jan. 1, 1766 in *Early American Imprints* (Worcester: American Antiquarian Society, 1963), 41663.

# South End Forever North End Forever

Extraordinary verses on Pope-night. or, A commemoration the fifth of November, giving a history of the attempt, made by the papishes, to blow up king and Parliament, A. D. 1588. Together with some account of the Pope himself, and his wife Joan: with several other things worthy of notice, too tedious to mention. Sold by the printers boys in Boston [1768].

1. HUZZA! brave Boys, behold the Pope,
   Pretender and Old-Nick,
   How they together lay their Heads,
   To plot a poison Trick?
2. To blow up KING and PARLIAMENT
   To Flitters, rent and torn:
   --Oh! blund'ring Poet, Since the Plot,
   Was this Pretender born.--
3. Yet, sure upon this famous Stage,
   He's got together now;
   And had he then, he'd been a Rogue
   As bad as t'other two.
4. Come on, brave Youths, drag on your Pope
   Let's see his frightful Phiz:
   Let's view his Features rough and fierce,
   That Map of Ugliness!
5. Distorted Joints, so huge and broad!
   So horribly drest up!
   'Twould puzzle Newton's Self to tell,
   The D--l from the Pope.
6. See I how He Shakes his tot'ring Head
   And knocks his palsy Knees;
   A Proof He is the Scarlet Whore,
   And got the soul Disease.
7. Most terrible for to behold,

He Stinks much worse then Rum:
Here, you behold the Pope, and here
Old Harry in his Rome.
8. D'ye ask why Satan Stands behind?
Before he durst not go,
Because his Pride won't let him Stoop,
To kiss the Pope's great Toe.
9. Old Boys, and young, be Sure observe
The Fifth Day of November;
What tho' it is a Day apast?
You still can it remember.
10. The little Popes, they go out First,
With little teney Boys:
In Frolicks they are full of Gale
And laughing make a Noise.
11. The Girls run out to fee the Sight,
The Boys eke ev'ry one;
Along they are a dragging them,
With Granadier's Caps on.
12. The great Ones next go out, and meet
With many a Smart Rebuf:
They're hall'd along from Street to Street
And call hard Names enough.
13. "A Pagan, Jew, Mahometan,
Turk, Strumpet, Wizzard, Witch;"
In short the Number of his Name's,
Six Hundred Sixty six.
14. "How dreadful do his Features show?
"How fearful is his Grin?
"Made up of ev'ry Thing that's bad;
He is the Man of Sin.
15. If that his deeden Self could see
Himself so turn'd to Fun:
In Rage He'd tear out His Pope's Eyes,
And scratch his Rev'rend Bum.
16. He'd kick his tripple Crown about,
And weary of his Life,
He'd curse the Rabble, and away
He'd run to tell his Wife.
17. [Some Wits begin to cavil here
And laughing seem to query,
"How Pope should have a Wife, and yet,
The Clergy never marry."
18. Laugh if you please, yet still I'm sure
If false I'm not alone;
Pray Critic, did you never hear
Not read of fair Pope-Joan.]
19. "Help Joan! see how I'm drag'd and bounc'd,
"Pursu'd, surrounded, -- Wife!
"And when I'm bang'd to Death, I shall
"Be barbacu'd alive."
20. Joan cry's, "Why in this Passion, Sir?
"And why so raving mad?
"You surely must mistake the Case,

"It cannot be so bad."
21. "You Fool! I saw it with my Eyes,
"I cannot be deceiv'd."
"Yes, but You told me t'other Day,
"Sight! must not be believ'd."
22. A sham'd, inrag'd, and mad, and vex'd,
He mutters ten Times more.
"I'll make a Bull, and my He-Cow
"Shall bellow, grunt and rear."
23. Oh! Pope, we pity thy sad Case,
So dismal and forlorn!
We know that thou a Cuckold art,
For thou hast many an Horn.
24. And eke sev'n Heads he has also.
Tho' but one on him flicks:
Ten Horns he in his Pocket puts,
And Heads no less than six.
25. His Pockets full of Heads and Horns,
In's Hand he holds his Keys;
So down He bends beneath their Weight,
With Age, Shame and Disease.
26. His End so near, each Cardinal
Quite old himself would feign:
He tries to stoop and cough that he
Might his Successor reign.
27. And now, their Frolick to compleat,
They to the Mill-Dam go,
Burn Him to Nothing first, and then
Plunge Him the Waves into.
28. But to conclude, from what we've heard,
With Pleasure serve that King:
Be not Pretenders, Papishes,
Nor Pope, nor t'other Thing.

-Sold by the Printers Boys in Boston.

# 1771, 1772, 1773, and 1774- LATIN VERSES PRESENTED BY STUDENTS OF WILLIAM AND MARY COLLEGE TO THE GOVERNOR OF VIRGINIA, 1771, 1772, 1773, and 17741

In the charter of the College, granted Feb. 8, 1693, a grant of twenty thousand acres of land was made by King William and Queen Mary, with the requirement that every year, in lieu of quit rent, two copies of Latin verses be presented: "on every fifth day of November, two copies of Latin verses yearly, at the house of our governor, or lieutenant governor of Virginia, for the time being, for ever, in full discharge, acquittance, and satisfaction of all quit-rents, services, customs, dues and burdens whatsoever,due, or to be due, to us, or our successors, for the said twenty thousand acres of land"

To His Excellency, The Right Honourable John Earl of Dunmore, His
Majesty's Lieutenant Governor General, Comander in Chief of the Colony
and Dominion of VIRGINIA, and Vice Admiral of the same.

Nonis Novembris MDCCLXXI.

Hinc procul 0 procul este profanii. Daedala Tellus
Submittat fruges, pro salvis dona maritis
Grata ferant sponsae, sertisque recentibus halet
Ara tibi, crebro Britonum celebrata per urbes
Hic et ubique Dies! Memori de pectore grates
Depromant cuncti pariter j uvenesque senesque.
Jam nox atra polo piceam detraxerat Umbram
Nec tamen aut roseis digitis Aurora refulget
Aureus aut Titan ostentat lampada terris;
Cuncta tenent tenebrae: Quin Sol trepidavit et ipse
Mundus ne rueret repetens compage soluta
Antiquum Chaos? En! pavor undique et undique lethum est.
Conscia fama volat; simul et [?] quisque pavendo
Dat vires illi ignotoque auctore malorum
Quod timuere fovent. Nec solum vulgus acerbo
Perculsum terrore tremit sed Curia et ipse.
Sedibus exiluere patres. Caelestia tangat
Dummodo corda stupor, stupuere. At fallere quicquam
Possit eum mare qui terras qui numine torquet
Caelum, qui motus animi sensusque latentes
Rimatur? Deus ipse Deus qua mole parentur
Insidiae quantumque caput sic fraude petatur
Vidit et ingemuit: Phoebum splendrescere clare
Praecipit, "Heus fiat factum": subitoque in apertam
Proripuit lucem quos strinxerat impius Error
Popicolas; ausus sontes patefecit ad auras,
Auctores stravit; nec enim sua dextera aberrat
Cum feriat candente manu. 0 Jupiter alme,
In quem tota hominum gens inclinata recumbit,
O columen Britonumque stator Britonumque nepotum,
Sis bonus: 0 felix, tuis [?] sic semper adesto,
Terrarum caelique parens! semperque placeto
Parcere subjectis et debellare superbos.

To his Excellency, The Right Honourable John, Earl of Dunmore, His Majesty's Lieutenant Governor General, Commander in Chief of the colony and Dominion of VIRGINIA, and Vice Admiral of the same,

Nonis Novembris MDCCLXXI.

Serus in Caelum redeas, diuque
Laetus intersis populo Quirini,
Neve te nostris vitiis iniquum
        Ocyor aura

Tollat

Ah! nimium nimiumque Colonia fortunata,
Hunc talem sortita virum, tam stemmate longo;
 Quodque homines raro norunt, tu Laudibus ipsa
Scis te felicem justis, et scire fateris.
Ne tamen, 0 cives, humanis fidite rebus;
 Nuper enim nemini vos (heu ludibria vitae)
Vidit Sol hilares: subito mors invida gressu
En! venit, ac tenebris carum caput illius urget,
Qui gentem hanc nostram patrio dilexit amore;
Cuncta gemunt late, lacrymarum flumina larga
Vultus humectant cunctos. Quis nomine Berklei
Temperet a lacrymis? Quin vanos sistite planctus.
Ecce uno avulso non deficit aureus alter!
Carpite dum fas est fugitivae gaudia vitae;
Nil oriturum unquam profitentes Principe recto
Pulchrius aut melius. Hic, hic, quod quaeritis adstat.
Talem Romulidae tranquilla pace fruentem
Numam habuere suum, talem te Anglique, Georgi,
Tu quoque Murrae ascriptus pars altera nostri,
Aoniis arvis semen des crescere largum,
Atque velis patrum lauris adnectere Olivam.
Obruit illustres titulos Proserpina nocte,
Obruit heroum sudores, nescia flecti:
Doctorum. monumenta virum tristem Phlegethonta
Vincere sola valent, atque Orci jura superbi.
I decus, i nostrum, monstretque viam tibi virtus,
Macte animi bonitate nova, meritusque referto
Egregias laudes, et justos de morte triumphos,
Sors ubi te quoque fert, Numa quo devenit et Ancus.


To His Excellency, The Right Honourable John, Earl of Dunmore, His Majesty's Lieutenant Governour General, Commander in Chief Of the Colony and Dominion Of VIRGINIA, And Vice-Admiral of the same,

Nonis Novembris MDCCLXXII

Aude, hospes, contemnere opes.

Fulmen uti rutilans annosas dejicit ornos,
  At frutices parvos praeterit ira Jovis;
Pauper in aere suo curas non sentit edaces,
  Quae circumvolitant et comitantur opes.


Hunc fortuna favens sublimem ad sidera tollit,
  Ast illum cumulo praegravat atra mali;
Ipse inconcussus cernit ridetque procellas,
  In tuto positus perfugio atque sinu.
Huic sylvae tegimen praebent, huic murmura rivus,
  Sollicitat somnos umbraque grata leves.
Stratus humi teneros luctantes cornibus haedos,
  Aut detondentes gramina spectat oves.
Ut juvat ex agris redeuntem vespere lassum
  Ridentem pura luce videre focum!
Utque videre juvat redeuntes nocte juvencos,
  Vomeribus versis, approperare domum!
Interea haerentes collo nati oscula jungunt,
  Demulcetque hilaris sponsa pudica virum.
At tu, qui celsa late dominaris in aula, et
  Divitias, quantas Attalus ipse, tenes,
Quod nondum es vitae casus expertus acerbos,
  Ne tumido fastu pectora plena geras;
Nam fortuna levis varios transmutat honores,
  Et certam praesens vix habet hora fidem.
Mane fuit Croesus gazis opibusque superbus,
  Ac gentes habuit sub ditione sua,
Nox piceo at nondum terras velarat amictu,
  Cogitur externo subdere colla jugo.
Sic rosa mane viget, vernoque colore renidet,
  Deciduas ponit pendula nocte comas.


To his Excellency, The Right Honourable John, Earl of Dunmore, His Majesty's Lieutenant & Governor General, Commander in Chief of the Colony and Dominion of VIRGINIA, and Vice Admiral of the same.
Nonis Novembris, MDCCLXXIII.

Nescio qua natale solum dulcedine cunctos
Ducit; et immemores non sinit esse sui . . . . Ovid.

Pertaesus patriae, valido correptus amore
  Mutandi caelum quo nova nulla videt,
Montibus excelsis descendit Cambro-Britannus,
  Italiae valles, laetaque rura petit.
Huc latus molli se percipit aere cinctum;
  Aurea poma vorat, mitia vina bibit.
Intentis oculis lustrat spectacula pulchra,
  Aedes miratur culminibus nitidis,

Aspectat turres celsas splendore micantes,
  Atque stupet templis, ac statuis inhiat.
Exclamat postremo; "Vix ea vita vocanda
  Quam degi vilem, cum populoque rudi.
At Veneres novitas tandem diffundere cessat:
  Mente sitit Patriam, sic queriturque gemens.
Hei mihi! quod nostros non possum cernere montes,
  Non possum pecudes cernere lanigeras,
Nec Haedos hirtos, pendentes rupibus altis.
  His nuper notis quam magis illa juvant!

Quando iterum pascam distentas lacte capellas?
  Quando iterum siccans ubera plena premam?
Vae mihi! non solito redolent mea viscera Porro,
  Caseus haud pinguis nunc mihi tostus adest.
Wallia, dulce solum! peream porrigine turpi,
  Si pateat toto gratior orbe locus.

Memoriae Gulielmi et Mariae Regis et Reginae, Angliae, Scotiae, Franciae et Hyberniae Sacrum;

Pierides, regem regni sociamque canamus,
  Quorum fausta manus carmina pensat agris;
Quique, novo ne vos erretis in orbe, ministris
  Mandant dilectis aedificare domum;
Aedibus atque indunt ipsorum nomina, mentis
  Quae maneant aequae pignora perpetua.
Quo studio comites cedunt tot dona Camenis?
  Quo crescat sibi laus? Quo patriaeve decus?
Pectore, ni fallor, votum miscetur utrumque,
  Ut crescat sibi laus, ut patriaeque decus.
Qui prospexerunt musis sedesque locarunt
  Sacrantes titulis nominibusque suis.
Norunt, quod virtus belli aut sapientia pacis,
  Plena viget musae non nisi culta manu.
Quin etiam norunt cantus, mercede minores
  Dum mentes mulcent, exstimulare bonos.
Qui forti populo scelerata pericula, turpe
  Dejecere animis corporibusque jugum,
Non sunt contenti geminis tria regna catenis
  Et subito miris eripuisse modis;
Regna volunt, firmis doctrinae fulta columnis,
  His terris nasci, libera, multa, pia.
Aggredimur frustra grates persolvere justas,
  Dii tantis factis praemia digna ferant.
Interea nobis praetensa exempla virorum
  Teda sit ardens, quae monstret in astra viam.
Pergant succendi reges dulcedine famae,
  Nec impar reddant ingenio pretium.

## NON DOMI.

Si te promeritus fui, Carine,
Et semper volui domi videre,
Sit sedes tua longius superba:
Sed sum proximus ad pyrum virentem
Eheu! civis ego, Jovem vetustum
Cernit rustica Flora qua tonantem.
Est vincenda mihi laboriosa,
 (Infamis meretricibus) Suburra;
Et gressu madido periculosa
Semper saxa; daturque vix onustos
Mulos vincere, quaeque fune multo
Cernis marmora sumptuosa duci.


Illud durius est adhuc, Labores
Quod post mille graves, Carine, saepe
Te non Janitor intus esse dicit.
Foedus terminus hic mei Laboris,
Ac udo togulae luto madentis!
Tanti cernere vix fuit Carinum.
Sed nunc esse vicarius recuso,
Et rex esse meus quidem superbus
Non, ni dormieris, potes, Carine.

To His Excellency, The Right Honourable JOHN Earl of DUNMORE
His Majesty's Lieutenant Governour General, Commander in Chief Of the Colony and Dominion of VIRGINIA and Vice Admiral of the same.
Nonis Novembris. MDCCLXXIV

## SOLIS INVOCATIO.

Sol qui perpetua mundum vertigine lustras,
Alme parens rerum, Caeli decus, et Stellarum
Princeps, aeterni fons luminis, undique cernens
Omnia, puniceo dum Persida linquis obortu,
Et pergens tandem occiduis absconderis undis,
Atque eadem rursus repetis vestigia semper.
Per te cuncta patent, noctis quibus umbra colorem
Abstulerat, tenebris tua non patientibus Ora.
Mundi oculus; qui transverso dum limite curris
Per duodena means animantum Idola, quaternis
Dispensas annum spatiis, et tempora mutas
Et cum temporibus quicquid generatur in orbe.
O sanctum jubar! 0 Divum pulcherrime salve!
Te colimus, tibi sincero de pectore laudes
Fundimus: at tu hodie laeto nos respice vultu
Et laetum concede diem, redeasque benignus.
Nubila diffugiant, aer sit ubique serenus,
Adventuque tuo ponti vada salsa quiescant,
Et sit iter tutum cupidis per caerula nautis.
Non segeti, non arboribus, non vitibus imber
Insanusve obsit turbo, lapidosave grando:
Sed blandas Pyrois afflet mortalibus auras,
Accipiantque tuo reditu, Deus, omnia pacem.
Salve praesidium et sacris Tutela Poetis!
Tu vatum mentes divino numine reples,
Ipsorumque moves ad dulcia carmina linguas;
Tu dignos lauroque facis famaque perenni.
Salve igitur dexterque mihi sis quaeso petenti,
Et faveas coeptis et nostros dirige Cursus.
Me non immerito tumr Dux Dumnorus amabit
Et tollet secum Bellator in Aethera Vatem.
Sic Aquila scindas subvectus Regule nubes.

   Format enim natura prius nos intus ad omnem
   Fortunarum habitum.

Aethereus simul ut genitalem spiritus ortum
Sustulit, accepit diversa elementaque vitae,
Affectus varii incendunt, quos Jupiter ipse
Optimus insevit, traherent feliciter ut nos
"Per varios casus, per tot discrimina rerum."
En demens tollit rutilum iracundia vultum.

En agitur Furiis, totoque ardentes ab ore
Scintillae absistunt, oculis micat acribus ignis.
Est alius vultus, vox horrida plena minarum,
Plenaque terroris, rauco de gutture fertur:
Neve preces iram flectant, mollissima verba
Non audit, surdus veluti maria humida Ponti,
Quae insanos fluctus pulsata ad littora volvunt.
   Invidia alterius macrescit rebus opimis,
Pectus felle vorat, nec grata est ulla voluptas,
Nec risus, nisi quem visi movere dolores;
Alterius bona perturbat fortuna quietem.
   Dissimili longe facie, pulcherrima visu
Spes graditur, ridet placide, summoque pudore
Sese offert, at saepe pedem referens, velut horret
Monstrum aliquod, juxta oppositum; lateque vagatur
Prospiciens oculus, vastumque amplectitur orbem,
Haec nos fida comes sequitur, vita fugiente,
Mortales placida nec fallit mente jacentes.
Pallidus hic timor est; steterunt in vertice crines;
Corda tremunt; moles labefactaque tota laborat,
Genua labant, crepitantque nova formidine dentes;
Corripit inde fugam subito, et cervice reflexa
Avolat ille, Noto citius volucrique sagitta.
   Jam converte oculos; en hic gratissima forma
Ridet amabiliter; quasi toto flore juventae
Purpureus resplendet honos; placidissima vultu
Nempe gratia inest; radiantia lumina late
Effulgent; quocumque velit sibi figere gressus,
Sub pedibus violae nascuntur; tangere quicquid
Sit placidum, roseum confestim spirat odorem,
Humani hinc generis cognoscere possis amantem.

-Transcribed from originals :New York Public Library.

# Norwich Conn. USA

Mrs. Daniel Lathrop Coit (b. 1767, d. 1848),

1792- Norwich [Conn.]
Mrs. Daniel Lathrop Coit (b. 1767. d. 1848), used to tell her grandchildren of the Guy Fawkes day, observed in Norwich in her childhood. An effigy of straw was carried through the streets, and afterward burned, and she remembered snatches of the doggerel sung : —

The fifth of November
You must always remembner;
The Gunpowder Plot
Must never be forgot.
Ding! Dong!

The Pope's come to town

- *The Weekly Register*, November, 1792.

## 1660-1800- Perkins, Mary E.: Old Houses of the Antient [sic] Town of Norwich,

With maps, illustrations, portraits, and genealogies., Publisher Press, Norwich Conn., 1895
Mass. U.S.A. Newburyport

The Fifth of November,
as you well remember
was Gunpowder treason and plot
and where is the reason
that gunpowder treason
should ever be forgot?
When James the First
the scepter swayed
this hellish powder plot was laid
they placed the powder down below,
all for old England's overthrow;
lucky the man, and happy the day,
that caught Guy Fawkes in the middle of his play.
Hark! our bell goes jink, jink, jink;
pray, madam, pray sir, give us something to drink;
pray, madam, pray, sir, if you'll something give,
we'll burn the dog and not let him live.
We'll burn the dog without his head,
And then you'll say the dog is dead.

Look here, from Rome
the Pope has come,
that fiery serpent dire.
Here's the Pope that we have got,
the old promoter of the plot --
we'll stick a pitchfork in his back
and throw him in the fire!

## Pope Night

Lay up the faggots neat and trim;
pile 'em up higher, set 'em afire!
The Pope roasts us and we'll roast him!
(old song)

## Ame's Almanac 1735

Gun Powder Plot
We ha'nt forgot.

## Ame's Almanac 1746

Powder-plot is not forgot
'Twill be observed by many a Sot

## Otis 1823

"Tudor in his "Life of Otis", (1823, Boston) gives an account of the observance of the day and its disagreeable features. He says the intruders paraded the streets with grotesque images, forcibly entered houses ringing bells, demanding money, and singing rhymes similar to those sung all over England:

"Don't you remember?
The Fifth of November,
The Gunpowder Treason and plot,
I see no reason
Why Gunpowder Treason
Should ever be forgot.

From Rome to Rome
The Pope is come,
Amid ten thousand fears,
With fiery serpents to be seen
At eyes, nose, mouth, and ears,
Don't you hear my little bell
Go Chink, chink, chink,
Please give me a little money
To buy my Pope some drink."

-Earle, Alice Morse, <u>Customs and Fashions in Old New England.</u>, New York, 1893. P. 230.

## 1845- Joshua Coffin

The fifth of November As you well remember,
Was gunpowder treason and plot;
I know of no reason Why the gunpowder treason,
Should ever be forgot.
When the first king James the sceptre swayed,
This hellish powder plot was laid.
Thirty-six barrels of powder placed down below,
All for old England's overthrow:
Happy the man, and happy the day,
That caught Guy Fawkes in the middle of his play.
You'll hear our bell go jink, jink, jink;
Pray madam, sirs, if you'll something give,
We'll burn the dog, and never let him live.
We'll burn the dog without his head,
and then you'll say the dog is dead.

From Rome, from Rome, the pope is come,
All in ten thousand fears;
The fiery serpent's to be seen,
All head, mouth, nose, and ears.
The treacherous knave had so contrived,
To blow king parliament all up all alive
God by his grace he did prevent
To save both king and parliament.
Happy the man, and happy the day,
That catched Guy Fawkes in the middle of his play.
Match touch, catch prime,
In the good nick of time.
Here is the pope that we have got,
The whole promoter of the plot.
We'll stick a pitchfork in his back,
And throw him in the fire

-Joshua Coffin, A Sketch of the History of Newbury, Newburyport, and West Newburyport (Boston, 1845). -- "Boston's Political Street Theatre: The Eighteenth-Century Pope Day Pageants", Sherwood Collins, Educational Theatre Journal, Vol. 25, No. 4 (Dec. 1973).

# 1856- Drake

"Three Strangers blaze amidst a bonfire's revel,

The Pope, and the Pretender, and the Devil"

- Samuel G. Drake, *The History and Antiquities of Boston* (Boston, 1856), 662.

# 1888- POPE-DAY IN AMERICA, By John Gilmary Shea.

New England, in the same way, resorted to "Cheshire Cheese," and by a happy device pleased Court and people. They would celebrate the 5th of November with all due noise and honor; but they had the Pope carried around in effigy, instead of Guy Fawkes, amid the noise of firecrackers, and finally committed it to the flames amid loud huzzas.

Thus, though they sang

"Let's always remember The fifth of November," the day became, on this side of the Atlantic, not Gunpowder Treason, but Pope-Day. The contrast between that annual insult of the last century, and the recent ovation of all loyal hearts, the tributes paid by the rulers of English-speaking lands, is striking enough. "Viva il Papa-re."

# 1899- William Barton

"Remember, Remember!
The Fifth of November!
Gunpowder treason and plot!
I know of no reason
Why gunpowder treason
Should ever be forgot!"

"Bold Freemen are we.
We'll drink no more tea
Though King and Gov'nor command.
The vile Bohea,
We'll pitch in the sea,
If ever it comes to land."

-Barton, William, Eleazar, <u>When Boston Braved the King,</u> 1899, P. 180.

# 1930, NOVEMBER 5- LATIN VERSES PRESENTED TO THE GOVERNOR OF VIRGINIA,

Viro Honestissimo Ioanni Garland Pollard Praefecto Rei Publicae Virginiae praeses, professores, discipulique Collegii Regis et Reginae Gulielmi et Mariae in Virginia, ex praescripto diplomatis antique collegii D. D. D.

Nonis Novembribus, Anno Domini MDCCCCXXX

0 felix, talem quae sis dignata saluti,
    Virginia, ipsa tuae praeposuisse virum!
qualem non regalis honos, non saeva cupido
    imperii a patriae dulcis amore vocat.
Civis enim est, civisque iugo te temperat aequo
    civibus et iusto iura dat ore suis.
Tullius alter adest; non inscius hic quoque legum.
    Hunc quoque custodem respicis, alma parens.
At tu, nostra salus, praeclarum imitare prioris
    temporis exemplar, sis patriaeque pater.
Ne tamen haec quaecumque iuvent; maiora sequaris
    et veterum certes exsuperare decus.
Te duce per populum redeant Saturnia regna,
    mox redeat virtus religioque patrum;
Pax iterum laetam lustret cum Virgine terram
    et teneant clausas Martia templa fores.
Tradidit ipse tibi clavum qui rexit in oras
    communem optatas per vada caeca ratem.
Hic tibi monstret iter, doceat quae flabra minentur,
    qua lateant scopuli, quaeque pericla maris.
Dique deaeque tibi faveant aurisque secundis
    ad Musas revehant Aoniumque nemus.
Namque tui desiderio correpta caterva
    doctorum reditus Pieridumque dolet.
Haec quae praesidibus patres sub rege dederunt
    munera, nunc eadem dantur, honeste, tibi;
non tamen ut gens serva usum renovamus avorum,
    regis at externi nescia ferre iugum,
Accipe dein nostri quam parva haec pignora amoris
    et studium populi spernere parce tui.

    This custom had been in discontinued since Lord Dunmore's time. On Nov. 5, 1930, it was revived and was to be be continued every year.

- "Latin Verses Presented to the Governor of Virginia November 5, 1930,", <u>The William and Mary Quarterly</u>, Vol. 11, No. 1 (Jan. 1931), p. 54.

# The Center for Fawkesian Pursuits: Linthicum Maryland

Remember Remember the fifth of November
        Gunpowder Treason and Plot!
  We See no Reason That Gunpowder Treason Ever should be Forgot!
Remember, Remember, that Pope's Day in Boston Lead to the Liberty Tree!
We See no reason that Pope's Day in Boston should be forgot by you or me!
      King Billy King Billy Toss Us an Orange
          You came to set us free!
       A Lemon a Lemon for Bigoted James
      Our Proud constitution he'll not re-arrange!
   Holla! boys Holla! boys, ring in the night (ring bells)
    Holla boys, Holla boys burn fires bright (stomp)

Verse Added Commemorative of 911.

Remember, Remember eleven September
Bin-laden, terror and plot
We see no reason that trade center terror should
Ever Be Forgot!

-11/2001

-The Official Chant/Prayer of the Center for Fawkesian Pursuits Bonfire Society Linthicum,, Maryland, U.S.A. Composed October, 1998 Center For Fawkesian Pursuits Chant

# Bonfire

## 1620-Captain John Smith

Recorded the first New World celebration in Bermuda:

"The fift[h] of No[v]ember the damnable plot of the powder treason was solemnized, with Praiers, Sermons, and a great Feast, whereto the Go[v]ernor in[v]ited the chiefe of the *Spaniards*, where drinking the Kings health, it was honored with a quicke volly of small shot, which was answered from the Forts with the great Ordnance, and then againe concluded with a second volley of small shot; neither was the afternoone without musicke and dancing, and at night many huge bone-fires of sweet wood.

-- Smith, John, *The Generall Historie of Virginia, New-England, and the Summer Isles [1584-1624]* . . . (London: I.D. and I.H. . . ., 1624), 197. For more on Bermuda (the Summer Isles) in this time, see Jean de Chantal Kennedy, Isle of Devils: Bermuda Inder the Somers Island Company (London: Collins, 1971). -

## 1623- Mariners celebrated the day in Massachusetts, at Plymouth

Plantation. Emmanuel Altham, an adventurer, wrote that "a sudden fire" had destroyed "one half of the plantation" on November 5. Governor /historian William Bradford, governor and historian, wrote that sailors on shore, seeking good cheer, had built a fire, had lit a shed on purpose, and had lost control of the blaze but had burnt only three or four houses, not half of the three-year-old settlement, to the ground. He complained that blasted the fire that a "rude company" had started: "This fire was occasioned by some of the seamen that were roistering in a house where it first began, making a great fire in cold weather, which broke out of the chimney into the thatch . . . The house in which it began was right against their storehouse, which they had much ado to save, in which were their common store and all their provisions, the which, if they had been lost, the plantation had been overthrown. But through God's mercy it was saved by the great diligence of the people and care of the [government] . . . But a trusty company . . . suspected some malicious dealing, if not plain treachery, and whether it was only suspicion or not, God knows; but this is certain, that when the tumult was greatest, there
was a voice heard (but from whom it was not known) that bid them look about them, for all were not friends that were near them . . . But God kept them from this danger, whatever was intended.

- Bradford, William, Of *Plymouth Plantation, 1620-1647*, ed. by Samuel Eliot Morison (New Brunswick, New Jersey: Rutgers University Press, 1952), 136-37. -

## 1662- Middlesex County Court

Convicted two servants, Thomas Facy and Paul Wilson, of charges of "disorderly carriage" and abusing "a day of publ[ic] thanksgiving" in Charlestown. They were found guilty of "abetting sundry young persons & others, gathering themselves into companies & kindling fires in the evening . . . & absenting themselves from their [masters] houses." They were charged with gathering firewood and bringing down a house. The court sentenced Facy and Wilson to five lashes of the whip each and. Their masters were fined the costs of the trial and 30 shillings.

-Pulsifer Transcript, *Middlesex County Court Records*, File 3 (Massachusetts State Archives), December 16, 1662, 274. -

## 1662- Samuel Maverick,

A royalist steadfast wrote Edward Hyde, criticizing the decision that the court had made, in the Facy-Wilson case.

"[The] Divers Youths [were] lately prsecuted att Boston for making bonefires on Gunpowder treason day at night, it being kept as a thankesgiving . . ., Ye Youth being Willing to Conforme to ye practice that Such a tyme affords in old England, for this the parents of the Youths were fined, but ye Children of ye Church Members Who Were guilty as much as Others . . . [escaped?] all Scott free."

-Maverick, Samuel Letter to the Earl of Clarendon, [date?], in The New-York Historical Society, *Collections of the New-York Historical Society for the Year 1869* (New York: The Society, 1870), 47. -

*"Mr. Allin preached Nov. 5. 1685 finished his Text 1 Jn? 1. 9. mentioned not a word in Prayer or Preaching that I took notice of with respect to Gun-powder Treason. . . . Although it rained hard, yet there was a Bonfire made on the Comon, about 50 attended it. Friday night [November 6] being fair, about two hundred hallowed about a Fire on the Comon."*

*"...After perambulating the town, and finishing their collections, they concluded their evening's entertainment with a splendid supper; after making with the exception of the wheels and the heads of the effigies, a bonfire of the whole concern, to which were added, all the wash tubs, tar barrels, and stray lumber, that they could lay their hands on. With them the custom was, to steal all the stuff. But those days have long since passed away... "*

*"...Chaps in this city had their annual blow-out on Guy Fawkes' night, and in parts of the city the toot of the horns was something terrific. Some grotesque pumpkin lanterns were seen, and altogether the celebration was evidently enjoyed by the boys. Portsmouth is not alone in this peculiar observance, for down at Marblehead the night of the 5th of November is remembered by a huge bonfire on the neck, around which the chaps with horns dance in fantastic glee. The blaze Saturday night on the M. N. was a bigger one than usual...."*

- Checkley, Samuel, "Diary of the Rev. Samuel Checkley", 1735 In: <u>Publications of the Colonial Society of Massachusetts Colonial Society of Massachusetts</u>, pp. 292-295.

"...In the evening, there was a bonfire on Dorchester neck, and several in this town; and there were a variety of fireworks played off upon this occasion, both on the land and on the water…"

-- Cressy, David., *Bonfires and Bells. "National Memory and the Protestant Calendar in Elizabethan and Stuart England.*, University of California Press, Berkeley,1989.

## 1704- In early 1704, the Common Council of New York

Requested that the treasury pay the mayor's office a sum of over £5 owed for the costs of the bonfire and the wine from the fall before.

-Osgood, ed., *Minutes of the Common Council of the City of New York,* II: 121. -

1711- Williamsburg, Virginia 1711, William Byrd, planter and lieutenant-governor Alexander Spotswood accompanied "several ladies" in enjoying a bonfire that "the boys" of William and Mary had made on campus.

- Wright, Louis B. and Marion Tinling, eds., *The Secret Diary of William Byrd of Westover, 1709-1712* (Richmond, Virginia: Dietz Press, 1941), 432-33. -

## 1714- New York,

The aldermen and the assistants of the council ordered: "there be a Bonfire that Night at the usual place" and for 7 gallons of wine be drunk for "the Kings health" on "Gunpowder Treason day".

-Osgood, ed., *Minutes of the Common Council of the City of New York,* II: 256-57, 452-53; III: 51, 77-78, 187-88, 192, 217-18. -

## 1731&1737- The legislature of Rhode Island

prohibited acts of "Mischief," including the "firing of Guns and Pistols" and the "throwing of Squibs, Fire-Works, &c." in the lanes, the streets, or the taverns, of the province, "on any Night whatsoever." And that, "Custom . . .notwithstanding," "no Bonfire [should] be made on the Fifth of November" unless a town had in fact authorized such a fire." Punishments ranged from twenty-shilling fines for first offenses to month-long prison terms for third offenses.

-Rhode Island, *The Charter, Granted by His Majesty, King Charles II. to the Governor and Company of the English Colony of Rhode-Island and Providence-Plantations, in New-England, in America* (Newport: Samuel Hall, 1767), 120-21. -

## 1735- Samuel Checkley wrote:

In 1735, Samuel Checkley wrote, "A great number of people went over to Dorchester neck where they made a great bonfire and plaid off many fireworks."

- Checkley, Samuel, "Diary of the Rev. Samuel Checkley", 1735 In: Publications of the Colonial Society of Massachusetts Colonial Society of Massachusetts, pp. 292-295.

## 1751-1752, George Washington

"The captain's name, if he had just debarked from it after several weeks on the "fickle & Mirciless Ocean" (p. 69). Also, it is not likely that a vessel arriving in port on 2 Oct. would be preparing to sail by 6 Oct. MRS. CLARKE & MISS ROBTS.: Mrs. Mary Clarke, wife of Gedney Clarke, and her niece Elizabeth Roberts. TO COME & SEE THE SERPTS. FIR'D: Serpents, or fireworks discharged in commemoration of Guy Fawkes Day, 5 Nov...."

-1751-1752- George Washington Diary from Barbados referring to Celebration of Guy Fawkes Day (see above).

## 1753- Anti-Bonfire Legislation

CHAPTER 18.
AN ACT FOR. FURTHER PREVENTING ALL RIOTOUS, TUMULTUOUS AND DISORDERLY ASSEMBLIES OR COMPANIES OF PERSONS, AND FOR PREVENTING BONFIRES IN ANY OF THE STREETS OR LANES "WITHIN ANY OF THE TOWNS OF THIS PROVINCE…

…And varies bonfires have been sometimes kindled in the streets, lanes and other parts of several of the towns of this province, to the endangering of the lives and estates of the inhabitants,
—
Be it further enacted, [Sect. 3.]

That if any person or persons shall set fire to any pile, or any combustible stuff, or be anyways concern[e]'d in causing or making a bonfire in any street or lane, or any other part of any town within this province, such bonfire being within ten rods of any house or building, every person so offending shall for each offence forfeit the sum of forty shillings or suffer imprisonment not exceeding one month, or if the offender shall be a negro servant, in lieu of the imprisonment, he may be whip'[t][d] not exceeding ten stripes, at the discretion of the justice before whom the trial shall be : the several fines in this act to be applied, when recovered, one half to the poor of the town where the offence shall be committed, and the other half to him or thorn that shall inform and sue for the same ; and all masters are hereby made liable to the payment of the several fines as afores[ai]d, for the offences of their servants, and all parents for the offences of their children under age, not being servants.

*(complete text is in the legislation chapter.)*
-Acts and Resolves, Massachusetts Bay Colony, 1742-1756, Vol. III (Boston, 1878.), pp. 647-48. 6 Court Files,
1765- The whole then proceeded to Liberty tree, under the shadow of which they refreshed themselves for a while, & then returned to ye Northward agreeably to their plan. They reached Cop's hill before 6 o'clock, where they halted, & having enkindled a fire, the whole pageantry was committed to the flames & consumed."

-*Boston Evening-Post* of 11 November 1765.

## 1768- New Hampshire Law

[Chapter 9.]

An Act To Prevent the Disorders Commonly Committed on the Fifth of November & the Evening following under pretence of celebrating the anniversary of the deliverance from the Gunpowder Plot.

[Passed Oct. 28, 1768. 9 George III. Original Acts. Vol. 6, p. 21: recorded Acts, vol. 3, p. 90. This act is revived and extended for ten years by the act of Jan. 10, 1771.]

Whereas it Often Happens that many Disorders & Disturbances are Occasioned and Committed by Loose Idle People under a Notion & Pretence of Celebrating and keeping a Memorial of the Deliverance from the Gunpowder Plot on the fifth of November & the Evening following as Servants & boys Tempted to Excessive Drinking & Quarreling – Surrounding Peoples doors with Clamor& rudely Demanding money or Liquor making mock Shows of the Pope & other Exhibitions making bonfires whereby buildings are in Danger in Populous places & Stealing Materials for such fires with many other Irregularities which Disturb the Peace of Such places & tend much to Corrupt the Manners of Youth – for Prevention whereof.

Be it enacted by the Governor Council and Assembly That Henceforth all Such Clubs Companies & Assemblies for Celebrating or Commemorating the Day aforesaid with the usual shows & mock representations of the Pope & other Exhibitions usually Carried from place to place with the Rude Noisy speeches & Demands of Money or Liquor frequently made at Peoples Doors and the making of bonfires are hereby Strictly forbidden to be done, on the said Day or evening following or any other on the Account of & for the Cause Aforesaid on pain of Imprisonment for the Space of forty eight hours of all concernd in perpetrating any of the Offences aforesaid.

## 1895- Mary Elizabeth Perkins

"Thanksgiving Day, Fast day, Election and Training days were the great holidays of the year. The Weekly Register of November, 1792, hopes that "the savage practice of making bonfires on the evening of Thanksgiving may be exchanged for some other mode of rejoicing, more consistent with the genuine spirit of Christianity."

--Perkins, Mary Elizabeth, Old Houses of the Antient Town of Norwich [Conn.] 1660-1800, 1895, p,19.

"…Pope Night — the anniversary of the discovery of the Papal incendiary Guy Fawkes, booted and spurred, ready to touch fire to his powder train under the Parliament House — was celebrated by the early settlers of New England, and doubtless afforded a good deal of relief to the younger plants of grace in the Puritan vineyard. In those solemn old days, the recurrence of the powder plot anniversary, with its processions, hideous images of the pope and Guy Fawkes, its liberal potations of strong waters, and its blazing bonfires reddening the wild November hills, must have been looked forward to with no slight degree of pleasure…

… The stranger who chances to be travelling on the road between Newburyport and Haverhill, on the night of the 5th of November, may well fancy that an invasion is threatened from the sea, or that an insurrection is going on inland; for from all the high hills overlooking the river tall fires are seen blazing redly against the cold, dark, autumnal sky, surrounded by groups of young men and boys busily engaged in urging them with fresh fuel into intenser activity. To feed these bonfires, everything combustible which could be begged or stolen from the neighboring villages, farm houses, and fences is put in requisition. Old tar tubs, purloined from the ship builders of the river side, and flour and lard barrels from the village traders, are stored away for days, and perhaps weeks, in the woods or in the rain gullies of the hills, in preparation for Pope Night. From the earliest settlement of the two towns the night of the powder plot has been thus celebrated, with unbroken regularity, down to the present time. The event which it once commemorated is probably now unknown to most of the juvenile actors. The symbol lives on from generation to generation after the significance is lost; and we have seen the children of our Catholic neighbors as busy as their Protestant playmates in collecting, by " hook or by crook," the materials for Pope Night bonfires. We. remember, on one occasion, walking out with a gifted and learned Catholic friend to witness the fine effect of the illumination on the hills, and his hearty appreciation of its picturesque and wild beauty — the busy groups in the strong relief of the fires, and the play and corruscation of the changeful lights on the bare, brown hills, naked trees, and autumn clouds…."

."… Increase Mather on November 5 1664 was *"at night much troubled to see the bonfires"*.

"…While conservatives could celebrate the continued actions of the hand of providence and salvation others would see in the bonfire the unexploded gunpowder left for us all by Guy Fawkes. The precedent of questioning authority from the street was just as important as its deliverance…."

- Cressy, David., *Bonfires and Bells." National Memory and the Protestant Calendar in Elizabethan and Stuart England.*, University of California Press, Berkeley, 1989.

# Fireworks

## 1731&1737- The legislature of Rhode Island

…prohibited acts of "Mischief," including the "firing of Guns and Pistols" and the "throwing of Squibs, Fire-Works, &c." in the lanes, the streets, or the taverns, of the province, "on any Night whatsoever." And that, "Custom . . .notwithstanding," "no Bonfire [should] be made on the Fifth of November" unless a town had in fact authorized such a fire." Punishments ranged from twenty-shilling fines for first offenses to month-long prison terms for third offenses.

-Rhode Island, *The Charter, Granted by His Majesty, King Charles II. to the Governor and Company of the English Colony of Rhode-Island and Providence-Plantations, in New-England, in America* (Newport: Samuel Hall, 1767), 120-21.

## 1735- Dorchester Neck

"In the evening, there was a Bonfire on *Dorchester* Neck, and several in this Town, and there were a variety of Fire-Works play'd off upon this Occasion, both on the Land and on the Water. The same Evening 4 young Men of this Town, went in a Cannoe (as we are told) to see the Bonfire on [the] Neck, and have not been heard of since; so that 'tis greatly feared they were drowned in their return home."

-Boston," *Boston Evening-Post*, November 10, 1735.

# Theatre

The first formal theatre to open in Boston was the Board Alley Theatre in 1792. A Massachusetts Bay Colony law of 1750 indicates a slightly earlier formal origin. Cultural or Folk/ informal theatre is a different matter. Theatre in forms such as mumming, guising, and ritual performance were integral parts of the folk cultures of Europe, brought with the first colonists. In 1686 Cotton Mather, in his *Testimony Against Profane and Superstitious Customs*, wrote "there is much discourse now of beginning stage plays in New England." In 1699, the Governor and Council banned, both variety acts and more formally theatrical activity. Laws in both 1753 and 1761 were specifically designed to ban Pope day theatre.

The law of 1753 states the prohibition of: "tumultuous companies of men, children and negroes, carrying about with them pageants and other shews through the streets and lanes of the town of Boston and other towns within this Province's"

## The Anti-Theatre/Pageantry Law of 1753

CHAPTER 18.
AN ACT FOR. FURTHER PREVENTING ALL RIOTOUS, TUMULTUOUS AND DISORDERLY ASSEMBLIES OR COMPANIES OF PERSONS, AND FOR PREVENTING BONFIRES IN ANY OF THE STREETS OR LANES "WITHIN ANY OF THE TOWNS OF THIS PROVINCE.

"Whereas many and great disorders have of late years been committed by tumultuous companies of men, children and negroes, carrying about with them pageants and other shews through the streets and lanes of the town of Boston, and other towns within this province, abusing and insulting the inhabitants, and demanding and exacting money by menaces and abusive language ; and besides the horrid profaneness, impiet}' and other gross immoralities usually found in such companies, a person has lately been killed when orderly walking in the streets of the town of Boston, by one or more belonging to such tumultuous company ; and the aforesaid practices have been found by experience to encourage and cultivate a mobbish temper and spirit in man}' of the inhabitants, and an opposition to all government and order.

---

\* These acts were only revived and continued by 1745-46, chap. 17; but they -were passed as in the margin.

Persons disguised to go about with pageants and armed with any weapons, exacting money, &c.,—
to be punished by fine or imprisonment.
Negroes, &c., may be punished by whipping.
Persons carrying pageants, &c., in the night, though unarmed, to be punished.

Bonfires in streets or lanes forbidden.
Penalty.
Masters and parents liable for their servants and children.
Limitation.

Be it therefore enacted by the Lieutenant-Governour, Council and House of Representatives, [Sect. 1.] That if an}- persons, being more than three in number, and being arm'd all or any of them with sticks, clubs or any kind of weapons, or disguised with vizards, so called, or painted or disco[u]lour[e]d faces, or being in any other manner disguis[e]'d, shall assemble together, having any kind of imager}' or pageantry with them, as a publick shew, in an}- of the streets or lanes of the town of Boston or any other town within this province, or if any person or persons being of or belonging to any company having any imagery or pageantry for a publick shew, shall, by menaces or otherwise, exact, require, demand or ask any money or other thing of value from any of the inhabitants or other persons, in the streets, lanes or houses of any town within this province, every person being of or assembled with such com)any, shall for each oftence forfeit and pay the sum of forty shillings, or suffer imprisonm[en]t not exceeding one month; or if the offender shall be a negro servant, in lieu of the imprisonm[e/i]t, he may be whip['t][j9ed] not exceeding ten stripes, at the discretion of the justice before whom the trial shall be.

And he it further enacted, [Sect. 2. J That if any persons to the number of three or more, between sun-setting and sun-rising, being assembled together in any of the streets or lanes of any town within this province, shall have any kind of imagery or pageantry for a publick shew, altho none of the company so assembled shall be arm'd or disguis[e]'d, or exact, demand or ask any money or thing of value, every person being of such company shall forfeit and pay the sum of forty shillings, or suffer imprisonment not exceeding one month, or if the offender shall be a negro servant, in lieu of the imprisonment he may be whip'[t][(dJ not exceeding ten stripes, at the discretion of the justice before whom the trial shall be. …

…[Sect. 4.] This act to continue and be in force for three years from the publication thereof, and to the end of the session of this court then next after, and no longer. \_Passed January 5 ; 2^ublished

January 6,

1753.

[2d Sess.] Province Laws.—1752-53. 64

*(Complete text can be found in the Legislation section)*

-Acts and Resolves, Massachusetts Bay Colony, 1742-1756, Vol. III (Boston, 1878.), pp. 647-48. 6 Court Files.

# 1761- Suffolk County Directive

In October of 1761, the authorities wrote in the directive:

This law acted to: "prevent the carrying of Pageantry or Imagery in any of the Streets and Lanes of the town of Boston."

"To the Sheriff of the County of Suffolk his Under-sheriff & Deputies, and to the Constables of the Town of Boston, & Each & Every of them Greetings."  The directive emphasized:
The danger of "tumultuous companies.., found by experience to encourage and cultivate a mobbish temper and spirit in many of the inhabitants, and an opposition to all government and order."

"These are therefore in His Majesty's Name to Direct and Require you and Each & Every of you, carefully to attend your Duties incumbent on you, by doing your utmost to prevent the practices aforesaid, & all Transgressions of the Laws now in force for prohibiting the same, and for that End, & for the better discovering the Breaches of the Law, and the offenders, you the Sheriff, Undersheriff & Deputy Sheriffs, & you & Each of you the Constables of the Town of Boston aforesaid, with your Staffs, are directed and requir'd, immediately upon the Setting of the Sun, on the fifth day of November next, to attend & wait at such places in Boston aforesaid, as carrying of any kind of Pageantry or Imagery in any of the Streets or Lanes in the Town of Boston aforesaid, & also prevent any person or persons making any Bonfires in said Streets or Lanes, & you are also required to give Information to all of His Majesty's Justices of the peace, of all such persons as shall offend in any of the particulars aforesaid, that so they may be punish'd as the Law in such Case directs. Hereof you are not to fail at your Perils. Dated at Boston the thirtyeth day of October, in the Second year of His Majesty's Reign Anno Dom 1761.

By order of the Court of General Sessions of the Peace begun & held at Boston the first Tuesday of October AD 1761.

Ezekiel Goldthwait, Clerk"

-Suffolk County, Vol. 487, August 1761-October 1761.

## 1877-Samuel Breck Describes "Antics"

Samuel Breck in: *Recollections* mentions Pope Day "Anticks" and the blackguards, who "disguised in filthy clothes and ofttimes with masked faces, went from house to house in large companies... obtruding themselves everywhere... ," He records a traditional Mummers play:

"There he lies But ere he dies
 A Doctor must be had."

He observed that there was more than one Mummers' company: "it happened not infrequently that the house would be filled by another gang when they [the first] had departed. There was no refusing admittance."

Samuel Breck, Recollections of..., ed. H. E. Scudder (Philadelphia, 1877), pp. 35-6.

## 1685, 1775, 1776- Samuel Sewell Observed

The last year of the Pope Day celebration was either 1775 or 1776, both in and around the other towns of the Commonwealth. It has been suggested that they were ended as not to offend Catholic France but it is more possible that the patriot participants were forced to leave the city.

Judge Samuel Sewell, in his diaries, noted bonfires in 1685 and 1692, and in 1709 wrote: "I walked the town with Col. Townsend... find the town quiet and in good order. Were jealous the 5th Novr might have occasioned disturbance."

- Collections of the Massachusetts Historical Society, Vol. VI, Fifth Series, *Diary of Samuel Sewell.*

# 1735- Samuel Checkley Wrote

In 1735, Samuel Checkley wrote, "A great number of people went over to Dorchester neck where they made a great bonfire and plaid off many fireworks." Also in 1735 the November 11th Weekly Journal noted, "On Wednesday last being the fifth of November, the guns were fired at Castle William and in the evening there were bonfires and other rejoycings." Pageants were not mentioned.

# 1766- John Rowe Observed

In 1753, authorities thought legislation against celebrations was necessary. In 1766, John Rowe complains in his diary:

"November 5. This is a day of great confusion in Boston occasioned by the foolish custom of carrying about the Pope & the devil &c on a large carriage thro' the streets of this town. Indeed three very large ones made their appearance today."

- John Rowe, Letters and Diaries of ..., ed. Anne Rowe Cunningham (Boston, 1903),, p. 114.

# 1845- Joshua Coffin Describes Performance

No scripts for the pageants exist. Collins suggests that they were related to surviving verses such as:

The fifth of November As you well remember,
Was gunpowder treason and plot;
I know of no reason Why the gunpowder treason,
Should ever be forgot.
When the first king James the sceptre swayed,
This hellish powder plot was laid.
Thirty-six barrels of powder placed down below,
All for old England's overthrow:
Happy the man, and happy the day,
That caught Guy Fawkes in the middle of his play.
You'll hear our bell go jink, jink, jink;
Pray madam, sirs, if you'll something give,
We'll burn the dog, and never let him live.
We'll burn the dog without his head,
and then you'll say thd dog is dead.

From Rome, from Rome, the pope is come,
All in ten thousand fears;
The fiery serpent's to be seen,
All head, mouth, nose, and ears.
The treacherous knave had so contrived,
To blow king parliament all up all alive
God by his grace he did prevent
To save both king and parliament.
Happy the man, and happy the day,
That catched Guy Fawkes in the middle of his play.
Match touch, catch prime,
In the good nick of time.
Here is the pope that we have got,

The whole promoter of the plot.
We'll stick a pitchfork in his back,
And throw him in the fire

-Joshua Coffin, A Sketch of the History of Newbury, Newburyport, and West Newburyport (Boston, 1845). -- "Boston's Political Street Theatre: The Eighteenth-Century Pope Day Pageants", Sherwood Collins, Educational Theatre Journal, Vol. 25, No. 4 (Dec., 1973).

## Isaiah Thomas c. 1749-1831, Describes One of the Larger Popes

On the front of these stages, was placed in proportion to the dimensions of the Stage, a large lantern framed circular at the top and covered with paper. Behind this lantern was placed an effigy of the pope sitting in an armed Chair. Immediately behind him was the imaginary representation of the Devil, standing Erect with extended arms.... The larger Effigies had heads placed on poles which went thro' the bodies & thro' the upper part of the stages which were formed like large boxes, some of them not less than 16 or 18 feet long, 3 or 4 feet wide and 3 or 4 feet in depth. Inside of the Stages and out of sight sat a boy under each effigy whose business it was to move the heads of the Effigies by means of the poles before mentioned, from one side to the other as fancy directed.

- Isaiah Thomas, *Three Autobiographical Fragments*, Worcester, Mass., 1962.

## 1973- Sherwood Collins Describes Popes Day Theatre

"A stage was built on a wagon and on this appeared effigies of the Pope, the Devil, assorted minor devils, and other characters associated in the public mind with the Gunpowder Plot.".." in the late 1760s and early 1770s, effigies of unpopular public figures (always Tories) also appeared. In the last years of the practice Boston had two Pope Day companies, possibly three, and these moved about the town during the day as well as at night."

"…we are told in one that the wagons were between twenty and forty feet long. Anyone familiar with the twisted streets and lanes of colonial Boston (and for that matter of today) would doubt how maneuverable a forty-foot wagon would be. Boston had several hills... The wagons were pulled by men and boys, though occasionally horses were used. It would not seem that men and boys could pull such wagons up hills, over bridges, and through the quagmires that passed as streets and lanes. A woodcut of 1769 suggests a wagon of springboard size, a point agreed on by an unsigned remembrance in the November 10, 1821 Columbian Centinel, which tells how "an oblong square box was made of a size ten to twelve feet long." the woodcut shows only one platform but most accounts indicate that there were two, the lower supporting a second some five or six feet higher. This upper level on which the effigies and any performers appeared was framed by a low railing, possibly to establish a stage area, more likely to give a small protection to the effigies on stage particularly when the wagons were moved from one station to the next.…

…the stage had to be elevated so that large street audiences would have better sight lines. Joshua Coffin, official historian for Newbury's bi-centennial celebration, suggests that the five or six feet between the two platforms allowed room for boys to hide on the lower one. Poles supporting the heads passed through the bodies of the effigies of the Pope and the Devil and into the space between the two platforms. The small boys hidden there would turn the poles in order to make the effigies face any desired direction "to give everyone a sight and to pay obeisance of the Popes.…

The front end of the stage nearest the drawbar of the wagon held a large paper lantern made of arched poles and covered with oiled paper to make it transparent. An unsigned recollection in the November 10, 1821 Columbian Centennial reported that this lantern was capable of holding several men, though we are not told to what purpose. Since the pageants were designed at first for nighttime viewing, candles or lanterns must have been placed within the large lantern providing some light for the stage. Possibly the men inside would be posed to create a shadow show on the transparent sides, possibly parodies of well-known Catholic statuary. Certainly, in the beginning the slogans painted on the sides of the lantern were derisive of Catholicism; later, patriotic slogans and portraits were often substituted….

Next on the platform and facing the lantern, the figure of the Pope was seated. His chair and table were the only pieces of furniture on the stage. Upon the table a large book lay and playing cards were scattered. Behind the Pope, at the far end of the wagon, stood the "gigantic" figure of the Devil holding a pitchfork. Curiously the Pope was always seated, the Devil always standing. Other characters might be present: Nancy Dawson (sometimes an effigy, sometimes a male dressed in female attire), Admiral Byng hanging from a gallows, and Guy Fawkes. Political figures who appeared in effigy at least once included Jacob Main (a Tory printer who had roused particular ire among the patriots), Governor Hutchinson, and the customs officials. Small boys frolicked and danced about, sometimes playing with the cards on the table, at other times sitting on the Pope's lap, kissing and fondling him as did the Nancy Dawson. The accounts also place dancers and musicians on this stage, though it would seem there would not be room for them unless the wagons were, after all, twenty to forty feet long. More than likely, the dancers performed on the ground before and around the wagon….

Both the Pope and the Devil were dressed as the eighteenth-century Bostonians pictured them. The Devil's costume was covered with tar and feathers with a very grotesque mask. Some accounts indicate that the minor devils (the small boys) occasionally wore costumes covered with tar and feather, though more often they were dressed as monks and friars. The Pope was dressed in brilliant red robes "with a large white bush wig on, over which was an enormous gold laced hat. The wigs procured for this occasion had often adorned the pulpits of Churches." The men pulling the wagons usually wore dunce hats and their regular street clothing."

-- "Boston's Political Street Theatre: The Eighteenth-Century Pope Day Pageants", Sherwood Collins, Educational Theatre Journal, Vol. 25, No. 4 (Dec., 1973), p. 408.

# Plays on Relevant Topics Performed in America

In the 19th century American theatre was closely linked to Britain. Players, plays and playwrights crossed the Atlantic along with published reviews. Guy Fawkes and the Gunpowder Plot were popular topics.

## 19th Century Performances of Plays relating to Guy Fawkes and the Gunpowder Plot in the United States

The New Chatham Theatre, New York City, between James and Roosevelt streets on Chatham Street, 1841-42: Guy Fawkes;

The Chestnut Street Theatre Company, also known as the Wignell and Reinagle Company, the Warren and Wood Company, and the Company of the New Theatre in Chestnut Street, Philadelphia
1822-23: Guy Fawkes;

Park Theatre Company. New York City
1822-23: Guy Fawkes; *or,* The Gunpowder Plot. 1/1/23

-Durham, Weldon, B., <u>American Theatre Companies, 1749-1887</u>, Greenwood Press, 1986.

1823, April-

Ben[efit of] Wed. 9 [The] Man[ager] in distress, 402.50 Warren Guy Fawkes* & [The King and] Miller of Mansfield [As the Miller. DP] fine, Guy Fawkes (*H*): 1823, April 9.

*- *Old Drury of Philadelphia: A History of the Philadelphia Stage, 1800-1835, Including the Diary Or Daily Account Book of William Burke Wood, Co-Manager with William Warren of the Chestnut Street Theatre, Familiarly Known as Old Drury,* Reese D. James, William Burke Wood; University of Pennsylvania Press, 1932.

January 1st, 1823.

The drama of " Guy Fawkes" was played for the first time, and with the following cast....
The latter lady was, this season, for the first time the sole representative of old women, Mrs. Barrett not having been re-engaged.

- Ireland, Joseph Norton, *Records of the New York stage, from 1750 to 1860,* 1866.

# Comprehensive List of Relevant British Plays

**Guy Fawkcs.** The promoter of the Gunpowder Plot is the central figure of several dramatic pieces :—(1) 1 Guy Fawkes: or, The Fifth of November:' a play produced at the Haymarket on November 5, 1793 (2) 'Guy Fawkes; or, The Gunpowder Plot:' a play in two acts, by GEORGE MACFARREN, produced at the Coburg in 1826, with "O." Smith in the title character and H. Beverley as *King James.* (3) 'Guy Fawkes:' a burlesque by ALBERT SMITH.brought out at the Marylebone Theatre at Easter, 1849, with Miss Charlotte Saunders in the title part. (4)' Guy Fawkes' Day:' a burlesque by F. C. BURN AND *(q.v.),* written at Eton about 1854 or 1855, printed at Windsor, and performed a few times in the provinces. (5)' Harlequin Guy Fawkes:' an "amateur pantomime," produced for the benefit of Angus Reach at the Olympic Theatre, London, on March 31, 1856, with a cast including T. K. Holmes as *Fawkes,* Albert Smith as *Catesby,* Arthur Smith as *Pantaloon,* J. Robins as *Clown,* Edmund Yates as "the lover," Miss Rosina Wright as *Columbine,* etc. The pantomime was repeated at Drury Lane shortly afterwards in aid of the Royal Naval Female School, with Samuel Bran dram as *Fawkes.* (6) 'Guy Fawkes:' a burlesque by HENRY J. BYRON, first performed at the Gaiety Theatre, London, on January 14,1874, with J. L. Toole as *Guy Fawkes,* Miss E. Farren as *Lord Monteagle,* Miss C. Loseby as *Tresham,* W. Maclean as *James I.,* R, Soutar as *Catesby,* Lionel Brough as *Patentlcatherby,* etc (7) 'Guy Fawkes; or, A New Way to Blow up a King:' an opera-bouffe in three acts, by JOHN THOMAS DOUGLAS, Standard Theatre, London, April 16, 1870. (8) 'Guy Fawkes, Esq. :* a burlesque in three acts, by "A. C. TORR" (Fred Leslie) and-HERBERT CLARKE, music by G. W. Byng; first performed at Theatre Royal, Nottingham, April 7,1890; produced at Gaiety Theatre, London, on the afternoon of July 26,1890, with Arthur Roberts in the title part, Miss Fanny Marriott as *Catesby,* etc. (0) 'Guy Fawkes the Traitor:' drama in four acts by CHARLES WHITLOCK, North Shields, July 15, 1901.

-P.621.

**Guido Fawkes**: or. The Prophetess of Ordsall Cave I A melodrama in two acts, by EDWARD STIRLING, first performed at the Queen's Theatre, Manchester, in June, 1840; afterwards played in London at the English Opera and the Queen's.

-p.618.

**Gunpowder Plot** (A). (1) A plav by JOHN OXENFORD *(Q.V..),* produced at the Lyceum Theatre, London, in Mav, 1836. (2) A farce by SYDNEY HODGES, Olympic Theatre, London, May 12, 1873.

-p.619.

-Adams, William, Davenport, <u>A Dictionary of the Drama: a guide to the plays, play-wrights, players, and playhouses of the United Kingdom and America, from the earliest times to the present,</u> Volume 1.

# 1823, January: American Performances

Mordecai Manuel Noah, editor of: National Advocate of New York, Mentioned performance of a new play about Guy Fawkes

New York theater house. Later the Rhode-Island American, and General Advertiser noted the next novel of Sir Walter Scott would be about the Gunpowder Plot.

In May the Baltimore Patriot wrote that a play "Guy Fawkes" was being rehersed at the Baltimore Theatre.

- "New Novel," [Providence] Rhode-Island American, and General Advertiser, April 15, 1823. Baltimore Patriot, May 17, 1823; May 19, 1823; May 21, 1823; May 27, 1823; May 28, 1823; May 31, 1823. Cited in: Doyle, Kevin Q. *"Rage and Fury Which Only Hell Could Inspire": The Rhetoric and the Ritual of Gunpowder Treason in Early America A Dissertation Presented to The Faculty of the Graduate School of Arts and Sciences.* Diss. Brandeis University, 2013.

# Mummers Plays

## Mummer's Poem In Newburyport, Massachusetts (1760 ?)

The Fifth of November,
As you well remember,
Was gunpowder treason and plot;
I know of no reason
Why the gunpowder treason
Should ever be forgot.

When the first King James the septre swayed,
This hellish powder plot was laid.
Thirty-six barrels of powder placed down below
All for old England's overthrow:
Happy the man, and happy the day
That caught Guy Fawkes in the middle of this play.
You'll hear our bell go jink, jink, jink;
Pray madam, sirs, if you' something give,
We'll burn the dog and never let him live.

We'll burn the dog without his head,
And then you'll say the dog is dead.
From Rome, from Rome, the pope is come,
All in ten thousand fears;
The fiery serpent's to be seen,
All head, mouth, nose and ears.
The treacherous knave had so contrived,
To blow king parliament all up alive.
God by his grace he did prevent
To save both king and parliament.
Happy the man, and happy the day,
That catched Guy Fawkes in the middle of his play.

Match touch, catch prime,
In the good nick of time.
Here is the pope that we got,
The whole promoter of the plot.
We'll stick a pitchfork in his back
And throw him in the fire.

After the verses were repeated, the purser stepped forward and took up his collection. Nearly all on whom they called, gave something. Esquire Atkins and Esquire Dalton, always gave a dollar apiece. After perambulating the town, and finishing their collections, they concluded their evening's entertainment with a splendid supper; after making with the exception of the wheels and the heads of the effigies, a bonfire of the whole concern, to which were added, all the wash tubs, tar barrels, and stray lumber, that they could lay their hands on. With them the custom was, to steal all the stuff. But those days have long since passed away.

-Publications of the Colonial Society of Massachusetts, XII (1909), 293-94. From an article by Henry W. Cunningham on the contents of a colonial diary. He quotes from Joshua Coffin's History of Newbury...1635-1845, Boston, 1845, 249-516. Coffin says that Guy Fawkes' Day was not celebrated in Newbury after 1775, in deference to the French"whose assistance was deemed so advantageous at that time.." cited in:
-Hennig Cohen and Tristram Coffin, eds. The Folklore of American Holidays (Detroit: Gale Research Company, 1987), 319

# The Memorial History Of Boston

ed. Justin Winsor
Vol. III
Boston, 1881

We have but scanty personal recollections preserved of this period relating to the common life within the town, and must have recourse again to the good natured Mr. Breck, who piques us by forgetting more important things than he remembered. His Childhood was spent in Boston: and he remembered well the old beacon which stood on the hill, and was blown down in 1789:-

"Spokes were fixed in a large mast, on the top of which was placed a barrel of pitch or tar, always ready to be fired on the approach of the enemy. Around this pole I have fought many battles, as a South End boy, against the boys of the North End of the town; and bloody ones, too, with slings and stones very skillfully and earnestly used. In what a state of semi-barbarism did the rising generations of those days exist! From time immemorial these hostilities were carried on by the juvenile part of the community. The school-masters whipt, parents scolded,--nothing could check it. Was it a remnant of the pugilistic propensities of our British ancestors; or was it an untamed feeling arising from our sequestered and colonial situation? Whatever was the cause, every thing of the kind ceased with the termination of our Revolutionary War....I forget on what holiday it was that the Anticks, another exploded remnant of colonial manners, used to perambulate the town. They have ceased to do it now; but I remember them as late as 1782. They were a set of the lowest blackguards who disguised in filthy clothes and oftimes with masked faces went from house to house in large companies; and, bon gré, mal gré, obtruding themselves everywhere, particularly into the rooms that were occupied by parties of ladies and gentlemen, would demean themselves with great insolence. I have seen them at my father's, when his assembled friends were at cards, take possession of a table, seat themselves on rich furniture, and proceed to handle the cards, to the great annoyance of the company. The only way to get rid of them was to give them money, and listen patiently to a foolish dialogue between two or more of them. One of them would cry out:--

"Ladies and gentlemen sitting by the fire,
Put your hands in your pockets and give us our desire."

When this was done, and they had received some money, a kind of acting took place. One feellow was knocked down and lay sprawling on the carpet, while another bellowed out:-

"See, there he lies!
But ere he dies,
A doctor must be had."

He calls for a doctor, who soon appears, and enacts the part so well that the wounded man revives. In this way they would continue for half an hour; and it happened not infrequently that the house would be filled by another gang when these had departed. There was no refusing admittance. Custom had licensed these vagabonds to enter even by force any place they chose. What should we say to such intruders now? Our manners would not brook such a usage a moment. Undoubtedly these plays were a remnant of the old mysteries of the fourteenth and fifteenth, centuries..

*(Note: activities are noted by contemporary newspaper accounts as being associated with the celebration of "Pope's Day" or the fifth of November.)*

- Winsor, Justin ed.,*The Memorial History Of Boston*, Vol. III, Boston, 1881.

# Food Ways

See also the Thanksgiving section.

## 1735: Diary of Samuel Checkley

[4] John Adams, attending court at Salem on Wednesday, November 5, 1766, says:

"Spent the evening at Mr. Pynchon's, with Farnham, Sewall, Sargeant, Col. Saltonstall &ct. very agreeably. Punch, wine, bread and cheese,"

4 Literary Diary, i. 182, 470.

...."After the verses were repeated, the purser stepped forward and took up his collection. Nearly all on whom they called, gave something. Esquire Atkins and Esquire Dalton, always gave a dollar apiece. After perambulating the town, and finishing their collections, they concluded their evening's entertainment with a splendid supper; after making with the exception of the wheels and the heads of the effigies, a bonfire of the whole concern, to which were added, all the wash tubs, tar barrels, and stray lumber, that they could lay their hands on."

- Checkley, Samuel, "Diary of the Rev. Samuel Checkley", 1735  In: <u>Publications of the Colonial Society of Massachusetts Colonial Society of Massachusetts,</u>  pp. 292-295.

## Wine

1704- In early 1704, the Common Council of New York requested that the treasury pay the mayor's office a sum of over £5 owed for the costs of the bonfire and the wine from the fall before.

-Osgood, ed., *Minutes of the Common Council of the City of New York,* II: 121. -

1714- New York, the aldermen and the assistants of the council ordered: "there be a Bonfire that Night at the usual place" and for 7 gallons of wine be drunk for "the Kings health" On "Gunpowder Treason day".

-Osgood, ed., *Minutes of the Common Council of the City of New York,* II: 256-57, 452-53; III: 51, 77-78, 187-88, 192, 217-18. -

1713- New York, November 3, the corporation ordered that seven gallons of wine be obtained for the celebration.

-Osgood, ed., *Minutes of the Common Council of the City of New York,* II: 256-57, 452-53; III: 51, 77-78, 187-88, 192, 217-18. -

1742- Georgia, then celebrated the holiday. Governor William Stephens directed "due observation" of the anniversary in Savannah, with a Church of England service and the raising of the British flag. The governor believed that "burning more powder, would be a needless waste, of what we might stand in Need of on a more urgent Occasion." The next year he proclaimed the Fifth an "annual Rejoycing day" of the territory, but he also called it "pretty antiquated". "The principal people of the Town" gathered at noon, for the firing of the guns at Fort Argyle, and the governor took part "drinking a few Glasses of Wine with the usual healths" to the monarchy in 1744 and 1745, and perhaps later.

- Coulter, E. Merton, ed., *The Journal of William Stephens* (Athens, Georgia: University of Georgia Press, 1958 and 1959), I: 134 and II: 36, 164, 248. For more on Stephens, see Julie Anne Sweet, *William Stephens: Georgia's Forgotten Founder* (Baton Rouge: Louisiana State University, 2010). -

1766- Wednesday November 5, John Adams

"Spent the Evening at Mr. Pynchons, with Farnham, Sewal, Sergeant, Coll. Saltonstall &c., very agreably. Punch, Wine, bread and Cheese, Apples, Pipes and Tobacco. Popes and Bonfires this Evening at Salem, and a Swarm of tumultuous People attending them."

-Diary and Autobiography of John Adams, Volume 1, 1755–1770. - Adams, John, Diary, November 5, 1766, in John Adams and Charles Francis Adams, *Works: With a Life of the Author,* Vol. 10 (Boston: Little, Brown, 1865), 201. -

## 1750-The diary of Captain Francis Goelet

New York merchant visiting Boston in 1750:
After dinner went with some of the company to the north end the towne. Bought Some Limes &c., where we saw the devil and the Pope &c. carried about by the mob, represented in effegy, very drole. Soone after see two more of them, but the justices, feareing some outrages may be committed, put a stop to them.

- Francis Goelet, *The Voyages and Travels of Francis Goelet, 1746–1758*, ed. Kenneth Scott (Queens, N.Y.: Queens College Press, 1970), "Diary," 5 November 1750.

## 1821- Supper

"The money collected on these occasions, was expended by each crew, in procuring a supper, where the combatants met to relate the feats of the day."

-1821- From *Columbian Centinel*, 10 November. Cited in: Benes, Peter, *Night Processions: Celebrating the Gunpowder Plot in England and New England, (unpublished Mss.).*

# 1864 Reminiscences by Gen. Wm. H. Sumner. P. 191

General Sumner, in his Reminiscences, published in the New England Historic Genealogical Register (vol. viii., April, 1854), gives an account of Governor Hancock's measures, through the mollifying influences of a dinner, to put an end to Pope Day in Boston a short time before more tragic hostilities broke out in 1775."

"While on the subject of Mrs. Scott's conversations, I will record one which she related to me some time since respecting the great zeal of the Grovemor, before the war, to do away the animosity which subsisted in Boston between the North and South enders, who, on Pope day, used to have a regular battle, the ill blood arising from which continued through the year, and showed itself in almost every private as well as public transaction. The Governor, wishing to heal this difference, and thinking it essential to a successful resistance of British aggression, exerted himself in every possible way to effect it without any avail. He then gave a supper at the Green Dragon Tavern, which cost him $1000, at which he invited all the leading men of both the Pope parties to be present. He addressed them at table in an eloquent speech, and invoked them, for their country's sake, to lay aside their animosity, and fully impressed upon them the necessity of their united efforts to the success of the cause in which they were engaged. There is nothing more productive of domestic union than a sense of external danger. With the existence of this the whole audience now became fully impressed, and shook hands before they parted, and pledged their united exertions to break the chains with which they were manacled. The happiest results attended this meeting, and since that time the North and South End Popes have not showed their heads in the streets, and a custom and celebration in which all the town participated, and which had long been established, was broken, as it were, by a charm, making the stories related of it by our fathers, who themselves were engaged in it, hardly credible hy their children."

- 1864 Reminiscences by Gen. Wm. H. Sumner. P. 191

- *Recollections of Samuel Breck, with passages from his note-books.* (1771–1862.), EDITED BY Horace. Elisha. SCUDDER.

# Chronology-Short Entries

1570- Regnans in Excelsis. Papal Bull issued by Pope Pius V encouraged British citizens to *revolt.*

1588- Spanish Armada defeated via storm off the coast of England.

1601- **Essex Rebellion** Essex's Rebellion an unsuccessful rebellion led by **Robert Devereux, 2nd Earl of Essex** in 1601 against **Elizabeth I of England,** It included many of the plotters of 1605 who were fined, forgiven and released.

1605, November 5 - Gunpowder plot followed by attempted revolt in the Midlands. Guy Fawkes, Sir Everard Digby; Henry Garnett, S.J. John Gerard, S.J.; Thomas Percy; Ambrose Rockwood; Oswald Tesimond, S.J.; Francis Tresham; Robert Winter; Thomas Winter; Christopher Wright; John Wright, led by Robert Catesby.

1600s and the 1700s, both military institutions and political institutions in Anglo-America advocated and furthered the memory of the Gunpowder Treason, from Georgia to Massachusetts. Governors hosted lavish parties, raised toasts to the king, and supported the lighting of bonfires; legislatures attended services at church; and soldiers stationed at forts gave loud military salutes. With fire and wine and more, individuals and organizations with authority in early America saw this festive culture as a means of promoting the empire, the holiday, and the nation.

1606-62 - Establishment of Guy Fawkes Day in England and Pope's Day in America. -

1612- John Speed, cartographer recommended that: the "roaill *Tent*" of James I as well as the "Gospell of *Iesus Christ*" expanded in "Virginea and also that the Fifth should be celebrated with "thanksgiuing, prayse and prayers" in the English world, "in memory" of the deliverance.

- Speed, John, *The Theatre of the Empire of Great Britaine Presenting an Exact Geography of the Kingdomes of England, Scotland, Ireland, and the Iles Adioyning* . . . (London: William Hall, 1612), 157, 894.

1619- General Assembly of Virginia proclaimed: "all ministers . . . duly read divine service, . . . according to the ecclesiastical laws." This would have included Gunpowder Treason.

-. Van Schreeven, William J and Reese, George H, eds., *Proceedings of the General Assembly of Virginia* July 30 - August 4, 1619 (Jamestown: Jamestown Foundation of the Commonwealth of Virginia, 1969), 59 (and 121, 131.

1620-Captain John Smith records the first New World celebration in Bermuda:

"The fift[h] of No[v]ember the damnable plot of the powder treason was solemnized, with Praiers, Sermons, and a great Feast, whereto the Go[v]ernor in[v]ited the chiefe of the *Spaniards*, where drinking the Kings health, it was honored with a quicke volly of small shot, which was answered from the Forts with the great Ordnance, and then againe concluded with a second volley of small shot; neither was the afternoone without musicke and dancing, and at night many huge bone-fires of sweet wood.

- Smith, John, *The Generall Historie of Virginia, New-England, and the Summer Isles [1584-1624]* . . .

(London: I.D. and I.H. . . ., 1624), 197. For more on Bermuda (the Summer Isles) in this time, see Jean de
Chantal Kennedy, *Isle of Devils: Bermuda Inder the Somers Island Company* (London: Collins, 1971).

1622- Patrick Copland, Independent minister of a Bermuda church, read *Virginia's God Be Thanked*, the sermon that he had written for the Virginia Company, in London. He asked that the audience to remember the "loving kindnesse" of God and "take to heart" the "dangers" from which the Lord had delivered England, including the Spanish Armada and "the *Gunpowder Treason*."

- Copland, Patrick, *Virginia's God Be Thanked, or a Sermon of Thanksgiving for the Happie Successe of
the Affayres in Virginia This Last Yeare. Preached . . . at Bow-Church in Cheapside, Before the Honorable Virginia Company, on Thursday, the 18. of Aprill 1622 . . .* (London: I. D., 1622), 14.

1623- Mariners celebrated the day in Massachusetts, at Plymoth Plantation. Emmanuel Altham, an adventurer, wrote that "a sudden fire" had destroyed "one half of the plantation" on November 5. Governor /historian William Bradford, governor and historian, wrote that sailors on shore, seeking good cheer, had built a fire, had lit a shed on purpose, and had lost control of the blaze but had burnt only three or four houses, not half of the three-year-old settlement, to the ground. He complained that blasted the fire that a "rude company" had started: "This fire was occasioned by some of the seamen that were roistering in a house where it first began, making a great fire in cold weather, which broke out of the chimney into the thatch . . . The house in which it began was right against their storehouse, which they had much ado to save, in which were their common store and all their provisions, the which, if they had been lost, the plantation had been overthrown. But through God's mercy it was saved by the great diligence of the people and care of the [government] . . . But a trusty company . . . suspected some malicious dealing, if not plain treachery, and whether it was only suspicion or not, God knows; but this is certain, that when the tumult was greatest, there was a voice heard (but from whom it was not known) that bid them look about them, for all were not friends that were near them . . . But God kept them from this danger, whatever was intended.

- Bradford, William, *Of Plymouth Plantation, 1620-1647*, ed. by Samuel Eliot Morison (New Brunswick,
New Jersey: Rutgers University Press, 1952), 136-37.

1630s - New England abandoned the calendar – and the holidays - of the Church of England.

1638- Rev. Thomas Hooker published for the first time the lecture that he had
given on the Plot in 1626, in London, as *The Church's Deliverances*. In the text he noted the "malice" of the plotters, who he considered "the enemies of God's grace and gospel."

- Hooker, Thomas, The *Church's Deliverances*, November 5, 1626, in George H. Williams, Norman
Pettit, Winfried Herget, and Sargent Bush, Jr., eds., *Thomas Hooker: Writings in England and Holland,
1626-1633* (Cambridge, Massachusetts: Harvard University Press, 1975), 53-88.

1641- Thomas Shepard, minister of the First Church of Cambridge, Massachusetts
mentioned the Plot in a sermon. In *The Sincere Convert*, he believed that many had
fallen from the "glorious profession to Popery." He wrote: "*Ignorance* is the first Rocke, or the first powder-plot," of damnation.

- Shepard, Thomas *The Sincere Convert Discovering the Paucity of True Beleevers and the Great
Difficulty of Saving Conversion* (London: T. P. and M. S., 1641), 124, 212.

1642- Thomas Lechford, Massachusetts lawyer, wrote that, even though the colony did
not keep "the fift[h] of November," should do so and also treat it like "the
dayes of Purim among the Jews" – and set aside time for "the moderate recreation of youth and servants." And "why not set fasting dayes & . . . feasts . . . in the Reformed Churches?"

- Lechford, Thomas, *Plain Dealing, or . . . a Short View of New-Englands Present Government, Both
Ecclesiastical and Civil, Compared With the Anciently-Received and Established Government of England
in Some Materiall Points . . .* (London: W. E. and I. G., 1642), 19-20.

1647- The Virginia assembly ordered the reading of the Book of Common Prayer.

- Van Schreeven, William J. and George H. Reese, eds., *Proceedings of the General Assembly of Virginia* July 30 - August 4, 1619 (Jamestown: Jamestown Foundation of the Commonwealth of Virginia, 1969)

1650- Thomas Shepherd wrote in the treatise *Theses Sabbaticae* published in England, Shepard contended that, just as "the whole fifth of November is sanctified"

Shepard, Thomas, Theses *Sabbaticae, or, the Doctrine of the Sabbath . . . Which [Was] First Handled More . . . in Sundry Sermons in Cambridge in New-England . . .* (London: Printed for John Rothwell, 1649, 1650), 63.

1659 - General Court in Boston banned festive activity "For preventing disorders arising in several places within this jurisdiction by reason of some still observing such festivalls, as were superstitiously kept in other countrys, to the, great dishonnor of God & offense of others, it is therefore ordered by this Court and the authority thereof, that whosoever shall be found observing any such day as Christmas or the like, either by forbearing of labour, feasting, or any other way, upon any such account as aforesaid, every such person so offending shall pay forevery such offense five shillings, as a fine to the county."

-Shurtleff, Nathaniel Bed, *Records of the Governor and Company of the Massachusetts Bay in New England* (Boston: William White, 1854), IV.1: 366.

1662 & 1667: John Hull of Boston recorded that the anniversary had been observed as a day of thanksgiving "throughout" Massachusetts.

-Hull, John, Diary [Transcript], 1628-82, in Richards-Childs Family Papers, Massachusetts Historical Society.

By 1662- November 5 became, in the New World, a day of humiliation and thanksgiving, honoring the preservation of church and state.

1662- Middlesex County Court convicted two servants, Thomas Facy and Paul Wilson, of charges of "disorderly carriage" and abusing "a day of publ[ic] thanksgiving" in Charlestown. They were found guilty of "abetting sundry young persons & others, gathering themselves into companies & kindling fires in the evening . . . & absenting themselves from their [masters] houses." They were charged with gathering firewood and bringing down a house. The court sentenced Facy and Wilson to five lashes of the whip each and. Their masters were fined the costs of the trial and 30 shillings.

-Pulsifer Transcript, Middlesex County Court Records, File 3 (Massachusetts State Archives), December 16, 1662, 274.

1662- Middlexex County court records:

"Thomas Facy and Paul Wilson who had also been caught and punished for Maying, were: "convicted of disorderly carriage on the fifth of November last, being a day of public thanksgiving in abetting sundry young person and others gathering themselves into companies and kindling fires in the evening, and absenting themselves from their master's houses and lodgings after nine at night to the disquiet of the inhabitants, sundry men having their fences by that occasion pulled up and burnt, and one house tumbled into a cove, and sundry guns shot of whereof Paul Wilson confesses he shot one of them."

-As Cited by: Cressy, David, "The English Calendar in Colonial America". pp. 190-206 of David Cressy, Bonfires and Bells."National Memory and the Protestant Calendar in Elizabethan and Stuart England. 1989.

1662- Samuel Maverick, a royalist steadfast wrote to Edward Hyde, criticizing the decision that the court had made, in the Facy-Wilson case.

"[The] Divers Youths [were] lately prsecuted att Boston for making bonefires on Gunpowder treason day at night, it being kept as a thankesgiving . . ., Ye Youth being Willing to Conforme to ye practice that Such a tyme affords in old England, for this the parents of the Youths were fined, but ye Children of ye Church Members Who Were guilty as much as Others . . . [escaped?] all Scott free."

-Maverick, Samuel Letter to the Earl of Clarendon, [date?], in The New-York Historical Society, *Collections of the New-York Historical Society for the Year 1869* (New York: The Society, 1870), 47.

1662- Charlestown- "a group of young men celebrated the Fifth by hauling down an old house and pulling up the fences around it; they then made a bonfire and discharged guns (it "being a public thanksgiving," explained the author)"

- Richard Frothingham, History of Charlestown, Massachusetts; quoted by Joseph B. Felt, Annals of Salem, Massachusetts, 2 vols. (Salem: Ives, 1845, 1849), 2:46. 1, Cited in: -Benes, Peter, "Night Processions: Celebrating the Gunpowder Plot in England and New England," in *New England Celebrates: Spectacle, Commemoration, and Festivity*, Dublin Seminar for New England Folklife Annual Proceedings 2000 (Boston: Boston University, 2002), p.14.

1664- Increase Mather, minister of the Second Church of Boston, noted recorded
On the anniversary, he had been "at night much troubled to see the bonfires" in the seaport".

- Mather, Increase, *Diary*, Reel One: [1659?], 1663, 1664-1667, Massachusetts Historical Society.

1664- Duke's Laws passed in which the Duke of York, the future James II, ordered that January 30 –the martyrdom of Charles I, May 20 the birthday and the restoration of Charles II, and, November 5 – "the Great deliverance from the Gunpowder Treason" – should "be observed." Clergy was "enjoyned to pray and Preach," the laity, was to "abstain from [its] Ordinary Laboure and Calling."

-New York State, Commissioners of Statutory Revision, . . . *The Colonial Laws of New York, From the Year 1664 to the Revolution: Including the Charters to the Duke of York, the Commissions and Instructions to Colonial Governors, the Duke's Laws, . . . and the Acts of the Colonial Legislatures From 1691 to 1775* (Albany: J. B. Lyon, 1894), 60.

1665- Petition sent by a four-man Royal commission from Massachusetts to Charles II and the General Court:

"[T]here ought to be inserted & ordeined to be kept the 5th of November, & the nine & twentyeth of May, as dayes of thanksgiving; the first for the miraculous preservation of our king & country from the gunpowder treason; the second for his majestyes birth, [and] miraculous & happy restauration to his crownes upon the same day; as also the thirtieth of January as a day of fasting & praying, that God would please to avert his judgments from our nations for that most barbarous & execrable murder of our late soveraigne, Charles the First."" Petition rejected by the colonial legislature.

- Hall, Michael G., Edward *Randolph and the American Colonies, 1676-1703* (Chapel Hill: University of North Carolina Press, 1960), x.

1665- The monarchy ordered in that the colony keep the Fifth of November in recognition of "the miraculous preservation of . . . King & country." The governor of Massachusetts Bay refused.

1665- Boston," the fifth of November" should be kept for thanksgiving for "the miraculous preservation of our king and country from the gunpowder treason"

-Massachusetts General Court, May 1665

1667- Mid-October. The governor/ general court of Massachusetts Bay declared the Fifth "a day of thanksgiving unto God for the continuance of our peace and liberties."
This may have been merely a harvest thanksgiving.

-Lucas, "Colony or Commonwealth," 90 ns. 6-7; Bernard Bailyn, *The New England Merchants in the Seventeenth Century* (Cambridge, Massachusetts: Harvard University Press, 1955) and Richard S. Dunn, *Puritans and Yankees: The Winthrop Dynasty of New England, 1630-1717* (Princeton: Princeton University Press, 1962).

Overcoming the opposition to what the English called Guy Fawkes Day required the joint effort of crown officials and colonial royalists, and the elite in Massachusetts still resisted the holiday. The ministry, too, hesitated to accept the Fifth (though it had no qualms with anti- Catholicism). After the Glorious Revolution, the Puritan distaste for the holiday faded, thanks in no small part to the new association of November 5 with the great triumph of, Protestantism under William III.

1667- November 5 established officially as a time of humiliation and thanksgiving in the urban North (first in Massachusetts Bay in 1667, then, in New York in 1700).

1667-Samuel Green and Marmaduke Johnson, two Massachusetts Bay printers, republished *Gods Terrible Voice in the City of London*, in which Thomas Vincent Referenced the Gunpowder Plot.

- Vincent, Thomas, *Gods Terrible Voice in the City of London: . . . the Narration of Two Late Dreadful Judgements of Plague and Fire . . .* (Cambridge, Massachusetts: Samuel Green, 1667, and Marmaduke Johnson, 1668), 22-23.

1668- Green printed *Tydings From Rome or England's Alarm* (printed the year before in London) In it John Flavel addressed the Gunpowder Plot: "O [people of God] be as zealous for the Protestant Interest as [the papists] are against it; if they dare to smite with the fist of wickedness, we hope You will not be afraid to smite them with the Sword of Justice. Remember what a matchless salvation was once given to our English Parliament, . . . the Powder Plot, that *Catholick Villany*, as one aptly calls it: Such a deliverance as ages past cannot parrallel in any Hystory, . . . Had it not been recorded . . .posterity would never believe it. [The papists] have indeed studiously endeavored [as of late] . . . to hide from [you] the goodness of God in [1605], that by forgetting [H]is goodness, they might bury in silence their own wickedness [but]
we hope that none of you acting against this enemy will be stained with lukewarmness."

- Flavel, John, *Tydings From Rome or England's Alarm. Wherein Several Grounds to Suspect the Prevalency of the Popish Interest Are Seasonably Suggested . . .* (Cambridge, Massachusetts: Samuel Green, 1668),

1669- Joseph Browne of Boston changed his almanack bringing it in line with the colony of Massachusetts, recording November 5 "Powder Treason".

- Browne, Joseph, *An Almanack of Coelestiall Motions for the Year of the Christian Aera, 1669 . . .* (Cambridge, Massachusetts: Samuel Green and Marmaduke Johnson, 1669).

1669- Thomas Bailey of Weymouth wrote the four page poem "In Quintum Novembris,"

"The Puritans, thought to Calumniate
O'th Plott and that they did participate...."

"Who sav'd us on 5th day of November
Which may us cause God still to remember.
. . .
But [?] Let us God celebrate
Who hath us freed from such a hellish fate.
To my exclaim that it shall bee
Praise be to God to all eternity.
Who hath thus far us kept, preserved always"
Render to him the glory and the praise.

- Bailey, Thomas, "In Quintum Novembris," November 5, 1669, Massachusetts Historical Society, MSS, Miscellaneous Bound Collection, 1657-1671.

1672- The first formal description of similar pageants  Pamphlet describing a "play" held on the Fifth of November in Poultrey, a square in London

- The Burning of the whore of Babylon as it was acted with great applause, in the Poultrey, London, on Wednesday night, being the fifth of November last, at six of the clock (London: printed by R. C., 1673). Cited in: -Benes, Peter, "Night Processions: Celebrating the Gunpowder Plot in England and New England," in *New England Celebrates: Spectacle, Commemoration, and Festivity*, Dublin Seminar for New England Folklife Annual Proceedings 2000 (Boston: Boston University, 2002), P.12.

1673-  Urian Oakes, the minister of the First Church of Cambridge, preached that firebrands pursued a "trade of Lying and calumn[i]ating" and "creeping" created "the very *Gun-powder-Plot* that threatens the destruction of Church and State"

- Oakes, Urian, *New-England Pleaded With, and Pressed to Consider the Things Which Concern Her Peace at Least in This Her Day, or, a Seasonable and Serious Word of Faithful Advice to the Churches and People of God, Primarily Those in the Massachusetts Colony, Musingly to Ponder, . . . What Will Certainly Be the Sad Issue, of Sundry Unchristian and Crooked Wayes . . . Delivered in a Sermon Preached at Boston. . ., May 7, 1673, . . .* (Cambridge, Massachusetts: Samuel Green, 1673), 42-43.

1676- Royal agent Edward Randolph had visited Boston and reported that that the Massachusetts government had given up conditions of its charter, allowed illegal trade, and committed tyranny; also that the colony kept "no days commanded by the laws of England to be observed or regarded."

- Tappan, Robert Noxon ed., *Edward Randolph; Including His Letters and Official Papers . . . 1676-1703*, Vol. 2 (Boston: Prince Society, 1898), 198-201.

1677- "George Joy, Mariner," referenced the Plot in the poem "Innocency's Complaint"

"Lament, *Newengland*, like a tender Mother!
To see thy Children one destroy another:
. . .
Those that in Conscience cannot wrong a Worm,
Are fined and whipt, because they can't conform;
And time hath been, which ne'er shall be forgot,
God's Servants have been hang'd, none knows for what,
Except for serving of their blessed Lord,
For Quaking and for Trembling at his Word.
Let those black Days [of oppression], like the fifth of *November*,
Be writ in Red, for Ages to Remember."

- Joy, George, Mariner, "Innocency's Complaint Against Tyrannical Court Faction in Newengland (S. I.: S. N., 1677; perhaps, Boston: John Foster, 1677).

1678- An imaginary conspiracy against the crown of Great Britain on the part of English Roman Catholics, fabricated by Titus Oates as a means of gaining power.

1679-81-**Exclusion Crisis,** 1679 through 1681 in the reign of King **Charles II of England, Scotland and Ireland**. The Exclusion Bill sought to exclude the King's brother and **heir presumptive**, **James, Duke of York**, from the thrones of **England**, **Scotland** and **Ireland** because he was Roman Catholic. The **Tories** were opposed to this exclusion while the "Country Party", who were soon to be called the **Whigs**, supported it.

1680- John Foster published the anniversary sermon that John Wilson, a former minister of the First Church of Boston, read first in Sudbury, Suffolk, in 1626.

*A Song of Deliverance…*

Now was November fifth at hand
when ore this hellish pit,
Both head and body to the Land
were all at once to sit.
When furious *Fauxe* with matches three
(for spickets) was provided,
The rest of this fraternity
were very closely sided….

Nor would they father by and by
the Plot, (though 'twere their own),
But meant the infamy should lye
where it was quite unknown.
If you would know what kind of man
they would have thus traduced,
Forsooth, it was the Puritan
(so in their stile abused.)
Indeed they meant the Protestants
should all be under guilt,
As if the blood of Popish Saints
at once they would have spilt.

- Wilson, John, *A Song of Deliverance from the Lasting Remembrance of Gods Wonderful Works* . . . (Boston: John Foster, 1680): 15-19, 23-25.

1682- February the Massachusetts legislature repealed the 1659 law prohibiting the observation of Christmas and "the like" possibly encouraged celebration.

-. Whitmore, William H., *The Colonial Laws of Massachusetts: Reprinted From the Edition of 1660, With the Supplements to 1672* . . . (Boston: Published by Order of the City Council of Boston, 1889), 291.

1682, November 5- Benjamin James, servant and others gathered people in Boston to light bonfires in the streets. Later in November, the Suffolk County Court sentenced James and others to pay prison fees. p.124.

1684, Boston- With the dissolution of the charter the region had to countenance the presence in Boston of a Church of England and put up with numerous English political institutions and practices. The region now had to think seriously about the Gunpowder treason as a national holiday."

--Benes, Peter, "Night Processions: Celebrating the Gunpowder Plot in England and New England," in *New England Celebrates: Spectacle, Commemoration, and Festivity*, Dublin Seminar for New England Folklife Annual Proceedings 2000 (Boston: Boston University, 2002), P.14.

1685- November 5, Boston, the people even lit large bonfire on town common. Samuel Sewel Sewall noted that, in a hard rain, about fifty people were at a bonfire on the Common. The next night a crowd of two hundred attended "hallowed about" A fire made on the same place.

1685- Samuel Green published, John Griffin sold in Boston *The Protestant Tutor*, written by Benjamin Harris. This edition did not include the commentary on "The Gun-powder Treason *Contrived by the* Papists"; "a Damnable Design, Contrived by some Priests, Jesuites, and other Papists, to Undermine the Parliament-House, and with Gunpowder to Blow up the King, Prince, Clergy, Nobles, Knights, and Burgesses, the very Confluence of all the Flower, Glory, Piety, Learning, Providence and Authority in the Land, Fathers, Sons, Brothers, Allies, Friends, Foes, *Papists*, and *Protestants*, all at one Blast." found in the 1679 English edition.

- Harris, Benjamin, *The Protestant Tutor* (London: Benjamin Harris, 1679), 63-64.

1686, November 5 - Boston assembled for an ordination ceremony. Charles Morton, pastor of the Charlestown church, gave a sermon on Romans 1:16, using the "occasion to speak of the 5th of November" giving a "very pithy" lecture, maintaining that the Church of Rome "taught and practiced" "the just contrary to that Epistle." Increase Mather preached "in praise of the Congregational way," Josias Clark directed a meeting of "the English Church" at the Town House and preached Presbyterianism.

- Sewall, Samuel, *Diary, 1674-1729*, ed. M. Halsey Thomas (New York: Farrar, Straus and Giroux, 1973), I: 81-82, 125. A.

ca. 1688- 1703- Glorious Revolution. The invasion fleet of William III, the Prince of Orange, in England on November 5, 1688.

1688- Before, The holiday focused on anti-popery.

1688- After, The holiday stressed the king and the kingdom.

1688- The Fifth also doubled as a celebration of the arrival, and the ascent, of William III.

After the Glorious Revolution, "the common sort" (apprentices, artisans, boys, farmers, laborers, sailors, servants, and slaves) took over the memory of the plot from the elite, keeping the anti-popery of Pope's Day and burning effigies of the devil, the pope, and other enemies of freedom.

1688- Boston, "Sewall (Samuel) and the rest of the Puritan elite continued subtle resistance to the holiday until after 1688."

-Sewall, Samuel, III, *The Diary of Samuel Sewall, 1674-1729,* MHS. Collections, 5th Ser., VII (Boston, 1882), 19.

1689- Jacob Leisler, new governor of New York supported the new regency and kept the Fifth, with bonfires and effigies. In the same month, Leisler wrote Edwin Stede, the governor of Barbados. He noted the celebration: "[T]he 4th Novem[ber] being the birth day of our gracious King which we did solemnise with bonefires & rosting one ox &c. the fifth was gun pouder treason which also we did solemnise with bonefires & burning the pope."

- Leisler, Jacob, Form of an Association Proposed to the Inhabitants, [June 3?] 1689, CO 5/1081, 70-7I, PRO; Declaration of Leisler and His Party Against Major Ingoldsby and His Council, March 16, 1691, in *The Documentary History of the State of New-York*, ed. O'Callaghan, II, 344; Jacob Leisler, Letter to Edwin Stede, the Governor of Barbados, November 23, 1689, in *Documents Relative to the Colonial History of the State of New-York*, ed. E. B. O'Callaghan (Albany: Weed, Parsons, & Co., 1853), II: 24-25. -

1692- New charter of the city of Boston creates two politically informed parts: North End and South End. North End was allied to the Mathers and royalism, supporting the charter. South End supported the Bradstreets and self-government and opposed royal government .

- Forbes, Esther, *Paul Revere and the World He Lived In* (Boston: Houghton Mifflin Harcourt, 1999), 94-95,

1689-1776- Warden wrote of how these "Ends" celebrated the 5th:

"[In] Boston the celebration was much more violent. Being so large a town, she fell into the habit of having two popes, two popes' carriages, and two escorting mobs [the mobs of the North End and the South End]. Whenever these two rival gangs, numbering "thousands," met, a ferocious battle was fought for the possession of the other side's pope and devils. People were killed and maimed for life. Paving stones, bricks, cudgels, were fair weapons, and great damage was done, both to human flesh and property. All night long through Boston's unlighted, cobbled streets, nothing was heard but "a confused medley of the rattling of the Carriages, the noise of the Popes Drums, and the infernal yelling of those who are fighting for possession of the Devil." For twenty-four hours Boston was in the hands of a mob [a mob that practiced "hell-raising"] which custom, if not law, had legalized."

-.Warden, G. B., *Boston, 1689-1776* (Boston: Little, Brown, and Company, 1970): 35.

1692, 1693, 1694- Benjamin Harris published almanacs that, instead of noting the landing of William III, noted the Fifth as the Gunpowder Plot day.

- Harris, Benjamin, *Boston Almanack for the Year of Our Lord God. 1692* . . . (Boston: Benjamin Harris and John Allen, 1691); Benjamin Harris, *Boston Almanack for the Year of Our Lord God. 1692* . . . (Boston: Benjamin Harris and John Allen, 1691).

1693- The charter of the College of William and Mary (1693 stipulated that, in exchange for twenty thousand acres of land, the administration and the faculty – "the President and masters or professors" – must provide two copies of Latin verses "every fifth day of November" to the house of the governor or lieutenant governor of Virginia. The college, the charter continued, not only "for the time being" but, in fact, "forever."

-- Jones, Julian Ward, "A 'New' Latin Quitrent Poem of the College of William and Mary," *Virginia Magazine of History and Biography* 96.4 (1988): 500.

1694- New York, the governor, Benjamin Fletcher, supported the anniversary of the landing of William III and ordered that the citizens celebrate by lighting a bonfire.

- Balmer, Randall, H., *A Perfect Babel of Confusion: Dutch Religion and English Culture in the Middle Colonies* (New York: Oxford University Press, 1989).

1700- November 5 as a time of humiliation and thanksgiving in the urban North (first in Massachusetts Bay in 1667, then, in New York in 1700).

1700- November 4, Massachusetts legislature banned lighting of fireworks in Boston.

1700- Common Council of New York supported the Fifth as a formal holiday, ordering that the mayoralty "provide firewood" for bonfires on the Fourth and the Fifth.

- Middleton, Simon, From *Privileges to Rights: Work and Politics in Colonial New York City* (Philadelphia: University of Pennsylvania Press, 2006).

1700- By November 5- In Boston, people started parading and torching, in effgy, representatives of the pope.

1701- The English Parliament passed the Act of Settlement, which barred members of the Catholic Church and their spouses from "inherit[ing], possess[ing], or enjoy[ing] the crown and [the] government of this realm."

-The Act of Settlement, 1701, The UK Statute Law Database, http://www.statutelaw.gov.uk/content.aspx? activeTextDocId=1565208.

1701, 1702, 1707, 1718, 1719- The diary of Manasseh Minor, a farmer, notes that Stonington, Connecticut, celebrated the Fifth as a day of thanksgiving.

- Minor, Manessah, *Diary, 1696-1720*, eds. Frank Denison Minor and Hannah Minor (Stonington, Connecticut: S. N., 1915), a, b, c, d.

1702- Alice Morse Earle wrote that Boston added James Francis Edward Stuart, the Prince of Wales, the son of James II, (the Pretender) and a Catholic – to be burnt in effigy.

- Earle, Alice Morse, *Customs and Fashions in Old New England* (New York: Charles Scribner's Sons, 1893), 230.

1702-mid-October- in Marblehead, Essex, Josiah Cotton, schoolmaster, noted that a "poor fellow" had made plans for practicing the English custom on the holiday by baiting a bull, slaughtering the thing, and giving the meat to the poor.

- Cotton, Josiah, Letter to Rowland Cotton, October 17, 1701, ed. Robert E. Moody, *Collections of the Massachusetts Historical Society* 80 (1972): 171.

1702, Marblehead: The fifth of November with bull baiting. The meat was given to the poor.

-"Josiah Cotton to Rowland Cotton, October 17, 1702," Massachusetts Historical Society, Collections, 80 (1972), 271. Joseph B. Felt, Annals of Salem, II (Salem, 1849), 50-55 and Joshua Coffin, History of Newbury (Boston, 1845), 288-289. Cited in: "Deliverance from Luxury: Pope's Day, Conflict and Consensus in Colonial Boston", 1745-1765, Francis D. Cogliano, *Studies in Popular Culture*, Vol. 15, No. 2 (1993), pp. 15-28.


1703- The Gunpowder Treason poem submitted to William and Mary College was on Francis Nicholson, the governor, co-founder of the college:

"What worthy thanks may I pour forth from a remembering heart,
Or what thanks may I ready to return, O most famous man, for your gifts
So great and so many, so readily heaped upon me by you?
You have won for me as a seat of the Muses two estates, great and rich,
Twice ten thousand fruitful acres of land,
And you have obtained for me a charter replete with generous benefactions.
. . .
And while many resisted, to me readily were rendered
Art, virtue, probity, and modest manners by you.
Henceforth it is not necessary to seek other lands lying under another sun
And at a distance across the sea from my native country,
. . .
But what have I said? May God turn this omen away from us!
Late may you return into the sky. For a long time may Virginia,
Its school, its clergy, and its church, possess you.
May you remain here, rejoicing in these, making the people happy all around."

- Jones, Julian Ward, "A 'New' Latin Quitrent Poem of the College of William and Mary," *Virginia Magazine of History and Biography* 96.4 (1988): 500.

1704, 1705, 1706, 1708, 1711, 1718, 1719 - Even though Quakers did not observe the days of the Church of England, one Quaker Jacob Taylor, proclaimed Fifth, in print specifically in almanacs. The same was done by Quaker-turned-Anglican publisher Daniel Leeds, in Newport and New York City, his almanac of 1713.

- Taylor, Jacob, An *Almanack for the Year of Our Lord* . . . (Philadelphia: Tiberius Johnson, et al., 1704, 1718, 1719); Taylor, Jacob, *Ephemeris Sideralis. A (Mathematical) Almanack for the Year of Our Lord* . . . (Philadelphia: Tiberius Johnson, et al., 1705, 1706); Taylor, Jacob, *An Almanack for the Year of Christian Account* . . . (Philadelphia: s.n., 1708, 1711). Leeds, Daniel, *Leeds 1713. The American Almanack for the Year of Christian Account 1713* . . . (Newport and New York: William Bradford, 1712).

1704- In early 1704, the Common Council of New York requested that the treasury pay the mayor's office a sum of over £5 owed for the costs of the bonfire and the wine from the fall before.

-Osgood, ed., *Minutes of the Common Council of the City of New York*, II: 121.

1704, November- Edward Hyde (the Earl of Clarendon, the Lord Cornbury) the governor of New York, wrote to the Lords of Trade, noting that the colony had run low on gunpowder because the city had, again, celebrated the day.

-Lord Corbury, Letter to the Lords of Trade – Details of Provincial Affairs, November 6, 1704, in

*Documents*, ed. O'Callaghan, IV: 1123.

1705- Williamsburg, Virginia, the anniversary of the failure of the plot, the Houses of Burgesses sxplained the need for oaths of allegiance and supremacy and that they would: "extinguishing the hopes of the pretended prince of Wales, all other
pretenders," and threats to church and the state.

- McIlwaine, H. R., ed., *Journals of the House of Burgesses of Virginia, 1702-3 to 1705, 1705 to 1706, 1710 to 1712* (Richmond: Colonial Press, E. Waddey Co., 1912), 43, 62.

1709- Williamsburg, Virginia, James Blair, Church of England minister and president of the college, celebrated the holy day, composing and delivering a quitrent-poem as required by the charter.

-Jones, "A 'New' Latin Quitrent Poem".

1709- November 5, Boston, Samuel Sewall walked at night and found the city "quiet and in good order" but had suffered "jealous[y]" that the day did not bring disturbance

- Thomas, M. Halsey, ed. *The Diary of Samuel Sewall. 1674-1729*. 2 Vols. New York: Farrar, Straus, and Giroux, 1973.920-21, 933, 936.

1710- The Rev. John Sharpe, the chaplain of New York noted that the Rev. William Vesey, rector of Trinity Church, gave an anniversary sermon on "Gunpowder Treason.

-Manuscript Division of the Historical Society of Pennsylvania, "Journal of Rev. John Sharpe," *Pennsylvania Magazine of History and Biography* 40.3 (1916): 257-97.

1710- New York City, in 1710, William Bradford printed the first copy of the Book of Common Prayer published in Anglo-America including the old "A Form of Prayer with Thanks-giving, to Be Used Yearly Upon the 5th Day *November*." Which offered thanks for "the happy Deliverance of King *James* the first" and the happy Arrival of King *William*." (Five years later, Bradford published it as an abridgement, "translated into the Mahaque Indian language." The Gunpowder section was not included)

-The Church of England, *The Book of Common-Prayer, . . .* (New York: William Bradford, 1710).

1711- Joshua Hempstead, (attorney, carpenter, deputy, farmer, militia-man, representative, selectman, and surveyor) noted the celebration of the 5th New London, Connecticut : "ye Saylors made a Bonfire in ye evening."

- Hempstead, Joshua, *Diary, 1711-58*, ed. New London County Historical Society (New London, Connecticut: New London County Historical Society, 1901), 3.

1711- Williamsburg, Virginia 1711, William Byrd, planter, and lieutenant-governor Alexander Spotswood accompanied "several ladies" in enjoying a bonfire that "the boys" of William and Mary had made on campus.

- Wright, Louis B. and Marion Tinling, eds., *The Secret Diary of William Byrd of Westover, 1709-1712* (Richmond, Virginia: Dietz Press, 1941), 432-33.

1712, November 4, Maryland, State.

p. 755  Carryed down to the House by Col Holland and Col Greenberry Col Addison & Col Tilghman


The Board adjourned until one of the Clock to morrowbeing the 5th Novem[r] and Gunpowder Treason Day

Wednesday November the 5th 1712

*-Proceedings and Acts of the General Assembly (Maryland), October 25, 1711-October 19, 1714.*

1712- "the whole House" of the Maryland assembly, in Annapolis, remembered "the Anniversary Day of Thanksgiving for the Delivery from the Gunpowder Plot."
It "repaired to the Church," returning after the Anglican service.

Browne, William H., and the Maryland Historical Society, *Archives of Maryland. 29. Proceedings and Acts of the General Assembly of Maryland, October 25, 1711–October 19, 1714* (Baltimore: Maryland Historical Society, 1909), 147.

> Proceedings and Acts of the General Assembly of Maryland
> October 23, 1711 - October 9, 1714
> Volume 29
> Preface
> Wednesday 5th Nov. 1712.
>   This being the Anniversary Day of Thanksgiving for the
>   Delivery from the Gunpowder Plot the Honble Speaker at
>   tended by the whole House repaired to the Church and after
>   Divine Service and Sermon ended The House met according p. 348
>   to Adjournment. Being called over were present as yesterday
>     Read what was done yesterday.
>     Matthew Mason's Petition again read and .debated.
>     Put to the Question whether the House will proceed therein
>   this Session or not? Resolved in the Affirmative and Leave
>   given to bring in a Bill as prayed
>     The Report of the Conferrees brought into the House

http://www.mdarchives.state.md.us/megafile/msa/speccol/sc2900/sc2908/000001/000029/html/am29--147.html

William Kilty's A report of all such English statutes as existed at the time of the first emigration of the people of Maryland, and which by experience have been found applicable to their local and other circumstances;...
Volume 143 The one-hundred and forty-third volume of the Archives of Maryland series was originally published in 1811.

> STATUTES NOT FOUND APPLICABLE........
>           STATUTES.
>   3 James 1.--A. D. 1605.
>           STATUTES.
>     CHAP. 1.  An act of a public thanksgiving to
>   Almighty God, every year on the fifth day of November.
>     CHAP. 6.  Merchants.
>     CHAP. 7.  Attornies.
>     CHAP. 8.  An act to avoid unnecessary delays
>   of executions.

http://www.mdarchives.state.md.us/megafile/msa/speccol/sc2900/sc2908/000001/000143/html/am143--88.html

1711- New York, mid-October, the city council told the Treasury that it was responsible for "providing all things Necessary" for the celebration.

-Osgood, ed., *Minutes of the Common Council of the City of New York,* II: 256-57, 452-53; III: 51, 77-78, 187-88, 192, 217-18.

1713- New York, November 3, the corporation ordered that seven gallons of wine be obtained for the celebration.

-Osgood, ed., *Minutes of the Common Council of the City of New York,* II: 256-57, 452-53; III: 51, 77. 78, 187-88, 192, 217-18. -

1713- Boston, Richard Steere published *The Daniel Catcher*, describing Catholicism as a religion of "*Rapine, Rebellion, Treason, Fire,* and *Blood,*" of "vip'rous Brood." He asked: Can *Eighty-Eight* [the Glorious Revolution], the Cursed *Powder Plot,* And STROMBOLIAN LONDON [the Great Fire of 1666] be forgot?

- Steere, Richard, *The Daniel Catcher. The Life of the Prophet Daniel: in a Poem. To Which is Added, Earth's Felicities, Heaven's Allowances,* . . . (Boston: John Allen, 1713), 18.

1713-1715- John Wise of Ipswich, Massachusetts, clergyman He wrote that the proposed change "smell[ed] so strong of the POPE's cooks and kitchen, where his broths are prepared, that they are strong enough to strangle a *Free-Born English Man.*" In: *The Churches Quarrel Espoused, or, A Reply in Satyre,* he noted that the proposal – or "design," was first presented on November 5, 1705, centennial of the Gunpowder Plot. In pushing the point, he suggested that "the CABAL" lead by the Mathers had purposefully chosen this date. Wise wanted people to remember the importance of the Fifth in the debate:

"The [day] has been as a *Guardian Angel* to the most Sacred Interest of the Empire: It has rescued the whole Glory of Church & State from the most fatal Arrest of Hell and *Rome.* . . . [W]e are *Every Man* [in New England] *Ruined*, being *Running Faux's Fate*! . . . [For, the cabal] intend[s] the Blowing up [of] the Churches, as *Faux's* did the Parliament".

- Wise, John, *The Churches Quarrel Espoused, or, A Reply in Satyre, to Certain Proposals Made, in Answer to This Question, What Further Steps Are to Be Taken, that the Councils May Have Due Constitution and Efficacy in Supporting, Preserving and Well Ordering the Interest of the Churches in the Country?* (New York: William Bradford, 1713; and Boston: Nicholas Boone, 1715),106-07, 141.

1714- New York, the aldermen and the assistants of the council ordered: "there be a Bonfire that Night at the usual place" and for 7 gallons of wine be drunk for "the Kings health" On "Gunpowder Treason day".

-Osgood, ed., *Minutes of the Common Council of the City of New York,* II: 256-57, 452-53; III: 51, 77-78, 187-88, 192, 217-18.

1716- New York, Long Island, Thomas Poyer Anglican minister delivered a sermon "Thanksgiving for the Failure of the Gunpowder Plot."

Onderdonk, Henry, ed., *Records kept by Rev. Thomas Poyer, Rector of Episcopal Churches at Jamaica, Newtown & Flushing, Long Island* (Brooklyn: S. N., 1913).

1716- New York City John Fontaine, traveler, watch-maker and Huguenot-Irish, drank "loyal healths" while in at the French club at what he then called "the tavern."

- Fontaine, James, Ann Maury, John Fontaine, and James Maury, *Memoirs of a Huguenot Family* (New York : G.P. Putnam & Co., 1872), 299.

1717- The *Boston News-Letter* covered stories from England that chronicled or referenced the Fifth of November. It published an account of the holy day in London in 1716:

"Yesterday being the Anniversary of the Gun-powder Plot, and of the Landing of the late King William, of Glorious Memory, to rescue these Nations from Popery and Slavery, the same was observed with the usual Solemnity."

-*Boston News-Letter*, May 27, 1717; *Boston News-Letter*, January 26, 1719.

1718- Boston, *The Practice of Piety*, a manual on godly living that Lewis Bayly, Anglican bishop first published in 1612, was re-published. It valued the Fifth of November, the date should be commemorated with charity, dancing, feasting, gift-giving, and psalm-reading.

- Bayly, Lewis, *The Practice of Piety: Directing a Christian How to walk, That He May Please God . . .* (Boston: B. Green, 1718), 269-70.

1718-1719- New York, the corporation again directed the commemoration in the streets of "the fifth day of November.

-Osgood, ed., *Minutes of the Common Council of the City of New York,* II: 256-57, 452-53; III: 51, 77-78, 187-88, 192, 217-18.

1719- Cotton Mather read *Mirabilia Dei*, the Fifth of November sermon in the Second Church of Boston. The sermon warns of the Papacy defeating the free world. -

1720- Franklin published a reprint of a work that Watts had written in 1719: *The Psalms of David, Imitated in the Language of the New Testament*, the pastor provided two psalms for the celebration, one identified as a critique for "Popish Idolatry" and another, "A Song for the 5th of November," that contained this quatrain:

We leap for Joy, we shout and sing,
Who just esape'd the fatal Stroke;
So flies the Bird with chearful Wing,
When once the Fowler's Snare is broke.

- Watts, Isaac, "Psalm 115" and "Psalm 124," *The Psalms of David, Imitated in the Language of the New Testament, and Apply'd to the Christian State and Worship.* . (Philadelphia: Benjamin Franklin, 1729), 239-40, 269.

1720- A Boston printing house published a new edition of *Hymns and Spiritual Songs. In Three Books* (1707-09) by minister Isaac Watts. It included "The Church Saved, and Her Enemies Disappointed," "a spiritual song, "composed on November 5, 1694, and stressed themes of antagonism, frustration, and salvation in this verse.

"Shout to the Lord, and let our Joys
Thro' the whole Nation run:
Ye *British* Skies, resound the Noise
Beyond the rising Sun.
Thee, Mighty God, our Souls admire,
Thee our glad Voices sing,
And join with the coelestial Choir,
To praise th' Eternal King.

Thy Pow'r the whole Creation rules,
And on the starry Skies
Sits smiling at the weak Designs
Thine envious Foes devise.
Thy Scorn derides their feeble Rage

And, with an awful Frown,
Flings vast Confusion on their Plots,
And shakes their Bable down.
[Their secret Fires in Caverns lay,
And we the sacrifice:
But gloomy Caverns strove in vain
To 'scape all-searching Eyes.
Their dark Designs were all reveal'd,
Their Treasons all betray'd:
Praise to the Lord, that broke the Snare
Their cursed Hands had laid.]
In vain the busy Sons of Hell
Still new Rebellions try,
Their Souls shall pine with envious Rage,
And vex away, and die.
Almighty Grace defends our Land
From their malicious Pow'r:
Let *Britain* with united Songs
Almighty Grace adore."

- Watts, Isaac, "The Church Saved, and Her Enemies Disappointed," *Hymns and Spiritual Songs. In Three Books. I. Collected From the Scriptures. II. Compos'd on Divine Subjects. III. Prepar'd for the Lord's Supper* . . . (Boston: s.n., 1720), 191-92.

1724
Concerning New England New York and Virginia

" It was complained in 1724 that the Virginians paid little attention to the two anniversaries of the gunpowder treason — the 5th of November and the 3oth of January. But the former of these was celebrated in some of the northern colonies by fire-works, by burning an effigy of Guy Fawkes, or by carrying about the village two hideous pumpkin faces, supposed to represent the Pope and the devil, and then consigning them to a bonfire. The pale shadow of this old celebration reaches to our time; boys in some New England coast towns still light their bonfires on the 5th of November, though quite unable to tell what for. In the region about New York forgetfulness has gone further; stacks of barrels are burned, not on the 5th, but on the evening of the November election day, by lads both Catholic and Protestant, none of whom have any interest in the gunpowder plot, or any suspicion that they are perpetuating in disguise a custom handed down to them from ancestors loyal to the throne and Parliament of England."

-Social Life in the Colonies, by Edward Eggleston: pp. 387-408  p. 400 The Century; a popular Quarterly. Volume 30, Issue 3 The Century Company   July 1885, New York.


1725- An almanac printed in Delaware first recorded Gunpowder Treason Day.

- Taylor, Jacob, *Taylor, 1726. A Compleat Ephemeris for the Year of Christ 1726* . . . (New Castle, Delaware: Samuel Keimer, 1725).

c. 1726- William G. Stanard wrote of Fifth in the Old Dominion: "On November 5th [the people] held a service of thanksgiving . . .

-Stanard, "Virginia Council Journals, 1726-1753," *Virginia Magazine of History and Biography* 32 (1924), 14.

1726- December – Along with ruling on a tax on liquor, the Commissioners for Trade and Plantations reviewing the1693 charter of the College of William and Mary, confirmed that the school must continue to "pay" the colony two Latin verses each Fifth of November. P. 181.

1728- Philadelphia. Samuel Keimer, founder of the *Pennsylvania Gazette*, printed and sold a translation of a history of Quakerism in Dutch, and first published in1688. It explained that, to prevent the birth of another Gunpowder Treason, the Oath of Allegiance passed in 1606 had had negative effect on the Society of Friends, and the Church of Rome, because Quakerism banned oath-taking and swearing. The oath had "continually" acted as "a Snare," bringing about imprisonment of many in the community, due to their refusal to swear loyalty to the kingdom and that the papacy had no authority in England. It also condemned the "malice" and the "wickedness" of this plot.

-- Sewel, William, *Histori van de Opkomste, Aanwas, en Vortgang der Christenen, Bekend by den Naam van Quakers* [*The History of the Rise, Increase, and Progress, of the Christian People Called Quakers: Intermixed with Several Remarkable Occurrences . . .*], trans. Samuel Keimer (Philadelphia: Printed and Sold by Samuel Keimer, 1728), 258.

1728- November 3- , Thomas Paine, minister of the Congregational Church of Weymouth, Massachusetts, gave a sermon giving thanksgiving for God, sparing New England of a real disaster in the earthquake that had hit the area on October 29. The sermon also noted that God had often saved the English world from "the alarmed Rage of *Hell*, and the *popish Powers* on Earth, at the Progress of the Reformation" in the face of "the invincible Armado" and, in the Gunpowder Plot, "a Cruelty black and vile enough to compare with the worst Intreagues of Hell."

- Paine, Thomas, *The Doctrine of Earthquakes: Two Sermons Preached at a Particular Fast in Weymouth, Nov. 3. 1727 . . .* (Boston: Printed for D. Henchman).

1728- William Byrd II, Virginia aristocrat, wrote the *History of the Dividing Line Betwixt Virginia and North Carolina* in 1728. In a survey of the border he noted that, with "the memory of the gunpowder treason-plot . . .still fresh in every body's mind and . . . [with] England too hot for papists to live in, without danger of being burnt with the pope, every 5th of November," Maryland had become a haven for Catholicism. "Not only the gunpowder treason, but every other plot, both pretended and real, that has been trumped up in England ever since, has helped to people".

- Byrd, William, *The Westover Manuscripts Containing the History of the Dividing Line Betwixt Virginia and North Carolina, . . .*, eds. Edmund Ruffin and Julian C. Ruffin (Petersburg, Viginia: E. and J.C. Ruffin, 1841).

1729- Boston, Benjamin Walker merchant, wrote in his journal: "some men brought through the North End . . . the Pope in a chair," raising this effigy around the city on the Fifth.

- Walker,Benjamin, Diary, Massachusetts Historical Society, November 5, 1729. See also Francis D. Cogliano, *No King, No Popery: Anti-Catholicism in Revolutionary New England* (Westport, Connecticut: Greenwood Press, 1995), 25.

Late 1730s- "The first sign that New Englanders were carrying and burning effigies of the pope and the devil came in the late 1730s, or about sixty years after these events had reached their height in London in 1680."

-Benes, Peter, "Night Processions: Celebrating the Gunpowder Plot in England and New England," in *New England Celebrates: Spectacle, Commemoration, and Festivity*, Dublin Seminar for New England Folklife Annual Proceedings 2000 (Boston: Boston University, 2002), p.11.

1730s and beyond- The crowd revitalized the anniversary, adding noise and violence
It was organized on behalf of an ideology of religion – an argument asserting the righteousness of Protestantism and the wickedness of Catholicism. The crowd that assembled on the Fifth re-politicized the day in the middle of the eighteenth century, stressing its hatred for absolutism in politics and religion. Marks beginning of gradual movement of this anniversary from assemblies, churches, and townhouses into the newspapers and, also, onto the streets.

1731&1737- The legislature of Rhode Island prohibited acts of "Mischief," including the "firing of Guns and Pistols" and the "throwing of Squibs, Fire-Works, &c." in the lanes, the streets, or the taverns, of the province, "on any Night whatsoever." And that, "Custom . . .notwithstanding," "no Bonfire [should] be made on the Fifth of November" unless a town had in fact authorized such a fire." Punishments ranged from twenty-shilling fines for first offenses to month-long prison terms for third offenses.

-Rhode Island, *The Charter, Granted by His Majesty, King Charles II. to the Governor and Company of the English Colony of Rhode-Island and Providence-Plantations, in New-England, in America* (Newport: Samuel Hall, 1767), 120-21.

1732- Philadelphia, Benjamin Franklin started printing *Poor Richard's Almanack* in which he noted that the Fifth of November was: "Powder Plot, 1605."

- Franklin, Benjamin, *Poor Richard, 1733. An Almanack for the Year of Christ 1733*, . . . (Philadelphia: Benjamin Franklin, 1732.

1732, November 4- Jonathan Belcher, governor of Massachusetts,
Proclaimed:

*"Whereas divers Persons have of late presumed to throw Squibs, Serpents and
Rockets, and other Fire-Works in the Streets of Boston, and from off the Houses
within the same, to the endangering [of] the Buildings of the Town, and great
Annoyance of Persons passing thro' the Streets thereof, in Violation of the Law of this Province,(1700) which
strictly forbids the throwing [of] all such Fire-works in the
Streets, Lanes, and Alleys of the Town . . . upon the Penalty of Twenty Shillings
Fine for every such Offense, or Corporal Punishment or Imprisonment."*

-*New-England Weekly Journal*, November 6, 1732.

1735- Nathaniel Ames, Sr. astronomer-innkeeper-physician and almanac publisher since 1725, entered in an almanac : "Gun Powder Plot/We ha'n't forgot." More than the
"Gun Powder Plot" or "Gun Powder Plot, 1605," of earlier editions.

- Ames, Nathaniel *An Astronomical Diary, or an Almanack for the Year of Our Lord Christ 1735* . . .
(Boston: Printed for the Booksellers and Sold at Their Shops, 1734).

1735 and 1742- Boston, Daniel Henchman, bookseller reprinted - *The Sincere Convert: Discovering the Small Number of True Believers and the Great Difficulty of Saving Conversion* (1641) by Thomas Shepard. Referred to the plot of 1605 that: "Ignorance" of God is "the first Rock, or the first Powder-Plot," of damnation.

- Shepard, Thomas, *The Sincere Convert: Discovering the Small Number of True Believers and the Great Difficulty of Saving Conversion. Newly Corrected and Amended* . . . (Boston: John Draper, Printed for Daniel Henchman, 1735, 1742), 132.

1735 -November 10- The *Boston Evening-Post* printed a history of the Powder Plot noting:

"[T]he 5th of this Instant *November*, the Guns were fired at Castle *William*, in Token of Joy for the happy Deliverance of our Nation from one of the most horrid and Damnable Conspiracies that ever was contrived by *Hell* and *Rome* . . . and [adopted by] a desperate Ruffian named *Guy Fawks*, . . . [whom in defeat] said, he was sorry it came not to Perfection, affirming, *That God would have concealed it, and the Devil only discovered it.*"

It also printed:

"In the evening there was a Bonfire on *Dorchester* Neck, and several in this Town, and there were a variety of Fire-Works play'd off upon this Occasion, both on the Land and on the Water. The same Evening 4 young Men of this Town, went in a Cannoe (as we are told) to see the Bonfire on [the] Neck, and have not been heard of since; so that 'tis greatly feared they were drowned in their return home."

-Boston," *Boston Evening-Post*, November 10, 1735.

1735- November,6: *Boston News-Letter*: "A large bonfire was made at Dorchester-Neck and many curious Fire-works played off; but by reason of thick Weather and a great Fall of Snow, the Splendor thereof was much diminish'd being scarce visible in Town."

1736- Thomas Prince, celebrity-historian, minister of the Old South Church in Boston, wrote *A Chronological History of New-England in the Form of Annals*. He included a three-paragraph history of the Powder Plot, stating that the plotters determined that, "when the Blast was made, it was to be charg'd on the Puritans." He condemned James I, stating that he had, on November 9, 1605, informed Parliament that he found the anti-popery of Puritanism as an evil "worthy of *Fire*."

- Prince, Thomas, *A Chronological History of New-England in the Form of Annals . . . From the Discovery by Capt. Gosnold in 1602, to the Arrival of Governor Belcher, in 1730. With an Introduction Containing a Brief Epitome of the Most Remarkable Transactions and Events Abroad, From the Creation: Including . . . the Gradual Discoveries of America, and the Progress of the Reformation to the Discovery of New-England* (Boston: Kneeland & Green, . . ., 1736), 16-17.

1736, November 12, Williamsburg Virginia- the College of William and Mary:

"[On] the Fifth . . ., the Presidents, Masters, and Scholars of *William* and *Mary* College, went, according to their Annual Custom, in a Body, to the Governor's [Palace], to present His Honour with Two Copies of *Latin* Verses, in Obedience to their Charter . . . Mr. President delivered the Verses to His Honour; and Two of the Young Gentlemen spoke them. It is further observed, that there were upwards of 60 Scholars present; a much great Number than has been in any Year before, since the Foundation of the College.

-Williamsburg, Nov. 12," *Virginia Gazette*, November 12, 1736.

1736- Williamsburg, Va. "Yesterday being the Anniversary Thanksgiving for the Gunpowder Treason Plot, when King, Lords and Commons were deliver'd from the bloody Designs of the Papists, was kept as usual."

-*Virginia Gazette*, Williamsburg, Feb. 4-11, 1736.

1737- The Boston papers noted that it being the Fifth of November, "Guns were fired at Castle William, in Commemoration of the happy and remarkable Deliverance of our Nation from Popery and Slavery, by the Discovery of the Gun Powder plot in the year 1605; and in the Evening there were Bonfires and other Rejoycings"

-Benes, Peter, "Night Processions: Celebrating the Gunpowder Plot in England and New England," in *New England Celebrates: Spectacle, Commemoration, and Festivity*, Dublin Seminar for New England Folklife Annual Proceedings 2000 (Boston: Boston University, 2002), p.16.

1737- Ames's *An Astronomical diary; or, an Almanack*: "Ere you pretend to burn the Pope / Secure the Papists with a Rope."

-Benes, Peter, *Night Processions: Celebrating the Gunpowder Plot in England and New England,*

(unpublished Mss.).

1737, 1738, and 1740: The selectmen of Boston directed John Savell to "take Effectual Care to prevent Spoil and Damage" to the fences, rails, the trees, of the Common, for "Bonfires &c." After all, with "it being the 5th. of Novr.," the town could not overlook that "large Numbers of Persons" would "meet there."

-Boston [MA] Registry Department, *A Report of the Record Commissioners of the City of Boston,* Vol. 15 (Boston: Rockwell and Churchill, City Printers, 1886), 81, 141, 259.

1737, Monday October 31- Saturday last, being the fifth of November, it was observed, here in Memory of the horrid and Treasonable Popish Gun-Powder Plot to blow up and destroy King, Lords and Commons, and the Gentlemen of his Majesty's Council, the Assembly and Corporation and other the principal Gentlemen and Merchants of this City waited upon his Honor the Leut. Governour at Port-George, where the Royal Health's were drank, as usual, under the Discharge of the Cannon, and at Night the City was illuminated.

-*New York Gazette* Monday October 31-Nov 7, 1737.

1737- The *Virginia Gazette* printed an editorial that had first appeared in a London paper in 1736; the text praised the deliverance of England, in 1605, from "the bloody designs of the Papists" and the rescue of 1688, from the "standing Armies [of James II] in Times of Peace." Again in 1737, the *Boston Gazette* printed a description of the holiday in Dublin, Ireland, in 1736:

When the Lord Justices had processed "in great State" to Christ Church, a cathedral of the Church of Ireland, the priest gave the congregation "an excellent Sermon, suitable to the Occasion." Later, the Lord Mayor and others, received a performance of *The Tragedy of Tamerlane* (1702), a drama used as commemoration of the landing of William III in 1688. Later just outside the gates of Trinity College:

"[T]he Constable of St. Andrew's Watch on Duty, being a very loyal Man, made a
Bonfire before the Effigie on College Green, and [setting] Candles in Lanthorns
above, . . . made a glorious Show, then paraded his Men, which were thirty in
Number, and he at the Head of them, . . . and [bearing] a half Pike . . ., he drank to
the immortal memory of King William, and made all his Men do the same, then
he march'd them in Ranks four men double, with their Candles lighted in their

Lanthorns and borne [atop] their Watch Pikes. At the end of this display, this cast had drunk healths in honor of the king and the House of Hanover, and, then, those keeping the day had "concluded the Night with all publick Marks of Joy."

-"London, Nov. 6," *Virginia Gazette*, February 11, 1737. "Kells, County of West-Meath, Oct. 31," *Boston Gazette*, January 31, 1737.

1737-"Gentlemen of his Majesty's Council, the Assembly and Corporation, and other principal Gentlemen and Merchants of this City waited upon" the lieutenant governor at Fort George, "where the Royal Healths were drank, as usual, under the Discharge of the Cannon and at Night the City was illuminated."

- Stokes, *Iconography,* IV, 554. From:*The Road to Mobocracy,* Paul A. Gilje, University of North Carolina Press, 1987.

1737- From: *An Astronomical Diary*:

"Ere you pretend
to burn the Pope
Secure the Papists
with a Rope."

- Ames, Nathaniel, An *Astronomical Diary, or an Almanack for the Year of Our Lord Christ . . .* , 1737-39).

1737- Monday October 31-Nov 7, New York Gazette,

Saturday last, being the fifth of November, it was observed, here in Memory of the horrid and Treasonable Popish Gun-Powder Plot to blow up and destroy King, Lords and Commons, and the Gentlemen of his Majesty's Council, the Assembly and Corporation and other the principal Gentlemen and Merchants of this City waited upon his Honor the Leut. Governour at Port-George, where the Royal Health's were drank, as usual, under the Discharge of the Cannon, and at Night the City was illuminated.

1738- George Whitefield, English celebrity-itinerant priest in the Church of England. In the 1730s, The Book of Common Prayer included the Gunpowder Treason Prayer. While crossing the Atlantic for a fund raising trip he felt the significance of the Fifth of November:

"This Day we rejoiced with trembling. For though we thereon commemorated our Deliverance from the *Gunpowder-Plot*, yet as our Circumstances call'd for Acts of Humiliation, I used Part of the Office of Commination, (besides solemn Prayer and Psalms three Times) and enlarged on these Words of St. *James*, "My Brethren, count it all Joy, when ye fall into diverse Temptations; [remembering] . . that the trying of your Faith worketh Patience: But let Patience have her perfect Work."

- Whitefield, George, *A Journal of a Voyage from Gibraltar to Georgia, . . . Containing Many Curious Observations* (Philadelphia: Printed and Sold by Benjamin Franklin, 1740), 17, 80-81.

1739, November 2- Governor Belcher of Massachusetts. At a meeting of the Governor's Council, condemned the "disorder" of the holiday and "other Days of publick Rejoycing," blaming "loose and dissolute People." He singled out the organization of companies, the "exacting" of money for the support of "diversions," and the "abuse" of homes and persons of those who would not contribute. The *Boston Evening Post* noted on the day of the Fifth that Belcher condemned the "Surprize and Terror" and "Violence" that this act of remembrance created. He called for the justices of the peace "take effectual Care" on the Fifth of November.

-"Boston," *Boston Evening Post*, November 5, 1739.

1739- Nathaniel Ames's Almanac: "Tho' the Plotters are rotten / the Plot's not forgotten."

-Benes, Peter, *Night Processions: Celebrating the Gunpowder Plot in England and New England*, (unpublished Mss.).

1740, September- Joseph Seccombe the pastor of the Congregational Church of Kingston, New Hampshire, presented a sermon: *A Plain and Brief Rehearsal of the Operations of Christ as God*, Deep in which he noted that God had spared the church of disaster referring to the Armada, the Gunpowder Plot and installation of William II.

- Seccombe, Joseph, A *Plain and Brief Rehearsal of the Operations of Christ as God* (Boston: Samuel Kneeland and Timothy Green, 1740), 10-11.

1740-

"Now for the Old Plot, the POPE goes to Pot.
The curst Pope stands in the Way, or I had told you the Day.
What heaven decrees, no Prudence can prevent."

- Ames, Nathaniel, An *Astronomical Diary, or an Almanack for the Year of Our Lord Christ* . . . , 1737-39).

1740s- The crowd exercised the politics in its ridicule of models of Charles Edward Stuart, the Pretender (i.e., the Catholic claimant to the throne), as well as those of the devil and the pope, warning Jacobites in British North America that the Glorious Revolution would not be reversed. And the inclusion of the Pretender in Pope's Day festivities revealed that the world of the crowd extended beyond the local; the people had some command of the politics of the Atlantic. The celebration moves into the Southeast. -

1740- Cambridge, Mass. Harvard College president and the trustees on November 5, decreed:
"(Considering the Disorders that have sometimes been [instituted] upon the 5th Day
of November) each Tutor shall charge his Pupils, that they should not throw
Squibs or Crackers within the College yard that Evening, & that They should
[not] dare to make destruction of any Fence . . . for any Bon-fire; and to be all at
their Chambers at nine a Clock, according to the Order of the College & that the
President be [advised?] to give like Direction[s] publicly after evening prayer[s]
on the Morrow." The college president, Edward Holyoke, did so on "the
morrow" at "the time abovementioned."

-Faculty Records, Harvard College, Vol. I: 1735-1752, Harvard University Archives, 132-33, 160-62.

1741- Cambridge, Mass. Harvard College ordered that the tutors must make sure that the pupils did not fire crackers "by Day or by Night." Every tutor heard the evening prayers, and the presidential warning, the next day. On November 7, the college tried and sentenced three students taking part in the firing of squibs in the College Yard. Each boy had to pay the school a five-shilling fine, offer "confessions" for the crimes, and undergo "a public Admonition" in Massachusetts Hall.

--Faculty Records, Harvard College, Vol. I: 1735-1752, Harvard University Archives, 132-33, 160-62.

1741- George Whitefield said that his regeneration was like an illumination like the ray of light that in 1605 shone from the "Eye" of God, "dart[ing] down into the Pit" under
Parliament saving England from "the Gun-Powder-Plot."

-Prescott, Benjamin, A *Letter to the Reverend Mr. George Whitefield, an Itinerant Preacher, With-in the Dominions of His Most Excellent Majesty George, II* . . . (Boston: D. Gookin, 1745), 7.

1742- In the almanac published in 1742, Nathanial Ames published "Tho' the Pope's burnt/he will be Pope still," for November 5.

- Ames, Nathaniel, Sr., *An Astronomical Diary, or, An Almanack for the Year of Our Lord Christ, 1743* . . . (Boston: John Draper, 1742).

1742- November 5, Friday, Georgia, Savannah,
The divine Service appointed for the day was duly observed, when Mr. Dobell read the prayers and after it one of the Church Homilies……Our Flag was hoisted in Commemoration of the day; but I was of Opinion, that burning more powder, would be a needless Waste, of what we might stand in Need of on a more urgent Occasion.

- Coulter, ed., *Journal of Wiliam Stephens*, I, p. 134.

1742- Georgia, then celebrated the holiday. Governor William Stephens directed
 "due observation" of the anniversary in Savannah, with a Church of England service and the raising of the British flag. The governor believed that "burning more powder, would be a needless waste, of what we might stand in Need of on a more urgent Occasion." The next year he proclaimed the Fifth an "annual Rejoycing day" of the territory, but he also called it "pretty antiquated". "The principal people of the Town" gathered at noon, for the firing of the guns at Fort Argyle, and the governor took part "drinking a few Glasses of Wine with the usual healths" to the monarchy in 1744 and 1745, and perhaps later.

- Coulter, E. Merton, ed., *The Journal of William Stephens* (Athens, Georgia: University of Georgia Press, 1958 and 1959), I: 134 and II: 36, 164, 248. For more on Stephens, see Julie Anne Sweet, *William Stephens: Georgia's Forgotten Founder* (Baton Rouge: Louisiana State University, 2010).

1743- Ames Almanac: "Tho' the Pope's burnt / he will be Pope still."

-Benes, Peter, *Night Processions: Celebrating the Gunpowder Plot in England and New England, (unpublished Mss.)*

1743- William Douglass, Scottish-born doctor-philanthropist noted in his almanac: that the "Papal Conspiracy" was a "festival" of the Church of England and wrote that "*King William* landed at Torbay, 1688." He listed the "Gun-Powder Plot" as one of the days
"observed in New-England."

- Douglass, William, Mercurius *Nov-Anglicanus: Or An Almanack Anno Domini 1743* . . . (Boston: Rogers and Fowle, 1743).

1743- Georgia, Savannah , "Expectations of our people in taking the usual notice" (re. 5th of November) the military tried in 1743 to limit celebration to flag raising…..not firing guns due to gunpowder shortage…people objected and he was forced to fire guns and joined in loyal toasts….

-Coulter, ed., *Journal of Wiliam Stephens*, Vol. II p. 36.

1745 -The Second Jacobite Rebellion.

1745- Nathaniel Ames wrote in his almanac that "Powder-Plot is not forgot;/'twill be observed by many a Sot."

-Ames, Sr., *An Astronomical Diary, . . .* 1746 (Boston: John Draper, 1745) .


1745 November 5, Boston- Residents of North End and South End built and paraded effigies of the Pope, at the same time "a vast Number of Negroes and white Servants, armed with Clubs, Staves, and Cutlashes," were "very abusive to the Inhabitants," they broke windows, demanded money (for liquor, etc.), and fired insults outside the homes of the wealthy. The companies of the two ends then met on Cornhill Street, and, there, the crowd was "so infatuated, as to fall upon each other with the utmost Rage and Fury." Bruising and injury occurred. The *Boston Evening-Post* wrote that some were "left for dead, and rendered incapable of any Business for a
long Time, to the great Loss and Damage of their respective Masters."

-"Boston," *Boston Evening-Post*, November 11, 1745.


1745, November 11- The *Boston Evening-Post* , "gentleman of character" wrote:

"What a *Scandal* and *Infamy* to a *Protestant Mob*, be it of the rudest and lowest *Sailor*; out of *Boston*, or even of the *Negroes* of the Town, to fall upon one another with *Clubs* and *Cutlasses*, in a Rage and Fury which only *Hell* could inspire, or *Devils* broke loose from their Chains there, could well represent! Is this a meet . . . Show of *Protestant Zeal* against *Popery*? Is this [act] to honour the Protestant Religion to the few *French Prisoners* of War that are left among us? or can our Children or Servants be *safe* in the Streets at such a Time, if such *Rioters* be permitted? Or (in a Word) what Madness must seize the *two Mobs*, . . . as they would appear against *Popery*, to fall upon *each other*, break one another's *Bones*, or dash one another's *Brains* out! Why *this Enormity*, above all others, should be winked at, and the Inhabitants of the Town, with their Dwellings, left to the Mercy of a rude and intoxicated Rabble, the very Dregs of the People, *black* and *white*; and why no more has been done to prevent or suppress such riotous Proceedings, which have been long growing upon us, and as long bewailed by all sober and orderly Persons, must be humbly left to our Betters to say.

A rebuttal was published November 21 in the *Boston Weekly News-Letter*, "that ancient Custom" maintained "the Aversion to Popery and Slavery" and wrote that ending the celebration in Boston, would be "a very invidious Affair." The author suggested that
the clergy stage an annual lecture series on the day noting that preaching, could just as well convey the "absurdity" and "impiety" of popery. The lecture series never happened.

- "Boston," Boston Evening-Post, November 11, 1745; Boston Weekly News-Letter, November 21, 1745.

1745- Nov'r 5., James Freeman- "Two Popes were made & carried thro the streets in the evening 1 from the N. & ye other from ye S. attended by a vast number of negroes & white servants w/ clubs &c., who were very abusive to ye inhab. insulting persons and breaking windows &c of such as did not give them money to their satisfaction, & even of those who had given them liberally, & ye 2 Popes meeting in Cornhill their followers fell upon one another w/ ye utmost rage & fury. Several were wounded & bruised & some left for dead, & rendered incapable of business for a long time. Fleets Evening Post"

-James Freeman notebook, 1745-1765. Massachusetts Historical Society

1745- Nov. 18, Boston.
"Tuesday last being the Anniversary of the Gunpowder Plot, two Popes were made and carried thro' the Streets in the evening, one from the North, the other from the South End of the Town, attended by a vast number of negroes and white servants, armed with clubs, staves and cutlashes, who were very abusive to the Inhabitants, insulting the Persons and breaking the windows,&c., of such as did not give them money to their satisfaction, and even many of those who had given them liberally; and the two Popes meeting in Corn-hill, their followers were so infatuated as to fall upon each other with the utmost Rage and Fury. Several were sorely wounded and bruised, some left for dead, and rendered incapable of any business for a long time to the great Loss and Damage of their respective Masters.….

I hope you will not suffer the grand fray, not to say bloody, that happen'd before your Door last Tuesday evening to pass off without a public rebuke; and such an one as becomes a person zealous as well for the Peace and Good Order of the State as the Church. What a scandal and Infamy to a Protestant Mob, be it of the rudest and lowest Sailors out of Boston, or even of the very negroes of the Town, to fall upon one another with Clubs and Cutlashes in a Rage and Fury which only Hell could inspire or the Devil broke loose from chains there could represent! Is this a meet or sufferable show of Protestant zeal against Popery? Is this to honor the Protestant religion to the few French prisoners of war that are left among us? Or can our children or servants be safe in the streets at such a time if such Rioters be permitted? Or in a word, what madness must seize the two mobs, united Brethren, as they would appear against Popery, to fall upon each other, break one another's Bones or dash one another's Brains out?
Why this enormity above all others should be winked at, and the Inhabitants of the Town with their Dwellings left to the mercy of a rude and intoxicated Rabble, the very Dregs of the People, black and white, and why no more has been done to prevent or suppress such Riotous proceedings, which have been long growing upon us, and as long bewailed by all sober Persons, must be humbly left to our betters to say."

- Weekly Post-Boy," Nov. 18, 1745.

1746- George Whitefield, itinerant minister in Marblehead, preached: "a very good sermon suitable" for "the fifth of November, that never to be forgotten day of thanksgiving," quoting Proverbs 14:28, reminded the church that "righteousness exalteth a nation."

- "Extract of a Letter From a Gentleman in Marblehead to One in This Place, Dated October 27, 1746,"
[Annapolis] *Maryland Gazette*, November 11, 1746, in Maryland Historical Society, *Early State Records Online*, MSA SC M 1278, pp. 363-64.

1746, May, Annapolis, Maryland, Alexander Hamilton spoke to the satire-social
Club, the Tuesday Club, on its one-year anniversary. He presented a history of holidays, including the Fifth. He observed that, even though the Roman Church denied the existence of the Gunpowder Plot, America, Britain, and Ireland observed this date "in commemoration of that Singular delivery from a horrid and bloody popish plot." He hoped that the celebration would continue.

- Hamilton, Alexander, *The History of the Ancient and Honorable Tuesday Club*, ed. Robert Micklus
(Chapel Hill: University of North Carolina Press, 1990), I: 214 and II: 306; Elaine G. Breslaw, *Records of the Tuesday Club of Annapolis, 1745-56* (Chicago: University of Illinois Press, 1988), 28-29, 292-98.

1746, February- Arthur Browne, missionary of the Society for the Propagation of the Gospel in Foreign Parts, Anglican church minister, Portsmouth, New Hampshire, recalled Treason in a sermon that attacked Catholicism and Jacobinism. The Church of Rome was described as "ravenous Wolves" a "savage" and he observed the "fit"-ness of the Fifth, and the importance that it be kept up due to the hellishness of the conspiracy.

- Browne, Arthur, *The Folly and Perjury of the Rebellion in Scotland, Display'd: In a Sermon Preach'd, . . . February the 23d 1745-6 . . .* (Boston: T. Fleet, 1746).

1746
"some of the Pope's attendences had some supper as well as Money given 'em at a House in Town. One of the Company happene'd to swallow a slilver spoon with his Victuals, Marked IHS. Whoever it was is desired to return it when it comes at hand"
-Boston Gazette
PDC


1748- November 1, - Boston, Justices of the peace proclaimed, that: disorder,"terror," and window-breaking of the celebration stop. They noted: rioting was a crime. The magistracy proclaimed that, on the Fifth, constables and justices would enforce the bill, keep the peace, and prosecute those who violated the law severity.

- *Boston Gazette, or Weekly Journal*, November 1, 1748.

That same month, in New York City, "a numerous Concourse of People" celebrated the day: The crowd carried the Devil, "his Un[holi]ness the Pope," and the Pretender in front of "the Gentlemen" in the city, then burnt them in the Commons.

At this point, the *New-York Gazette, Revived in the Weekly Post- Boy* learned of the the government's proclamation posted in Boston, and, on November 11, it concluded:

"[I]t seems the Magistrates of [Boston] have resolved . . . to put a Stop to a riotous
and tumultuous Assembly that annually parades [through] that Town, on the
Evening of the 5th of November; whilst we, 'tis feared, are just a going to begin
that *silly* Practice"

The *Gazette* wrote of a procession that occurred in the city earlier in that week, noting that a "grand" march, "the first of the Kind in these Parts," had traveled the streets, smashing windows that were not illuminated. Not liking this action one bit, the paper wrote that no good could come from the festivity and encouraged that it end. New York City was "a Part of the World too much already deviated from the Rules of true Christianity."

- "New-York," *New-York Weekly Journal*, November 7, 1748; "New-York, November 7," *New-York Gazette, Revived in the Weekly Post-Boy*, November 11, 1748.

1748- Until this time the holiday was celebrated as an official holiday. Then New Yorkers adopted the custom as practiced in Boston- "parading and then by burning effigies of the pope, the Pretender, and the devil"

-*Weekly Journal*, Nov. 7 1748, *Gazette: Post-Boy*, Nov. 7,1748, in: Gilje, Paul A., *The Road to Mobocracy*, , University of North Carolina Press, 1987 .

1749- NOVEMBER. IX Month., Poor Richard improved: Being an Almanack and Ephemeris ... for the Year of our Lord 1749

The 5th of this month, NOVEMBER, seems to be a lucky day to the English church and British liberty; for on that day 1604, the popish gunpowder treason was detected; and on the same day in 1688, our glorious deliverer from popery and slavery, King WILLIAM, landed at Torbay. Eighty-eight seems likewise a lucky year; for in 1588 was the Spanish Armada defeated.

-Poor Richard improved: Being an Almanack and Ephemeris ... for the Year of our Lord 1749. ... By Richard Saunders, Philom. Philadelphia: Printed and Sold by B, Franklin, and D. Hall.).

1749- William Douglass almanac writer, appreciated the evil of the plot and that the papacy was responsible. He noted that the celebration "for some Years past" had become more intense in Massachusetts. "Several *Mobs*" had performed "*Pageants*" of the Pope, Devil, and Pretender. The government did not approve of "increase" in the mob activity and, had responded and had passed "some more severe Acts against *Riots, Mobs,* and *Tumults*". The "mobile vulgus" he maintained was a cause of danger. He saw "the most numerous and outrageous Muster of this *Mob*," in Boston, on November 5, 1747, which he thought caused the Knowles impressment riots (November 1621, 1747) that had brought out "several thousands" protesting a factor of the Royal Navy. However, he thought that the mob had "very good" cause.

- Douglass, William, A *Summary, Historical and Political, of the First Planting, Progressive Improvements, and Present State of the British Settlements in North-America* (Boston: Rogers and Fowle, 1749), 225-26, 239.

1749- Dr. William Douglass, physician, historian, and cartographer, writing about New England, compared these pageants to press gangs which were used by British naval officers to provide seamen for their vessels. "For some years past, upon the 5th of Nov. being the anniversary Gunpowder Treason Day, several Mobs have carried about pageants of the Pope, the Devil, and Pretender; these gunpowder Treason Mobs yearly increase: a few days after the gun-powder Treason Pageantries or Mobs, an Impress in Boston harbor with the recent accident of two Men in Boston, being murdered by a Press-gang, occasioned a very great Tumult in Boston."- Douglass, *Op.cit.*

-Benes, Peter, *Night Processions: Celebrating the Gunpowder Plot in England and New England,*

*(unpublished Mss.).*

1749- Following the holiday that year, a Bostonian advertised in the *Gazette*, noting that a silver spoon had been lost after "some of the Pope's Attendance" had had supper and had "happen'd to swallow" the thing. The author requested the spoon be returned.

-Advertisement, *Boston Gazette*, November 14. 1749.

c. 1749-1831- Isaiah Thomas, printer, remembered the 5th in Boston, suggesting that "in no part of the British dominions" had "the 5th" been "carried to greater length than in Boston." As a youth, he, too, had joined the crowd in honoring this date, remembered how stages no less than "16 or 18 feet" in length, "3 or 4 feet" in width, and "3 or 4" deep were "placed on cart wheels and Drawn by horses" on the streets of this city. He had observed as the pageantry unfolded:

"Men to boys of all sizes and ages exhibited [a host of] Effigies [of the Devil and the Pope] . . . Little boys had [the effigies] placed on shingles, bigger Boys [atop] a piece of a board no bigger than one boy could carry in his hands, others would require 2 or more boys, and so on. On the front of these stages [stood] . . . a large lantern framed circular at the top and covered with paper. Behind this Lantern was placed . . . the pope sitting in a . . . chair . . . [and] immediately behind him, . . . the Devil. . . . Inside the Stages and out of sight sat a boy under each effigy whose business it was to move the heads of the Effigies by means of . . . poles . . . from one side to another as fancy directed. . . . The Devil was . . .

tarred in order to hold a thick coat of feathers . . . that extended from his neck to his heels. . . . The Great Lanthorn . . . was 6 or 9 feet high, as wide as the stage, covered with . . . paper, on which were various labels, ugly and uncouth figures, on the sides, but on the front . . . was wrote or painted in as large Letters as the biggness of the Lanthorn would permit, "The Devil takes the Pope."
He was struck in the head with "a piece of brick" aimed at a lantern of the "competition" between the two ends, Otis described a romantic portrait of this event. He remembered that, on each team, a captain gave orders in "the harsh sound of a Boatswain of a Man of War," and he noted the "free use" of brickbats, clubs, fists, and stones notwithstanding, "persons were," "but seldom killed."

- Thomas, Isaiah, Three *Autobiographical Fragments; Now First Published Upon the 150th Anniversary of the Founding of the American Antiquarian Society* (Worcester: American Antiquarian Society, 1962), 22-25., Thomas, Isaiah and Benjamin Franklin Thomas, "Memoir of Isaiah Thomas," *The History of Printing in America: With a Biography of Printers, Vol. 1*, in *Transactions and Collections of the American Antiquarian Society*, Vol. V (Worcester: Printed for the Society, 1874), xxviii-xxxi., Marble, Annie Russell, *From 'Prentice to Patron: The Life Story of Isaiah Thomas* (New York: D. Appleton-Century, 1935); and, also, Clifford K. Shipton, *Isaiah Thomas: Printer Patriot and Philanthropist, 1749-1831* (Rochester, New York: Hart, 1948).


1750s - 1760s- The legislatures outlawed the street theater of the Fifth. Due to the Fifth of November giving "the common sort" agency, confraternity, expression, and power.
Some forms of crowd action on the Fifth were criminalized. -

1750-The diary of Captain Francis Goelet, New York merchant visiting Boston in 1750: After dinner went with some of the company to the north end the towne. Bought Some Limes &c., where we saw the devil and the Pope &c. carried about by the mob, represented in effegy, very drole. Soone after see two more of them, but the justices, feareing some outrages may be committed, put a stop to them.

- Francis Goelet, *The Voyages and Travels of Francis Goelet, 1746–1758*, ed. Kenneth Scott (Queens, N.Y.: Queens College Press, 1970), "Diary," 5 November 1750.

-Benes, Peter, *Night Processions: Celebrating the Gunpowder Plot in England and New England*,

(unpublished Mss.)

-Anonymous, "Extracts From Captain Francis Goelet's Journal, Relative to Boston, Salem and Marblehead, &c., 1746-1750," *New-England Historical and Genealogical Register and Antiquarian* 24.1 (Jan. 1870): 60-63. -

1750, October- The magistracy wrote the *Boston Gazette observed that* people, armed, "disguis'd," and rude, were fined "several Hundred Pounds" for their crimes of November 5, 1749. To warn the "audacious" and reassure the anxious, the magistracy proclaimed that constables and "substantial Householders" would keep watch.

-*Boston Gazette, or Weekly Journal*, October 30, 1750. -

1750- Two silver beakers, three inches tall and wide, by silversmith Daniel Christian Fueter and engraver Joseph Leddel, Jr., engraved in New York City Described by Ian M. G. Quimby:

"(1) [the] head of [a] beast with jaws agape, flame emerging from mouth, smoke from eyes and nostrils; amid flames: "Hell" in roman letters
(2) [a] full-length male figure with [a] hairy body, cloven feet, horns, and snakes for hair, a serpent entwined around his body; his left hand holds a flail with 3 snakes emerging from the end; the flail is directed toward the fires of hell; chain leads from this figure back through a gate of 2 fluted columns and an arch with a

death's head and inscription: "DEATH" in roman letters
(3) the chain from the gate is attached to the nose of a standing male figure, wearing a mi-ter and ecclesiastical garments, who carries a cross in his right hand and a rope in his left;
(4) the rope runs from the mitered figure through a gallows to the neck of a standing male figure attired in tam-o'-shanter, plaid shawl, knee breeches, shoes, and a sword."

This poem is below the rim:

I WISH THEY WERE ALL HANG'D IN A ROPE
THE PRETENDER DEVIL AND THE POPE.
THREE MORTAL ENEMIES REMEMBER.
THE DEVIL THE POPE AND THE PRETENDER.
MOST WICKED DAMNABLE AND EVIL.
THE POPE THE PR[E]TENDER AND THE DEVIL.

-Ian M. G. Quimby, *American Silver at Winterthur* (Winterthur: Henry Francis du Pont Museum, 1995), 230-32.

A inscription on one cup may indicate that the Samuels, a Jewish family of New York, owned it. Neil Kamil, historian writes: "America and England [become] harnessed by the neck to Charles Stuart as their monarch, it would be the equivalent of marching in lockstep behind the damned" to the belly of the beast.

-Neil Kamil, *Fortress of the Soul: Violence, Metaphysics, and Material Life in the Huguenot's New World, 1517-1751* (Baltimore: Johns Hopkins University Press, 2005), 912.

- Quimby, Ian M. G., *American Silver at Winterthur* (Winterthur: Henry Francis du Pont Museum, 1995), 230-32.

1751- Annapolis, Maryland, The Tuesday Club. describing a local evening robbery, accomplished with a lantern and a pistol, as "unmatched villainy, [that] can
scarce be paralleled in history, or meet with its equal in the annals of time, nay, not even ... Guy Fox, that Infernal Tool of the Gunpowder Treason with his dark Lanthorn, can match the barbarity of this att[empt]."

- Hamilton, Alexander, *The History of the Ancient and Honorable Tuesday Club*, ed. Robert Micklus (Chapel Hill: University of North Carolina Press, 1990), I: 214 and II: 306; Elaine G. Breslaw, *Records of the Tuesday Club of Annapolis, 1745-56* (Chicago: University of Illinois Press, 1988), 28-29, 292-98.

1751
George Washington Diary from Barbados referring to celebration of Guy Fawkes Day Voyage to Barbados 1751--52 Page 36

the captain's name, if he had just debarked from it after several weeks on the "fickle & Mirciless Ocean" (p. 69). Also, it is not likely that a vessel arriving in port on 2 Oct. would be preparing to sail by 6 Oct. MRS. CLARKE & MISS ROBTS.: Mrs. Mary Clarke, wife of Gedney Clarke, and her niece Elizabeth Roberts. TO COME & SEE THE SERPTS. FIR'D: Serpents, or fireworks discharged in commemoration of Guy Fawkes Day, 5 Nov. This remark enables us to correct the dating of the diary entries made during this period.

-From: The Diaries of George Washington. Vol. 1. Donald Jackson, ed.; Dorothy Twohig, assoc. ed. The Papers of George Washington. Charlottesville: University Press of Virginia, 1976.
(editor's Note: that is he got the date wrong!).

1752-*Boston Post Boy,* November 6:"in order to prevent any Disturbances within the Town of Boston, This Evening, by carrying about what is commonly called the Pope (in Commemoration of the 5th of November) and demanding Money of the Inhabitants, and breaking the Windows of such as refuse to give them any, or by inkindling Bonfires," masters and heads of families should "to retain their Children and Servants, more especially their Negroes, from being abroad in the Evening.

-Benes, Peter, *Night Processions: Celebrating the Gunpowder Plot in England and New England, (unpublished Mss.)* .

1752- A force of "his Majesty's Justices of the Peace" - and, "a very considerable Number of the Inhabitants" – informed the city of Boston that it would police with "more than common Care" in the evening, to stop breaking windows, demanding money, "inkindling" of bonfires, and injury or intimidation. It announced that transgressions these rule prohibitions would incur "the strictest Rigour" of the law, and it closed noting that that heads-of-households and masters must "retain" children, servants, and "more especially . . . Negroes," from "being abroad" at night, on the 5th.

-*Boston Post Boy*, November 6, 1752.

1752- A sailor John Crabb, was killed in a fight related to the celebration of Pope's Day by "a lad named Chubb and a Negro Fellow. w." Thomas Chubb, a sailor, and Abraham, a slave of William Pitman, clubbed Crabb to death. Chubb was branded on the hand and imprisoned for twelve months for his part.

-*The Boston Weekly News-Letter*, November 23,1752. Cited in: "Deliverance from Luxury: Pope's Day, Conflict and Consensus in Colonial Boston", 1745-1765, Francis D. Cogliano, *Studies in Popular Culture*, Vol. 15, No. 2 (1993), pp. 15-28.

1752- November 23- Governor's Council noted that "many grievous disorders have been committed in the town of Boston on the evening of the fifth of November and the Pageants or Show generally made use of on that occasion having of late years been greatly multiplied the disorders have proportionally increased." A committee was created to consider legislation to stop the disorders.

- Massachusetts Archives, MA 47:357-359. Cited in: "Deliverance from Luxury: Pope's Day, Conflict and Consensus in Colonial Boston, 1745-1765", Francis D. Cogliano, *Studies in Popular Culture*, Vol. 15, No. 2 (1993), pp. 15-28.

1753- The *Boston Evening Post* published a report of the day what is now Ghana, "tis great pity [November 5] ever should pass without very sensibly affecting the Mind." In the paper regretted that the "common sort" celebrate the day with a "sensible" mind

-"Extract of a Letter from Cape Coast Castle, Dated June 4. 1752," *Boston Evening Post*, January 22, 1753.

1753- Charleston  A newspaper wrote "The anniversary of our happy Deliverance from a most horrid Popish Plot, and the glorious Revolution...was observed here as usual.

-South Carolina Gazette, Nov. 16, 1753.

1753- General Court of Massachusetts  banned  "pageants" in the streets for purposes  of "demanding and exacting money":

Whereas . . . tumultuous companies of men, children and negroes [have as of late] .
. . abus[ed] and insult[ed] the inhabitants, . . . be it therefore enacted . . . [t]hat if
any persons, being more than three in number, and being arm'd all or any of them
with sticks, clubs or any kind of weapons, or disguised with vizards, . . . or painted
or disco[u]lour[e]d faces . . . shall assemble together, having any kind of imagery or

pageantry . . . shall, by menaces or otherwise, exact, require, demand or ask any money or other thing of value from any[one], in the streets, lanes or houses of any town [in] this province, each person being assembled with such company, shall for each offence forfeit and pay the sum of forty shillings, or suffer imprisonm[en]t not exceeding one month; or if the offender shall be a negro servant, in lieu of the imprisonm[en]t, he may be whip['t] not exceeding ten stripes, at the discretion of the justice before whom the trial shall be.

- Shurtleff, Nathaniel B. M.D., ed., *Records of The Governor and Company of the Massachusetts Bay in New England* (Secretary of the Commonwealth, 1878), 211-12; *Acts and Resolves, Massachusetts Bay Colony*, 1742-1756, Vol. III (Secretary of the Commonwealth, 1878), 647-48.

1753- November 16
"The anniversary of our happy Deliverance from a most horrid Popish Plot, and the glorious Revolution...was observed here as usual."

- South Carolina Gazette, Nov. 16, 1753.
PDC

1754- James Freeman wrote that reason for taking pageantry through the streets was that "the vulgar might impress them [the wealthy] with a sense of deliverance from luxury."

- Freeman Notebook, Cited in:"Deliverance from Luxury: Pope's Day, Conflict and Consensus in Colonial Boston, 1745-1765," Francis D. Cogliano, *Studies in Popular Culture*, Vol. 15, No. 2 (1993), pp. 15-28.

1754- Harvard College banned the firing of crackers and squibs, destruction of fences for firewood and conveying that violation would invite "peril."

-Harvard College, Copies of Faculty Minutes/Records, Harvard University Archives, Vol. II: November 4, 1754.

1754- William Brogden, rector of Queen Anne Parish, Prince George's County, Maryland, delivered a Anglican fifth of November sermon at St. Barnabas' Church, in Queen Anne Parish. It was published as:"Popish Zeal Inconvenient to Mankind, and Unsuitable to the Laws of Christ." It was preached that "popery is always the same – always bent upon amassing wealth and power, upon ruling men's consciences, sense and reason, and upon extirpating all that oppose its errors." Brogden maintained that the people would hold "*zeal in a good cause* – zeal both in maintaining the *true* and in guarding against . . . a *false* religion."

- Allen, Ethan, Rev "The Rev. William Brogden, Rector . . .," Part II of American Ecclesiastical History, Sketches of the Colonial Clergy of Maryland, in *The Church Review, and Ecclesiastical Register*, Vol. IX, 1856-57 (New Haven: George B. Bassett & Co., 1857), 114.

1754-63- Seven Years War

1755- "A large Body of the Mobility" of New York City celebrated by moving on "biers" "hideously formed, and as humorously contrived" representations of the Devil, the Pope, and the Pretender. The Devil stood next to the Pope, "seemingly paying compliments" to the latter, while holding a threepronged pitchfork poking "his Holiness on the Back." The Devil carried a lantern, the Pope stood in front of the Pretender, instructing. Before The crowd burnt the three to "cinders," it stopped at the "lodgings" of, Baron Dieskau, a prisoner-of-war and French general captured in the Battle of Lake George (September 8, 1755). A guard was assigned to prevent "mischief," but, the "mobility" harassed the baron from below. The baron, knew the custom, and sent down some silver to paciffy the mob.

-*New-York Gazette: or, the Weekly Post-Boy*, November 10, 1755; "NEW-YORK," *Maryland Gazette*, December 4, 1755.

1755- Pope Day effigies were carried around the city on a bier at night: "hideously formed, and as humorously contrived, the Devil standing close behind the Pope, seemingly paying his compliments to him, with a three pronged Pitchfork...on the Back....(was ) the young Pretender standing before the Pope waiting his commands." "The procession stopped before the lodgings of the captured French general, Baron Dieskau, to reinforce the anti-Catholic message. The baron knew how to defuse a potentially dangerous situation and paid homage to the celebr atns by sending down some silver. The crowd recognized the traditional concession, returned the favor with three huzzahs, and then "march'd off to a proper Place," where they "set Fire to the Devil's Tail, burning the Three to Cinders." (no direct evidence exists for Pope Day processions for every year there are references to the dates - 1748,1755, 1757,1765, so that it is believed that processions were held each year from 1748-1764.

-*Weekly Journal*, Nov. 7, 1748, *Gazette: Post-Boy,*Nov.7,1748, Nov. 10, 1755, Nov.7,1757, Stokes, *Iconography*, IV, 673,675;*Murcury*, Nov.7, 1757; G.D. Scull, ed, *The Montresor Journals* (New York Historical Society,Collections, XIV, (New York, 1881), 338-339.) From:*The Road to Mobocracy,* Paul A. Gilje, University of North Carolina Press, 1987 .


1755- December 4

Maryland

"the Devil, the Pope, and the Pretender, at night were carried about the city on a bier, their three effigies hideously formed, and as humorously contrived, the Devil standing close behind the Pope, seemingly paying his compliments to him, with a three-pronged pitchfork in one hand, with which at times the was made to thrust his Holiness on the Back, and a lanthorn in the other, the young Pretender standing before the Pope, waiting his commands."

"In their route through the Streets, they stop't at the French General's Lodgings,"--this was General Dieskau, then lying wounded and a prisoner in Boston,--"where a guard was ordered to prevent mischief by the Mob. The General sent down some silver by the carriers, with which after giving three huzzas, they marched off to a proper place, and set fire to the Devil's tail, burning the three to cinders."

-Annapolis Gazette," Dec. 4, 1755.
PDC

1756-, "the common sort" in Boston the "mobility" gathered, "as usual," on this occasion and made its target Admiral John Byng. He had been court-martialed for the loss of the battle, and the island, of Minorca (May 20, 1756) to France, therefore the crowd in Boston included effigies of the Devil, the Pope, and the Pretender as well as one of the Admiral. They hung Byng on a "gibbet" and pierced the figure of the traitor, with a steel sword and a wooden sword. On the front of the stage, the gallows was placed a message, in block letters, issued a challenge:

Come hither brave Boys, be jolly and sing,
Here's Death and Confusion to Admiral B---g.

-*Boston Gazette, or Weekly Journal*, November 8, 1756; *New-Hampshire Gazette*, November 11, 1756..

1758- John Leach, Boston called the celebration: "an annual custom . . . not to be forgotten" in America or Britain.

- Leach, John, *Diary*, Manuscript, Massachusetts Historical Society, Ms. N-1567.

1760

Mummer's Poem In Newburyport, Massachusetts (1760 ?)

The Fifth of November,
  As you well remember,
  Was gunpowder treason and plot;
 I know of no reason
Why the gunpowder treason
Should ever be forgot.

When the first King James the scepter swayed,
This hellish powder plot was laid.
Thirty-six barrels of powder placed down below
All for old England's overthrow:
Happy the man, and happy the day
That caught Guy Fawkes in the middle of this play.
You'll hear our bell go jink, jink, jink;
Pray madam, sirs, if you' something give,
We'll burn the dog and never let him live.

We'll burn the dog without his head,
And then you'll say the dog is dead.
From Rome, from Rome, the pope is come,
All in ten thousand fears;
The fiery serpent's to be seen,
All head, mouth, nose and ears.
The treacherous knave had so contrived,
To blow king parliament all up alive.
God by his grace he did prevent
To save both king and parliament.
Happy the man, and happy the day,
That catched Guy Fawkes in the middle of his play.

Match touch, catch prime,
In the good nick of time.
Here is the pope that we got,
The whole promoter of the plot.
We'll stick a pitchfork in his back
And throw him in the fire.

3.Notes that when the term "boys" is used that it may refer as much to adults of a lower status as to the age of the individual Newberryport Mass. 1775.

  - Hennig Cohen and Tristram Coffin, eds. <u>The Folklore of American Holidays</u>., Detroit: Gale Research Company, 1987, 319.

1760, November 5- The army of Massachusetts celebrated the conspiracy, encamped, on Lake Champlain, at the British fort at Crown Point, New York.

At Fort St. Frederic in 1760, the provincial army celebrated the day. Sergeant David Holden, cooper and farmer from Groton, wrote in his journal that he that, following "a mighty firing" held by soldiers in celebration of the 5th a corporal and "a file of men" patrolled the camp, to "confine" and discipline those responsible. Captain Samuel Jenks, blacksmith from Chelsea, also took interest in this commemoration. He termed the day "Pope Night" and "Powder Plot," he wrote that "the provincials" had "kept firing all over the camps." He noted that "all possible care" had was taken to "detect" those responsible and "suppress the fire," he noted that, the men had kept up "a constant fireing and squibing in different the encampments till bedtime." Holden nor Jenks described whether a provincial force or a regular force was responsible, but it is helpful to note that Major General Jeffery Amherst, a man with was not fond of the provincial army, commanded the fort. If he ordered the "confinement" on November 5, then he, favored discipline over revelry.

- Davenport, James, Quoted in William B. Sprague, *Annals of the American Pulpit: Or, Commemorative Notices of Distinguished American Clergymen of Various Denominations*, Vol. III (New York: Robert Carter & Bros., 1863?), 91.

-Green, Samuel A, in "June Meeting, 1889 . . . Journal of Sergeant Holden . . .," *Proceedings of the Massachusetts Historical Society* 24 (1887-89): 384-86, 405.

- Jenks, Henry F,. in "March Meeting, 1889 . . . Journal of Captain Jenks . . .," *Proceedings of the Massachusetts Historical Society* 25 (1889-90): 352-53, 388.

- Woodwell, P. M. ed., *The Diary of Thomas Moody: Campaign of 1760 in the French and Indian War* (South Berwick, Maine: Chronicle Print Shop, 1976), 39.

1760- Boston, a paper suggested that the city, celebrated only by sounding guns at the batteries and the castle.

-*Boston Evening Post*, November 10, 1760.

c. 1760- The South & North ends of Boston were, in old times, (that is that exceedgly wise & important [?] portion of the Population the boys) in decided and unceasing opposition to each other. In celebration of that immortal day the fifth of Nov. each Party had its Pope accompanied by the "gentleman in black"—there were thus the South End Pope & the North End Pope.

These two parties always continued to meet at some half way spot where a regular fight ensued (an annual battle)—which lasted until one Party drove off the other & took possession of its Pope—the victorious Party then took both Popes to some particular place—generally the Mill Pond, & then burnt them both together.

On the present occasion, one of the wheels which supported the Platform of the South End Pope came off—or broke down—this, of course, would tend to Slide off his Holiness into the Street or at least compel him to lower his head before the rival Pope which would be regarded as a Sign of Submission.

To prevent this awful catastrophe, Knox immediately placed his Shoulder under the platform & kept the Sacred image erect until the fight was over. Which way the victory turnd Mr. Hayward does not remember.

Knox at the time was not—properly speaking—a boy, but rather as Mr. Chamberlain said, a dashing young man, about 18 or so. The belligerents—by the way—on these occasions were not by any means mere boys only, but were composed also of young men.

The South End Party was then commanded by a certain Abraham Foley—usually known as Niddy-Noddy, a nickname given him from a peculiar motion of the head. This man afterwards became a Servant and at last died in the Hospital [i.e., was poor and possibly insane]. Knox as Pope man was Subject to his orders—among others of the South End Party. And here, as the Showman says, is the illustration which the anecdote affords—Foley the comander, dying in the Hospital—Knox, the dashing young man, at last the Major-General.

- Bell, J. L., "Henry Knox on Pope Night," November 3, 2010, http://boston1775.blogspot.com/search/label/Henry%20Knox?updated-max=2011-01-29T08:34:00-05:00&max-results=20&start=20&bydate=false; and Francis S. Drake, Life and Correspondence of Henry Knox : Major-General in the American Revolutionary Army (Boston: Samuel G. Drake, 1873).

1760-1775- James Otis, patriot, lawyer, defended "some thoughtless young men" who were responsible for "a great deal of noisy turbulence" on the Fifth. They broke windows that were lit in Plymouth. He represented them pro bono in court. "Thinking the prosecution to have been illnatured and vindictive," Otis used "humour and argument," to portray *Pope day* as "a common, annual frolic, undertaken without malice." The defense won.

- Tudor, William, *The Life of James Otis, of Massachusetts : Containing Also, Notices of Some Contemporary Characters and Events, From the Year 1760 to 1775* (Boston: Wells and Lilly, 1823), 25-29.

1761- October 30, the General Court of Massachusetts reminded constables and sheriffs of the importance of peace-keeping on this holiday. The Court ordered that, immediately at sunset on November 5, 1761, law enforcement must "attend & wait" at specified locations to help the magistracy and to prevent bonfire-raising, "imagery," and "pageantry."

-General Court, *Court Files, Suffolk County* Vol. 487, page x.

1761, October 7- Harvard College again issued a general order prohibiting the firing of squibs, "by Day or by Night, either within the College Walls or in the College yard or in any other Part" "under Pain of the severest Punishment that may be inflicted by the College Law." An onlooker saw an effigy of the Pope, wearing "a very antique dress" and "a really Roman nose," and an effigy of the Devil, nearby complisance," with a longer beak holding a key in one hand and a pitchfork in the other.

-Harvard College, Copies of Faculty Minutes/Records, Harvard University Archives, Vol. II: October 7, 1760.

1764- Savannah, One newspaper noted without detail the "usual".

-"SAVANNAH, NOVEMBER 8," *Georgia Gazette*, November 8, 1764.

1763- Treaty of Paris

1763- Thomas Hutchinson:

(Gov. Thomas) Hutchinson wrote, July 27, 1763, "Four of the commissioners of the customs thought themselves in danger, and took shelter in the castle. Some people were so foolish as to say that they might be taken from thence, and we have had the castle surrounded ever since with men-of-war. We have such people among us: but an attempt upon the castle would be the most consummate piece of Quixotism; and, mad as we are, I cannot think we are mad enough for it, if there had not been a man-of-war in America. Mobs, a sort of them at least, are constitutional, and we have reason enough to fear mobs; and our misfortune is, that the authority of Government is so weak, that we are not able to check them when they rise, but are forced to leave them to their natural course. We cannot continue a great while in this state. Government must be aided from without, or else it must entirely subside."

-Cited in: Frothingham, Richard, *life and Times of Joseph Warren,* 1865, p.74.

1764

Newberryport Mass. "in addition to the images of the pope and his company" on a cart 40 feetx10 feet "there might be found on the same platform, half a dozen dancers and fiddlers." As Cited by Peter D. Apgar in: <u>Festivals of Colonial America from Celebration ot Revolution</u>. Masters Thesis, 1995, Texas Tech. pp. 52-67.
- Cohen and Coffin, <u>Folklore of American Holidays</u>. 319).


1764- November 8.
"Savannah November 8 Monday last the fifth inst. being the anniversary of the Gunpowder Treason, was observed here as usual."

-*The Georgia Gazette* 894 Nov 8, 1764.

1764- Boston, November 5- In the north end a boy, a child of a "Mr. Brown" five to nine years of age, fell under a wheel of one of the carriages carrying, an effigy of the Devil. The boy was crushed under the cart, which was just "setting off," and died. At the batteries and castle, the government held its commemoration, firing its guns at one. The government the magistracy and the militia ordered the destruction of the popes in both ends. A of justices, officers, and sheriffs, who knew "the respective Places of . . . Rendezvous," went to work "demolishing" stages and "pull[ing] to pieces" the figure of the pope in the North End. It proved unable to inflict the same damage on the flotilla in the South End. It was unable to do so and was unable to prevent the North End from rebuilding its pope. At around eight, the two neighborhood groups gathered at the Mill Bridge and, began a battle, using brickbats, clubs, and staves. A half hour later the South End obtained "a compleat Victory." It then brought its popes and stages, and those of its rival, to the gallows on the Neck, where it was burnt. During the skirmish, law enforcement showed up. It arrested a "Negro" and the captain of the South End, shoemaker Ebenezer Mackintosh. Not surprisingly, given the death and the violence of the celebration. John Rowe, English-born merchant of Boston, called the death of Brown "a sorrowful accident." The *Providence Gazette* suggested that "several" had been killed. The *Boston Post Boy* wrote that only the child had died. The November 8, 1764, *Boston News-Letter and New-England Chronicle* confirmed the event was a lower-class celebration. Blacks and servants did the heavy transport of the "carved" effigies of the Pope and his "attendants" through the town. It noted that the anniversary "impress'd" a sense of "Deliverance from Popery" on "the Minds of the Vulgar," the paper suggested that the "Party-Affair" had a purpose and the approval of "the better sort." The author said, the city had also seen the bad side of the holiday, in "melancholy Accident." The crowd was described as "the Champions of both Ends of the Town" and "the Rabble," bruised, maimed, and wounded arms and the heads. It had left some of the spectators not "so well as they could wish." It would have been worse it would, the newspaper wrote have done even more damage had the moon not been out. The *News-Letter* ended with a comment, which noted that "these Parties do not subsist much at any other Time. Several thousand were "hallowing" on their way to the gallows, with clubs and torches, opposing the authorities.

-*Boston News-Letter and New-England Chronicle*, November 8, 1764; "Newport, November 8,"
*Newport Mercury*, November 8, 1764; *Boston Post Boy*, November 5, 1764; Anne Rowe Cunningham, ed., *Letters and Diary of John Rowe, Boston Merchant, 1759-1762, 1764-1779* (New York: New York Times and Arno Press, 1969), 67-68; James Freeman, Notebook on November 5, 1764, Massachusetts Historical Society. Cunningham, ed., *Letters and Diary of John Rowe*, 67-68.

-*Providence Gazette and Country Journal*, November 10, 1764; "Boston, November 8," *Boston Post Boy*, November 12, 1764.

-*Boston News-Letter and New-England Chronicle*, November 8, 1764.

1764-1776- Coronet Joyce who arrested Charles I before the execution was added as parade effigy. Custom continues beyond independence.

-Matthews, "Joyce Junior Once More," in: Colonial Society of Massachusetts, <u>Publications,</u> XI, 294n.

1764, Nov 8-  Savannah November 8 Monday last the fifth inst. being the anniversary of the Gunpowder Treason, was observed here as usual.

- The Georgia Gazette 894 Nov 8, 1764.

1764- Newberryport, Mass. Cites observation of a spectator: "in addition to the images of the pope and his company" on a cart 40 feetx10 feet "there might be found on the same platform, half a dozen dancers and fiddlers."

-Cohen and Coffin, Folklore of American Holidays. 319.

1764, Nov 8- The Georgia Gazette 894, Savannah November 8 Monday last the fifth inst. being the anniversary of the Gunpowder Treason, was observed here as usual.

1764, 5 November-James Freeman writes: "It was formerly a custom on these anniversaries for ye lower class of people to celebrate the evening in a manner peculiar to themselves, by having carried images erected on stages, representing the Pope, his attendant, &c. and these were generally carried thro' the streets by negroes & other servants, that ye minds of ye vulgar might be impressed w/ a sense of their deliverance from popery, & money was generally given to them, to regale themselves in the evening, when they burnt the images. But of late those who are concerned in this pageantry make a party affair of it, & instead of spending the evening agreeably, the champions of both ends of the town prepare to engage each other in battles under the denomination of S. end & N. end. In ye afternoon the magistrates & other officers of the town went to the respective places of their rendezvous, & demolished their stages, to prevent any disorders, which they did without opposition. Notw/standing which as soon as it was dark, they collected again, & mended their stages, which being done they prepared for a battle, & about 8 o'clock the two parties met near the mill bridge where they fought with clubs, staves, brick bats, &c for about half an hour, when those of ye S. end gained the victory, carrying off not only their own, but their antagonist's stages &c which they burnt on Boston neck. In the fray many were much bruised & wounded in their heads & arms, some dangerously. It should be noted that these parties do not much subsist at any other time."

-*Boston Evening-Post* of 12 November 1764.

1765- November 7, *Massachusetts Gazette*,"….these shews of late years had been continued in the evening, and we have often seen the bad effects attending them at such a time; the servants and negroes would disguise themselves, and being armed with clubs would engage each other with great violence, whereby many came off badly wounded."

-Benes, Peter, *Night Processions: Celebrating the Gunpowder Plot in England and New England, (unpublished Mss.)*.

1765- November, 4 , Boston- Last Friday being the day the stamp-Act was to take Place, the Public were not much alarmed or displeased at the Morning's being ushered in by the Tolling of Bells in several Parts of the Town, and the Vessels in the Harbour displaying their Colors half-mast high, in token of Mourning: and tho' some previous Steps had been taken by Authority to prevent any Pageantry, fearing lest Tumult and Disorder might be the Consequence yet the People were soon informed that the Great Tree at the South part of the Town (known by the Name of the Tree of Liberty ever since the memorable 14th of August) was adorned with the Effigies of the two famous or rather infamous enemies of American Liberty; G—ge G—nv—e and J–hn H–sk–.

The Figures continued suspended without any Molestation till about 3 o'clock in the Afternoon, when they were cut down in the View and amid the Acclamations of several Thousand People of all Ranks, and being placed in a Cart, were with great Solemnity and Order followed by the Multitude, formed into regular Ranks, to the Court House, where the Assembly was then sitting; from thence proceeding to the North End of the Town and then returning up Middle Street, they pass'd back thro' the Town to the Gallows on the Neck, where the

Effigies were again hung up, and after continuing some Time were cut down, when the Populace, as a token of their utmost Detestation of the Men they were designed to represent, tore them in Pieces and flung their Limbs with Indignation into the Air.—

This being done, three Cheers were given, and every Man was desired to repair to his Home, which was so punctually performed, that the Evening was more remarkable for Peace and Quietness than common; a Circumstance that would at any Time redound to the Honour of the Town, but was still more agreeable, as the Fears of many were great least it should prove another 26th of August; for the horrid Violences of which Night we hope the good Order of this will in some measure atone, as it is a Proof such Conduct was not agreeable to the Sentiments of the Town, but was only the lawless Ravages of some foreign villains, who took Advantage of the overheated Temper, of a very few people of this place, and drew them in to commit such violences and disorders as they shuddered at with horror in their cooler hours.

… Notwithstanding the Insinuations of those who would represent the Inhabitants of this Town as Mobbish, it has no doubt given Pleasure to the General Assembly now sitting, to find it quite otherwise; and that the spirited Endeavours of those who would picture the Betrayers of their invaluable Liberties in a just and ridiculous View, are attended with the greatest Order and Decorum. . . .

We are well assured, and we have Reason to think, that the Inhabitants are satisfied in it, that if any Exhibitions are made, as usual, on the 5th of the Month, the same unexceptionable Behaviour will be observed; those true Sons of Liberty having agreed to unite as Brethren, in preventing Disorders of every Kind, and in promoting the COMMON CAUSE.

-*Boston Gazette*

1765, November 18- (Boston), An entertainment was made last week by the heads of the south and north Parties of the — and a great number of Persons of character had tickets sent them and most of them were Present and such a junction is thought to be the only way to preserve the town from further outrages.5 The riots at N York have given fresh spirits to the rioters here. An uniformity of measures it is said will be effectual and join or die is the motto. When you and I were at Albany ten years ago we did not Propose an union for such Purposes as these.

-Letter, "To Benjamin Franklin from Thomas Hutchinson, 18 November 1765, From Thomas Hutchinson", Letterbook copy: Massachusetts Archives.

1765- James Freeman, "It has long been the custom in Boston on ye 5th of Nov'r for Nos. of persons to exhibit on stages some pageantry denoting their abhorrence of popery & the horrid plot which was to have been executed on that day in the year 1605. These shows have of late years, been continued in the even'g, & we have often seen the bad effects attending them at such a time; the servants & negroes would disguise themselves & being armed with clubs would engage each other with great violence whereby many came off badly wounded. In short, they carried it to such lengths that two parties were created in ye town under the appellation of N. end & S. end. But the disorders which had been committed from time to time induced several gentlemen to try a reconciliation between the 2 parties; accordingly the chiefs met on the 1st of this inst., & conducted the affair in a very orderly manner. In ye even'g the commander of ye N. & after making general overtures they reciprocally engaged in an Union, & the former distinctions to subside, at the same time the chiefs with their assistants engaged their honour no mischief should arise by their means, & that they would prevent any disorders on ye 5th. When the day arrived about noon the pageantry representing the Pope, the Devil, & several other effigies signifying tyranny, oppression, slavery, &c. were brought on stages from the N. & S. & met in Kings Str. where the union was established in a very ceremonial manner, & having given three huzzas, they interchanged ground, the S. marched to ye N. & the N. to the S. parading thro' ye streets until they again met near ye Court House. The whole then proceeded to Liberty tree, under the shadow of which they refreshed themselves for a while, & then returned to ye Northward agreeably to their plan. They reached Cop's hill before 6 o'clock, where they halted, & having enkindled a fire, the whole pageantry was committed to the flames & consumed."

*-Boston Evening-Post* of 11 November 1765.

1765- Nov. 7, Georgia Gazette Thurs. American Intelligence Savannah November 7

Tuesday last being the anniversary of the Gunpowder Plot, the same was observed here by firing of the great guns, &c. A number of sailors having assembled together in order to parade through the streets, as is usual on that day, one of them, representing a Stamp-master, was placed upon a scaffold supported by six others, having a paper in his hand, and a rope fastened under his arms and round his neck; at certain stages they made a stand, where this pretended Stamp-master was obliged by several severe blows with a cudgel to call out in a pitiful tone, No Stamps, No riot act, Gentlemen, &c. After thus sufficiently exposed him to the view of the inhabitants, and used him with every indignity they could think of, they conducted him to the Machenry's tavern before which they concluded the whole by hanging him up for a little while, and afterwards cut him down, in the presence of a crowd of spectators, who were highly diverted with the humour of the tars.—In all they exhibitions here of this kind, private as well as publick property has remained.

1765- Monday November 11, *Boston Gazette*, #55 Boston.

Tuesday last being the Anniversary of the Commemoration of the happy Deliverance of the English Nation from the Popish Plot, commonly called The Powder Plot, the Guns at Castle William and at the Batteries in Town were fired at One o'clock; as also on board the Men of War in the Harbor.

It has long been the Custom in this Town on the Fifth of November for Numbers of Persons to exhibit on Stages some Pageantry, denoting their Abhorrence of POPERY and the horrid Plot which was to have been executed on this Day in the Year 1605; these Shews of late Years has been continued in the Evening, and we have often seen the bad Effects attending them at such a Time; the Servants and Negroes would disguise themselves, and being armed with Clubs would engage each other with great Violence, whereby many came off badly wounded; in short they carried it to such Lengths that two Parties were created in the Town, under the Apellation of North End and South-End: But the Disorders that had been committed from Time to Time induced several Gentlemen to try a Reconciliation between the two Parties; accordingly the Chiefs met on the First of this Instant, and conducted that Affair in a very orderly Manner; in the Evening the Commander of the South entered into a Treaty with the Commander of the North, and after making several Overtures they reciprocally engaged in an UNION and the former Distinctions to subdue; at the same Time the Chiefs with their Assistants engaged upon their Honor no Mischiefs should arise by their Means, and that they would prevent any Disorders, on the 5th—When the Day arrived the Morning was all Quietness, --about Noon the Pageantry, representing the Pope, Devil, and several other Effigies signifying Tyranny, Oppression, Slavery, &c. were brought on Stages from the North and South, and met in King Street, where the Union was established in a very ceremonial Manner, and having given three Huzzas, they interchanged Ground, the South marched to the North ,and the North to the South, parading thro the Streets until they again met near the Court-House.

The whole then proceeded to the Tree of Liberty, under the Shadow of which they refreshed themselves for a while, and then retreated to the Northward, agreeable to their Plan;--they reached Copp's Hill before 6 o' Clock, where they halted, and having enkindled a Fire, the whole Pageantry was committed to the Flames and consumed: This being finished every Person was requested to retire to their respective Homes.—It must be noticed to the Honor of all those concerned in this Business that every Thing was conducted in a most regular Manner, and such Order observed as could hardly be expected among a Concourse of several Thousand People—all seemed to be joined, agreeable to their principal Motto Lovely Unity- The Leaders, Mr. McIntosh from the South, and Mr. Swift from the North, appeared in Military Habits, with small Canes resting on their Left Arms, having Musick in front and Flank: their Assistants appeared also distinguished with small Reeds, then the respective Corps followed among whom were a great Number of Persons in Rank: These with the

Spectators filled the Streets; not a Club was seen among the whole, nor was any Negro allowed to approach near the Stages;-after the Conflagration the Populace retired, and the Town remained the whole Night in better Order than it had ever been on this Occasion—Many Gentlemen seeing the Affair so well conducted, contributed to make up a handsome Purse to entertain those that carried it on.-This Union, and one other more extensive, may be look'd upon as the (perhaps the only) happy Effects arising from the S—p A—t.

Nov. 7, 1765
"American Intelligence Savannah November 7

Tuesday last being the anniversary of the Gunpowder Plot, the same was observed here by firing of the great guns, &c. A number of sailors having assembled together in order to parade through the streets, as is usual on that day, one of them, representing a Stamp-master, was placed upon a scaffold supported by six others, having a paper in his hand, and a rope fastened under his arms and round his neck; at certain stages they made a stand, where this pretended Stamp-master was obliged by several severe blows with a cudgel to call out in a pitiful tone, No Stamps, No riot act, Gentlemen, &c. After thus sufficiently exposed him to the view of the inhabitants, and used him with every indignity they could think of, they conducted him to the Machenry's tavern before which they concluded the whole by hanging him up for a little while, and afterwards cut him down, in the presence of a crowd of spectators, who were highly diverted with the humour of the tars.—In all they exhibitions here of this kind, private as well as publick property has remained unmolested, and no outrages have been committed."

-<u>Georgia Gazette</u> Thurs. Nov. 7, 1765 PDC.

1765, Nov,5- Lt. Gov. Cadwallader Colden of New York reported to London that an angry crowd was besieging him in Fort George with the province's stamped paper.

To the Marquess of Granby, Colden wrote, "I expect the Fort will be stormed this night—everything is done in my power to give them a warm reception."

Capt. John Montresor of the Royal Artillery, who was strengthening the fort, wrote in his journal:

*November 5- Advertisements and many papers placarded throughout this city declaring the storming of the Fort this Night under cover of burning the Pope and pretender unless the Stamps were delivered.*

The next day Colden updated his messenger:

*In the forenoon yesterday the Common Council of the City presented an Address to me Requesting that in order to restore Peace to the City & to prevent the effusion of Blood, I would deliver the Stamp'd Paper into the care of the Corporation, who in that case undertook to protect them. I was surprised at the Proposition, but upon their adding a Clause whereby the Mayor & Corporation became engaged for the full amount of the Paper &c and Duty, in case they were lost, destroyed or carried out of the Province, I consented to take the advice of his Majesty's council upon it.*

New York's provincial noted: "the City appeared to be in perfect annarchy, and the power of Government either Military or Civil insufficient—that the defense of the Fort would involve the destruction of the City. 5 November evening the lieutenant governor conveyed the stamped paper in Fort George to a committee led by Mayor John Cruger

.Cruger signed this receipt:

*Received of the Honble. Cadwallader Colden, Esq. his Majesty's Lt. Govr. and Commander in Chief of the Province of New York, Seven Packages containing Stamp'd Paper & Parchment all marked No. 1, J. McE., New York which I promise in behalf of the Corporation of the City of New York to take charge & care of, and to be accountable in case they shall be destroyed, or carried out of the Province as particularly set forth and declared in the Minutes of the Common Council of the said Corporation of this Day. Witness my hand in the City of New York this fifth day of November 1765.*

1765, November 4- Boston Gazette:

*Notwithstanding the Insinuations of those who would represent the Inhabitants of this Town as Mobbish, it has no doubt given Pleasure to the General Assembly now sitting, to find it quite otherwise; and that the spirited Endeavours of those who would picture the Betrayers of their invaluable Liberties in a just and ridiculous View, are attended with the greatest Order and Decorum. . . .*

*We are well assured, and we have Reason to think, that the Inhabitants are satisfied in it, that if any Exhibitions are made, as usual, on the 5th of the Month, the same unexceptionable Behaviour will be observed; those true Sons of Liberty having agreed to unite as Brethren, in preventing Disorders of every Kind, and in promoting the COMMON CAUSE.*

1765, New Hampshire

"Three effigies, representing, according to the Rev. Mr. Rogers, the pope, the devil and a stamp master, but according to another eye witness, Lords North and Bute as two of the characters, were carried about the streets of the town, and finally taken across the river, to the front of where the jail afterwards stood and set fire to and burnt to ashes."

- Charles Bell, *History of Exeter*, 1765.

1765 Savannah- A paper wrote in 1765 about sailors taking part in "usual" or Customary Pope day celebrations.

-As Cited by Peter D. Apgar in: Festivals of Colonial America from Celebration ot Revolution. Masters Thesis, 1995, Texas Tech. pp. 52-67 . (Source cited: Georgia Gazette, Nov. 7, 1765.

1765- Thurs. Nov. 7, Georgia Gazette, American Intelligence Savannah November 7
Tuesday last being the anniversary of the Gunpowder Plot, the same was observed here by firing of the great guns, &c. A number of sailors having assembled together in order to parade through the streets, as is usual on that day, one of them, representing a Stamp-master, was placed upon a scaffold supported by six others, having a paper in his hand, and a rope fastened under his arms and round his neck; at certain stages they made a stand, where this pretended Stamp-master was obliged by several severe blows with a cudgel to call out in a pitiful tone, No Stamps, No riot act, Gentlemen, &c. After thus sufficiently exposed him to the view of the inhabitants, and used him with every indignity they could think of, they conducted him to the Machenry's tavern before which they concluded the whole by hanging him up for a little while, and afterwards cut him down, in the presence of a crowd of spectators, who were highly diverted with the humour of the tars.—In all they exhibitions here of this kind, private as well as publick property has remained unmolested, and no outrages have been committed.

- *Georgia Gazette* Thurs. Nov. 7, 1765

1765- Monday November 11, Boston Gazette, #55 Boston
Tuesday last being the Anniversary of the Commemoration of the happy Deliverance of the English Nation from the Popish Plot, commonly called The Powder Plot, the Guns at Castle William and at the Batteries in Town were fired at One o'Clock; as also on board the Men of War in the Harbor.

It has long been the Custom in this Town on the Fifth of November for Numbers of Persons to exhibit on Stages some Pageantry, denoting their Abhorrence of POPERY and the horrid Plot which was to have been executed on this Day in the Year 1605; these Shews of late Years has been continued in the Evening, and we have often seen the bad Effects attending them at such a Time; the Servants and Negroes would disguise themselves, and being armed with Clubs would engage each other with great Violence, whereby many came off badly wounded; in short they carried it to such Lengths that two Parties were created in the Town, under the Apellation of North End and South-End: But the Disorders that had been committed from Time to Time induced several Gentlemen to try a Reconciliation between the two Parties; accordingly the Chiefs met on the First of this Instant, and conducted that Affair in a very orderly Manner; in the Evening the Commander of the South entered into a Treaty with the Commander of the North, and after making several Overtures they reciprocally engaged in an UNION and the former Distinctions to subdue; at the same Time the Chiefs with their Assistants engaged upon their Honor no Mischiefs should arise by their Means, and that they would prevent any Disorders, on the 5th—When the Day arrived the Morning was all Quietness, --about Noon the Pageantry, representing the Pope, Devil, and several other Effigies signifying Tyranny, Oppression, Slavery, &c. were brought on Stages from the North and South, and met in King Street, where the Union was established in a very ceremonial Manner, and having given three Huzzas, they interchanged Ground, the South marched to the North ,and the North to the South, parading thro the Streets until they again met near the Court-House.

The whole then proceeded to the Tree of Liberty, under the Shadow of which they refreshed themselves for a while, and then retreated to the Northward, agreeable to their Plan;--they reached Copp's Hill before 6 o' Clock, where they halted, and having enkindled a Fire, the whole Pageantry was committed to the Flames and consumed: This being finished every Person was requested to retire to their respective Homes.—It must be noticed to the Honor of all those concerned in this Business that every Thing was conducted in a most regular Manner, and such Order observed as could hardly be expected among a Concourse of several Thousand People—all seemed to be joined, agreeable to their principal Motto Lovely Unity- The Leaders, Mr. McIntosh from the South, and Mr. Swift from the North, appeared in Military Habits, with small Canes resting on their Left Arms, having Musick in front and Flank: their Assistants appeared also distinguished with small Reeds, then the respective Corps followed among whom were a great Number of Persons in Rank: These with the Spectators filled the Streets; not a Club was seen among the whole, nor was any Negro allowed to approach near the Stages;-after the Conflagration the Populace retired, and the Town remained the whole Night in better Order than it had ever been on this Occasion—Many Gentlemen seeing the Affair so well conducted, contributed to make up a handsome Purse to entertain those that carried it on.-This Union, and one other more extensive, may be look'd upon as the (perhaps the only) happy Effects arising from the S—p A—t.

-*Boston Gazette,* Monday November 11, 1765 #55 Boston.

1765- Boston, Nineteen men were tried in the Suffolk County Court, after being indicted for rioting on the Fifth of November before. All of the defendants, one of which was a mulatto servant: the owner of the barn where the North End pope was built, were of "the lower sort" "the middling sort." Most worked in the leather trades (3), the maritime trades (8), or provision handling (4). Ebenezer Mackintosh – a twenty-seven year- old veteran of the Seven Years War, a cobbler, and a member of Engine Company 9, located in the South End – and Henry Swift – a shipwright from the North End, the two captains of the two ends of the town, were included. The chief justice of Massachusetts Thomas Hutchinson, presented the charge to a jury, and called the 1764 event "a most scandalous and notorious Riot" a violation of "Common Law" and "Natural Law, that is, the Law which every man has implanted in him" and a law of the colony. He defined the activity as any criminal activity of "any Number not less than three," and told the jury that the magistracy and others had tried to prevent the "Insult upon Government" that the commemoration of 1764 caused in Boston. He believed that the activity was of "that lawless Mob" that had "most atrociously broke[n] the Peace, put every Member of this Town in Confusion, and many in the utmost Hazard of their Lives," and he stressed that, if anyone had died, every participant would have been placed on trial, and, received the death penalty, for murder. The charges were eventually dropped.

- Cogliano, Francis D., *No King, No Popery: Anti-Catholicism in Revolutionary New England* (Westport, Connecticut: Greenwood Press, 1995), 29, 32; Hoerder, Dirk, *Crowd Action in Revolutionary Massachusetts, 1765-1780* (New York: Academic Press, 1977),

94, 96; Young, ,Alfred F., "Ebenezer Mackintosh: Boston's Captain of the Liberty Tree," in *Revolutionary Founders: Rebels, Radicals, and Reformers in the Making of the Union*, eds. Alfred F. Young, Gary B. Nash, and Ray Raphael, eds. (New York: Alfred A. Knopf, 2011), 22-23. Suffolk County Court Files, 70058, 70433, 100493, 100494, MA – and Council Records, 15:339., Samuel M. Quincy, ed., *Reports of Cases Argued and Adjudged in the Superior Court of Judicature of the Province of Massachusetts Bay, Between 1761 1772, by Josiah Quincy, Jr. . . .* (Boston: Little, Brown, and Company, 1865),112-14. Anderson, George P., "Ebenezer Macintosh: Stamp Act Rioter and Patriot," "A Note on Ebenezer Macintosh," in Colonial Society of Massachusetts *Publications* (1924-26): 15-64. 348-61; Young, "Ebenezer Mackintosh," 15-33; Young, Alfred F., *Liberty Tree: Ordinary People and the American Revolution* (New York: New York University Press, 2006), 341.

1765- Stamp Act incited anguish and resistance.

1765, August 14, Boston: An effigy of "A.O.," Andrew Oliver, the distributor of stamps for Massachusetts, and effigy of a devil in a boot, were both hung in the South End from a great elm, eventually known as deemed Liberty Tree. The boot was a play on words, representing John Stuart, the third Earl of Bute (pronounced: "boot"), former prime minister. The boot had a "green-vile" sole, a green-painted bottom, which referred to George Grenville, the prime minister at the time, author of the Stamp Act. An imp placed next to the devil pointed a pitchfork at Oliver as if intending spear the man, and the devil held a copy of this bill. A poem, a mock suicide note, was placed with the effigy of the distributor:

Fair freedom's glorious cause I've meanly quitted,
For the sake of pelf [money].
But ah! The devil has me outwitted,
And instead of *stamping* others, I've *hang'd* myself.

The ridicule continued, as a crowd of several thousand – Francis Bernard, the governor, claimed that "the greatest Part of the Town" had "engaged" in in this assembly – formed a large procession, giving the devil and the stampman a mock funeral. The Loyal Nine put Mackintosh in charge, the cobbler brought together the two ends of town, the two gangs that had bats and clubs in the November 5 affair of 1764. On the way by the town house, the crowd shouted "Liberty, Property, and No Stamps". Moving onward, it flattened the office and vandalized the home of Oliver, before decapitated and "stamping" (stomping on), burning the effigy of "A. O." on a bonfire on Fort Hill. On August 26, a mob built another bonfire in the city on the Charles. It ransacked the mansion home of the Hutchinson family. The sheriff arrested Mackintosh and six other men the next day, for rioting. Soon the cobbler was soon released, after "a leading citizen" informed the sheriff that "no one would patrol the streets to keep order" if the captain of the South End was jailed. Later crowds in both Massachusetts Bay and other colonies would imitate this expression as they protested acts of Parliament – and burned effigies of officials and taxmen.

- Hoerder, *Crowd Action in Revolutionary Massachusetts, 1765-1780*, 94-96 ff, Young, "Ebenezer Mackintosh: Boston's Captain of the Liberty Tree," 22-24 ff. Robert Blair St. George, "Attacking
Houes," *Conversing by Signs: Poetics of Implication in Colonial New England Culture* (Chapel Hill: University of North Carolina Press, 1998), 205-96.

1765, mid-October- John Adams wrote: (under the pseudonym "Humphrey Ploughjogger,") in the October 14 edition of the *Boston-Gazette*:

"I Han't rit nothing to be printed a great while: but I can't sleep a nights, one wink
hardly, of late. – I hear so much talk about the stamp act and the governor's
speech, that it seems as if 'twould make me crazy. – The governor has painted a
dreadful picture of the times after the first of November – I hate the thoughts of
the first of November. – I hope twill be a great storm, and black and gloomy
weather, as our faces and hearts will all be. – Tis worse than all the fifth of

Novembers that ever was – The Pope never did half so much mischief as that stamp act will do, if the world stands as long as the Pope has done —"

- Ploughjogger, Humphrey. Messieurs Edes & Gill," *Boston-Gazette, and Country Journal*, October 14, 1765.

1888 (1765)- Charles Henry Bell, Exeter, New Hampshire

The feeling of the citizens of Exeter was well expressed by the Rev. Daniel Rogers, pastor of the Second church, who wrote in his diary under date of November 1, 1765, the day when the law went into effect : " The infamous Stamp Act, abhorred by all the British Colonies, took place." The fifth of the same month used in many places in New England to be observed as "pope's day," in commemoration of the discovery of Guy Fawkes's gunpowder plot. This year it was made the occasion of a display of popular feeling in Exeter against the Stamp Act. Three effigies, representing, according to the Rev. Mr. Rogers, the pope, the devil and a stamp master, but according to another eye witness, Lords North and Bute as two of the characters, were carried about the streets of the town, and finally taken across the river, to the front of where the jail afterwards stood, and there set fire to and burnt to ashes. We may safely assume that the exhibition was witnessed by the citizens with abundant tokens of approbation.

-Bell, Charles Henry, *History of the Town of Exeter, New Hampshire*,1888.

1765- The governor of Massachusetts, Francis Bernard, upheld the Stamp Act.
On October 29 he told the council that on November 1 (i.e., the launch of the Act) "a
great parade" of heated protest of the bill, including effigy-burning and pageantry would be held.  Bernard warned the Council of "the probable consequences of the usual
riots" on "the 5th of Novr." They agreed that the "mob" could, cause mayhem. In pursuit of "the Peace of the Town," this government ruled, it had to police the city with more vigilance, keeping "a Military Watch" of artillerymen and cadets "day & night" from October 31 to November 6. The force was doubled on the nights of the fourth and the fifth. The government hoped that the joint effort would prevent "shows & pageants" that might "draw the people together" to oppose the Act. On November 1, a parade  commanded by Mackintosh formed.  It marched effigies of merchants, and officers, from the Liberty Tree to the whipping post to the gallows. Following hanging and tearing "images" of General Thomas Gage and other villains at this site, the mob followed the order of its "ringleader", dispersing before dark.

- Young, *Liberty Tree*, 334, 340, 342., Francis Bernard, Letter to John Pownall [Secretary to the Board of Trade], November 1, 1765, in Colin Nicholson, ed., *The Papers of Francis Bernard, Governor of Massachusetts, 1760-1769*, Vol. II: 7 January 1764 to 22 December 1765 (Boston: Colonial Society of Massachusetts, 2012), 396., Colin Nicolson, *The RLINK "http://www: Francis Bernard and the Origins of the American Revolution* (Boston: Northeastern University Press, 2001).

1765- Boston, early November, The militia failed to muster.  In a letter to the Board of Trade in London, Bernard Admitted  that Mackintosh, artisan had, in the first week of the month, trained "150 or 200 men," and took command of the mob – which numbered "at least2,000 men" – and had, essentially, obtained  "full" control of the city. Bernard
Noted that a Council member had joined Mackintosh the "captain-general," walking
"arm in arm" along the street, complementing the cobbler on the power that he had obtained. While two men walked around the town house, the assembly deliberated inside on matters of state. Bernard noted that the citizens had put on its shows, dragging "sevral Stages with Images of popes & Devils & hanging Stampmen" through the town. They stopped at the town house while the Court met in session inside, and, finally, collected tribute from Bernard. Bernard said that the mob had, "subverted" the government, but, it had brought about so much change that the system of government could not recover. Criticizing the "Wickedness" of the crowd's leaders, and the mob's "Madness"  fearing that things could get worse, the governor thought about resigning and going to Britain. But he remained. Isaac Winslow, a Tory merchant of Boston, composed  a similar observation on mob rule, criticizing the lack of government "interference" in the rioting in 1765, both  August and  in November. He approved  that, on "the 5th of November," the mob, "dress'd out in a very gay manner,"

had done little vandalism and violence. In this collective action, Bernard and Winslow, knew the weakness of the state, and seemed ill at ease. Both seemed concerned that cooperation between the two ends of town held.

- Winslow, Isaac Letter to [Unknown], November 15, 1765, in Robert Newsome, ed. and trans., *Family Memorial: The Winslows of Boston*, Vol. I: Winslow, Isaac and Margaret Catherine Winslow, 1837? – 1873? (University of California, Irvine, and Massachusetts History Society, 2009-10), 66. Bernard, Letter to John Pownall, November 26, 1765, in Nicholson, ed., *The Papers of Francis Bernard,* II: 423. Bernard, Francis, Letter to John Pownall, November 5, 1765, in Nicholson, ed., *The Papers of Francis Bernard,* Vol. II, 399.

1765- Bernard observed: Being "dresst in blue & red, in a gold lace Hat & a gilt Gorget on his breast, with a Rattan Cane hanging at his wrist," Mackintosh led the militia parade of two thousand, shouting orders from a megaphone, supervising a march that united both ends to protest of the Act. "Trumpet" in hand, the "general" led a mock officialdom carrying hats and wands through the streets of the town, ensuring that "no one else" in the procession carried sticks or weapons – and that "no Negro was suffered" to be in the ranks of this protest. Hancock financed the uniforms

- Winslow, Isaac, Letter to [Unknown], November 15, 1765, in Robert Newsome, ed. and trans., *Family Memorial: The Winslows of Boston*, Vol. I: Isaac Winslow and Margaret Catherine Winslow, 1837? – 1873? (University of California, Irvine, and Massachusetts History Society, 2009-10), 66. Bernard, Letter to John Pownall, November 26, 1765, in Nicholson, ed., *The Papers of Francis Bernard,* II: 423.

1765-72- The North End and the South End reconciled in the parading, of Union popes. On November 5, 1765 the team met for refreshments "under the shadow" of the Liberty Tree, then set depictions of the devil, the pope, and "stamp men" on fire. And, at the end of November, Bernard stated that he "fear[ed]" that the reconciliation of the two neighborhoods was done for "other Purposes . . . than burning a Pope."

-Young, *Liberty Tree,* Ibid.; Bernard, Letters to John Pownall, November 1, 5, and 26, 1765, Sparks Mss. Harvard, Letterbook 5: 16-23, 43-46; Douglass Adair and John Schutz, eds., *Peter Oliver's Origin and Progress of the American Rebellion: A Tory View* (San Marino, California: Huntington Library, 1961), 54; Peter Orlando Hutchinson, ed, *The Diary and Letters of Thomas Hutchinson,* 2 vols. (Boston: Houghton Mifflin, 1884-86. 1884-86), 2:71. See also Nathaniel Ames, Diary, November 5, 1765, *Dedham Historical Register* II (date): 27.

1765, November 5- Boston, The Bernard administration celebrated the anniversary officially by firing the guns at batteries and the castle and on board the men-of-war rolling in the surf.

- Bernard, Letter to John Pownall, November 26, 1765, in Nicholson, ed., *The Papers of Francis Bernard,* Vol. II, 423.

1765- Boston- Supporting the celebration of "the happy Deliverance of the English Nation from the Popish Plot, commonly called THE POWDER PLOT," the *Gazette* and the *News-Letter* both noted that the union of the neighborhoods had brought the Fifth respectability.

1. First, the papers reviewed Pope's Days in the past:

"It has long been the Custom in this Town on the Fifth . . . for Numbers of Persons to exhibit on Stages some Pageantry, denoting their Abhorrence of POPERY and the horrid Plot . . . these Shews of late Years [have] been continued in the Evening, and we have often seen the bad Effects attending them . . .; the Servants and [the] Negroes would disguise themselves, and being armed with Clubs would engage each other with great Violence, whereby many came off badly wounded; in short they carried it to such Lengths that two Parties were created in the Town, under the Apellation [sic] of *North-End* and *South-End*."

2. The papers reviewed the development of the alliance crafted by Mackintosh and Swift:

"But the Disorders that had been committed from Time to Time induced several Gentlemen to try a Reconciliation between the[se] two Parties; accordingly the Chiefs met on the First of this Instant, and . . . in a very orderly Manner; the Commander of the South entered into a Treaty with the Commander of the North, and after making several Overtures they reciprocally engaged on a UNION . . . [barring] Mischiefs . . . and . . . Disorders, on the 5th.

3. The papers considered the Pope's Day of 1765:

"When the Day arrived the Morning was all Quietness, – about Noon, the Pageantry, representing the Pope, [the] Devil, and several other Effigies signifying Tyranny, Oppression, Slavery, &c. were brought [forward] on Stages from the North and [the] South, and met in King-Street, where the Union was established in a very ceremonial Manner, and having given three Huzzas, they interchanged Ground, the South marched to the North, and the North to the South, parading thro' the Streets until they met near the Court-House . . . and [later] they retreated to the Northward, . . . they reached Copp's Hill before 6 o'Clock, . . . they halted, and having enkindled a Fire, the whole Pageantry was [at last] committed to the Flames and consumed; . . . [and] every Person was requested to retire to their respective Homes."

After the celebration the press marveled that "a Concourse of several Thousand People," following "Music in Front and Flank" and parading in front of the crowd that "filled the Streets," had kept such "Order" and "Unity." The *Gazette* and the *News-Letter* noted that in 1765 not a single club was seen in the parade and no person of Africandescent was allowed to come near the stages. The press concluded that "this Union, and one other more extensive"– "may be look'd upon as the (perhaps the only) happy Effects arising from the S---p A-t."

- "Boston," *Boston News-Letter and New-England Chronicle*, November 7, 1765; and "Boston," *Boston Gazette, and Country Journal*, November 11, 1765.

1765- Peter Oliver, Tory jurist of Boston, later remembered that Mackintosh, a figure of manliness and sensibility, had a command of the crowd such that he could quiet it completely. He obtained "punctual" obedience when he sent the participants home. Merchant Winslow approved of the union, noting that the attainment of order and "quiet" represented a big improvement of the two "contending bodies," the two parts, of the town had been "at swords points" with each other.

- Winslow, Letter to [Unknown], November 15, 1765, in Newsome, ed. and trans., *Family Memorial*, Adair and Schutz, eds., *Peter Oliver's Origin and Progress*, 54.

1765- Isaac Winslow Jr: [My father] says "The 5th of November happily disappointed ones fears, a union was formed between the South and North, by the mediation of the principal gentlemen of the town" – The Popes (meaning probably, the South end and north end processions) ["] paraded the Streets together, all day, and after burning them at the close of it, all was quiet in the evening. There were no disguises of visages, but the two leaders, M'cIntosh of the South, and Swift of the North, (the same who was so badly wounded last year, were dress'd out in a very gay manner, The authorities["] he says ["]did not interfere at all in the matter["] (MacKintosh was one of the most active of the mob which destroyed Governor Hutchinsons house in North

Square 26 August 1765, and was arrested by the Sheriff, but could not be committed on account of the popular interference)...."

"...On the anniversary of "Pope day" on the 5th of November, there had always existed a bitter rivalry between the South and North parts of the town, which party should capture and destroy each other's Pope – the effigies of whom accompanied by others of the Devil and his Imps were carried about in procession on that day & he added by a distinguished fighting character from each Section – the Northern procession going to the South, and vice versa accompanied each other with a vast concourse of people – They usually met each other in or about Dock Square where the contest took place – These conflicts were very severe, but this year (1765) the popular leaders had excited in the minds of the people such a determined opposition to the Stamp act, that they succeeded in making peace, between the two parties who had before always been at swords points with each other."

- Isaac Winslow Jr., *Winslow Family Memorial.*

1765, New York- November 1, An anonymous representative of the mob gave Cadwallader Colden, lieutenant governor, a letter from "the People of this City and Province of New York." The letter stated that the enforcement of the Act would make Colden "the Chief Murderer of [the] Rights and [the] Privileges" of the city and colony. The correspondence considered the new tax a breach of liberty. Signed "New York," the protest stated that, if Colden ordered those at Fort George to put down a potential popular disturbance, the government would meet a quick, and humiliating, end by the community. That night, a crowd of two thousand, vandalized property in New York, using "the upcoming Pope Day celebration" as a model for collective action. It made grotesques of Colden, destroying the coach of the governor, assaulted the fort with bricks and stones and sacked the home of the mayor. Four days later, on the holiday, the crowd met, again, threatening to commit violence. Colden surrendered custody of the stamps to the crowd at city hall and saved the city and the fort.

- Anonymous, "To the Honourable Cadwallader Colden Esq. Lieut. Governor of the City of New York," November 1, 1765, in F. L. Engleman, "Cadwallader Colden and the New York State Act Riots," *William and Mary Quarterly* 10.4 (Oct. 1953): 561-62.

1765- Portsmouth, The *New-Hampshire Gazette wrote* that, less than a week after "some Hundreds of Persons" of the countryside marched toward the capital, coming less than two miles of the state-house, the royal government in Portsmouth worried that the citizenry might lead a revolt, to protest of the Stamp Act. The *Gazette* wrote, on the Fifth, this government had organized a hundred-man watch that prevented the "disorder" of the crowd and destruction of private property. Feeling that its audience would not act out due to "Prejudice" or "Spleen" on this date or any other, the paper requested the people of New Hampshire to uphold the ideas of Christianity, law, reason, and sensibility, and it congratulated the order that had prevailed on the Fifth.

-"Porstmouth, Nov. 7," [Portsmouth] *New-Hampshire Gazette, and Historical Chronicle*, November 8, 1765.

1765- Savannah, Georgia, the government and seamen celebrated the holiday. The former fired "great guns" and the latter made one man a living dummy, a representative of the customs office in town. He was supported on a scaffold that six other men transported. The sailor-stampman tied a rope "under his arms and round his neck," and held a paper symbolic of the act, and underwent theforce of "several severe blows with a cudgel," while chanting, "No Stamps, No riot act, Gentlemen, &c. No Stamps, No riot act, Gentlemen." While the rest of the group kept the man outside a local tavern. The *Georgia Gazette* observed that no vandalism, or violence, occurred.

- *Georgia Gazette*, November 7, 1765. "SAVANNAH, in Georgia, October 24," [Philadelphia] *Pennsylvania Gazette*, January 2, 1766.

1766- English merchant from England, John Rowe, visiting Boston:

"This is a Day of Confusion in Boston occasioned by a foolish Custom of Carrying about the pope & the Devill &c on a large carriage thro' the streets of this Town. Indeed three very large ones made their appearance this day."

-John Rowe, *Letters and Diary of John Rowe, Boston Merchant, 1759–1762, 1764–1779*,

ed. Anne Rowe Cunningham (Boston: W. B. Clarke, 1903), 5 November 1766. -Benes,

Peter, *Night Processions: Celebrating the Gunpowder Plot in England and New England*,

unpublished Mss.

1760s Annually in Boston, shoemaker Ebenezer Mackintosh led a South End force into battle against shipwright Henry Swift and a North End contingency on November 5. Both sides carried a model of the pope. Sometimes the South End stole the effigy of its rival; sometimes it did not. Nevertheless, both "civil" institutions often watched both popes, like sacrifices, go up in flames. The holiday changed form in the 1760s as a result of the imperial crisis that came as a result of the Seven Years War. Celebrations of Pope's Day explode in the mid-Atlantic and the South, and New England. Parliament became the focus: "the new papacy" -.

- Robinson, David, Letter to William Preston, November 5, 1761, *Massachusetts Historical Society Publications* 32 (1918-19): 184.

1766- Pepperell, Massachusetts, a sermon was presented by pastor Joseph Emerson on the deliverance of the England from the Armada, Plot, and the Stamp Act. The pastor argued that: "sacred history" had shown the "wisdom" of God acting for the English nation and against the "violence" of its enemies. In 1605, he noted, the Lord rescued the kingdom from "the hellish schemes of Rome," and, in 1688, in the Glorious Revolution, he saved it from "popery and slavery." Emerson reflected on the Watts psalter, reading "A Hymn of Praise for Three Great Salvations":

"Then, might GOD, the Earth shall know
And learn the Worship of the Sky:
Angels and *Britons* join below,
To raise their *Hallelujahs* high.

- Emerson, Joseph, *A Thanksgiving-Sermon Preach'd at Pepperrell, July 24th. 1766. A Day Set Apart by Public Authority as a Day of Thanksgiving on the Account of the Repeal of the Stamp-Act . . .* (Boston: Edes and Gill, 1766), 18ff; , Watts, Isaac, *Horae Lyricae. Poems, Chiefly of the Lyric Kind, in Three Books. Sacred I. To Devotion and Piety. II. To Virtue, Honour and Friendship. III. To the Memory of the Dead ..* . (Boston: Rogers and Fowle, 1748), 16-19.

1766- Boston, November 5

Pope Day, celebrations:
"Thinking our Dehverance from the Stamp-Act somewhat analogous in its Consequences to the Escape from the Popish Plot, it was thought necessary by the Conductors of the Pageantry, to increase the Pope's Retinue, by adding thereunto, in Effigy... Advocates of the late Stamp-Act."

-Boston Gazette, Nov. 10, 1766.

1766- Citizens of Boston paraded, torched and beheaded "a Variety of very droll as well as ridiculous effigies" of "the Advocates of the late Stamp Act," the Pope, and "Friends" of autocracy and slavery. The people viewed the "Deliverance" of the colony from the tax "somewhat analogous to the Escape from the Popish Plot" (i.e., Gunpowder Plot), the crowd propelled a number of stages and "Retinue" of the pope and "Dictator and Supporter of both Plots" (1605 and 1765), an enemy "calculated to overturn" the British Constitution and "deprive the Subject of his Liberty,". The mob sent "the Bodies to the Flames" it carried lanterns marked "Liberty" and *The Lovely Unity.*" The *News-Letter* noted that the celebration avoided "Disorder." The government, celebrated the day, firing the cannons at the batteries in Charlestown, North End, South End, and from "the Ramparts" at Castle William.

-"Boston, Nov. 6," *Boston Evening Post*, November 6, 1766; [Portland, Maine?] *New-Hampshire* "Boston, Nov. 6," *Boston Evening Post*, November 6, 1766; [Portland, Maine?] *New-Hampshire.*

1766- Boston, John Rowe, merchant, was disgusted, and called the Fifth "a Day of Confusion in Boston" and act of carrying the Devil and the Pope "a foolish custom."

- Pierce, Edward Lillie ed., *Letters and Diary of John Rowe, Boston Merchant, 1759-1762, 1764-1779* (Boston: W. B. Clarke, 1903), 114.

1766- Wednesday November 5, John Adams

"Spent the Evening at Mr. Pynchons, with Farnham, Sewal, Sergeant, Coll. Saltonstall &c., very agreably. Punch, Wine, bread and Cheese, Apples, Pipes and Tobacco. Popes and Bonfires this Evening at Salem, and a Swarm of tumultuous People attending them."

-Diary and Autobiography of John Adams, Volume 1, 1755–1770. - Adams, John, Diary, November 5, 1766, in John Adams and Charles Francis Adams, *Works: With a Life of the Author,* Vol. 10 (Boston: Little, Brown, 1865), 201.

1766- The government of Charleston again celebrated "the happy delivery" of King and Parliament from "the horrid gunpowder treason The light infantry company went at three in the morning, fourteen miles in the dark over "very sandy road" to the Goose Creek estate of Peter Manigault, Speaker of the Royal Assembly (critic of the Stamp Act), to receive,"elegant" entertainment for several hours, and marched back again the same day.

-"CHARLESTOWN NOVEMBER 7 . . .," *South Carolina and American General Gazette*, November 7, 1766.

1766- Savannah "duly observed" November 5 in 1766, one year later,
the royal government in that city had "the flag . . . displayed at the fort, the colours of the vessels" on the Ashley River "hung out," and the cannons "fired" at one in the afternoon.
(The city fired the cannons again in 1768.)

-"Savannah, November 12," [Savannah] *Georgia Gazette*, November 12, 1766; "Thursday; Gunpowder; Plot . . .," [Savannah] *Georgia Gazette*, November 11, 1767; "Savannah, November 9," [Savannah] *Georgia Gazette*, November 9, 1768.

1767- North End Cart in Boston carried a British Flag and the British dissident John Wilkes an ally to colonists anti taxation efforts.

-Matthews, "Joyce Junior Once More," in: Colonial Society of Massachusetts, Publications, XI, p. 301.

1767- Anglican preacher, Charles Woodmason preached a sermon at a Quaker meetinghouse South Carolina, outside of the city of Charleston perhaps the first sermon on the Plot in that colony – its lessons including the Plot the evils of popery.

- Hooker, Richard J. ed., *The Carolina Backcountry on the Eve of the Revolution: The Journal and Other Writings of Charles Woodmason, Anglican Itinerant* (Chapel Hill: University of North Carolina Press, 1953), 29-30.

1767- Citizens of Boston burned effigies of the Devil, the Pope, the Pretender, and taxmen, pulling and pushing carts carrying the effigies, while wearing costumes and hats, blowing horns. Pierre Eugéne Du Simitiére, Swiss portraitist visited Boston that Fall, and drew "Boston Affairs," two fine sketches of Pope's Day processions. Du Simitiere described effigies, floats, participants, and props that he saw. He explained the politics of the anniversary in the imperial crisis. Many carts and effigies demonized the papacy and Parliament. These had labels which read "liberty & property & no commissioners" and "The Loyal Arms," "TERROR/DESPAIR" and "the true American." Du Simitiére revealed that, the North End presented its approval of the radical Whig John Wilkes ("No. 45 / LOVE / AND / UNITI / the / north briton [sic]"). In its cart, the South End presented its dislike for both the customs officialdom and the Townshend Acts. In the margins, the artist noted that, "the North End Pretender [bears] a drum; the South End says more with a gallows." The procession portrayed in this image included the blowing of conch shells, a small child wearing a big, conical hat , and a small version of a Pope's Day wagon, carried on a handheld platform. Henry Hulton, customs official who arrived in the city on the 5th noted "twenty Devils, Pope's, & Pretenders".

- Bell, J. L., "Du Simitiére's Sketches of Pope Day in Boston, 1767," in *The World of Children, 1620-1920*, ed. Peter Benes (Boston: Boston University Press, 2002), 209-20, esp. 210, 212-13, 215-16. Hulton, Ann [sister], *Letters of a Loyalist Lady* (Cambridge, Massachusetts: Harvard University Press, 1927), 8.

1767- "A Friend to Peace" wrote of the holiday, in Boston in the *News-Letter*, recognizing "the happy Deliverance of the British Nation from the Popish Plot." This work emphasized "Animosity," and "Folly" of Pope's Day in the city. "A Friend of Peace" condemned the festivity for generating immorality and irreligion, forsaking "Kindred and Friendship" for parading of "clumsy Image[s]" in "Rags." Observing the violence, and the "hellish Malice," of Pope's Days, the author wrote:

"Can any Thing be more absurd, than [the act of] Men . . . [abandoning] every
Sentiment of Morality and Religion . . . and . . . commit[ting] such cruel Ravages
upon one another as even the evil Spirits would be asham'd of? . . . I do not urge
the Scandal that is bro't on the Town, no the Pretence [sic] which it gives our
Enemies to inculcate the Necessity of Quartering Troops upon us to restrain
Licentiousness. — Murder has been sometimes committed in these ignominious
Quarrels, and probably may be again . . . and . . . the Man who has countenanced
[these quarrels], tho' he may escape the Punishment of [the] Law, will ever
remain guilty in the Sight of Heaven.

"A Friend of Peace," was upset by the Quartering Act of 1765 but he was also upset by
 "fighting under the Standard of Infatuation." "He did not approve of a fête, an "absurdity"that had intensified the anger of Parliament. He thanked the men who "two Years past" brought "Order" and "Unity" to Boston. He hoped that celebrations would not again get the "Passions" of this port town "work'd up to such a Pitch of Madness."

-"Boston, November 5," *Boston News-Letter, via Supplement to the Massachusetts-Gazette*, November 5, 1767.

1767-Boston

"By November 1767, the Pope rarely made any appearances at all to further politicize the event. Advocates of the Townshend duties and the Tea Act became common Pope Day targets instead of the Pope."

- Hoerder, "Boston Leaders," 248, Cited In: Peter D. Apgar, FESTIVALS OF COLONIAL AMERICA: FROM CELEBRATION TO REVOLUTION, 1995.

1767- Newport, the General Assembly of Rhode Island reviewed the royal charter of 1663, and reissued many laws including prohibitions on the "firing of Guns and Pistols," the "throwing of Squibs, Fire-Works, &c. in the Streets," the lighting of bonfires on "Gunpowder-Treason Day.

-Rhode Island [Assembly], *The Charter, Granted by His Majesty, King Charles II. to the Governor and Company of the English Colony of Rhode-Island and Providence-Plantations, in New England, in America* (Newport: Printed and Sold by Samuel Hall, 1767), 120-21. -

1767- November, 5th. Effigies of the Pope, &c. carried about town, as commemorative of gun powder treason.

-Joseph B. Felt, *Annals of Salem,* 1827.

1767- William Cooper, town clerk of Boston, supported the nonimportation agreement of this city, and asked that the town "take all proper Measures," by keeping indoors "Children and Servants" and "other Ways to prevent such Disturbances as have sometimes happened on or about the 5th Day of November."

-[No Title], *Boston Evening Post*, November 2, 1767.

1768-New Hampshire Legal Action
New Hampshire Law
1768

An Act To Prevent the Disorders Commonly Committed on the Fifth of November & the Evening following under pretence of celebrating the anniversary of the deliverance from the Gunpowder Plot.

[Passed Oct. 28, 1768. 9 George III. Original Acts. Vol. 6, p. 21: recorded Acts, vol. 3, p. 90. This act is revived and extended for ten years by the act of Jan. 10, 1771.]

Whereas it Often Happens that many Disorders & Disturbances are Occasiond and Committed by Loose Idle People under a Notion & Pretence of Celebrating and keeping a Memorial of the Deliverance from the Gunpowder Plot on the fifth of November & the Evening following as Servants & boys Tempted to Excessive Drinking & Quarreling – Surrounding Peoples doors with Clamor & rudely Demanding money or Liquor making mock Shows of the Pope & other Exhibitions making bonfires whereby buildings are in Danger in Populous places & Stealing Materials for such fires with many other Irregularities which Disturb the Peace of Such places & tend much to Corrupt the Manners of Youth – for Prevention whereof.

Be it enacted by the Governor Council and Assembly That Henceforth all Such Clubs Companies & Assemblies for Celebrating or Commemorating the Day aforesaid with the usual shows & mock representations of the Pope & other Exhibitions usually Carried from place to place with the Rude Noisy speeches & Demands of Money or Liquor frequently made at Peoples Doors and the making of bonfires are hereby Strictly forbidden to be done, on the said Day or evening following or any other on the Account of & for the Cause Aforesaid on pain of Imprisonment for the Space of forty eight hours of all concernd in perpetrating any of the Offences aforesaid. And it shall be Lawful for any Justice of the peace Judge of the Superior Court of Judicature Inferior Court of Common pleas or the Sheriff of the Province upon their own View, or the Information of any Credible Witness to Cause any such Offenders or Offender to be brought before him & on Conviction to Commit the Offender for the space aforesaid unless they shall upon warning & being forbid to proceed therein which shall be first given by any householder, they shall Immediately Disperse & Retire.

.... "Be it enacted by the Governor Council and Assembly that henceforth all such clubs and companies and assemblies for celebrating or commemorating the day aforesaid with the usual shows and mock representations of the Pope and other exhibitions usually carried from place to place with the rude noisy speeches and demands of money or liquor frequently made at peoples doors and the making of bonfires are strictly forbidden to be done."

1768- Charles Paxton, customs commissioner who collected taxes on British manufactures, thought that the folly, or malevolence, of the day had gotten out of hand.
He wrote Lord Townshend on November 6, to complain that he had suffered on
November 5, "the indignity of being burnt in Effigie" in Boston.

- Paxton, Charles, Letter to Lord [Charles?] Townshend, November 6, 1768, in George G. Wolkins, ed., "Letters of Charles Paxton," *Proceedings of the Massachusetts Historical Society* 56 (1923): 350.

1768- Boston, Fifth of November. Celebrated with play and politics, maintaining
order and peace. Apprentices in Boston adopted the title "the printer boys" wrote and printed a poem "South End Forever. North End Forever. Extraordinary Verses on Pope-Night." The poem, a broadside, portrayed the spirit of the day. In a series of quatrains, the "printer boys" remembered the history of the Plot and invited others to celebrate:

HUZZA! brave Boys, behold the *Pope*,
*Pretender* and *Old-Nick*,
How they together lay their Heads,
To plot a poison Trick?
To blow up KING and PARLIAMENT
To Flitters, rent and torn:
. . .
Come on, brave Youths, drag on your *Pope*
Let's see his frightful Phiz:
Let's view his Features rough and fierce,
That Map of Ugliness!

They called the pope: "the Man of Sin,"

Others should join in:

*Old Boys*, and young, be Sure observe
The *Fifth* Day of *November*;
What tho' it is a Day apast?
You still can it remember.
The little *Popes*, they go out First,
With little teney Boys:
In Frolicks they are full of Gale
And laughing make a Noise.
The Girls run out to fee the Sight,
The Boys eke ev'ry one;
. . .

They also said the pope was: "the Beast of the Sea" of the Book of Revelation. The "boys" of Boston told the crowd that it should meet at the Mill Dam, and burn "the Man of Sin" to a crisp, and then, "plunge" the body into the sea.

- The Printer Boys in Boston, "South End Forever. North End Forever. Extraordinary Verses on Pope-Night . . ." (Boston: The Printer Boys in Boston, 1768) -

1768- Spring, the *Gazette; and Country Journal* of Providence reissued "Innocency's Complaint," the poem by George Joy written in 1677. Three couplets have special meaning in this time:

The making [of] laws for to ensnare the just,
Of God is hated, and to be accurst,
The Massachusetts is alike for crime
Unto Judea, in Christ Jesus' Time:
. . .
Let these black days, like the fifth of November,
Be writ in red, for ages to remember.

1768- Ashley Bowen, rigging business owner and veteran of the Siege of Quebec in 1768, and a member of the Church of England, wrote that "the boys" in Marblehead, Massachusetts, considered the Fifth as a red-letter day.

-[No Headline], *Providence Gazette; and Country Journal*, June 18, 1768. "Providence, November 11," *Providence Gazette; and Country Journal*, November 11, 1769.

1768- The assembly of New Hampshire enacted "a most excellent law." Due to disorder in Portsmouth, banned "Apprentices, Boys, &c. from carrying Effigies, representing the Pope, Devil, &c." around this town in thanksgiving for the frustration of "the Powder Plot.
-"Portsmouth, Nov. 4," *New-Hampshire Gazette, and Historical Chronicle*, November 4, 1768.

1768- The town council of New London, Connecticut, noted that November 5 had in recent years produced "very bad consequences, and pregnant mischief and much disorder," the Fifth had to be controlled. Effigy-burning would result in a fifteen-shilling fine.

-Frances Manwaring Caulkins, *History of New London, Connecticut, From the First Survey of the Coast in 1612 to 1860* (New London: H. D. Utley, 1852), 480-81.

1769- The royal government in New Hampshire noted its displeasure of Pope's Day, as the House of Representatives condemned the "Pretence" of celebrating the discovery of the Plot.

-New Hampshire Government], *Journal of the House of Representatives for the Province of New Hampshire, Conven'd the 21st Day of February 1769* . . . (Portsmouth: Daniel and Robert L. Fowle, 1769), 94-95.

1769- August 1770, Sgt. Thomas Thornley of the army's 14th Regiment told a Boston magistrate that the 5th of November before he was been:

"oblig'd to go through a large mob to the relief of the Sentries, the mob called him and his party Lobster scoundrels, what business had they there, & damn'd Governor [Francis] Bernard, the Commissioners, and the rest of the scoundrels of Ministers that ordered the Soldiers to Boston, on which he the Deponent was obliged to order his party to charge their bayonets to make way through the mob, all the while receiving a great deal of abusive language." When Thornley testified the conflict between citizens and soldiers had led to the shootings near the Old State House known as the Boston Massacre.

- Thornley deposition dated 25 Aug 1770, Colonial Office Transcripts, 5:88:412, Manuscripts Division, Library of Congress. http://display.5thofnovember.us/2007/10/bostons-gangs.html.

1769- "A Description of the Pope, 1769." Published. It replicated imagery of the Pope's Day processions used in 1768, it approved of the "Love" and the "Unity" that the union of the two ends then yielded. ( November 5 fell on a Sunday in 1769, therefore government and people celebrated the Fifth on Monday, the sixth The government fired the guns.) This broadside supported the abuse of the man-made-villain, John Mein. Scottish-born bookseller and printer, a transplant, and a violent critic of the nonimportation agreement who had disclosed names of merchants who first signed and then violated the agreement. In late October, a mob had attacked the man with a cane and a shovel, shouting "Kill him, kill him!." He later attacked the Whig leadership of Boston in the *Chronicle*. (After hiding, he had fired into the mob.)

"A Description of the Pope" used an acrostic of "J-O-H-N M-E-I-N" that had been used in the parade: "Mean is the Man, M--N is his Name,"

Now shake, ye Torries! See the Rogue behind,
Hung up on a Scarecrow, to correct Mankind.
Oh had the Villain but received his Due,
Himself in Person would here swing in View:
But let the Traitor mend [?] within the Year,
Or by the next he shall be hanging here.

- Anonymous, "Description of the Pope, 1769," Boston: S.N., 1769; and "From Tuesday, November 7 to Tuesday, November 14, 1769.

1769- The paraded at one large carriage and at one large lantern.It offered toasts to "the American Whig," "Confusion to the Torries,"and "a total Banishment to Bribery and Corruption." The called The Tory community as: "infernal Crew" of "Slaves," and it stated its intent to spill "honest Blood" and "purge the Land" of the enemy. Carriages; effigies of the Devil and the Pope, with crucifixes and pitchforks; and horn blowing were part of the procession. They thought Lord Bute, adversary of 1765, "the veriest monster on earth." They proclaimed : "WILKES and LIBERTY, No. 45." The crowd called those supporting the bookseller "A Bunch of Tom-Cods." It hung Mein in effigy including, "Johny Dupe Esq." (the name the printer had given John Hancock, merchant-patriot). They attacked an effigy of the Mein printing press. That evening, the crowd "retired" to Copp's Hill, and burned the effigies. Mein sailed for London on November 17.

- Anonymous, "Description of the Pope, 1769" (Boston: S.N., 1769); "Boston Intelligence," [Salem, Massachusetts] *Essex Gazette*, November 14, 1769.

1769- January, the *Evening-Post* reflected on "the resolution of 1765" that formed the union, and commended the "decency" and "decorum" that the celebration produced in. In October, an unknown gentleman of Boston wrote a letter to the *Gazette*, noting that, "ever since the UNION in 1765," the celebration had been "observ'd" with dignity and modesty. He noted a culture of violence in the city, year round, and, he requested that the legislature proceed with caution, making "any appearance of *authority*," or sign of the power of the government over crowds noting "*alarming* Attacks" on estates and persons, and the aggression of the British Army in Boston, the author hoped that this government would keep the city from becoming a war zone. He hoped that the Hutchinson administration would keep the peace and keep "the *Tragedy of St. George's Fields*" (a 1768 London riot in which troops shot into a crowd protesting the imprisonment of the Whig hero Wilkes) from being "[re-en]acted in the Streets." He wanted the government to do more than fight and outlaw the "Pageantry" of the Fifth. Noting that, "if the Pageantry usually made on the Fifth of November, *was not* an actual Breach of the Peace, it had a Tendency to it," and admitting that the army was a source of concern in the town, another writer noted that "the UNION" might collapse on the Fifth.

- "Pleasure; November; Decorum; Time; Persone; Evening; Faces," *Boston Gazette, and Country*

*Journal*, October 30, 1769, "People; Thousands; Inhabitants; Lights; Notice; Commanding Officer; Majesty; Town," [Portsmouth] *New-Hampshire Gazette, and Historical Chronicle*, November 3, 1769.
c. 1771 (?) Recollections of Samuel Breck, with passages from his note-books. (1771–1862.).

1769- John Rowe, diarist, recorded on November 5 "A wet Rainy Day. Pope weather!."

The Boston Gazette noted that "no Man's 'Person or Property was in the least Degree injur'd'" and: "those few who were in hopes to make out a Riot, were sadly disappointed." A fight in wherein a civilian "drub'd on" a soldier when the soldier tried to stop him from celebrating with "some Pageantry" in the area of the state house.

-Pierce, ed., *Letters and Diary of John Rowe*, 145. "Boston, November 13," *Boston-Gazette, and Country Journal*, November 13, 1769.

1769- "a great Concourse of People" met in Providence, R.I, to celebrate "the Anniversary of the Popish Plot, commonly called Gunpowder Treason," and burn effigies of "the Pope, Devil, &c."

-"Providence, November 11," *Providence Gazette; and Country Journal*, November 11, 1769.

1769- Marblehead, Massachusetts, celebrated the Fifth as a red-letter day. Men "carried a Pope about the town" and made this date "a grand holiday" in 1770.

- Smith, Philip Chadwick Foster ed., *The Journals of Ashley Bowen (1728-1813) of Marblehead, Publications of the Colonial Society of Massachusetts*, Vol. 44: Collections (Boston: *Colonial Society of Massachusetts*, 1973), 225, 258.

1770- Boston, The Hutchinson administration celebrated the holiday by holding a church service at King's Chapel, and firing guns, on land, at the batteries and the castle and, at sea, from the frigates and the ships of His Majesty.

-"Boston, November 12," *Boston Post Boy*, November 12, 1770.

1770- Casco Bay, Samuel Deane, the minister of the First Parish Church in Portland, Maine, saw: "several popes and devils" being paraded on the 5th.

- Samuel Deane, Diary, November 5, 1770, in William Willis, ed., *Journals of the Rev. Thomas Smith, and the Rev. Samuel Deane: Pastors of the First Church in Portland: With Notes and Biographical Notices: And a Summary History of Portland* (Portland: Joseph S. Bailey, 1849), 329.

1770- Some called the Boston massacre a new gunpowder plot on March 15, the *Connecticut Courant*, patriot newspaper from New Haven, linked the Fifth of March with the Fifth of November. It suggested investigation would "lay open such a plot as will render the Fifth of November below the notice even of boys and children."

- "Boston, March 15," [New Haven] *Connecticut Courant*, March 23, 1770.

1770- Appearance of Joyce Jr. as effigy.

"By 1770, a new character arrived on the scene in Pope Days Joyce Jr., the same "individual" who "signed" the notice from the Boston Committee of Tarring and Feathering. Joyce was the arresting officer and one of the executioners of King Charles. This event in 1649 ushered in an 11-year period when no monarch ruled. In 1821 a Boston newspaper printed a series of articles titled Reminiscences that described Joyce's role in Pope Day. The paper explained:

"[Joyce] used to ride on an ass . . . His office was to assemble men and boys in mob style, and ride in the middle of them, and in such company to terrify adherents to the Royal Government, before the Revolution."

- Hennig Cohen and Tristram Coffin, eds.. The Folklore of American Holidays (Detroit: Gale Research Company, 1987), 319.

The appearance of Joyce, a regicide, as a symbol of authority whose main role was to terrify officers and supporters of the Crown further pushed Pope Day festivities closer to revolution."

- Apgar, Peter D., FESTIVALS OF COLONIAL AMERICA: FROM CELEBRATION TO REVOLUTION, 1995.

1770
Boston Celebrations
Cited in: Hennig Cohen and Tristram Coffin, eds. The Folklore of American Holidays (Detroit: Gale Research Company, 1987)

1821-"Reminiscences" "A man used to ride on an ass, with immense jack boots, and his face covered with a horrible mask, and was called Joyce, Jr. His office was to assemble men and boys in mob style, and ride in the middle of them, and in such company to terrify adherents to Royal Government, before the Revolution. The tumults which resulted in the Massacre, 1770, was excited by that means. -Joyce Junior was said to have a particular whistle which brought his adherents, &c. whenever they were wanted."

-Publications of the Colonial Society of Mass. VIII , 1903. 90-91. and Boston Daily Advertiser, Nov 9 1821.

1771, February- The *Essex Gazette* of Salem noted that America, like Britain, was a place of "haters of popery" and the "sons of Belial." It also wrote that America defended liberty and Protestantism. The paper argued that the Fifth of March now trumped the Fifth of November, because Britain had "formed a plan to blow up all the liberties of the Americans."

- "From the Essex Gazette, Feb. 22, 1771," *Newport Mercury*, March 6, 1771.

1771- November 5. No popes nor devils here to-night at my house. 26. Pearson Jones married (to Betty, daughter of Enoch Ilsley, afterwards married to Samuel Freeman.) This has been, on the whole, an extraordinary warm and pleasant fall.

- Samuel Deane, Diary, November 5, 1770, in William Willis, ed., *Journals of the Rev. Thomas Smith, and the Rev. Samuel Deane: Pastors of the First Church in Portland: With Notes and Biographical Notices: And a Summary History of Portland* (Portland: Joseph S. Bailey, 1849), 329.

c. 1771- 18-We stayed a few months in Philadelphia, and then removed to Taunton in Massachusetts, in order to be ready to enter Boston as soon as the British should evacuate the town. It was here at Taunton that I distinctly recollect seeing the procession of the Pope and the Devil on the 5th of November, the anniversary of the Gunpowder Plot. Effigies of those two illustrious personages were paraded round the Common, and this was perhaps the exhibition of the kind in our country.† Sentiments of great liberality and toleration, together with an entire absence of colonial or English feeling, have contributed to abolish the custom heretofore annual, and to root out all violent prejudices against the good bishop of Rome and the Church which he governs. † The celebration of Pope Day in Boston was always accompanied by violence. There were rival popes from the North End and the South End—the Avignon and Rome of Boston—and the followers of each fought to get possession of the opposition pope. General Sumner, in his Reminiscences, published in the New England Historic Genealogical Register (vol. viii., April, 1854), gives an account of Governor Hancock's measures, through the mollifying influences of a dinner, to put an end to Pope Day in Boston a short time before more tragic hostilities broke out in 1775. In due time we returned to Boston, and having been nursed, as I said before, at Lexington,…..
"They were a set of the lowest blackguards, who, disguised in filthy clothes and ofttimes with masked faces, went from house to house in large companies, and, *bon gré, mal gré,* obtruding themselves everywhere,

particularly into the rooms that were occupied by parties of ladies and gentlemen, would demand themselves with great insolence. . . .

"The only way to get rid of them was to give them money, and listen patiently to a foolish dialogue between two or more of them. . . . In this way they continue for half an hour; and it happened not unfrequently that the house would be filled by another gang when these had departed."

- Breck, Samuel, *Recollections of Samuel Breck, with passages from his note-books.* (1771–1862.).

1771- Stephen Hawley, pastor, Congregational Church in Bethany, Connecticut, highlighted the evils of the Gunpowder Plot in a discussion he read on theodicy and weather. He remembered that God "with a Blast," overcame "Instruments and Weapons of Blood and War" of the Church of Rome preserving, in England, "the Rights of Reason, Conscience, and Religion." God had, he maintained, stopped the "Fooleries" and the "Fopperies" of that church.

Vincent, Thomas *Gods Terrible Voice in the City of London: . . . the Narration of Two Late Dreadful Judgments of Plague and Fire . . .* (New London: T. Green, 1770), 19-20.

1771- Williamsburg, The College of William and Mary satisfied its 1693 charter that required the school "pay" the government Latin verses "every fifth day of November.", it presented a poem, written in honor of king George III, and Lord Dunmore, governor of Virginia, that emphasized the base nature of Catholicism and the virtues of Protestantism. It remembered, that God had "laid low" "the papists" – "authors" of the Plot – in 1605, hitting Catesby, Fawkes, and others with a "blazing hand" of justice and violence.

- Jones, Julian Ward, "A 'New' Latin Quitrent Poem of the College of William and Mary," *Virginia Magazine . . .* 96.4 (1988): 500; Counsell, E. M., "Latin Verses Presented by Students of William and Mary College to the Governor of Virginia, 1771, 1772, 1773, and 1774," *William and Mary Quarterly* 10.3 (Jul. 1930): 269-70.

1771, November 5- Narragansett Bay, Ezra Stiles, minister of Second Congregational Church of Newport, observed "Powder Plot, - Pope, &ct carried about".

- Stiles, Ezra, Diary, November 5, 1771, in Franklin Bowditch Dexter, ed., *The Literary Diary of Ezra Stiles,* Vol. I: Jan. 1, 1769 - Mar. 13, 1776 (New York: C. Scribner's Sons, 1901), 182.

1771, January- Colonial legislature of New Hampshire extended, the law of 1769 that forbid "the licentious practices" of the holiday for a decade. It noted concerns for "peace and safety."

-New Hampshire, *An Act to Authorise the Treasure to Issue an Extent Against the Purchaser of the Excise . . .* (Portsmouth: Daniel and Robert Fowle, 1773), 44. The 1769 law was renewed ("revived") on
January 10, 1771.

1772-November 5- Narragansett Bay, Ezra Stiles, minister of Second Congregational Church of Newport, observed . . . . . . This afternoon three popes &c. paraded thro' the streets, & in the Evening they were consumed in a Bonfire as usual —among other were Ld. North, Gov. Hutchinson & Gen. Gage.

-- Stiles, Ezra, Diary, November 5, 1771, in Franklin Bowditch Dexter, ed., *The Literary Diary of Ezra Stiles*, Vol. I: Jan. 1, 1769 - Mar. 13, 1776 (New York: C. Scribner's Sons, 1901), 470.

1772- Dedham, Massachusetts, almanac-maker Nathaniel Ames published an almanac that contained:

"To burn the Pope, is now a joke,

for a design he miss't on,
to sap that mansion
which dares pension
your famous Butcher *Preston*!"

- Ames, Nathaniel, *An Astronomical Diary; or Almanack for the Year of Our Lord Christ 1772* (New London: Timothy Green, 1771).

1773- The Tea Act and the Quebec Act aggravated the old street warfare in Boston on the Fifth. -

1773- November 5:

"This accursed Tea is the very Match that is appointed to set fire to a Train of Gunpowder that has been long, tho'
secretiy, laid by our Ministry and your Governor,"

-*The Massachusetts Spy.*

1773- Boson, November 5, The patriot corps met at Faneuil Hall, to protest of the new Tea Act, six weeks before the "Destruction of the Tea." December 20.

- Cooper, William, "Notification. The Freeholders and Other Inhabitants of the Town of Boston,
Qualified as the Law Directs, Are Hereby Notified to Meet at Faneuil-Hall, on Friday the 5th Day of
November Instant . . . [Regarding] the Report That the East-India Company in London Are About Shipping a Cargo or Cargoes of Tea Into This and the Other Colonies; and That They Esteem It a Political Plan of the British Administration" (Boston: S. N., 1773).

1773- Boson, November 5, Manhattan, a handbill to "the friends of liberty and commerce" was distributed in favor of a nonimportation agreement.

-"New York, Nov. 3, 1773," *Rivington's New-York Gazetteer*, November 11, 1773.

1773- November 5- Boston, "the Union of 1765" collapsed, fighting between the North End and the South End returned. The *Massachusetts Spy* noted that, after
the old game of "*Blows* and *Knocks*," the North End was victorious and won the pope of the South End.

-"Thursday, November 11. Boston," *Massachusetts Spy Or, Thomas's Boston Journal*, November 11,
1773.

1773- November 5- Boston, John Rowe wrote that November 5, was a "very quiet" occasion for a Pope Night," he may have missed it as he had attended a ball.

-Pierce, ed., *Letters and Diary of John Rowe*, 254.


1774-New-York, June 16. Last night a gallows with the figure of three men suspended by the neck, intended to represent Lord N-- , Governor H—, and Solicitor W--, with another figure representing the devil, were carried through the principal streets the city attended by several thousand people, and- burnt before the coffee-house door. They were decorated with suitable emblems, devices and inscriptions.

- *Hampshire Chronicle* - Monday August 8, 1774.

1773-November 5, New York.
"[A] vast multitude of the Inhabitants of all ranks paraded" -effigies were burned in a bonfire.

- New York Journal, Nov. 15, 1773.

1774-Charleston S.C.

1774- Charleston, a person represented the devil: "curiously tarred and feathered," and with a sign- "HOWL-Ye! Prepare my Way.-Lie on one Side, then on the other; and proclaim hyour Candour on each. You are my Beloved-be dilligent in your calling."

- South Carolina Gazette, Nov. 21, 1774.

"Saturday last, being the Anniversary of the Nation's happy Deliverance from the infernal Popish POWDER-PLOT in 1605, and also of the glorious REVOLUTION by the Landing of King William in 1688, two Events which our Brethern in England seem of late to have too much overlooked, the Morning was ushered in with Ringing of Bells, and a "Magnificent Exhibition" of Effigies, designed to represent Lord North, Gov. Hutchinson, the Pope, and the DEVIL, which were placed on a rolling stage, about eight feet high and fifteen feet long, hear Mr. Ramadge's Tavern in Broad street, being the most frequented place in town. The Pope was exhibited in a chair of state superbly drest in all his priestly Canonicals; Lord North (with his Star, garter, & showing the Quebec Bill) on his right hand , and Governor Hutchinson on his left, both chained to stakes; the Devil with extended ARms, behind the Thre, and elevated above them, holding in one Hand a Javelin directed at the Head of Lord North, and in the other a scroll, inscribed" Rivington's New York Gazetteer;" on his arm was suspended a large Lanthorn, in the shape of a Tea Cannister, on the side of which was writ in Capitals, "Hyson, Green, Congo and Bohea Teas." The Exhibition was constantly viewed by an incredible Number of Spectators, among whom were most of the Ladies and Gentlemen of First Fortune and Fashion. The Pope and the Devil, were observed frequently to bow, in the most complaisant manner, to sundry individuals, as if in grateful Acknowledgement of their past services. About 8 o'clock, A.M. the whole was moved to the square before the State-House, and back again to Mr. Ramadge's, where Devine services began in St. Michael's Church; in which situation it remained throughout the day without the least Appearance of Opposition, Tumult, or Disorder. The figure Representing Lord North, was reckoned a tolerable Likeness, and that of Governor Hutchinson a very striking one; both their heads having been carved from very good Designs. IN the Evening the whole Machinery was carried thro' the principle (sic) streets, to the Parade, without the Town Gate, when a pole 50 feet high was erected, strung with and surrounded by a great numnber of Tar Barrels. The tea collected by young Gentlemen the Tuesday before, being placed between the Devil and Lord North, was set on fire, and brought on our Enemies in Effigy, that Ruin they had designed to bring on us in Reality. The whole was consumed in a short time, in the Presence of some Thousands who rejoiced to see the Abbertors of American Taxation consumed, By that very Engine of Oppression. It is remarkable, that during the whole Transaction not the least Disorder Happened; and by 8'o clock at Night the Town was in a great a Quiet as on a Sabbath Evening... Besides the above exhibition, the young Gentlemen from the schools, prepared another Pope and Devil, which they also burnt in the Evening, after parading all the Streets with them throughout the Day. Their Devil was a most grotesque figure, curiously tarred and feathered. Their Pope was also in a fitting Posture, which a large lLanthorn before him , on the Front of which was writ- Liberty, Prosperity, and Carolina Forever--on one side was drawn, a large Cannister of Tea in Flames- on the other the Figure of America hurling a Spear at the Lord North, Kneeling upon a chest of tea, and bound with a cord, held by a hand representing Magna Charta...

-*South Carolina Gazette, Nov. 21, 1774.* cited in: -Hennig Cohen and Tristram Coffin, eds. The Folklore of American Holidays (Detroit: Gale Research Company, 1987).

1774-November

Charleston

"We had great diversion the 5th instant in seeing the effigies of Lord North, Governor Hutchinson, the Pope and the Devil, which were erected on a moving machine, and after having been paraded about the town all day, they were in the evening burnt on the common with a large bonfire, attended by a numerous crowd of people".

- New York Journal," Dec. 15, 1774. PDC.

1774- October 24,

The town of Newburyport (Mass.) voted, "that no effigies be carried about or exhibited on the 5th of November, only in the day-time." Motives of policy afterwards induced the discontinuance of this custom which has now become obsolete. This year (1774) the celebration went off with a great flourish. In the day-time companies of little boys might be seen in various parts of the town, with their little popes dressed up in the most grotesque and fantastic manner, which they carried about, some on boards and some on little carriages for their own and others' amusement. But the great exhibition was reserved for the night, in which young men as well as boys participated. They first constructed a huge vehicle, varying at times, from 20 to 40 feet long, 8 or 10 wide, and 5 or 6 high, from the lower to the upper platform, on the front of which they erected a paper lantern, capacious enough to hold in addition to the lights, five or six persons. Behind that as large as life sat the mimic Pope and several other personages, monks, friars and so forth. Last but not least stood an image of what was designed to be a representation of old Nick himself, furnished with a pair of huge horns, holding in his hands a pitchfork and otherwise accoutred, with all the frightful ugliness that their ingenuity could devise. Their next step after they had mounted their ponderous vehicle on four wheels, chosen their officers, captain, first and second lieutenant, purser and so forth, placed a boy under the platform to elevate and move around at proper intervals the movable head of the Pope.

- History of Newburyport PDC.

1775- Newberryport Mass.

"In the day time, companies of little boys might be seen, in various parts of the town, with their little popes, dressed up in the most grotesque and fantastic manner, which they carried about, some on boards, and some on little carriages, for their own and other's amusement. But the great exhibition was reserved for the night, in which young men, as well as boys, participated. They first constructed a huge vehicle, varying at times, from twenty to forty feet long, eight or ten wide, and five or six high, from the lower to the upper platform, in the front of which they erected a paper lantern, capacious enough to hold, in addition to the lights five or six persons. Behind that, as large as life, sat the mimic pope, and several other personages, monks, friars and so forth. Last, but not least, stood an image of what was designed to be a representation of old Nick himself, furnished with a pair of huge horns, holding in his hand a pitchfork, and otherwise accoutered, with all the frightful ugliness that their ingenuity could desire. Their next step, after they had mounted their ponderous vehicle on four wheels, chosen their officers, captain, first and second lieutenant, purser and so forth, placed a boy under the platform, to elevate and move round, at proper intervals, the moveable head of the pope and attached, ropes to the front part of the machine, was to take up their line of march through the principal streets of the town. Sometimes in addition to the images of the pope and his company, there might be found, on the same platform, half a dozen dancers and a fiddler, whose "Hornpipes, jigs, strathspeys, and reels Put life and Mettle in their heels,
Together with a large crowd who made up a long procession. Their custom was, to call at the principal houses in various parts of the town, ring their bell, cause the pope to elevate his head, and look round upon the audience, and repeat the following lines…

-*Publications of the Colonial Society of Mass.*, XII (19809), 293-4. also Henry W. Cunningham on the Contents of a colonial Diary quoting from Joshua Coffin's History of Newbury…1635-1845, Boston, 1845, 249-516. cited in: Hennig Cohen and Tristram Coffin, eds. The Folklore of American Holidays (Detroit: Gale Research Company, 1987) - Cited by Peter D. Apgar in: Festivals of Colonial America from Celebration ot Revolution. Masters Thesis, 1995, Texas Tech. pp. 52-67.

1775- November 5. George Washington , November 5, 1775, General Orders

The Writings of George Washington from the Original Manuscript Sources, 1745-1799. John C. Fitzpatrick, Editor. --vol. 04

Head Quarters, Cambridge, November 5, 1775.

Parole Montgomery. Countersign Chamblee.

Samuel Huntington, and John Englis, soldiers in the 34th Regt. of foot, tried at a late General Court Martial for "Mutiny"--The Court upon mature consideration, are of opinion that the Evidence against the prisoners, is not sufficient to convict them ofMutiny, but they are each of them guilty of assisting and encouraging Mutiny, therefore adjudge that each of them pay a fine of fifteen Shillings, and suffer each of them fifteen days fatigue. The General approves the Sentence and orders it to be put in execution.

As the Commander in Chief has been apprized of a design form'd for the observance of that ridiculous and childish custom of burning the Effigy of the pope--He cannot help expressing his surprise that there should be Officers and Soldiers in this army so void of common sense, as not to see the impropriety of such a step at this Juncture; at a Time when we are

solliciting, and have really obtain'd, the friendship and alliance of the people of Canada, whom we ought to consider as Brethren embarked in the same Cause. The defence of the general Liberty of America: At such a juncture, and in such Circumstances, to be insulting their Religion, is so monstrous, as not to be suffered or excused; indeed instead of offering the most remote insult, it is our duty to address public thanks to these our Brethren, as to them we are so much indebted for every late happy Success over the common Enemy in Canada. PDC

1775- After 1775, In the new nation, the evocation of the Gunpowder Treason it helped elucidate the reframing of the federal government during the drafting and the ratification of the Constitution, and the debate of the merits of aristocracy and democracy.

1771- Boston, the Hutchinson administration celebrated the Fifth, "the happy Deliverance of the British Nation from the Popish Powder Plot," by firing the guns at the forts and the nine men-of-war in the harbor.

-"Boston, November 7," *Boston News-Letter*, November 7, 1771. -

November 5 after 1783

1783- Fletcher, John, 1783

6. Sometimes the plainest *prophecies,* the most public *miracles,* and the *annals* of kingdoms, well known when those books were first received, wonderfully concur to demonstrate their authenticity. Take one instance out of many. A prophet out of Judah, above 300 years before the event, thus foretold the pollution of Jeroboam's altar at Bethel, before Jeroboam himself, who was attended by his priests, his courtiers, and, no doubt, a vast number of idolatrous worshippers: *O altar, altar, thus says the Lord, Behold a child shall be born unto the house of David, Josiah by name, who shall burn mens bones upon thee:* and *this is the sign: Behold,* this very day, *the altar shall be rent, and the ashes that are upon it scattered.* King Jeroboam, enflamed with anger, *stretched forth his hand against the man of God, saying* to his guards, *Lay hold on him*; but his extended hand *was dried*

*up so that he could not pull it in again to him*; the rending of the altar, and scattering of the fire, instantly took place; and the capital prophecy was exactly fulfilled by pious king *Josiah,* as you may see by comparing 1 Kings xiii. 1, &c. with 2 Kings xxiii. 15, &c.—Can we reasonably suppose, that books, containing accounts of such public events, would have been received as *divine,* by a *divided* people, if their authenticity had not been confirmed by indubitable matter of fact? Nay, is it not as absurd to assert it, as it would be to affirm, that the offices for the 5th of November, and the 30th of January, were forged by crafty priests; and that the Papists, Puritans, and Royalists of the last century, agreed to impose upon the world the history of the gun-powder plot, and of king Charles's decollation, with which those parts of our liturgy are so inseparably connected?

7. This scattered, despised people, the irreconcileable enemies of the Christians, keep with amazing care [*] the old testament, full of the prophetic history of Jesus Christ, and by that means afford the world a striking proof that the new testament is true; and Christians in their turn show, that the old testament is abundantly confirmed and explained by the new. The earl of Rochester, the great wit of the last century, was so struck with this proof, that upon reading the 53d chapter of Isaiah, with floods of penitential tears he lamented his former infidelity, and warmly embraced the faith, which he had so publicly ridiculed

-Fletcher, John, An appeal to matter of fact and common sense. Or A rational demonstration of man's corrupt and lost estate. Bristol: printed, Philadelphia: re-printed by Melchior Steiner, in Race-Street, near Third-Street., M.DCC.LXXXIII. [1783], pp.140-141.

1785, November 5, Portsmouth, New Hampshire,

A "greasy and dirty," two-faced dummy of the arch-traitor, Benedict Arnold rather than "Guy Fox and his companions, as usual," was paraded with "a rusty sword".

- "Portsmouth, Nov. 11," [Portsmouth] *The New-Hampshire Gazette; or State Journal, and General Advertiser*, November 11, 1785.


1786, 4 November- Thomas Brand Hollis to Abigail Adams

The 4th of November
The day of deliverance from Popery and Tyranny. 1786

Mr Brand Hollis presents his compliments to Mrs Adams and desires her acceptance of two medals one on the execution of the counts Egmont and Horne two Dutch Patriots contrary to faith-given!

The other on the Murder of the first Prince of Orange
Base acts of a Tyrant!
Three common wealth coins to record, what England once was.
Mrs Adams had the only copy of the right hand of Fellowship which was printed at that time otherwise more would have been sent.
-Adams Papers

1787- 23 November, Massachusetts Gazette,

The enemies of the new constitution have discovered their modesty in *one circumstance*—they have not had the assurance to offer any system of their own, in lieu of the excellent one they attempt to depreciate.

A correspondent observes, that the source of opposition, at present, in this place, to that glorious fabrick of republicanism, the FEDERAL CONSTITUTION, is derived from two characters, who, if they had their just des[s]erts, would be carted about and hooted at, as the effigies of the devil and the pretender formerly were, in this town.13 One of the characters, as some one has remarked before, *crept into office* by means of a most glaring deception practised upon his fellow-citizens,14 and the other, for some of his *good deeds*, in the town to which he belongs, was, some time since, *promoted* to the *high* and *important office* of—*Hog-Reeve.*

1789- July, William Maclay of Pennsylvania, Senator expressed a lack of faith in the Judiciary. He had genuine "fear" that the bill, "a so confused and so obscure" law, would be "the gunpowder plot of the Constitution."

- Maclay, Edgar S., ed., *The Journal of William Maclay, United States Senator From Pennsylvania, 1789-1791* (New York: D. Appleton and Company, 1890/1891), 101. –

1792- Norwich [Conn.]
Thanksgiving day, Fast day, Election and Training days were the great holidays of the year. The Weekly Register of November, 1792, hopes that "the savage practice of making bonfires on the evening of Thanksgiving may be exchanged for some other mode of rejoicing, more consistent with the genuine spirit of Christianity." Mrs. Daniel Lathrop Coit (b. 1767. d. 1848), used to tell her grandchildren of the Guy Fawkes day. observed in Norwich in her childhood. An effigy of straw was carried through the streets, and afterward burned, and she remembered snatches of the doggerel sung : —

The fifth of November
You must always remember;
The Gunpowder Plot
Must never be forgot.
Ding! Dong !
The Pope's come to town.

- *The Weekly Register*, November, 1792.

1795- Reverend William Bentley of Salem, Massachusetts, minister of the East Parish in Salem, Massachusetts:

"The fifth of November. Not all the revolutions which have passed over our Country can yet efface the remembrance of this anniversary. The boys must have their bon fire."

- Bentley, William, *The Diary of William Bentley, D.D., Pastor of the East Church, Salem, Massachusetts* (1905–1914; reprint ed., Gloucester, Mass.: Peter Smith, 1962), 5 November 1795, 5 November 1802, 5 November 1819.
-Benes, Peter, *Night Processions: Celebrating the Gunpowder Plot in England and New England, (unpublished Mss.)*.

1801, November- William Bentley wrote that, in Salem, "the old day of Pope & Devil" did not have "the bare recollection of the antient festivity" of England.

-Bentley, *The Diary of William Bentley, D.D., Pastor of the East Church, Salem, Massachusetts*, Vol. II: 402.

1802- William Bentley witnessed "rudeness" come back to the streets of Salem on the Fifth.

-Bentley, *The Diary of William Bentley, D.D., Pastor of the East Church, Salem, Massachusetts*, Vol. II: 456.

1802- November 5

.... The children cannot entirely forget pope day. Tho' there was no exhibition, the rudeness of the Streets discovered in the evening that the old practices were not entirely forgotten.

- Bentley, William, D.D., <u>The Diary of William Bentley, D. D.: Pastor of the East Church, Salem, Massachusetts</u> ,1907.

1804- The Fifth was considered an Independence Day in Boston. The *National Intelligencer* called it: "Glorious Anniversary." An account on the speeches, and the toasts, the Democratic-Republican Party had given at Faneuil Hall was published. A day of "decorum," and "genuineness" of patriotism, a gathering of two hundred plus in Boston, a hub of Federalism, promoted "the spirit of '75." It maintained that the Federalist Party had, recently "contrived to blow up" its competition on the Fifth of November. The group requested that the Fifth, as the Fourth, be maintained as a day of "joy and Triumph to the People" – a day of "disappointment and disaster" for their enemies.

-"Boston, July 5, 1804. Glorious Anniversary," [Washington, D.C.] *The National Intelligencer and Washington Advertiser*, July 13, 1804-

1804- more so than In an article from mid-October, the *Democrat* of Boston headlined:

*Citizens of Massachusetts!*
*" ::::::::::: REMEMBER –*
*The 5th OF NOVEMBER."*

*The article encouraged a revival of the celebration.*

-"Citizens of Massachusetts ! Remember the 5th of November," [Boston, MA] *Democrat*, 10-17-1804. -

1811

Maryland

William Kilty's A report of all such English statutes as existed at the time of the first emigration of the people of Maryland, and which by experience have been found applicable to their local and other circumstances;...

Volume 143 The one-hundred and forty-third volume of the Archives of Maryland series was originally published in 1811.

STATUTES NOT FOUND APPLICABLE........

STATUTES.
3 James 1.--A. D. 1605.

STATUTES.

CHAP. 1.  An act of a public thanksgiving to
Almighty God, every year on the fifth day of November.
CHAP. 6.  Merchants.
CHAP. 7.  Attornies.
CHAP. 8.  An act to avoid unnecessary delays
of executions.

http://www.mdarchives.state.md.us/megafile/msa/speccol/sc2900/sc2908/000001/000143/html/am143--88.html

1813- November 5, William Bentley noted that a "wicked artifice" of "superstition" (i.e.,lighting of "several bonfires") had embarrassed Salem, noting that the day was for Britain, and not America, a "political occasion." He wrote that the "mortals" of the city should "learn" from this error, noting that it was time that this city have independence.

-Bentley, *The Diary of William Bentley, D.D., Pastor of the East Church, Salem, Massachusetts*, Vol. IV:

213.

1814, November 6- William Bentley wrote:

"[T]he fifth of November is entirely forgotten. This base artifice which maintained itself till [sic] the Am. Revolution, spent all its force upon its inventors, & the people whom it was intended to delude employed it against its contrivers. It was an opportunity for vulgar mirth upon all British friends & influence. Some few efforts were made by ignorance to revive it, but the Pope & the Devil were left to the recollection of European politicians."

--Bentley, *The Diary of William Bentley, D.D., Pastor of the East Church, Salem, Massachusetts*, ?.

1814, December 17-John Adams, "…We curse the Inquisition, and the Jesuits and yet the Inquisition and the Jesuits are <, Start deletion, are restored. We curse religiously the Memory of Mary for burning good Men in Smithfield, when if England had the been democratical She would have burned many more, and We murder many more by the Guilotine, in the latter Years of the Eighteenth Century. We curse Guy Faulks for thinking of blowing Up Westminster Hall, Yet Ross blows up the Capitol, the Palace and the Library at Washington and would have done it With the same sang froid had Congress and the Presidents Family been within the Walls. Oh! my soul! I am weary of these dismal Contemplations! When will Mankind listen to reason, to NATURE or to Revelation?"

-Letter- "From John Adams to John Taylor, 17 December 1814."

Adams Papers, Washburn Collection

1819- fifth of November, -  Reverend William Bentley of Salem, Massachusetts, minister of the East Parish in Salem, Massachusetts:

"We have had this evening the full proof of the obstinate power of superstition and habit…Tho we have lost all connection with Great Britain & have detected the fraud & the purpose, yet our common people still keep- the 5 of Nov. and we had a roaring fire on the Neck on this occasion."

- Bentley, William, *The Diary of William Bentley, D.D., Pastor of the East Church, Salem, Massachusetts* (1905–1914; reprint ed., Gloucester, Mass.: Peter Smith, 1962), 5 November 1795, 5 November 1802, 5 November 1819.

-Benes, Peter, *Night Processions: Celebrating the Gunpowder Plot in England and New England, (unpublished Mss.)*.

1821- November 5: "A curious scene unfolded on the streets of Boston. In what can only be compared to an improptu outdoor museum that probably filled at least two city blocks, scores of people assembled to display the mementos that marked an annual celebration that had last taken place on this date about fifty years earlier. As described in the *Columbian Centinel* later that week.

More than a hundred vehicles called Popes were on this anniversary exhibited in the streets, of different sizes, from those constructed of shingles, and carried in the hands of children, to those drawn by horses, and owned by brawny mechanics.

Called "Popes" because they carried effigies of the pope, the devil, and other eighteenth-century representations of forces of evil, these images were literally made from anything that came to hand. The faces of those carried by children were made from potatoes; larger ones, which were mounted on handcarts, wheelbarrows, or large wheeled stages, were carved from wood. These larger vehicles —they would now be called "floats"—were furnished with tables, chairs, gigantic paper lanterns, lots of attendants, and one or two musicians. They were not likely to have been entirely authentic. …the heads of some effigies may indeed have dated to the eighteenth century…."

-Benes, Peter, "Night Processions: Celebrating the Gunpowder Plot in England and New England," in *New England Celebrates: Spectacle, Commemoration, and Festivity*, Dublin Seminar for New England Folklife Annual Proceedings 2000 (Boston: Boston University, 2002) p. 9.

1821-November 5, *Columbian Centinel*

More than a hundred vehicles called *Popes* were on this anniversary exhibited in the streets, of different sizes, from those constructed of shingles, and carried in the hands of children, to those drawn by horses, and owned by brawny mechanics.

- *Columbian Centinel*, November 10, 1821

-Benes, Peter, *Night Processions: Celebrating the Gunpowder Plot in England and New England,*

(unpublished Mss…)

1821- Columbian Centinel

An anonymous 70 year old man is cited as he wrote to the Columbian Centinel about a popes day celebration. in 1821:

"On the stage was music and something to drink-also boys, clad in frocks and trousers well covered with tar and feathers who danced around the Pope and frequently climbed up and kissed the devil"

-PDC

1821- From *Boston Daily Advertiser*, 8 November

All those of our ancient fellow citizens who remember the pageantry of the 5th of November, before British troops were among us, can well appreciate the anecdote, though it may appear as uninteresting circumstance to those who never saw the Pope and Pretender and his Sattanick majesty carried through the streets on a state, and in effigies twice as big as life.

-Benes, Peter, *Night Processions: Celebrating the Gunpowder Plot in England and New England,*

(unpublished Mss..)

1821-Boston

"Reminiscences"
"A man used to ride on an ass, with immense jack boots, and his face covered with a horrible mask, and was called Joyce, Jr. His office was to assemble men and boys in mob style, and ride in the middle of them, and in such company to terrify adherents to Royal Government, before the Revolution. The tumults which resulted in the Massacre, 1770, was excited by that means.-Joyce Junior was said to have a particular whistle which brought his adherents, &c. whenever they were wanted.

-"Publications of the Colonial Society of Mass. VIII (1903). 90-91. and *Boston Daily Advertiser*, Nov 9 1821. PDC.

1821- From *Boston Daily Advertiser*, 9 November.

The Fifth of November

Mr. Hale — The reminiscences with which you have amused the public, so calls to mind the celebration of this day, as one of the grand gala days, in this town, which formerly attracted great attention, but has deservedly been consigned to oblivion since the year 1772. It is known to those who are conversant with English history, that in the year 1605, when James the First was on the throne, the Catholics were charged with a plot to blow up the Parliament house by an explosion of gunpowder, while the king should be in both houses assembled therein, and re-establish [their religion] in that country. This was to have been executed on the fifth of November. It was said to have been discovered by means of one of the House of Lords receiving a billet requesting him not to go to the parliament on that day: and accompanied by such hints as induced an examination of the vaults under the parliament house. These had been leased to some Catholics for the purpose of storing coals. Upon searching them, thirty six barrels of powder were found. The Catholics have uniformly denied the existence of such a plot: and asserted that it was only one fiction among others to render them obnoxious and to excuse the persecution to which they were subjected. Let it be true or false, it is certain that one *Guy Fawkes*, a poor fanatic, suffered death, as the chosen instrument for the perpetration of this crime. It has been observed as a religious festival in England, and a form of prayer was establish to be used upon it, in the Liturgy of their church; and it has been denominated the *gun powder treason*. In this country it was called Pope day.

Our ancestors brought with them other prejudices into this land. For many years exhibitions were made in the evening. A very large stage was drawn, sometimes by horses, sometimes by men, from the north end through the town, to the furthest part of the south end — it returned to the north after passing Middle Street, was carried to Copp's Hill and burnt. Persons carrying small bells, as a commission, visited all the houses to collect contributions, with the proceeds of which, a grand entertainment was made for those who belonged to the *Pope*. Upon the front of the stage was displayed a lanthorn of transparent paper, capable of holding a number of men, on which were scrawled uncouth figures, and rhymes in derision of the Pope and his gunpowder plot. In the middle was an effigy of the Pope in an armchair, dressed in gorgeous attire, with a large white bush wig on, over which was an inormous gold laced hat. The wigs procured for this purpose, had often adorned the pulpits of churches. Before his holiness was a table on which was a large book, and play cards scattered over it. In the extreme rear was a gigantic figure to represent the Devil; of hideous form, with a pitchfork in his hand, and covered with tar and feathers. On the stage was music and something to drink—also, boys clad in frocks and trowsers, well covered with tar and feathers, who danced about the Pope, played with the cards and frequently climbed up and kissed the Devil. These were called the Devil's imps. For many years all this was carried on peacably. But in process of time, another Pope was built on the south end. This raised the resentment of the north-enders, as an encroachment upon their patent right; and so much confusion followed, that the government of the town put a stop to all exhibitions of the kind in the evening. After this, the whole day was devoted to it. The foregoing was the work of men. — When the frolic was carried on by day-light, the elder apprentices of mechanics exhibited a pageantry of similar kind called a tender* on a smaller scale. The younger apprentices still smaller; and so it descended in gradations to boys in petticoats, who swarmed in the streets and ran from house to house with little Popes in their hands, on pieces of board and shingle, the heads of which were carved out of small potatoes. The heads of the large figures were moveable by means of poles which went through the bodies down into the box of the stage, and were turned round occasionally by boys within, in order to give every one sight and to pay the obeisance of the Pope. At sun-down the north-end Pope and tender was carried to Copps Hill and burnt, and the south end Pope and tender to Fort Hill. At length a competition arose—formidable mobs collected, and furious battles were fought with fists, clubs, stones and other missiles. Through the greater part of the day, they avoided each other, and collected as much cash as they could. Towards night they sought a meeting and each endeavored to gain the right hand side of the street. This was a signal for the battle—much bruising and in one instance death, was the consequence. The victorious part would seize the pageantry of their opponents, and bear it in triumph to Copps Hill or Fort Hill; as the case might be, and burn the two together. — When the dissention with Great Britain took place, the leading political characters, seeing the necessity of uniting all interest prevailed with the head men of the Popes to unite in one pageantry, which was to be built and burnt alternatively at the north and south end. It was first done at the north — but the next year the north enders fell from the agreement — got up their old Pope and the animosity revived. After this it assumed a political aspect. When the board of Commissioners of Customs was established in Boston, their effigies were complimented with seats at the table placed between the Pope and the Devil. At another time, the same attention was paid to Mein and Flemming, printers of an obnoxious Tory newspaper, and every years there was made some display of a political cast. A figure of a man suspended from a gibbet, was called admiral Byng, but meant as a memento of the commanding naval officer who duty it was understood to be to enforce the revenue laws. A man in femail attire was always on the stage dancing, caressing the Pope and kissing the Devil. He was called *Nancy Dawson*. In 1774 a British Army was quartered in Boston. Great apprehensions were entertained regarding this spectacle. It was threatened that effigies of Lord North, Lord Hillsborough, and other obnoxious persons should be placed on the stage, which probably would have caused bloodshed. To prevent anything of this kind required much address — After much exertion, it was determined that there should be but one large Pope; that it should be built and destroyed in the north-end. A very inoffensive man from the south end was the captain. Respect was paid to General Gage who was governor of the Province, at his quarters in the province house. He received the officers of the Pope at the door, and presented a gratuity to the treasurer. The soldiers were kept in their quarters; and all things were conducted in peace and quietness. This was the last celebration of the day in this town. Most of the present generation probably know nothing of it.

* A corruption we presume of *Pretender*, whose name had been long associated in the minds of all loyal subjects with the abominations of Popery.

-Benes, Peter, *Night Processions: Celebrating the Gunpowder Plot in England and New England*, (unpublished Mss.).

1821- From *Columbian Centinel*, 10 November.

Pope Day. Mr. Russell – Monday last, Nov 5th, being "Pope Day," brought to my recollection scenes of former days. – Some of them I have placed on paper. To three fourths of your readers they may be new, and perhaps amusing to others. Yours. A BOSTONIAN

The fifth of November was an anniversary which excited considerable interest among the lower orders of people, in Boston, previous to the American Revolution. It was called "Pope Day," in consequence of a conspiracy of the Roman Catholics to blow up King James, and his Parliament, on the 5th of Nov 1605. – More than a hundred vehicles called *Popes* were on this anniversary exhibited in the streets, of different sizes, from those constructed of shingles, and carried in the hands of children, to those drawn by horses, and owned by brawny mechanics.

A pope of a large size was constructed in the following manner: - an oblong square box was made of the size intended, which varied from ten to twelve feet long, and those which were sufficiently large were placed on a carriage with wheels. On the top of this box, which had a railing, was erected (at one end) a hideous figure, meant to represent the Devil, in human form, the body and limbs of which were composed of stuffed canvas, *tarred and feathered*, and the countenance of carved wood, most terrifically caricatures. He held in his hands labels, on which were printed in large letters, his affectionate regard for the *Pope*, the *Pretender*, and the *Tories*, and his gratitude for their services. He was generally attended on the stage, within the railing, by one or two little devils, who were small boys, in dresses and ferocious masks, to correspond to his own. Immediately before him was placed an arm chair, a figure to represent the *Pope of Rome*. He was dressed in a large flowing wig, with a gold laced hat, and his robes were covered with a profusion of tinsel, and gilt paper in strips, to imitate gold lace. In his hands were also placed labels alluding to the supposed Roman Catholics which were in power, such as Bute and Mansfield, &c. An invariable attendant on his holiness was a man in a cloak and boots, and a dark lantern to represent *Guy Fawkes*, the incendiary, who was taken with the matches and combustibles in his pocket, when the discovery of the conspiracy was made. – There were also various other figures usually introduced, according to the taste or sentiments of the owners. Governor Hutchinson was often represented, with *two faces*, to denote his duplicity, and with Judge Oliver, Lords North, Bute, and Mansfield, hung in effigy, with labels on their breasts, appropriate to their characters.- The following extract from the tragedy of Cato, I remember seeing on the breast of one of the figures of governor Hutchinson:

"Is there not some chosen curse
Some hidden thunder in the stores of Heav'n
Red with uncommon wrath, to blast the man
Who owes his greatness to his country's ruin?"

In front of the *Pope*, there was a projection of four to five feet, on which was erected, what was called the Lantern, arched on the top and formed with hoop poles, and covered with oiled paper, to make it transparent; on which were painted, patriotic inscriptions, and the portraits of Chatham, Camden, Barre, Wilkes, and Liberty No. 45, Hancock – and some were painted caricatures of the Tories. I recollect one, which represented Lord Bute in a Highland dress, pulling out the teeth of the British Lion.

Each *Pope* had a Captain, Lieutenant, and crew like a ship. As they passed through the streets, they civilly asked for money of the passengers, and at the doors of the houses and shops. – Those who were appointed to collect money carried a small bell, which was rung by way of warning, and then began repeating about a dozen doggerel verses which commenced with:

"Don't you remember, the fifth of November
The gunpowder treason, and plot?
I see no reason, why the gunpowder treason,
Should ever be forgot."

The money collected on these occasions, was expended by each crew, in procuring a supper, where the combatants met to relate the feats of the day.

Severe battles were fought with clubs and bludgeons, between the crews of the North and South End *Popes*. I am told this contention originated many years ago. In consequence of the South part of the town, being the most wealthy, the largest sums were collected in that quarter. The crews of the South End *Popes* endeavored to prevent their opponents from crossing either of the bridges and entering their territory; but the crews of the North were much more athletic and robust, and generally gained the victory, though not without hard fighting.

Our people became veterans in this pugilistic warfare, so that when the British troops were quartered in the town, the inhabitants were invariable victorious in the frequent squabbles which occurred between them, even when the soldiers were double their number. And in one instance, about seventy rope makers and ship carpenters, fought with more than two hundred soldiers of the 29th Reg. With the sargent-major at their head, in what is now called Pearl-street, and drove them to their barracks, on what is now called Foster's-wharf, which battle was one of the causes of the massacre of 5th March.

-Benes, Peter, *Night Processions: Celebrating the Gunpowder Plot in England and New England,* (unpublished Mss.).

1821- "Brawny mechanics" and horses had helped transport "[m]ore than a hundred" images up and down the streets of Boston.

-"Recollections of a Bostonian," [Boston] *Columbian Centinel*, November 10, 1821, A BOSTONIAN,"Miscellany. Pope Day," [Boston] *Columbian Centinel*, November 10, 1821.

1821, Nov. 9 *Boston Daily Advertiser* wrote:

Boys in petticoats...swarmed in the streets and ran from house to house with little Popes in their hands, on pieces of board and shingle, the heads of which were carved out of small potatoes.

1826-November, "A Watchman" wrote in the *Christian Observer*, a Protestant Episcopal Church magazine from Boston, suggesting that the Gunpowder Treason Prayer of the Church of England was an eternal reading that kept its integrity in "modern times."

"Within the year of Christ our Lord
Sixteen-hundred and five,
Then suddenly to have blown them up,
Not leaving one alive,
With houses both of Parliament,
And all that royal court,
With gun-powder; to church and realm
To work the deadly hurt……"

…And therefore do ascribe unto
His own most holy name
All honour, glory, laud and thanks
With praises for the same;
And do retain in memory
This joyful happy day,
Of that most rare deliverance
To praise of God alway."

-A Watchman, "To the Editor of the Christian Observer," [Boston] *Christian Observer, Conducted by Members of the Established Church*, November 1826.

1841, November- The *Journal of Literature and Politics* of Portsmouth, New Hampshire, wrote that the youth of that city, revived "the customs of their great grandfathers," had celebrated the Fifth as "Pope Night," carried an effigy of the Pope "round in a crate on a pole," lighting "a host of Guy Fawkes lights, in the shape of pumpkin lanterns," blew horns, and rang bells. "The old rhyme,"
was sung:
"Chink, chink, chink,
Give me some money to buy me some drink."

The *Journal* did not approve, writing that the holiday was an "unmeaning and absurd" occasion and asked that, parents keep children in bed off the streets.

-"Pope Night," *Portsmouth Journal of Literature and Poltlics*, November 6, 1841. -

1842- The (Columbia) *South Carolina Temperance Advocate* printed a letter from "P. D." The letter-writer remembered a town drunkard with a fondness for "celebrating the 5th day of November annually." He would, in hard times, earn money by chopping wood for neighbors to support the celebrations. After purchasing rum, he would make a bonfire, dance and drink, singing:

"Remember, remember, the fifth of November,
That happy and glorious day, O! Moll, Moll, Moll, O!"

-P. D., Letter to the Editor, [Columbia] *South Carolina Temperance Advocate and Register of Agriculture and Literature*, September 29, 1842.

1843- Letter from Margaret G. Cary to George Blankeren Cary, March 09, 1843

Yes, my father had arrived, and preparation was soon made for the nuptials. Dresses were already in advance, furniture was soon purchased for the house at Chelsea, and on the evening of the 5th of November they were married. That day was always one of confusion in Boston while under the British government. It was the celebration of the anniversary of "Gunpowder Treason and Plot." The South Enders and North Enders, each carrying about a representation of Guy Fawkes with a lantern in a cart, were in the habit of meeting at the mill bridge, and what began in ridicule ended in fight. On that occasion my uncle Captain Cary joined in the frolic, directly after the wedding, and in the course of the evening was brought in senseless. There was, however, no fatal consequence and no …lasting inconvenience. The winter was passed very pleasantly by my parents. There were a number of young couples with whom they associated intimately; and though they were occasioally at Chelsea, they were a great deal in Boston."

-Margaret Gary, Letters.

1849- The *Salem Gazette* wrote that "the annual bonfire" people of Salisbury, Massachusetts, lit to celebrate of "Pope's night" had, in 1849, "caus[ing] an alarm of fire." Engines, and firemen, were left in "a covering of mud."

-"The 5th of November," *Salem Gazette*, (*Newburyport Herald*), November 9, 1849.

1851, January 2- "J. G. W." ( the editor-poet Whittier?) published a piece in the *National Era*: "Pope Night." This author criticized the revival of the Fifth in Britain, and considered the celebration "a grim piece of Protestant sport" including parading, and creating, "straw and pasteboard" effigies of bishops, cardinals, and popes. In early New England, "the younger plants of grace in the Puritan vineyard" celebrated the holiday, as well, as a "saturnalia," parading "hideous images of the Pope and Guy Fawkes," consuming "liberal potations of strong waters," burning the Pope with tar, and "blazing bonfires" that "redden[ed] the wild November hills," with activity and with bigotry. On November 5, 1850, "J. G. W." noted that, the citizens of northern Essex County, Massachusetts, had celebrated in this way marking the day such that it seemed that "an invasion was threatened from the sea" or "an insurrection was going on i[n]land." This essayist hoped that the "hatred" and the "intolerance" of the celebration would decline, and that citizens would unite at a "common altar" of "the one universal church."

-J. G. W., "Pope Night," [Washington, D.C.] *National Era*, January 2, 1851.

1852, November- The *Semi-Weekly Eagle* of Brattleboro, Vermont wrote that the Fifth was not "in vogue" and had, "fallen into utter desuetude."

-"English; Church; Liturgy; Parliament; Guido; Fawkes; Old," [Brattleboro, Vermont] *Semi-Weekly Eagle*, November 11, 1852.

1854- Boston, Episcopalian poet-translator Thomas William Parsons wrote:

"Fifth of November, Guy Fawkes' Day, at Howe's Tavern [the Wayside Inn of Longfellow fame], in Sudbury"

One fifth of November, when meadows were brown,
And the woods were all withered, – in Sudbury town
Four lads from the city, by special request,
At an old tavern met for a whole day of rest.
There was Henry and Austin and William and John,
And the glasses went round as the oak-wood went on,
And the spirit was kindly, the water was hot, –
Why then should Guy Fawkes and his day be forgot?

-Thomas Williams Parsons, "Fifth of November, Guy Fawkes' Day, at Howe's Tavern, in Sudbury," *Poems . . .* (Boston: Ticknor & Fields, 1854), 184-85.

1859, November- *New York Times* wrote "old fogyism" had, "for the past one hundred and seventy-five years," "the ancient town" of Bristol, Rhode Island, had celebrated with bonfires and illuminations.

-"Matters in Rhode Island . . .," *New York Times*, November 12, 1859.

1860s and 1890s- American branches of the Orange Order – the Protestant fraternal organization of Northern Ireland –celebrated the Fifth in Chicago and Manhattan, with meetings and addresses, which proclaimed loyalty to America, and mocked a "Protestant gunpowder plot," and condemned "Jesuitism," worldwide.

-"Anniversary of the Gunpowder Plot," *New York Times*, November 6, 1869; "Guy Fawkes Day – Orangemen Celebrate the Fifth of November," [Chicago] *Daily Inter Ocean*, November 6, 1891.

late 1800s- Towns on the New England celebrated the day as "Pope Night," with "small bands" on the North Shore of Massachusetts (e.g., Marblehead, Newburyport) and the seacoast of New Hampshire (e.g., New Castle, Portsmouth) building bonfires, dancing, parading "pumpkin lanterns," and, with "glee" and "mischief," blowing "tin horns. Some in this area called the holiday "Pork Night."

-*Marblehead Messenger*, November 9, 1872; "Guy Fawkes Remembered in America," *New York Times*, November 11, 1883; "An Old English Custom: How Pope Night Is Celebrated in Portsmouth . . .," *New York Times*, November 15, 1891; *Portsmouth Republican News*, November 7, 1892; *Portsmouth Daily Evening Times*, November 7, 1892; John Albee, "Pope Night in Portsmouth, N. H.," *Journal of American Folklore* 5.19 (Oct.-Dec. 1892): 335-36; "Guy Fawkes Day in New England," *Bangor [ME] Daily Whig &Courier*, December 23, 1893; "Guy Fawkes Day in New England," *Emporia [KS] Gazette*, January 13, 1894, and February 8, 1894; John Albee, "Pope Night: Fifth November," *Journal of American Folklore* 6.20 (Jan.-Mar. 1893): 68-69.

1881

We have but scanty personal recollections preserved of this period relating to the common life within the town, and must have recourse again to the good natured Mr. Breck, who piques us by forgetting more important things than he remembered. His Childhood was spent in Boston: and he remembered well the old beacon which stood on the hill, and was blown down in 1789:-

"Spokes were fixed in a large mast, on the top of which was placed a barrel of pitch or tar, always ready to be fired on the approach of the enemy. Around this pole I have fought many battles, as a South End boy, against the boys of the North End of the town; and bloody ones, too, with slings and stones very skillfully and earnestly used. In what a state of semi-barbarism did the rising generations of those days exist! From time immemorial these hostilities were carried on by the juvenile part of the community. The school-masters whipt, parents scolded,--nothing could check it. Was it a remnant of the pugilistic propensities of our British ancestors; or was it an untamed feeling arising from our sequestered and colonial situation? Whatever was the cause , every thing of the kind ceased with the termination of our Revolutionary War....I forget on what holiday it was that the Anticks, another exploded remnant of colonial manners, used to perambulate the town. They have ceased to do it now; but I remember them as late as 1782. They were a set of the lowest blackguards who disguised in filthy clothes and oftimes with masked faces went from house to house in large companies; and, bon gré, mal gré, obtruding themselves everywhere, particularly into the rooms that were occupied by parties of ladies and gentlemen, would demean themselves with great insolence. I have seen them at my father's, when his assembled friends were at cards, take possession of a table, seat themselves on rich furniture, and proceed to handle the cards, to the great annoyance of the company. The only way to get rid of them was to give them money, and listen patiently to a foolish dialogue between two or more of them. One of them would cry out:

"Ladies and gentlemen sitting by the fire,
Put your hands in your pockets and give us our desire."

When this was done, and they had received some money, a kind of acting took place. One feellow was knocked down and lay sprawling on the carpet, while another bellowed out:-

"See, there he lies!
But ere he dies,
A doctor must be had."

He calls for a doctor, who soon appears, and enacts the part so well that the wounded man revives. In this way they would continue for half an hour; and it happened not infrequently that the house would be filled by another gang when these had departed. There was no refusing admittance. Custom had licensed these vagabonds to enter even by force any place they chose. What should we say to such intruders now? Our manners would not brook such a usage a moment. Undoubtedly these plays were a remnant of the old mysteries of the fourteenth and fifteenth, centuries..

( Transcriber notes: activities are noted by contemporary newspaper accounts as being associated with the celebration of "Pope's Day" or the fifth of November.)

-Memorial History of Boston

- The Memorial History Of Boston ed. Justin Winsor Vol. III Boston, 1881.

November 7, 1892

"The celebration of the anniversary of Guy Fawkes' night on Saturday by the young people of this city was not so extensive as in former years, no doubt owing to the condition of the streets, but nevertheless small bands paraded the streets and made the early part of the evening hideous with music (?) from the tin horns they carried for the occasion. Some carried the usual pumpkin lanterns. The ringing of door-bells was also extensively indulged in. Very few of the paraders knew that the celebration was in keeping of the old English custom of observing the anniversary of the discovery of the famous gunpowder plot to blow up the House of Commons.

- Portsmouth Republican News, Nov. 7 1892.
PDC


1888- John Gilmary Shea wrote the first known history of Pope's Day, a
seven-page pamphlet accentuating the mayhem of November 5 in mid-eighteenth century urban America and arguing that the War of Independence discontinued the Fifth.

-Shea, John D. Gilmary. *Pope-day in America*. New York, 1888. -


1892-Portsmouth/New Castle New Hampshire

"It is said there are only three places left in New England in which Pope Night continues to be celebrated. These are Newburyport, in Massachusetts, and Portsmouth and Newcastle, in New Hampshire. In regard to Newburyport I can only speak from common report; but of Portsmouth and New Castle I can bear eye-witness, or rather ear-witness, for it is a celebration in which noise is the main element. It is boys, however, and rather young boys who maintain a custom once pretty general in the cities and larger towns of New England, and the small boy's enjoyment and way of manifesting himself is and ever has been by making a noise helping himself thereto by every sort of instrument that will produce the loudest sound with the least music. It has been said that human beings in the various stages of growth, from infancy to manhood, pass through and typify the progressive stages in the development of races. The so-called music of the barbarian and half-civilized man corresponds to the strange and rude sounds which seem to delight the ears of boyhood. Pope Night, in Portsmouth and new Castle, which is a seaside village below and very near to Portsmouth, is at present celebrated by boys from six to fourteen years of age by the blowing of horns and the carrying of lights of all kinds. They march through the streets in procession, or in small bands, gathering in, as they march, single groups, or dividing again and sending off detachments, so as to leave no street unvisited. The horns are of all sorts, from the penny whistle to those of two and three feet in length. Whence the origin of the custom of blowing horns on Pope Night I am uncertain. But the lanterns and other devices for lighting the darkness of the November night have evidently something to do with the discovery of Guy Fawkes under the chambers of Parliament in the act of blowing them up with gunpowder. In childhood I remember well looking at pictures of the scene which represented armed men with lanterns searching about in a subterranean place while the dwarfish Guy crouched among great casks of supposed gunpowder. Formerly the lights used by the boys in their observance of Pope Night were candles set in hollowed-out pumpkins, the light showing through holes in the shells of the pumpkins, cut to represent a very squat human face. To the lighted pumpkin heads have now been added all sorts of illuminations, chiefly lanterns and torches.

There is no doubt that in Portsmouth at least Pope Night has been observed from the earliest times, and formerly by older boys than at present; those indeed who knew what they were celebrating and in which they took a serious interest. It is doubtful if the children who now take a part in it know what their own act signifies or commemorates. I shall presently produce a curious proof of this in the case of the boys of New Castle. It is a very singular fact that in Portsmouth, hwich long since outgrew its early local boundaries, the observance of Pope Night is entirely confined to the ancient portion of the town. This portion has remained substantially unchanged since the colonial period; and along with its antique houses, streets, alleys and docks, there remain the remnants of old families, many local names and traditions, and this historic survivor of the observance of the Gunpowder Plot. But it will not apparently survive much longer in Portsmouth. Every year the interest grows less and less and the boys who take part in it fewer and of a younger age.

The same may be said of New Castle, where even the name, Pope Night, has been confounded and the whole meaning of the celebration obliterated. I sufficiently attests, the easy loss of the primitive significance of customs and observances and the complete transformation of their names, to note that in this obscure village the name Pope Night has undergone the absurd change to Pork Night"

- *Journal of American Folklore*, V (1892), 335-36 and VI (1893), 68-69. *John Albee of New Castle contributed two newspaper cuttings and the "eye-witness or rather ear witness" accounts.* -Cited in -Hennig Cohen and Tristram Coffin, eds. The Folklore of American Holidays (Detroit: Gale Research Company, 1987).

1892-Marblehead Mass.
"Portsmouth is not alone in this peculiar observance, for down at Marblehead the night of the 5th of November is remembered by a huge bonfire on the Neck, around which the chaps with horns dance in fantastic glee. The Blaze Saturday night on the Marblehead Neck was a bigger one than usual." "It's a queer custom for the youths of Portsmouth and Marblehead have.

- *Portsmouth Daily Evening Times,* November 7, 1892.

1892- John Albee

Pope Night in Portsmouth, N. H. — I inclose two slips from two Portsmouth newspapers in regard to "Pope Night" in 1892. I send them that you may have authentic witness of such celebration in one place. I think Newburyport may be also included in the list of places where Pope Night is remembered.

In addition, I can vouch for the similar celebration in this town, New Castle, for twenty-six years past, or ever since I became resident. Doubt less the reason for such celebration is long since lost to the "chaps" who still keep it up.

In this town, not only is the reason lost, but there the name also, — the boys call it Pork Night. But this is in accordance with the general fortune of popular festivals; as soon as the meaning is lost, the names suffer strange and often grotesque transformations.

-John Albee, New Castle, N. H.

"The celebration of the anniversary of Guy Fawkes' night on Saturday by the young people of this city was not so extensive as in former years, no doubt owing to the condition of the streets, but nevertheless small bands paraded the streets and made the early part of the evening hideous with music (?) from the tin horns they carried for the occasion. Some carried the usual pumpkin lanterns. The ringing of door-bells was also extensively indulged in. Very few of the paraders knew that the celebration was in keeping of the old English custom of observing the anniversary of the discovery of the famous gunpowder plot to blow up the House of Commons."

— From the *Portsmouth Republican News*, November 7, 1892.

"Chaps in this city had their annual blow-out on Guy Fawkes' night, and in parts of the city the toot of the horns was something terrific. Some grotesque pumpkin lanterns were seen, and altogether the 'celebration' was evidently enjoyed by the boys." Portsmouth is not alone in this peculiar observance, for down at Marblehead the night of the 5th of November is remembered by a huge bonfire on the Neck, around which the chaps with horns dance in fantastic glee. The blaze Saturday night on the M. N. was a bigger one than usual. "It's a queer custom the youths of Portsmouth and Marblehead have."

— From the *Portsmouth Daily Evening Times*, November 7, 1892.

1895- Portsmouth, N.H.

It is said that in Portsmouth, N. H., November 5th is still observed by the boys with bonfires. Miss Caulkins mentions that Washington, in one of his

Thanksgiving barrel burning on Jail Hill Clarence E. Spalding

army orders, prohibited the soldiers from any demonstrations on Guy Fawkes or Pope-day out of deference to our French allies, and that the New London boys, or the same reason, were persuaded during the war to give up their usual celebration.

After the Revolution was over, Pope-day revived again, and the New London authorities then prevailed upon the populace to substitute Sept. 6th, the day that Arnold burnt the town, and to burn the traitor in effigy instead of the Pope. Patriotic motives may have also influenced the Norwich boys to transfer their annual barrel burning to our New England festal day, and long may they keep up this custom, peculiar to the town.

-Perkins, Mary Elizabeth, *Old Houses of the Antient Town of Norwich [Conn.] 1660-1800*, 1895, p,19.

# Dissolution~Spin Offs

## See Also: Discussion of Thanksgiving Above

Guy Fawkes/Bonfire becomes Election Celebration in the U.S.A.

Many scholars believe that one of the ways that Guy Fawkes Day / Bonfire Night was translated to American tradition was via the celebration of Election night. This is understandable because election night is scheduled to occur either on or within days of Guy Fawkes Day- November 5. Additionally, elections are after all just another way of removing the head of state and isn't that just what the conspirators wanted to do?
(image above A campaign parade at night from Ingersoll -see below)
Celebrations in New York

# 1896- Election Day in New York

Ernest Ingersoll
pp. 3-16  p. 8 1 The Century; a
Popular Quarterly. / Volume 53, Issue 1,The Century Company  Nov 1896  New York

"The moment the polls close the liquor-saloons open, but the excessive drunkenness and brawling common in former years are not now seen. Five o'clock editions of the news- papers are issued, but have little to tell, for everywhere the clerks are still busily counting the votes. The streets overflow with boys who hardly wait for the earliest dark- ness to institute their picturesque part of the day's doings. The New York citizen begins to break election-day laws as soon as he can toddle about the block. Bonfires are strictly prohibited, yet thousands of them redden the air and set all the windows aglow before seven o'clock. Antiquarians inform us that this custom is nothing but a survival in America of the old English celebration of burning Guy Fawkes on the 5th of November, in recollection of the Gunpowder Plot of 1605, which the children have transferred to the movable feast of our election day. Maybe so. At any rate, for weeks beforehand the lads, large and small, rich and poor, have begged, borrowed, or stolen every burnable thing they could lay their hands on, and have kept their treasure as well as they could. Knowing by sad experience the untruth of the aphorism, "There is honor among thieves," they usually persuade someone to let them store these combustibles in his back yard or still safer cellar. From hundreds of such repositories the lads bring their treasures, heap them up in the middle of the street, and fight off raiders until they are safely blazing. Women and children swarm out of the huge tenements and cluster about the scene, where the youngsters are leaping and whooping and waving brands, like the true fire-worshipers they are. The smallest boys and girls have saved a box and a board or two, or beg some fuel from good-natured big brothers, and start little blazes of their own, with a headless ash-barrel for a chimney. Everywhere are dancing, merriment, singing, and shouting. The great heaps throw out a terrific heat, glare upon the highest windows, and illuminate the whole sky, while showers of sparks whirl up and down the narrow streets in the autumn wind, yet rarely do serious damage. But boxes and barrels are slight, and the flames die down long before the enthusiasm of the boys and their applauding friends is exhausted. Now begins criminal foraging and senseless waste. Lumber-piles, scaffolding, new buildings, kitchen chairs, wheelbarrows, and sometimes even serviceable wagons, are seized by marauders and thrown on the fires, unless carefully guarded, so that each year sees not only a great waste of good fuel among the poor, but the destruction of much valuable timber and household furniture. This work of hoodlums cannot easily be stopped, because just then nearly all the police are in the polling-places watching the canvass."

- Ingersoll, Ernest, *"Election Day in New York"*,: pp. 3-16  p. 8 1 *The Century, a popular quarterly.* / Volume 53, Issue 1,The Century Company  Nov 1896  New York.

# 1954--From "The Yearbook of English Festivals"

English colonists brought the Guy Fawkes tradition with them to the New World. In 1665, according to New York State laws, every minister had to preach a sermon to commemorate deliverance from the Gunpowder Plot. And in the United States, as in England, November 5 was once observed with bonfires, mummery and anti-Popish ditties. Although the custom has died out now, some vestiges of it may continue, here and there, in the election bonfires and in the traditional 'Lection Day cake, which old-fashioned New England housewives still bake. Some British experts even maintain that the ragamuffin habit of begging for "something for

Thanksgiving," and the mummers' parades of Philadelphia and New York originated in Guy Fawkes's Day. It was natural, they reason, for the early settlers to perpetuate the customs of November 5 in their own new November holiday!

- <u>Yearbook of ENGLISH FESTIVALS</u>  Dorothy Gladys Spicer  THE H. W. WILSON COMPANY NEW YORK 1954.

# Commentary

Pope Day, just like Guy Fawkes Day in Britain, has elicited much commentary. Writers either love the celebrations or hate them. Those writing against the celebrations in Britain have even been incorporated into the ritual with their own effigies as "Enemies of the Bonfire." Over all, most commentaries are written by those not directly involved in the tradition. Such commentaries must be assessed with care along with a detailed knowledge of the structures and purposes of the celebration as:

*Nova Britannia: Offering Most Excellent Fruites by Planting in* obtained from within the traditions. It is important to fully understand the original function, structure and intent of the celebrations before tracing their ecolutionary path and determining how they reflect their host cultures.

## 1609- Robert Johnson

*The deputy-treasurer and propagandist of the Virginia Company*

*Virginia: Exciting All Such as Be Well Affected to Further the Same* (London: John Windet, 1609), 4, 13-14.

"Touching which, I doe earnestly admonish you to beware and shunne three kindes of people: the first, a most vile minded sort, and for the most part badde members of this Citie, by some meanes shaken out of their honest courses, and now shifting by their wittes, will bee alwaies de|uising some vnhappines to wrong the plantation: such as daily beate their braines, and séeke by lying suggestions; vnder colour of good pretence to the Common-wealth to infringe our auncient liberties, and would (if they were not mette withall and curbed by authoritie) make a monopoly to themselues, of each thing after other, belonging to the free|dome of euery mans profession, the very wrack of Merchandizing.

The second sort are papists, professed or Recusant of which I would not one, seasoned with the least taint of that leauen, to be setled in our plantation, nor in any part of that country, but if once perceiued, such a one, wéede him out, and ship him home for England, for they will euer bee plotting and conspiring, to root you out if they can, howsoeuer they sweare, flatter, and equiuocate, beleeue them not: keepe onely these two examples in minde.

Watson the Seminarie priest in his printed Quodlibets: he, of all other men protesteth the greatest truth and fidelity to his Prince and countrey; obiecting all the bloudy plottes and treasons, to haue come from the combination of Iesuits, and from Parsons that Arch-Atheist in chiefe, but as for himselfe, hee wished no longer to liue and breath, then the thoughts of his hart should be true and vpright to his prince and Countrey: Notwithstanding, this Watson was the very first wretch of all other, that had his hand in treason a|gainst our King, and reapt his reward according to his wish.

The other example is a Popish Pamphlet, called the Lay Catholikes Petition, offered to his Maiestie for tolleration of Popery, protesting likewise their fidelitie and vnfained loue to his Maiestie, offering to be bound life for life with good suerties for their loyall behauiour: happy men had we béene to haue taken their bonds, (no doubt) for euen at that instant, when this petition was exhibiting, the chiefe heads of those lay Catholikes, were then labouring with all their might, to vndermine the Parliament house, to shake the Pillers, and the whole frame of the Kingdome to shiuers·

And which is more, there is newly dispersed an idle discourse against an honorable personage of this Land, by a Papist, that termes himselfe a Catholike Diuine, defending Garnet the popish Priest; saying, there was nothing against him at his arraignement, but onely his acquaintance with the Powder-plotte: which (saith hee) beeing reuealed vnto him in auricular confession, hee might not therefore by the lawe and right of Catholike religion, disclose nor make it knowne.
How like you these Catholikes and this diuinitie? if they grow so bold and desperate in a mighty setled State, howe much more dangerous in the birth and infancie of yours? Therefore if you will liue and prosper, harbor not this vipe|rous broode in your bosome, which will eat out and consume the wombe of their mother.

The third sort to auoide, are euill affected Magistrates, a plague that God himselfe complaines of by the Prophet Isaiah: O my people, they that leade thee, cause thee to erre. Touching which, I am no way able to speake enough, for herein lies the very life of all: let no partialitie preferre them, vnlesse they be worthy men; if they be papists or popishly minded; if prophane Atheists, contemning God and his word, turning religion to policy, vnchaste, idle, ambitious, proud and tyrannous, forgetting their allegiance to their King, and duety to their country, neglecting their com|mission of imployment, aduancing vile and vitious persons like themselues, and basely vsing those that bee vertuous, godly, and well affected: then looke for no blessing nor assi|stance of God, but misery, crosses, and confusions in all wée take in hand: but in men of knowledge, and religious education, there is euer found true humilitie, temperance and iu|stice, ioyned with confidence, valour and noble courage, such as was in Moses the man of God, whose iustice excéeded, and courage was incomparable, and yet the méekest man that went vpon the earth: tenne of such will chase an hundred: no aduersitie can make them despayre, their prouident care wil euer be to repulse iniuries, and represse the insolent, to encourage the paineful and best minded, to employ the idle to some honest labours, and to releeue with mercy and com|miseration, the most feeble, weakest and meanest member."

- Robert Johnson, *Nova Britannia: Offering Most Excellent Fruites by Planting in Virginia: Exciting All Such as Be Well Affected to Further the Same* (London: John Windet, 1609), 4, 13-14.

# 1742- William Stephens

## Coulter, ed., *Journal of William Stephens, I*, p. 134

Secretary of Georgia, Savannah

1742 November 5, Friday

"The divine Service appointed for the day was duly observed, when Mr. Dobell read the prayers and after it one of the Church Homilies……Our Flag was hoisted in Commemoration of the day; but I was of Opinion, that burning more powder, would be a needless Waste, of what we might stand in Need of on a more urgent Occasion."

p.76

Vol. II p. 36 (Coulter)

"Expectations of our people in taking the usual notice" *(re. 5th of November) He tried in 1743 to limit celebration to flag raising…..not firing guns due to gunpowder shortage…people objected and he was forced to fire guns and joined in loyal toasts….*

p. 272

*1764-1776 Coronet Joyce who arrested Charles I before the execution added as parade effigy. Custom continues beyond independence.*

-Matthews, "Joyce Junior Once More," in: Colonial Society of Massachusetts, <u>Publications,</u> XI, 294n.

-p. 301

1767 North End Cart in Boston carried a British Flag and the effigy of British dissident John Wilkes an ally to colonists anti taxation efforts.

## 1748- James Burgh

*Britain's remembrancer. Being some thoughts on the proper improvement of the present juncture. : The character of this age and nation. : A brief view [sic] from history, of the effects of the vices which now prevail in Britain, upon the greatest empires and states of former times. : Remarkable deliverences this nation has had in the most imminent dangers; with suitable reflections. : Some hints, shewing what is in the power of the several ranks of people, and of every individual in Britain, to do toward securing the state from all its enemies.*

"…The Winds in their Courses fought for England. He that is mighty hath done glorious Things for us; he hath scattered the Proud in the Imagination of their Hearts. He hath taken our Enemies in the very Snare themselves had laid for us.

In the Year 1605, when that infernal Power, who has long been drunk with the Blood of Saints and Martyrs, found her cursed Machinations against us disappointed; ever thirsting, ever insatiable of Protestant Blood, she resolved to strike a Stroke, which might at once cut off the Hopes of all who opposed her Interest in this Land, by hurrying our King, and some Hundreds of the principal Men and chief Rulers of the Nation, out of the World by one Explosion of a Mine of Gunpowder. Deeply was the Plot laid, and dark and secret was the hellish Contrivance: But that Eye, from which the Darkness hides no more than the Light, before which Hell is naked and Destruction uncovered, saw all their horrid Combinations, confounded their Devices, and brought them in Ruin and Vengeance upon their own Heads."

## 1765- November 11, Boston Gazette, Monday #55 Boston

"Tuesday last being the Anniversary of the Commemoration of the happy Deliverance of the English Nation from the Popish Plot, commonly called The Powder Plot, the Guns at Castle William and at the Batteries in Town were fired at One o'Clock; as also on board the Men of War in the Harbor.

It has long been the Custom in this Town on the Fifth of November for Numbers of Persons to exhibit on Stages some Pageantry, denoting their Abhorrence of POPERY and the horrid Plot which was to have been executed on this Day in the Year 1605; these Shews of late Years has been continued in the Evening, and we have often seen the bad Effects attending them at such a Time; the Servants and Negroes would disguise themselves, and being armed with Clubs would engage each other with great Violence, whereby many came off badly wounded; in short they carried it to such Lengths that two Parties were created in the Town, under the Apellation of North End and South-End: But the Disorders that had been committed from Time to Time induced several Gentlemen to try a Reconciliation between the two Parties; accordingly the Chiefs met on the First of this Instant, and conducted that Affair in a very orderly Manner; in the Evening the Commander of the South entered into a Treaty with the Commander of the North, and after making several Overtures they reciprocally engaged in an UNION and the former Distinctions to subdue; at the same Time the Chiefs with their Assistants engaged upon their Honor no Mischiefs should arise by their Means, and that they would prevent any Disorders, on the 5th—When the Day arrived the Morning was all Quietness, --about Noon the Pageantry, representing the Pope, Devil, and several other Effigies signifying Tyranny, Oppression, Slavery, &c. were brought on Stages from the North and South, and met in King Street, where the Union was established in a very ceremonial Manner, and having given three Huzzas, they interchanged Ground, the South marched to the North, and the North to the South, parading thro the Streets until they again met near the Court-House.

The whole then proceeded to the Tree of Liberty, under the Shadow of which they refreshed themselves for a while, and then retreated to the Northward, agreeable to their Plan;--they reached Copp's Hill before 6 o' Clock, where they halted, and having enkindled a Fire, the whole Pageantry was committed to the Flames and consumed: This being finished every Person was requested to retire to their respective Homes.—It must be noticed to the Honor of all those concerned in this Business that every Thing was conducted in a most regular Manner, and such Order observed as could hardly be expected among a Concourse of several Thousand People—all seemed to be joined, agreeable to their principal Motto Lovely Unity- The Leaders, Mr. McIntosh from the South, and Mr. Swift from the North, appeared in Military Habits, with small Canes resting on their Left Arms, having Musick in front and Flank: their Assistants appeared also distinguished with small Reeds, then the respective Corps followed among whom were a great Number of Persons in Rank: These with the Spectators filled the Streets; not a Club was seen among the whole, nor was any Negro allowed to approach near the Stages;-after the Conflagration the Populace retired, and the Town remained the whole Night in better Order than it had ever been on this Occasion—Many Gentlemen seeing the Affair so well conducted, contributed to make up a handsome Purse to entertain those that carried it on.-This Union, and one other more extensive, may be look'd upon as the (perhaps the only) happy Effects arising from the S—p A—t."

## 1768- New Hampshire Legal Action

New Hampshire Law
1768

[Chapter 9.]

"An Act To Prevent the Disorders Commonly Committed on the Fifth of November & the Evening following under pretence of celebrating the anniversary of the deliverance from the Gunpowder Plot.

[Passed Oct. 28, 1768. 9 George III. Original Acts. Vol. 6, p. 21: recorded Acts, vol. 3, p. 90. This act is revived and extended for ten years by the act of Jan. 10, 1771.]

Whereas it Often Happens that many Disorders & Disturbances are Occasioned and Committed by Loose Idle People under a Notion & Pretence of Celebrating and keeping a Memorial of the Deliverance from the Gunpowder Plot on the fifth of November & the Evening following as Servants & boys Tempted to Excessive Drinking & Quarreling – Surrounding Peoples doors with Clamor& rudely Demanding money or Liquor making mock Shows of the Pope & other Exhibitions making bonfires whereby buildings are in Danger in Populous places & Stealing Materials for such fires with many other Irregularities which Disturb the Peace of Such places & tend much to Corrupt the Manners of Youth – for Prevention whereof.

Be it enacted by the Governor Council and Assembly That Henceforth all Such Clubs Companies & Assemblies for Celebrating or Commemorating the Day aforesaid with the usual shows & mock representations of the Pope & other Exhibitions usually Carried from place to place with the Rude Noisy speeches & Demands of Money or Liquor frequently made at Peoples Doors and the making of bonfires are hereby Strictly forbidden to be done, on the said Day or evening following or any other on the Account of & for the Cause Aforesaid on pain of Imprisonment for the Space of forty eight hours of all concernd in perpetrating any of the Offences aforesaid. And it shall be Lawful for any Justice of the peace Judge of the Superior Court of Judicature Inferior Court of Common pleas or the Sheriff of the Province upon their own View, or the Information of any Credible Witness to Cause any such Offenders or Offender to be brought before him & on Conviction to Commit the Offender for the space aforesaid unless they shall upon warning & being forbid to proceed therein which shall be first given by any householder, they shall Immediately Disperse & Retire.

Provided that the Punishment of Imprisonment shall not be Inflicted on Boys under twelve years of Age.

This Act to Continue and be in force for three years and no Longer."

## 1770-1882- Boston, Isaiah Thomas

At another time, on the Evening of the annual celebration of the 5th of November, to commemorate the discovery of Guy Fawkes, who [entered?] the Gunpowder plot to blow up King James and his parliament, which celebration perhaps in no part of the British dominions was carried to greater length than in Boston; it had grown into custom. Effigies of the Pope and

Isaiah Thomas

the Devil, the imputed instigators of the plot, were placed on a Stage, placed on cart wheels and Drawn by horses, at least some of them, for there were numerous exhibitions of this kind annually on that day in Boston. Some [were] drawn by men and others carried about by white men [and] boys indeed from Men to boys of all sizes and ages exhibited these kind of Effigies, and the effigies were as various in their magnitude as the Men and boys who exhibited them. Little boys had them placed on shingles, bigger Boys on a piece of a board some no bigger than one boy could carry in his hands, others would require 2 or more boys, and so on. On the front of these stages, was placed in proportion to the dimensions of the Stage, a large lanthern framed circular at the top and covered with paper. Behind this Lanthern was placed an effigy of the pope sitting in an armed Chair. Immediately behind him was the imaginary representation of the Devil, standing Erect, with extended arms. In one hand was placed another small Lanthorn. The other grasped a pitchfork. The larger Effigies had the heads placed on poles, which went thro' the bodies & thro' the upper part of the stages which were formed like large boxes, some of them not less than 16 or 18 feet long, 3 or 4 feet wide and 3 or 4 in depth. Inside the Stages and out of sight sat a boy under each effigy whose business it was to move the heads of the Effigies by means of the poles before mentioned from one side to another as fancy directed. Other Effigies beside those of the pope and Devil decorated the Stages. Conspicuous characters who had merited public censure or indignation, were placed on a gibbet or gallows. Admiral Byng who was shot for cowardice, was for many years after noticed in this way. Lord Bute and Lord North in the unpopular part of their administrations were thus exhibited, &c. Along side of his Holiness, after the memorable Battle of Colleden, the unfortunate Charles Stuart, commonly called the Pretender to the British Crown, had a seat. The Effigy of the Devil was always well tarred in order to hold a thick coat of feathers. The tar and feathers extended from his neck to his heels. Why tar and feathers were selected as proper clothing for his satanic Majesty I have never learned. The Stage, the Pope, Devil, and all the Contents was emphatically called a Pope. The Great Lanthorn of the large Ones was 6 or 9 feet high, as wide as the stage, covered with oiled paper, on which were various labels, ugly and uncouth figures, on the sides, but on the front invariably was wrote or painted in as large Letters as the biggness of the Lanthorn would permit, 'The Devil take the Pope,' and then followed the part of the town, either north or south, where the paper belonged, viz, North (or South) End for Ever.

A competition, it seems, early arose between the inhabitants of each part of the town which made the best Popes and Devils. Hostilities soon commenced, and in process of time, the original design of this Pageantry was lost, and was annually [unclear] up to procure money and to try the Skill of the north with the South at fists and clubs, &c. The great aim of the one party was to destroy the Popes of the other. To accomplish this purpose strategy was sometimes used when [unclear] endeavors were frequently used by going secretly in the night sometimes the week or more before the 5th of November to the [place where the] popes were building and destroy them. This caused furious attacks [to be] made on one side and warm resistance on the other whenever the appropriate parties met on the 5th of Nov. In those Battles, stones and brick bats, besides Clubs and fists were freely used, and altho' persons were but seldom killed, yet broken heads and bones were not infrequent.

But these battles were most frequently fought after dark when men and boys who had to work in the Day were then freed from labor and eagerly joined the force of their respective parties. After having assembled, and expended in liquour the money that had been begged in the day, the great lanthorn on the stage and the one in the hand of the Devil were lighted up. The chief, for there was always a

Captain and other officers, gave the command in the harsh sound of a Boatswain of a Man of War, to move on. His orders were conveyed thro' a speaking trumpet. IUmult immediately commenced, the horrid noise of blowing Conk shells, whistling between the fingers, huzzaing, s[?]curing, hollowing, beating with clubs against houses, &c, with everything horrid in a mob now took place. Numbers continually vocifercating North End for Ever! (or South End forever! as the party was). The line of division between north end and south was the Mill Creek. Whichever party first reached this line, gave 3 cheers and with increased noise and tumult proceded on to meet their antagonists, their numbers encreasing with their noise.

On one of these nights, I [came?] out of the house, when the North End Pope passed the door with its multitude of followers.     They had been as far South as where the Great Elm Trees formerly stood, one of which was afterwards known by the Name of Liberty Tree, and were on their return not having met with opposition, excepting now and then a stone or brick bat would be thrown from some persons insulted at the great lanthorn on the stage of the pope. Having no prudence but much curiosity, to see the labels on the great lantern, I had gotten thro' the thick and thin of the multitude near the Stage when unluckily a piece of brick aimed at the lantern hit me on the head, and I fell to the ground. It was surprising, I was not killed by people's trampling over me. The velocity of the brick was weakened before it reached [me], or that would have been sufficient to have prevented my seeing the light of another day. As it was I was badly wounded, and bled very freely. A person who stumbled over me, hearing me grown, took me up, a large crowd gathered round, and some had lights. A person in the crowd luckily knew me, and I was carried home, a surgeon sent for, my wound dressed and pronounced not mortal, and in short time it was healed. The Officers of these popes, were commonly distinguished by gold or brass leaf stuck on paper with su[?]ing, cut out to the width of lace, and sewed on their coats and waistcoats and around the brims of their [hats.] [unclear] powdered hair, with a sword or cutlass. Those In the begging, went into every house, and attacked every person who had the appearance of having any money in pocket. Each had a hand bell, which was frequently rung. The address was in poetry and always the same, and as nearly as I can recollect as follows,

> "Sir, Don't you remember, the fifth of November
> The gunpowder treason and plot — Sir Is there a reason, gunpowder plot treason Should ever be forgott.
> Guy Fawkes, Guy, who was [unclear] was going to his pray,
> With a dark lanthorn by his side."

- Thomas, Isaiah, *"Three Autobiographical Fragrnents; Now First Published Upon the 150th Anniversary of the Founding of the American Antiquarian Society*, (Worcester, Mass.: American Antiquarian Society, 1962), 22—25. Submitted by Ross W. Beales Jr -p. 218. Note in: Bell, J. L. "Du Simitière's Sketches of Pope Day in Boston, 1767." *The Worlds of Children, 1620-1920* (2002): 209-217.

**Isaiah Thomas** (January 19, 1749 – April 4, 1831) was an American newspaper publisher and author. He performed the first public reading of the Declaration of Independence in Worcester, Massachusetts, and reported the first account of the Battles of Lexington and Concord. He was the founder of the American Antiquarian Society. Thomas was born in Boston, Massachusetts. He was apprenticed on July 7, 1756 to Zechariah Fowle, a Boston printer, with whom, after working as a printer in Halifax, Portsmouth (New Hampshire) and Charleston (South Carolina), he formed a partnership in 1770. From 1775 until 1803, Thomas published the *New England Almanac*, continued until 1819 by his son, Isaiah Thomas, Jr. .. He was engaged at Walpole, New Hampshire, in book publishing and printing the *Farmer's Museum*, and in 1788 opened a bookstore in Boston under the firm name of Thomas and Andrews, also establishing branches of his publishing business in several parts of the United States. The monthly *Massachusetts Magazine* was published by the firm, with Ebenezer T. Andrews, in eight volumes, from 1789 until 1796. At Worcester, he printed a folio edition of the Bible in 1791, Watts' *Psalms and Hymns*, and most of the Bibles and school books that were used in the U.S. at that date -Wikipedia, verified.

# 1792- Norwich [Conn.]

## Perkins, Mary Elizabeth, Old Houses of the Antient Town of Norwich [Conn.] 1660-1800, 1895, p,19.

Thanksgiving Day, Fast day, Election and Training days were the great holidays of the year. The Weekly Register of November, 1792, hopes that "the savage practice of making bonfires on the evening of Thanksgiving may be exchanged for some other mode of rejoicing, more consistent with the genuine spirit of Christianity." Mrs. Daniel Lathrop Coit (b. 1767. d. 1848), used to tell her grandchildren of the Guy Fawkes day. observed in Norwich in her childhood. An effigy of straw was carried through the streets, and afterward burned, and she remembered snatches of the doggerel sung: —

The fifth of November
You must always remember;
The Gunpowder Plot
Must never be forgot.
Ding ! Dong !
The Pope's come to town.

It is said that in Portsmouth, N. H., November 5th is still observed by the boys with bonfires. Miss Caulkins mentions that Washington, in one of his

Thanksgiving barrel burning on Jail Hill Clarence E. Spalding

army orders, prohibited the soldiers from any demonstrations on Guy Fawkes or Pope-day out of deference to our French allies, and that the New London boys, or the same reason, were persuaded during the war to give up their usual celebration.

After the Revolution was over, Pope-day revived again, and the New London authorities then prevailed upon the populace to substitute Sept. 6th, the day that Arnold burnt the town, and to burn the traitor in effigy instead of the Pope. Patriotic motives may have also influenced the Norwich boys to transfer their annual barrel burning to our New England festal day, and long may they keep up this custom, peculiar to the town.

-Perkins, Mary Elizabeth, <u>Old Houses of the Antient Town of Norwich [Conn.] 1660-1800</u>, 1895, p,19.

## c. 1771- Samuel Breck

*Recollections of Samuel Breck, with passages from his note-books. (1771–1862.)*

EDITED BY Horace Elisha SCUDDER

p.19

Samuel Breck

"My parents have often told me how hospitably we were received in that city, where, in common with all the colonies, a strong sympathy was entertained for the sufferers in Boston. I, of course, have few recollections of that period. One thing only can I remember, and that is the inoculation of my sister and myself for the small-pox.*

* The reader will recall the frequent references, as in the letters of John and Abigail Adams, to the personal discomfort caused by the precautions taken against small-pox through inoculation before the introduction of vaccination.

We stayed a few months in Philadelphia, and then removed to Taunton in Massachusetts, in order to be ready to enter Boston as soon as the British should evacuate the town. It was here at Taunton that I distinctly recollect seeing the procession of the Pope and the Devil on the 5th of November, the anniversary of the Gunpowder Plot. Effigies of those two illustrious personages were paraded round the Common, and this was perhaps the last exhibition of the kind in our country.† Sentiments of great liberality and toleration, together with an entire absence of colonial or English feeling, have contributed to abolish the custom heretofore annual, and to root out all violent prejudices against the good bishop of Rome and the Church which he governs.

† The celebration of Pope Day in Boston was always accompanied by violence. There were rival popes from the North End and the South End—the Avignon and Rome of Boston—and the followers of each fought to get possession of the opposition pope. General Sumner, in his Reminiscences, published in the New England HistoricGenealogical Register (vol. viii., April, 1854), gives an account of Governor Hancock's measures, through the mollifying influences of a dinner, to put an end to Pope Day in Boston a short time before more tragic hostilities broke out in 1775."

p.117.

"cooled off, and I was now again a Protestant. I had the consent of my family to aid the new priest in establishing his chapel, which was done with all manner of solemnity and without the smallest opposition, for persecution in Boston had wholly ceased. We fitted up a dilapidated and deserted meeting-house in School street that was built in 1716 by some French Huguenots, and it was now converted into a popish church, principally for the use of French Romanists. A subscription put the sacristy or vestry-room in order, erected a pulpit and purchased a few benches. A little additional furniture and plate was borrowed. At length, everything was prepared to solemnize the first public mass that was ever said in Boston—in a town where thirteen years before the Pope and the Devil were annually promenaded through the streets and finally burned together, leaving it doubtful then which was the greater rascal of the two. I attended the mass and carried round the begging-box as quéteur. This was the commencement of the Roman Catholic Church in Boston. Thayer was succeeded by M. Martignon, and he by the celebrated Cheverus, now archbishop of Bordeaux.

-Beck, Samuel, *Recollections of Samuel Breck, with passages from his note-books. (1771–1862.),* Ed.: Horace. Elisha. Scudder,1877.

**Samuel Breck** (July 17, 1771 – August 31, 1862) was a member of the U.S. House of Representatives from Pennsylvania. Samuel Breck (brother of Daniel Breck) was born in Boston, Massachusetts. He attended the Royal Military School of Loreze, France. He moved to Pennsylvania and settled in Philadelphia in 1792, where he engaged in business as a merchant. He served as corporal during the Whiskey Rebellion. Breck was a member of the Pennsylvania House of Representatives from 1817 to 1820, and served in the Pennsylvania State Senate from 1832 to 1834. Breck was elected as an Adams-Clay Federalist to the Eighteenth Congress. He withdrew from active business pursuits and lived in retirement until his death in Philadelphia in 1862. Interment in St. Peter's Churchyard. -Wikipedia, verified.

## 1774- Rokeby, Matthew Robinson-Morris, Baron

*Considerations on the measures carrying on with respect to the British colonies in North America. Rokeby, Matthew Robinson-Morris.*
[Boston] : London: printed. Boston, re-printed and sold by Edes and Gill, in Queen-Street., M, DCC, LXXIV. [1774], p. 59-63.

But let us take this matter, in another light—Suppose a Prince to have been the subject of these letters instead of a People and his conduct and character to have therein been so freely treated and censured instead of theirs and the divesting him of his power and dignity so plainly mentioned and recommended, instead of the depriving them of their rights and privileges and the taking him off proposed instead of the taking off some of them, what would have been the consequence?—High Treason—But might not these have been private letters of friendship and the receiver have secreted and concealed them?—There is no such thing as private letters in the case. No civilities sent to the fairest Lady in the land can make them so. The person receiving must at his over peril carry them to a Secretary of State or to a Justice of the Peace or to some other Magistrate; we don't otherwise want a word for him, which is misprision of treason.—But who would take notice of such a thing?—Let Mr. Attorney or Mr. Solicitor answer that—But on what ground is all this?—Because the Prince is supposed to be the public person and to represent the whole people and that what relates to him may affect them—But there are bad Princes and writing against them is sometimes writing in support and in the interests of the Public and of the People—No such plea or proposition is ever suffered. It would on the contrary be an additional crime even to make or to offer it. —But does anyone by representing a body acquire more prerogatives than belong to that body itself or are the Publick more affected through a third person than immediately in themselves? —Yes, just so. Say a word against a Prince and beware of informations, indictments, fines, prisons, scaffolds and gibbets. These are the strongest arguments in the world and I never knew any man get the better in disputing with them. But abuse a people from morning till night and every one knows, that the rule and the law is; let them mend their manners, if it is true; let them despise it and leave it to fall on the author, if it is not—I am at the feet of Gamaliel, I desire only to learn. I shall not contradict the doctrine concerning a Prince and I subscribe heartily to that about a People. Should these commonwealths of America ever become as strong and independent, as they are now weak and dependant and should they in their greatness and glory remember word of the humblest and the meanest, but not the lea•• sincere or the least disinterested of their friends and advocates, it will be, never to employ force and power against reason and argument; to leave those instruments to such as chuse to make use of them, but to believe truth to be ever the real interest of the People and the Public and that no other incense or sacrifice should ever be offered at the altars of that Goddess, but the pure oblation of a freedom of thinking speaking and writing. But here it cannot will fail to be observed; that should these people, whose distresses are now pleaded, ever come to be masters both of themselves and of others to be glutted with power and riches, that they will certainly run the race of the rest of mankind and learn in their turn tyranny and injustice, as their betters and their predecessors have done before them—I answer, no man perhaps believes this, more than myself; however that is not now the case. But it is hoped, that neither will there in that day be wanting some honest man who will endeavour to make them blush at such a conduct, if he shall not be able to disswade and divert them from it. However, I would willingly in my turn now ask, whether this last observation is also local and confined to America or whether it extends itself likewise to Great Britain?

It is not reason and argument; it is this locality which operates on the present occasion. It is this only that makes many men easy and indifferent in the case about right and wrong justice and injustice. Were my countrymen now in England dipped once in the River Delaware. I dare say, that it would make an almost miraculous change in their opinions. If some, who might be named were transposed into Assembly Men, they would perhaps be as ready to repeal certain late laws as ever they were to pass them. However, I will not go back again to topicks, which seem sufficient to awake the most lethargic Englishman out of his soundest sleep; but I desire to put a case relating to this locality itself and its power and effects.

At the beginning of the last century, there lived a gentleman of the name of Fawkes He hired a house and some cellars and other apartments in Westminster. We will suppose that he had a lease of them; a lease is for the time as good as a purchase; it might not indeed be stamped, but stamps were not then in fashion, it was good without. He bought some gunpowder. It is to be believed, that he paid honestly for it. He could perhaps have produced a receipt for it. He placed it in the cellars or other apartments hired by him He had indeed a mind to amuse himself with blowing up the Legislature of Great Britain. He met with his reward. But suppose that he and Garnet and the rest of their associates, instead of falling into the hands of an English Jury, had been tried at Rome before the Consistory Court or any other Court there, they would no doubt have found an advocate. That is no other than the duty of the profession. I won't take upon me to say, whether he would in this case have flourished about private property, trespass or forcible entry; but whatever turn the Italian council had thought proper to give the cause of his clients, has any one seriously the least doubt, but that they would have been cleared and acquitted and probably by the Court of Rome itself in good time preferred and promoted. As it happened, nothing remained for them but the honour of Martyrdom, which however some of them are said to have attained. So much can a difference of climate do and such force have prejudice, prepossession and locality. But Garnet and Fawkes and their friends were fools, Jesuits as some of them were. They did not understand their trade. A certain northern Prince of our time and perhaps some others, have found better ways of blowing up Legislatures than with gunpowder; which don't make a quarter of the crack and combustion, but which are ten times more effectual.

But our colonies might be well enough, were it not for Dr. Franklin, who has with a brand lighted from the clouds set fire to all America—No Governments care ever to acknowledge the people to be fairly against them. For whatever may be the case with the opinions of the multitude in abstruse and refined matters, which but little concern them nor do they much trouble themselves about; yet the end and therefore the touchstone and trial of all Government being their welfare and happiness, there is hardly common modesty in affecting to despise and refuse their sense concerning their own good and evil, their own feelings, benefits or sufferings. It is in these things that the voice of the People is said to approach that of their Maker. The sycophants of Ministers endeavor therefore to throw on the artifice and influence of individuals all discontent or dissatisfaction of the Public. Mr. Wilkes moves England and Dr. Franklin America; as if we had here no feeling, but through the first and they had there neither eyes or ears, but by the latter. It were happy for mankind, if Administrations procured their own votes and majorities with as much fairness, as the voice of the People is commonly obtained. I wonder, whether we should then have ever heard of any government in Europe indebted in the sum of a hundred and forty million sterling or be at this moment under the alarm of a parent state attacking its own colonies or of a great empire setting at work its fleets and armies only to throw the parts of itself into mischief and confusion. It is idle and childish to be crying out against this or that private person. The truth is that whenever governments heap up combustibles, there will always be found a hand to put the match to them or these would heat and fire of themselves, if there were not.

But is not Mr. W.'s Philipick against the Doctor a capital performance? —I am sure that I have not the least inclination to depreciate the ingenuity of that learned Gentleman, whose argument I have been making so free with. But the being charmed with spruce expressions or a smartness of invective, where the subject makes against the privileges or the liberties of a People, what is it better, then if a parcel of prisoners or of galley-slaves were so abject as to take a pleasure in the rattling, or as it were, in the music of their own chains?

I am drawing towards an end of my career. However, I will first say something to the Americans themselves. I observe them to charge sometimes on the British subjects in general the measures, with which they are aggrieved. Herein they do us wrong. I may venture to affirm, that there would not be hurt the hair of the head of an American, where it to be voted by all our country. Everyone must remember, the universal satisfaction produced by the repeal of the Stamp Act and it would no doubt be the same again were the present measures discharged and remitted. But it often happens, that Representatives and their Constituents are in the most essential and the most important points directly and diametrically opposite to one another. I don't pretend to account for this. It is a fatality. But the Americans should consider, that two different parts of a country may be oppressed by one and the same hand. Administrations have been squandering and running us in debt at home, until our whole substance is wasted and consumed. It may now be coming to their turn. But procul a Jove, procul a fulmine. Great Britain is first brought to its extremity. Let any of our dependencies compare their burthens with ours and then complain of the nation, if they shall find that ours are the lighter. I don't mean to make a merit of this; but let them suppose the same strong hand to be upon us both, when they shall have been convinced, how little we are in this respect to be envied……

- Rokeby, Matthew Robinson-Morris, *Considerations on the measures carrying on with respect to the British colonies in North America. [Six lines from Phillippe de Commines],* [Boston]: London: printed. Boston, re-printed and sold by Edes and Gill, in Queen-Street., M, DCC, LXXIV. [1774], p. 59-63.

## 1852- Nathaniel Hawthorne

Nathaniel Hawthorne

The dark superstition of former days had not yet been so far dispelled as not to heighten the gloom of the present times. There is an advertisement, indeed, by a committee of the Legislature, calling for information as to the circumstances of sufferers in the "late calamity of 1692," with a view to reparation for their losses and misfortunes. But the tenderness with which, after above forty years, it was thought expedient to allude to the witchcraft delusion, indicates a good deal of lingering error, as well as the advance of more enlightened opinions. The rigid hand of Puritanism might yet be felt upon the reins of government, while some of the ordinances intimate a disorderly spirit on the part of the people. The Suffolk justices, after a preamble that great disturbances have been committed by persons entering town and leaving it in coaches, chaises, calashes, and other wheel-carriages, on the evening before the Sabbath, give notice that a watch will hereafter be set at the "fortification-gate," to prevent these outrages. It is amusing to see Boston assuming the aspect of a walled city, guarded, probably, by a detachment of church-members, with a deacon at their head. Governor Belcher makes proclamation against certain "loose and dissolute people" who have been wont to stop passengers in the streets, on the Fifth of November, "otherwise called Pope's Day," and levy contributions for the building of bonfires. In this instance, the populace are more puritanic than the magistrate. The elaborate solemnities of funerals were in accordance with the sombre character of the times.

-Hawthorne, Nathaniel, (1804-1864): *The Snow-image and Other Twice-told Tales,* (1852), p164.

**Nathaniel Hawthorne** born **Nathaniel Hathorne**; July 4, 1804 – May 19, 1864) was an American novelist, Dark Romantic, and short story writer. He was born in 1804 in Salem, Massachusetts, to Nathaniel Hathorne and the former Elizabeth Clarke Manning. He entered Bowdoin College in 1821, and graduated in 1825. Hawthorne published his first work, a novel titled *Fanshawe*, in 1828; he later tried to suppress it, feeling it was not equal to the standard of his later work. He published several short stories in periodicals, which he collected in 1837 as *Twice-Told Tales*. The next year, he became engaged to Sophia Peabody. He worked at the Boston Custom House and joined Brook Farm, a transcendentalist community, before marrying Peabody in 1842. *The Scarlet Letter* was published in 1850, followed by a succession of other novels. A political appointment as consul took Hawthorne and family to Europe before their return to Concord in 1860. Hawthorne died on May 19, 1864, and was survived by his wife and their three children.

Much of Hawthorne's writing centers on New England, many works featuring moral allegories with a Puritan inspiration. His fiction works are considered part of the Romantic movement and, more specifically, Dark romanticism. His themes often center on the inherent evil and sin of humanity, and his works often have moral messages and deep psychological complexity. -Wikipedia, verified.

## 1854- John Greenleaf Whittier,

*Literary Recreations and Miscellanies.* p. 151.

# POPE NIGHT

" Lay up the fagots neat and trim;
Pile 'em up higher;
Set 'em afire!
The pope roasts us, and we'll roast him! "

-Old Song.

John Greenleaf Whittier

The recent attempt of the Romish church to reestablish its hierarchy in Great Britain, with the new cardinal, Dr. Wiseman, at its head, seems to have revived an old popular custom, a grim piece of Protestant sport, which, since the days of Lord George Gordon and the "no Popery " mob, had very generally fallen into disuse. On the 5th of the eleventh month of this present year all England was traversed by processions, and lighted up with bonfires, in commemoration of the detection of the "gunpowder plot" of Guy Fawkes and the Papists in 1605. Popes, bishops, and cardinals, in straw and paste board, were paraded through the streets and burned amid the shouts of the populace, a great portion of whom would have doubtless been quite as ready to do the same pleasant little office for Henry of Exeter, or his grace of Canterbury, if they could have carted about and burned in effigy a Protestant hierarchy as safely as a Catholic one.

In this country — where every sect takes its own way, undisturbed by legal restrictions, each ecclesiastical tub balancing itself, as it best may, on its own bottom, and where bishops Catholic and bishops Episcopal, bishops Methodist and bishops Mormon, jostle each other in our thoroughfares — it is not to be expected that we should trouble ourselves with the matter at issue between the rival hierarchies on the other side of the water. It is a very pretty quarrel, however, and good must come out of it, as it cannot fail to attract popular attention to the shallowness of the spiritual pretensions of both parties, and lead to the conclusion that a hierarchy of any sort has very little in common with the fishermen and tent makers of the New Testament.

Pope Night — the anniversary of the discovery of the Papal incendiary Guy Fawkes, booted and spurred, ready to touch fire to his powder train under the Parliament House — was celebrated by the early settlers of New England, and doubtless afforded a good deal of relief to the younger plants of grace in the Puritan vineyard. In those solemn old days, the recurrence of the powder plot anniversary, with its processions, hideous images of the pope and Guy Fawkes, its liberal potations of strong waters, and its blazing bonfires reddening the wild November hills, must have been looked forward to with no slight degree of pleasure. For one night at least, the cramped and smothered fun and mischief of the younger generation were permitted to revel in the wild extravagance of a Roman saturnalia or the Christmas holidays of a slave plantation. Bigotry — frowning upon the May pole, with its flower wreaths and sportive revellers, and counting the steps of the dancers as so many steps towards perdition — recognized in the grim farce of Guy Fawkes's anniversary something of its own lineaments, smiled complacently upon the riotous young actors, and opened its close purse to furnish tar barrels to roast the pope, and strong water to moisten the throats of his noisy judges and executioners.

Up to the time of the revolution the powder plot was duly commemorated throughout New England. At that period the celebration of it was discountenanced, and in many places prohibited, on the ground that it was insulting to our Catholic allies from France. In Coffin's History of Newbury it is stated that, in 1774, the town authorities of Newburyport ordered " that no effigies be carried about or exhibited only in the daytime." The last public celebration in that town was in the following year. Long before the close of the last century the exhibitions of Pope Night had entirely ceased throughout the country, with, as far as we can learn, a solitary exception. The stranger who chances to be travelling on the road between Newburyport and Haverhill, on the night of the 5th of November, may well fancy that an invasion is threatened from the sea, or that an insurrection is going on inland; for from all the high hills overlooking the river tall fires are seen blazing redly against the cold, dark, autumnal sky, surrounded by groups of young men and boys busily engaged in urging them with fresh fuel into intenser activity. To feed these bonfires, everything combustible which could be begged or stolen from the neighboring villages, farm houses, and fences is put in requisition. Old tar tubs, purloined from the ship builders of the river side, and flour and lard barrels from the village traders, are stored away for days, and perhaps weeks, in the woods or in the rain gullies of the hills, in preparation for Pope Night. From the earliest settlement of the two towns the night of the powder plot has been thus celebrated, with unbroken regularity, down to the present time. The event which it once commemorated is probably now unknown to most of the juvenile actors. The symbol lives on from generation to generation after the significance is lost; and we have seen the children of our Catholic neighbors as busy as their Protestant playmates in collecting, by " hook or by crook," the materials for Pope Night bonfires. We remember, on one occasion, walking out with a gifted and learned Catholic friend to witness the fine effect of the illumination on the hills, and his hearty appreciation of its picturesque and wild beauty — the busy groups in the strong relief of the fires, and the play and corruscation of the changeful lights on the bare, brown hills, naked trees, and autumn clouds.

In addition to the bonfires on the hills, there was formerly a procession in the streets, bearing grotesque images of the pope, his cardinals and friars; and behind them Satan himself, a monster with huge ox horns on his head, and a long tail, brandishing his pitchfork and goading them onward. The pope was generally furnished with a movable head, which could be turned round, thrown back, or made to bow, like that of a china ware mandarin. An aged inhabitant of the neighborhood has furnished us with some fragments of the songs sung on such occasions, probably the same which our British ancestors trolled forth around their bonfires two centuries ago: — "

The 5th of November,
As you well remember,
Was gunpowder treason and plot;
And where is the reason
That gunpowder treason
Should ever be forgot? "

" When James the First the sceptre swayed
This hellish powder plot was laid;
They placed the powder down below,
All for Old England's overthrow.
Lucky the man, and happy the day,
That caught Guy Fawkes in the middle of his play! "

" Hark! our bell goes jink, jink, jink ;
Pray, madam, pray, sir, give us something to drink;
Pray, madam, pray, sir, if you'll something give,
We'll burn the dog, and not let him live.
We'll burn the dog without his head,
And then you'll say the dog is dead."

" Look here! from Rome
The pope has come,
That fiery serpent dire;
Here's the pope that we have got,

The old promoter of the plot;
We'll stick a pitchfork in his back,
And throw him in the fire! "

There is a slight savor of a Smithfield roasting about these lines, such as regaled the senses of the virgin Queen or "bloody Mary," which entirely reconciles us to their disuse at the present time. It should be the fervent prayer of all good men that the evil spirit of religious hatred and intolerance, which on the one hand prompted the gunpowder plot, and which on the other has ever since made it the occasion of reproach and persecution of an entire sect of professing Christians, may be no longer perpetuated. In the matter of exclusiveness and intolerance, none of the older sects can safely reproach each other ; and it becomes all to hope and labor for the coming of that day when the hymns of Cowper and the Confessions of Augustine, the humane philosophy of Channing and the devout meditations of Thomas a Kempis, the simple essays of Woolman and the glowing periods of Bossuet, shall be regarded as the offspring of one spirit and one faith — lights of a common altar, and precious stones in the temple of the one universal church.

**John Greenleaf Whittier** (December 17, 1807 – September 7, 1892) was an American Quaker poet and advocate of the abolition of slavery in the United States. Frequently listed as one of the Fireside Poets, he was influenced by the Scottish poet Robert Burns. Whittier is remembered particularly for his anti-slavery writings as well as his book *Snow-Bound*. John Greenleaf Whittier was born to John and Abigail (Hussey) at their rural homestead in Haverhill, Massachusetts, on December 17, 1807.. Although he received little formal education, he was an avid reader who studied his father's six books on Quakerism until their teachings became the foundation of his ideology. Whittier was heavily influenced by the doctrines of his religion, particularly its stress on humanitarianism, compassion, and social responsibility.
-Wikipedia, verified.

# 1907- Martin I.J. Griffin, Pope Day in the Colonies

*Ed. Note: Washington's order did not end Pope Day.*

*The American Catholic Historical Researches.*
Apr. 1907,3,2, pg.132.

"Pope Day in the Colonies"

GENERAL WASHINGTON PROHIBITS THE "RIDICULOUS AND CHILDISH CUSTOM OF BURNING THE EFFIGY OF THE POPE"—1775.

Prior to the Revolution Pope Day, November 5th, was annually very generally celebrated throughout New England. It was a day known in England as Guy Fawkes Day, intended to commemorate "The Gunpowder Plot," 1588, or the Papists' Conspiracy, when it was alleged "some Roman Catholics" had made preparations to blow up the Parliament House when the King, James I, with the Lords, would be present, but the plot, it was alleged, was discovered by means of a letter to a Catholic Lord, warning him not to be present. The vaults were searched and the gunpowder discovered, of course, and Guy Fawkes, the chief conspirator, seized and executed. This "fiendish plot" and "providential delivery" was not so generally celebrated in the other Colonies as in New England, though there are records showing "the timely discovery of the plot" was not passed by in the southward colonies.

When John Adams, on the evening of July 2, 1776 (not 4th), wrote his wife that the Resolution for Independence had that day been passed, he prophesied that the day, 2nd, would be celebrated by bonfires, fireworks and other demonstrations of delight; he was but transferring the carryings on of November 5th each year at Boston to the day he believed would be commemorated as the Day of American Independence. But the Day of the Declaration, July 4th, and not the Day of the Resolution, became the Day of Independence.

However, the boys' antics on July 4th are but the counterpart of the doings of the 'prentice boys of Boston and elsewhere, before Independence came.

"Boston being a city of great cultivation and refinement took the lead in celebrating Pope Day. An effigy of the Pope was made and generally one of the devil; these were placed on a platform and carried by the crowd, who kept firing crackers, home-made at first, but when New England enterprise opened with China the Chinese firecrackers were imported for use on Pope Day."-

-(U.S.C.H. Mag., Vol. II, p. 3).

The revolutionary War brought not only Civil Liberty, but Religious Liberty as well. So Washington, who won both for the Nation, was the destroyer of Pope's Day by his General Order of November 5, 1775 prohibiting his soldiers from celebrating it and
rebuking them as "devoid of common sense," for undertaking to do
so at that time. His order reads :... *(ed. note text of order -available elsewhere in this volume...)*

....So not afterwards did the boys and senseless men demonstrate by public manifestation that they continued to

"Remember, remember,
The fifth of November."

In course of time, one quarter of Boston thought itself badly treated in the arrangements for the procession. Then North End and South end each had a Pope and the procession generally met on Union street, where a fight took place for the possession of all the figures, the North Enders burning them on Copp's Hill if they won the day; while their antagonists, when successful, burned the Pope on the commons.

 -- (U.S.C.H. Mag., Vol. II, P.3).

In 1745:--Tuesday last being the Anniversary of the Gunpowder Plot, two Popes were made and carried through the streets in the evening, one from the North, the other from the South end of the town, attended by a vast number of negroes and white servants, armed with clubs, staves and cutlasses, who were very abusive to the inhabitant, insulting the persons and breaking the windows, etc., of such as did not give them money to their satisfaction, and even many of those who had given them liberally; and the two Popes meeting in Cornhill, their followers were so infatuated as to fall upon each other with the utmost rage and fury. Several were sorely wounded and bruised, some left for dead and rendered unfit of any business for a long time, to the great loss and damage of their respective masters.

--(U.S.C.H. Mag., Vol. II, p.4).

Charleston, S.C.--"We had a great diversion the 5$^{th}$ instant. The Pope and devil, which were erected on a moving machine, and after having been paraded about the town all day, they were in the evening burnt on the Common, with a large bonfire, attended by a numerous crowd of people.

--New York Journal, Dec. 15, 1774, quoted in U.S.C.H. Mag., Vol. II, p. 6).

Other instances, cited by Rev. T.J. Shahan, D.D., now of the Catholic University, may be read in the United States Catholic Historical Magazine, April, 1888). *(Also in this Volume)*

After Washington's exorcism of "The Pope and devil," the progress of the war debarred a continuance of so ridiculous, childish and senseless a custom. The Canadians were so friendly, in 1776, that continuance would have been damaging to the endeavor that year to secure an alliance on their neutrality. When the alliance with France was secured, a renewal of the folly would have been resented. So, ceased "The Pope and the devil" effigy burning and head breaking encounters of the unruly upholders of the Act of Parliament which declared "The Gunpowder Plot" to have been caused by "many malignant and devilish Papists, Jesuits and Seminary priests, much enjoying the true and free possession of the Gospel by the Nation, under the greatest, most learned and most religious monarch who had ever occupied the throne."

In "Reminiscences of Gen. Wm. H. Sumner" in the New England Historical and Genealogical Register, Vol. 8, April 1854, p. 191, it is related concerning John Hancock, when Governor of Massachusetts, "respecting his great zeal, before the Revolutionary War, to do away with the animosity which subsisted in Boston between the North and Southerners, who, on Pope day, used to have a regular battle, the ill-blood arising from which continued through the year, and showed itself in almost every private as well as public transaction. The Governor, wishing to heal this difference, and thinking it essential to a successful resistance to British aggression, exerted himself in every possible way to effect it, without any avail. He then gave a supper at the Green Dragon Tavern, which cost him $1,000, at which he invited all the leading men of both the Pope parties to be present. He addressed them at the table in an eloquent speech and invoked them, for their country's sake, to lay aside their animosity, and fully impressed upon them the necessity of their united efforts to the success of the cause in which they were engaged. There is nothing more productive of domestic union than a sense of external danger. With the existence of this the whole audience now became fully impressed and shook hands before they parted, and pledged their united exertions to break the chain with which they were manacled. The happiest results attended this meeting, and since that time the North and South Popes have not showed their heads in the streets, and a custom and a celebration, in which all the town participated and which had long been established, was broken as it were by a charm making the stories related of it by our fathers, who themselves were engaged in it, hardly credible by their children.

-Also in: Griffin, Martin, I.J, *Catholics and theAmerican Revolution*, 1907. Volume I

## Martin Ignatius Joseph Griffin

Journalist, historian, b. at Philadelphia, 23 Oct., 1842; d. there, 10 Nov., 1911. In early manhood, he was associated as contributor and editor with various Catholic publications. Appointed in 1872 secretary of the Irish Catholic Benevolent Union he founded and edited its organ from 1873 to 1894, first with the title the "I.C.B.U. Journal", and then as "Griffin's Journal". His articles on local Catholic history printed in this "Journal" led to the founding, 22 July, 1884, of the "American Catholic Historical Society" of Philadelphia, of which he was librarian at his death. In January, 1887, he began the publication of the "American Catholic Historical Researches", which he continued to edit till he died. An indefatigable delver into the byways of the past, he collected a large amount of original data that will be of much value and assistance to the historian of the development of the Church in the United States. His most important publications are the "History of Commodore John Barry" (Philadelphia, 1903), and "Catholics and the American Revolution" (3 vols., Philadelphia, 1907-1911). Monographs on the history of old St. Joseph's and several other Philadelphia churches (1881-1882), on Bishop Michael Egan, O.S.F. (1885), Thomas FitzSimons (1887), and "The trial of John Ury" (1899) preserve many details otherwise neglected. Mr. Griffin was also very active in the promotion of the cause of total abstinence, and of the building and loan associations that did so much good in the industrial community of his native city. -Catholic Encyclopedia

# 1933- R.S Longley, Pope Day, Massachusetts

"Massachusetts also had Pope Day mobs. Each November fifth was celebrated as the anniversary of the discovery of Guy Fawkes and his lighted torch, ready to blow up James I and his Parliament. This Gunpowder Plot was considered a union between the Pope and the Devil; after 1701, the Pretender was added to the enemies of liberty. Boston's Pope Day parade took the form of carting through the streets effigies of the Devil, the Pope, and the Pretender. The effigies were decorated during the evening with lanterns and figures drawn on oiled paper. Small boys were often placed in the carts to make the effigies take ludicrous and grotesque shapes. The parade ended with a celebration at the Neck, where

Three Strangers blaze amidst a bonfire's revel,
The Pope, and the Pretender, and the Devil.[4]

For many years, Boston was divided into two factions. The boys of the North and South Ends often fought on Beacon Hill; their elders clashed on Pope Day. In the course of time there was a North and South End Pope. In conformity with European, as well as Bostonian history, these Popes were rivals. Each had its own organization and leaders. A mechanic, Mackintosh, later noted for other riotous activities, led the South End. The North End leader was another mechanic, Swift. In 1764 the carriage on which the North End Pope was fixed ran over a boy, who died instantly. When this news reached the authorities, they ordered both papal effigies destroyed. The sheriff and his helpers pulled the North End Pope to pieces, but the South End crowd proved too great. The latter, when they saw the sheriff coming, seized their Pope and started the usual parade. Meanwhile, the North End repaired its Pope and moved to meet its rival. The factions met at the Mill Bridge, where a spirited fight ensued, resulting in many broken heads. Finally, the South End captured the rival Pope and moved to the Neck for the bonfire. Several thousand people witnessed this exhibition and added their cheers to the excitement and the noise.[5]

[4] Samuel G. Drake, The History and Antiquities of Boston (Boston, 1856), 662. 5 John Rowe, Letters and Diary (Boston, 1903), 67-68.

During the Pope Day evenings, it was not uncommon for ruffians to appear on the streets disguised with masks and armed with clubs. They demanded money of pedestrians and threatened the lives and property of those who resisted.[6] Other groups, disguised in filthy clothes and horrid masks, went from house to house, intruding everywhere, acting a form of an old mystery play, and demanding money as a reward.[7] The year before the Stamp Act, Boston had two minor riotous disturbances. A man and his wife were placed in the stocks for ill-treating their child. A mob gathered and pelted the man cruelly for several hours.[8] In September, a mob destroyed a wooden horse on the Common, and freed a soldier who had been sentenced to ride it for insubordination to his officer.[9] In fact, any excitement, such as the use of the whipping post or the pillory, was sufficient to bring together a rough and turbulent audience, often armed with rotten eggs and other repulsive kinds of garbage.[10] Such was the material from which the Massachusetts radicals made a political mob. They justified its use on the ground that "Tumults never happen except thro' Oppression and Scandalous Abuse of Power."[11] Hence, in their eyes, if riots led to revolution, it was unfortunate, or, perhaps, fortunate, according to the point of view, but always justifiable, because the end

[6] Boston Gazette, October 30, 1769.
[7] Breck's Recollections, quoted in Justin Winsor, Memorial History of Boston (Boston, 1880-1881), III, 172.
[8] Rowe's Diary, 65.
[9] Ibid. 61.
[10] Breck's Recollections, Winsor, Boston, III, 173.
[11] Boston Gazette, August 29, 1768. These words are taken from a New York dispatch reporting riots in London.

of revolution was always greater freedom for the common man. Or, as it was phrased more poetically:

Shall at this Era all our hopes expire,
And weeping Freedom from her fanes retire?
Shall proud Oppression still our peace pursue,
From the pain'd eyebrow drink the vital dew?

Thus, mobs on both sides of the Atlantic were encouraged to act in the name of that "Liberty" of which John Wilkes became the symbol. Old London organized "Forty-Five" Liberty Parties; New London drank the toast,

"May we never want a Wilkes and may Wilkes never want Liberty,"'

Boston drank his health at every "Sons of Liberty" banquet, and hung forty five lanterns from the branches of the Liberty Tree in honor of the condemned copy of the *North Briton*.[12]

[12] Boston Gazette, August 29, 1768. "

- Longley, R. S., "Mob Activities in Revolutionary Massachusetts" <u>The New England Quarterly</u>, Vol. 6, No. 1 (Mar., 1933), pp. 98-130.

*We should consider the "political" mob an essential layer of government.*

## 1962- Edmund s. & Helen M. Morgan

*Stones and Barrel Staves in Boston* From: <u>The Stamp Act Crisis.</u> Edmund s. & Helen M. Morgan, Collier, *1962*.

"Bostonians sometimes seemed to love violence for its own sake. Over the years there had developed a rivalry between the South End and the North End of the city. On Pope's Day, November 5, when parades were held to celebrate the defeat of Guy Fawkes' famous gunpowder plot, the rivalry between the two sections generally broke out into a free-for-all with stones and barrel staves the principal weapons. The two sides even developed a semi-military organization with recognized leaders, and of late the fighting had become increasingly bloody. In 1764 a child was run over and killed by a wagon bearing an effigy of the pope, but even this had not stopped the battle. Despite the efforts of the militia, the two sides had battered and bruised each other until the South End finally carried the day."

-Notes: Massachusetts Gazete and Boston News-Letter, November 8, 1764, Governor Bernard to Jon Pownall, November 26, 1765, Bernard Papers, V, 43-46, Harvard College Library.

*Was this ritual-"violence for its own sake?*

## 1979- Gary B. Nash

Nash, Gary B. *The Urban Crucible: Social Change, Political Consciousness, and the Origins of the American Revolution* (Cambridge: Harvard University Press, 1979).

"The Northern Seaports and the Origins of the American Revolution", Harvard, 1986, Abridged pp.164-5.

Standing in contrast to these important harbingers of the breakdown of paternalistic labor relations in Philadelphia was the persistence of traditional cultural practices in Boston. The leather apron men were the most remarkable of Boston's inhabitants in perpetuating the highly symbolic and ritualistic culture of the laboring classes. The Pope's Day celebration in Boston provides the best glimpse of their universe. Held every November 5 to commemorate the thwarting of the Catholic conspiracy in England, when Guy Fawkes attempted to blow up the Houses of Parliament in 1605, Pope's Day had become the high point of antipopery in New England. Also, called Gunpowder Plot Day, this annual festival had special appeal on both sides of the Atlantic among urban artisans, especially of the lower ranks.

*A strong case can be made for involvement of all classes.*

In the 1730's or earlier, Boston's artisans began to commemorate the day with a parade and elaborate dramaturgical performances that mocked popery and the Catholic Stuart pretender. For several years artisans from the North End dominated the elaborate mummery. But South Enders soon began competing with them, parading through the streets with their own stage. What started out as friendly competition soon turned into gang battles. The victorious party won the right to carry the opposition's pageantry to the top of a hill and to burn it at night along with their own stage. As the years passed, artisans from both areas formed paramilitary organizations with elaborate preparation preceding the annual event. Though not so intended, Pope's Day became a school for training lower-class leaders, for organizing men who worked with their hands and for imparting to the lower element a sense of its collective power.

*There was considerable involvement of upper classes in organizing especially as celebrations became more political*

Boston's Pope's Day also involved the ritual of status reversal so well known throughout Europe. November 5 became the day when youth and the lower class ruled, not only in controlling the streets of the town but also in going from house to house to collect money from the affluent for financing the prodigious feasting and drinking that went on from morning to night. These "forced levies" were handed up during the morning by well-to-do households as a matter of course for, as Isaiah Thomas, a young printer's apprentice, recalled some years later, "but few thought it quite safe to refuse."

*House visitation and threshold crossing was an ancient important and widespread, respectable artifact of celebration assisting the "socal safety net" although a vocal few objected and some used it commercially.*

Authorities in Boston made attempts to control the violence and indisipline of Pope's Day, especially after melees in which fatal injuries were inflicted, but in general they were powerless to change its character.

*Nash highlights noted a growing class conflict and intensification "street politics" in the 18th century claiming that, with the beginning of the Awakening, the Northern, urban "proletariat" organized illegal societies, "mass meetings," and protests and thus "force[d] [its] way into the political arena" and "assumed" power for a while, only to give up this power in the organization of the revolution. It might be considered that Pope Day represented a pre-reformation, pre-awakening structure for conflict resolution and even political innovation operating in the street. It was taken over by revolution and went out with the bathwater of the flood of presumed utopian change. The fragmenting Awakening was in direct opposition supporting teoligigical evolution over adaptation.*

## 1973- Alfred F Young

Notes: Alfred F. Young, "Pope's Day, Tar and Feathers, and "Cornet Joyce, jun. From Ritual to Rebellion in Boston, 1745-1775," pts. I and II (manuscript/unpublished).

"The seaport crowds of 1765 can best be understood, however, as large groups of disaffected citizens, drawn heavily but not entirely from the laboring ranks, who worked in purposeful and coordinated ways to protest British policies and express opposition to local oligarchies. Leadership of the crowds varied from port to port. In Boston, where poverty was endemic and where the Pope's Day tradition and recurrent street demonstrations since the late 1730s had taught the laboring classes the basic lessons of organization and protest, the crowd leaders emerged from the lower social ranks and were tenuously tied to those above them. In New York, where poverty had arrived only in the wake of the Seven Year's War and there was no recent history of crowd protests, the Stamp Act demonstrators were led by men somewhat higher up the social ladder --ship captains, master craftsmen, and even lawyers."

Pope's Day, Tar and Feathers and Cornet Joyce, Jun.: from Ritual to Rebellion in Boston, 1745-1775.

The paper is a section of a book on the mechanics in the making of the American nation in the revolutionary and early national eras. The focus is on Boston in the generation before the revolution and the revolutionary decade (1765-1775). I use the term mechanic to embrace all segments of the urban working population, the master artisans and the journeymen in the craft system, and apprentices, indentured servants and wage labourers below them. My concern in the paper is in exploring the role of ritual and tradition in shaping ideology and activity among the lower classes of mechanics.

I. Pope's Day in England and New England. Pope's Day in Boston was a distinctly lower class observance every November 5th for at least a generation before the revolution in a form that combined a popular Protestant anti-Stuart anti-Popery with a kind of urban gang warfare. Boston's Pope's Day telescoped elements from two different English celebrations: November 5th, the anniversary of the Gunpowder Plot, and November 17th, Accession Day, the anniversary of the accession of Queen Elizabeth to the throne. The evolution of the English observance of November 5th to the politically empty 19th century boys' 'Guy Fawkes' holiday is obscure. So is the Pope procession of accession day. But the 'cavalcades' sponsored by Whig politicians, 1679 ff. and c. 1710-15 suggest that there existed in England by the early 18th century all the features of Boston's 'Pope's Day'. In Boston from the mid-1740s to the mid-1750s the ritual assumed its 'mature' pattern: a procession with stages and effigies of the Devil, Pope and Pretender, forced levies from bystanders and householders, and in the evening a bone-breaking battle between two 'companies' coming from the north and south end of town, ending with effigy burning.

II. Pope's Day: an analysis. 1) Composition was unmistakably of the lower strata of the mechanics and from youth. 2) The north-south rivalry was expressed by working men and older youth on Pope's Day alone, but for young boys was a year-round affair. The antagonism was long-lived and tenacious. 3) Leadership came from within the group and was organized along quasi-military lines. 4) The ideological content of the anti-Popery was more 'political' than 'religious', to oversimplify. The day was not observed until it could be turned against the Stuarts. It took shape in the context of the rebellions of the 'old' Pretender and 'young' Pretender and of two wars in North America against the French Papist enemy in which Bostonians participated ardently. 5) It drew on and embodied the flavour of many English customs, for example Lords of Misrule and Plough Monday with its forced levies from the better sort as 'of right'. As such, it bears some resernblance to English village ritual processions in which, as Rude and Hobsbawm have suggested in Captain Swing, 'the customary order of social relations was briefly stood on its head' and which provided the 'experience of organization' and 'collective activity' for the lower classes.

III. The Stamp Act resistance. 1765-66. The first year of resistance to British imperial policy, it is argued, was built on the scaffolding of Pope's Day: the leadership, tiie constituency, and the rituals. Five major crowd events of 1765 are re-examined with an eye to the ritual elements they exhibited: the famous riots of August 1 4 and 16, and the less famous mock funeral November 1st, the Pope's Day procession of November 5th. and the forced resignation of the Stamp Act Commissioner, December 18th.

On Pope's Day, the north and south end companies united, under their own leadership, parading anti-British effigies and slogans. The mocking derisive spirit of the crowds was especially pronounced in the 'funeral' and public 'execution' of effigies. And the Devil, the prompter of the Pope and Pretender on Pope's Day, was omnipresent in the demonstrations as the inspirer of political evil.

IV. Pope's Day, 1766-1775. For the next few years Pope's Day remained a unified, politicized celebration, with effigies and inscriptions adjusted each year to the target of the moment. The middle-class Whig leadership, however, was never at ease with the observance and after the traumatic Boston massacre moved to supplant Pope's Day with a commemoration of the massacre in which fervent oratory and horrifying illuminations predominated. Perhaps because of this, on 5 November 1973, the old north end-south end warfare erupted with all its fury. In 1774 in the midst of British occupation the leadership kept the celebration under control and the following year the city was under military siege. This was the end of Pope's Day - although the north-south rivalry of young boys continued for at least twenty years after the war.

V. Tar and feathering. The ritual of tarring and feathering a political enemy was first practised by the same class we have identified as the Pope's Day constituency, and owes something to the example set on Pope's Day when the Devil and his imps were tarred. The custom, while thought of tiien as 'modem' and 'American', was British and ancient. As best as can be made out, it was primarily although not exclusively a punishment of the sea, not only by authority but by sailors as a means of moral enforcement. When it emerged in America in the late 1760s it did so first in New England ports where 'Jack Tars' very likely were the carriers.

More important, the practice filled a function similar to other rituals of official public punishment in which the lower classes traditionally played a lju-ge role. It combined public identification, humiliation, painful punishment, confession and repentance. Tlie only new element was banishment (abandoned in New England after the 17th c) and the crowd usurping the role of the magistrates to dispense justice.

VI. 'Joyce, Jun' and the tradition of regicide. The most notorious incident of tar and feathering (John Malcolm, 1774) prompted the Whig leadership to put forward a 'Committee for Tarring and Feathering' whose 'chairman' was 'Joyce, Jun'. 'Joyce' very likely was John Winthrop Jr, scion of the famous family; of that we are reasonably certain. And 'Joyce, Jun' was meant to invoke the name of Cornet George Joyce, the tailor of humble rank in Cromwell's army who had audaciously seized Charles I in 1647. For the latter there is less proof. Oral tradition we know kept alive the lore of the three regicide judges who escaped to New England, and possibly a good deal more of the traditions of the Good Old Cause.

'Joyce', whatever his historic origins, established himself as a public avenger in 1774 and at his second appearance in 1777 as a leader of the crowd in enforcing public laws on price control, carting violators out of town. The Whig leadership thus identified themselves with tar and feathering, regicide, and then banishment — symbolic of the way in which they had been radicalized by their quest for popular support.

VII. 'Bring me up Oliver Cromwell'. From the fall of 1774 the popular mind was saturated with the same sort of anti-Stuart anti-Popery expressed by the symbolism of the Pope's Day observances and of 'Joyce, Jun'. The stimulus was the Quebec Act establishing Catholicism in Canada. The 'common word' as men marched off to battle after Lexington and Concord was 'No King, No Popery'. For this there is evidence from a variety of sources: doggerel verse, the fusing of tar and feathering with anti-Popery, Tory burlesques, and a new kind of pamphlet of wide circulation. In the American Chronicle of the Times, written in biblical form, the prophet Jedidiah summons up Cromwell to topple the 'usurper'; Cromwell appears as 'Lord Protector of the Commonwealth of Massachusetts'.

As Boston's shipwrights, shoemakers and servants sat around camp fires singing hymns, one feels they were fighting as beleaguered Cromwellian Protestants, rather than as 18th-century Whigs, and that Pope's Day, tar and feathers and 'Joyce, Jun' were rituals and symbols that had brought them to rebellion. [I am especially interested in any suggestions from English scholars on the 17th-18th-century history of the three English elements in my picture: Guy Fawkes' Day, tar and feathering, and the reputation of Comet Joyce.] ALFRED F. YOUNG (Northern Illinois University) -Bulletin -- *Society for the Study of Labour History*, September 1, 1973.

-Manuscript provided by the author.

"My first was into ritual, custom, and tradition epitomized in the title to the paper, "Pope's Day, Tar and Feathers, and Coronet George Joyce, Jun.: From Ritual to Rebellion in Boston," which has enjoyed an underground circulation. The popular side of the resistance to the Stamp Act was built on the scaffolding, symbolism, and leadership of the North-End and South-End gangs, active for thirty years in the annual observance of the American Guy Fawkes day.'9 I attempted to puzzle out a theoretical framework for this transmission of plebeian culture from England to New England and from one century to another. Drawing on Herskovits's hypotheses for the survival of African culture, I suggested several underlying processes: a straightforward carry over and retention; the thawing of something frozen in an earlier era; and a reaching back, borrowing, and syncretism that amounts to innovation. (20 "English Plebeian Culture and Eighteenth Century American Radicalism," in Margaret Jacob and James Jacob, eds., The Origins of Anglo-American Radicalism (London, 1984), 185-212.).

- Young, Alfred F., "An Outsider and the Progress of a Career in History," *The William and Mary Quarterly*, Vol. 52, No. 3 (Jul., 1995), pp. 499-512.

## 1981-Peter Shaw

Shaw, Peter, *American Patriots and The Rituals of Revolution*, 1981.

*Shaw focuses upon the complex artifacts of celebration which have been curated and archived, available "off the shelf" for adaptive re-use. Many of these take the form of pan cultural rituals of great antiquity as suggested by the work of Sir James George Frazer (1854–1941) as referenced in The <u>Golden Bough: A Study in Magic and Religion.</u> 1890-1915, and other works.*

> "*The Golden Bough* attempts to define the shared elements of religious belief and scientific thought, discussing fertility rites, human sacrifice, the dying god, the scapegoat, and many other symbols and practices whose influences have extended into 20th Century culture. Its thesis is that old religions were fertility cults that revolved around the worship and periodic sacrifice of a sacred king. Frazer proposed that mankind progresses from magic through religious belief to scientific thought" -Wikipedia, verified.

"In England "guys"--effigies of the leader (*Ed. Note: incorrect: the leader was Robert Catesby*) of the plot-were carried in processions and then burned. In New England the Catholic Guy Fawkes was replaced by the pope, and accompanied by the devil. These substitutions reflected an American religious bias: a plot against the king almost automatically suggested a popish conspiracy, and hence the devil. A third figure was sometimes added in America: the pretender to the throne, James III, who had invaded Scotland in 1715, and whose son, James

IV, still alive in the 1760s, had led a similar invasion in 1745. The Pretender figure represented a suggestive updating of the earlier powder plot against the king"

*Research shows that the first effigies were devils then came popes, then Fawkes. In Britain figures from current events replaced Fawkes from an early date. Even when the effigy was Fawkes his image was changed from agent of the devil/terrorist to Freedom fighter to Pantomime Harlequin clown as appropriate for the received view of the time. The plot did not have to be interpreted as to "suggest" a popish conspiracy- it was one. The pope was not regarded in a biased manner. He appears as a real political threat to liberty and freedom. Due to Papal politics, he remained a politically appropriate evil doer throughout the period. His continued relevance as such influenced children in Britain and in America to call all effigies: "Popes"*

-pp.16-17.

"The insurrectionary potential in this rowdy holiday was evident. Its threats to peace officers, together with a certain wantonness of symbolism, breathed defiance of authority in general. In substituting the pope for Guy Fawkes, moreover, Americans had put their own anti-Catholic concerns ahead of the holiday's concern with treason against the king."

*The theological foundations for the celebrations call for fervent extreme though righteous behavior carried out to the point of pain as sacrifice. None the less, the celebrations were remarkably safe often self-policed.*
p.18.

"The patriot conception of the Revolution as a familial drama has been perpetuated both by historians of the Revolution and by writers of fiction up until the present-with all concurring in a picture of the break from England as a kind of national coming of age."

*This assumes that revolution was an original intent*

-p.18.

"Yet another incident from Otis's past serves to indicate the sympathy that he felt with regard to the symbolism implicit in these origins. As a young lawyer he defended a second group of youths, this time in Plymouth, Massachusetts, after a frolic on Pope Day. In the traditional manner the young men of the town had forced homeowners to illuminate their windows, and then had gone on a window-breaking spree (presumably of unlit windows). Otis's biographer reports the story from family tradition: "Thinking the prosecution [of the young men] to have been ill-natured and vindictive, [Otis] kindly engaged in their defense, exerted all his powers of humour and argument, described it as a common, annual frolic, undertaken without malice, and conducted without substantial injury; obtained their acquittal and refused all fees.""

*Exactly: approved well founded ritual not insurrection.*

-p. 105

"Festival and revolutionary practices alike frequently harked back to an actual victim. Boys in England dressed themselves as the villain, Guy Fawkes, just as in America they dressed as tar-covered devils. And just as effigies were designed to resemble persons, the published cartoon of an effigy could depict that person as actually hanging from a bough. Similarly, on one occasion instead of a Guy Fawkes effigy a real person was seized and carted through the usual proceedings. Andrew Oliver's effigy, when it was burned by the August 16 Stamp Act crowd, was termed a "Burnt-Offering.""

p.216.

*In theological terms, it was an offering-a message to god rather than personal attack.*

"The scapegoat ceremony symbolized this national process, and at the same time was itself the reflection of political revolution in the distant past. In the earliest times, after all, the victim himself was a substitute-most likely for a king or other leader. The original ceremony, therefore, had amounted to a transmission of political power by means of regicide, and so was itself an act of political revolution. Since a new king replaced the old, giving rebirth to the kingly powers, the ceremony celebrated both overthrow and legitimate succession"

p.216.

*Fawkes was captured- he never was in power. The monarch does not appear-was not reinstated in the ritual"*

"Today, studies of crowds and revolutions tend to accept the notion that the dying god described in the Golden Bough lies behind the ubiquitous burning of effigies in revolutionary demonstrations. This symbolism, however, is taken as illustrative rather than operative.

-p.215.

*This does not explain how the "pre-defeated" "already executed" Fawkes appears and how he was for a time uplifted or "chaired" as freedom fighter (following the publication of Ainsworth's work)*

"so the original Guy Fawkes-Pope Day procession had focused on two figures, the pope and the devil, and in its political adaptations on one or another paired arrangement of figures. The mummers' play had a cast of several characters, but when the proceedings resolved themselves into a marching pageant, two figures dominated, consisting either of two paraded effigies or two men carrying crosses. On Guy Fawkes Day the procession might feature two Guys and on Pope Day two popes or the pope and a devil. Oliver's effigy appeared alongside Bute as a boot in August 1765, Grenville's alongside Huske on November 1, Governor Colden's alongside a devil on November 5, and in 1774 Hutchinson appeared beside Wedderburne. (In the French Revolution the human heads on poles came in pairs.)"

-p.217.

*The mummers play is a ritual of threshold crossing and house visitation. It is comparable not to the procession but rather the ritual of boys going door to door with popes collecting money. In Britain, this was done both as substitute commercial activity and poor relief/alms giving. The presence of duality is to convey the known disclosure of evil to a new entity by association.*

"Pope Day began as the commemoration of a historical event, the Gunpowder Plot, and a would-be regicide, Guy Fawkes.

*Not exactly. It conveys deliverance.*
The holiday evolved by assimilating later attempts at overthrow and later regicidal figures, such as Cornet Joyce. When the American patriots chose their symbols and ritual from Pope Day, therefore, they brought into their political movement a holiday that had itself arisen out of and evolved in response to politics. In doing so they departed from the contemporary English practice with regard to ritualization, which in other respects they copied. For in England as on the continent, protesters tended to adopt the practices of the nearest convenient holiday in the calendar."

*The British holiday made wide use of "off the shelf" artifacts derived from many seasons especially that of house visitation which occurs in all seasons. The seasonality of the celebration was derived arbitrarily by the unfolding of the plot itself.*

Because of religious and cultural peculiarities that touched on the character of the American Revolution, Pope Day was the only adaptable New England holiday in existence at the time of the Stamp Act. English and American Puritans alike had disapproved of holidays, all of which to them smacked of Catholicism and paganism. In England, the Puritans had been able to enforce a ban on such holidays and folk observances during the twenty years of their revolution from the 1640s to the 1660s."

*That ban did not hold.*

p.197-198.

"As a result of the Puritan hegemony, in eighteenth-century New England the only holiday that continued to include popular folk practices was Pope Day. Banned were Christmas, New Year's, Easter, May Day, and All Souls. As for Sunday, the English day for games and recreation, this was turned into a sober occasion for going to church-twice. New Englanders were granted a certain latitude for recreation on a number of holidays: Artillery Day, Election Day, and college Commencement Day, all of which took place in the spring."

*The holiday survived because it was Not! Religious, but more Judicial.*

-p.198.

"…New England legislatures proclaimed Pope Day, actually a time of riot and disorder,

*Note: Behaviors "extreme" but if righteous, they were then theologically underwritten. To say otherwise betrays the judgement of outsiders- the true revolutionaries.*

to be a serious memorial of the popish plot having as its purpose the instilling of "an Abhorrence of Popery & Forming a Spirit of Loyalty in the Youth of the Town. Yet despite their formula of approval, New England elders were acutely aware of the disorderly content of Pope Day. As holidays approached they grew apprehensive of violence, which often involved apprentices.

*Apprentices required approval of masters and were available in sufficient numbers and were more trusted than slaves who were excluded.*

*Shaw concludes:*

" OVER THE CENTURIES the festivals of mankind have undergone profound changes, adopting new dates, new names, and, where a performance is involved, new casts of characters. Yet no matter how far corrupted or co-opted, festivals have tended to retain their identity. Above all, their spirit of subversion never seems to remain suppressed for long. The very festivals that appear to have been successfully prohibited or taken over for official use may be those whose irrepressible elements will burst forth in the service of revolution."

-p.204.

…" The rituals of the American Revolution, then, were of two kinds: public and private. They were enacted both by crowds and in the minds and hearts of the patriots. The rituals were what might be termed prospective or prophetic rites of transition. That is, they predicted, anticipated, and even encouraged revolution-were "rehearsals" of revolution-without being the thing itself. Carrying with them all the ambiguities attendant on the process of dawning revolutionary consciousness, the rituals celebrated a passage from one state of being to another: from the reign of a king to that of the American people."

p.231.

*Shaw's account is of great interest and deserves close reading.*

# 1982 - Robert Middlekauff

1982-*The Glorious Cause: The American Revolution, 1763-1789*, Oxford, 1982, pp. 89, 157, 189, 683.

(The Loyal Nine of Boston)…..To do the rough work of rioting they turned to experience, the recently united North and South End mobs. These groups had entertained themselves for years, most notably in a session on Guy Fawkes Day, November 5, which the two mobs usually commemorated by brawling, a peculiar but apparently satisfying way of celebrating the frustration of an explosion. The fights between the two mobs were not gentle affairs; they used clubs, bricks, stones, and fists on one another, and in the fracas of 1764 a child who got in the way had been killed.

*It is important to recognize participants as specialists.*

Understandably, neither mob kept a roster of its members, but we know that most were craftsmen, workers of lesser skills, sailors, apprentices, and boys. After the fight of 1764, some sort of rough agreement was apparently worked out between the two groups, and the leader of the South Enders, Ebenezer MacIntosh, a cobbler by trade and a man of commanding presence, assumed leadership of the combined group. Persuading Macintosh and his followers to enlist against the Stamp Act probably was not very difficult. All the Loyal Nine had to do was to induce the mob to substitute one local enemy for another -- instead of the opposing mob, the enemy was Andrew Oliver and the crew of placemen who had gobbled up offices for years. Oliver was well known; he and his ilk stood to profit by the stamp tax, and current gossip had it that Oliver's brother-in-law, Thomas Hutchinson, had recommended the tax. Striking a blow for liberty meant hitting such creatures.

The identification of English and local tyranny was made evident early on the morning of August 14. The town awoke to find an effigy of Oliver hanging in a tree; beside it hung a large boot, representing the Earl of Bute, a play on his name. Bute, of course, was no longer in office in England, but he was remembered as an evil man, symbolic of, if not responsible for, the recent dangerous encroachments upon colonial liberties…. "

*To protect liberty*

…..A week later the Customs commissioners arrived from England. Their arrival had been expected -- they were already odious figures -- but its timing was a stroke of bad luck: November 5, Guy Fawkes Day, a day ordinarily of riotous behavior. Somehow they avoided all abuse, though they were greeted by a large crowd parading with effigies of "Devils, Popes, & Pretenders", all with labels on their breasts reading "Liberty & Property & no Commissioners". …..

….The American Board of Customs Commissioners, designed to bring order and honesty, never performed as expected, nor did the new vice admiralty courts established by order in council the year after to stiffen the law. The board contained at least one able man, John Temple, but be was soon on the outs with the others; John Robinson was upright but stubborn and unimaginative; Henry Hulton had abilities but he did not bring them to bear; Charles Paxton disliked the colonists from that unfortunate day of arrival -- Guy Fawkes Day -- when he suffered the "indignity" of seeing his effigy burned. Little is known of Burch. Together the commissioners led a style of life that set them apart from the people they had to deal with, and together they never seemed to be able to conceive of any solution to their difficulties that did not involve the use of troops against the Americans. …

*Stamp act protests were new artifacts borrowed from tradition but not Pope Day itself.*

# 1987- Gilje, Paul, A.

*The Road To Mobocracy,* University of North Carolina Press, 1987.

From: *The Road to Mobocracy,* Paul A. Gilje, University of North Carolina Press, 1987.

(p. 22)

"During the Pope Day pagent, revelers carted effigies about town in the same manner as officials had criminals carted through the streets, they enforced a general illumination by smashing unlit windows, and they collected money to support their efforts in a kind of unofficial tax."

*House visitation rituals were commonly associated with British Guy Fawkes Celebrations as well as with other customs such as Wassail. While at times commercial thir most important function was to serve the "social safety net"*

*Gilje interprets the significance of Pope's Day Celebrations as follows:*

"The meaning of this ritual is complex: it expressed faith in the standing order and simultaneously questioned. it. On the surface, Pope Day was a patriotic holiday, celebrating the Protestant succession. All levels of society shared this patriotism, which was of particular importance to New York's disparate Protestants, who were united only in their ardent anti Catholicism. But there are deeper meanings behind the ritual--meanings that suggest that the Pope Day ceremony after 1748 also acted as an implicit challenge to the social hierarchy. In other words, patriotic ritual served as a screen to hide the more subtle shadows of social conflict."

*It is important to remember that the challenge of Catholicism was primarily political in this period.*

*(here Gilje cites Max Gluckman and Victor Turner as informing his analysis)*

"The intricacies of the symbolic meaning of the Pope Day ritual are evident when we examine the New York crowd's selection of effigies. Although the procession occurred on the anniversary of Guy Fawke's attempted misdeed, that Catholic fanatic held little significance for New Yorkers in the mid-eighteenth century. The crowd, instead, chose its own anti-catholic symbols. The patriotic message of all three effigies is clear. The pope naturally represented the hated Romanism, and after the failed invasions of 1715 and 1745, the Pretender epitomized the popular fear of the arbitrary and Catholic monarchy in the Stuart mold. The devil, leading, whispering or hovering about the scene, was a common motif representing evil in eighteenth-century iconography."

*Acoording to the concept of heteroglossia many interpretations can coexist. It is important to see the generalized Pope and Devil effigies as establishing a "lineage of evil" leading to specific named effigies.*

*(here Gilje cites Shaw, American Patriots and U.S. Library of Congress, The American Revolution in Drawings and prints...., David H. Crestwell comp.)*

"The submerged challenge to social authority is less evident. The attack on popery may have represented, in the popular mind, a criticism of all church hierarchy. More important is the central role of the Pretender's effigy. It is granted, of course, that its desecration represented an explicit statement of loyalty to the current regime. But there may have been other, even contradictory meanings to the effigy. The Pretender despite all his faults, was also a member of the aristocracy. Engraved silver beakers of the New York Pope Day effigies (see above) portray the Pretender as a Scottish lord. With sword at his side, the effigy may have stood as a muted symbol of the aristocracy. Under the guise of patriotism, the common folk could denigrate and humiliate this effigy, which represented an individual ordinarily untouchable. Moreover, there is another possible meaning to the ritual which almost negates the loyalism of the holiday. The prominence of the effigy of the Pretender-- who lost his claim to the throne because of the perfidy of James II--may have acted also as a reminder to the monarchy of what might become of the Hanoverian dynasty if it behaved to arbitrarily, if it got too close to the Catholics, or if it betrayed the people.

*I would suggest that the most important qualities being promoted wewe Freedom and Liberty from outside powers. Both slogans were painted on Pope Day wagons.*

The evidence that these effigies served as a type of challenge to authority is tenuous, but this interpretation becomes more compelling when placed in the context of the commencement of the Pope Day parades. The political and economic conditions of the 1740s and 1750s certainly were conducive to a New York plebeian challenge to the standing order. During these years a bitter factional rivalry divided the provincial elite who charged one another with failing to protect the welfare of all......Thus, as New York filled with men returning from war in 1748, the Pope Day effigy procession long practiced in Boston, offered itself as a means to express contrasting emotions---clearly hatred for French papists was dominant, but perhaps also this new ritual expressed dissatisfaction with the colonial leadership, the peace, and , subliminally , the king. Class antagonism confused factional politics, the rise of a market economy, and conventional and official celebration to a special plebeian holiday from 1748 to at least
1765.....The Pope Day processions that began in 1748, the New Year's frolics practiced throughout the century, the less regular rowdyism accompanying official celebrations, and the sporadic rioting against impressment and over issues like the coinage controversy of 1754--all were plebeian activities. Youths, seamen, mechanics, laborers, and black slaves were the main participants. The patrician might stroll across the plebeian state and might even participate in the drama. He too, after all, was a member of the community and shared to some degree, in the popular culture. But if he did join in or lead the tumult, he was only temporarily entering a world in which he might exert some influence, but a world he could never completely control. His presence did not alter the basic plebeian character of the rioting..."

*This Analysis is interesting however, it leaves me wondering- Why November? -What happened to traditional Guy Fawkes celebrations from the earliest times when the holiday must have been in the cultural baggage of more than a few, and what is the relationship of the celebration not only to the veterans returning from the war but to the countryfolk who have by November 5 just freed themselves temporarily from the land and the harvest? '*

*I find the observation that Guy Fawkes is not mentioned of interest. I would think that he always represented the Devil as in the phrase "devil in the vault."*

# 1989- David Cressy

"The English Calendar in Colonial America". pp. 190-206 of David Cressy., Bonfires and Bells."National Memory and the Protestant Calendar in Elizabethan and Stuart England.

"Bringing The Celebration of Bonfire Night/Guy Fawkes Day to Colonial America"
Being a reflection upon Chapter 12.

To be sure 17th century Colonial America was not 17th century England. There were many differences. For example, there were no bells to ring on the 5th of November. Other local holidays recording local events added new holidays to the calendar. One can even cite the different rhythm of the seasons. In tobacco country there was not one date which could be associate with the harvest as the crop was prepared and processed the year round. There was also a strong feeling that cultural life in the colonies should create a new beginning. This feeling was helped along to reality by conservative churchmen who eliminated the Celebration of central holidays such as Christmas and even went so far as to rename the months of the year. None the less the holiday of the 5th of November did arrive in the cultural baggage of the English colonists along with an awareness of the political lessons which the holiday taught. At Jamestown settlers had to take a strong oath designed to eliminate Popish plots and one of the first celebrations appears to be that which resulted in a fire at Plymouth. Eventually the holiday took a solid root in the large trade centers of Boston and New York. Little is heard of the celebration elsewhere. But, can we be sure that we have the full picture? Perhaps the celebration is simply better recorded in the urban areas. Cressy notes that celebrations were not as well recorded in the Colonies as they were in contemporary England.

There were not many diarists in the colonies. Those that did write did not say much about celebrations. One would have thought that as in England, the maintenance of celebrations would have been a hot topic at court or in diaries or in polemic and other correspondence. This is however not the case and references are few and far between. Perhaps the creation of a new culture of America prevailed adapting to the new seasonal round and substituting new historical celebrations for the old.. Or, perhaps we have simply not looked hard enough at the personal correspondence that exists from the period or the peripheral references to the celebration which might exist in the form of subtle effects of the celebration upon daily life, commercial activities and legal judgments.

Cressy notes that the maintenance of religious routine was also weak or nonexistent. Without the prayerbook as a guide some celebrations could be easily lost. Surely the tensions of the frontier and the demands of survival would be factors which would dim the quality of any celebration. Even after the restoration and the return of many celebrations Gunpowder Treason Day had to wait until the Williamsburg era for its reintroduction from England to Virginia. It is mentioned in *The Virginia Gazette,* 4-11, F February 1736-7 and December 1774; and the *Virginia Almanack* (Williamsburg, 1743,1764,1774). In Maryland we encounter a colony which was not inclined to "cherish" any one faction of religion, however, with individual freedom to practice traditions of choice one would however, expect to see Gunpowder Treason Day in the cultural baggage and in the practice of more than a few colonists. Here again researchers point to an absence of documentation in the written record. Perhaps we should take our questions to archeologists.

The new colonial seasonal round did however occasionally cause many to celebrate on the 5th of November. This occurred because official celebrations of Thanksgiving Day often fell on that date. In Connecticut, the celebration of the first Wednesday as Thanksgiving often resulted in the celebration occurring on November 5. Thanksgiving would also tie in very well with the intent of the celebration of Gunpowder Treason Day.

Due to Puritan influences early American almanacs did not specially mark the date of November 5.

The custom of red letter days was unknown. Eventually after James II almanacs such as John Tullley's of Boston in 1687 brought back the custom of recording the old holidays. It was not until 1689 that Powder Plot Day was recorded in Tulleys work. However, when puritans again cracked down and other days were eliminated from the calendar Tully made two important exceptions in 1697 for the Birthday of King William III and for the Gunpowder Plot. While this is strong evidence for the continued celebration ministers with the exception of a few such as Thomas Hooker and John Wilson still did not deliver sermons to mark the holiday in New England. Even though strict Protestants did recognize that the Gunpowder had signaled God's deliverance they regarded its celebration to be superstitious. We cannot however, tar the entire colonial society with the same puritanical, revisionist brush. There was always an undercurrent of the "reprobate masses" who were unwilling to follow the "saints" in the censorship of tradition.

Emmanuel Altham for example on a visit to Plymouth notes that carousing sailors had built a fire at the Plymouth Plantation in 1623 which ran out of control to destroy three our four houses in 1623. William Bradford notes that *"this fire was occasioned by some of the seamen that were roystering in a house where it first began, making a great fire in very cold weather, which broke out of the chimney into the thatch"*. Of course, this celebration was frowned upon by the saintly classes and discouraged however, its survival is of significance.

Later in 1662 Samuel Maverick (a royalist) noted complaining: "divers youths (were) lately prosecuted at Boston for making bonfires on Gunpowder Treason day at night, it being kept as a thanksgiving for the return of the New England agents, the youths being willing to conform to the practice that such a time affords in old England; for this reason the parents of the youths were fined, but the children of the church members who were guilty as much as others scraped all scot-free".

Middlesex County court records of 1662 show more. Thomas Facy and Paul Wilson who had also been caught and punished for Maying, were :*"convicted of disorderly carriage on the fifth of November last, being a day of public thanksgiving in abetting sundry young person and others gathering themselves into companies and kindling fires in the evening, and absenting themselves from their master's houses and lodgings after nine at night to the disquiet of the inhabitants, sundry men having their fences by that occasion pulled up and burnt, and one house tumbled into a cove, and sundry guns shot of whereof Paul Wilson confesses he shot one of them."*.

So here was evidence of celebration escaping the cultural baggage to run in the community.

Unofficial celebrations continued throughout the rest of the 17th century in New England. America had to wait until the 18th Century for more elaborate celebrations in the English style to become popular. Increase Mather on November 5 1664 was *"at night much troubled to see the bonfires"*. Therefore, we must recognize the persistence of the celebration even though the celebrants were not of the dominant class. Perhaps it was the influence of mariners, who had recently witnessed the extravagant English celebrations, upon the youth which we must credit for the development of an interest in the celebration. Perhaps also the celebration by its very nature is most successful in urban rather than in rural areas. The celebration is infact a group and community celebration often associated with societies which could not be so organized in less populated rural areas. But here again our information of the isolated farms and communities is limited. Certainly, the time and resources for celebration would have also been greater as time passed, population grew and basic subsistence became less of a central concern. Renewed celebration may well be a result of prosperity and urban growth.

At last in 1665 Anglicans including Samuel Maverick petitioned the General Court of Massachusetts to make the laws of the colony conform with those of England.

"There ought to be inserted and ordained to be kept the fifth of November, and the nine and twentieth of May, as days of thanksgiving; the first for the miraculous preservation of our king and country from the Gunpowder Treason; the second for his majesty's birth (and) miraculous and happy restoration to his crowns upon the same day; as also the thirtieth of January as a day of fasting and praying, that God would please to avert his judgment from our nations for that most barbarous and execrable murder of our late sovereign, Charles the first"

This proposal was rejected. It was however a very important statement reflecting common heritage and linked traditions. The desire to break clean with England in America was not entirely successful. Infact, the later emphasis upon the celebration in Boston and New York was to demonstrate that the tradition was not only restored but an integral part of American political life in these urban centers.

November 5, 1667 was, however, declared" a day of thanksgiving unto God for the continuance of our peace and liberties" Of course this could be done because it was also to be celebrated as the traditional Thanksgiving day which just happened to fall upon the 5th. So here it appears that American Thanksgiving Day Commemorations and Gunpowder Treason Day Celebrations are in competition for the same date. This is however, not the case as both days were considered to be celebrations of thanksgiving and could be celebrated together without conflict.

Thomas Bailey of Massachusetts wrote a four-page poem in 1669: *In Quintum Novembris"*. In this poem he praised Jehovah: *"Who sav'd us on the 5th day of Novermber/ Which may us cause God still to remember."* Here again the importance and the shared traditions of the day emerges from the cultural baggage as a real concern.

The people of Boston were treated to a publication of John Wilson's *Song of deliverance for the lasting remembrance of God's wonderful works*. This work was originally written in England in the 1620s. It was reprinted in Boston in 1680 and is seen to be an influence across the ocean of the fear of another Catholic succession which had lead in London to mock pope burnings. Wilson had infact re-located from England to Massachusetts where he became a minister. New Englanders could reflect upon his words:

Never since world began was thought plot more abominable
Never Deliverance was wrought more strange and admirable

It is no doubt however, that the new generation had seen the celebration in the cultural baggage of their parents and grandparents. Perhaps in rural areas it had never been discontinued as a part of their own seasonal round. The puritans did, after all, recognize the deliverance from the treason of the Gunpowder as an important part of the pattern of providences. They preached the celebration but simply refrained from celebrating beyond the pulpit.

There was a significant demand for sermons on the topic. Perhaps this demand stems from the perpetuation of the old calendar in the more conservative countryside.

Samuel Sewal for example noted his disappointment on 5 November 1685 in his diary: *"Mr. Allin preached.... mentioned not a word in prayer or preaching that I took notice of which respect to Gunpowder treason."* The next year he was a bit happier to note as Mr. Morton, preaching at Charlestown, *"took occasion to speak of the 5th of November very pithily"*. The pattern of providences continued to link the heritage of New England to that of England. Just as this link was seen in the pulpit once the time was right for its rebirth it was also seen in the streets. Is it possible that the later street activity was encouraged by a movement of practitioners of the celebration from rural (poorly recorded) settings to the urban (better recorded) settings?
In November 1682 Benjamin James and a few others were taken to Suffolk County Court because he had gathered people together to start a bonfire in Boston. On 5 November 1685 *"although it rained hard, yet there was a bonfire made on the common. About fifty people attended it."* The next night with better weather: "about two hundred hallowed about a fire on the common". There was no violence but merchants and magistrates

worried about the disturbances. Most 17th century celebrations of the 5th were infact not violent. There was bull-baiting at Marblehead in 1702 for the celebration. The poor were given the meat.

William III accomplished much to save the celebration. First he was born on the 4th of November and then he arrived in England on the 5th to rid the country of the tyrant king James II. This made the period of days even more important. This complimented the concurrent celebration of the American holiday of Thanksgiving. Guns were fired on the king's birthday in 1697: *"At night great illuminations made in the Town House governor and council and many gentlemen there. About eight Mr. Brattle and Newman let fly their fireworks from Cotton Hill, Governor and Council went thither with a trumpet sounding"* With more days to celebrate in the same week it was possible to escalate the celebration over a period of days with a climax on the 5th itself. It was also possible to avoid bad weather. The logistics of being able to hold a festival over a long period of time may have also aided in its success. Eventually a fully developed carnival and fire-festival developed. Its climax was the ritual burning of an effigy of the pope. Within 50 years the celebration had returned to life in America as a major holiday.

The Boston Almanac for November 1735 noted:

*"Gunpowder-Plot*
*We hna'n't forgot"*

The Boston Evening Post of that year retold the tale of Guy Fawkes and of the conspiracy:

"for the information of such of our readers who are not furnished with the history of this surprising attempt" The paper reported on 10 November 1735: "Wednesday last, being the 5th of this instant November, the guns were fired at Castle William, in token of joy for the happy deliverance of our nation from one of the most horrid and damnable conspiracies that ever was contrived by hell and Rome...In the evening there was a bonfire on Dorchester neck, and several in this town; and there were a variety of fireworks played off upon this occasion, both on the land and on the water." Some apprentices who had gone out to watch the festivities on boats drowned on their way back. Eventually the growth of the celebration would bring competitive processions, effigies and bonfires. Rival gangs (North Vs. South) parading their popes caused death and destruction in Boston in 1764. Some see the celebrations as a way of blowing off social steam. The urban furnace produced high tensions as well as noise, light license, festivity and danger. Anti-Catholicism merged with anti-authoritian philosophies. Gunpowder Treason day was re-named Pope's day. The Effigy of Lord North and tea in 1774 in Boston demonstrated that the celebration had fused onto the processes which were to lead to the birth of a new nation via the American revolution. The celebration had resisted attempts to fully Americanize the new world and it had found a place in the seasonal round arm and arm with Thanksgiving. The transference of politics from the courts of kings and churches of the clergy to rival societies of ordinary people on the street turned the celebration completely inside out the plot became emplematic of the power of the people and an occasion for the celebration of that power more in celebration of Fawkes than in the celebration of the preservation of the elite.
While some see the transformations of the celebration in America to be the harnessing of a celebration by an Ideological tradition I believe that it is just as important to see the continuity of a multidimensional holiday in the celebration. As is pointed out elsewhere on these pages the many dimensions of the holiday provide many handles for its use by a wide variety of groups for a wide variety of purposes.

While conservatives could celebrate the continued actions of the hand of providence and salvation others would see in the bonfire the unexploded gunpowder left for us all by Guy Fawkes. The precedent of questioning authority from the street was just as important as its deliverance.

I would maintain that the celebration itself continued throughout the 17th century as a part of the cultural baggage of colonists-perhaps in the unrecorded or poorly recorded rural areas. I am confident that if we look carefully both in subtle textual references and in the archeological record we will find those bonfires of celebration on the new frontier and throughout the colonies where English men and Women maintained this very important celebration of the continuity of political and social development from one side of the Atlantic to the other. Perhaps the migration of practitioners or of their thoughts and philosophies from rural areas to the urban centers lead to the late 17th and early 18th century revival of celebration. The continuation of the celebration is strong evidence for the defiance of the American climate and the agricultural seasonal round- a triumph over the wilderness . The celebration in urban centers would symbolize a triumph of the people and political partys of the streets over the institutions of government and of religion. Robert Catesby and Guy Fawkes would have been quite proud.

- Cressy, David.,Bonfires and Bells."National Memory and the Protestant Calendar in Elizabethan and Stuart England.,University of California Press, Berkeley,1989.

## 1995- Francis D. Cogliano

In *No King No Popery* Francis D., Cogliano (Greenwood Press, London 1995) provides us with a chapter: "#2 Deliverance from Luxury:Pope's Day, Social Conflict, and the Anti-papal Persuasion".

"The Anti Papal Persuasion "Deliverance from Luxury: Pope's Day"

"The celebration of Pope's Day gave Boston's common people a voice with which to assert their participation in and agreement with the very foundation of New England culture, Protestantism. The aversion to Catholicism, which colonial New Englanders termed "popery" was at the heart of New England Protestantism." P.15.

-- Cogliano, Francis D., "Deliverance from Luxury: Pope's Day, Conflict and Consensus in Colonial Boston, 1745-1765", *Studies in Popular Culture*, Vol. 15, No. 2 (1993), pp. 15-28.

*Although it is impossible to know if any or all were on the same page it can be accurately asserted tht the primary concern regarding "papacy" was political. This fear was justified by the fact that the Pope and serogates such as France and Spain represented real threats to the freedoms and liberties of the colonists.*

Cogliano wishes to demonstrate that anti-popery extended beyond lectures and sermons to grand popularr rituals. Again events in New England are noted. One still must wonder what if anything occurs outside of Boston, New York and New England. He notes that " the elite appreciated the stabilizing impact of anti-papal rhetoric which unified and bound a socially disparate people together. The pope was thought to be a good lightening rod to direct anger away from them. (p.24) .Cogliano finds that the celebrations link the common people with the mainstream Protestant culture and provide a chance to vent anxieties and frustrations. Cogliano notes the first celebration of Pope's day in the new world as occurring in Plymouth in 1623 when rowdy sailors let their bonfire get out of control and burn several homes. The involvement of sailors and ports in the celebration is seen as significant. Ports with celebrations included: Newport, Salem, Marblehead and Portsmouth. There was Bull-baiting for the celebration in Marblehead in 1702. The Meat was given to the poor. The plebeian nature and focus of the festivities and participants is noted. The Boston celebrations were singled out as most vigorous. The burning of the pope and the devil in effigy is noted. The beginning of the parade custom in Boston in 1720's is noted. Sometimes several popes were paraded through the streets with fighting occuring when paths crossed. Drinking was noted as being associated with the event. In 1735 four apprentices drowned while canoeing from Boston Neck after burning their pope there. Cogliano lists the three elements of the celebrations: 1. procession of the effigy of the pope through the streets and exacting of tribute from the populace 2. Violent confrontation between rival processions. 3. The burning of the popes. The celebrations began in afternoon or early evening. Large floats which took many weeks to construct followed young boys who carried their own pope effigies. The ballad of the "Printshop Boys" dating from the 1760s is cited:

*"The little Popes they go out first With little teney Boys: In frolics they are full gale And make a laughing noise."* p.25. -North End South End Forever (Boston 1768)

Another verse from another song is cited in the notes #18, p.36.

*"You'll hear our bell go jink, jink, Pray madam, sirs, if you'll something give, We'll burn the dog (the pope) and never let him live."*

-Joshua Coffin, *History of Newbury (Boston, 1845).*

Observations of a Printer's Apprentice Isaiah Thomas are cited in regard to celebrations in the 1750's and 1760's "Little boys had them (popes) placed on shingles, bigger boys on a piece of board, some no bigger than one boy could carry in his hands, others would require two or more boys and so on." p.25

Larger parades came after the boys parades. Pope "gangs" were defined by Geography. In boston the rival neighborhoods were the North end and South end- these groups had rival popes.

Isaiah Thomas' account of one of the larger popes is cited:

*"On the front of these stages, was placed in proportion to the dimensions of the Stage, a large lantern framed circular at the top and covered with paper. Behind this lantern was placed an effigy of the pope sitting in an armed Chair. Immediately behind him was the imaginary representation of the Devil, standing Erect with extended arms...The larger Effigies had heads placed on poles which went thro' the bodies and thro' the upper part of the stages which formed like large boxes, some of them not less than 16 or 18 feet long, 3 or f4 feet whide and 3-4 feet in depth. Inside of the Stages and out of sight sat a boy under each effigy whose business it was to move the heads of the effigies by means of the poles before mentioned, from one side to the other as fancy directed"* pp.25-26.

An anonymous 70-year-old man is cited as he wrote to the *Columbian Centinel* in 1821: *"On the stage was music and something to drink-also boys, clad in frocks and trousers well covered with tar and feathers who danced around the Pope and frequently climbed up and kissed the devil"*-p26. The relationship between the pope and the devil in the concerns of New Englanders is noted. David Robinson a Philadelphian is cited as he wrote about his experiences in Boston in 1761- *"His Holiness was in a very antique dress and had a really Roman nose. The Devil, out of compliance wore one about two inches longer and had a key in one hand and a pitch fork in the other."* p.26.

Isaiah Thomas is cited remembering that *"The Effigy of the devil was always well tarred in order to hold a thick coat of feathers."*

Peter Oliver is cited as agreeing: *"sometimes both of the (the pope and the devil) are tarred and feathered, but it was generally the Devil's luck to be singular."*

It is noted that the pope is shown as the servant of Satan. The Hierarch of celebrants is noted. Officers were elected to oversee construction of the pope and to lead the procession. Ebenezer Mackintosh, a shoemaker who had risen from poverty is mentioned as such an elected officer. He was known as "General" Mackintosh and is described leading the South End Pope wearing a blue and gold uniform with a lace hat and holding a rattan cane and speaking trumpet (1760s). p.26.

The election of leadership by the Pope's Day groups is considered significant as a parallel for the more traditional power structure of the city.

The Printshop Boy's Broadside is again cited as it describes the ridicule given the popes by the crowd:

*"The great ones next go out, and meet With many a smart rebuff, Theyu're hall'd along the street And called bad names enough."* p.27.

When the procession came to the home of a wealthy individual a "purser" collected tribute to pay for expenses of the celebrations. It is suggested that a form of mummers play was provided in exchange for money. Celebrants would hit the sides of houses with staves or clubs implying a threat of violence. A bell and a poem are noted by Isiah Thomas as being rung and recited at the homes of the wealthy. The Bostonian James Freeman is cited noting that the procession: was

*"very abusive to inhabitants, insulting persons and breaking windows of such who did not give them money and even of those who had given liberally."*

The object of the violence between groups was the capture of the pope of the other side. Isaih Thomas is cited as remembering: *"A competition it seems early arose between each part of town which made the best Popes and Devils. Hostilities soon commenced...In those battles stones, brickbats, besides clubs were freely used and altho' persons were seldom killed, yet broken heads were not infrequent."* p.27

James Freeman is cited as noting that a meeting of popes in 1745 was particulary bloody . The years of 1750's and 1760's are cited as being particularly violent. In 1752 A sailor John Crabb died-clubbed to death. Since in Boston the celebration reached its climax with the burning of Popes on Boston Neck, the site of the public gallows, the popes were often given a mock trial and execution there. Following the trial and execution the winning side burned the floats of the other as well as all available lumber. Then there was hearty drinking as the evening ended.

For the author the importance of Pope's day celebrations is that they were both anti papal and anti-authority. The plebeians rejoiced that they were free of the papal tyranny which oppressed so many others in foreign lands. The Aristocracy could tolerate the anti-authority aspect because the focus remained upon the pope. Eventually they were to gain the upper hand as the plebialn's lost the aspects of pope's day unrule which were traditionally their own. Violence was eliminated and destruction limited. While legislated attempted to limit the festivities incidents such as the death of a young boy under the wheel of a North End Pope and excessive rioting (1764) gave authorities direct cause to crack down.

Employing Ebenezer Maddintosh and his followers the Whig elite helped keep order in 1765. The Plebiean nature of the event had been changed:

James Freeman is cited as observing: *"about noon the pageantry....were brought on stages and met at King Street where the Union was established in a very ceremonial manner, and having given huzzas they interchanged ground, the South marched to the North and the North to the South until they again met...the whole proceeded to the Liberty Tree...they refreshed themselves for a while and returned to the northward agreeable to plan. They reached Copp's Hill before six o' clock where they halted. Having kindled a fire, the whole pagentry was committed to the flames."* -p.33

The author notes that the pope's day mobs began to focus their attention toward Britain as the 18th century progressed. The British it was felt were drifting too close to papist ways and tolerance. In this way the pope's day celebrations plugged right into the anti British sentiments which fueled the revolution.

The author cites an example of one of the revelers eating at the house of one of the upper classes. It seems a spoon was missing: *"some of the Pope's attendences had some supper as well as Money given 'em at a House in Town. One of the Company happene'd to swallow a silver spoon with his Victuals, Marked IHS. Whoever it was is desired to return it when it comes at hand"*-Boston Gazette 1746, p.30.

# 1995- Peter D. Apgar

## Cited by Peter D. Apgar in: Festivals of Colonial America from Celebration ot Revolution. Master's Thesis, 1995, Texas Tech. pp. 52-67.

Pope's Day in Boston

1. Notes spectators observance that a boy was "placed under the platform to elevate and move round, at proper intervals, the moveable head of the pope."-(Source=Cohen and Coffin, Folklore of American Holidays, 319)

2. Notes that signs reading "The devil take the pope" and "Terror. Despair," were seen in Boston on Pope's day cart fronts (Source given-Lahvis, "Icons of American Trade," 223)

3. Notes that bonfires consumed effigies on Fort Hill. (Source-Lahvis, "Icons of American Trade." 223.)

4. Notes the competition between the gangs "North Enders and South Enders" and the battle over the effigy of the Pope resulting in injury and death. (Source Shaw, American Patriots, 16-18)

Boston Celebrations Cited in: Hennig Cohen and Tristram Coffin, eds. The Folklore of American Holidays (Detroit: Gale Research Company, 1987)

1821-"Reminiscences" "A man used to ride on an ass, with immense jack boots, and his face covered with a horrible mask, and was called Joyce, Jr. His office was to assemble men and boys in mob style, and ride in the middle of them, and in such company to terrify adherents to Royal Government, before the Revolution. The tumults which resulted in the Massacre, 1770, was excited by that means.-Joyce Junior was said to have a particular whistle which brought his adherents, &c. whenever they were wanted.

-*Publications of the Colonial Society of Mass. VIII (1903). 90-91.* and *Boston Daily Advertiser*, Nov 9 1821.

## Newberryport Mass.

as Cited by Peter D. Apgar in: Festivals of Colonial America from Celebration ot Revolution. Master's Thesis, 1995, Texas Tech. pp. 52-67.

1. Cites observation of a spectator: (1764) "in addition to the images of the pope and his company" on a cart 40 feetx10 feet "there might be found on the same platform, half a dozen dancers and fiddlers." (Source cited: Cohen and Coffin, Folklore of American Holidays. 319)

2. Provides the following:

    Mummer's Poem In Newburyport, Massachusetts (1760 ?)

The Fifth of November,

As you well remember,
Was gunpowder treason and plot;
I know of no reason
Why the gunpowder treason
Should ever be forgot.

When the first King James the septre swayed,
This hellish powder plot was laid.
Thirty-six barrels of powder placed down below
All for old England's overthrow:
Happy the man, and happy the day
That caught Guy Fawkes in the middle of this play.
You'll hear our bell go jink, jink, jink;
Pray madam, sirs, if you' something give,
We'll burn the dog and never let him live.

We'll burn the dog without his head,
And then you'll say the dog is dead.
From Rome, from Rome, the pope is come,
All in ten thousand fears;
The fiery serpent's to be seen,
All head, mouth, nose and ears.
The treacherous knave had so contrived,
To blow king parliament all up alive.
God by his grace he did prevent
To save both king and parliament.
Happy the man, and happy the day,
That catched Guy Fawkes in the middle of his play.

Match touch, catch prime,
In the good nick of time.
Here is the pope that we got,
The whole promoter of the plot.
We'll stick a pitchfork in his back
And throw him in the fire.

-Hennig Cohen and Tristram Coffin, eds. The Folklore of American Holidays (Detroit: Gale Research Company, 1987), 319.

3. Notes that when the term "boys" is used that it may refer as much to adults of a lower status as to the age of the individual   Newberryport Mass. 1775

"In the day time, companies of little boys might be seen, in various parts of the town, with their little popes, dressed up in the most grotesque and fantastic manner, which they carried about, some on boards, and some on little carriages, for their own and other's amusement.  But the great exhibition was reserved for the night, in which young men, as well as boys, participated.  They first constructed a huge vehicle, varying at times, from twenty to forty feet long, eight or ten wide, and five or six high, from the lower to the upper platform, in the front of which they erected a paper lantern, capacious enough to hold, in addition to the lights  five or xix persons.  Behind that, as large as life, sat the mimic pope, and several other personages, monks, friars and so forth.  Last, but not least, stood an image of what was deisgned to be a represntation of old Nick himself, furnished with a pair of huge horns, holding in his hand a pitchfork, and otherwise accoutred, with all the frightful ugliness that their ingenuity could desire.  Their next step, after they had mounted their ponderous vehicle on four wheels, chosen their officers, captain, first and second lieutenant, purser and so forth, placed a boy under the platform, to elevate and move round, at proper intervals, the moveable head of the pope and attached, ropes to the front part of the machine, was to take up their line of march through the principal streets of the town. Sometimes in addition to the images of the pope and his company, there might be found, on the same platform, half a dozen dancers and a fiddler, whose "Hornpipes, jigs, strathspeys, and reels Put life and Mettle in their heels,

Together with a large crowd who made up a long procession. Their custom was, to call at the principal houses in various parts of the town, ring their bell, cause the pope to elevate his head, and look round upon the audience ,and repeat the following lines...(see above)--*Publications of the Colonial Society of Mass.,* XII (19809), 293-4. also Henry W. Cunningham on the Contents of a colonial Diary quoting from Joshua Coffin's History of Newbury...1635-1845, Boston, 1845, 249-516. cited in: Hennig Cohen and Tristram Coffin, eds. The Folklore of American Holidays (Detroit: Gale Research Company, 1987)

# Charleston S.C.

as Cited by Peter D. Apgar in: Festivals of Colonial America from Celebration ot Revolution. Masters Thesis, 1995, Texas Tech. pp. 52-67 .

1. Notes that in 1753 a Charleston newspaper wrote: "The anniversary of our happy Deliverance from a most horrid Popish Plot, and the glorious Revolution...was observed here as usual." (Source cited-South Carolina Gazette, Nov. 16, 1753.

2. Notes that in Charleston a person represented the devil: "curiously tarred and feathered," and with a sign- "HOWL-Ye! Prepare my Way.-Lie on one Side, then on the other; and proclaim hyour Candour on each. You are my Beloved-be dilligent in your calling."-(Source cited: South Carolina Gazette.,Nov. 21, 1774

"Saturday last, being the Anniversary of the Nation's happy Deliverance from the infernal Popish POWDER-PLOT in 1605, and also of the glorious REVOLUTION by the Landing of King William in 1688, two Events which our Brethern in England seem of late to have too much overlooked, the Morning was ushered in with Ringing of Bells, and a "Magnificent Exhibition" of Effigies, designed to represent Lord North, Gov. Hutchinson, the Pope, and the DEVIL, which were placed on a rolling stage, about eight feet high and fifteen feet long, hear Mr. Ramadge's Tavern in Broad street, being the most frequented place in town. The Pope was exhibited in a chair of state superbly drest in all his priestly Canonicals; Lord North (with his Star, garter, & showing the Quebec Bill) on his right hand , and Governor Hutchinson on his left, both chained to stakes; the Devil with extended Arms, behind the them, and elevated above them, holding in one Hand a Javelin directed at the Head of Lord North, and in the other a scroll, inscribed" Rivington's New York Gazetteer;" on his arm was suspended a large Lanthorn, in the shape of a Tea Cannister, on the side of which was writ in Capitals, "Hyson, Green, Congo and Bohea Teas." The Exhibition was constantly viewed by an incredible Number of Spectators, among whom were most of the Ladies and Gentlemen of First Fortune and Fashion. The Pope and the Devil, were observed frequently to bow, in the most complaisant manner, to sundry individuals, as if in grateful Acknowledgement of their past services. About 8 o'clock, A.M. the whole was moved to the square before the State-House, and back again to Mr. Ramadge's, where Devine services began in St. Michael's Church; in which situation it remained throughout the day without the least Appearance of Opposition, Tumult, or Disorder. The figure Representing Lord North, was reckoned a tolerable Likeness, and that of Governor Hutchinson a very striking one; both their heads having been carved from very good Designs. In the Evening the whole Machinery was carried thro' the principle (sic) streets, to the Parade, without the Town Gate, when a pole 50 feet high was erected, strung with and surrounded by a great number of Tar Barrels. The tea collected by young

Gentlemen the Tuesday before, being placed between the Devil and Lord North, was set on fire, and brought on our Enemies in Effigy, that Ruin they had designed to bring on us in Reality. The whole was consumed in a short time, in the Presence of some Thousands who rejoiced to see the Abbertors of American Taxation consumed, By that very Engine of Oppression. It is remarkable, that during the whole Transaction not the least Disorder Happened; and by 8'o clock at Night the Town was in a great a Quiet as on a Sabbath Evening... Besides the above exhibition, the young Gentlemen from the schools, prepared another Pope and Devil, which they also burnt in the Evening, after parading all the Streets with them throughout the Day. Their Devil was a most grotesque figure, curiously tarred and feathered. Their Pope was also in a fitting Posture, which a large Lanthorn before him, on the Front of which was writ- Liberty, Prosperity, and Carolina Forever--on one side was drawn, a large Cannister of Tea in Flames- on the other the Figure of America hurling a Spear at the Lord North, Kneeling upon a chest of tea, and bound with a cord, held by a hand representing Magna Charta..

-South Carolina Gazette, Nov. 21, 1774. cited in: -Hennig Cohen and Tristram Coffin, eds. The Folklore of American Holidays (Detroit: Gale Research Company, 1987).

# Savannah

As Cited by Peter D. Apgar in: Festivals of Colonial America from Celebration ot Revolution. Masters Thesis, 1995, Texas Tech. pp. 52-67.

1. Notes that a Savannah paper wrote in 1765 about sailors taking part in "usual" or Customary Pope day celebrations. (Source cited: Georgia Gazette, Nov. 7, 1765.

*Apgar provides a good account of how the celebrated at all levels of society and of its wide distribution in North America. Most importantly he sets the celebration in context with other contemporary celebrations.*

"Within a highly stratified colonial society that traditionally
precluded the populace from poltical involvement, crowd action in pre
Revolutionary America became a potent force in successfully obtaining
poltical goals. Participation in festivals contributed to this new sense
of popular empowerment. The festivals of May Day, New England
Election Day, Pinkster, the King's Birthday, Pope Day, and New Year's
Eve allowed the populace forums to build dynamic group relationships,
to gain experience in organization, and to publcly express opinions.
Revolutionary leaders recognized the importance of festivals and drew
on their rituals, objects, and symbols to energize the public, and the
public responded by further adapting festive elements for protest"

-p. IV.

"By 1775, the original meanings of many festive elements
used by colonists were no longer recognizable, yet festive rituals,
objects, and symbols proved vital in pubhc expression. Festivals had
undergone a metamorphosis as forums of celebration to that of
revolution."

-p. 309

## 2002- Peter Benes

*A completeand innovative survey,*

Benes, Peter, "Night Processions: Celebrating the Gunpowder Plot in England and New England," in *New England Celebrates: Spectacle, Commemoration, and Festivity*, Dublin Seminar for New England Folklife Annual Proceedings 2000 (Boston: Boston University, 2002) p. 9.

"On the surface of things, these celebrations are one more example of the transfer of popular culture from the Old World to the New. Begun as anti-Catholic street pageantry in England in the third quarter of the sixteenth century, the parading of the pope was originally one of several New England customs that marked the fall and early winter seasons through bonfire nights.

*Note: The celebrations originated as theologically informed political rituals which took pains not to condemn religions or individuals. Through time, interest in the celebrations was inspired by political acts by the secular aspect of the church: The Vatican/" Papal" state*
*(s). Labeling political acts clouds analysis and derails explanation.*

"It also served as a sectarian riposte against Spain and France in a region of eastern New England that concentrated English Protestants still mindful of the Catholic presence. However, a closer look at these nighttime events reveals elements in the Anglo-Saxon political character that persisted in the United States for generations. The participants were always made up of men and boys working in gangs. Sometimes they were hooded. And sometimes they exhibited blatant sexual imagery both in the masquerade characters they reenacted and in the emblemism that surrounded them. Although there was widespread talk that the participants were primarily apprentices, mechanics, servants, and blacks, their leaders belonged to an aspiring elite who sometimes used them for their own ends. It was a formula later repeated in American history by leaders who mixed sexisrn, racisrn, and violence to promote personal and political gain." -p.9.

"Representing equal measures of patriotism, prejudice, and pageantry, they revived and kept alive religious bigotry while feeding on overt chauvinism and lingering fears of the supernatural. In the end, they became caught in the vortex of outright political retribution.", p.10.

*It is easy to fall into the trap of historical naysayers who had little regard for the theological basis for ritual celebration. It is like considering church services "riot". These should not be considered "ordinary "street altercations. Granted, that the "supernatural" aspect had diminished, none the less, the sanctioning of the celebrations was founded by higher values.*

# 2006- Brendan McConville

## Brendan McConville, *The King's Three Faces*, 2006.

"Pope's Day Established," p.56.

*McConville makes a case for the "imposition" of Pope's Day celebrations by "Empire" over the colonists. He sees it as san "imperialization of public time in British America" and the "reconciliation of the colonial past and the cosmopolitan future." It is very important to note that for English colonists arriving after 1605 the round of calendar customs always included celebration of Guy Fawkes Day on the Fifth of November each year. This was also always a state holiday celebrated as dictated by the Book of Common Prayer with official sermons, local expenditures for firewood and bell ringing as well as drink. The holiday had a wide range of public manifestations which complimented official rituals. If there was an "Colonial version" it was that which developed with the evolution of Stamp Act Protests.*

*McConville sees the holiday as an imperial imposition- a mechanism for extending power and belonging to empire. While it cannot be disputed that the celebration contributed to national solidarity and belonging it is also true that the holiday arrived with the colonists and was not imposed upon them. Without any prompting other than that of an almanac or prayer book they would have looked forward to if not insisted upon the celebration as was seen in Georgia below. The fact that a diverse population of those of many national origins and religious persuasions is more evidence of the general enculturation of all the colonists than it is evidence of an imposition of the ritual. It is likely that non-English colonists were won over to the reality of English cultural, political and linguistic dominance as a matter of practicality. McConville is correct that the celebration is not so much a product of a specifically colonial "mobocracy" or "popular culture." It was the product of the continuity of English culture and enculturation of non-English colonists. Yes, it was recognized by the state/empire and tolerated but other than via the requirements of the prayer book it was not necessarily always imposed.*

p.56.

"Yesterday being the Anniversary Thanksgiving for the Gunpowder Treason Plot, when King, Lords and Commons were deliver'd from the bloody Designs of the Papists, was kept ass usual."

-Virginia Gazette, Williamsburg, Feb. 4-11, 1736.

p.56

""the fifth of November" should be kept for thanksgiving for "the miraculous preservation of our king and country from the gunpowder treason"

-Massachusetts General Court, May 1665.

An annual Holiday recognized on November 5 by the Massachusetts legislature for public thanksgiving and humiliation.

-Shurtleff, Nathaniel, B, ed. Records of the bovernor and Company of the Massachusetts Bay in New England, VI (Boston, Mass, 1854), part 2 211-212, 346.

p.57

"Sewall (Samuel) and the rest of the Puritan elite continued subtle resistance to the holiday until after 1688."

-Sewall, Samuel, III, The Diary of Samuel Sewall, 1674-1729, MHS. Collections, 5th Ser., VII ( Boston, 1882), 19.

*McConville claims a special appeal of the Calvinists in the Colonies for the holiday because they saw it as "providential intervention that upheld a Protestant ruler and referred, at least early in the eighteenth century, to the Glorious Revolution's triumph over a Catholic, popish ruler." This awareness also pre-dated colonial America and is often cited as foundation for the continued celebration of the holiday in England despite political transitions.*

p. 57

1689 – Jacob Leisler reports the burning of a apope effigy in New York City.

Leisler, Jacob, "Papers of Jacob Leisler, placed on H- Net by David Voorhees, associate editor: " Jacob Leisler to Edwin Stede, Nov. 23,1689.

p.75.

# 2013-Kevin Q. Doyle

Doyle, Kevin Q. *"Rage and Fury Which Only Hell Could Inspire": The Rhetoric and the Ritual of Gunpowder Treason in Early America.* A Dissertation Presented to The Faculty of the Graduate School of Arts and Sciences. Diss. Brandeis University, 2013.

*Kevin Doyle has created the most thorough and complete study of Pope Night ever written. It is noteworthy that he has documented the way the Great Deliverance and Plot has permeated our culture on so many levels, proving instrumental throughout our history from 1605.*

"…at times, I conduct a comparative history of these two holy days, analyzing the relationships between empire, holiday-making, and Protestantism while doing so. At other times, I advance vignettes of individuals who bridged two "worlds" of the anniversary, such as Benjamin Harris (England, America), Samuel Sewall (animosity for holidays, reverence for the Fifth), and Isaiah Thomas (participation in Pope's Day and the print culture of the 1800s). I close read almanacs, diaries, instructionals, letters, newspapers, novels, sermons, and textbooks as a means of understanding the process by which the memory of November 5 was appropriated, reconstructed, and re-politicized."

-viiii

*It is indeed essential to consider "personal" evidence as so much work to date has centered on print media sources and legislation. It is hoped that future work will extend outward from urban centers via sources such as letters and personal communication. It is amazing to follow the path of the celebration acroxx the ocean. So much remained the same including the dismantling of both holidays due to a fading understanding of underwriting padadigms and the rise of "utopian" reformed states as well as the growth of a community of literate vocal nay-sayers.*

"I investigate what became of November 5 after 1783, and I scrutinize the many ways in which the creative arts and the partisan press made frequent use of the memory of the events of 1605. I consider both how that memory arose in new places after the war and in what ways the parties of the republic, like the crowds of the colonies, evoked the Fifth as a warning against absolutism. I question the retention of English culture – and also English history – in the new nation."

-viii

*The ocean of cultural memory is a critical dynamic fource that must not be overlooked.*

"I close this project with a review of the very heightened referencing of the Gunpowder Treason in what was a very apt time for remembrance – the lead-up to the Civil War. But, throughout, I attempt to demonstrate that the Fifth of November, like the Fourth of July, deserves attention in the study of early America. For, in this country, the Fifth was both a critical occasion and a critical subject, long before and long after the Revolution."

*Pope Night studies have long suffered an incomplete chronological approach. As sources expand it is hoped that this wider view might intensify.*

-VIII – IX

"Sometimes, as in 1685 Boston, the people even lit large bonfires on town commons. Yet "the better sort" retained control of the day in the 1680s.... But this crowd was no ordinary crowd, for, unlike its counterparts in America, it was organized on behalf of an ideology of religion – an argument asserting the righteousness of Protestantism and the wickedness of Catholicism. The crowd that assembled on the Fifth re-politicized the day in the middle of the eighteenth century, stressing its hatred for absolutism in politics and religion. In doing this, it unknowingly laid a foundation for the violent activity (e.g., the Stamp Act Crisis) that would later culminate in the American Revolution."

*Once-strong ties between the theological underwriting and the celebration deteriorated due largely to the further deterioration and fading from memory of the Great Chain of Being the collection of aartifacts of celebration became fair game and were snatched up by the forces of Renaissance and Reformation which had initiated the process. Unfortunately trusting in new utopian government, functions in the area of street justice were neglected. The next step is an an analysis of the mechanisms behind these adaptations-hopefully some progress will be found in this volume.*

-2

"In this manner, Calhoun, Davis, Garrison, Lincoln, and others became regarded as new Fawkeses, and the story of "gunpowder, treason, and plot" did far more than offer invective and perspective. It was more than a mere article of rhetoric. And only in some writings was it tamed as either a subject of antiquity or a source of comedy. For, in the mid-nineteenth century, the Plot remained, throughout much of the North, the South, and the West, very much a thing of relevance and substance."

*The ability to interchange other targets for Fawkes is an important aspect of the celebration. It has helped it to retain relevance.*

-440

"of what Charles A. Beard called "the Second American Revolution."
The Fifth and the Plot continued to attract considerable interest in both the festive
culture and the literary culture of the United States well after the conclusion of the
American Civil War. In the late 1860s and again in the late 1890s, American branches of the Orange Order –
the Protestant fraternal organization based in Northern Ireland –
celebrated the Fifth in Chicago and Manhattan, holding meetings and reading addresses,
while emphasizing loyalty to America, mocking the idea of a "Protestant gunpowder plot," and rebuking
"Jesuitism," across the globe. Meanwhile, in the late 1800s, towns
along the New England coast kept the day as "Pope Night," with "small bands" on both
the North Shore of Massachusetts (e.g., Marblehead, Newburyport) and the seacoast of
New Hampshire (e.g., New Castle, Portsmouth) building bonfires, dancing, parading
"pumpkin lanterns," and, with much "glee" and much "mischief," blowing "tin horns."
A holiday of boys from ages six to fourteen with little to no knowledge of the history of
the Plot, it was an occasion that some in this area called "Pork Night."

*Relevance continues today particularly in the Orange Order.*

-442

"Hundreds of years after the conspiracy of Catesby and Fawkes ended in awesome
failure, the Treason survives in the collective memory of both the United Kingdom and

the United States. Here, in America, it seems that few know much about the motivation, or the undoing, of the Plot, but the recurrence of the mask, and the showing of V for Vendetta, does impart some of the story… Examination of this practice fosters the study of American history and that of current events, yet, with Fawkes now made a hero, one wonders what the future will bring the reminiscence of 1605. Regardless, the memory of "gunpowder, treason, and plot," or at least some aspects of this story, remains in good standing in the United States, in the twenty-first century. And, today, it appears that that memory, perhaps given another rhetoric or another ritual, might well be an active element of the American national imaginary for quite some time to come."

-448

*Not to worry! Fawkes survived being both a hero and a clown in the past. Further understanding of the internal structure and function of the celebration will help to maximize its contued utility. This is the next step.*

# Revival

## The Center For Fawkesian Pursuits Bonfire Society

A revival bonfire society in Linthicum, Maryland, U.S.A. It is the only Bonfire Society in North America. Celebrations occurred through 2016. Celebrations have included components of Pope Day celebrations such as devils and pope carts as well as elements of British celebrations. The society maintains close links with Hastings Bourough Bonfire Sosiety, Hastings, England. The two societies exchange bonfire wood each year.

The audience is regional and all ages attend. The valiudity of all points of vew is highlighted with the foundation being the unifying function of disclosure of the universal Dark Folkloric Landscape. Effigies include Guy Fawkes, Devil, Pope and individuals from current events. The admission is free. Particapants donate food and drink. The history of the plot is told. There is an emphasis on our continued deliverance from terror.

Attendance ranges from 50-130 in number.

From the Center's web page:

"The Center For Fawkesian Pursuits is dedicated to the celebration of the Fifth of November worldwide! There is no reason it should be forgot! By anyone, anywhere!

The Center For Fawkesian Pursuits Bonfire Society is Dedicated to the concept that no matter what year, what age, what people, or what place-

*We See NO reason that the 5th of November Shall EVER be forgot! By anyone! Any where! For Any reason!*

Join us in the enrichment, encouragement and celebration of the triumph of law over tyranny. Good and democracy over evil! and the warmth of bonfire over the cold and dark of night. "

"No Faux Fawkes! Video Rideo!
Remember! Remember the 5th of November!"

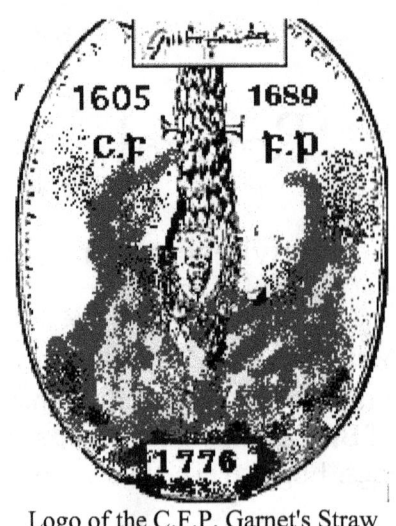

Logo of the C.F.P. Garnet's Straw
with Fawke's Signature on top

"Organized in 1993, the Center For Fawkesian Pursuits Bonfire Society is dedicated to the pursuit of all things Fawkesian! We are dedicated to all things relating to the Celebration of November 5 as Guy Fawkes Day. We also pursue the interpretation of the history of the plot and the preservation of structures, sites, objects and information related to it. We are a Bonfire Society. To the best of our knowledge the first in North America.

Our missions include the encouragement of the perpetuation and documentation of the ancient Folk customs of the celebration and assistance of those who wish to remember through celebration the bravery and circumstances described by the history of the plot. We support no political groups nor do we wish to sanction any terrorist act. Yet, it is our firm belief that the spirit of Fawkes lives on in the soul of every free man, woman and child and that it conditions our every relationship with government. We believe that while this spirit survives that tyranny will never again come to dominate our lives. We believe that the universality of the plot is uniquely reflected by the fact of its discovery, and the divine intervention which saved both king and parliament--that is the mother parliament of our American Congress. Were it not for its discovery history would have taken a different turn. The dominance of Roman Catholicism and the absolutism with which it has been so closely associated, would have projected a profound tyranny. This event would have placed the British Isles and its institutions on the path to absolutism traveled by the other Catholic nations. So therefore we celebrate the triumph of the King, State and Parliament just as we celebrate the bravery of the plotters. Had the state not prevailed the concept of separation of state and church as well as that of the constitutional monarchy, the ancestor of contemporary Democracy might all never have come to be. Had the concept of challenging of the government championed by the plotters faded, we would have never had the steps toward democracy brought by the Glorious Revolution. We also, therefore, celebrate the eventual triumph of William of Orange which occurred with his landing in England on November 5. For more on William of Orange and the Glorious Revolution which ended forever the tyranny of absolutist rule in the British Isles and which was founded upon the separation of church and state please contact our other web pages.

Let each and every one take the time to light up the November evening sky with this spirit in remembrance of the bravery of those who were prepared to risk all for their beliefs and for their freedom. Let us, in their memory, detonate the powder which their matches were kept from lighting as a symbol of our ability to so challenge our institutions when called upon to do so. Let us also give thanksgiving for the divine protection of the forerunner of our democracy, :Parliament, King, and State. Let us also rejoice in the changing of the seasons and in fellowship with one another as we give thanks for our very being from one year to the next beside the Bonfire.

Composed in 1998, our Bonfire Prayer or Chant has been designed to include all of the major aspects of bonfire celebration of the 5th of November. It has been composed in the traditional style.

The Chant shall be performed with loud and hearty voices and shall be followed by a toast giving thanks for our general deliverance from terror in the past year and hope for the year to come.

Remember Remember the fifth of November
Gunpowder Treason and Plot!
We See no Reason That Gunpowder Treason Ever should be Forgot!
Remember, Remember, that Pope's Day in Boston Lead to the Liberty Tree!
We See no reason that Pope's Day in Boston should be forgot by you or me!
King Billy King Billy Toss Us an Orange
You came to set us free!
A Lemon a Lemon for Bigoted James
Our Proud constitution he'll not re-arrange!
Holla! boys Holla! boys, ring in the night (ring bells)
Holla boys, Holla boys burn fires bright (stomp)

-The Official Chant/Prayer of the Center for Fawkesian Pursuits Bonfire Society

Our official Badge, pin, button and rosette!

October 10, 1998- Conrad Bladey, Center Director, sent a piece of American Oak
an official proclamation and chant to the Hastings Borough Bonfire Society just prior to a procession through the American Ground the proclamation was formally read out by a town crier. A wonderful photo was taken by Graham George which shows bonfire chairman Keith Leech and other officials presiding. Many thanks to Gerry Glenister for his assistance. We are always glad to link up with other bonfire societies.

The Philosophy of the Center for Fawkesian Pursuits:

Folk celebration is best done by the folk and where everyone can afford to attend without exception.

1998

Wood from our bonfire is presented by HBBS at the American Ground, Hastings, UK. just before it went on the bonfire. We exchange wood with HBBS each year.

-C.F.F.P Web Page: http://www.cbladey.com/guy/html/center.html#The%20Center%20ForFawkesian%20Pursuits

# 1997-Bonfire Celebration, Linthicum, Maryland, U.S.A

## The Center For Fawkesian Pursuits-America's Only Bonfire Society! Linthicum,Md. 1997

"It was a wet and sloshy night.....The fire the night before struggled with the elements. The keg was ready to sustain and all worked hard to keep the fire burning over the rocks in the pit. The Guys were readied- photos soon! Tony Blair was the favorite with a few heads he had taken in the recent elections in his chariot (a baby carriage) with its wheel run over a stop sign! The Union flag fluttering from the sun cover- he wore no poppy. Guy stepped out in his pink legs and short pants with black coat and demonic grin- the children liked him the best. The turkey made it into the ground on time and then we set to roasting potatoes and baking bread and steaming the puddings. The rain had ended by the time the crowd of some 30 had gathered. (the faux Fawkeses always deterred by the traditional weather) Incense filled the air from the shrine built a top the turkey pit which was presided over by the Jack-O-Lantern. As the crowd drank beer and wine and ate peanuts the children ran amok in the fall leaves wondering where their food was coming from. The Period music of Byrd and Italian composers of the time filled the air mixed with English Style brass band music and fanfares. Soon with the wife herself growing hungry and the crowd demanding to be fed I was forced to begin the ritual of the evening. The light was lit over the crowd and three teams were formed for the chants. All did a fine job shouting at the top of their lungs to proclaim the annual remembrance. The team representing Worchestershire did the best and pounded the ground right well! It was then time to go over to the pit. When all assembled the steamy earth was torn apart in search of the grand bird! The steam rose up and the air was sage, wine and orange. The turkey was excavated -well done! Just Right. All went inside conveyed by the rich aromas of the earth oven. Carefully without loosing track of the least grain of sand the bird of 35 lbs was carefully excavated cleanly from its shroud of collard leaves and mesh wire. Not a speck of dirt was reported this year! The new Fawkesians looked on in absolute wonder that a turkey should be so well done in the pit. Plates of steamy succulent meat made their way down to the assembled and hungry party. During dinner the crowd watched a video of last years Lewes, Sussex, UK events complete with the Pope and the jeers! With guests filled with turkey and good sweet beer- a honey lager time for dessert was upon us. (Image left:" Behold the Pudding. Image right: Garnet's Straw) We all

moved upstairs for the ceremonial reading of the page from Dickens which described the Cratchet's Xmas pudding as the pudding was slid from its pot. Success! The steaming pudding was placed on its tray and ceremoniously paraded out into the yard along with brandy. On the way a sprig of fresh ripened holly was picked and placed on it as a crown.  Then it was onward to the cast iron stove out back where the chimney has carved in it a likeness of Guy which spouts fire from the eyes nose mouth and beard. The brandy was heated then flamed then poured over the pudding which became as blue as a police car light in the dark. The crowd went wild and demanded several lightings! Then to the shout "behold the Pudding" all passed by into the house to the dessert table which contained the hard sauce, the saxon pudding and the cakes brought by the guests.  As time went on the weaker departed one by one. The bonfire raged in the pit as children made somemores from chocolate graham crackers and marshmallows. Once the children had had their sweets we gathered them together for the traditional Fawkes day message.  We talked of the bravery and dedication of those who as plotters held their values high. Then we talked of the plot and the meaning of Terrorism and the need to remember that taking the law into your own hands is an unwise choice. We talked of Father Garnet and of the Jesuit mission. We learned of his bravery in the face of certain death and torture. But we also learned that he did not follow the law but relied too much on his religion and the government of the church. We all were thankful that the plotters were defeated and that the English government continued to improve over the years and that we were relatively free of terrorism in our country. One by one the children selected "corns" from the Jack-O-Lantern container until one got the corn with the  face of Garnet upon it- they got the candy reward for listening  to be passed out to all! Once the children had gone their way the music of the Whisky Priests filled the air and the men worked on re-cycling the aluminum out back!  Then in the morning the job still not quite done.... resumed again...

# Arch of Torches 2010

Pit Turkey 2010

Bonfire Sermon-Conrad Bladey 2007

Conrad Bladey, addressing devil 2009

Guy effigy 2010

Pudding 2010

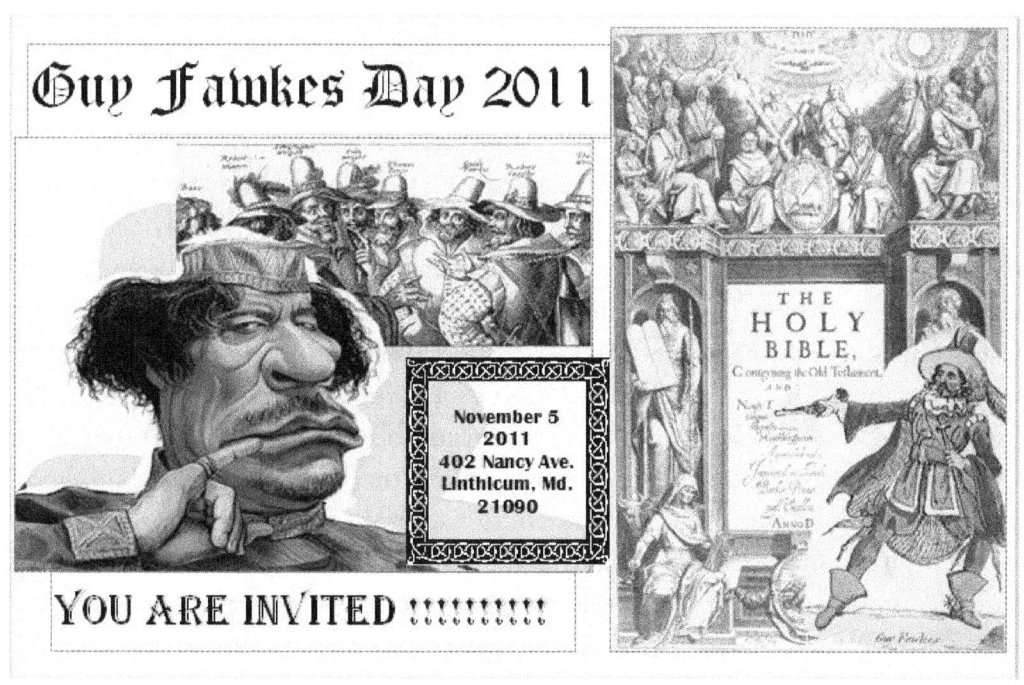

Invitation 2011-effigy: Khaddafi. Also celebrated: King James Bible

-Conrad Bladey, The Center for Fawkesian Pursuits, Linthicum, Md. 1997.

# Conclusion

The Gunpowder Plot and the miraculous deliverance of 1605 confronted cultures and peoples who were well prepared. There was a stable, unified Church and State which despite Reformation and Renaissance had maintained the Great Chain of Being which still linked the natural world via the Divine Monarch through his religious diplomats the Theologians to God and Heaven. The theologians still relatively unified, were as essential as political diplomats to God. The connection with God was "Live." The need to react properly was absolute. Thanksgiving and Celebration were serious essential obligations. Immediately the Theologians analyzed then sermonized. The King proclaimed and then the real wonder occurred. Skilled organized networks of specialists sprang into action. Another bonfire had to happen. Wood had to be obtained. The traditional fire sites had to be made ready. Effigies and their transport had to be constructed. Skilled troupes of players would be readied, lights, costumes scripts for mummers plays-done. Rhymes and chants were to be composed. Then came crowd control. Commercial activity was stoked. The entire society was on one page with one purpose. The artifacts of celebration were hauled out, restored or improved. They had all done this before. Accession days, royal birthdays great victories…..and if not done right no more would come. For Britain, such unity would probably never be seen again. The rest of the century was traumatic and what remained of the old order was to be turned upside down in the next. The nature of the celebration of the Great Deliverance was created within the context of the culture of the historical "period" of its arrival.

The Early Modern Period (c. 1450-1750) was a time of transition from the Middle Ages to the Industrial Revolution. When the celebration of the Great Deliverance of 1605 was assembled and then brought to the American Colonies this transition was far from complete. Although it barely evaded the Puritains of New England who generally opposed any celebration, it arrived as a complex Artifact of Celebration of the old way of thinking. We can consider it to be Pope Day only as long as it served its original function of disclosing the dark folkloric landscape on behalf of the entire culture. As the period progressed, belief in the Great Chain of Being declined its critics triumphed, and the foundation of the celebration deteriorated. Eventually the American Revolution installed a utopian state for which "Mobocracy" would be thought to be obsolete. The revolution acted as an internal parasite, falsely disclosing as evil the very institution that it had used for its inception. The glue holding all of the artifacts of celebration was dissolved. They were carted off as the marbles of the ancient Roman forum by the "barbarian" hordes. While some were recycled into Stamp Act Protests, Election bonfires, Thanksgiving celebrations and Fourth of July fireworks displays others were lost, some like the Guy Fawkes mask were stored (only to re-emerge in the 21[th] century via *V For Vendetta*).

The commemoration of the Great Deliverance of 1605 as a significant cultural institution for the disclosure of the dark folkloric landscape became a significant negative consequence of revolution.

I hope that this work has begun the process of assembling the information required for the restoration of thanksgivings and celebrations to their maximum positive potential.

Significant work needs to be done especially in the area of personal, household and rural celebrations, especially early ones. This work will be advanced by expanded consultion of personal papers such as letters, diaries and court records.

Importantly:

> "We see no reason why Disclosure of Gunpowder Treason,
> Should Ever Be Forgot!"

# Bibliography

Abbott, W. W., ed. The Papers of George Washington, Revolutionary War Series, Vol. 2: September-December 1775. Charlottesville: University Press of Virginia, 1987.

Abrahams, Roger D. "Antick Dispositions and the Perilous Politics of Culture: Costume and Culture in Jacobean England and America." Journal of American Folklore 111.444 (Spring 1998): 115-32.

Acts and Resolves Passed by the General Court of Massachusetts, 1742-1756. Boston: Secretary of the Commonwealth, 1878.

Adair, Douglass and John Schutz, eds. Peter Oliver's Origin and Progress of the American Rebellion: A Tory View. San Marino, California: Huntington Library, 1961.

Adams, Charles Francis et al. "March Meeting, 1895. Will of Dr. George E. Ellis; A Century of the United States Senate; Diary of John Rowe; Samuel Skelton; Alice Blower." Proceedings of the Massachusetts Historical Society, vol. 10, 1895, pp. 1–115. www.jstor.org/stable/25079778.

Albanese, Catherine L. Sons of the Fathers: The Civil Religion of the American Revolution. Philadelphia: Temple University Press, 1976.

Albee, John. "Pope Night: Fifth November." Journal of American Folklore 6.20 (Jan. – Mar. 1893): 68- 69.

Alexander, Edward Porter, ed. The Journal of John Fontaine: An Irish Huguenot son in Spain and Virginia, 1710-1719. Charlottesville, Virginia: University Press of Virginia, 1972.

Alexander, John K. "Unwelcome Americans: Living on the Margin in Early New England." The Journal of American History 89.1 (2002): 199-200.

Ames, Nathaniel. An Astronomical Diary, or, an Almanack for the Year of Our Lord Christ. Boston: John Draper, 1735 and ff.

Anonymous (Charles Willson Peale). A Representation of the Figures Exhibited and Paraded Through the Streets of Philadelphia, on Saturday, the 30th of September 1780. Philadelphia: John Dunlap, 1780.

Anderson, Benedict R. O'G. Imagined Communities: Reflections on the Origin and Spread of Nationalism. New York: Verso, 1991.

Anderson, George P. "Ebenezer Mackintosh: Stamp Act Rioter and Patriot." Publications of the Colonial Society of Massachusetts, Transactions 26 (1927): 15-64, 346-61.

"The Anti-Catholic Spirit of the Revolution." American Catholic Historical Researches 6 (Oct. 1889):146-78.

Andrews, Charles M. Colonial Folkways: A Chronicle of American Life in the Reign of the Georges. New Haven: Yale University Press, 1919.

Andrews, Charles. The Colonial Period of American History. 4 vols. New Haven: Yale University Press, 1934-38.

Apgar, Peter D. Festivals of Colonial America: from celebration to revolution. Diss. Texas Tech University, 1995.

Arrom, Silvia M. and Servando Ortoll. Riots in the Cities: Popular Politics and the Urban Poor in Latin America, 1765-1910. Wilmington: Scholarly Resources, 1996.

Atherton, Herbert M. "The 'Mob' in Eighteenth-Century English Caricature." Eighteenth-Century Studies 12.1 (Autumn 1978): 47-58.

Ayer, Mary Farwell. Boston Common in Colonial and Provincial Days. Privately printed, 1903.

Ayer, Mary Farwell. Early Days on Boston Common. Priv. Print., 1910.
Bailey, Thomas. "In Quintum Novembris." Massachusetts Historical Society, MSS. Miscellaneous Bound, 1657-1671.

Bailyn, Bernard. The Origins of American Politics. New York: Alfred A. Knopf, 1968.

Baldwin, Loammi. Papers (Diary Extracts, Letters, and Other Documents), 1740-1807. Houghton Library, Harvard College Library, Harvard University.

Baldwin, Samuel. A Sermon Preached at Plymouth, December 22, 1775. Being the Anniversary Thanksgiving, in Commemoration of the First Landing of the Fathers of New-England, .
Boston: Powars and Willis, 1776.

Barber, Samuel. Boston Common: A Diary of Notable Events, Incidents, and Neighboring Occurrences. Christopher Publishing House, 1916.

Barnard, Thomas. A Sermon Preached Before His Excellency Francis Bernard . . . Boston: Richard Draper, Printer to His Excellency the Governor and the Honourable His Majesty's Council, 1763.

Bastian, Peter. "Celebrating the Empire in the Changing Political World of Boston, 1759-1774." Australasian Journal of American Studies 16.1 (1997): 26-44.

Bell, J. L. "Du Simitière's Sketches of Pope Day in Boston, 1767." In The World of Children, 1620-1920. Peter Benes, ed. Boston: Boston University Press, 2002, 209-20.

Bellah, Robert N. "Civil Religion in America." Journal of the American Academy of Arts and Sciences 96.1 (1967): 1–21.

Beneke, Chris. "The New, New Political History." Reviews in American History 33.3 (Sep. 2005): 314-24.

Benes, Peter, "Night Processions: Celebrating the Gunpowder Plot in England and New England," in New England Celebrates: Spectacle, Commemoration, and Festivity, Boston University Press (2002).

Benes, Peter, and Jane Montague Benes. The Worlds of Children, 1620-1920. Boston University, 2004

Bentley, William. The Diary of William Bentley, D.D., Pastor of the East Church, Salem, Massachusetts (1784-1819). 4 Vols. Gloucester, Massachusetts: Peter Smith, 1962.

Bercovitch, Sacvan. The Rites of Assent: Transformations in the Symbolic Construction of America. New York: Routledge, 1993.

Bernard, Francis. "Letter to John Pownall [Secretary to the Board of Trade], November 1, 1765." In Colin Nicholson, ed., The Papers of Francis Bernard, Governor of Massachusetts, 1760-1769, Vol. II: January 1764 to 22 December 1765 (Boston: Colonial Society of Massachusetts, 2012.

Bickerstaff, Isaac. An Astronomical Diary or Almanac, for 1785. Hartford: Barlow & Babcock, 1784.

Bickerstaff, Isaac. Bickerstaff's Genuine Boston Almanack for 1786. Boston: E. Russell, 1785.

Bickerstaff, Isaac. Bickerstaff's Plymouth Almanack for 1786. Plymouth, Massachusetts: Nathaniel Coverly, 1785.

Billington, Ray Allen. The Protestant Crusade, 1800-1860: A Study of the Origins of American Nativism. New York: Rinehart, 1952.

Bodnar, John. Remaking America: Public Memory, Commemoration, and Patriotism in the Twentieth Century. Princeton: Princeton University Press, 1992.

Boller, Paul F. "George Washington and Religious Liberty." The William and Mary Quarterly 17.4 (1960): 486-506.

Borger, Philip M. The People's Pope: Effects of Audience Orientation on News Content Following the Death of Pope John Paul II. Diss. Ohio University, 2010.

Borsay, Peter "All the Town's a Stage: Urban Ritual and Ceremony 1660-1800," The Transformation of English Provincial Towns 1600-1800, ed. Peter Clark (London: Hutchinson & Company, 1984), 235.

Boston [MA] Registry Department, A Report of the Record Commissioners of the City of Boston, Vol. 15 (Boston: Rockwell and Churchill, City Printers, 1886Resolution of the Council of Massachusetts Bay. November 4, 1778.

Bourne, Russell. Cradle of Violence: How Boston's Waterfront Mobs Ignited the American Revolution. Hoboken, New Jersey: John Wiley & Sons, Inc., 2006.

"Boyle's Journal of Occurrences in Boston, 1759-1778." New England Historical and Genealogical Record 84 (1930): 142-71, 248-72, 290; 357-82, and 85 (1931): 5-28, 117-33, 290? (159, 259-60, 266).

Bradford, William, The Book of Common Prayer. "A Form of Prayer With Thanksgiving, to be Used Yearly Upon the 5th Day November, for the Happy Deliverance . . . From the Most Traitorous & Bloody Massacre by Gun-powder." New York: William Bradford, 1710.

Brattle, William. An Almanack of the Coelestiall Motions, Aspects and Eclipses, &c. . . . Boston: B. Green, . . . , 1693.

Breen, T. H. "An Empire of Goods: The Anglicization of Colonial America, 1690-1776." Journal of British Studies 25 (1986): 467-99.

Brewin, Mark W. Celebrating Democracy: The mass-mediated ritual of election day. Vol. 2. Peter Lang, 2008.

Brewin, Mark. "The History and Meaning of the Election Night Bonfire." Atlantic Journal of Communication 15.2 (2007): 153-169.

Bridenbaugh, Carl. Cities in Revolt: Urban Life in America, 1743-1776. New York: Oxford University Press, 1971.

Brown, Gayle K. "The Impact of the Colonial Anti-Catholic Tradition on the Canadian Campaign, 1775–1776." Journal of Church and State 35.3 (1993): 559-575.

Brown, Wallace, and Henry Hulton. "An Englishman Views the American Revolution: The Letters of Henry Hulton, 1769-1776." The Huntington Library Quarterly (1972): 1-26.

Browne, J. An Almanack of Coelestiall Motions for 1669. Cambridge: S. G. and M. J., 1668.

Burke, Peter. Popular Culture in Early Modern Europe. New York: New York University Press, 1978.

Burne, Charlotte S. "Guy Fawkes' Day." Folklore 23.4 (Dec. 1912): 409-26.

[Cambridge] Abstract and Index of the Inferior Court of Pleas (Suffolk Co.) . . . , November 1682. M.A. book.

Caner, Henry. Letter-book of the Rev. Henry Caner, Society for the Propagation of the Gospel. November 5, 1770. Massachusetts Historical Society.

Capp, Bernard S. English Almanacs, 1500-1800: Astrology and the Popular Press. Ithaca, New York: Cornell University Press, 1979.

Carey, Edith H. "The Fifth of November and Guy Fawkes." Folklore 19.1 (Mar. 30, 1908): 104-05.

Carp, Benjamin L. "Fire of Liberty: Firefighters, Urban Voluntary Culture, and the Revolutionary Movement." The William and Mary Quarterly, vol. 58, no. 4, 2001, pp. 781–818. www.jstor.org/stable/2674500.

Carp, Benjamin L. Rebels Rising: Cities and the American Revolution. New York: Oxford University Press, 2007.

Carter, Michael S. "Mathew Carey and the Public Emergence of Catholicism in the Early Republic." PhD Thesis, University of Southern California, 2006.

Carty, Thomas J. "Popish Plots, Religious Liberty, and the Emerging Face of American Catholicism before 1928." A Catholic in the White House. Palgrave Macmillan US, 2004. 11-25.

Caudle, Joseph. "Measures of Allegiance: Sermon Culture and the Creation of a Public Discourse of Obedience and Resistance in Georgian Britain, 1714-1760" (PhD Thesis, Yale University, 1996

Caulkins, Frances Manwaring. History of New London, Connecticut, From the First Survey of the Coast in 1612 to 1860. New London: H. D. Utley, 1895.

Chaplin, James Patrick. Rumor, Fear and the Madness of Crowds. Courier Dover Publications, 2015.

Chapman, Alison A. "Whose Saint Crispin's Day Is It?: Shoemaking, Holiday Making, and the Politics of Memory in Early Modern England." Renaissance Quarterly 54.4.2 (Winter 2001): 1467-1494.

Clark, Gregory and S. Michael Halloran. Oratorical Culture in Nineteenth-Century America: Transformations in the Theory and Practice of Rhetoric. Carbondale, Illinois: Southern Illinois University Press, 1993.

Clarke, John. A Discourse, Delivered at . . . the Interment of the Rev. Charles Chauncy, . . . Boston: James D. Griffith, and Edward E. Powars, 1787.

Cogliano, Francis D. "Deliverance from Luxury: Pope's Day, Conflict and Consensus in Colonial Boston, 1745-1765." Studies in Popular Culture 15.2 (1993): 15-28.

Cogliano, Francis D. No King, No Popery: Anti-Catholicism in Revolutionary New England. Westport, Connecticut: Greenwood Press, 1995.

Cogliano, Francis D. "Nil Desperandum Christo Duce: The New England Crusade Against Louisbourg, 1745," Essex Institute Historical Collections 128 (Jul. 1992): 180-207

Cohen, Charles L., and Richard L. Bushman. "Crowning Assumptions." (1986): 61-67.

Colley, Linda. Britons: Forging the Nation, 1707-1837. New Haven: Yale University Press, 1992.

Collier, John Payne. An Old Man's Diary: Forty Years Ago. Vol. 2. T. Richards, 1871.

Collins, Sherwood. "Boston's Political Street Theatre: The Eighteenth-Century Pope Day Pageants." Educational Theatre Journal 25.4 (1973): 401-409.

Colman, Benjamin. A Sermon Preach'd at Boston in New-England on . . . the 23d. of August. 1716. Boston: T. Fleet and T. Crump, 1716.

Conroy, David W. In Public Houses: Drink & the Revolution of Authority in Colonial Massachusetts. Chapel Hill: University of North Carolina Press, 1995.

Coulter, E. Merton, ed. The Journal of William Stephens, 1741-1743. Athens, Georgia: University of Georgia Press, 1958-59.

Countryman, Edward. Review Article: "The Problem of the Early American Crowd." Journal of American Studies 7 (1973): 77-90.

Countryman, Edward. A People in Revolution: The American Revolution and Political Society in NewYork, 1760-1790. Baltimore: Johns Hopkins University Press, 1981.

Cressy, David. Bonfires and Bells: National Memory and the Protestant Calendar in Elizabethan and Stuart England. Berkeley: University of California Press, 1989.

Crocker, Matthew H. "No King, No Popery: Anti-Catholicism in Revolutionary New England." Historical Journal of Massachusetts 27.1 (1999): 101.

Cullen, Maurice R. "Benjamin Edes: Scourge of Tories." Journalism and Mass Communication Quarterly 51.2 (1974): 213.

Cunningham, Anne Rowe, ed. Letters and Diary of John Rowe, Boston Merchant, 1759-1762, 1764-1779. Boston: W. B. Clarke, 1903.

Cunningham, Henry Winchester, ed. "Diary of the Rev. Samuel Checkley, 1735." Publications of the Colonial Society of Massachusetts 12: Transactions (1908-09): _____.

Daboll, Nathaniel, ed. Freebetter's Almanac for 1774. New London, Connecticut, 1773.

Dadk, Wojciech. "Pope's Day in New England." Revere House Gazette 73 (2003): 1-3.

Da Matta, Robert. "Carnival in Multiple Planes." In Rite, Drama, Festival, Spectacle: Rehearsals Toward a Theory of Cultural Performance. John J. MacAloon, ed. Philadelphia: Institute for the Study of Human Issues, 1984.

Daniels, Bruce C. "Parties for the Common Good: Civic Socializing In Puritan New England." The Cultures of Celebrations (1994): 93.

Daniels, Bruce D. Puritans at Play: Leisure and Recreation in Colonial New England. New York: St. Martin's Press, 1995.

Davis, Natalie Zemon. "Some Tasks and Themes in the Study of Popular Religion." In The Pursuit of Holiness in Late Medieval and Renaissance Religion: Papers From the University of Michigan Conference. Charles Trikans and Heiko A. Oberman, eds. Leiden: Brill, 1974.

Davis, Natalie Zemon. Society and Culture in Early Modern France: Eight Essays. Stanford: Stanford University Press, 1975. (esp. "The Reasons of Misrule")

Davis, Susan G. Parades and Power: Street Theatre in Nineteenth-Century Philadelphia. Philadelphia: Temple University Press, 1985.

Davis, Susan G. "Strike Parades and the Politics of Representing Class in Antebellum Philadelphia." The Drama Review: TDR, vol. 29, no. 3, 1985, pp. 106–116. www.jstor.org/stable/1145657.

Dayton, Cornelia H., Sharon V. Salinger, Robert Love's Warnings: Searching for Strangers in Colonial Boston, University of Pennsylvania Press, Feb 18, 2014.

Deane, Samuel. Journal, 1761-1814 (The Journals of the Rev. Thomas Smith, and the Rev. Samuel Deane .. . Portland, Maine: J. S. Bailey, 1849.

De La Roche, Roberta Senechal. "Collective Violence as Social Control." Sociological Forum 11.1 (Mar. 1996): 97-128.

Dexter, Franklin Bowditch, ed. The Literary Diary of Ezra Stiles . . . (1769-1795). 3 Vols. New York: C. Scribner's Sons, 1901, 1973.

Dickinson, H. T. The Politics of the People in Eighteenth-Century Britain. New York: St. Martin's Press,1995.

Doyle, Kevin Q., "The Fifth of November in Colonial America" In: We Are What We Remember: The American Past Through Commemoration (2013): 288.

Doyle, Kevin Q. "Rage and Fury Which Only Hell Could Inspire": The Rhetoric and the Ritual of Gunpowder Treason in Early America. A Dissertation Presented to The Faculty of the Graduate School of Arts and Sciences. Diss. Brandeis University, 2013.

Drake, Samuel Adams. Old Landmarks and Historic Personages of Boston. 1873.

Du Simitiére, Pierre Eugéne. "Boston Affairs," A Drawing of a Hand-drawn Wagon in Boston. November 5, 1767. Library Company of Philadelphia.

Duncan, Jason K. Citizens or Papists?: The Politics of Anti-Catholicism in New York, 1685-1821. New York: Fordham University Press, 2005.

"South End Forever. North End Forever. Extraordinary Verses on Pope-Night . . ." Boston: The Printer Boys in Boston, 1768.

"Description of the Pope, 1769." Boston: S. N., 1769.
Earl, Alice Morse. Customs and Fashions in Old New England. New York: C. Scribner's Sons, 1893.

Ellsworth, Samuel. An Astronomical Diary or Almanack, for 1785. Bennington: Haswell & Russell, 1784.

Emerson, Joseph. A Thanksgiving-Sermon Preach'd at Pepperrell . . . Boston: Edes and Gill, 1766.

Etherington, Jim. Lewes Bonfire Night: A Short History of the Guy Fawkes Celebrations (Seaford, England: S. B. Publications, 1993), p. 14.

Etzioni, Amitai and Jared Bloom, eds. We Are What We Celebrate: Understanding Holidays and Rituals. New York: New York University Press, 2004.

Eustace, Nicole. Passion is the Gale: Emotion, Power, and the Coming of the American Revolution. Chapel Hill: North Carolina Press, 2008.

Feist, Tim. The Stationers' Voice: The English Almanac Trade in the Early Eighteenth Century. Philadelphia: American Philosophical Society, 2005.

Fell, Sister Marie Leonare, M.A. "The Foundations of Nativism in American Textbooks, 1783-1860." PhD Thesis, Catholic University of America, 1941.

Ferguson, Robert A. Reading the Early Republic. Cambridge, Massachusetts: Harvard University Press, 2004.

Fliegelman, Jay. Declaring Independence: Jefferson, Natural Language, & the Culture of Performance. Stanford: Stanford University Press, 1993.

Forbes, Esther. Paul Revere and the World He Lived In. Boston: Houghton Mifflin, Co., 1942.

Franchot, Jenny. Roads to Rome: The Antebellum Protestant Encounter With Catholicism. Berkeley: University of California Press, 1994.

Fraser, Antonia. Faith and Treason: The Story of the Gunpowder Plot. New York: Doubleday, 1996.

Freeman, Joanne B. Affairs of Honor: National Politics in the New Republic. New Haven: Yale University Press, 2001.

Fearnow, Mark. "American Colonial Disturbances as Political Theatre." Theatre Survey 33 (1992): 53-64.

Ferguson, Robert A. The American Enlightenment, 1750-1820. Harvard University Press, 1994.
Ferraiuolo, Augusto. Religious Festive Practices in Boston's North End: Ephemeral identities in an Italian American Community. SUNY Press, 2012.

Fitch, Elijah. A Discourse . . . Following the Precipitate Flight of the British Troops From Boston, . . . Boston: John Boyle, 1776.

Foster, J. MDCLXXIX: An Almanack of Coelestiall Motions for 1679. Boston: J. Foster, 1678.

Foxcroft, Thomas Grateful Reflexions on the Signal Appearances of Divine Providence for Great Britain and Its Colonies in America, Which Diffuse a General Joy: A Sermon Preached in the Old Church in Boston, October 9, 1760: Being the Thanksgiving-Day, on Occasion of the Surrender of Montreal, and the Complete Conquest of Canada . . . Boston: S. Kneeland, 1760

Franklin, Benjamin. Poor Richard, 1733, An Almanack For the Year of Christ 1733. Philadelphia: B. Franklin, 1732 and ff.

Freebetter, Edmund. The New-England Almanack; and Gentleman's and Lady's Diary for 1777. New-London, Connecticut: T. Green, 1776.

Freeman, James. The Notebook of James Freeman of Boston, . . . 1745-1765. MS N-1567, Massachusetts Historical Society.

Freiberg, Malcolm. "Going Gregorian, 1582-1752: A summary view." The Catholic historical review 86.1 (2000): 1-19.

Furley, O. W. "Pope-Burning Processions of the Late Seventeenth Century." History 44 (1959): 16-23.

Gilje, Paul A. "Boston Riots: Three Centuries of Social Violence. By Jack Tager. (Boston: Northeastern University Press, 2001. xii, 289 pp. Cloth, 45.00, ISBN 1-55553-461-9. Paper, 17.95, ISBN 1-55553-460-0.)." The Journal of American History 89.1 (2002): 200-201.

Gilje, Paul, "The Mob Began to Think and Reason: Recent Trends in Studies of American Popular Disorder, 1700-1850," Maryland Historian 12 (1981), 25.

Gilje, Paul A. Rioting in America. Indiana University Press, 1996.

Gilje, Paul A. Liberty on the Waterfront: American Maritime Culture in the Age of Revolution. Philadelphia: University of Pennsylvania, 2004.

Gilje, Paul A. The Road to Mobocracy: Popular Disorder in New York City, 1763-1834. Chapel Hill: University of North Carolina Press, 1987.

Gillis, John R., ed., Commemorations: The Politics of National Identity. Princeton: Princeton University Press, 1994.

Glassberg, David. "History and Memory," in Karen Haltttunen, ed., A Companion to American Cultural History. Malden, Massachusetts: Blackwell Publishing, 2008), 371-80.

Glassberg, David. Sense of History: The Place of the Past in American Life. Amherst: University of Massachusetts Press, 2001.

Golden, Morris. "The Imagining Self in the Eighteenth Century." Eighteenth-Century Studies 3.1 (1969) : 4-27.
Granger, Bruce Ingham. "The Stamp Act in Satire." American Quarterly 8 (1956): ___. (378)

Green, Samuel A., ed. Diary by Increase Mather, March, 1675--December, 1676. Together Extracts From Another Diary by Him, 1674-1687. J. Wilson, 1900.

Greenberg, Douglas, and Peter Shaw. "American Patriots and the Rituals of Revolution." (1981): 345-348.

Greene, Jack P. Imperatives, Behaviors, and Identities: Essays in Early American Cultural History. Charlottesville, Virginia: University of Virginia Press, 1992.

Greene, Jack P. Pursuits of Happiness: The Social Development of Early Modern British Colonies and the Formation of American Culture. Chapel Hill: University of North Carolina Press, 1988.

Greenspan, Jesse. "Guy Fawkes Day: A Brief History." History 5 (2012).

Griffin, Edward M. Old Brick: Charles Chauncy of Boston, 1705-1787. Vol. 11. U of Minnesota Press, 1980.

Griffin, Emma. England's Revelry: A History of Popular Sports and Pastimes, 1660-1830. New York: Oxford University Press, 2005.

Habermas, Jurgen. The Structural Transformation of the Public Sphere: An Inquiry Into a Category of Bourgeois Society. Cambridge, Massachusetts: MIT Press, 1989.

Haddow, Swapna. Dave Pigeon. Faber & Faber, 2016.

Hall, David D. Lived Religion in America: Toward a History of Practice. Princeton: Princeton University Press, 1997.

Hall, David D. Worlds of Wonder, Days of Judgment: Popular Religious Belief in Early New England. Cambridge, Massachusetts: Harvard University Press, 1990.

Hammerbacher, George. "Restoration and 18th Century Theatre Research Bibliography for 1973." Restoration and Eighteenth Century Theatre Research 13.2 (1974): 1.

Handelman, Don. Models and Mirrors: Towards an Anthropology of Public Events. New York: Cambridge University Press, 1990.

Hanson, Charles P. Necessary Virtue: The Pragmatic Origins of Religious Liberty in New England. Charlottesville: University Press of Virginia, 1998.

Harris, Benjamin . Boston Almanack for 1692. Boston: Benjamin Harris, and John Allen, 1691.

Harris, Tim, ed. Popular Culture in England, c. 1500-1850. New York: St. Martin's Press, 1995.

Hawley, Stephen. The Agency of God in Snow, Frost, &c., . . . New Haven: Thomas and Samuel Green, 1771.

Hawthorne, Nathaniel. "My Kinsman, Major Molineaux." In The Token and Atlantic Souvenir: A Christmas and New Year's Present, edited by S. G. Goodrich. Boston: Gray and Bowen, 1833.

Hempstead, Joshua. Diary of Joshua Hempstead (1711-1758). New Haven: New London County Historical Society, 1970.

Hobsbawm, Eric and Terence Ranger, eds., The Invention of Tradition. New York: Cambridge University Press, 1983.

Hoerder, Dirk. "Boston Leaders and Boston Crowds, 1765-1776." In The American Revolution:

Explorations in the History of American Radicalism. Alfred F. Young, ed. DeKalb, Illinois: Northern Illinois University, 1976.

Hoerder, Dirk. Crowd Action in Revolutionary Massachusetts, 1765-1780. New York: Academic Press, 1977.

Hoerder, Dirk People and Mobs: Crowd Action in Massachusetts During the American Revolution Berlin: Free University of Berlin, 1971

Hoffer, Peter Charles. Law and People in Colonial America. Baltimore: Johns Hopkins University Press, 1992.

Hoffman, Ronald and Peter J. Albert, eds. The Transforming Hand of Revolution: Reconsidering the American Revolution as a Social Movement. Charlottesville: University Press of Virginia, 1996.

Hoftstadter, Richard. The Paranoid Style in American Politics and Other Essays. New York: Alfred A. Knopf, 1965.

Hooker, Richard J., ed. The Carolina Backcountry on the eve of the Revolution: The Journal and Other Writings of Charles Woodmason, Anglican itinerant. Chapel Hill: University of North Carolina Press, 1953.

Horton, James Oliver. "Urban Alliances: The Emergence of Race-Based Populism in the Age of Jackson." African American Urban Experience: Perspectives from the Colonial Period to the Present. Palgrave Macmillan US, 2004. 23-34.

Howe, John. Language and Political Meaning in Revolutionary America. Amherst: University of Massachusetts Press, 2004.

Hulton, Anne. Letters of a Loyalist Lady. Cambridge, Massachusetts: Harvard University Press, 1927.

Hunt, James B. The Crowd and the American Revolution: A Study of Urban Political Violence in Boston and Philadelphia, 1763-1776. PhD Thesis, University of Washington, 1973.

Hurstfield Joel, "Gunpowder Plot and the Politics of Dissent, In: Reinmuth, Howard S. Jr. Ed, Early Stuart studies; essays in honor of David Harris Willson.1970.

Hutchins, William Norman. "Moral Values in National Holidays." The Biblical World 49.3 (Mar. 1917): 168-70.

Hutchinson, Peter Orlando, ed. The Diary and Letters of His Excellency Thomas Hutchinson . . . 2 Vols. New York: AMS Press, 1973.

Hutton, Ronald. The Stations of the Sun: A History of the Ritual Year in Britain. New York: Oxford University Press, 1996.

Ingram, Martin, "Ridings, Rough Music, and the Reform of Popular Culture" Past and Present (1984) 105 (1): 79-113.

Irvin, Benjamin H. Clothed in the Robes of Sovereignty: The Continental Congress and the People Out of Doors. New York: Oxford University Press, 2011.

Irvin, Benjamin H. "Tar, Feathers, and Enemies of American Liberties, 1768-1776." New England Quarterly 76 (June 2003): 197-238.

James, Anne, Poets, Players and Preachers, Remembering the Gunpowder Plot in Seventeenth Century England, University of Toronto Press, 2016, p.252.

James, Sydney V., Jr., ed. Three Visitors to Early Plymouth: Letters About the Pilgrim Settlement in New England During Its First Seven Years. Stinehour Press, 1963.

Johnson, Richard. Adjustment to Empire: The New England Colonies, 1675-1715 (New Brunswick, New Jersey: Rutgers University Press, 1981.

Kammen, Michael. A Season of Youth: The American Revolution and the Historical Imagination. New York: Alfred A. Knopf, 1978.

Kammen, Michael. Mystic Chords of Memory: The Transformation of Tradition in American Culture. New York: Alfred A. Knopf, 1991.

Kaser, James, and David E. Shi. "Facing Facts: Realism in American Thought and Culture, 1850-1920." (1997): 116-118.

Kennedy, William H. J. "Catholics in Massachusetts before 1750." The Catholic Historical Review 17.1 (1931): 10-28.

Kern, John. "The Politics of Violence: Colonial American Rebellions, Protests, and Riots, 1676-1747." PhD Thesis, University of Wisconsin-Madison, 1976.

Kidd, Thomas S. "'Let Hell and Rome Do Their Worst': World News, Anti-Catholicism, and International Protestantism in Early-Eighteenth-Century Boston." New England Quarterly 76.2 (June 2003): 265-290.

Kidd, Thomas S. "Recovering the French Convert: Views of the French and the Uses of Anti-Catholicism in Early America." Book History 7 (2004): 97-111.

Kidd, Thomas S. God of Liberty: A Religious History of the American Revolution. New York: Basic Books, 2010.

Kidd, Thomas S. The Great Awakening: The Roots of Evangelical Christianity in Colonial America. New Haven: Yale University Press, 2007.

Kidd, Thomas S. The Protestant Interest: New England After Puritanism. New Haven: Yale University Press, 2004.

Knott, Sarah. Sensibility and the American Revolution. Chapel Hill: University of North Carolina Press, 2009.

Krugler, John D. "Beyond Toleration: The Religious Origins of American Pluralism. By Chris Beneke.(New York: Oxford University Press, 2006. xii, 305 pp. 35.00, ISBN 978-0-19-530555-5.)." The Journal of American History 94.3 (2007): 914-915.

Labaree, Leonard W. Royal Government in America: A Study of the British Colonial System Before 1783. New Haven: Yale University Press, 1930.

Lahvis, Sylvia Leistyna. "Icons of American Trade: The Skillin Workshop and the Language of Spectacle." Winterthur Portfolio, vol. 27, no. 4, 1992, pp. 213–233. www.jstor.org/stable/1181434.

Lake, Peter and Michael Questier. "Puritans, Papists, and the 'Public Sphere' in Early Modern England: The Edmund Campion Affair in Context." Journal of British Studies 36.4 (Sep. 2000): 587-627.

Lake, Peter and Steven C. A. Pincus. "Rethinking the Public Sphere in Early Modern England." Journal of British Studies 45 (2006): 270-92.

Lake, Peter and Steven Pincus, eds. The Politics of the Public Sphere in Early Modern England. New York: Manchester University Press, 2007.

Lane, Roger, and Paul A. Gilje. A Trip Through Riot, Rout, and Tumult in New York. (1988): 380-384.

Leach, Eugene E. "Mental Epidemics: Crowd Psychology and American Culture, 1890-1940." American Studies 33 (1992), 8.

Leach, John. The Diary of John Leach (1757-1776). MS N-1567, Massachusetts Historical Society.

Le Bon, Gustave. Psychologie des Foules [The Crowd: A Study of the Popular Mind]. Paris: Presses Univeritaries de France, 1895.

Leisler, Jacob. "Letter to Edwin Stede, the Governor of Barbados. November 23, 1689." In Documents Relative to the Colonial History of the State of New-York, edited by E. B. O'Callaghan. Vol. III. Albany: Weed, Parsons, & Co., 1853.

Lemisch, Jesse "The American Revolution Seen from the Bottom Up," in Towards a New Past: Dissenting Essays in American History, ed. Barton J. Bernstein. New York: Vintage Books, 1968, 3-45

Lemisch, Jesse "Jack Tar in the Streets: Merchant Seamen in the Politics of Revolutionary America," William and Mary Quarterly 25 (1968): 371-407

Lemisch, Jesse. Jack Tar vs. John Bull: The Role of New York's Seamen in Precipitating the Revolution. New York: Garland Publishers, 1997.

Leverenz, David, and Peter Shaw. "American Patriots and the Rituals of Revolution." (1981): 285-287.
Levy, Barry. Town Born: The Political Economy of New England from Its Founding to the Revolution University of Pennsylvania Press (2009): 175.

Lewis, James R. "Fantasies of Abuse and Captivity in Nineteenth-Century Convent Tales." Sexuality and New Religious Movements. Palgrave Macmillan US, 2014. 213-230.

Lewis, Theodore B. "Massachusetts and the Glorious Revolution, 1660-1692." PhD Thesis, University of Wisconsin, 1967.

Łodej, Sylwester. "Concept-driven Semasiology and Onomasiology of Clergy." Middle and Modern English Corpus Linguistics: A multi-dimensional approach 50 (2012): 93.

Łodej, Sylwester. "Semantic Change in Sociolinguistic Perspective: The Term Pope." ANGLICA-An International Journal of English Studies 18 (2009): 83-96.

Lodej, Sylwester. "Semantic change in the domain of the vocabulary of Christian clergy." English Historical Linguistics 2008: Selected papers from the fifteenth International Conference on English Historical Linguistics (ICEHL 15), Munich, 24-30 August 2008. Volume II: Words, texts and genres. Vol. 324. John Benjamins Publishing, 2012.

Longley, Ronald Stewart. "Mob Activities in Revolutionary Massachusetts." The New England Quarterly 6.1 (1933): 98-130.

Love, W. DeLoss, Jr. The Fast and Thanksgiving Days of New England. Boston: Houghton, Mifflin, and Company, 1895.

Lovejoy, Jack P. The Glorious Revolution in America. New York: Harper and Row, 1972.
MacDonald, Edward. Old Copp's Hill and Burial Ground: With Historical Sketches. Industrial School Press, 1894.

MacGregor, Alan Leander. "Tammany: The Indian as Rhetorical Surrogate." American Quarterly, vol. 35, no. 4, 1983, pp. 391–407. www.jstor.org/stable/2712877.

Macinnes, Allan I. and Arthur H. Williamson, eds. Shaping the Stuart World, 1603-1714: The Atlantic Connection. Boston: Brill, 2006.

Malcom, Allison O'Mahen. "Anti-Catholicism and the Rise of Protestant Nationhood in North America, 1830-1871." PhD Thesis, University of Illinois at Chicago, 2011.

Magra, Christopher P., et al., Revolutionary Founders: Rebels, Radicals, and Reformers in the Making of the Nation. (2011): 737-740.

Maier, Pauline, Dirk Hoerder, and John Phillip Reid. Class, Law, and Revolutionary Violence. (1979): 70-78.

Maier, Pauline. "The Charleston Mob and the Evolution of Popular Politics in Revolutionary South Carolina." Perspectives in American History 4 (1970): 173-96.

Maier, Pauline. "The Pope at Harvard: The Dudleian Lectures, Anti-Catholicism, and the Politics of Protestantism." Proceedings of the Massachusetts Historical Society 97 (1985): 16-41.

Maier, Pauline. "Popular Uprisings and Civil Authority in Eighteenth-Century America." The William and Mary Quarterly, vol. 27, no. 1, 1970, pp. 4–35. www.jstor.org/stable/1923837.

Marshall, Douglas A. "Behavior, Belonging, and Belief: A Theory of Ritual Practice." Sociological Theory 20.3 (Nov. 2002): 360-80.

McConville, Brendan. "Pope's Day Revisited, 'Popular' Culture Reconsidered." Explorations in Early American Culture 3 (Dec. 2000): 258-80.

Massachusetts Council Records, Vol. 19. November 27, 1752. Vol. 47. November 23, 1752.

Mather, Cotton. Diary of Cotton Mather (1681-1724). 2 Vols. New York: Frederick Ungar Publishing Co., 1957.

Mather, Cotton Mirabilia Dei: An Essay on the Very Seasonable & Remarkable Interpositions of the Divine Providence, to Rescue & Relieve Distressed People, Brought Unto the Very Point of Perishing; Especially Relating to That Twice-Memorable Fifth of November . . . (Boston: B. Green, Printer to His Excellency the Governour & Council), 1719

McConville, Brendan. "Pope's Day Revisited, 'Popular' Culture Reconsidered." Explorations in Early American Culture 4 (2000): 258-280.

McConville, Brendan. The King's Three Faces: The Rise & Fall of Royal America, 1688-1776. Chapel Hill University Press (2006): 351-353.

McConville, Brendan. "A World of Kings." Historically Speaking 8.5 (2007): 5-8.

McGreevy, John T. Catholicism and American Freedom: A History. New York: W. W. Norton, 2003.

Mein and Fleeming's Massachusett's Register for 1767. Boston: Mein and Fleming, 1766.

Metzger, Charles H. "Bigotry of the Founding Fathers." Thought 12.1 (1937): 132-134.

Monti, Daniel J., "Violence as Social Intervention." Journal of Intergroup Relations 9 (1981), 33-34

Moore, Nina, and Susan I. Lesley, eds. Letters of James Murray, Loyalist. Boston: S. N., 1901.

Morgan, David and Sally M. Promey. Exhibiting the Visual Culture of American Religions. Valparaiso, Indiana: Brauer Museum of Art, Valparaiso University, 2000.

Morgan, Edmund S. Inventing the People: The Rise of Popular Sovereignty in England and America. New York: Norton, 1988.

Morgan, Edmund S. A Prologue to Revolution. Chapel Hill: University of North Carolina Press, 1959.

Morison, Samuel Eliot, ed. [William Bradford's History] Of Plymouth Plantation, 1620-1647. New York: Knopf, 1963.

Mullen, Lincoln. "Debating the Hartford Convention: Newspaper Politics, Political Opposition, and the Paranoid Style." MA Thesis, Bob Jones University, 2007.

Murrin, John. "Anglicizing an American Colony: The Transformation of Provincial Massachusetts." PhD Thesis, Yale University, 1966.

Nadir, William. Mercurius Nov-Anglicanus. or an Almanack for 1747. Boston: Rogers and Fowle, 1746

Nash, Gary B. "The Transformation of Urban Politics, 1700-1765." Journal of American History 60.3 (Dec. 1973): 605-32.

Nash, Gary B. Class and Society in Early America. Englewood Cliffs, New Jersey: Prentice-Hall, 1970.

Nash, Gary B. First City: Philadelphia and the Forging of Historical Memory. Philadelphia: University of Pennsylvania Press, 2002.

Nash, Gary B. The Unknown American Revolution: The Unruly Birth of Democracy and the Struggle to Create America. New York: Viking, 2005.

Nash, Gary B. The Urban Crucible: Social Change, Political Consciousness, and the Origins of the American Revolution. Cambridge: Harvard University Press, 1979.

New-Hampshire Gazette, and Historical Chronicle. November 4, 1768.

New York City, Minutes of the Common Council of the City of New York. March 7, 1803, 3: 228.

Newman, Henry. News From the Stars. An Almanack for 1691. Boston: R. Pierce for Benjamin Harris, 1690.

Newman, Simon P. Parades and the Politics of the Street: Festive Culture in the Early American Republic. Philadelphia: University of Pennsylvania Press, 1997.

Nicholls, Mark. Investigating Gunpowder Plot. New York: St. Martin's Press, 1991.

Nicolson, Colin. "'McIntish, Otis & Adams Are Our Demagogues': Nathaniel Coffin and the Loyalist Interpretation of the Origins of the American Revolution." Proceedings of the Massachusetts Historical Society 3.108 (1996): 72-114.

Nissenbaum, Stephen W. Christmas in Early New England, 1620-1820: Puritanism, Popular Culture, and the Printed Word. Worcester: American Antiquarian Society, 1996.

Nobles, Gregory H. "'Yet the Old Republicans Still Persevere': Samuel Adams, John Hancock, and the Crisis of Popular Leadership in Revolutionary Massachusetts, 1775-1790." In The Transforming Hand of Revolution: Reconsidering the American Revolution as a Social Movement.

Nowak, T. S. "Remember, Remember the Fifth of November: Anglocentrism and Anti-Catholicism in the English Gunpowder Sermons, 1605-1651." PhD Thesis, State University of New York at Stony Brook, 1992.

North, Selah. An Oration Delivered at Goshen, July 4th, 1817, . . . Hartford: F. D. Bolles, & Co., 1817.

O'Callaghan, E. B., ed. Documents Relative to the Colonial History of the State of New-York. 15 Vols. Albany: Weed, Parsons, & Co., 1853.

O'Donnell, James H. History of the Diocese of Hartford. DH Hurd Company, 1900.

Ormond, Barbara. "Pedagogy and pictorial evidence: interpreting Post-Reformation English prints in context." The Curriculum Journal 22.1 (2011): 3-27.

Orsi, Robert A. The Madonna of 115th Street: Faith and Community in Italian Harlem, 1880-1950. New Haven: Yale University Press, 1985, 2002.

Orsi, Robert A. "Parades, Holidays, and Public Rituals." Encyclopedia of American Social History 3 (1993).

Osborne's New-Hampshire Register: With an Almanack, for 1788. Portsmouth, New Hampshire: George Jerry Osborne, 1787.

Osgood, Herbert L. The American Colonies in the Seventeenth Century. 3 vols. New York: Columbia University Press, 1904-1907.

Osgood, Herbert L. The American Colonies in the Eighteenth Century. 4 vols. New York: Columbia University Press, 1924-1925.

Osgood, Herbert L., Austin Baxter Keep, and Charles Alexander Nelson, eds. Minutes of the Common Council of the City of New York, 1675-1776. New York: Dodd, Mead, and Company, 1905.

Palmer, Bryan D. "Discordant Music: Charivaris and Whitecapping in Nineteenth-Century North America." Labour/Le Travail (1978): 5-62.

Pasley, Jeffrey L. "The Tyranny of Printers": Newspaper Politics in the Early American Republic. Charlottesville: University of Virginia Press, 2001.

Pasley, Jeffrey L.; Andrew W. Robertson, and David Waldstreicher, eds. Beyond the Founders: New Approaches to the Political History of the Early American Republic. Chapel Hill: University of North Carolina Press, 2004.

The Patriots of North-America: A Sketch With Explanatory Notes . . . New York: James Rivington, 1775.

Peabody, Andrew P. "Boston Mobs before the Revolution." Atlantic Monthly 62 (1888): 321-333.

Peacock, M. "The Fifth of November and Guy Fawkes." Folklore 18.4 (Dec. 1907): 449-50.

Pencak, William. "Play as Prelude to Revolution: Boston, 1765-1776." In Riot and Revelry in Early America. William Pencak, Matthew Dennis, and Simon P. Newman, eds. University Park, Pennsylvania: Pennsylvania State University Press, 2002.

Pencak, William. "Revolutionary Play: Inlaws/Outlaws Twenty Years Later." New approaches to semiotics and the human sciences: essays in honor of Roberta Kevelson 13 (1998): 165.

Pencak, William, Matthew Dennis, and Simon P. Newman, eds. Riot and Revelry in Early America. University Park, Pennsylvania: Pennsylvania State University Press, 2002.

People v. Jonathan Burke Murphy. Court of General Sessions, MARC. December 23, 1818.

People v. Peter O'Brien, et al. New York Court of General Sessions. April 16, 1802.

Perkins, Mary Elizabeth, Old Houses of the Antient Town of Norwich [Conn.] 1660-1800, 1895.

Perry, Eliakim. The Vermont Almanack, for 1785. Bennington: Haswell & Russell, 1784.

Peskin, Lawrence A. "American Sailors, American Freedom: Jack Tar and the Meaning of Liberty." Reviews in American History 32.3 (2004): 341-346.

Pfau, William Michael. The Political Style of Conspiracy: Chase, Sumner, and Lincoln. East Lansing: Michigan State University Press, 2005.

Phythian-Adams, C. "Ceremony and the Citizen: the Communal Year at Coventry, 1500-1700" in Peter Clark and Paul Slack (eds.), Crisis and Order in English Towns

Picker, Greg. "'A nation is governed by all that has tongue in the nation': Newspapers and political expression in colonial Sydney, 1825-1850." Journal of Australian Studies 23.62 (1999): 183-189.

Pincus, Steven C. A. Protestantism and Patriotism: Ideologies and the Making of English Foreign Policy, 1650-1668. New York: Cambridge University Press, 1996.

Poole, Robert. "Give Us Our Eleven Days!": Calendar Reform in Eighteenth-Century England." Past and Present 149 (Nov. 1995): 95-139.

Poyer, Thomas. "Thanksgiving for the Failure of the Gunpowder Plot," in Henry Onderdonk, ed., Records Kept by Rev. Thomas Poyer, rector of Episcopal churches at Jamaica, Newtown & Flushing, Long Island. Brooklyn: ___, 1913.

Price, Benjamin Lewis, and Brendan McConville. "The King's Three Faces: The Rise and Fall of Royal America, 1688-1776." (2007): 99-100.

Prude, Jonathan. "To Look upon the 'Lower Sort': Runaway Ads and the Appearance of Unfree Laborers in America, 1750-1800." The Journal of American History 78.1 (1991): 124-159.

Purcell, Richard J. "Judge William Gaston: Georgetown University's First Student." Geo. LJ 27 (1938): 839.

Purcell, Sarah J. Sealed With Blood: War, Sacrifice, and Memory in Revolutionary America. Philadelphia: University of Pennsylvania Press, 2002.

Pye, Lucian W. "Political Culture Revisited." Political Psychology 12.3 (Sep. 1991): 487-508.

Quint, David, Epic and Empire: Politics and Generic Form from Virgil to Milton, 1993.

Raphael, Ray. A People's History of the American Revolution: How Common People Shaped the Fight for Independence. New York: New Press, 2001.

Ray, Mary Augustina, B. V. M., American Opinion of Roman Catholicism in the Eighteenth Century. New York: Octagon Books, 1936

Raynolds, Peter. The Kingdom Is the Lord's, or, God the Supreme Ruler and Governour of the World . . .New London: John Green, Printer to the Governor, & Company, 1757.

Reay, Barry. Popular Cultures in England, 1550-1750. New York: Longman, 1998.

Rediker, Marcus and Peter Linebaugh. The Many-Headed Hydra: Sailors, Slaves, Commoners, and the Hidden History of the Revolutionary Atlantic. Boston: Beacon Press, 2000.

Reed, Peter P. "Performing Patriotism: National Identity in the Colonial and Revolutionary American Theater (review)." Early American Literature 43.3 (2008): 734-738.

Resolution of the Council of Massachusetts Bay, November 4, 1778, copy. Lord/Sexton Papers. Archives of the Archdiocese of Boston.

Reynolds, Graham. "The Road to Mobocracy: Popular Disorder in New York City, 1763-1834, by Paul A. Gilje." Canadian Journal of History 23.3 (1988): 417-419.

Riley, Arthur J. Catholicism in New England to 1788. Washington, D.C.: Catholic University of America,1936.

Robertson, Andrew W. The Language of Democracy: Political Rhetoric in the United States and Britain, 1790-1900. Ithaca, New York: Cornell University Press, 1995.

Rogers, Nicholas. Crowds, Culture, and Politics in Georgian Britain. New York: Oxford University Press, 1998.

Rowe, John, and Edward Lillie Pierce. Letters and Diary of John Rowe: Boston Merchant, 1759-1762, 1764-1779. WB Clarke Company, 1903.

Rudé, George. The Crowd in History: A Study of Popular Disturbances in France and England, 1730- 1848. New York: John Wiley & Sons, 1964.

Rudé, George. "Ideology and popular protest." Historical Reflections/Réflexions Historiques (1976): 69-77.

Rudolph, Lloyd I. "The Eighteenth Century Mob in America and Europe." American Quarterly 11.4 (Winter 1959): 447-469.

Russell, D. An Almanack of Coelestiall Motions for 1671. Cambridge: S. G. and M. J., 1670.

St. George, Robert Blair. Conversing by Signs: Poetics of Implication in Colonial New England Culture. Chapel Hill: University of North Carolina Press, 1998.

Saltman, Helen Saltzberg. "John Adams's Earliest Essays: The Humphrey Ploughjogger Letters." The William and Mary Quarterly: A Magazine of Early American History (1980): 125-135.

Savage, Edward Hartwell. A Chronological History of the Boston Watch and Police: From 1631 to 1865; Together with the Recollections of a Boston Police Office, Or, Boston by Daylight and Gaslight, from the Diary of an Officer Fifteen Years in the Service. The author, 1865.

Schlesinger, Arthur Meier. "Political Mobs and the American Revolution, 1765-1776." Proceedings of the American Philosophical Society 99.4 (Aug. 30, 1955): 244-250.

Schnell, Scott. "Ritual As an Instrument of Political Resistance in Rural Japan." Journal of Anthropological Research 51.4 (Winter 1995): 301-28.

Scott, Kenneth, ed. The Voyages and Travels of Francis Goelet, 1746-1758. Queens, New York: Queens College Press, 1970.

Scudder, H. E., ed. Recollections of Samuel Breck, With Passages From His Note Books, 1774-1862. Philadelphia: Porter & Contes, 1877.

Scull, G. D., ed. The Montresor Journals. New York: The New-York Historical Society, 1882.

Seccombe, Joseph. A Plain and Brief Rehearsal of the Operations of Christ as God . . . Boston: S. Kneeland and T. Green, 1740.

Select Essays, With Some Few Miscellaneous Copies of Verses Drawn by Ingenious Hands. Boston: S. N.,1714.

Shaffer, Jason. Performing Patriotism: National Identity in the Colonial and Revolutionary American Theater. Philadelphia: University of Pennsylvania Press, 2007.

Shank, Theodore. "Political Theater in England." Performing Arts Journal 2.3 (Winter 1978): 48-62.

Sharpe, James. Remember, Remember: A Cultural History of Guy Fawkes Day. Cambridge, Massachusetts: Harvard University Press, 2005.

Shaw, Peter. "Hawthorne's Ritual Typology of the American Revolution." Prospects 3 (1978): 483-498.

Shaw, Peter. The American Patriots and the Rituals of Revolution. Harvard University Press, 1981: 100-101; 218.

Shea, John Gilmary. Pope-day in America. publisher not identified, 1888.

Sherman, Roger. An Astronomical Diary, or, an Almanack for 1760. Boston: Printed for D. Henchman, J. Webb, M. Dennis, J. Winter, T. Leverett, and S. Webb, 1759.

Shoemaker, Robert B. "The London 'Mob' in the Early Eighteenth Century." Journal of British Studies 26.3 (Jul. 1987): 273-304.

Shurtleff, Nathaniel B., ed. Records of the Governor and Company of the Massachusetts Bay in New England . . . Boston: W. White, printer to the commonwealth, 1854.

Skerry, Janine E. and Jeanne Sloane. "Images of Politics and Religion on Silver Engraved by Joseph Leddel." Antiques 141 (Mar. 1992): 490-99.

Smith, Mark M. "Culture, Commerce, and Calendar Reform in Colonial America." William and Mary Quarterly 55.4 (Oct. 1998): 557-584.

Smith, Philip Chadwick Foster. The Journals of Ashley Bowen (1728-1813) of Marblehead. Portland, Maine: Peabody Museum of Salem in Conjunction with the Colonial Society of Massachusetts, 1973.

Smith, William A. "Anglo-Colonial Society and the Mob, 1740-1775." PhD Thesis, Claremont Graduate School, 1966.

Sponsler, Claire. Ritual Imports: Performing medieval drama in America. Cornell University Press, 2004.

Stabile, Susan M. Memory's Daughters: The Material Culture of Remembrance in Eighteenth-Century America Ithaca, New York: Cornell University Press, 2004.

Stafford, Hosea. Stafford's Almanac, for 1778. New-Haven: Thomas and Samuel Green, 1777.

Stanwood, Owen. "The Protestant Moment: Antipopery, the Revolution of 1688-1689, and the Making of an Anglo-American Empire." Journal of British Studies 46.3 (Jul. 2007): 481-508.

Stanwood, Owen. The Empire Reformed: English America in the Age of the Glorious Revolution. Philadelphia: University of Pennsylvania Press, 2011.

Steere, Richard. The Daniel Catcher. The Life of the prophet Daniel in a poem . . . Boston: John Allen, 1713.

Stephens, Frederick George. Catalogue of Political and Personal Satires, Preserved in the Department of Prints and Drawings in the British Museum. Vols. London: British Museum Publications, Ltd., 1978.

Stowell, Marion Barber. Early American Almanacs: The Colonial Weekday Bible. New York: B. Franklin, 1977.

Suffolk County Court Files. Suffolk County Court House, Boston.

Suffolk County Court of General Sessions of the Peace, Docket Book, 1759-54. Suffolk County Court House, Boston.

Suffolk County, Court Files,. Vol. 487. August 1761 – October 1761. The Office of the Clerk, Supreme Judicial Court, Suffolk County Court House, Boston.

Sumner, William H. "Reminiscences by General William H. Sumner." New England Historical and Genealogical Register 8 (1854): 187-91.

Tager, Jack. Boston Riots: Three Centuries of Social Violence. Northeastern University Press, 2001.

Tappan, Robert Noxon, ed. Edward Randolph, Including His Letters and Official Papers From the New England, Middle, and Southern Colonies in America and the West Indies. 2+ Vols. Boston: Prince Society, 1898-1909.

Taylor, Antoinette. "An English Christmas Play." The Journal of American Folklore 22.86 (1909): 389-394.

Teachout, Woden. Capture the flag: A political history of American patriotism. Basic Books, 2009.

Thelen, David. "Memory and American History." Journal of American History 75.4 (Mar. 1989): 1117-29.

Thomas, Isaiah. Thomas's Massachusetts, Connecticut, Rhode-Island, New-Hampshire & Vermont Almanack . . . Worcester, Massachusetts: Isaiah Thomas, 1785, 1786.

Thomas, Isaiah. Three Autobiographical Fragments. Worcester, Massachusetts: American Antiquarian Society, 1812.

Thomas, M. Halsey, ed. The Diary of Samuel Sewall. 1674-1729. 2 Vols. New York: Farrar, Straus, and Giroux, 1973.

Thompson, E. P. The Making of the English Working Class. London: V. Gollancz, 1980.

Thompson, E. P. "The Moral Economy of the English Crowd in the Eighteenth Century." Customs in Common: Studies in Traditional Popular Culture. New York: New Press, 1993.

Thompson, E. P. "Rough music reconsidered." Folklore 103.1 (1992): 3-26.

Thompson, Roger. "Adolescent Culture in Colonial Massachusetts." Journal of Family History 9.2 (1984): 127-44.

Tilly, Charles. "Collective Action in England and America, 1765-1775." In Tradition, Conflict, and Modernization: Perspectives on the American Revolution. Richard Maxwell Brown and Don E. Fehrenbacher, eds. New York: Academic Press, 1977.

Tomlins, Christopher L. and Bruce H. Mann, eds. The Many Legalities of Early America. Chapel Hill: University of North Carolina Press, 2001.

Towner, Lawrence William. A Good Master Well Served: Masters and Servants in Colonial Massachusetts, 1620-1750. Taylor & Francis, 1998.

Travers, Len. Celebrating the Fourth: Independence Day and the Rites of Nationalism in the Early Republic. Amherst, Massachusetts: University of Massachusetts Press, 1997

Travis, Daniel. An Almanac of Coelestial Motions and Aspects, for . . . the Year of . . . 1717. Boston: Bartholomew Green, 1716.

Tudor, William, ed. Deacon Tudor's Diary, Or . . . a Record Or More Or Less Important Events in Boston, From 1732 to 1793, By an Eye Witness. Boston: Press of Wallace Spooner, 1896.

Tudor, William. The Life of James Otis, of Massachusetts. . . Boston: Wells and Lilly, 1823.

Tulley, John. An Almanack for the Year of Our Lord . . . Boston: B. Green, & J. Allen, . . . 1687, 1689, 1692-99, 1701-02.

Tumbleson, Raymond D. Catholicism in the English Protestant Imagination: Nationalism, Religion, and Literature, 1600-1745. New York: Cambridge University Press, 1998.

Underdown, David. Revel, Riot, and Rebellion: Popular Politics and Culture in England, 1603-1660. New York: Oxford University Press, 1987.

Veltri, Stephen C. "Nativism and Nonpreferentialism: A Historical Critique of the Current Church and State Theme." U. Dayton L. Rev. 13 (1987): 229.

Vickers, Daniel. "Competency and Competition: Economic Culture in Early America." The

William and Mary Quarterly, vol. 47, no. 1, 1990, pp. 3–29. www.jstor.org/stable/2938039.

Wade, Melvin, "Shining in Borrowed Plumage: Affirmation of Community in Black Coronation Festivals of New England," Western Folklore 40 (1981), 211.

Waldstreicher, David. In the Midst of Perpetual Fetes: The Making of American Nationalism, 1776-1820. Chapel Hill: University of North Carolina Press, 1997.

Waldstreicher, David. "Rites of Rebellion, Rites of Assent: Celebrations, Print Culture, and the Origins of American Nationalism." The Journal of American History, vol. 82, no. 1, 1995, pp. 37–61. www.jstor.org/stable/2081914.

Walker, Benjamin. The Diary of Benjamin Walker. 1726-1749. MS N-1719, Massachusetts Historical Society.

Warden, G. B. "The Caucus and Democracy in Colonial Boston." The New England Quarterly, vol. 43, no. 1, 1970, pp. 19–45. www.jstor.org/stable/363694.

Warner, Michael. The Letters of the Republic: Publication and the Public Sphere in Eighteenth-Century America. Cambridge, Massachusetts: Harvard University Press, 1990.

Watts, Isaac. Horae Lyricae. Poems, Chiefly of the Lyric Kind, in Three Books. Sacred. . . . Boston: Rogers and Fowle, 1748, 1772, 1781.

Weatherwise, Abraham. Weatherwise's Boston Almanack, for 1786. Plymouth: Nathaniel Coverly, 1785.

Weatherwise, Abraham. Weatherwise's Town and Country Almanack, for 1786. Boston: James D. Griffith, 1785.

West, Elliott. Growing Up in Twentieth-Century America: A History and Reference Guide Westport, CT London: Greenwood Press, (1997)

White, Shane. "'It was a proud day': African Americans, festivals, and parades in the North, 1741-1834." The Journal of American History 81.1 (1994): 13-50.

Whitehouse, David. "Origins of the Police." Works in Theory (2014).

Wilson, John. A Song of Deliverance From the Lasting Remembrance of Gods Wonderful Works. Boston: John Foster, 1680.

Wilson, Kathleen. "Inventing Revolution: 1688 and Eighteenth-Century Popular Politics." Journal of British Studies 28.4 (Oct. 1989): 349-86.

Winsor, Justin ed., The Memorial History of Boston, Vol. III, Boston, 1881.

Winthrop, Robert C. et al. "October Meeting, 1877. Tribute to Hon. George T. Davis; Letter of Mr. A. M. Harrison; Journal of Governor Hutchinson; Diary of Mr. Thomas Newell; Memoir of Dr. Appleton; Memoir of Governor Clifford." Proceedings of the Massachusetts Historical Society, vol. 15, 1876, pp. 307–379. www.jstor.org/stable/25079519.

Wise, John. The Churches Quarrel Espoused, or, a Reply in Satyre, to Certain Proposals Made . . New York: William Bradford, 1710, 1713.

Wood, Gordon S., and Peter Shaw. Histrionics and Hysteria in the American Revolution, (1981): 476-480.

Wood, Gordon. "A Note on Mobs in the American Revolution." William and Mary Quarterly 23 (Oct. 1966): 635-42.

Wright, Louis B. and Marion Tinling, eds. The Secret Diary of William Byrd of Westover, 1709-1712. Dietz Press, 1941.

Yirush, Craig Bryan, and Brendan McConville. The King's Three Faces: The Rise and Fall of Royal America, 1688-1776, (2007): 320-322.

Young, Alfred F. The American Revolution: Explorations in the History of America Radicalism. Northern Illinois University Press, 1976

Young, Alfred F. "The Crowd and the Coming of the American Revolution: From Ritual to Rebellion in Boston" (Unpublished Paper, Presented at the Shelby Cullom Davis Center for Historical Studies, Princeton University, 1976)

Young, Alfred F. "English Plebeian Culture and Eighteenth-Century American Radicalism." In The Origins of Anglo-American Radicalism. Margaret C. Jacob and James R. Jacob, eds. London: Allen & Unwin, 1984.

Young, Alfred F. Liberty Tree: Ordinary People and the American Revolution. New York: New York University Press, 2006.

Young, Alfred F. "An Outsider and the Progress of a Career in History." The William and Mary Quarterly, vol. 52, no. 3, 1995, pp. 499–512. www.jstor.org/stable/2947305.

Young, Alfred F. "Pope's Day, Tarring and Feathering, and Cornet Joyce, jun.: From Ritual to Rebellion in Boston, 1745-1775." Unpublished manuscript prepared for the Anglo-American Conference of Labor Historians, Rutgers University. 1973.

Young, Alfred F. The Shoemaker and the Tea Party: Memory and the American Revolution. Beacon Press, 1999

Zwierlein, F. J. "End of No-Popery in the Continental Congress." Thought 11 (1936): 357-77

Осипова, Е. В. "GUY FAWKES NIGHT OR BONFIRE NIGHT." Редакционная коллегия (2015): 85.

# Appendix I - Papal Wars

Timeline

Crusades

The Crusades were military campaigns sanctioned by the Latin Roman Catholic Church during the High Middle Ages and Late Middle Ages. In 1095 Pope Urban II proclaimed the First Crusade with the stated goal of restoring Christian access to holy places in and near Jerusalem. Many historians and some of those involved at the time, like Saint Bernard of Clairvaux, give equal precedence to other papal-sanctioned military campaigns undertaken for a variety of religious, economic, and political reasons, such as the Albigensian Crusade, the

Aragonese Crusade, the Reconquista, and the Northern Crusades. Following the First Crusade there was an intermittent 200-year struggle for control of the Holy Land, with six more major crusades and numerous minor ones. In 1291, the conflict ended in failure with the fall of the last Christian stronghold in the Holy Land at Acre, after which Roman Catholic Europe mounted no further coherent response in the east.

GERMAN ATTACK ON ROME (1081-1082)

PART OF THE GERMAN CIVIL WAR OF 1077-1106)

GERMAN ATTACK ON ROME (1090-1092)

PART OF THE GERMAN CIVIL WAR OF 1077-1106)

NORMAN-PAPAL WAR OF 1053

BATTLE OF CIVITELLA--POPE LEO IX CAPTURED BY THE NORMANS, LED BY HUMPHREY GUISCARD.

HOLY ROMAN EMPIRE-PAPACY WAR (1081-1084)

HOLY ROMAN EMPIRE-PAPACY WAR (1228-1241)

HOLY ROMAN EMPIRE-PAPACY WAR (1243-1250)

THE FERRARA WAR (1482-1484)

VENICE AND THE PAPAL STATES VS. FERRARA, GENOA, SIENA, FLORENCE, MILAN, AND NAPLES

FLORENTINE-PAPAL WAR (1485-1486)

NEOPOLITAN WAR OF 1494-1495

FRANCO-ARAGONESE WAR (1499-1504)

WAR OF THE LEAGUE OF CAMBRAI (1508-1509)

WAR OF THE HOLY LEAGUE (1510-1516)

FERRARA-PAPAL WAR OF 1512 (PART OF THE WAR OF THE HOLY LEAGUE)

SACK OF ROME (1527)

CARAFA WAR (1556-1557)

NAVAL BATTLE OF LEPANTO (AS PART OF A COALITION DEALING WITH THE OTTOMANS) (1571)

WAR OVER PARMA (1641-1644)

FRANCO-PAPAL WAR (1660-1664)

AUSTRO-PAPAL WAR (WAR OF SPANISH SUCCESSION) (1707-1709)

FRENCH OCCUPATION OF AVIGNON AND THE VENAISSIN (1791)

FIRST WAR OF THE COALITION, PARTS OF PAPAL STATE OCCUPIED BY THE FRENCH REVOLUTIONARIES (1792-1797)

REVOLUTION AND FRENCH OCCUPATION (1797-1798)

INVASION OF THE PAPAL STATE BY NAPLES (1798)

SECOND WAR OF THE COALITION (NAPOLEONIC WARS) (1799-1802)

FRANCO-ITALIAN ANNEXATION OF THE PAPAL STATE (NAPOLEONIC WARS) (1808-1809)

LIBERAL REVOLUTION (PAPAL STATES AIDED BY AUSTRIAN TROOPS) (1831)

AUSTRIAN OCCUPATION OF BOLOGNA, FRENCH OCCUPATION OF ANCONA (1832-1839)

REBELLION OF SAVIGNO/IMOLA (1843)

REVOLT OF RIMINI (1845)

REVOLUTION (1848-1849)

GARIBALDI'S EXPEDITION AGAINST SICILY (1860-1861)

INVASION OF ITALIAN PATRIOTS (1867)

France

Cardinal Richelieu
Armand Jean du Plessis, Cardinal-Duke of Richelieu and of Fronsac (English pronunciation: /ˈrɪʃəluː/; French pronunciation: [ʁiʃəljø]; 9 September 1585 – 4 December 1642) was a French clergyman, noble and statesman. He was consecrated as a bishop in 1607 and was appointed Secretary of State for Foreign Affairs in 1616. Richelieu soon rose in both the Catholic Church and the French government, becoming a Cardinal in 1622, and King Louis XIII's chief minister in 1624. He remained in office until his death in 1642; he was succeeded by Cardinal Mazarin, whose career he had fostered.

The Cardinal de Richelieu was often known by the title of the King's "Chief Minister" or "First Minister". He sought to consolidate royal power and crush domestic factions. By restraining the power of the nobility, he transformed France into a strong, centralized state. His chief foreign policy objective was to check the power of the Austro-Spanish Habsburg dynasty, and to ensure French dominance in the Thirty Years' War that engulfed Europe. Although he was a cardinal, he did not hesitate to make alliances with Protestant rulers in attempting to achieve his goals. While a powerful political figure, events like the Day of the Dupes show that in fact he very much depended on the King's confidence to keep this power.

Cardinal Mazarin

Jules Mazarin

Jules Mazarin (French: [ʒyl mazaʁɛ̃]; July 14, 1602 – March 9, 1661), born Giulio Raimondo Mazzarino [ˈdʒuljo raiˈmondo maddzaˈrino] or Mazarini, was an Italian cardinal, diplomat, and politician, who served as the chief minister of France from 1642 until his death. Mazarin succeeded his mentor, Cardinal Richelieu. He was a noted collector of art and jewels, particularly diamonds, and he bequeathed the "Mazarin diamonds" to Louis XIV in 1661, some of which remain in the collection of the Louvre museum in Paris. His personal library was the origin of the Bibliothèque Mazarine in Paris.

Details:
1375–July 1378

War of the Eight Saints

Result  Peace treaty concluded at Tivoli

The War of the Eight Saints (1375–1378) was a war between Pope Gregory XI and a coalition of Italian city-states led by Florence, which contributed to the end of the Avignon Papacy.
1460–1462

Skanderbeg's Italian expedition
Result  Ferdinand regains most of his lost territories
Skanderbeg's Italian expedition (1460–1462) was undertaken to aid his ally Ferdinand I of Naples, whose rulership was threatened by the Angevin Dynasty. George Kastrioti Skanderbeg was the ruler of Albania (Latin: dominus Albaniae) who had been leading a rebellion against the Ottoman Empire since 1443 and allied himself with several Western European monarchs in order to consolidate his domains. In 1458, Alfonso V of Aragon, ruler of Sicily and Naples and Skanderbeg's most important ally, died, leaving his illegitimate son, Ferdinand, on the Neapolitan throne; René d'Anjou, the French Duke of Anjou, laid claim to the throne. The conflict between René's and Ferdinand's supporters soon erupted into a civil war. Pope Calixtus III, of Spanish background himself, could do little to secure Ferdinand, so he turned to Skanderbeg for aid.

1463–1479
Ottoman–Venetian War (1463–79)
Result  Albanian defense victory until 1478 Ottoman victory , Treaty of Constantinople (1479)

The Eastern Mediterranean in 1450, just before the Fall of Constantinople. Venetian possessions are in green and red. By 1463, the Ottoman dominions would have expanded to include the Byzantine Empire (purple), and most of the smaller Balkan states.
The First Ottoman–Venetian War was fought between the Republic of Venice and her allies and the Ottoman Empire from 1463 to 1479. Fought shortly after the capture of Constantinople and the remnants of the Byzantine Empire by the Ottomans, it resulted in the loss of several Venetian holdings in Albania and Greece, most importantly the island of Negroponte (Euboea), which had been a Venetian protectorate for centuries. The war also saw the rapid expansion of the Ottoman navy, which became able to challenge the Venetians and the Knights Hospitaller for supremacy in the Aegean Sea. In the closing years of the war however, the Republic managed to recoup its losses by the de facto acquisition of the Crusader Kingdom of Cyprus.

1482–1484

War of Ferrara

Result        Venetian victory

The War of Ferrara (also known as the Salt War, Italian: Guerra del Sale) was fought in 1482–1484 between Ercole I d'Este, duke of Ferrara, and the Papal forces mustered by Ercole's personal nemesis, Pope Sixtus IV and his Venetian allies. Hostilities ended with the Treaty of Bagnolo, signed on 7 August 1484

1494–98

Italian War of 1494–98

First Italian War

Result --League of Venice victory

The First Italian War, sometimes referred to as the Italian War of 1494 or Charles VIII's Italian War, was the opening phase of the Italian Wars. The war pitted Charles VIII of France, who had initial Milanese aid, against the Holy Roman Empire, Spain, and an alliance of Italian powers led by Pope Alexander VI.

Pope Innocent VIII, in conflict with King Ferdinand I of Naples over Ferdinand's refusal to pay feudal dues to the papacy, excommunicated and deposed Ferdinand by a bull of 11 September 1489. Innocent then offered the Kingdom of Naples to Charles VIII of France, who had a remote claim to its throne because his grandfather, Charles VII, King of France, had married Marie of Anjou[2] of the Angevin dynasty, the ruling family of Naples. Innocent later settled his quarrel with Ferdinand and revoked the bans before dying in 1492, but the offer to Charles remained an apple of discord in Italian politics. Ferdinand died on January 25, 1494, and was succeeded by his son Alfonso II.[3].

16th Century

1508–16

War of the League of Cambrai

Result-    French and Venetian victory

The War of the League of Cambrai, sometimes known as the War of the Holy League and by several other names, was a major conflict in the Italian Wars. The principal participants of the war, which was fought from 1508 to 1516, were France, the Papal States and the Republic of Venice; they were joined, at various times, by nearly every significant power in Western Europe, including Spain, the Holy Roman Empire, England, Scotland, the Duchy of Milan, Florence, the Duchy of Ferrara, and Swiss mercenaries.
Pope Julius II, intending to curb Venetian influence in northern Italy, had created the League of Cambrai, an anti-Venetian alliance that included, besides himself, Louis XII of France, Holy Roman Emperor Maximilian I and Ferdinand II of Aragon. Although the League was initially successful, friction between Julius and Louis caused it to collapse by 1510; Julius then allied himself with Venice against France.
The Veneto–Papal alliance eventually expanded into the Holy League, which drove the French from Italy in 1512; disagreements about the division of the spoils, however, led Venice to abandon the alliance in favor of one with France. Under the leadership of Francis I, who had succeeded Louis to the throne, the French and Venetians would, through their victory at Marignano in 1515, regain the territory they had lost; the treaties of Noyon and Brussels, which ended the war the next year, would essentially return the map of Italy to the status quo of 1508.

1517
War of Urbino

Result Negotiated peace

The War of Urbino (1517) was a secondary episode of the Italian Wars.

The conflict ensued after the end of the War of the League of Cambrai (1508–16), when Francesco Maria I della Rovere decided to take advantage of the situation to recover the Duchy of Urbino, from which he had been ousted in the previous year.

In the early 1517 he presented himself under the walls of Verona to hire the troops which had besieged the city, now to be returned to the Republic of Venice. Della Rovere set off with an army of some 5,000 infantry and 1,000 horses which he entrusted to Federico Gonzaga, lord of Bozzolo, reaching the walls of Urbino on January 23, 1517.

He defeated the Papal condottiero Francesco del Monte and entered the city hailed by the population.

Pope Leo X reacted by hastily hiring an army of 10,000 troops under Lorenzo II de' Medici, Renzo di Ceri, Giulio Vitelli and Guido Rangoni and sending it against Urbino. Lorenzo was wounded by a bullet from an arquebus on April 4 during the siege of the Mondolfo castle, and returned to Tuscany. He was replaced by Cardinal Bibbiena. The latter was however unable to control the troops, and, defeated with relevant losses at Monte Imperiale, was forced to retreat to Pesaro.

1521–26
Italian War of 1521–26

Result-         Spanish-Imperial victory

The Italian War of 1521–26, sometimes known as the Four Years' War, was a part of the Italian Wars. The war pitted Francis I of France and the Republic of Venice against the Holy Roman Emperor Charles V, Henry VIII of England, and the Papal States. The conflict arose from animosity over the election of Charles as Emperor in 1519–20 and from Pope Leo X's need to ally with Charles against Martin Luther.

The war broke out across Western Europe late in 1521, when a French–Navarrese expedition attempted to reconquer Navarre while a French army invaded the Low Countries. A Spanish army drove the Navarrese forces back into the Pyrenees, and other Imperial forces attacked northern France, where they were stopped in turn.

The Pope, the Emperor, and Henry VIII then signed a formal alliance against France, and hostilities resumed on the Italian Peninsula; but, with the attention of both Francis and Charles focused on the battleground in northeast France, the conflict in Italy became something of a sideshow. At the Battle of Bicocca on 27 April 1522, Imperial and Papal forces defeated the French, driving them from Lombardy. Following the battle, fighting again spilled onto French soil, while Venice made a separate peace. The English invaded France in 1523, while Charles de Bourbon, alienated by Francis's attempts to seize his inheritance, betrayed Francis and allied himself with the Emperor. A French attempt to regain Lombardy in 1524 failed and provided Bourbon with an opportunity to invade Provence at the head of a Spanish army.

1526–1530

War of the League of Cognac

Result - Spanish-Imperial victory

The War of the League of Cognac (1526–30) was fought between the Habsburg dominions of Charles V—primarily Spain and the Holy Roman Empire—and the League of Cognac, an alliance including France, Pope Clement VII, the Republic of Venice, England, the Duchy of Milan and Republic of Florence.

Shocked by the defeat of the French in the Italian War of 1521, Pope Clement VII, together with the Republic of Venice, began to organize an alliance to drive Charles V from Italy. Francis, having signed the Treaty of Madrid, was released and returned to France, where he quickly announced his intention to assist Clement. Thus, in 1526, the League of Cognac was signed by Francis, Clement, Venice, Florence, and the Sforza of Milan, who desired to throw off the Imperial hegemony over them. Henry VIII of England, thwarted in his desire to have the treaty signed in England, refused to join.

## 1540
### Salt War (1540)

The Salt War of 1540 was a result of an insurrection by the city of Perugia against the Papal States during the pontificate of Pope Paul III (Alessandro Farnese). The principal result was the city of Perugia's definitive subordination to papal control.

Pope, Julius III gave the Perugians back a semblance of local rule in 1559, the city became part of the Papal States and remained so until Italian unification in 1860.

One curious note about the war is that Perugian legend holds that as part of a popular protest against the new papal tax in 1540, citizens stopped putting salt in their bread (unsalted bread is the norm to this day). Recent research suggests that this is an urban legend developed after 1860.

## 1570–1573
### Ottoman–Venetian War (1570–73)

Result-    Ottoman victory/rule

The Fourth Ottoman–Venetian War, also known as the War of Cyprus (Italian: Guerra di Cipro) was fought between 1570–1573. It was waged between the Ottoman Empire and the Republic of Venice, the latter joined by the Holy League, a coalition of Christian states formed under the auspices of the Pope, which included Spain (with Naples and Sicily), the Republic of Genoa, the Duchy of Savoy, the Knights Hospitaller, the Grand Duchy of Tuscany, and other Italian states.
The war, the preeminent episode of Sultan Selim II's reign, began with the Ottoman invasion of the Venetian-held island of Cyprus. The capital Nicosia and several other towns fell quickly to the considerably superior Ottoman army, leaving only Famagusta in Venetian hands. Christian reinforcements were delayed, and Famagusta eventually fell in August 1571 after a siege of 11 months. Two months later, at the Battle of Lepanto, the united Christian fleet destroyed the Ottoman fleet, but was unable to take advantage of this victory. The Ottomans quickly rebuilt their naval forces, and Venice was forced to negotiate a separate peace, ceding Cyprus to the Ottomans and paying a tribute of 300,000 ducats.

## 18 July 1579 – 11 November 1583

### Second Desmond Rebellion

Result-    English victory

Famine throughout Munster

Plantation of Munster

The Second Desmond rebellion (1579–1583) was the more widespread and bloody of the two Desmond Rebellions launched by the FitzGerald dynasty of Desmond in Munster, Ireland, against English rule in Ireland. The second rebellion began in July 1579 when James FitzMaurice FitzGerald, landed in Ireland with a force of Papal troops, triggering an insurrection across the south of Ireland on the part of the Desmond dynasty, their allies and others who were dissatisfied for various reasons with English government of the country. The rebellion ended with the 1583 death of Gerald FitzGerald, 15th Earl of Desmond and the defeat of the rebels. The rebellion was in equal part a protest by feudal lords against the intrusion of central government into their domains, a conservative Irish reaction to English policies that were altering traditional Gaelic society; and a religious conflict, in which the rebels claimed that they were upholding Catholicism against a Protestant queen who had been pronounced a heretic in 1570 by the papal bull Regnans in Excelsis.

The result of the rebellions was the destruction of the Desmond dynasty and the subsequent Munster Plantations – the colonisation of Munster with English settlers. In addition the fighting laid waste to a large part of the south of Ireland. War-related famine and disease are thought to have killed up to a third of Munster's pre-war population.

# 17th century

1639–49

Wars of Castro

Result

Farnese defeat and the destruction of Castro

The Wars of Castro were a series of conflicts during the mid-17th century revolving around the ancient city of Castro (located in present-day Lazio, Italy), which eventually resulted in the city's destruction on 2 September 1649. The conflict was a result of a power struggle between the papacy – represented by members of two deeply entrenched Roman families and their popes, the Barberini and Pope Urban VIII and the Pamphili and Pope Innocent X – and the Farnese dukes of Parma, who controlled Castro and its surrounding territories as the Duchy of Castro.

1684–1699

Morean War

Part of the War of the Holy League
and the Ottoman–Venetian Wars

Result-Venetian victory

The Morean War (Italian: La guerra di Morea, Turkish: Mora Savaşı) is the better-known name for the Sixth Ottoman–Venetian War. The war was fought between 1684–1699, as part of the wider conflict known as the "Great Turkish War", between the Republic of Venice and the Ottoman Empire. Military operations ranged from Dalmatia to the Aegean Sea, but the war's major campaign was the Venetian conquest of the Morea (Peloponnese) peninsula in southern Greece. On the Venetian side, the war was fought to avenge the loss of Crete in the Cretan War (1645–1669), while the Ottomans were entangled in their northern frontier against the Habsburgs and were unable to concentrate their forces against the Republic. As such, the Morean War holds the distinction of being the only Ottoman–Venetian conflict from which Venice emerged victorious, gaining significant territory. Venice's expansionist revival would be short-lived however, as their gains were reversed by the Ottomans in 1715.

# 18th Century

## 1714–18

### Ottoman–Venetian War (1714–18)

The Seventh Ottoman–Venetian War was fought between the Republic of Venice and the Ottoman Empire between 1714 and 1718. It was the last conflict between the two powers, and ended with an Ottoman victory and the loss of Venice's major possession in the Greek peninsula, the Peloponnese (Morea). Venice was saved from a greater defeat by the intervention of Austria in 1716. The Austrian victories led to the signing of the Treaty of Passarowitz in 1718, which ended the war.

This war was also called the Second Morean War, the Small War or, in Croatia, the War of Sinj.

## 1717

### Holy League

The Holy League of 1717 was one of many coalitions organised by the Papal States to deal with the Ottoman threat. This last one comprised Portugal, the Republic of Venice and Malta. Throughout the 17th century several Holy Leagues were organised by Rome, the most famous of which finally managed to defeat the Ottoman fleet at the third Battle of Lepanto. However the resurgent threat of the Ottoman fleet continued until the early 18th century, and came again to the fore in the Seventh Ottoman–Venetian War of 1714–1718. As with the previous Leagues, Rome organized the expedition, Venice financed it and a third party - usually a Catholic kingdom - was to provide the backbone of the fleet. Given that Spain was exhausted from the War of the Spanish Succession, the Pope appealed to Portugal which ended up sending a fleet to the Mediterranean. The efforts came to fruition in late July, when a combined fleet of Portuguese, Venetian, Papal and Maltese ships defeated the fleet of Kapudan Pasha Ibrahim Pasha[disambiguation needed] in the Battle of Matapan.

The outcome of 1717 as well as of the prior battles with the same goal, was that of restricting the Ottoman naval dominance to the eastern Mediterranean.

# Appendix II The Gunpowder Plot Prepares the Colonists at Jamestown

The oath below was administered to the 1607 Jamestown Island settlers-it adequately demonstrates the fear of the Papacy Not as a religion but as a political threat. Religion is mentioned only as a political force and threat to national security. Only two years afte the plot the political and social awareness which it shaped had been installed in America.

II. King and Privy Council. Oaths of Supremacy and Allegiance Administered to Colonists 1607
*Manuscript Records of the Virginia Company*, Volume III, Part i, Pages 20, 20a Document in the Library of Congress List of Records No. 5

1. The oath of Supremacie Allegiance

I, M        doe vtterlie testifie & declare in my conscience yt ye kings highnes ye onlie supreame Gouernor of great Brietaine and of all the Collony of        1

A blank space in the manuscript.

and all other his highnes Dominions & Countries, as well in all spirituall [and] ecclesiasticall things (or causes) as temporall. And that no forreine [prince] person—prelate state or potentate hath or ought to haue, any fur power, supreortie preheminence or authoritie Ecclesiasticcall or sperituall        wthin theise his Realmes And therfore I doe vtterlie renounce & for forreine Jurisdiction, Powers, supreorties & Authorities, And doe pmise henceforth I shall beare faith & true Allegeance to ye Kings highnes        lawfull successors & (to my power,) shall assist & defend all Jurisdiction        preheminence & Authoritie graunted & belonging to ye kings highnes,        and vnited & annexed to his Imperall crowne & so helpe me my god

[20a] 2. The oath of Allegeance Supremacye

I   M        doe trulie and sincerely acknowledge, professe testifie and declare in my Conscience before God & the world, That our Soueraigne Lord King James §Charles§ ys lawfull and rightfull King of great Britaine and of the Colony of Virginia, and of all other his Maiesties Dominions and Countrics. And that ye pope neither of himselfe, nor by any Authoretie of the Church or See of Rome, or by any other meanes (wth any other) hath any power or authoritie to dispo §depose§ the King or to dispose any of his Maties Kingdomes or Dominions, or to authorise any forreine prince, to inuade or anoy him in his Countries, or to discharge any of his subiectes of ther Allegeance and obedience to his Maiesty or to giue licence or leaue to any of them to beare Armes, raise, tumult, or to offer any violence, or hurt to his Maiestie royall person, state, Gouerment, or to any of his Maiesties subiectes wthin his Maiesties Dominions. Also I doe sweare frõ my hart, that notwthstanding any declaration or sentence of Excomunication, or depriuation made or granted, or to be made or granted by ye pope or his successors, or by any authoritie deriued, or pretended to bee deriued from him, or his Sea against the king his heires or successors, or any absolution of the said subiects from ther obedience: I will beare faith & true Allegeance to his Matie his heires and successors and him and them will defend to the vttermost of my power, against all Conspiracies and attempts whatsoeu9 wch shall be made against his or ther persons, ther Crowne and dignitie, by reason or Color of any such sentence or declaracon, or otherwise, and will doe my best Endeauors to disclose and make knowne vnto his Maiestie, his heires & successors, all treason and trayterous Conspiracies, wch I shall heare or knowe of to bee against him or any of them, And I doe further sweare, That I doe frõ my hart abhorr, Detest & abiure as ympious and hereticall, this damnable doctrine and position That Princes wch be excomunicated or depriued by the pope, may be deposed or murthered of ther subiects or any other whatsoeur And I doe belieue, and in conscience am resolued, That neither the pope nor any other person whatsoeur hath power to absolue me of this Oath or anie parte therof, wch I acknowledge by good & full Authoritie is to bee lawfullie ministred vnto mee, and doe renounce all pardones & dispensations to ye contrarie, And theise things I doe plainely and sincerely accknowledge & swere according to theise expresse words by me spoken. And according to ye plaine & comõn sense & vnder- standing of the same worde wthout any equivocation or mentall evation, or secret reseruation whatsoeu9, And I doe make this Recognition & accknowledgment hartilie willinglie & trulie vpon the true faith of a Christian So helpe me God;

### III. King and Privy Council. Oath of the Secretary of the Colony Administered by Governor and Council in Virginia 1607

Manuscript Records of the Virginia Company, Volume III, Part i, Page 20a Document in the Library of Congress List of Records, No. 6

The oath administred by the Governor and counsell after mr Secretarie Dauison death to Edward Sharples

You shall keepe all secret all matter Comĩtted & reuealed vnto you, and all things that shall be treated secretlie at ye Counsell table vntill such time, as by the Consent of his Maties Gouvnor & Capt generall & the full consent of the Counsell of state then resident, or the more parte of them publication shalbe made therof And you shall most exactlie & faithfullie to yor vtmost power record all acte & matters to be recorded & kept frõ tyme to tyme, wch shall be resolued vpon by the Gou9nor & Counsell of state, or the maior part of them, & you shall not deliu9 any thing con- cerning the affaires of the Counsell to any other person to bee coppied out or ingrossed, wth out first makeing the Gouvnor accquainted therwith and leaue obtayned. so hepe you God & the Contents of this Booke "

-Records of the Virginia Company, Vol III, 1933, pp 4-5. Library of Congress; Edited by Susan Myra Kingsbury, PhD.

# Appendix III. 1760 Price "Great Town of Boston" Map.

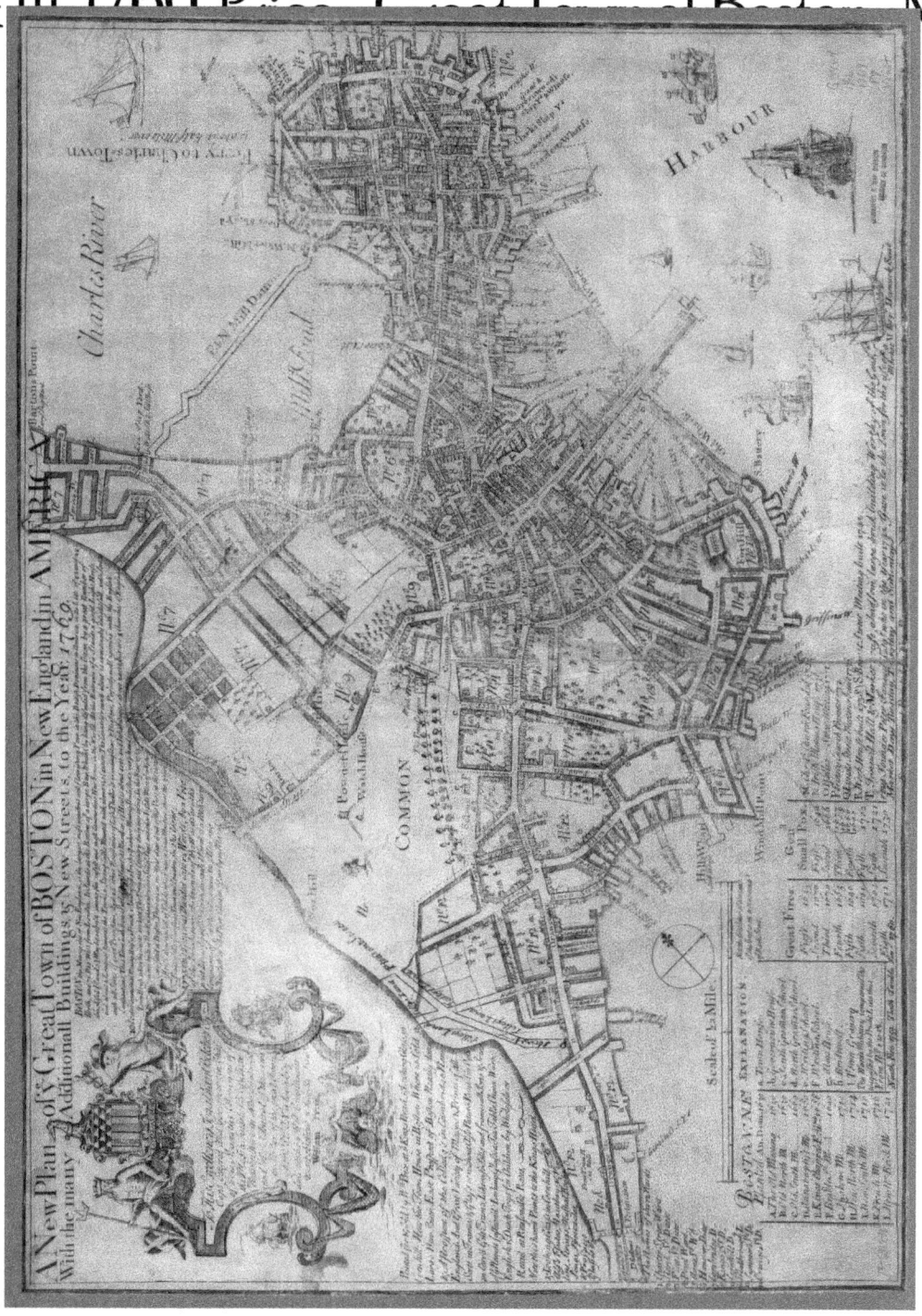

Back Cover Illustrations: Bottom-"South End Forever North End Forever", Broadside, Boston, 1768, Library of Congress Top-: Pierre Eugene Du Simitière, Pope Day in Boston, 1767, sketch of the South End cart company, detail, The Library Company of Philadelphia. Below: Pierre Eugene Du Simitière, Pope Day in Boston, 1767.

www.ingramcontent.com/pod-product-compliance
Lightning Source LLC
Chambersburg PA
CBHW080357170426
43193CB00016B/2740